GUITAR SCALE CHORD
&ARPEGGIO PRACTICE ROUTINES

THE COMPLETE THREE-BOOK COLLECTION

The Ultimate Chord, Scale & Arpeggio Workout in a 30-Week Guided Guitar Course

LEVI CLAY

FUNDAMENTAL CHANGES

Guitar Scale, Chord & Arpeggio Practice Routines

The Ultimate Chord, Scale & Arpeggio Workout in a 30-Week Guided Guitar Course

ISBN: 978-1-78933-462-3

Published by www.fundamental-changes.com

Copyright © 2025 Levi Clay

Edited by Joseph Alexander and Tim Pettingale

The moral right of this author has been asserted.

All rights reserved. No part of this publication may be reproduced, stored in a retrieval system, or transmitted in any form or by any means, without the prior permission in writing from the publisher.

The publisher is not responsible for websites (or their content) that are not owned by the publisher.

www.fundamental-changes.com

@fundamentalchanges

Join our free Facebook Community of Cool Musicians

www.facebook.com/groups/fundamentalguitar

For over 350 free guitar lessons with Videos, check out:

www.fundamental-changes.com

Cover Image Copyright: Author photo used by permission.

Contents

Book 1: Guided Guitar Scale Practice Routines

Introduction 4

How To Use This Book 5

Get the Audio 7

Primer – Scale Fingering Systems 8

Routine One – Major Scale Workout 16

Routine Two – Natural Minor Scale 26

Routine Three – Mixolydian Mode 35

Routine Four – Dorian Mode 45

Routine Five – Pentatonic Scales 56

Routine Six – Harmonic Minor 67

Routine Seven – Phrygian Dominant 74

Routine Eight – Melodic Minor 82

Routine Nine – Melodic Minor Modes 91

Routine Ten – Chromatic Scale 101

Conclusion 109

Book 2: Guided Guitar Chord Practice Routines

Introduction 113

How To Use This Book 114

Get the Audio 115

Routine One – Chord Grips 116

Routine Two – Major Triad Workout 123

Routine Three – Minor Triads & Beyond 131

Routine Four – Chord Scales 141

Routine Five – Open Voiced Triads & Inversions 151

Routine Six – 7th Chords & Triad Mutation 159

Routine Seven – Drop 2 Voicings 171

Routine Eight – Drop 3 & Beyond! 181

Routine Nine – Chord Naming Rules & Extensions 189

Routine Ten – Slash Chords 199

Conclusion 210

Book 3: Guided Guitar Arpeggio Practice Routines

Introduction 214

How To Use This Book 215

Get the Audio 216

Routine One: Right Hand Technique 217

Routine: Two Vertical Triads 225

Routine Three: Horizontal Triads 235

Routine Four: Triad Progression Workouts 243

Routine Five: Diatonic 7th Arpeggios 254

Routine Six: 7th Chord Progression Workouts 263

Routine Seven: Chord Scale Arpeggios 275

Routine Eight: Combining Arpeggios & Scales 284

Routine Nine: Extended Arpeggios 295

Routine Ten: Putting It All Together Etudes 307

Conclusion 321

Foreword to the Compilation

First of all, thank you so much for checking out this compilation of my three bestselling books: Guided Guitar Scale, Chord, and Arpeggio practice routines. What you have here are 30 progressive routines across three subjects that will help you to develop a bulletproof knowledge of the fretboard.

It's recommended that you start at the beginning and work your way through this book in order, because we'll start laying the foundations of an interval based approach by looking at scales, which in turn will help us to build our chords and find our arpeggios.

Each routine has the full audio of every example, along with the routine played in its entirety with me speaking over the top to give you further guidance and motivation. All in all there's over 12 hours of audio for this book. Take full advantage of it.

Take your time with each routine. Spend a week on each one before moving on and allow your mind the time to take on the ideas and shift them into your subconscious.

What's in the Book?

Here's a summary of the ground we'll cover in this compilation:

Book 1: Guided Guitar Scale Practice Routines

In this book, you're not just practicing scales, you are building core skills and fretboard knowledge to break through to a new level of musicianship.

- **Primer on Scale Fingering Systems:** Begin with foundational knowledge to ensure you're on solid ground

- **Major Scale Workout:** A comprehensive exploration of the major scale, laying the cornerstone for future scale practice regimes

- **Modes Unveiled:** Delve into the Dorian, Phrygian, Lydian, and Mixolydian modes, unlocking the secrets of modal playing

- **The Beauty of Pentatonics:** Master pentatonic scales and learn to weave them creatively into your musical expression

- **Beyond Basics:** Explore Harmonic Minor, Phrygian Dominant, Melodic Minor, and gain a new understanding of their musical applications

Book 2: Guided Guitar Chord Practice Routines

Dive into essential guitar chords, harmony, theory and application in this ground-breaking 10-week course. You'll master:

- **Foundation of Chord Shapes:** Starting with fundamental chord shapes, learn the three essential "master patterns" that will help you to break barre chord forms into triads to play chord voicings anywhere on the fretboard

- **Triads and Chord Theory:** Master closed voiced major and minor triads, explore other essential triad types, and understand the theory behind chord construction
- **Chord Scales and Diatonic Harmony:** Learn to connect chords within scales and understand their diatonic relationships for smoother transitions and progressions. Learn to play chord scales for every key using multiple triad voicings
- **Advanced Voicings and Inversions:** Explore open voiced triads, chord inversions, drop 2 and drop 3 voicings for richer harmonic textures and advanced chord structures.
- **Extensions and Alterations:** Understand chord naming conventions, learn how to create and accurately name any chord, then use chord extensions, alterations, and slash chords effectively in various musical contexts

Book 3: Guided Guitar Arpeggio Practice Routines

Here you'll discover an intense, laser-focused 10-week training program designed to take your arpeggio skills from beginner to pro. You'll master every essential arpeggio, from simple triads to advanced extended chords, while developing the precision and technique needed to stand out as a creative guitarist.

- **Complete mastery of all major and minor triads**, 7th chords, and extended arpeggios (9th, 11th, 13th) to revolutionize your playing
- **Advanced applications** that get you playing the rich, higher intervals in musical etudes that you can bring into your playing immediately
- **Master both vertical and horizontal arpeggios** in one easy system, allowing your playing to flow over the entire fretboard with confidence
- **A detailed method to combine arpeggios and scales** musically, helping you create seamless, melodic solos that flow effortlessly and creatively
- **Real-world applications** with dozens of full etudes and exercises that teach you to apply arpeggios over real chord progressions

Good luck, and feel free to reach out with any questions you might have!

Levi

Get the Audio

The audio files for this book are available to download for free from **www.fundamental-changes.com.** The link is in the top right-hand corner. Click on the "Guitar" link then simply select this book title from the drop-down menu and follow the instructions to get the audio.

We recommend that you download the files directly to your computer, not to your tablet, and extract them there before adding them to your media library.

For over 350 free guitar lessons with videos check out:

www.fundamental-changes.com

Join our free Facebook Community of Cool Musicians

www.facebook.com/groups/fundamentalguitar

Tag us for a share on Instagram: **FundamentalChanges**

GUIDED GUITAR SCALE PRACTICE ROUTINES

Master Every Essential Guitar Scale in this Comprehensive 10-Week Course

LEVI CLAY

FUNDAMENTAL CHANGES

Guided Guitar Scale Practice Routines

Master Every Essential Guitar Scale in this Comprehensive 10-Week Course

www.fundamental-changes.com

@fundamentalchanges

Join our free Facebook Community of Cool Musicians

www.facebook.com/groups/fundamentalguitar

For over 350 free guitar lessons with Videos, check out:

www.fundamental-changes.com

Cover Image Copyright: Author photo used by permission.

Contents

Introduction 4

How To Use This Book 5

Get the Audio 7

Primer – Scale Fingering Systems 8

Routine One – Major Scale Workout 16

Routine Two – Natural Minor Scale 26

Routine Three – Mixolydian Mode 35

Routine Four – Dorian Mode 45

Routine Five – Pentatonic Scales 56

Routine Six – Harmonic Minor 67

Routine Seven – Phrygian Dominant 74

Routine Eight – Melodic Minor 82

Routine Nine – Melodic Minor Modes 91

Routine Ten – Chromatic Scale 101

Conclusion 109

Introduction

Teaching has always been a fascinating profession to me. There are so many things we need to learn in this life, and a teacher's job is about guiding us through the learning process in a concise and manageable way.

Unfortunately, that creates its own set of problems! There are many schools of thought regarding the most effective or "correct" way to teach, and also what order to teach things in. As I write this, I have a notebook next to me that I've been writing/sketching in for a solid two months, because I wanted to get this process right for *you*.

Those readers who have followed my writing over the last eight years will know that I tend to write my books in groups of three, and off the back of the incredibly successful *Guided Practice Routines for Guitar* series, I knew I wanted to move beyond surface level material and really dig deep into the fundamental skills of fretboard knowledge and guitar technique. So, the next three books will focus on:

- Scales
- Chords
- Arpeggios

Why are these three things so important?

Music is a combination of melody, rhythm, and harmony. We hear melodies in relation to chords, so we need a solid understanding of those key ingredients. We could describe scales as a horizontal or linear expression of music, while chords are a vertical expression. The problem is, which should come first?

It's a chicken and egg situation. I think of scales as things that connect the notes of chords, but at the same time chords are built from the notes of a scale! In the end, I decided to start with scales, and I've taken this approach because I want you to think of scales like an *alphabet* and chords like the *words* you can form from the letters.

The focus of this book is therefore to give you a real workout in all essential scales, so that when you pick up the next book, you'll be well prepared to tackle the material it contains and extend your knowledge and practical use of chords.

How To Use This Book

This book isn't just another guitar book full of licks and exercises. After an introductory chapter on fingering systems, there are 10 complete week-long routines here, and the goal is to play each one along with me. Each exercise is presented individually in the notation and TAB, but there aren't 120 audio files to download – just 10. What sets this series of books apart from other guitar books is that you'll play each entire practice routine along with me, and this is a proven way of *really* accelerating your playing progress.

On the accompanying audio, I play all of the examples and repetitions while talking you through what we're playing and what's coming next. For the next 10 weeks (at least!), these should be all you hear in your practice sessions.

Over the last two years, the most common email I've received goes something like this:

"Hey Levi, really enjoying the book! I'm trying to spend just one week on each routine. But by the end of the week, I've learned everything but can't get it up to speed. Should I move on or stay on this week?"

I've thought a lot about this and wanted to make it really clear how to use this book, based on my philosophy of practice.

The first thing I want draw your attention to is the difference between *learning* and *practice*.

While you can absolutely use this book to learn about scales, that's not its main purpose. At Fundamental Changes we have lots of books that teach musical concepts in depth, and while I'll cover the basic concept of each scale, I'm writing with the assumption that you already know the majority of scales in this book.

That might seem like a strange thing to say! Why would you want a book full of things you already know?

Because *practice* is not the same as *learning*.

You can't practice a thing until you've learned it. If that's your approach, both your practice and learning will suffer. Instead, practice should involve working on, and refining, things you've already learned, moving them from short- to long-term memory.

Think of a sport like tennis or boxing (both activities I'm keen on!). When I go to my tennis training sessions, I repeat my serve over and over – not because I can't learn anything new, but because I've learned a thing and now need to practice it until it becomes second nature.

The same applies to my right hook! I've spent untold hours in the gym focusing on shifting my weight from the back to the front as I execute the motion. I don't expect to learn something new every time I practice – I just learn a thing, then I practice it.

So, ideally, you'll know the scales contained in this book, so that together we can practice them until they become as automatic as breathing. However, if you've picked up this book and are now thinking, *I don't know the Phrygian Dominant scale very well!* that's OK! You'll just need to adjust your expectations and plan to spend longer on that week's routine to get the fundamentals in place. (One of the core reasons for frustration in the practice room stems from putting unrealistic expectations on ourselves that we find difficult to meet).

If you know the content of a routine, you should be able to master it in one week. If you need to learn the scale, then do so before starting the routine and allow yourself more time. Remember that learning and practice are investments you're making in your future. Taking shortcuts means you'll be short-changing yourself. Consistency is key. One hour of practice per day is better than seven hours of practice on a Sunday.

I play all the routines here at a medium tempo, but if some still feel too quick, software like *Transcribe!* or *The Amazing Slowdowner* will allow you to adjust the tempo, and you can tackle them at a speed more comfortable for you.

Finally, when I sat down to write this book, I thought about practicing every scale in every key – a noble idea, but one I immediately realised would result in a 500-page book. So, instead, we have a routine dedicated to each scale.

For example, we'll play patterns and sequences for the major scale, then do the same for the minor scale, then modes, etc. The serious students among you can use this material to expand your routines and cover other keys. Or, you can take any pattern you've learned and apply it to any other scale. There's nothing to stop you experimenting with these ideas, in fact, it's encouraged!

So, buckle up… let's talk about scales!

Get the Audio

The audio files for this book are available to download for free from **www.fundamental-changes.com.** The link is in the top right-hand corner. Click on the "Guitar" link then simply select this book title from the drop-down menu and follow the instructions to get the audio.

We recommend that you download the files directly to your computer, not to your tablet, and extract them there before adding them to your media library.

For over 350 free guitar lessons with videos check out:

www.fundamental-changes.com

Join our free Facebook Community of Cool Musicians

www.facebook.com/groups/fundamentalguitar

Tag us for a share on Instagram: **FundamentalChanges**

Primer – Scale Fingering Systems

Many of you know that as well as being a guitarist, I've also been studying piano for years now. Learning the piano at a later point in my musical journey has allowed me to really think about how the guitar differs so greatly from most other instruments.

On the piano, for example, the key of Bb Major is just a collection of notes – Bb, C, D, Eb, F, G, A – that's it. When I sit at the piano to play that, there's only one way to play those notes, so not much stands in the way of learning what a scale contains and then playing it.

On the guitar, things are a little different, right? When I listed the notes of the Bb Major scale, more than a few readers will have taken my word for it. As guitarists, it's quite easy for us to play just about anything and never consider the names of the notes involved. Instead, if we want, we can rely entirely on shapes.

This is really cool, because it creates a low barrier of entry for aspiring guitar players. If you can play a Bb Major scale on the guitar, then you can play a B Major scale too. You just move everything up one fret.

A pianist (or horn player, or most other instruments), however, has to know that B Major contains the notes B, C#, D#, E, F#, G#, A#, B. That's *completely* different!

So it's all upside for us then?

Well… not really!

Because the guitar has six (or more) strings, it's like having six little pianos. If I take just three consecutive notes (C, E, G), I can play them in many ways on the guitar. Here are just eight ways to do that and this is by no means exhaustive!

Example 1a

The possibilities of where we can play things on guitar grow exponentially as the number of notes increases. I wouldn't even begin to know how to calculate the total possible fingerings for something like the C Major scale, for instance. Here are just two. One is very common; the other is so obtuse you'd almost certainly never play it.

Example 1b

In order to limit inevitable *option paralysis*, guitarists tend to adopt proven fingering systems in order to learn the fretboard in the most practical way possible. In this chapter we're going to look at a few of those, but I want to address something important first: no one system is "the best" – they all have their pros and cons.

Most importantly, using one system doesn't mean that you can't play something written in another. I want you to take a "system agnostic" approach to the content in this book. The TAB shows how *I* finger things, but I'm not trying to show you the "correct" fingering. True mastery of the instrument means reaching the place where we can play the *notes* not just the *fingering*.

Now, let's look at some of those systems.

Three-Note-Per-String System

The three-note-per-string system is a method of organising scales with the same number of notes on each string.

This system is popular because it's visually easy to grasp and also has the benefit of consistent string crossing mechanics from pattern to pattern.

Here's a C Major scale played with the three-note-per-string system. We'd call this Shape 1 because it starts on the first note of the C Major scale.

Example 1c

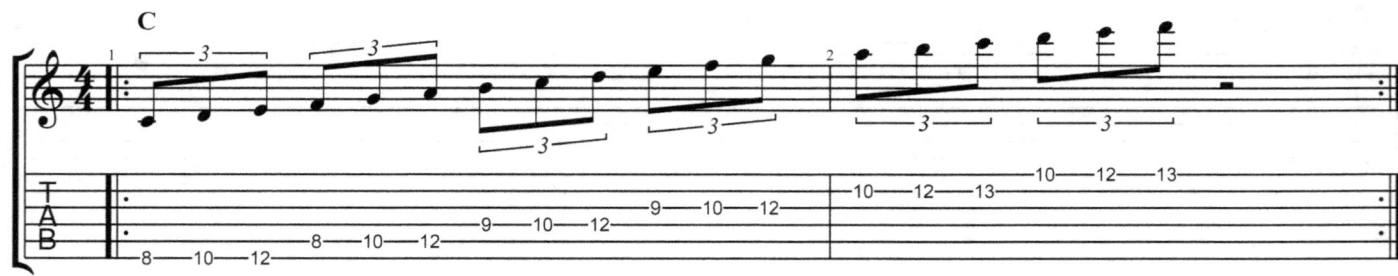

We can start a three-note-per-string scale pattern from any of the notes of the major scale, which means this system contains seven patterns to learn. Here's another C Major scale, this time starting on the note B (we would call this Shape 7).

Example 1d

One of the major upsides of this system is that we can take a pattern in one position then easily move it to another. Here's a melody played in Shape 7, then moved up into Shape 1.

Example 1e

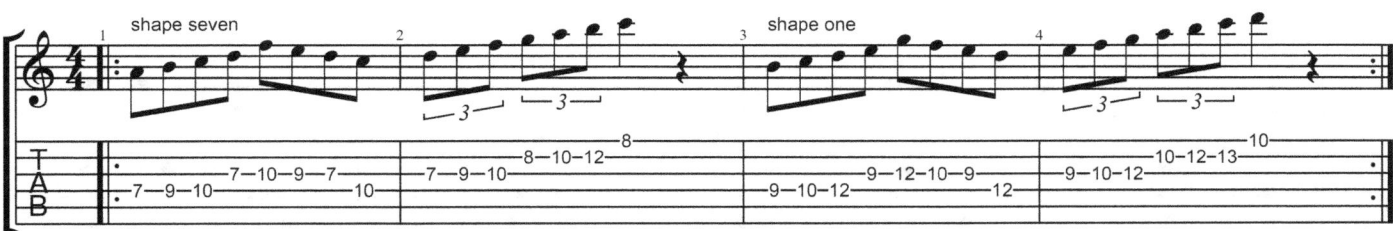

The three-note pattern of this system naturally lends itself to triplet phrasing. For that reason, it's important to work on these patterns as groups of two or four. While we can put accents on the triplet, we should also be able to accent it like this.

Example 1f

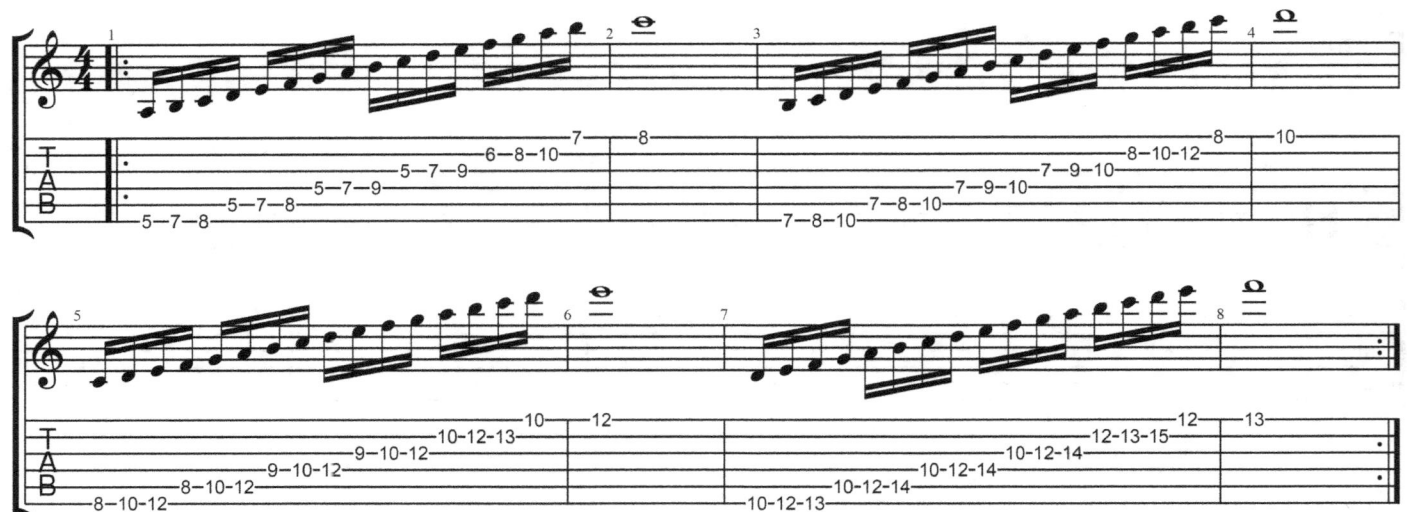

As mentioned, one of the downsides of the system is having to learn seven shapes that all overlap one another. If I express them all as diagrams, they look like this:

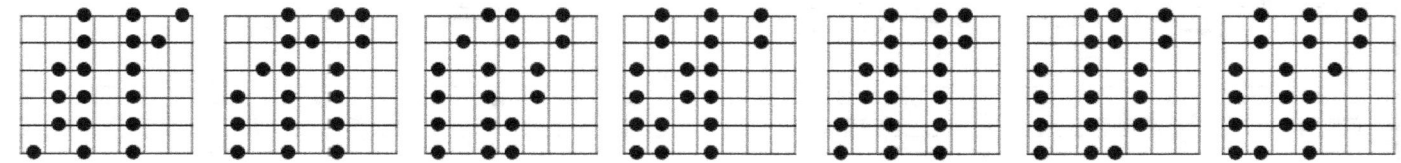

Or, as a fretboard map, they look like this.

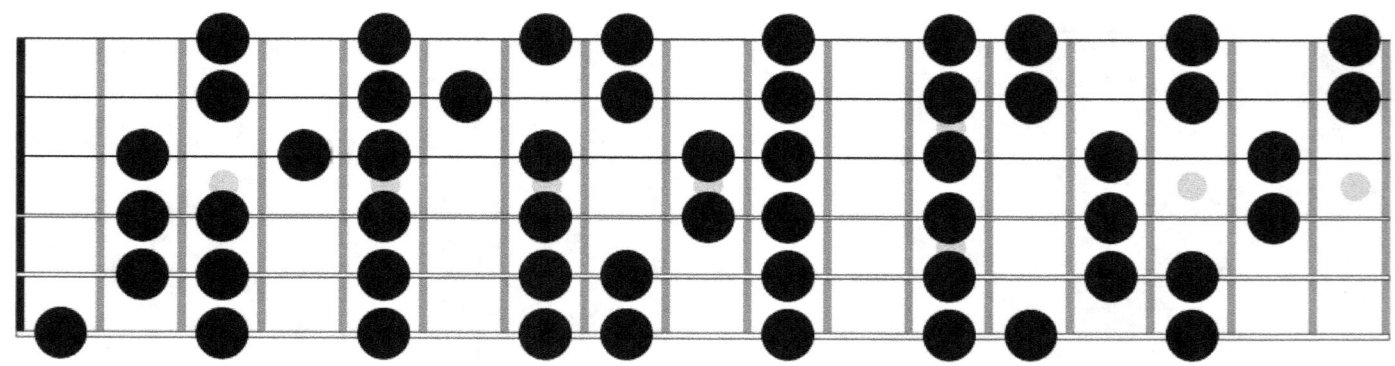

This is a lot of information to take in, and it can become confusing because of the overlapping and perceived similarities between positions. The only real way to track which pattern you're playing is either to see each shape in relation to a master shape (usually Shape 1) and know where the root notes are in every pattern, or to always remember what number shape you're playing in.

I'm not being down on this system – this is how I learned the guitar and played for many years. I still know this system well, and slip into it when I need to play faster triplet patterns, legato, or ideas that move along the neck.

CAGED System

Coined in the mid- to late-seventies and widely attributed to the teacher Keith Allen, the CAGED system is a fingering system derived from chordal positions, which places an emphasis on harmony and things that are easy to finger on the guitar.

You might wonder, if the system wasn't common currency until the mid-70s, why teachers like me talk about famous guitarists like Hendrix (who died in 1970) being users of the CAGED system when it hadn't been invented!

The truth is, nobody really "invented" CAGED, just like no-one really invented the three-note-per-string system. We are pattern-seeking mammals and we like to process large chunks of information in as manageable a way as possible. The observations of Keith Allen were likely not made in isolation.

As for me, I learned a *lot* from players like Albert Lee and Brent Mason. I'm almost certain neither player has ever mentioned CAGED, but they've both described how they see the fretboard and arrange licks, and it's textbook CAGED. It's entirely possible that separate parties will reach the same conclusions independently of each other. CAGED is just a nice little umbrella under which we place these approaches.

The CAGED system is based on the five open guitar chords of C, A, G, E and D, and moves them up the neck using barre forms. These five basic forms create the framework from which scales, chords and arpeggios are built.

Here's an example based on the open E chord. We move it up the neck using barre shapes to C, then play the C Major scale based around that chord form.

Example 1g

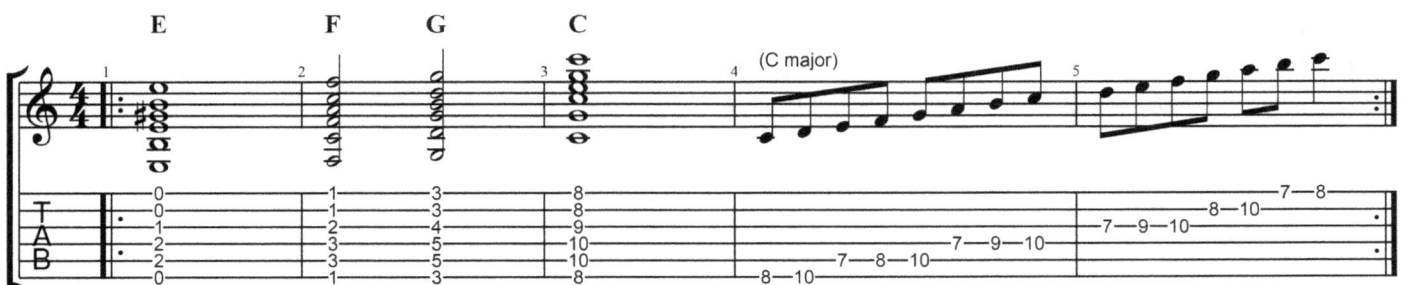

One of the best aspects of the CAGED system is that you'll *never* have to play two consecutive whole step movements on the same string (a key feature of the three-note-per-string system). The CAGED system will never make you stretch your hand more than three frets.

Example 1h

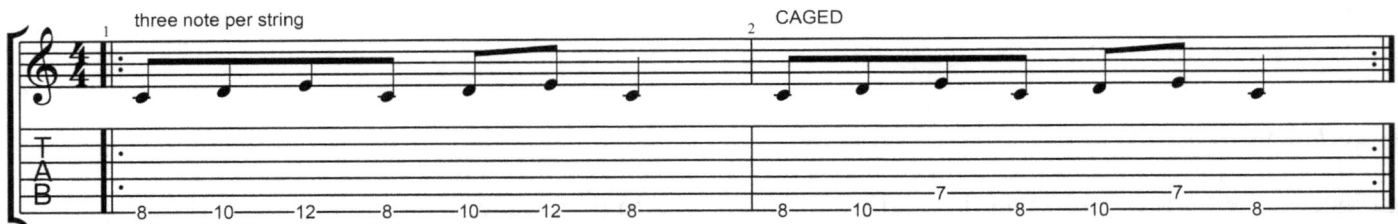

This makes the system *perfect* for beginners, young guitarists, or anyone with small hands, as it doesn't demand the same level of stretching with the fretting hand.

It has the added benefit that we only need to learn *five* patterns rather than seven, plus those patterns all relate to underlying chord shapes, so they are easier to spot quickly.

Here are the five CAGED major scale patterns laid out in diagrams.

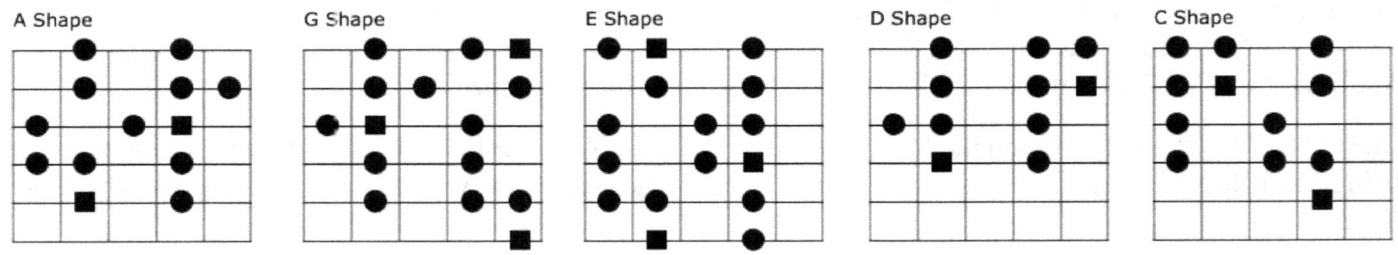

So, if I'm playing around the 8th fret, and I want to play an Eb Major scale, using CAGED I can quickly spot the Eb root note located at the 11th fret on the sixth string, and play the scale using the "G shape" above.

To achieve the same thing with the three-note-per-string system would require us to shift our fretting hand to a completely different position, or to do some quick mental calculations to slip into the appropriate shape at the right point. Here are both of those approaches laid out.

Example 1i

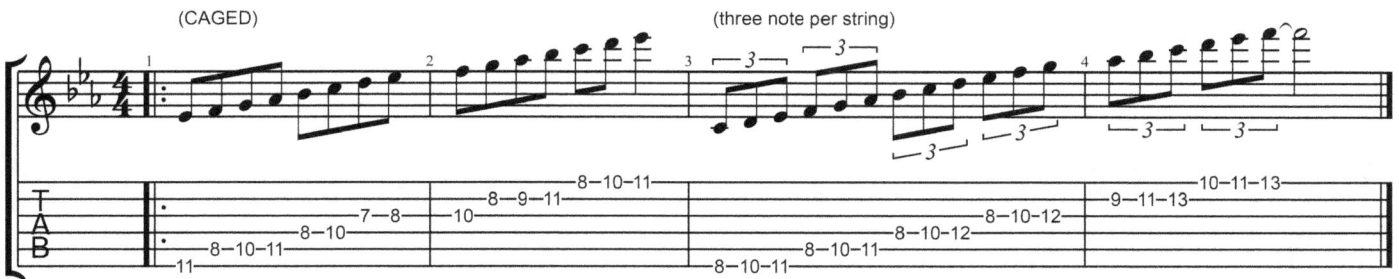

One of the perceived cons of the CAGED system is the inconsistency of notes per string. Because the patterns aren't organised with playing technique in mind, the CAGED system is a little less suitable if, for instance, your goals are pushing speed and technique to crazy levels.

I tend to rely on a CAGED-based approach in 90% of my playing/teaching when melody matters, and switch to a three-note-per-string approach when I want to inject some speed.

Anyone reading this who has studied privately with me will know that I really use my own little system for the fretboard which could be called ACE, because it uses triad forms that only cover three of the five CAGED shapes. But, I guess that really just makes it a subset of CAGED!

Four-Note-Per-String System

I'm not going to bore you with all the possibilities here, but yes, it's entirely possible to learn the neck with any number of notes per string.

Here's a C Major scale played with a four-note-per-string pattern. When tackling something like this, you could use four individual fingers on each string, but I'd be more inclined to play three notes, then shift up to the next note to play it with the same finger.

Example 1j

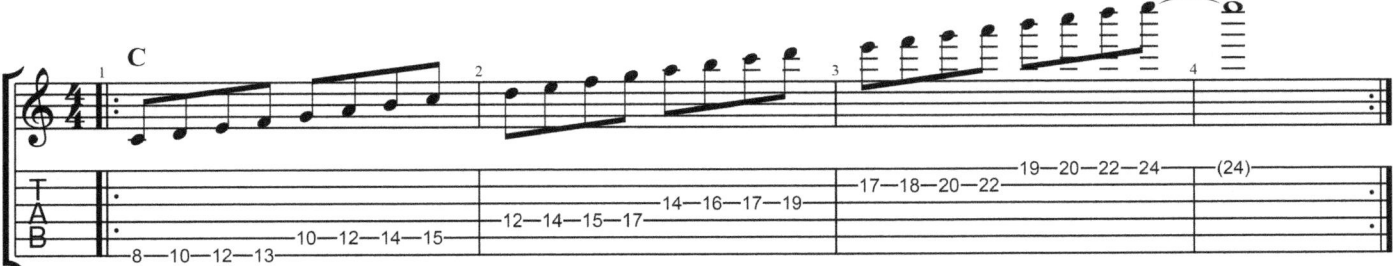

Fingering scales like this creates a tremendous amount of horizontal motion. I don't feel it's very practical in the long term, but hey, if it works for you, awesome!

We could also finger our scales with just two notes on each string, which forces us to move in a horizontal direction, but now towards the guitar's nut.

Example 1k

Again, I don't think this is hugely practical in the long run, but it's entirely possible.

Just Notes

The last option, which is the most fascinating to me, is to not use any consistent system. I've met a few people who play like this, and maybe you're one of them.

The "just notes" guys don't really exist in a pattern-based system. They've either learned the names of all the notes on the neck, or they hear the interval distance between the notes they want to play then just play them. They tend to have had a more classical education, maybe starting on piano, and didn't learn the guitar as much as they just learned music.

Whichever type you are, or if you're someone else, that's fine! Let's take our systems and learn the music. Because you'll find that the more you learn, the more you'll break out of the barriers of your system and become the "just notes" guy. So, let's do it!

Routine One – Major Scale Workout

The major scale could be considered the most vanilla of scales. It's like water. It's the building block of just about everything in music, and the measuring stick by which we compare everything that isn't the major scale.

For this reason, it's incredibly important that we have a deep understanding of the major scale down to the atomic level, so let's talk about it.

To construct the major scale we take a root note and apply a series of tones (two fret distance) and semitones (one fret distance).

The pattern of the major scale can be written/remembered as:

Tone Tone Semitone Tone Tone Tone Semitone (or TTSTTTS).

Our first exercise is to play this pattern starting on the note C, then again from F, Bb and Eb.

As you're doing this, you should be saying (or at least thinking!) "TTSTTTS".

Example 2a

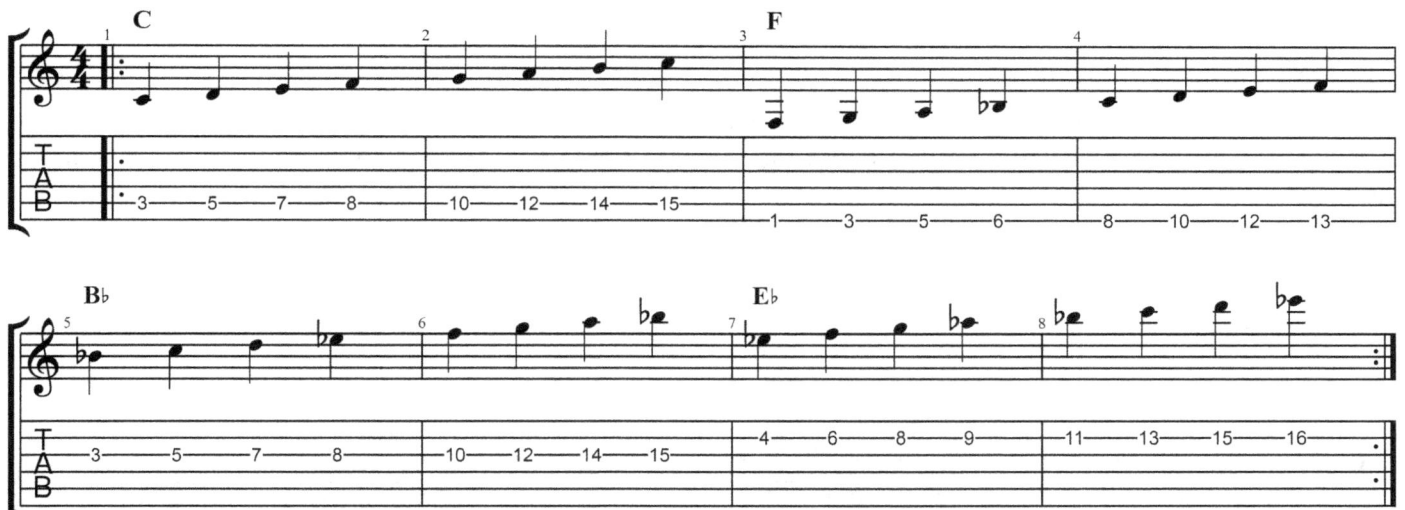

Why these random keys, Levi?

Well, they're not random at all! One of the best habits I've picked up from learning the piano is that it's good practice to play everything in all twelve keys. On the piano, that's essential, because each key looks different. On the guitar, getting into this habit will help remove some of the fear we might have of playing in different keys.

To keep our practice balanced, we can work our way through the Circle of 5ths (or 4ths depending on where we begin). Moving through this cycle starting on C gives us:

C – F – Bb – Eb – Ab – Db – Gb/F# – B – E – A – D – G – C.

That pattern was the ultimate conclusion of the Foundation Level practice routines book, but here we're getting straight into it!

Before we do, now that we have our major scale structure, we can focus on identifying the *intervals* in the scale in relation to the root note. Remember, the major scale is the scale to which all other scales are compared, so it's incredibly important we know what intervals are in it.

Thankfully, this is easy, because we can assign each note of the major scale a number that equals its interval.

C = 1, D = 2, E = 3, F = 4, G = 5, A = 6, B = 7.

Let's play the C Major scale from the root note on the sixth string. As we play through it, really focus on the numbers assigned to each note. I'll say these out loud the first few times I play it.

Example 2b

As a further exercise, you can play through the scale and pick a particular number, such as 3 or 6, and as you're playing, identify whenever that interval is played. Remember, we're challenging the brain, not just the fingers.

Now let's play the same major scale, this time starting with our first finger on the fifth string.

Example 2c

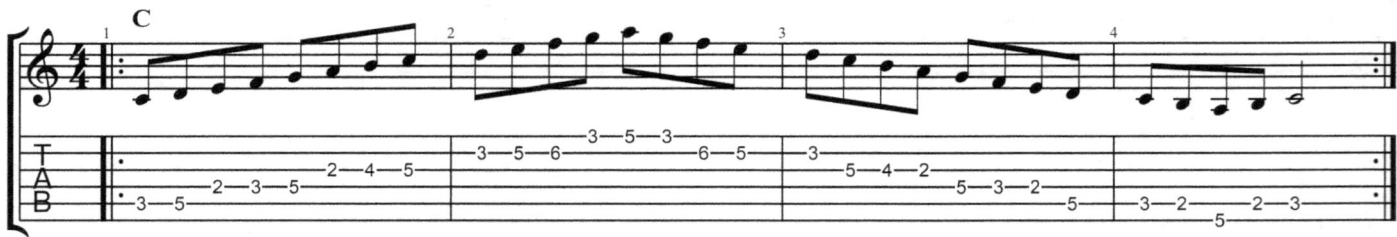

I like to think of these as "forward shapes". I.e., I have a root note and all my notes are in front of that note. My focus is being able to see the root note and build the scale shape around it. So, no matter what major scale I want to play, I can simply move my first finger to that note on the sixth or fifth string, and the scale shape will fit around it.

I also want to be able to do the same with a "backwards shape" – one where I play the root note and all the other scale notes are behind it. For example, here I'm playing a "C shape" C Major scale. The root note is played on the fifth string from my fourth (pinkie) finger.

Example 2d

I could do the same thing on the sixth string too, which would look like this.

Example 2e

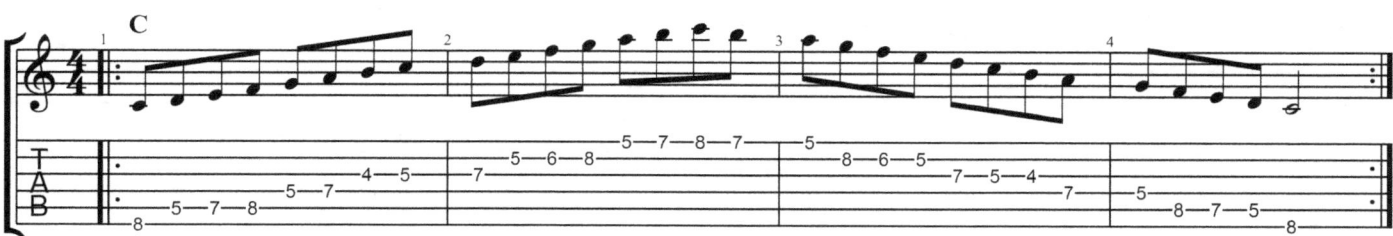

I can't stress enough that unless you *know* the last few examples, playing the next example will be hard work, so don't rush ahead. When playing scales through 12 keys, you can't possibly memorise the exercise as dozens of separate notes. While I'm playing the C Major scale, I'm looking at the fretboard to locate the F note I'll be targeting. And when I'm playing F Major, I'm looking for the Bb, and so on.

It doesn't matter if you don't play the same patterns as me – the exercise is just designed to help you practice thinking ahead.

Example 2f

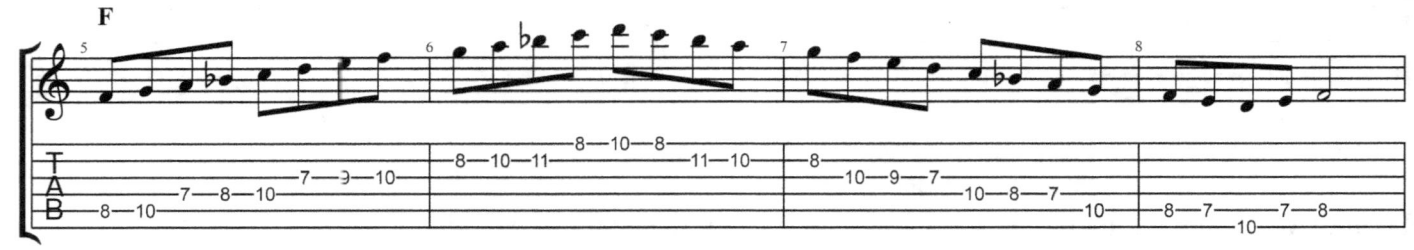

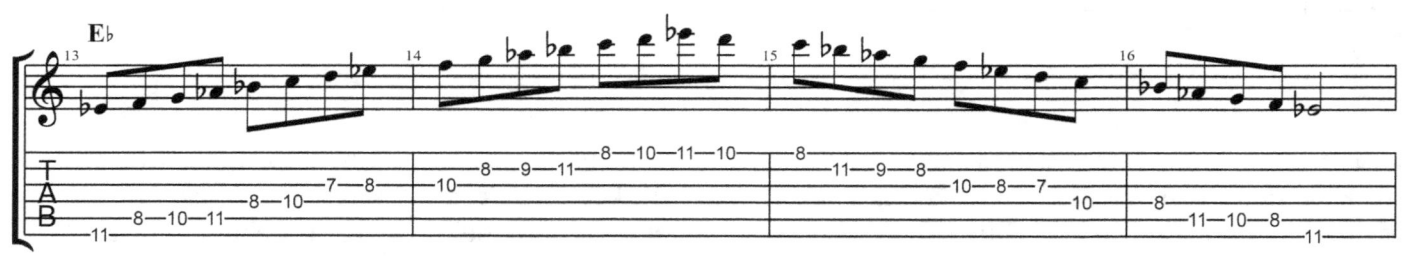

19

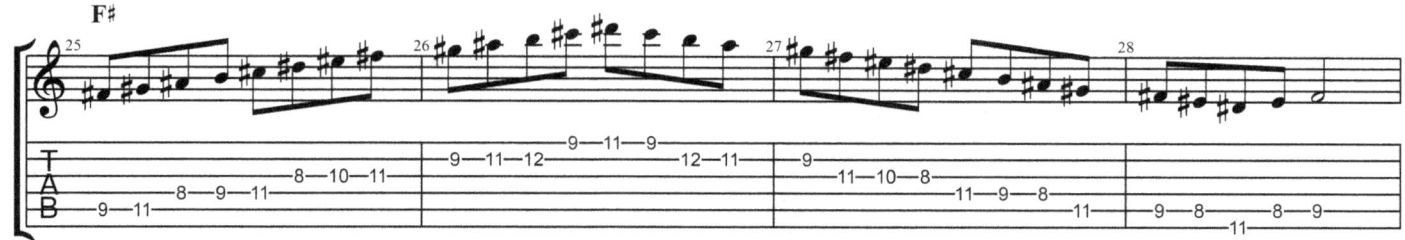

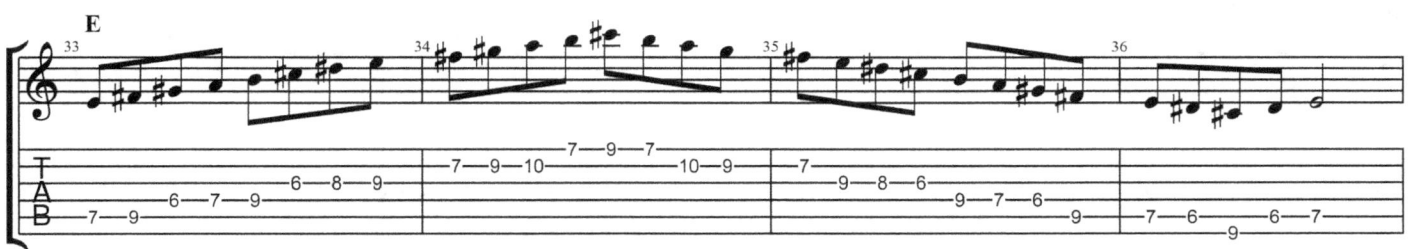

Wow, that was one hell of a workout! Where do we go from here? Well, scales are not always played in ascending fashion from the root note, so now we'll challenge ourselves by looking at the scale in descending form.

We'll mix things up a little by doing this in A Major with the root note on the first string. We won't descend to the root on the low string here, we'll keep to the top four strings.

Example 2g

Here's another descending scale, this time in the key of B, with the root note on the second string.

Example 2h

Now let's play another descending major scale, this time in the key of E, with the root note on the first string, played with the fourth finger.

21

Example 2i

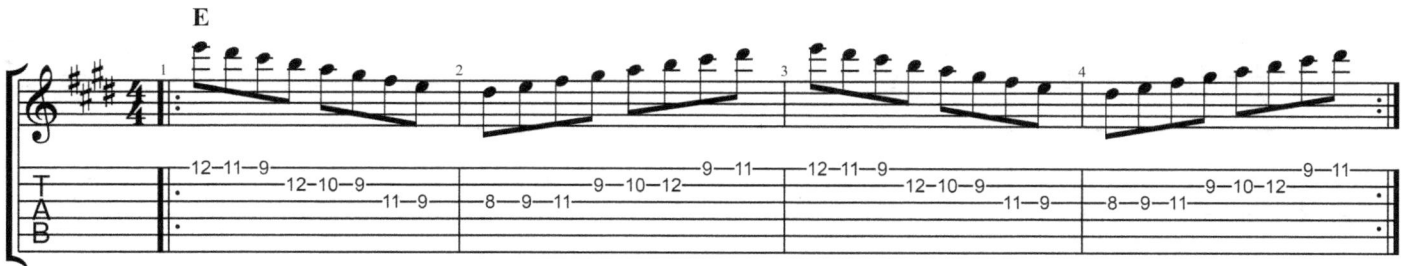

I'm a huge fan of working sequence pattens through scales as a way to keep our technique sharp, but also to mix up and explore some of the melodic capabilities of the scale pattern.

Sticking with the previous position, this time we'll start with the E root note, then skip down a third to C#, then move up a scale step to D#, then down a third to B, up a scale step to C#, then down a third to A, and so on.

This sequence of thirds is wonderfully musical!

Example 2j

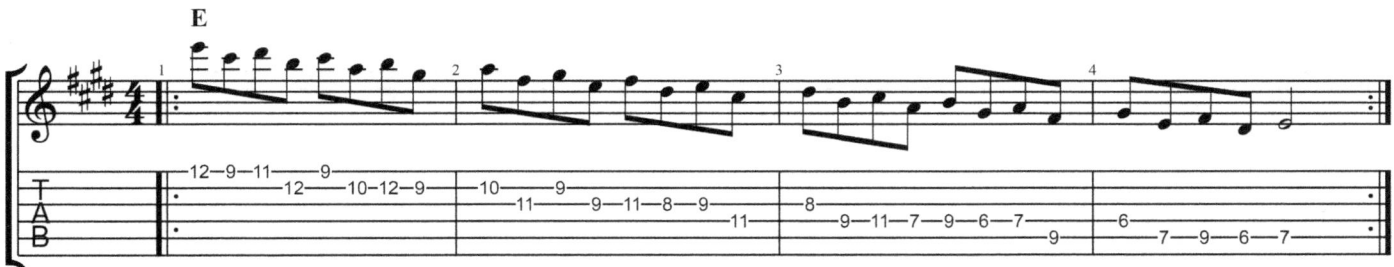

You may have noticed that we broke out of position a little when playing the previous example, and moved down the neck by playing four notes on the fourth string. Being comfortable with position shifts like this is a great way to keep exploring the fretboard.

Here's another example of that in C, transitioning from the "A shape" up to the "G shape".

Example 2k

I took a mind-bending way to practice this idea from the incredible Carl Verheyen. Here, we'll start down in F on the sixth string and play an ascending major scale all the way up the neck until we can't go much further. There are obviously limitless pathways to achieve this, and the exercise is really about looking for new ways each time you try it, but here's a good start.

Example 2l

Now let's do that in Bb.

Example 2m

You know where I'm going with this! Carl will do this as a warmup in all twelve keys, ascending and descending. For the sake of saving the rainforest, I won't write out the whole thing, but it's something you should absolutely take a stab at.

This isn't something that comes easily, but since we understand the concept, we shouldn't ignore the application. I know firsthand that feeling of, "I don't want to do that right now" because it means confronting a weakness we have. I could have fixed so much about my playing and saved years of work later, if I'd not given in to that feeling! Please, don't be like 20-year-old Levi!

OK, onto the final few exercises that are going to set us up for the rest of the book.

Earlier, we looked at the interval pattern of the major scale. Knowing where these intervals are located on the fretboard is going to be fundamental moving forward, especially when we begin comparing other scales to them, so let's do some work on embedding them now.

We'll start by playing a C root note on the sixth string, played with the first finger, then on the audio I'll call out a series of numbers. These are intervals, so when I say "3" you'll play the 3rd of the scale (7th fret of the fifth string, or 9th fret on the third). When I say "6", you'll play the 6th of the scale (7th fret, fourth string, or 10th fret, second string), and so on.

Example 2n

Now we're going to look at the same idea, but with a root note on the fifth string. This time I'll call out multiple intervals to find, so start out by reminding yourself of the numbers that identify each note, then follow the audio.

Example 2o

We've just scratched the surface here. This is the sort of thing we could spend weeks or months working on. I've been working to improve this skill for over a decade and it's still something I'm looking to get better at. All chords, arpeggios, and scales are just a collection of intervals, and if we can see those intervals effortlessly, then we'll be able to play any sound easily.

Interval recognition is a skill we're going to come back to again and again in this book, so don't be afraid to return to this section and keep testing yourself by going for different scale positions, different tempos, different notes… The more you do it, the easier it becomes!

Routine Two – Natural Minor Scale

If the major scale is the fundamental building block of music, the minor scale is its brother – it's closest relative.

The first term that comes up when thinking about the natural minor scale is "relative minor". In other words, the minor scale can be found within the major scale, and we locate it by starting on the 6th degree.

C Major = C, D, E, F, G, A, B, C

A Minor = A, B, C, D, E, F, G, A

These scales contain identical notes, and we call A Minor the *relative minor scale* of C Major.

This formula will always be true, regardless of which major scale we're using.

Bb Major = Bb, C, D, Eb, F, G, A, Bb

The 6th degree of Bb Major is G, so the relative minor of Bb Major is G Minor.

G Minor = G, A, Bb, C, D, Eb, F, G

You'll have probably also heard the natural minor scale referred to as the Aeolian mode. We can play the major scale starting from any of its seven notes, and each of these scales is referred to as a different mode.

I like to think of modes as different "states". A light switch has just two states or modes – on or off. A dice has six possible states/modes it can rest in. Similarly, the major scale has seven modes. It's the same notes, but from seven different perspectives.

That said, although A Minor has the same collection of notes as C Major, if I'm playing over an A Minor groove, it doesn't sound great if I'm thinking/playing C Major. Why? Because I'll phrase the melodies differently, emphasising certain notes when I'm thinking from a C perspective. It's far better to treat each mode as a sound in its own right, so that when we're playing over an A Minor vamp, we're using an A Minor sound.

Thinking about modes in terms of the parent scale and viewing them as "all the same sound from different starting points" is called *derivative modal theory*. It's quite common to see scales taught this way, because it's quick and sounds simple, but the truth is, it's a shortcut. It will get some quick results, like learning to drive a car without changing gears. But although you might get driving quicker, you can't drive around in first gear forever!

For this reason, I don't like to compare A Minor to C Major. I can't – they're the same thing!

It's far more helpful to compare the C Minor scale to C Major. When we do this, we can really understand the difference between the major and minor scales, and we also get a meaningful formula.

C Major contains the notes C, D, E, F, G, A, B

C Minor contains the notes C, D, Eb, F, G, Ab, Bb

Viewed like this, it becomes clear that the minor scale is like a major scale but with a b3, b6 and b7. This yields the minor scale formula of 1, 2, b3, 4, 5, b6, b7.

This method of comparing scales is called *parallel modal theory* – comparing scales from the same root note.

Like any sound in music, the minor scale is a collection of ingredients that work together, and the characteristic sound of the minor comes from its b3, b6 and b7 ingredients.

Out first step in practicing the minor scale is to play it ascending and descending while saying the intervals out loud. To highlight the sound of the minor, we'll play the C Major scale first, followed by the C Minor scale, really focusing on where the b3, b6 and b7 intervals are located.

Example 3a

Let's explore this position a bit more by playing a sequence through the scale. Remember, sequences are a wonderful way to test your scale pattern knowledge, and you can work at applying them to all of your scales/positions over time.

This sequence starts on the root, jumps up to the b3, down to the 2nd, then back to the root. Then we move down and repeat this motif, this time starting on the b7 (b7, 2nd, 1, b7), and then from the b6 (b6, 1, b7, b6), and finally from the 5th (5th, b7, b6, 5th) and so on.

Example 3b

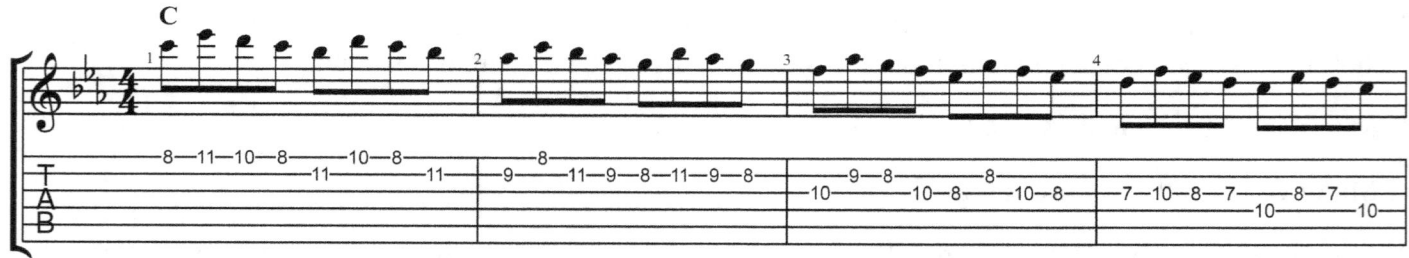

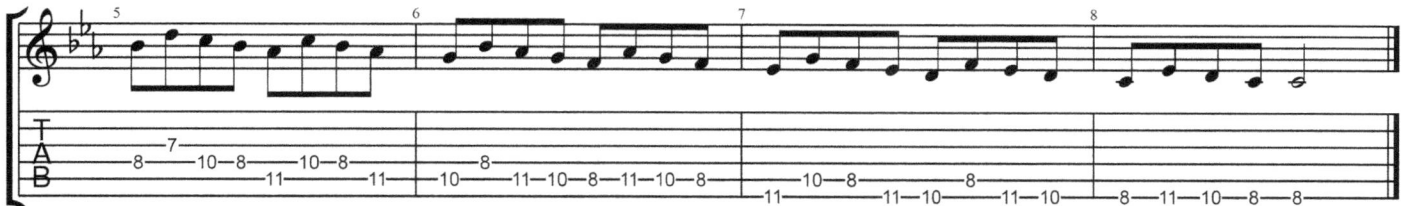

As with our major scales, we should be able to play our minor scales without hesitation in various positions. For example, with the root note on the fifth string.

As you play this, I want you to compare it to the C Major scale in the same position. Look at the pattern and notice when you're playing the b3, b6 and b7 intervals.

Example 3c

How about the C Minor scale in the higher register, still with the root on the fifth string, but now in backward form?

Example 3d

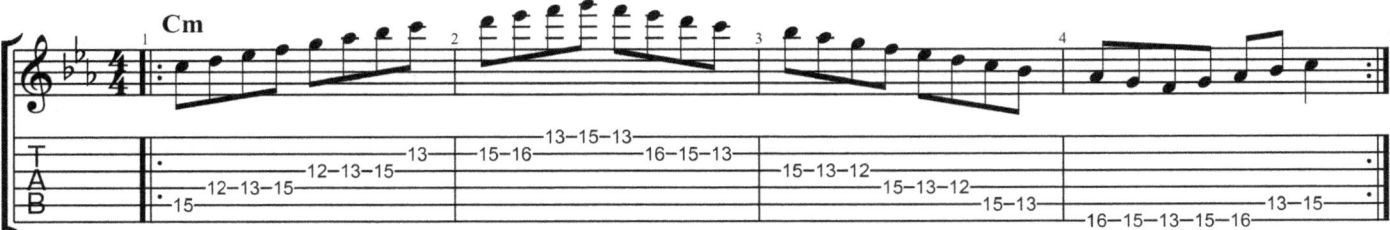

Or, with the root on the sixth string in backward form?

Example 3e

I find that one of the best ways to train the sound of scales into my fingers is to play simple melodies that include the key intervals of the scale. We know that the b3, b6 and b7 are the minor "character" intervals and the tones that distinguish it from the major scale, so here is a line constructed from root, b3, 2nd, 4th and b3, played in different areas of the neck.

An exercise like this helps to train our fingers and focus on what the b3 sounds like played over a minor chord.

Example 3f

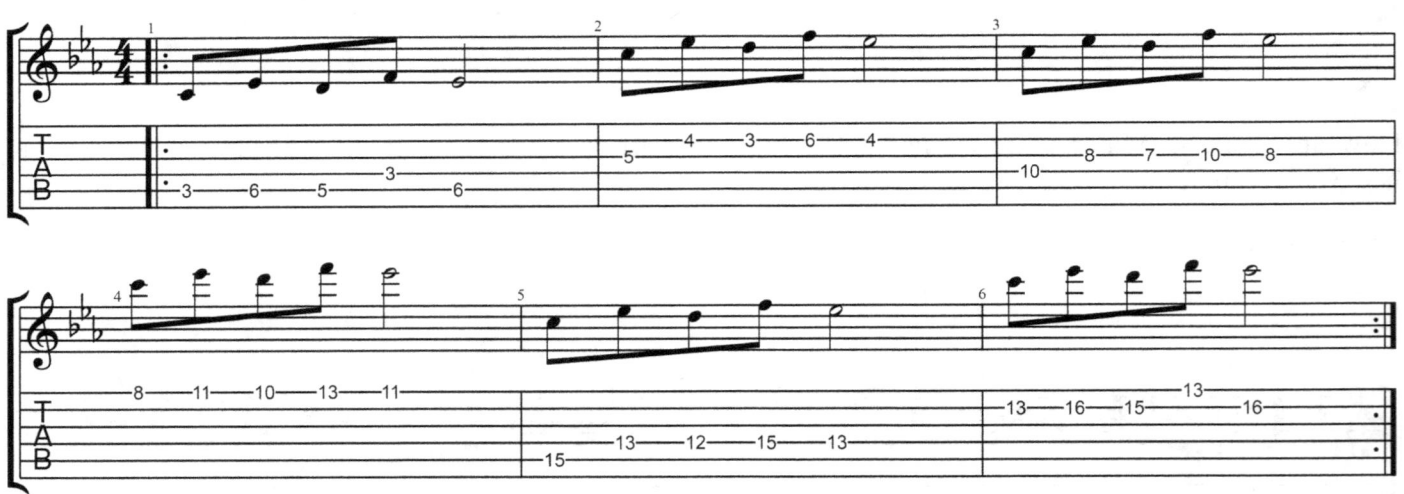

We can take the same melody and move it through all twelve keys. This is a great exercise that requires us to be able to do two things: first, to visualise the melody, and secondly to locate it in the next key ahead of time.

Knowing the melody is essential, because if you need to commit all your brain power to remembering its shape, then you won't have the capacity to think about what's coming next. We want to be able to do both things well, so apply them to the instrument slowly.

Remember, this isn't about learning the exact fingering I'm using, it's just about learning to play one thing twelve times – as opposed to remembering 60 notes!

Example 3g

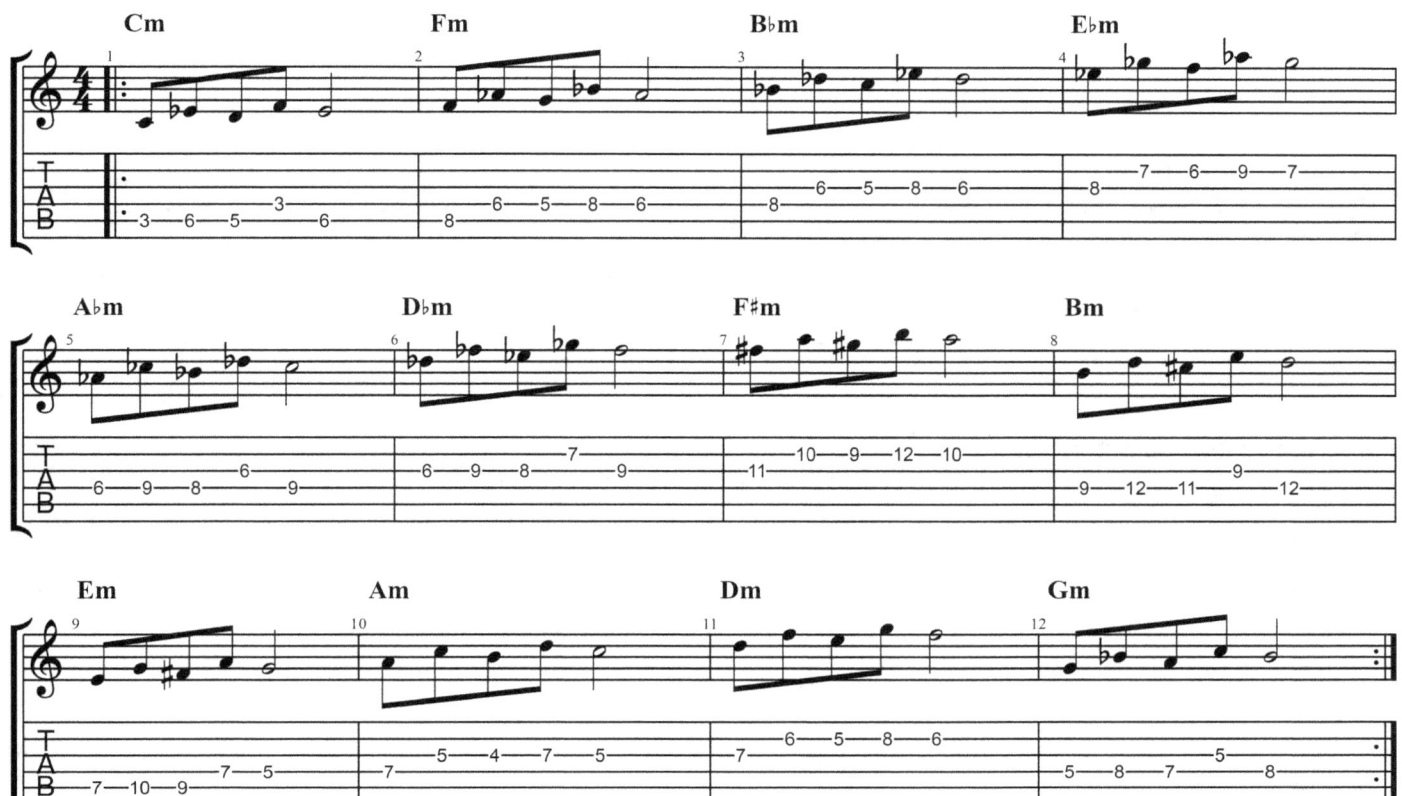

Here's another melody, this time ascending the minor scale from the root, moving up to the b6 and coming down to the 5th. The b6 naturally wants to pull down to the 5th, so this is a great thing for us to practice.

Example 3h

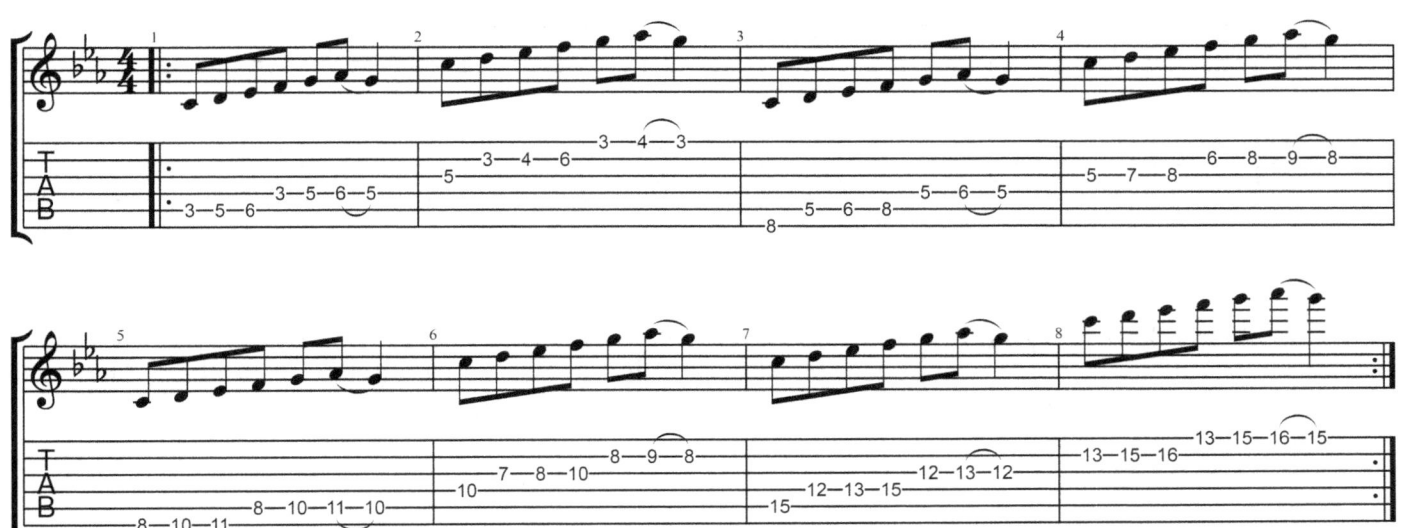

Now we've located the key intervals, it's worth us looking at some longer melodic etudes using minor scale patterns that cover more of the fretboard. Here I'm using some three-note-per-string ideas and even a four-note-per-string idea on the fourth string as a way of transitioning down the neck.

Example 3i

Another great way to develop scale knowledge is to abandon string crossing altogether and explore the scale in single-string fashion.

The minor scale has a TSTTSTT pattern, but rather than thinking about that, I find it more helpful to focus on the note intervals and how they relate to one another.

Here is the C Minor scale laid out on the second and third strings.

Example 3j

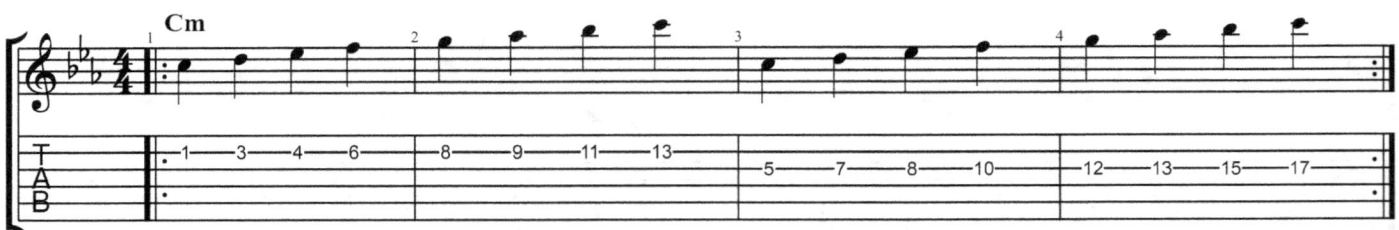

If you spend some time studying that pattern, you'll learn that the distance between the root and the 2nd is a tone. From the 2nd to the b3 is a semitone. The b3 to the 4th is a tone. The 4th to the 5th is a tone. The 5th to the b6 is a semitone. The b6 to b7 is a tone. And the b7 to the root is a tone.

We can intellectualise that, but what we really need to do it hear it and anticipate it. Play Example 3j again slowly, this time with your eyes closed. Play the first note, then slide your first finger up to the next note. Don't open your eyes and read the TAB, just use your ears to hear what the next note should be and get a feel for how far away it is. Do this for the whole scale, ascending and descending.

Now, here are two sequences on the first string using the notes of C Minor. I really want you to try and hear these in your head clearly before you play them, and build a connection between the sound you expect to hear and how you move your hand to play that sound.

Example 3k

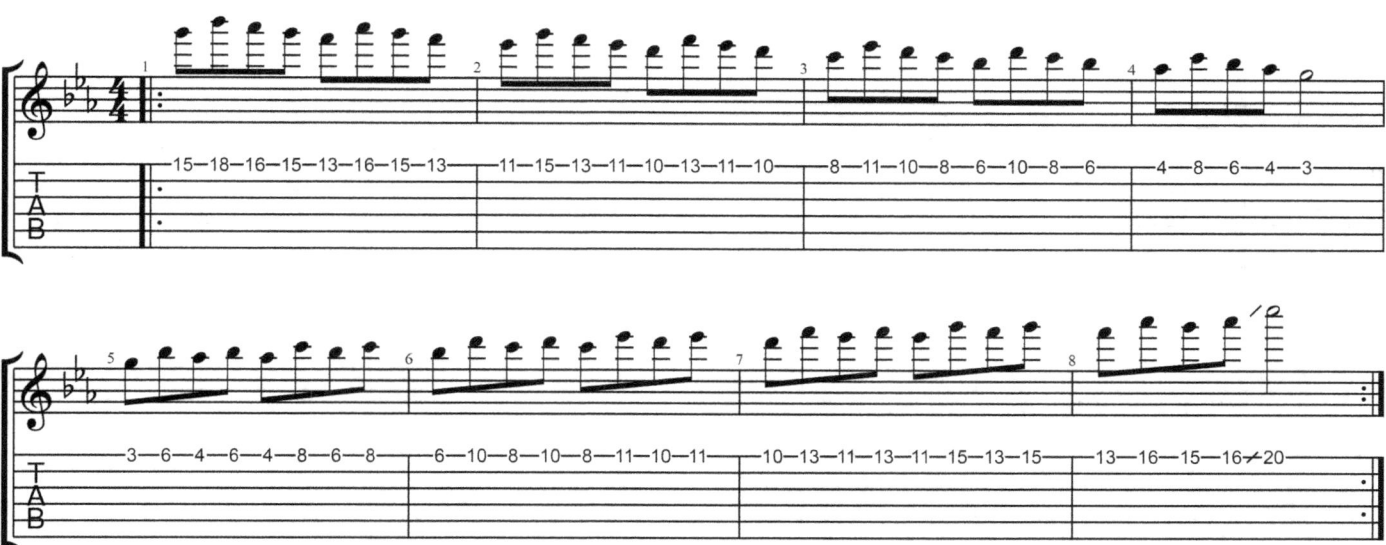

Here's a longer idea moving from C Minor low down on the neck into the higher register. This time, we're combining some position-based ideas with single-string movements for position changes.

Example 3l

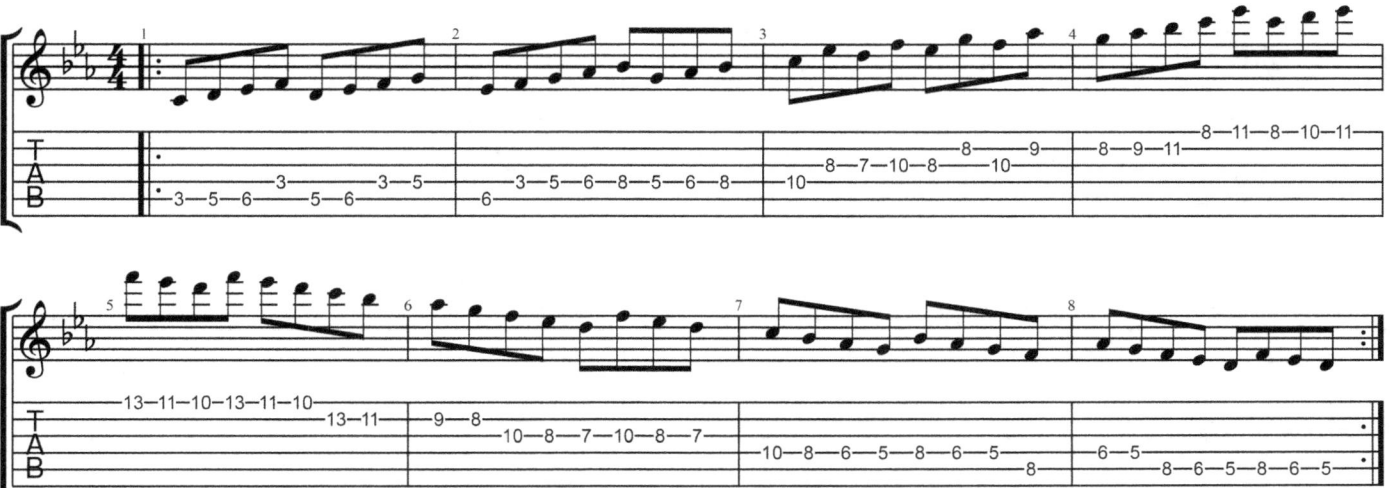

Like the previous routine, I want to end here by taking root notes on the sixth and fifth strings, and finding the intervals as I call them out on the audio.

To make things a little harder though, we'll combine all of the intervals we've learned so far. That is:

1, 2 b3, 3, 4, 5, b6, 6, b7, 7

Here's that idea played from the sixth string. In the notation below I've added some intervals, and these are for you to work out. I'll reveal the answers on the audio, then continue the exercise so you can continue to find intervals on your own.

Example 3m

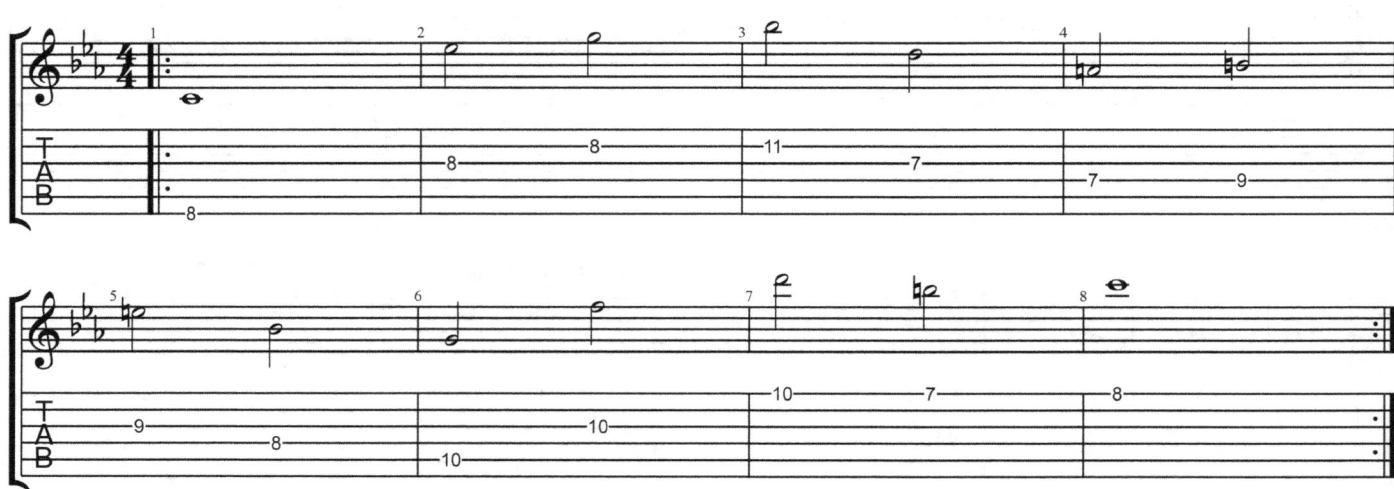

Now let's do the same thing from a root note on the fifth string, played with the first finger. Again, I've notated some for you and will continue the exercise on the audio.

Example 3n

Finally, here's a root note on the fifth string, with intervals placed behind the root note.

Example 3o

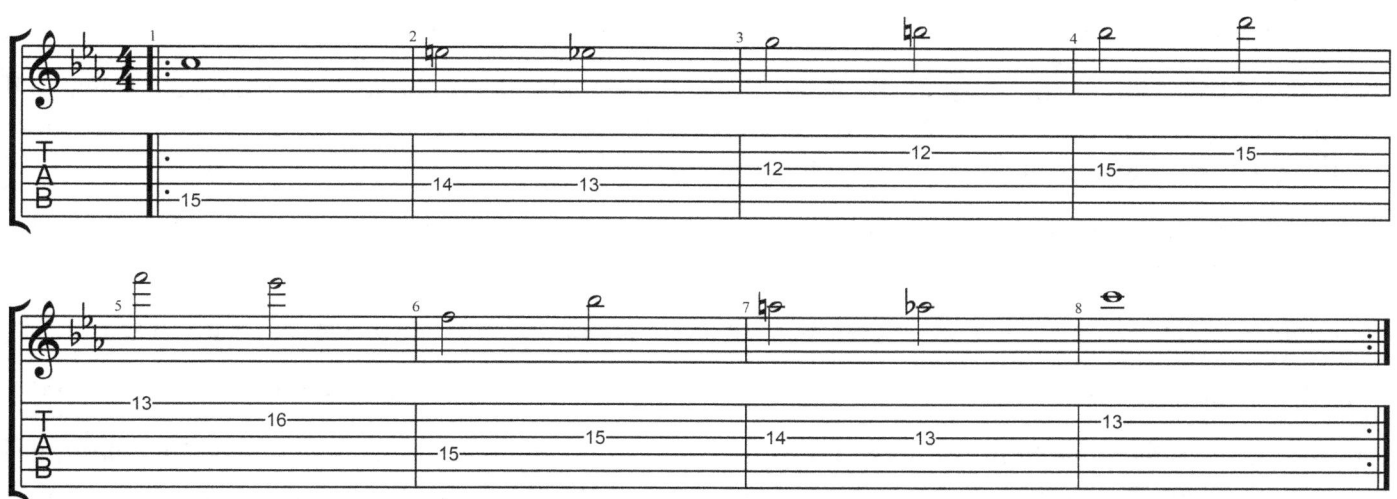

With the major and minor scales under your belt, you've learned 10 of the 12 intervals that exist in the Western tonal system of music. Before we learn the others, we're going to look at some modes we can play with the intervals we already know.

You may want to consider how valuable theory and note names will be for your future. To be clear, this isn't for everybody, but if you're looking to become a professional musician (where you'll likely be working with musicians who aren't guitarists!), knowing your keys, scales and intervals really well can't hurt.

We've put a lot of work in C Major and C Minor, but knowing how to navigate these ideas around the Circle of 5ths is something you may want to stop and devote some time to before moving on.

Routine Three – Mixolydian Mode

So far, we've looked at the major and minor scales. We've played them all over the neck and have a good understanding of the intervals they contain. We know that the intervals in each scale are like the ingredients in a meal – they add up to a particular flavour, which can elicit certain emotions.

It's often said that the major scale sounds happy or upbeat, while the minor scale sounds sad. If that's all you have to say about them, that's fine, but that feels too broad to me. I'd rather you made your own, more meaningful associations with these sounds, but here are mine!

To me, the major scale sounds predictable, like nursery rhymes, but pleasing in a clichéd way; folky at times and, at worst, bland.

The minor scale sounds yearning, neoclassical, dark and dramatic, somewhat cheesy but rewarding.

That's how I think of these particular scales. Having your own way of thinking about them is encouraged!

You may have noticed that "bluesy" wasn't a word I used to describe either of those scales. I wouldn't use them when playing in that context, because they don't sound very bluesy and neither do the chords built from them – that's where the Mixolydian mode comes in.

The Mixolydian mode is the fifth mode of the major scale. Using derivative modal theory, we can take the F Major scale and play it from its 5th degree to create the C Mixolydian mode… but you know I don't like that approach.

Considered from a parallel modal point of view, here's how C Mixolydian compares to C Major:

C Major = 1, 2, 3, 4, 5, 6, 7

C Mixolydian = 1, 2, 3, 4, 5, 6, b7

Ah! So, the Mixolydian mode is like a major scale but with a b7? Yes, it's as simple as that.

The Mixolydian mode is the scale we use over dominant chords, because a dominant chord is a major triad with an added b7.

When we talk about the Mixolydian I'm with Ted Green's approach. What does the term "Mixolydian" even mean? It sounds like some old Greek word that needs translating before we can understand it. Instead, it makes sense to call the Mixolydian mode "the dominant scale" like Ted, because it's a scale that perfectly fits dominant chords!

Let's check it out.

Here is the C Mixolydian scale played ascending and descending. Remember that it's almost identical to the major scale, we've just got a b7 instead of a natural 7. But that "new note" isn't new, right? We encountered the b7 interval in the minor scale.

Example 4a

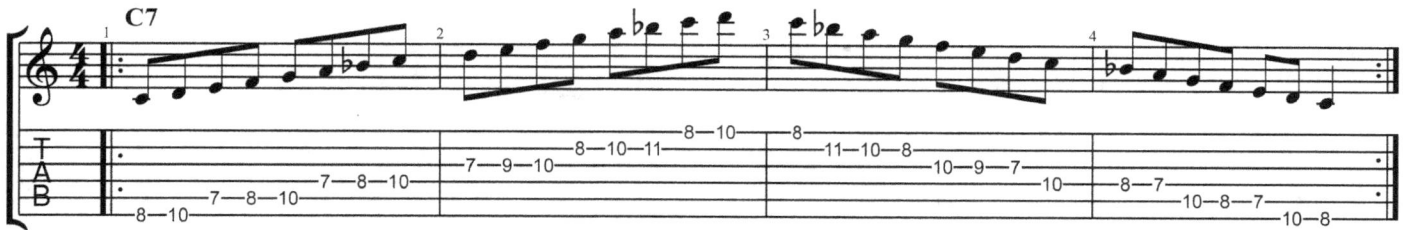

Let's play that in a few more places on the neck. Here's the scale rooted on the fifth string at the 3rd fret.

Example 4b

And here's that same scale played up at the 15th fret on the fifth string.

Example 4c

So, I guess that means the key ingredient of the Mixolydian mode is just the b7, right?

Well, not quite. Since it has a b7, what sets it apart from the minor scale, which also has a b7?

The two most important "character" notes in the Mixolydian are the b7 that distinguish it from the major scale and the natural 3rd that tells us it's a major-sounding mode, not a minor one.

Here's a simple melody that ascends the Mixolydian and uses a 3rd – 4th – 3rd movement before ascending to the b7. We're playing it in six different places on the neck.

Example 4d

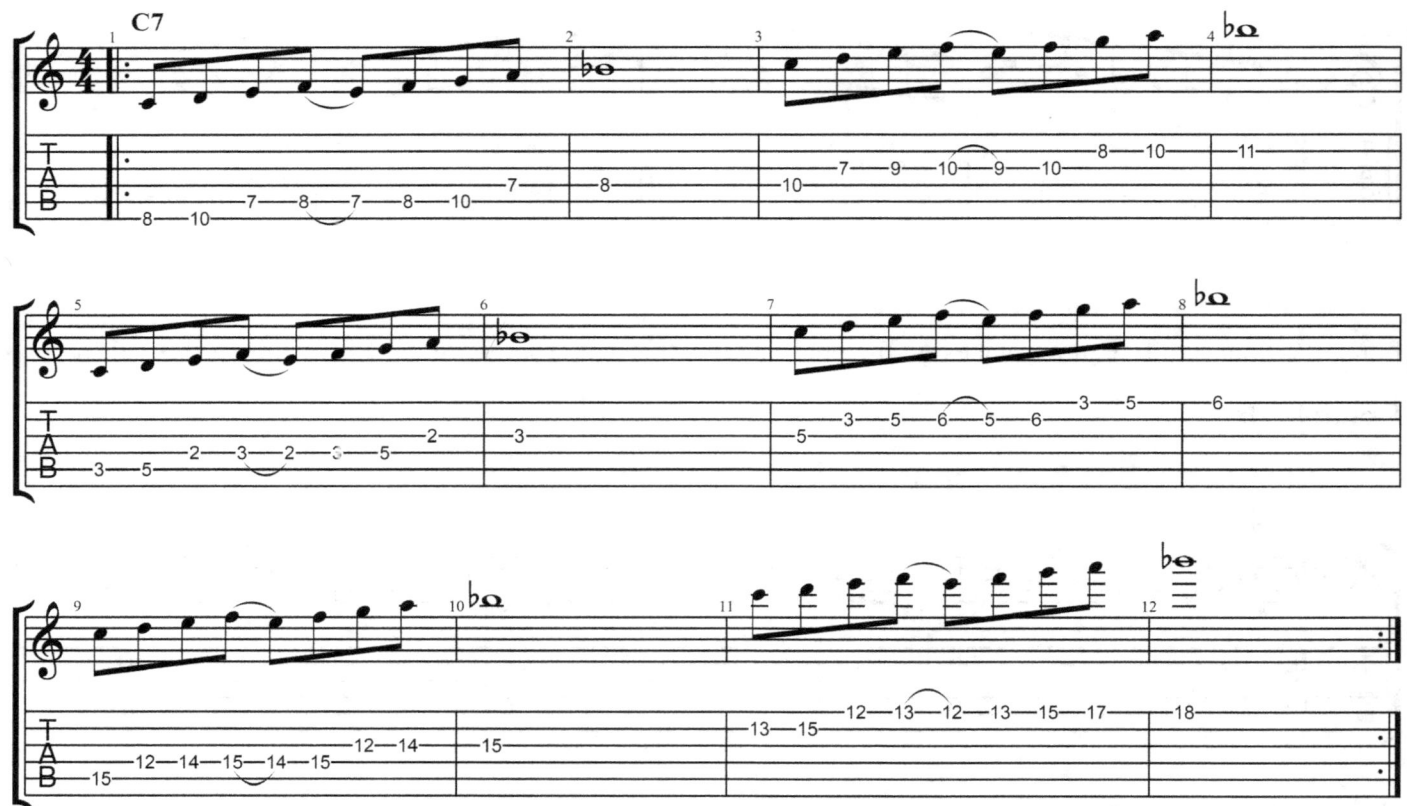

Now let's return to playing the scale along a single string… but with a twist. As in the previous chapter, I want you to play the first note of the scale then close your eyes. Work your way up the scale by listening to the intervals and anticipating each note. The aim is to "hear" the note clearly before you play it. Bonus points if you can sing it – and keep those eyes closed!

To begin with, it will sound just like the major scale, but when we play the 6th and we're anticipating the next note, we're looking for the b7 – a very different sound to the major scale, and we don't have to move far to get it. The big question is… can you hear it?

After playing that, let's apply the melody from Example 4d to a single string too.

Example 4e

Let's talk for a second about application. Although we can move major and minor scales through all twelve keys, we never have to do that when playing real music. Dominant chords, however, are a staple of blues, rock, gospel, jazz and more, where it's common to see a series of dominant chords in a progression that move through several keys.

Take the 12-bar blues, for example. It's a sequence made from three dominant chords.

A 12-bar blues in A contains A7, D7 and E7 chords.

These aren't pop progressions, where it's common to have one scale that fits all the chords. All three dominant chords belong to different keys, so ideally when playing a blues, we want to draw from three different Mixolydian modes:

A7 = A Mixolydian

D7 = D Mixolydian

E7 = E Mixolydian

Let's apply them as scales now.

Example 4f

Let's try the same concept, but over a different chord progression. This time we'll do C7 – D7 – F7 – C7 and play the Mixolydian associated with each chord. Let's also mix things up a little bit by switching positions between repeats.

Example 4g

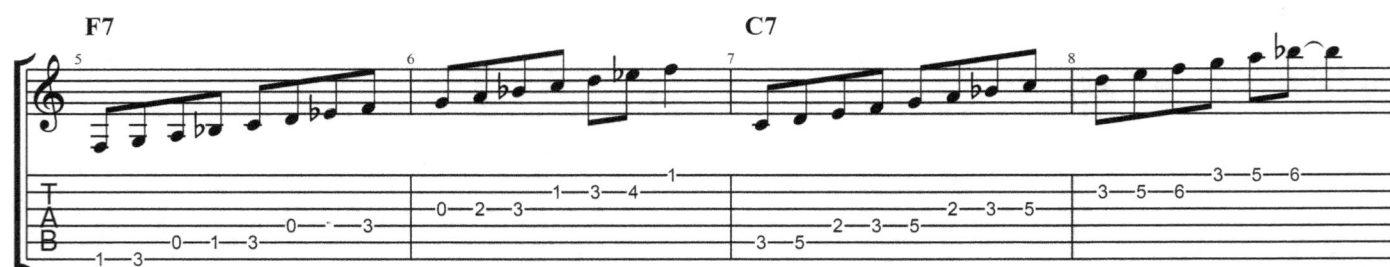

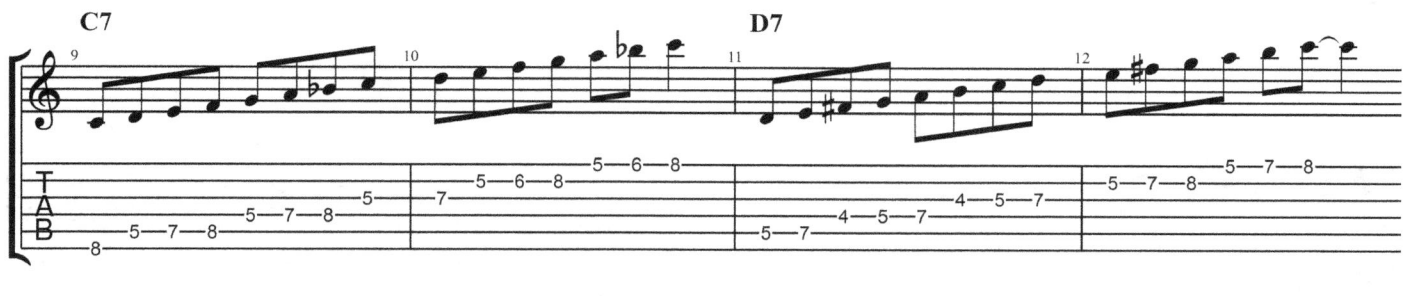

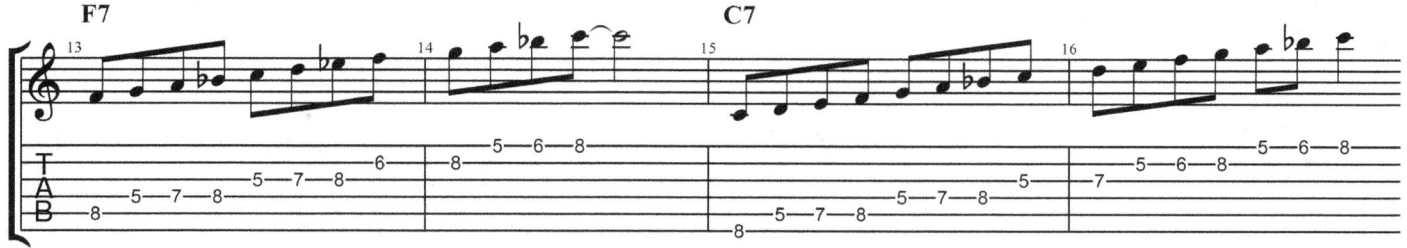

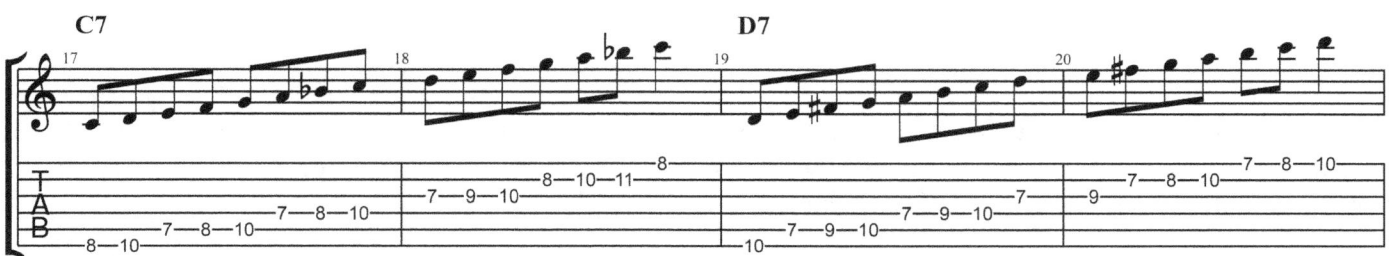

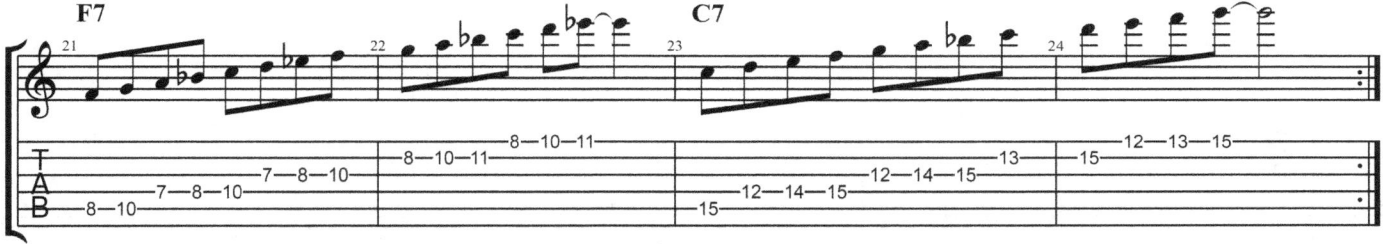

Another way I love to practice my scales is to break them down into smaller melodic cells and play them around the neck and through key changes.

The two primary cells I use from the Mixolydian mode are:

1, 2, 3, 5

1, b7, 6, 5

This is what they look like on the fretboard.

Example 4h

These cells are great for practicing in all twelve keys moving around the Cycle of 4ths. No matter which cell we play, we always start on the root note and we always end on the 5th. In other words, we only need to move down a tone from where we end, and we'll be at the next key/chord.

Here's that idea applied, but with some space between each cell to allow you some thinking/processing time.

Example 4i

This exercise becomes a real head-melter (but also strangely therapeutic when you start to get it) if we move it to a higher position and change chord every two beats.

In my own practice, exercises like this are a battle where I'm trying to work out if I'm using my head ("I'm playing C, so next I'll go to F and ascend…" etc) or trusting the connection I've built between my hands and ears. I know I want it to be the second scenario, but the only way to get there is to slow things down and engage with the former!

Example 4j

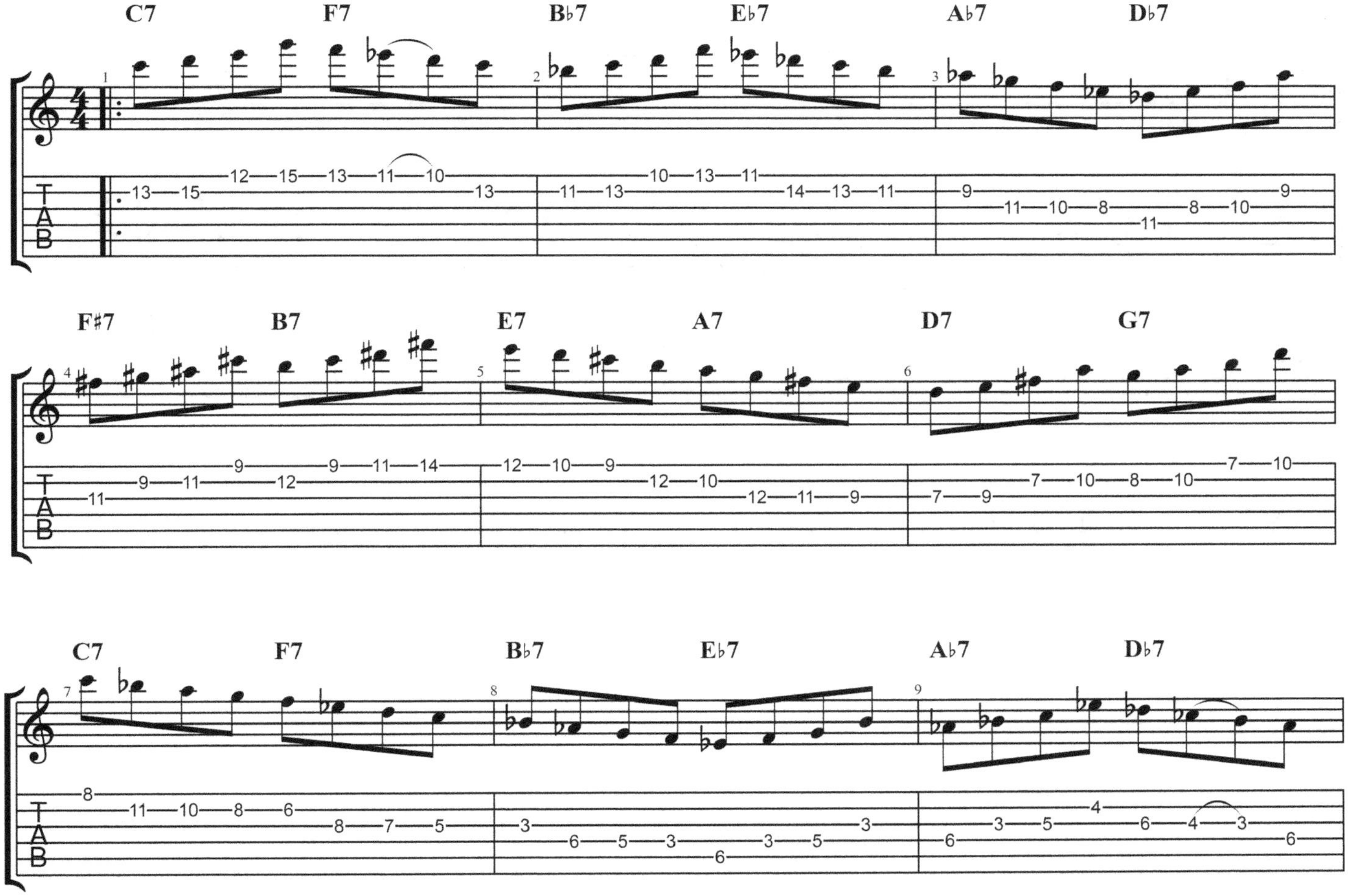

Now let's try a couple of Mixolydian examples that span the whole neck. Like the single-string ideas we've looked at so far, I want you to focus on anticipating the next note and feel how far you need to move to play it.

Example 4k

Here's one more long 1/8th note run, but this time we'll move from G Mixolydian to C Mixolydian.

Example 41

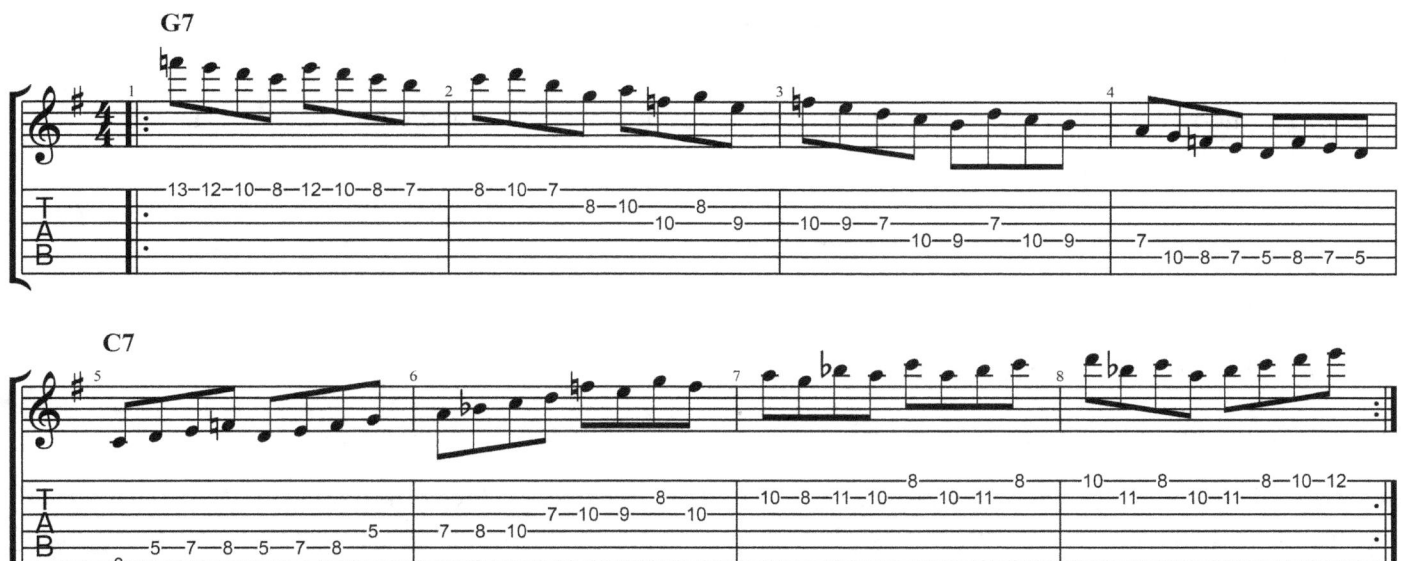

We won't go any further with the dominant scale sound in this chapter, but remember, when you learn the new patterns and ideas contained in the chapters that follow, you should come back and apply those concepts to the Mixolydian mode (or any scale you've learned).

Right, get to work!

Routine Four – Dorian Mode

This week it's time to look at a new mode and, as we learned last week, the best way of doing that is to first look at its pattern of intervals.

The Dorian mode is the second mode of the major scale and has the following interval structure:

1, 2, b3, 4, 5, 6, b7

We could view this as a Mixolydian mode but with a b3.

Or, we could view it as a minor scale with a natural 6th.

So, what's the best way to understand it?

Dorian is a *minor* mode because it has a b3, so it makes most sense to compare it to the minor scale.

In terms of the mood it creates, it has many of the characteristics of the minor sound but with a brighter, funkier edge, because we no longer have that mournful b6. Instead, Dorian adds a very sweet sounding natural 6th. That note is the difference between dark neoclassical minor and upbeat sounding minor blues-rock. Randy Rhoads vs Carlos Santana, if you like.

Let's start by running up and down the natural minor scale, then switch to the Dorian mode. As you do this, really focus on where the 6th is and how it sounds, compared to the b6 of the natural minor.

Example 5a

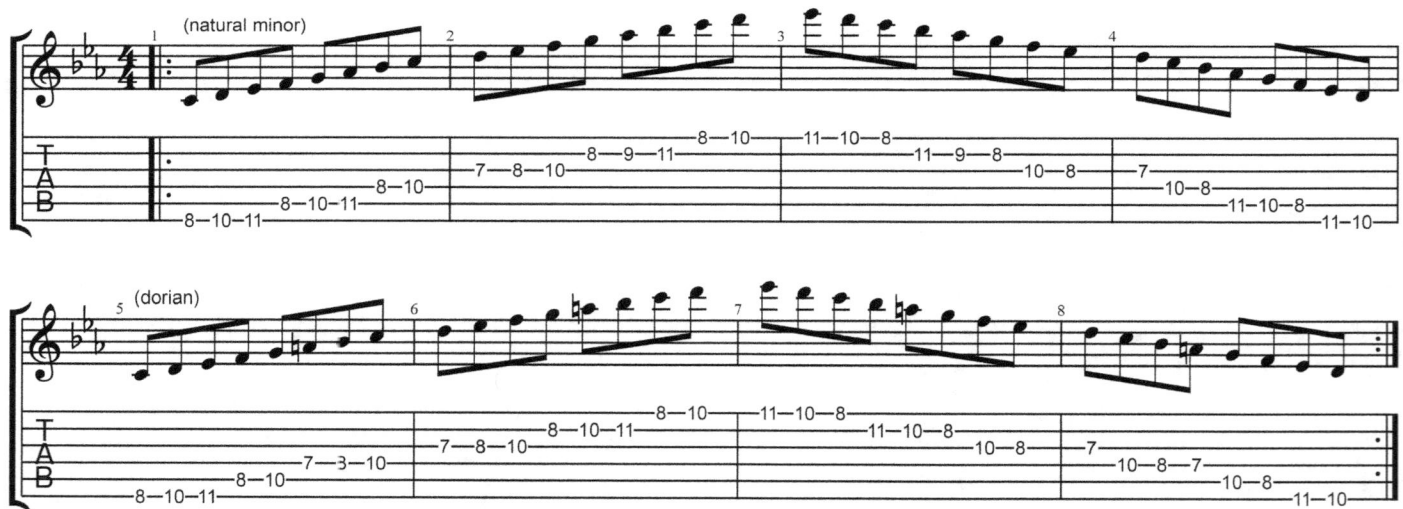

The b6 of the natural minor sounds a little unstable and wants to resolve down to the 5th. The 6th of the Dorian mode is much more stable.

Since the b3 tells us that the scale is minor and the 6th sets it apart from the natural minor, these are the most important "character" notes of Dorian.

Here's the Dorian mode played in the same position in an ascending and descending fashion, but using a sequence of diatonic thirds.

Example 5b

As with every scale, it serves us best if we're able to play it in different places on the neck. Here's the C Dorian mode played from the fifth string root, first as an ascending scale, then descending in a sequence of thirds.

Example 5c

We could also reverse that idea by descending the scale, then ascending the sequence of thirds.

Example 5d

Now let's play the same idea moved up to play the root note on the fifth string with the fourth finger.

Example 5e

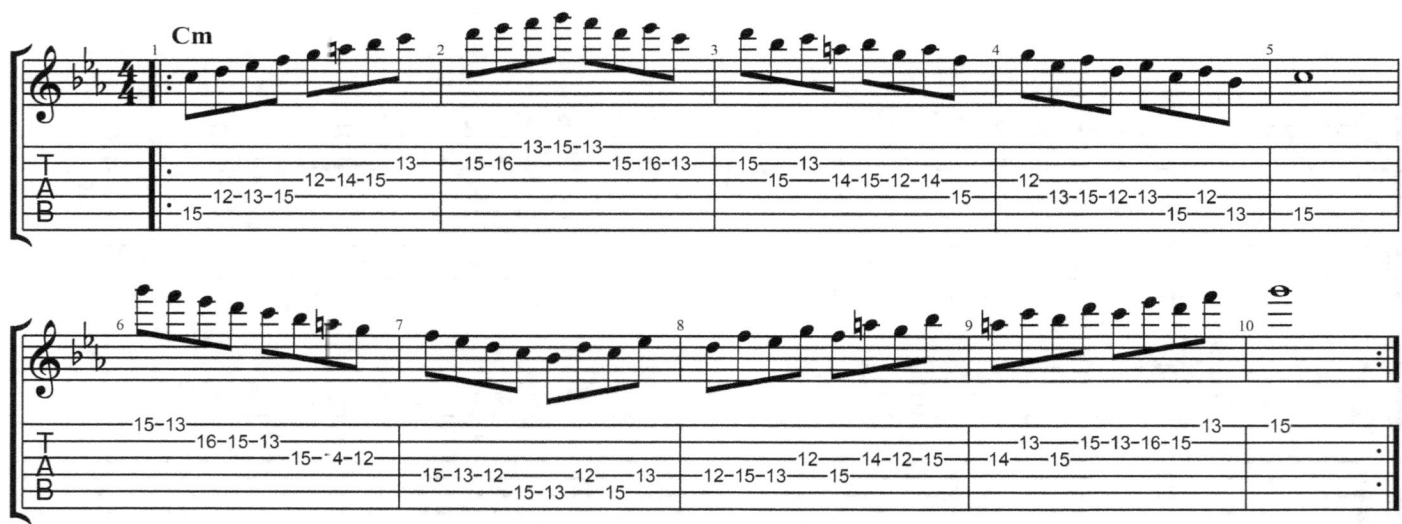

Next, we want to start covering the whole neck with a five-position based system. So, in the following example we'll ascend C Dorian from the 3rd fret (A shape) and when we reach the top of that position we'll shift up to the next one (G shape) and descend. Then we'll ascend the E shape, descend the D, ascend the C, then we're back at the A shape an octave higher.

Example 5f

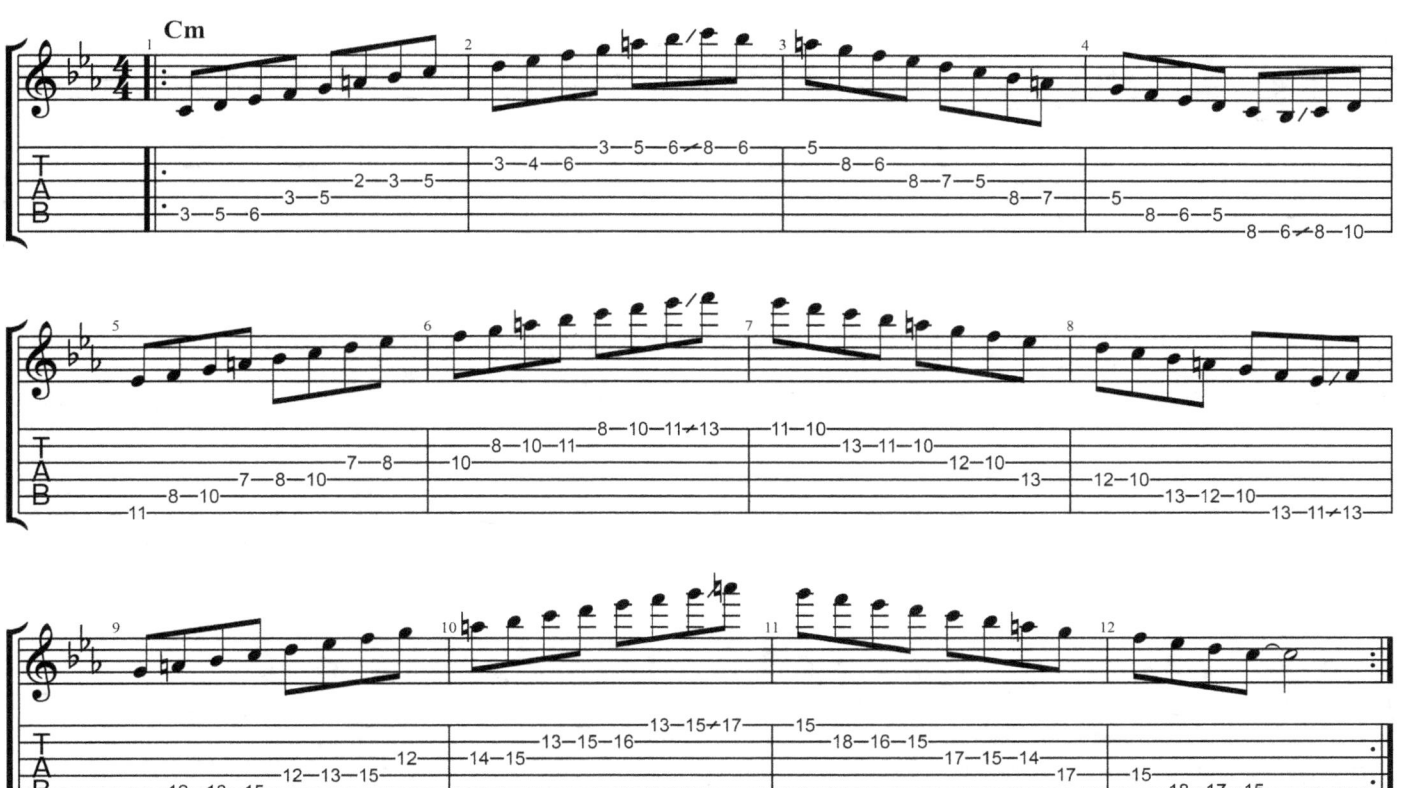

The Dorian mode is one of the staples of the rock-fusion sound, with guitarists like Greg Howe and Guthrie Govan using it extensively in compositions. A common chord progression in this context has minor 7 chords moving up in minor 3rd intervals, such as,

Cm7 – Ebm7 – F#m7 – Am7

This is a great progression to work on because it's both musical and lays out well on the fretboard.

In the next exercise we'll play over this chord progression, but we'll keep our hand around the 8th fret area.

Example 5g

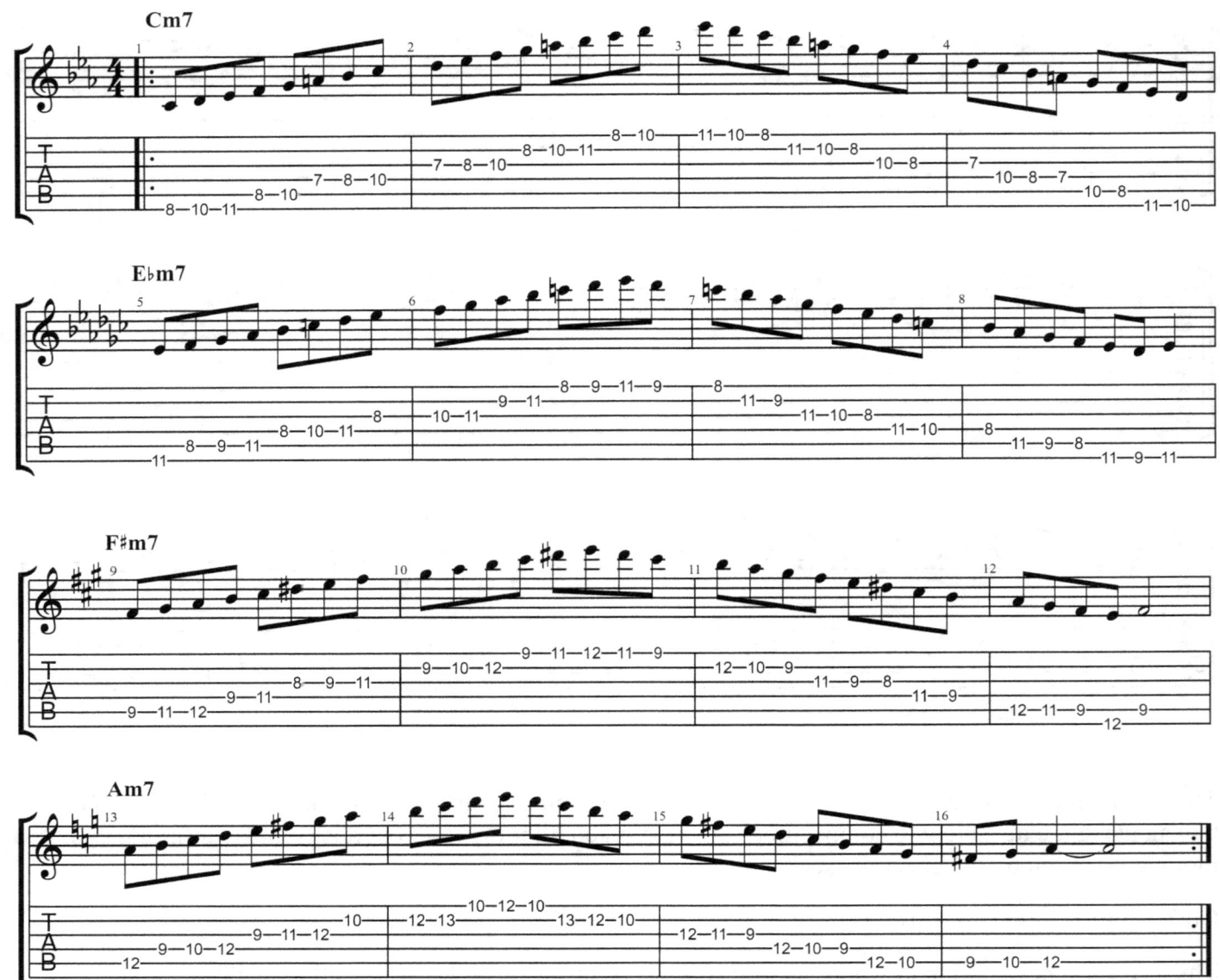

We could play this same progression in any area of the neck, like here in the 3rd fret zone.

Example 5h

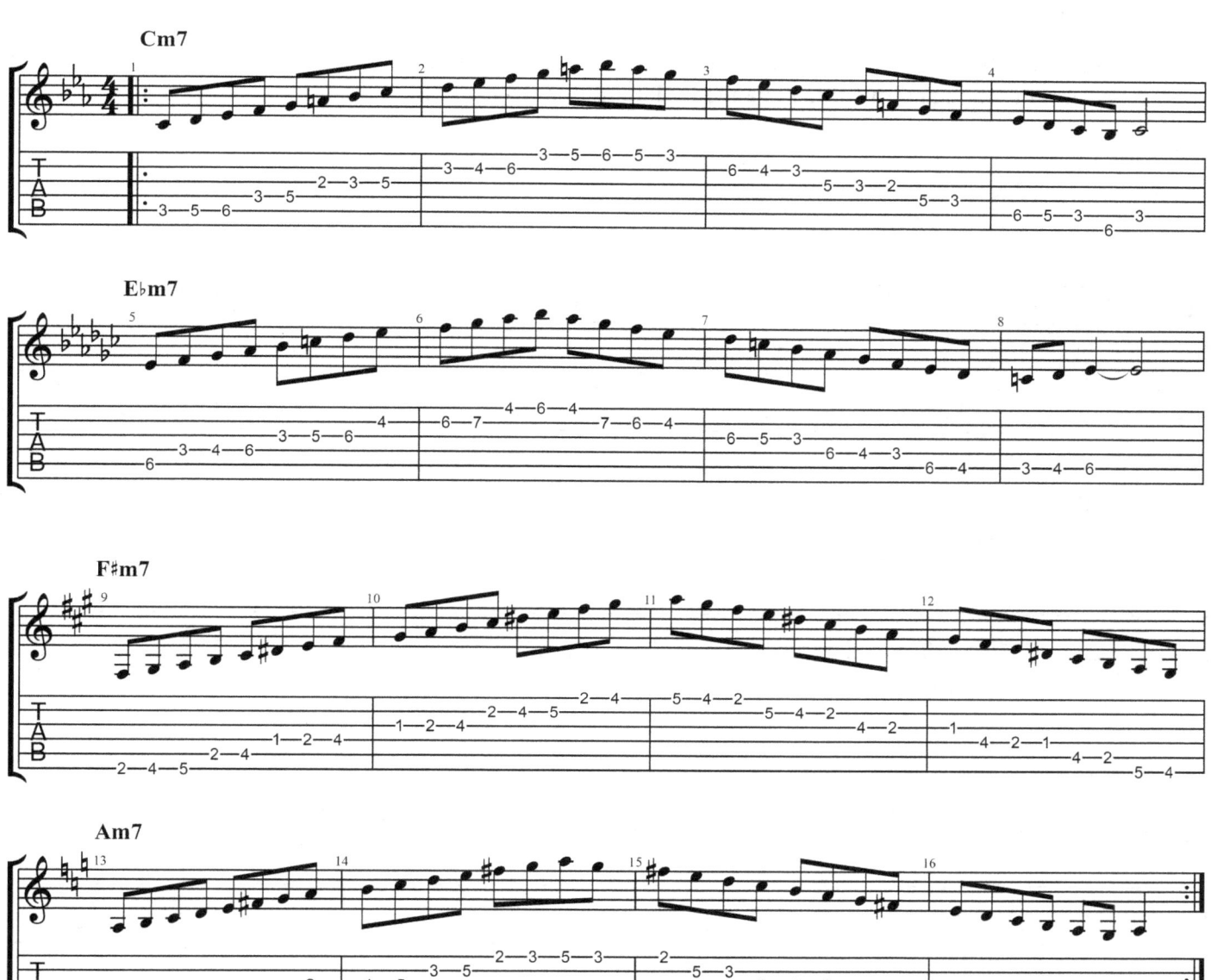

Now we're going to make it harder… much harder!

Using the same chord progression, we could work at connecting each Dorian mode by the *next closest note* instead of just changing when we get to the bottom of the scale.

To work on this, we'll start by giving our brains the best chance we can. We'll play nine notes, one on each beat moving up the scale and ending in bar three. When we're there, we'll leave two whole bars to work out where the next note is.

So, for example, we ascend the C Dorian mode and come to rest on the 2nd. Now we're looking at the fretboard and trying to map out the upcoming Eb Dorian mode, so we can see where the closest note is. In this case, we can actually move up one fret to land on the root of Eb Dorian.

As we ascend the Eb Dorian scale, we come to rest on the b7. Again, we're giving ourselves two bars to map out the F# Dorian mode and make the change by landing on its 4th, etc.

Example 5i

When I teach this idea, I always liken it to the RAM in a computer. The tech savvy among you will know the pain of needing your computer to do multiple tasks while struggling with 8 or even 4GB of RAM.

In the early stages of learning the fretboard, our brain struggles to complete multiple tasks simultaneously, but that's what we need it to do. So, we have to work on this method of creating stress on the brain while practicing. This is the only way we're going to see real results.

We must keep tweaking things to keep the pressure on – change positions, start at the top and come down, play for three bars rather than two (giving yourself half the time to try and see the change) or even increase the tempo. But the *real* challenge comes when we remove the long note. Here's the same exercise, but now we'll just play 1/4 notes through the changes without pausing.

Example 5j

Another approach is to place a restriction on yourself and, at the same time, limit the note options you're looking for. For example, we can play the same exercise in 1/8th notes, which increases the difficulty, but when we need to change scale, we'll just aim for the root, b3 of 5th of the next chord – the strong notes.

Notice that we're staying on the top four strings (apart from one note) in this exercise – a further limitation that narrow our options.

Example 5k

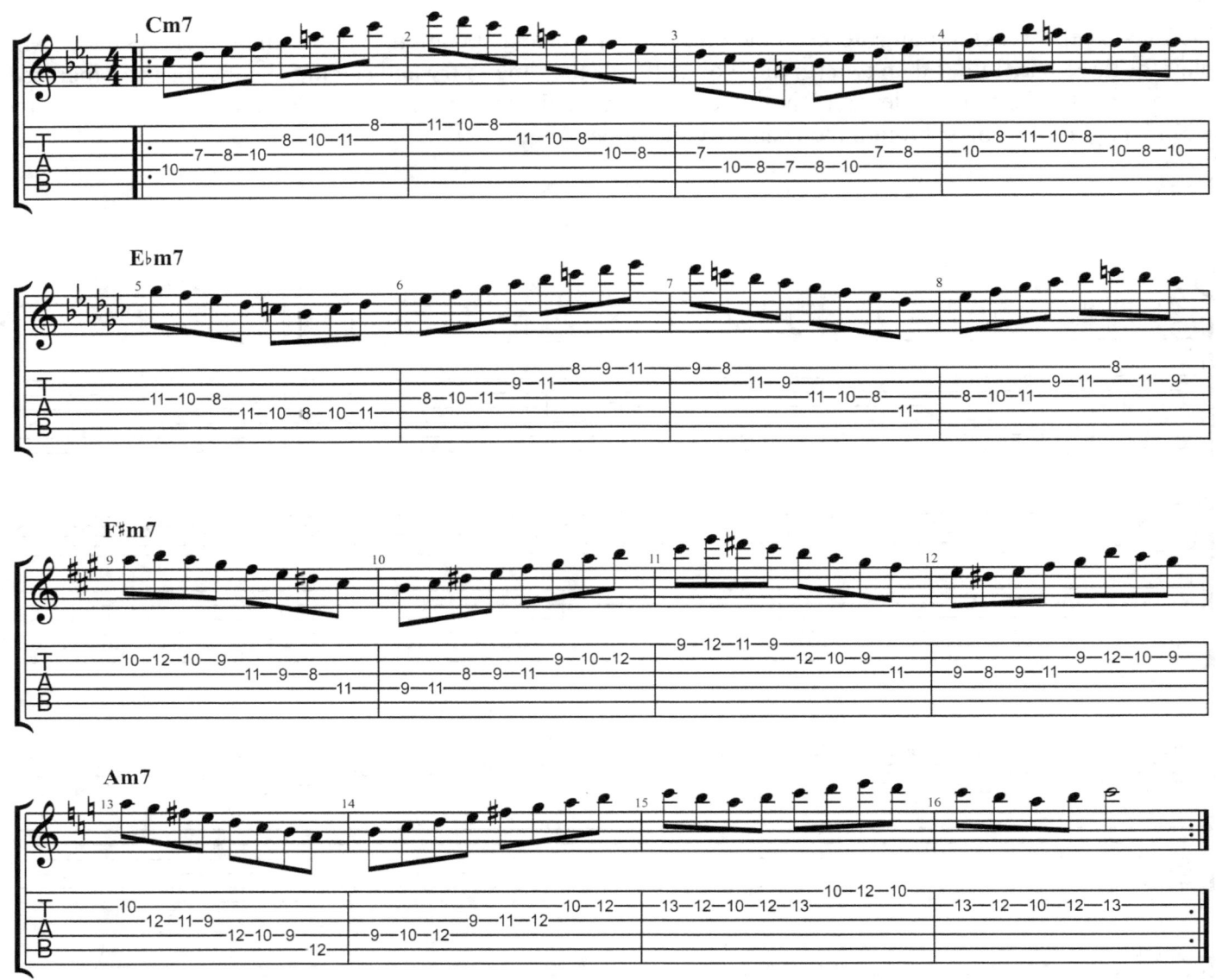

I can't stress this enough, but remember that this exercise is not about memorising and repeating exactly what I play here. Sure, learn that first, but ultimately, it's about learning to apply a concept. If it helps, sit down with a pen and paper and write your own pathway through the scales. When you're fluent at playing that, put it away and write a new one. Then look for a different way, and so on. Keep flexing that brain and you'll be fast-tracking your RAM upgrade!

Let's finish this routine with another good exercise to help us break away from lines that start on the root and ascend – one that also forces us to think about and visualise the intervals.

Here, we'll start by playing the C root note, then jump up to the b3 an octave higher. This is training us to be able to see key notes in each of our scale positions. To me, the b3 is the best note in any of the minor modes!

Example 5l

Now let's take that same melodic idea and apply it to the modulating minor 7 chords from the previous exercises.

Example 5m

The previous exercise is such a fun one to apply to all the previous scales, but you can also do it by moving up to other intervals. So, in the final example we'll jump up to the 5th each time instead of the b3.

Example 5n

OK, get to work and I'll see you on the next routine!

Routine Five – Pentatonic Scales

When planning this three-book series on scales, chords and arpeggios, I did a lot of thinking about what to do with pentatonic scales. Pentatonics are described as scales, but since they only contain five notes they have more in common with arpeggios than scales.

I could easily devote an entire book to pentatonic scales, as our own Shaun Baxter did recently with *just* the dominant pentatonic scale! Instead, I've included pentatonics here as a way of presenting to you something we've been secretly working on all along, and to show you where we'll be going with it, moving forward.

Many years ago, I was lucky enough to get some one-on-one time with the amazing modern jazz guitarist Wayne Krantz – then based in New York, now residing in Buenos Aires. For those who don't know, Wayne is *really* into intervals. After he'd been playing for some time, he began to think of every seven-note scale as just a collection of seven different intervallic ingredients. That led him to produce his book, *An Improviser's OS*, in which he presents every possible combination of interval collections that contain between two and eleven notes. In other words, for those looking for the ultimate resource, the book contains *everything* found in the Western twelve-tone system – every two-note interval, every triad, every arpeggio, every pentatonic scale, and so on – it's all there.

I say this to make the point that pentatonic scales are *just another collection of intervals* like any scale. You'll have almost certainly learned them as a series of shapes and patterns on the fretboard, but I want to encourage you to learn the formulas for these scales and begin to identify the intervals on the fretboard. This may feel like a backward step and harder at first, but in the long run it's going to open many doors in your playing.

Let's start by looking at the major pentatonic scale, which has the formula,

1, 2, 3, 5, 6

That's an interesting collection of notes. It's a major scale that's missing its 4th and 7th. It's also the Mixolydian mode minus its 4th and b7, which makes the major pentatonic a wonderfully versatile tool that will work in either context.

Here is the G Major Pentatonic scale laid out in three positions on the fretboard to get you started. As you play through this, think about the intervals rather than the pattern, and test how confidently you can visualise these notes as intervals that belong to scales you've already worked on.

Example 6a

It's most common to see pentatonic scales presented in two-note-per-string patterns and there are lots of sequences you can work on to keep yourself on your toes with these patterns.

For example, starting on the root note, you can ascend four notes of the scale, then go back to the second note in the scale and ascend four notes again. Then ascend four notes from the third note in the scale, and so on.

Here's that sequence ascending and descending in the first pattern. There are times when there are two notes on the same fret on adjacent strings, so you'll quickly realise that you need to sharpen up your "finger rolling" technique i.e., play both notes using the same finger, rolling from one string to the next. The notes shouldn't ring into each other, so be careful with that detail.

Example 6b

Here's the same idea played from a fifth string root. Here, we ascend in that position, then move up and descend the next position.

Example 6c

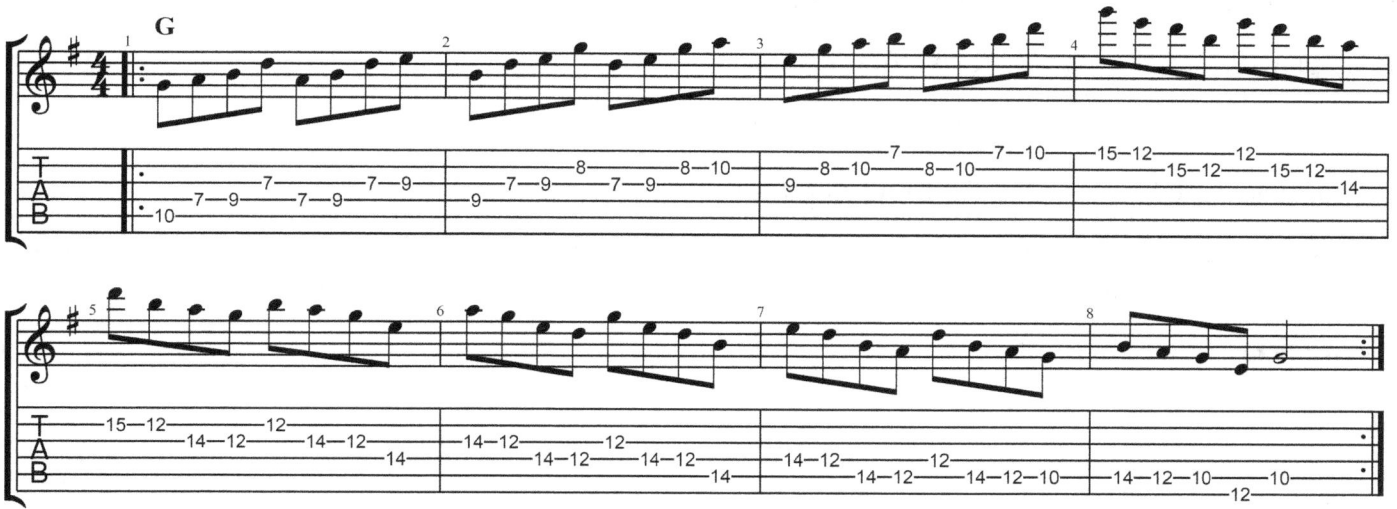

Another great sequence that is both musical and a great technical workout is to split these two-note-per-string patterns into lower and higher notes. We can play the two lower notes on adjacent strings, followed by the higher two, as below.

Note how we ascend one position, descend the next, then ascend the final one. This keeps us working on both the scale and the technique.

Example 6d

It's great to know these two-note-per-string patterns, but now let's work on breaking out of them using what I call the "if this, therefore this" approach.

What I mean by that is, as we develop an understanding of our intervals and their relationship to each other, we can use the location of one thing we know to tell us the location of something we're looking for.

For example, any time we play the root note, the 2nd will always be two frets higher.

If we play the 5th, the 6th will be two frets higher.

If we play the 6th, the root will be three frets higher.

We can also learn these relationships on adjacent strings.

Here's a G Major Pentatonic scale played ascending and descending from the bottom of the neck to the top and back again. It's good to work on ideas like this slowly enough that your brain can keep up!

Example 6e

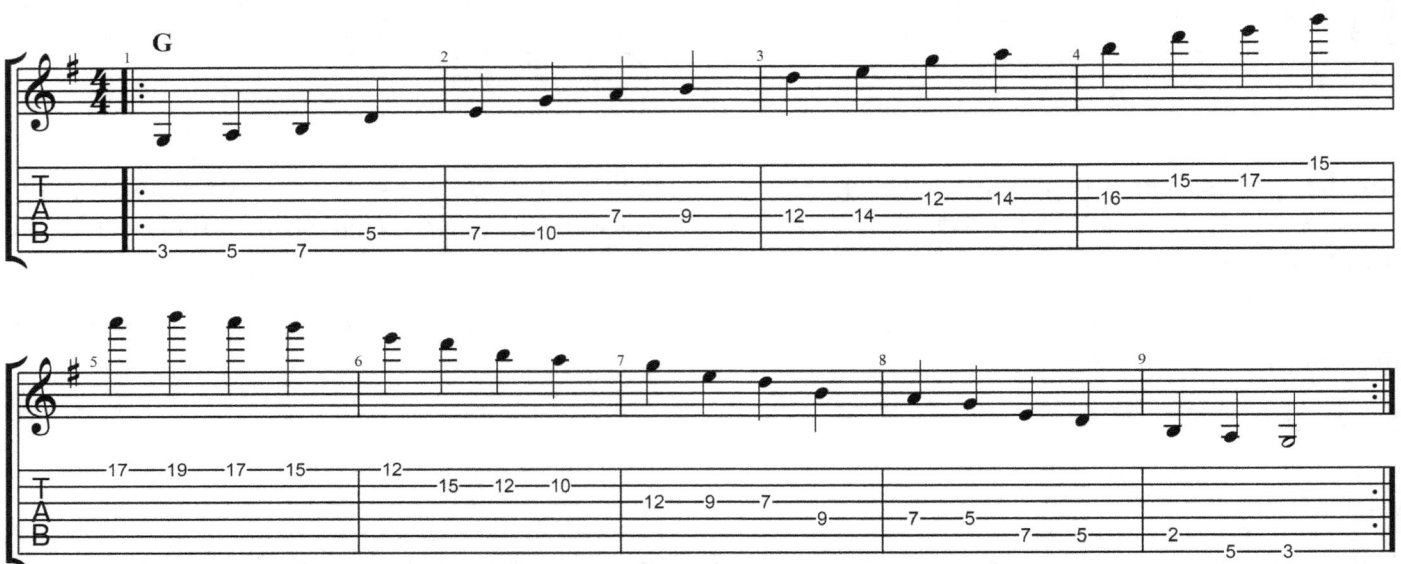

Now let's take a look at the minor pentatonic scale. As with the major, if you take the time to learn the intervals, you'll know this stuff better than ever. The intervallic formula for the minor pentatonic scale is,

1, b3, 4, 5, b7

It's the minor scale but missing its 2nd and b6. It's also the Dorian mode without its 2nd and natural 6th. The minor pentatonic works well in both those musical contexts.

There are lots of ways we can play the scale, but the following positions are a good start.

Example 6f

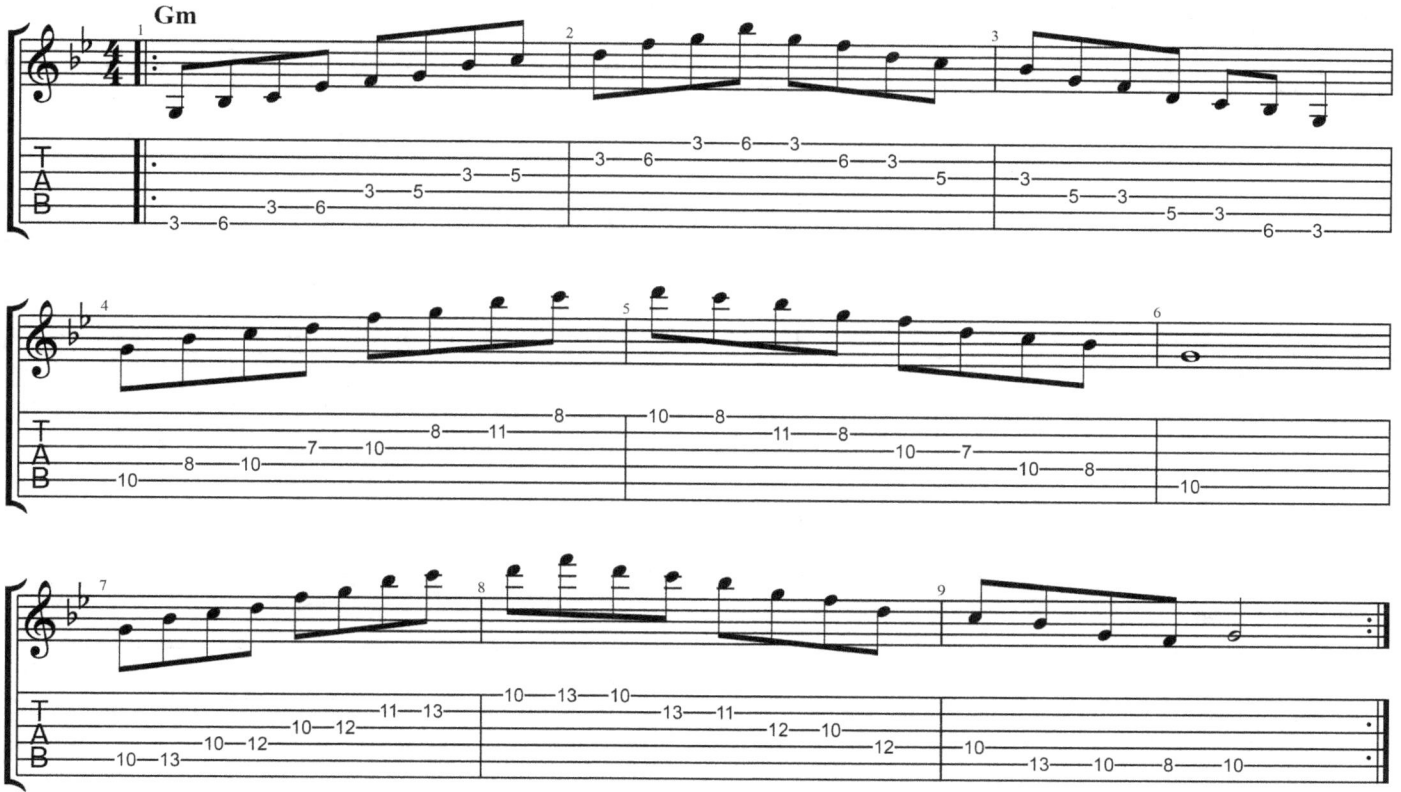

We want to really know our positions inside out, so here are the five positions broken down in the "low–high" sequence.

Example 6g

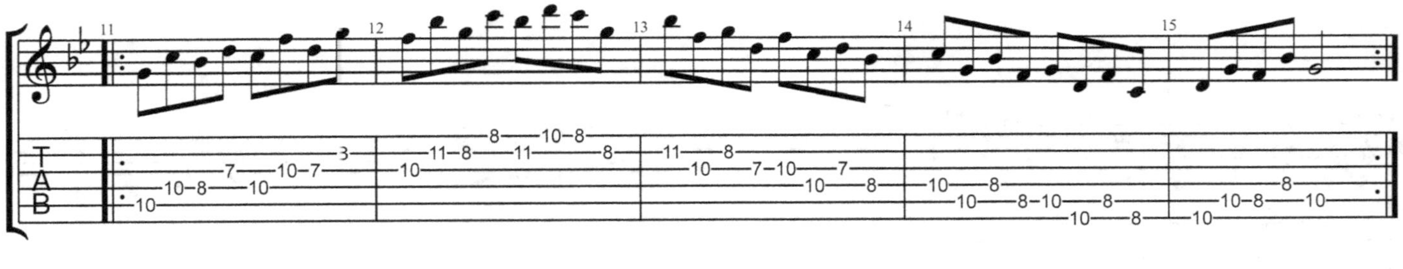

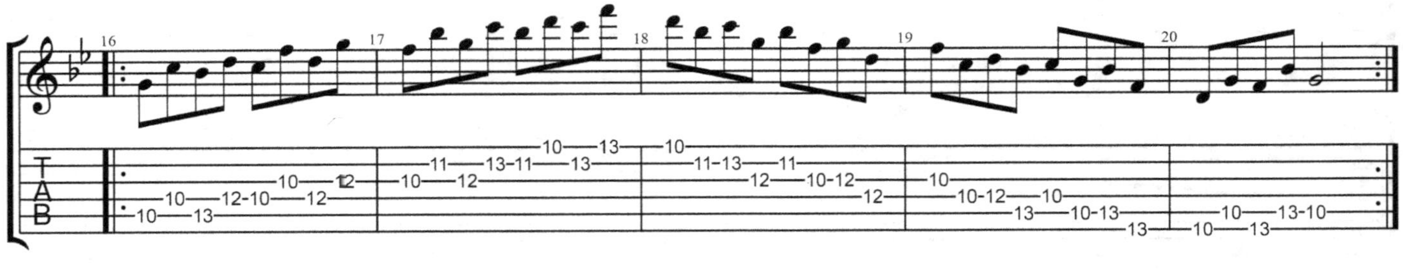

One of my favourite pentatonic patterns to work with is an Eric Johnson inspired series of descending fives. We start on the first string and descend five notes. This takes us down to the third string. Then we move back to the second string, play the higher of the two notes on that string, then descend five notes again, etc.

At the moment, our aim is not to be able to play this at blistering speed like Eric, we're just concerned with perfecting the finger rolling technique and focusing on getting our heads around the five-note pattern offset against the 4/4 rhythm.

Example 6h

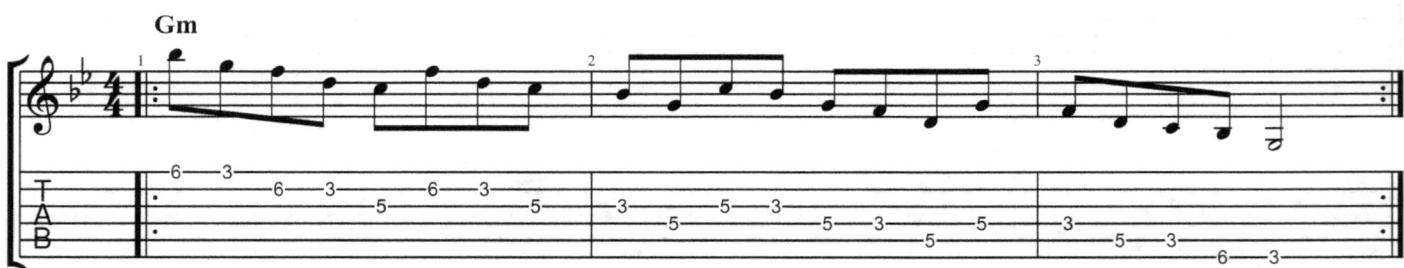

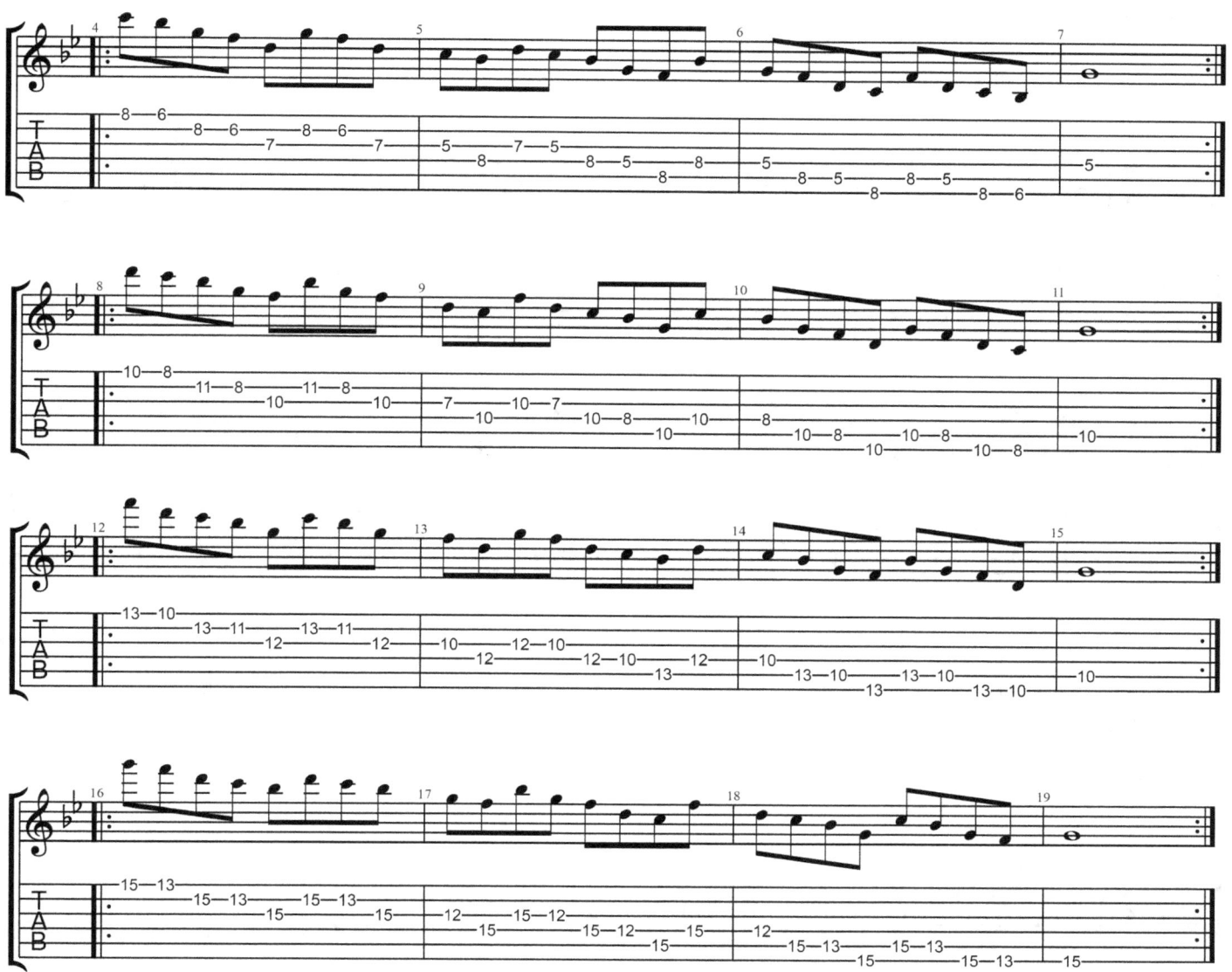

One of the more influential lessons I've had was when Guthrie Govan talked about how he views modes. He made the point that they don't have to be a binary thing, i.e., on or off. We can treat them more like a dimmer switch. In other words, we can play something that sounds *really obviously* Dorian, or we can ease off on the Dorian flavours and use the mode in a more subtle way.

Pentatonics are a great vehicle for doing this, because they can give us a nice skeleton of each mode without necessarily committing to the colourful notes. Then, when we want to add flavour, we can add other intervals around our pentatonic phrases to bring the spice.

For example, we could play the minor pentatonic scale, but each time we play the b3, add the 2nd after it, like this.

Example 6i

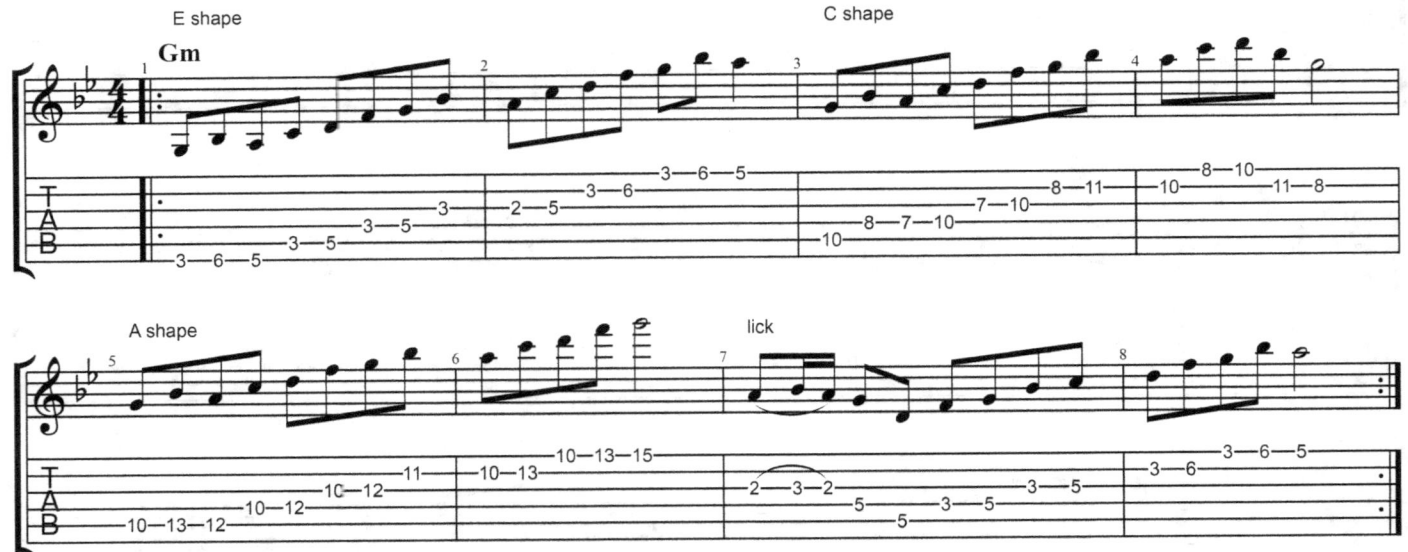

Here's another approach, where we add in the 6th interval around the minor pentatonic to give it some Dorian funkiness.

Example 6j

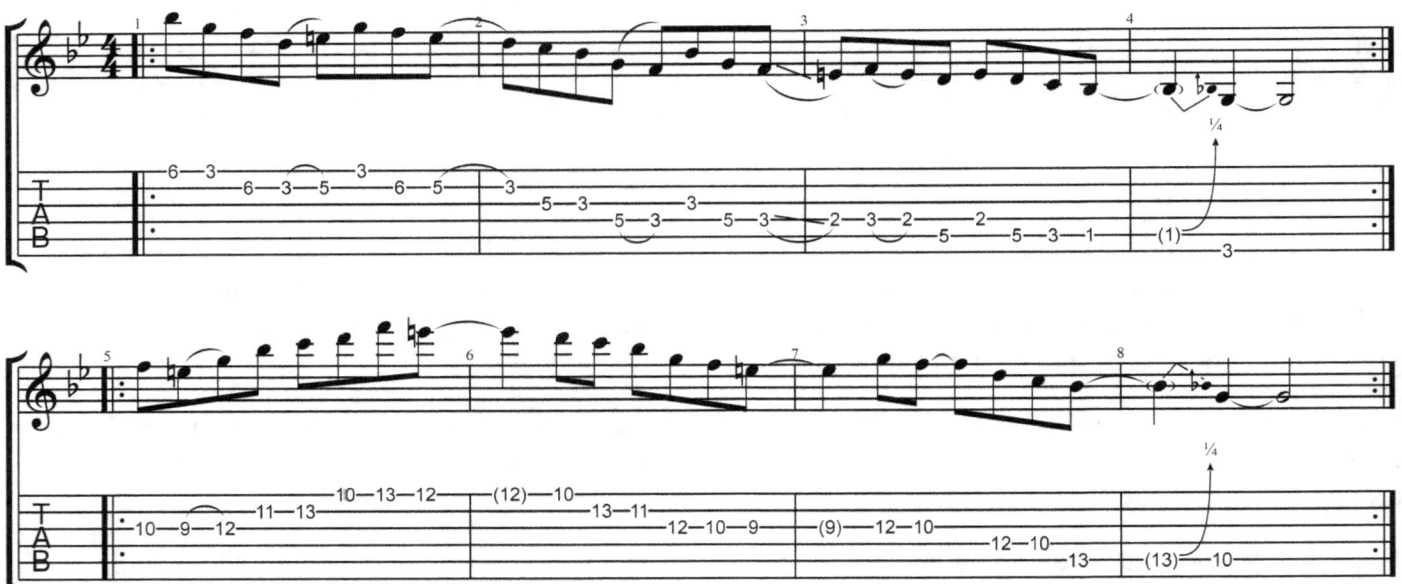

We can do this with the major pentatonic too! Here's a melody using the C Major Pentatonic scale, where we're adding the b7 to emphasise the Mixolydian sound.

Example 6k

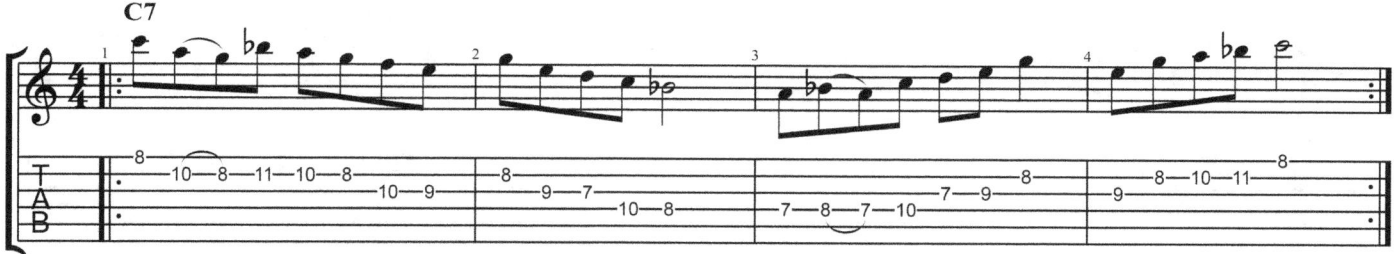

And here's another melody using C Major Pentatonic where we add the 7th to create a major scale sound.

Example 6l

To finish this chapter, I want us to consider a few other options that come under the category of pentatonic scales. This is a big topic in its own right, so this is just an overview.

First is the "dominant pentatonic" scale. This is like the major pentatonic scale, but with its 6th interval raised to a b7 to make it perfectly fit a dominant 7 chord.

Example 6m

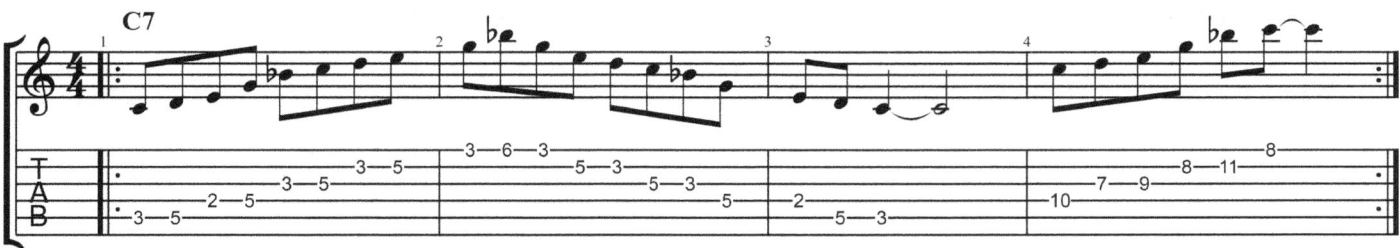

A cool alternative to this idea is to take the minor pentatonic scale and raise its b3 to a natural 3rd to give us 1, 3, 4, 5, b7. I've not seen anyone agree on a name for this scale, but it's another option for dominant chords.

Example 6n

Another nice variant of the minor pentatonic scale is one where we switch the b7 for a 6th (1, b3, 4, 5, 6).

Example 6o

And finally, here is a collection of scales often referred to as the Japanese pentatonic scales (however inaccurate that statement may be!), which includes the Akebono (1, 2, b3, 5, b6), Hirajoshi (1, b2, 4, 5, b6) and Kumoi (1, b2, 4, b5, b7). These are all wonderful sounds you can work on all over the neck.

Example 6p

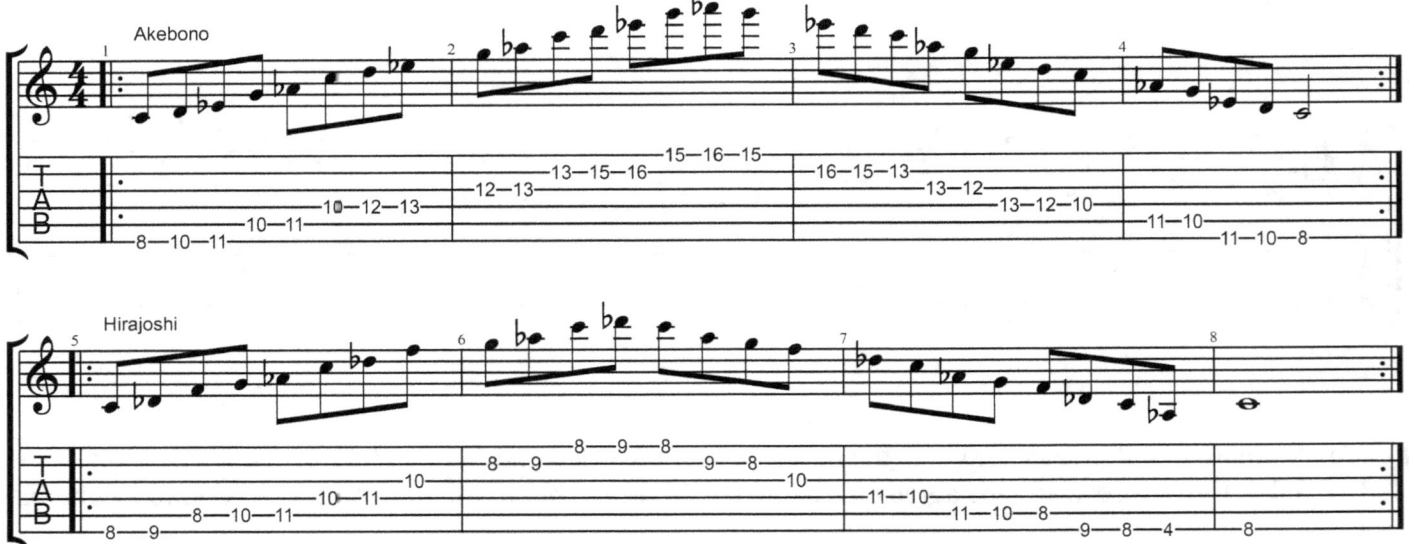

I hope you've grasped the idea that our plain major and minor pentatonic scales provide a great framework around which we can pinpoint and add certain intervals to bring out different colours, depending on the musical context and the sound we're going for.

There is a lot of information here and huge potential for developing ideas that may take many years of practice, but hopefully, the idea of intervals simply being building blocks for all our scales will be something you'll see value in and continue to develop moving forward.

Routine Six – Harmonic Minor

With major scale harmony and its most important modes out of the way, I wanted to devote a little time to some other common collections of notes, and the logical place to look after the major scale is the harmonic minor scale.

The harmonic minor scale gets its name from the way it is used – as the basis for creating much of the harmony in minor keys.

The harmonic minor is identical to the natural minor scale, but the b7 is raised to a natural 7th.

Natural Minor = 1, 2, b3, 4, 5, b6, b7

Harmonic Minor = 1, 2, b3, 4, 5, b6, 7

This single note difference means that, whereas chord V in the key of A Natural Minor is Em7, in the key of A Harmonic Minor it's E7.

That dominant V chord is often used to create a strong resolution in minor key music, so it's common to see the harmonic minor used in that context.

With its formula of 1, 2, b3, 4, 5, b6, 7, in the key of C that gives us the notes C, D, Eb, F, G, Ab, B. Let's play the scale and listen to how it sounds. We'll start on a single string, as we've done before, so we can clearly see the interval distances between the notes.

Example 7a

The first thing you should notice here (aside from the striking sound of the scale!) is that we now have a tone and a half gap between the b6 and the 7. This leap is immediately apparent when you hear the scale being used. Some say it has a very classical sound, but it's also a sound heard in lots of Eastern European folk music.

Let's play the scale with a root note at the 8th fret. There are two distinct fingering approaches. The first features that tone and a half gap on the second string in a three-note-per-string fashion that requires more of a hand stretch; the second fits more into the CAGED framework.

67

Example 7b

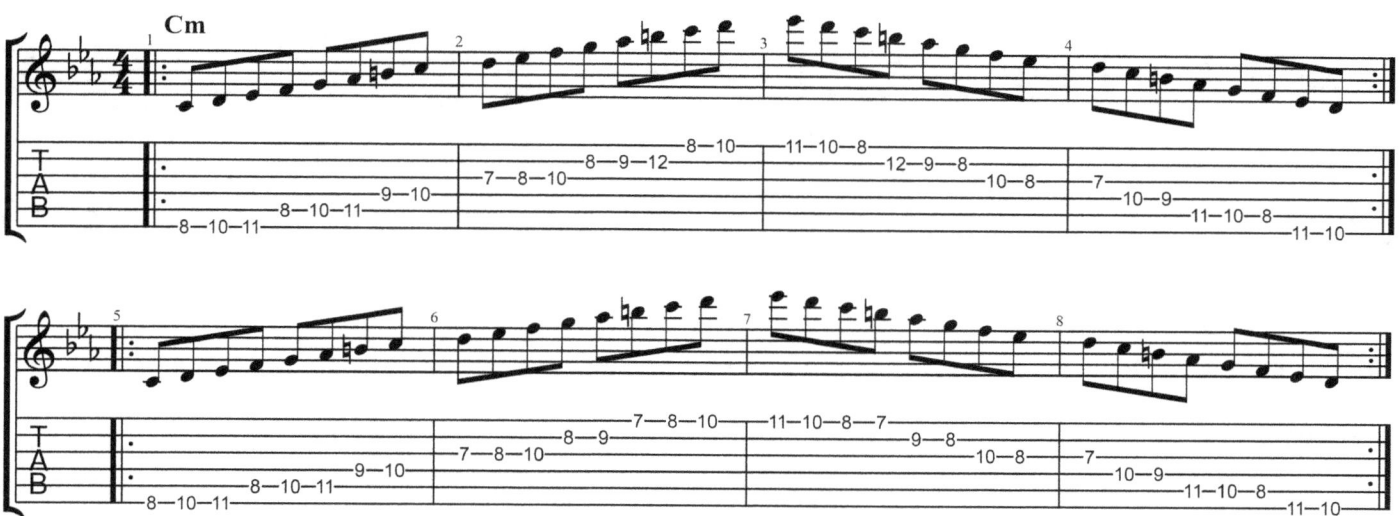

Both approaches have their drawbacks. While the stretch is harder on the hand, the CAGED approach requires us to be confident playing four notes on a string sometimes. This demands good control on shift slides.

A shift slide is where we play two notes on the same string using the same finger by shifting position. Both notes are still picked (unlike a legato slide) and the goal is to not even hear that we've used the shift slide. Here's the upper octave of the previous example with shift slides notated. We always shift using the last possible finger, so that's the fourth finger when ascending and the first finger when descending.

Example 7c

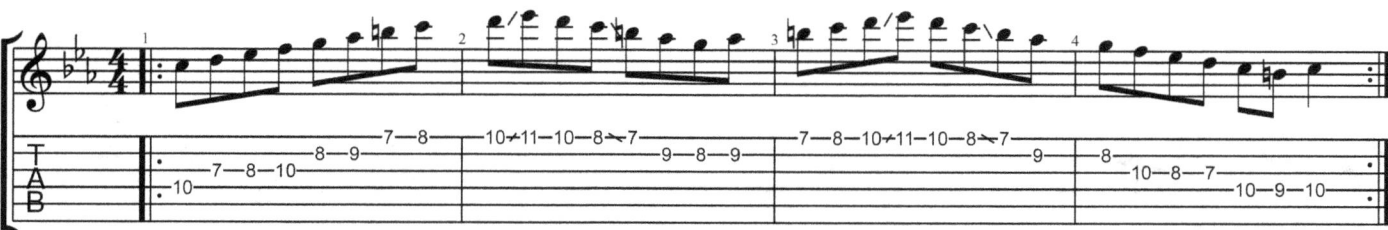

The nature of the guitar means that sometimes you have to play the pattern you least prefer. For example, when I play C Harmonic Minor around the 3rd fret, I must play a stretch on the first string.

Example 7d

Here's the same scale, now played with the fourth finger up on the 15th fret.

Example 7e

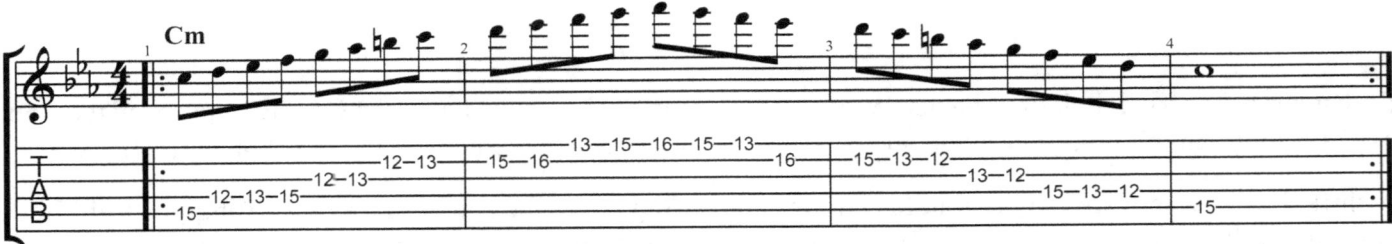

It's possible to organise your harmonic minor lines so that you don't have to deal with the stretch or shift slides, and you'll see a lot of rock players doing things like Example 7f.

Example 7f

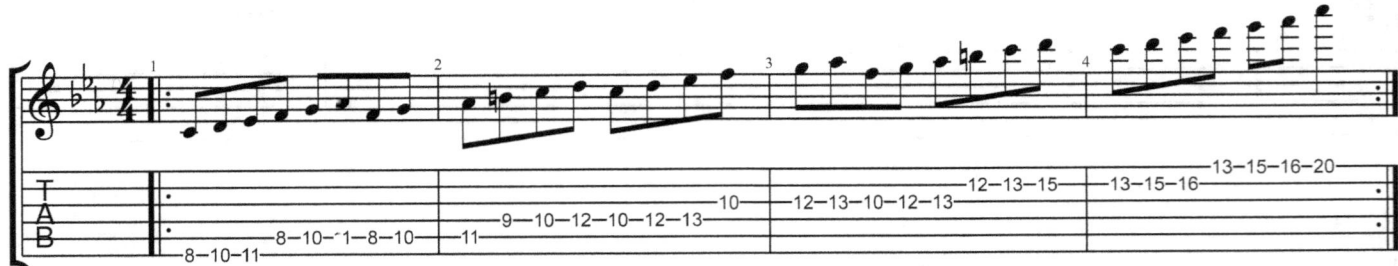

You'll see Malmsteen using a pattern like this on songs like *Trilogy*, although here we're playing in C Harmonic Minor.

Example 7g

The harmonic minor scale is an interesting little beast, because unlike everything we've covered in these routines so far, we can't play this scale around either of the basic pentatonic patterns.

The 3rd of the major pentatonic clashes with the b3 of the harmonic minor, and the b7 of the minor pentatonic clashes with the natural 7th of the harmonic minor.

This means there's no great pentatonic solution for the harmonic minor scale, so it demands that we put time into learning sequences. For example, here's a pattern of "4s" played ascending and descending.

Example 7h

How about applying the same sequence, but now descending then ascending.

Example 7i

Now I want to take our 3rds pattern, work it up and along the neck, and then down again. Once again, real mastery of a scale is being able to *hear it*, not just knowing where to put your fingers because you've played patterns over and over.

Example 7j

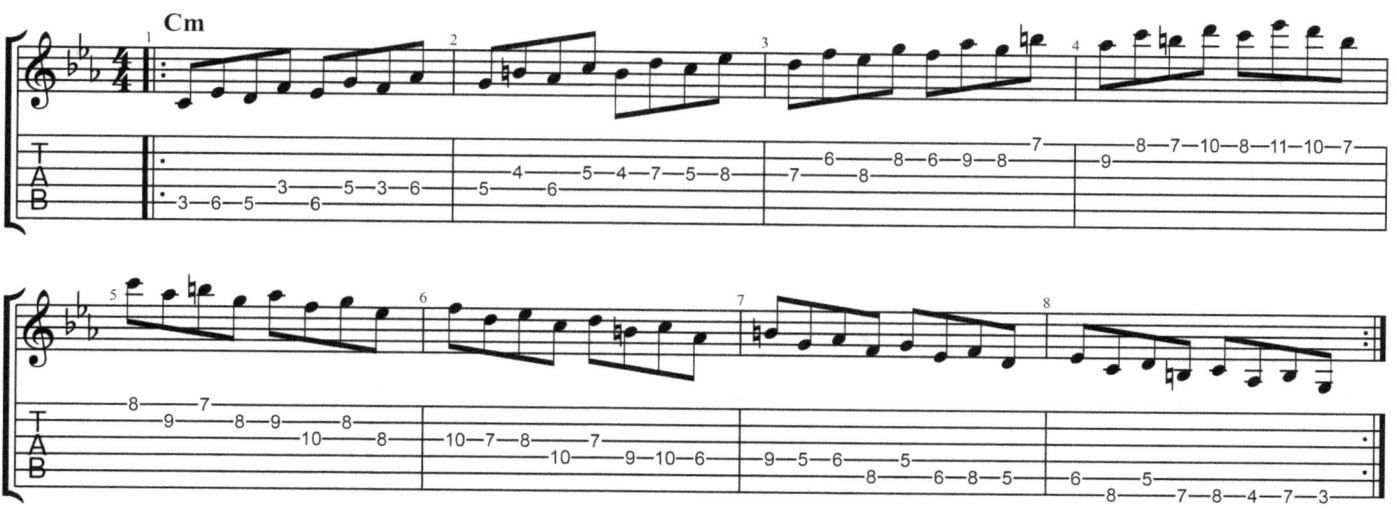

For our last few exercises, I want us to look the first steps of actually using the harmonic minor scale in chord progressions. This will force us to practice switching into and out of this new sound.

As mentioned, the first place we'll tend to use the harmonic minor is over a V – I sequence in a minor key. For a progression that goes Cm – Abmaj7 – G7 – Cm, the C Natural Minor scale will work great over the Cm and Abmaj7 chords, but over the G7 we really want to be playing C Harmonic Minor.

Here's a simple scalic approach over those chords.

Example 7k

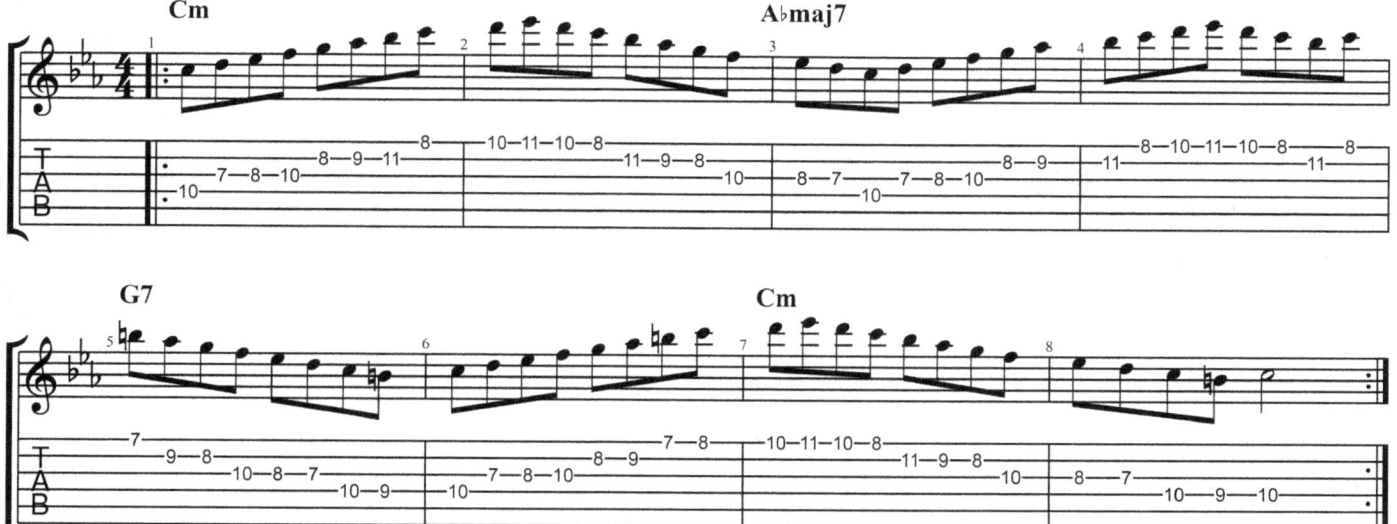

Of course, we can do this anywhere on the neck.

Example 7l

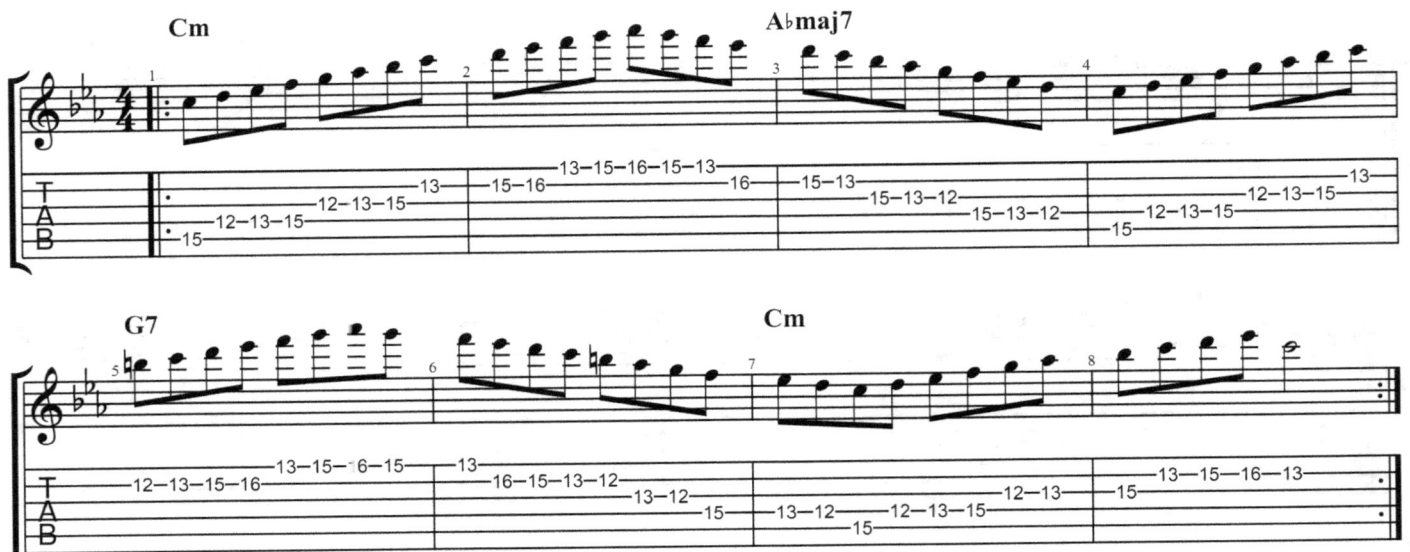

But not all melodies are just runs of 1/8th notes, so here's a little melody using some scale patterns over that progression.

Example 7m

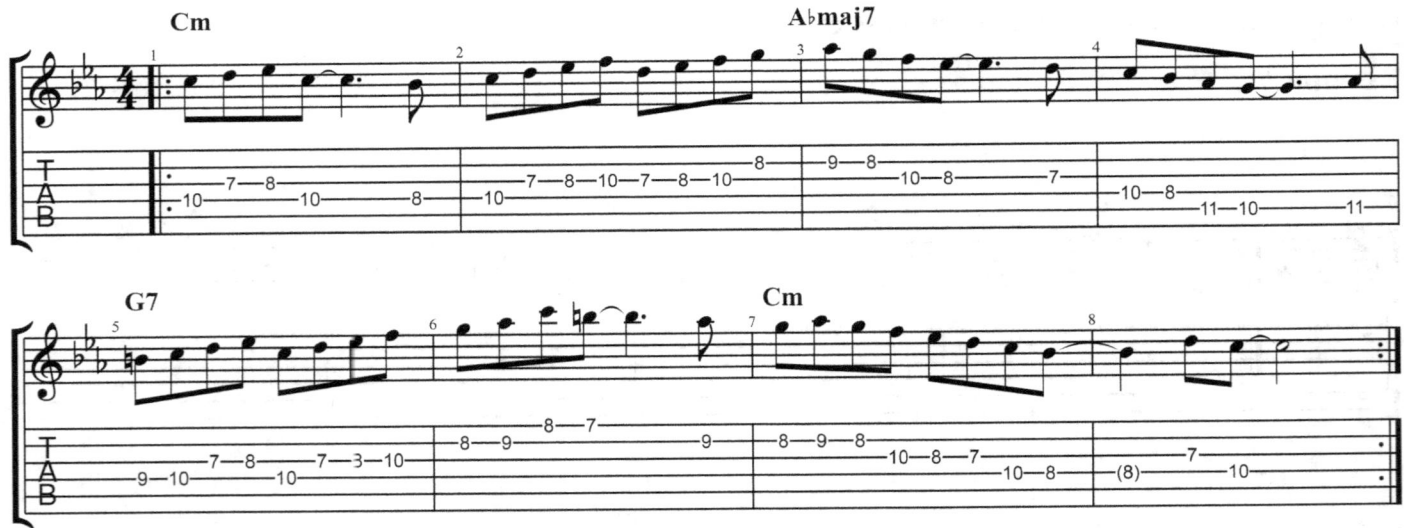

Some of you might be wondering exactly why C Harmonic Minor works over G7. We'll look at this in more detail next week. In the meantime, spend your time playing nothing but harmonic minor. Remember, there are no new intervals here! You already know them – we're just applying them in a specific way.

See you then!

Routine Seven – Phrygian Dominant

When planning a 10-week course on scales, the idea of it being completely comprehensive went out of the window quite quickly. For starters, the major scale has seven modes, so why have we only learned four of them? And the harmonic minor also has seven modes, right?!

Here's the logic behind the approach:

First, if you really know your intervals and understand the ingredients of each scale, I should be able to give you the recipe to *any* scale you don't know yet, and you'll find it much easier to pick up. Second, the other three scales of the major scale (Phrygian, Lydian and Locrian) aren't as useful to us in day-to-day playing as the scales we've covered.

Trying to cover everything gets messy real quick, so my aim here is to save you putting in countless hours working on things you'll never need.

I've been a full-time musical educator for about 15 years, and I can't recall a time where I've used any of the modes of the harmonic minor scale except for the one we're about to cover in this chapter!

The phrygian dominant is the fifth mode of the harmonic minor scale. In the previous chapter, I mentioned that the V chord of the harmonic minor is a dominant 7 (as opposed to the minor 7 of the natural minor). The mode associated with that dominant 7 chord is the most important harmonic minor mode to know – arguably more important than the parent scale!

The phrygian dominant consists of the following intervals:

1, b, 2, 3, 4, 5, b6, b7

In the key of C, that is:

C, Db, E, F, G, Ab, Bb

The phrygian dominant scale is really the phrygian mode of the major scale (mode three) with a natural 3rd instead of a b3. It has all the important notes of a dominant 7 chord (1, 3, 5, b7) but with much darker b2 and b6 intervals that you won't find in the Mixolydian mode.

Let's start by comparing C Mixolydian to C Phrygian Dominant over a C7 chord.

Example 8a

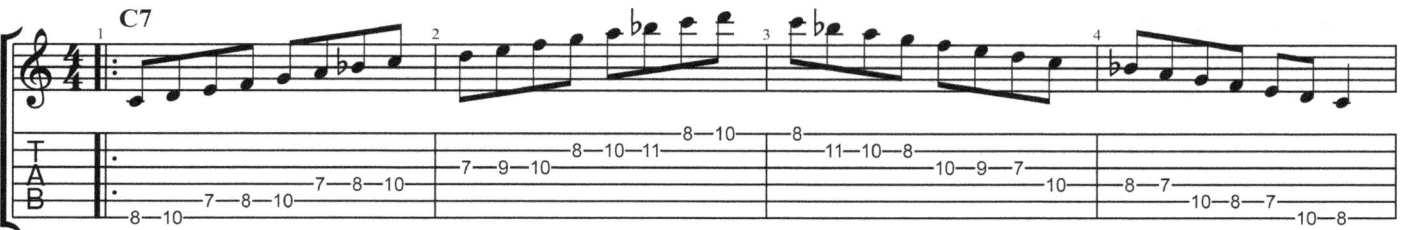

As with every other scale in this book, we need to be able to play it anywhere on the neck, so here's C Phrygian Dominant around the 3rd fret.

Example 8b

Here's the same scale, now played up at the 15th fret.

Example 8c

Let's jump back to a concept we looked at back in our Mixolydian routine and see how we can apply "cells" to this scale to create melodic information.

For Mixolydian, we learned that if we start on the root note we can always play:

1 2 3 5 or 1 b7 6 5 cellular patterns.

Would that approach work here if we just changed those intervals to fit the scale? I.e.,

1 b2 3 5 and 1 b7 b6 5

Absolutely!

Here's a selection of those cells applied to a static C7 chord. You'll notice that due to the three-fret gap between the b2 and 3rd, we never play those on the same string. Work smarter, not harder!

Example 8d

Of course, dominant chords are at their best when they're resolving! So now, we need to resolve the C7 chord to F minor. We can do this by playing either of these cells then moving down a tone to hit that chord change.

Once we know how to do this for a C7 chord, we can take the idea around the Cycle of Fourths. Let's do that now. We'll begin by resolving C7 to Fm, then F7 to Bbm, then B7 to Ebm, and so on. Here is that exercise using an ascending cell.

Example 8e

Here's the same progression, but now using the descending cell.

Example 8f

Remember, while you can learn this as a series of places to put your fingers, the real skill is in developing a sense of melodic anticipation with your ears. You should be able to hear the melody you want to play before you play it. And when you've got it clear in your mind, close your eyes and see if your fingers can follow.

Here's the same progression, now combining ascending and descending cells.

77

Example 8g

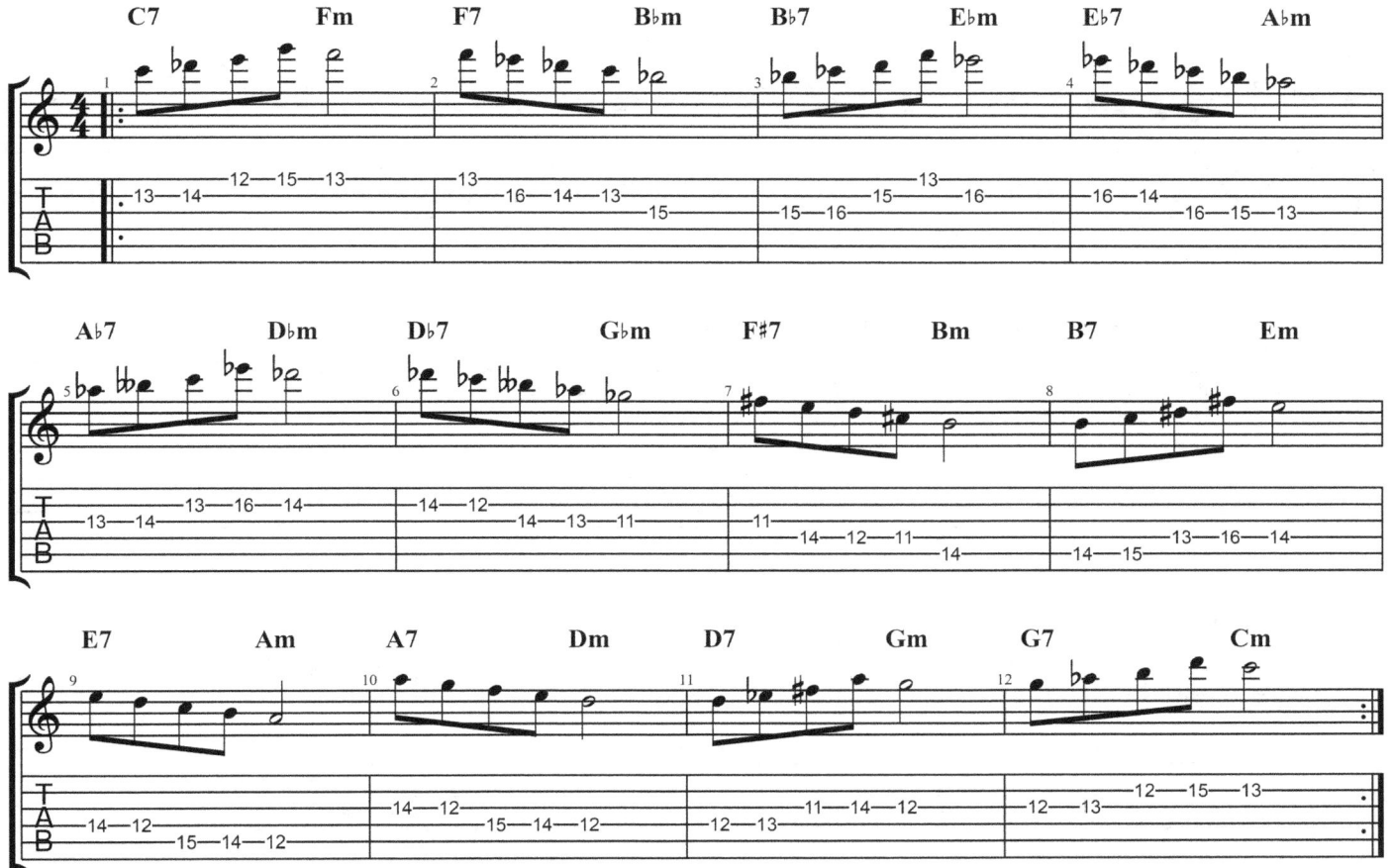

It's easy to work with a scale like the phrygian dominant and come up with melodies over static dominant vamps, because it naturally lends itself to that context. But we also need to work on developing melodic ideas that resolve the phrygian dominant scale over a dominant 7 chord, to the natural minor scale over a minor 7.

Let's look at some longer melodic examples using our scale patterns that do just that, using the progression C7b9 – Fm.

This example uses the first scale pattern we learned and plays a long scalic passage to begin with, then breaks up the pattern with more melodic ideas.

Example 8h

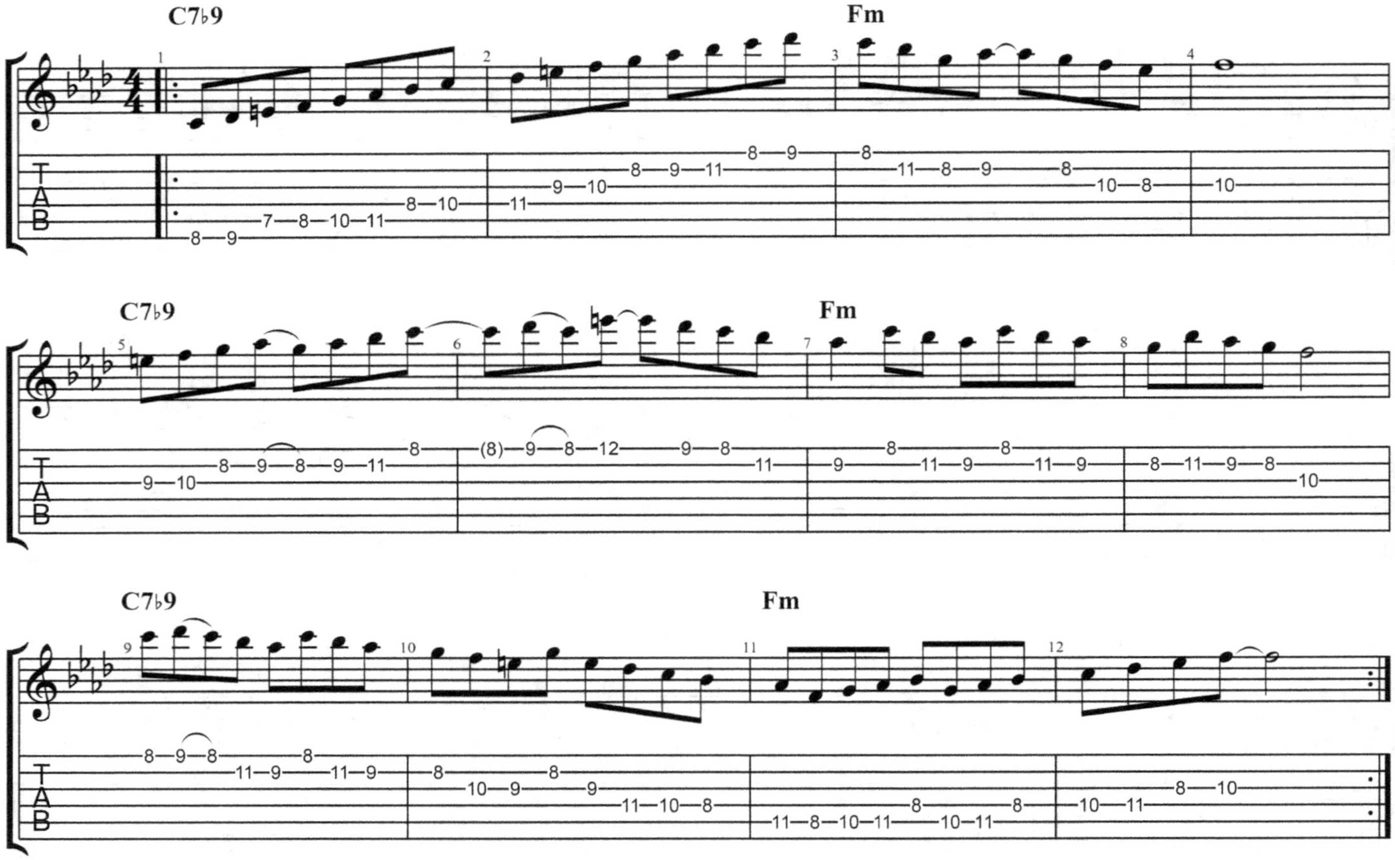

Here's the same idea but played around the 3rd fret area.

Example 8i

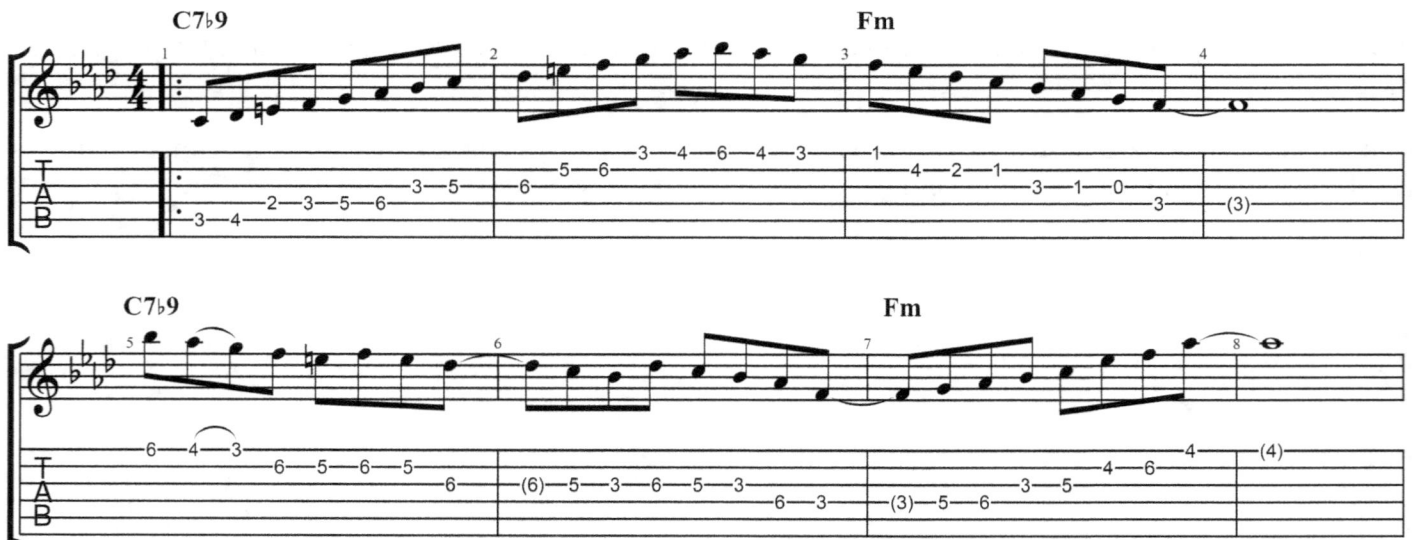

Finally, three more examples up at the 15th fret.

These examples are just ideas to get you inspired. Learn them, but then work on some of your own. The skill here is training your brain to play one scale while looking for the next one.

Example 8j

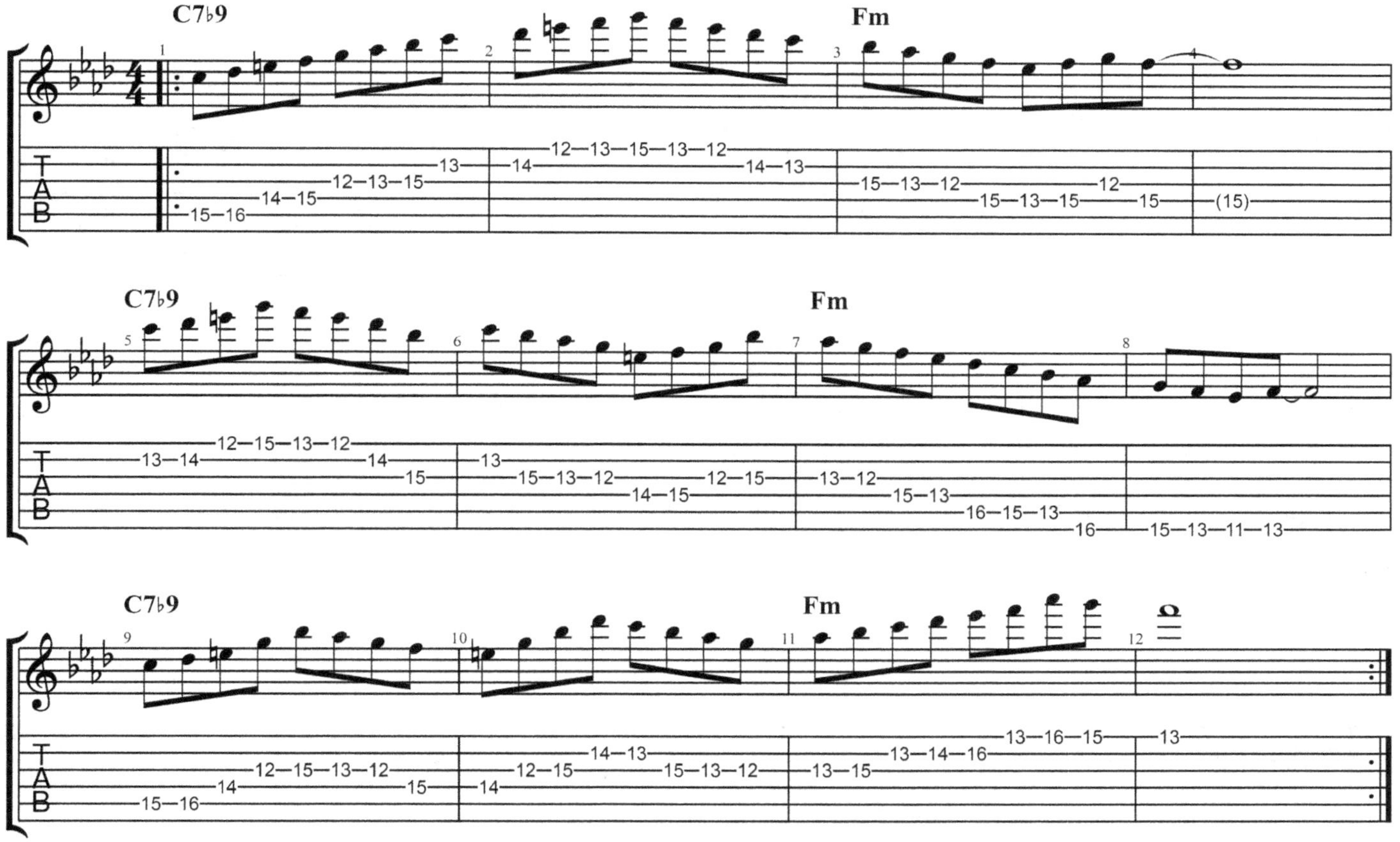

A cool little offshoot of phrygian dominant is the double harmonic major scale (sometimes known as the Byzantine or gypsy major scale). This is created by starting with the phrygian dominant scale then raising the b7 to a natural 7. It has the formula,

1, b2, 3, 4, 5, b6, 7

Example 8k

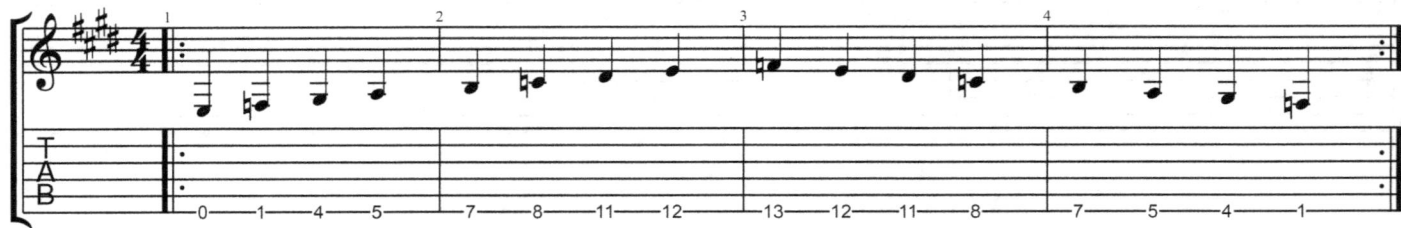

What a cool sound! This is the first time we've seen a scale that contains three consecutive semitone jumps. While the fingerings for this might not be all that easy to play physically, you should be at a point in your studies where they make sense.

Example 8l

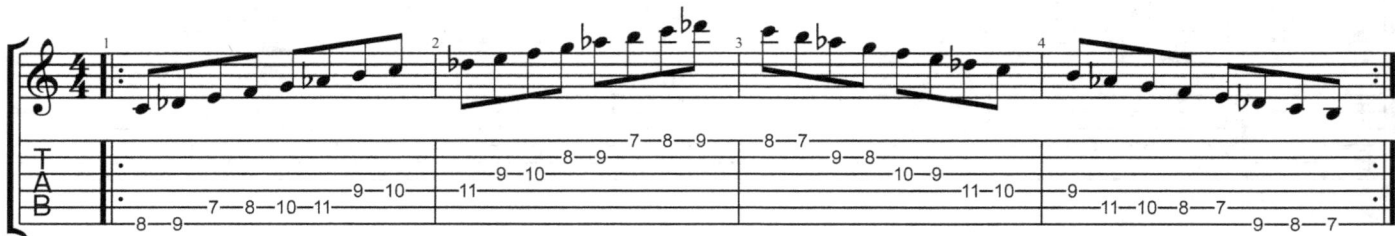

I'm won't write out every position for this scale, because based on the knowledge you now have, you should understand it. I.e., use the phrygian dominant scale, but play a 7th instead of a b7.

If we apply a sequence pattern such as 3rds to this, it creates some cool stuff that travels along the neck.

Example 8m

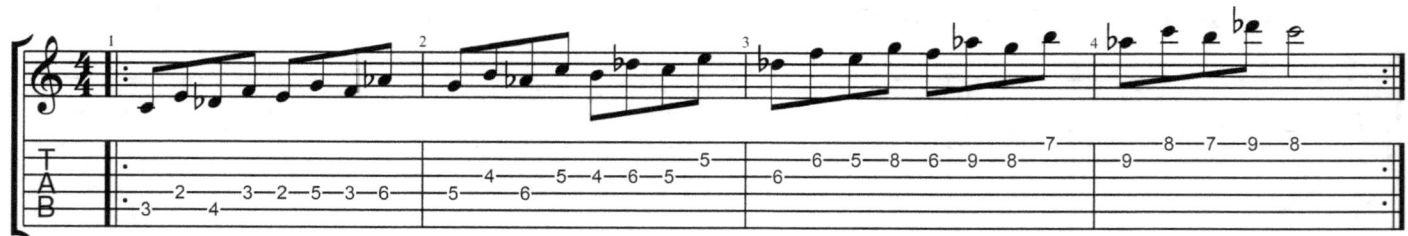

Spend some time getting familiar with these exotic sounding scales. Later, we'll come back and look at smoothing out that eastern sounding tone and a half gap found in the scale.

Routine Eight – Melodic Minor

If you asked me, "Levi, what's your favourite scale" I would, without hesitation, tell you it's the melodic minor scale. To me, there's a sense of beauty found in this scale that is mysterious enough to make it interesting, without veering too far away from the major scale harmony people expect to hear.

So, what's melodic minor? Interval-wise, it has the formula,

1, 2, b3, 4, 5, 6, 7

You could say, so it's a major scale but with a b3, right? Well, yes… but not really.

The theory books will tell you that the harmonic minor scale is a natural minor with a raised 7th, and the melodic minor is a natural minor with a raised 6th and 7th.

It's a minor sound, so it makes sense to compare it to the minor scale. But, at the same time, it's the minor scale with *two* changes, when we could view it as a major scale with *one*, so I can see why some people prefer that approach.

However, I have a better method of thinking about this scale. In musical application, we don't use the melodic minor in the same context as the natural minor – it's nearly always used as a substitute for the Dorian mode. So, literally anytime I would naturally play Dorian, I'll also play melodic minor.

Viewed from a Dorian perspective, the melodic minor scale is the Dorian mode with a natural 7th rather than a b7.

This is absolutely the way to think about it. Not only does it require a minimal change to something you already know, it's suited for the exact same musical context.

So what does it sound like? Here's the scale played around the 8th fret.

Example 9a

One thing people will love to tell you about the melodic minor (which is a sign they've read a lot of books but not played much music!) is that it is played this way when ascending, but you're supposed to switch to the natural minor when descending.

This is rubbish for a couple of reasons.

It's the done thing when practicing scales in a classical music context, but we're not using it to play classical music, and we're not just playing ascending and descending scale passages.

The classical thought process is that the melodic minor doesn't sound minor when descending until we reach the b3. However, we want to celebrate its unique sound, not avoid it!

Jazz musicians play this scale the same ascending and descending (it's often referred to as the "jazz minor") and I promise you, out there in the real world, nobody plays this scale differently on the way down.

Here's another C Melodic Minor fingering, lower on the neck.

Example 9b

The melodic minor is smoother than the harmonic minor in its execution as it doesn't contain that big interval jump in the scale.

What's fun about this scale is the whole tone scale flavour that comes from its consecutive whole steps between the b3, 4th, 5th 6th and 7th intervals. That's four whole tones in a row, which sounds pretty mysterious!

Example 9c

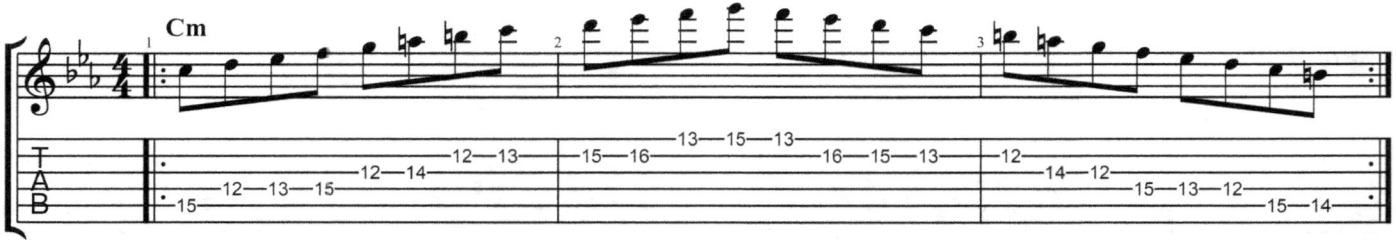

Next, here is C Melodic Minor played in five positions, starting down at the 3rd fret. We need these patterns to be completely automatic. I've added shift slides in the TAB to help you see how I'm moving between positions.

Example 9d

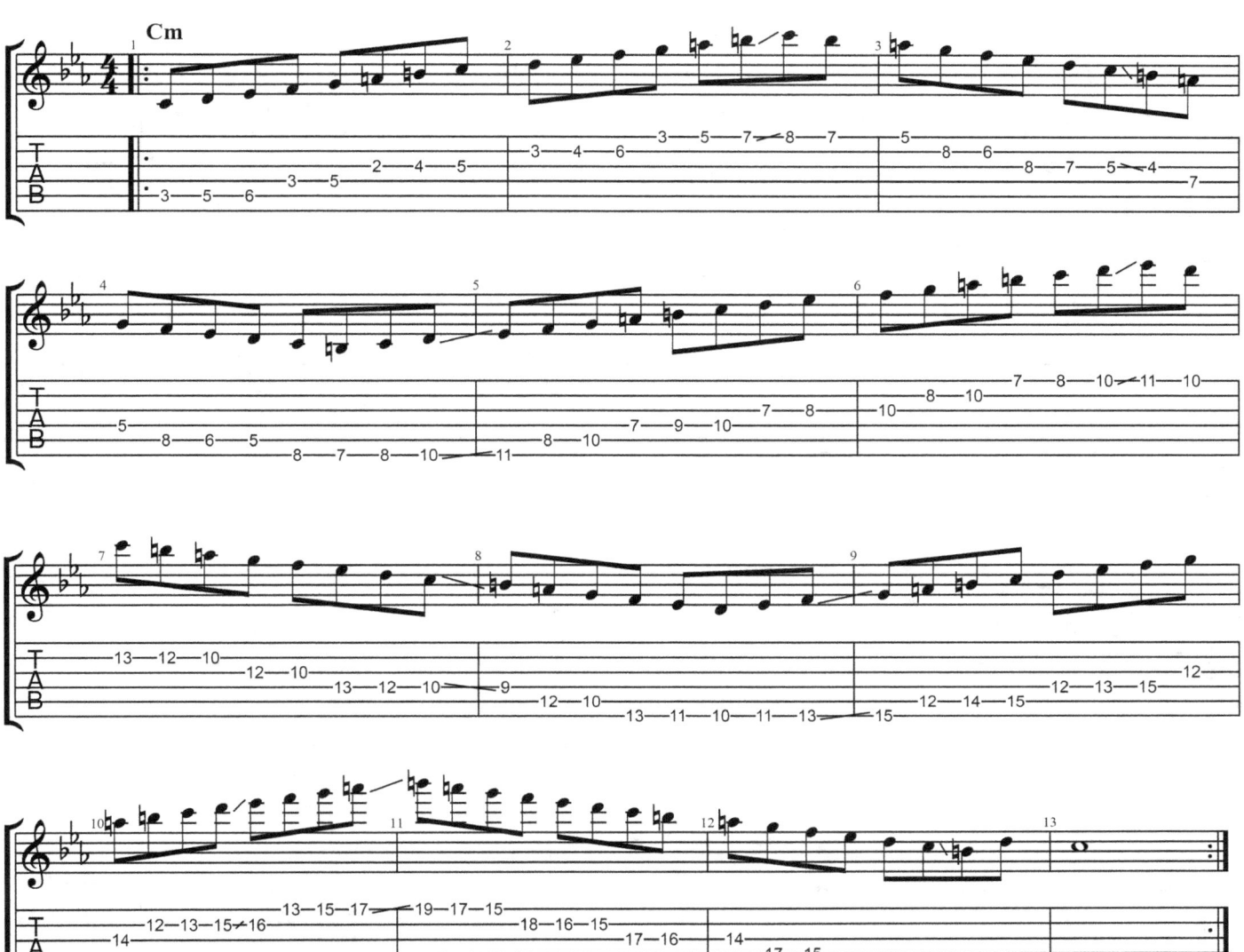

Here's the same idea, but now applied to the G Melodic Minor scale.

Example 9e

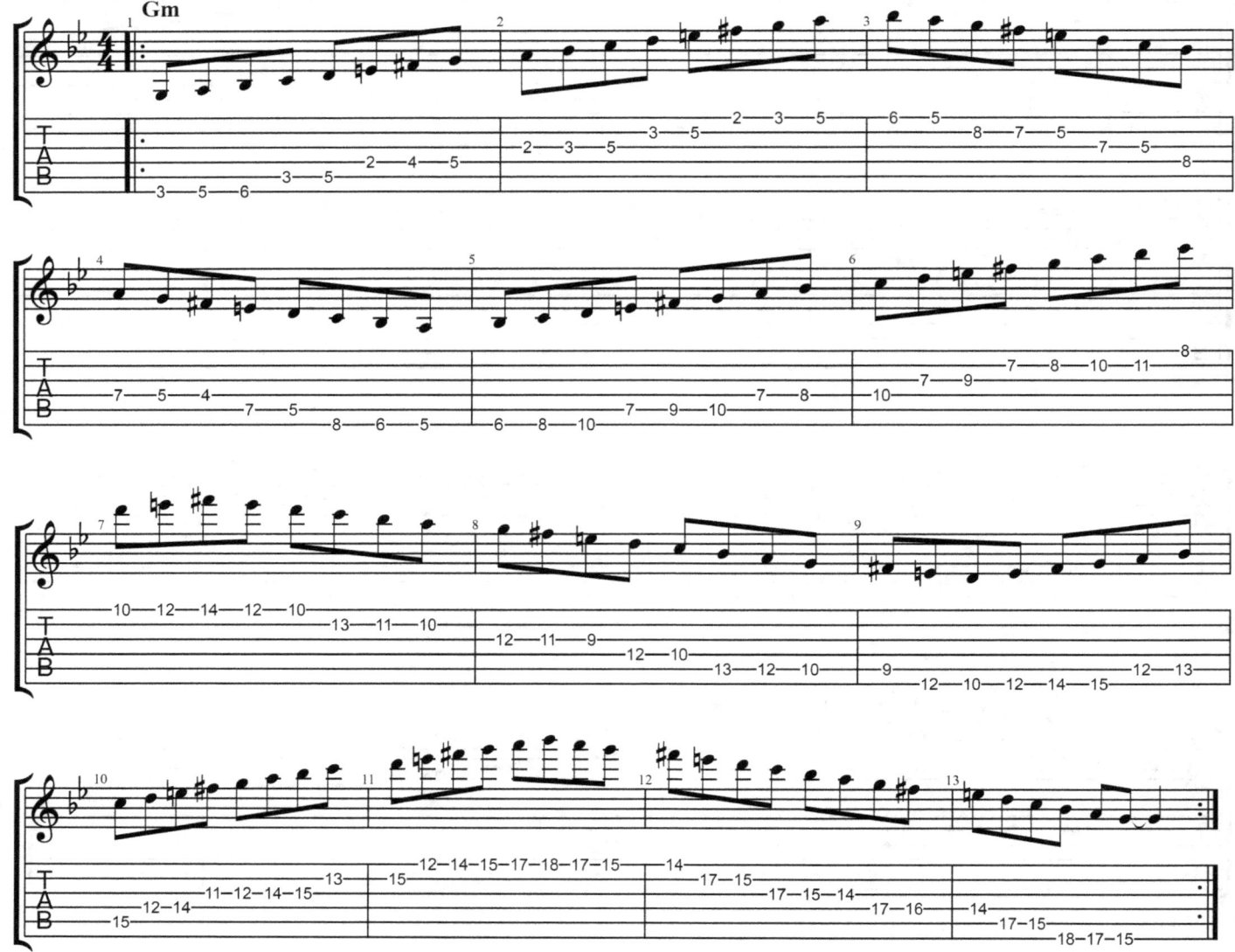

While it's true that, technically, there are "correct" places to use the melodic minor scale – such as over a min(Maj)7 chord (1, b3, 5, 7) – those musical settings are so few and far between that you'll want to find other places to use the scale. One such obvious place to me is to create a slightly outside sound on a minor 7 chord.

A great way to start learning this sound is to combine the minor pentatonic scale with the melodic minor. The skill we want to develop here is the ability to slip in and out of the melodic minor very smoothly.

Here's an example of that.

Example 9f

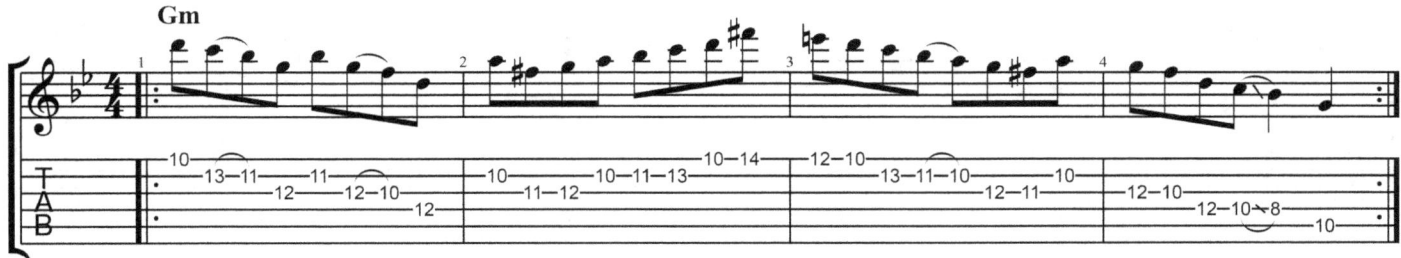

And here's another, again playing some minor pentatonic ideas then slipping into melodic minor and returning to the minor pentatonic to end.

Example 9g

We should be able to do this anywhere on the neck. For example, here's an idea at the 3rd fret.

Example 9h

The only way to learn how to slip in and out of the melodic minor and play something cool, is to first have a bunch of scale sequence ideas up your sleeve. Let's look at a couple now, beginning with 3rds.

Example 9i

And now in groupings of four notes.

Example 9j

While I now expect you to work on these ideas in as many positions as possible, I also want this chapter to be the one where we start breaking up scales into less predictable patterns. So, while it might be nice to be able to calculate what you're going to practice, here's an etude in G Melodic Minor that relies more on physical patterns than mathematical ones.

Example 9k

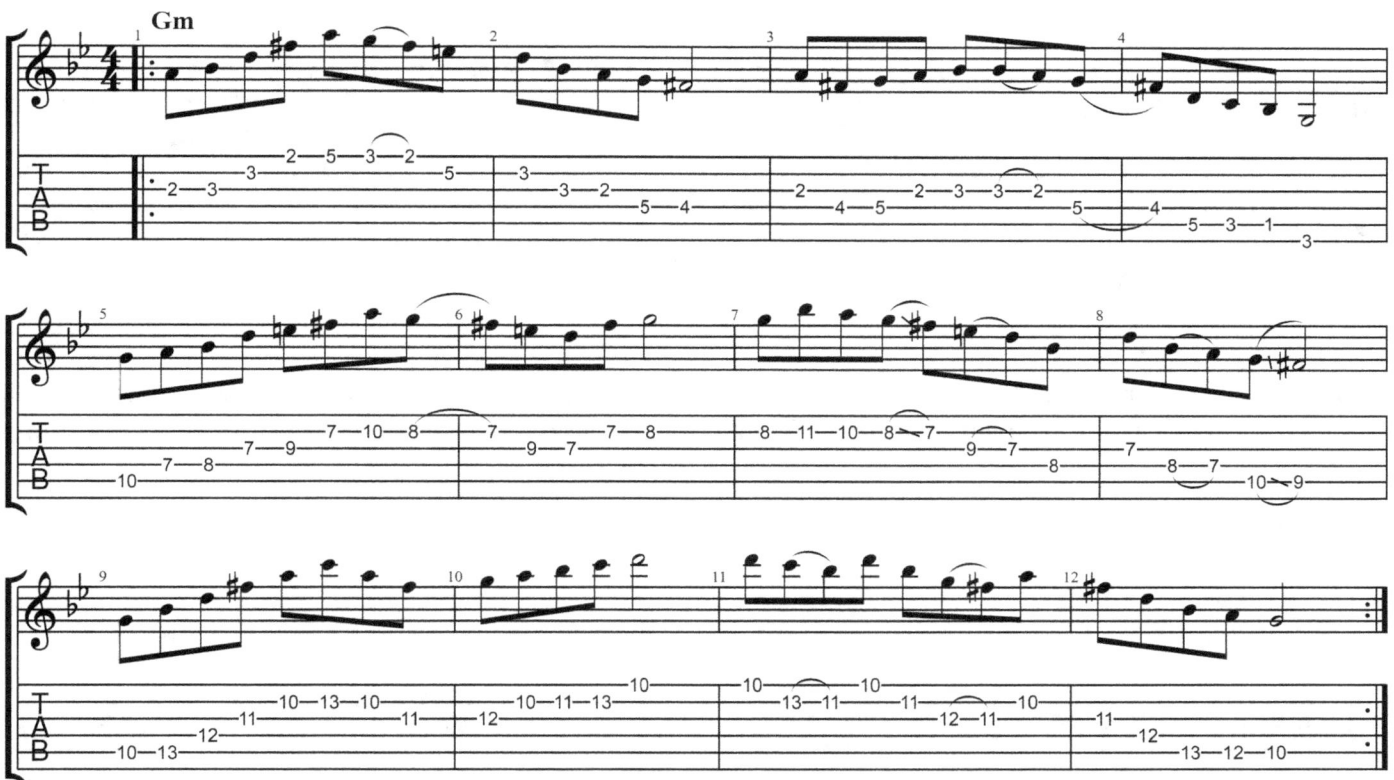

These ideas can be played in any of our twelve keys. If you can see the scale positions, you should be able to see the same licks. Here they are in C Melodic Minor.

Example 9l

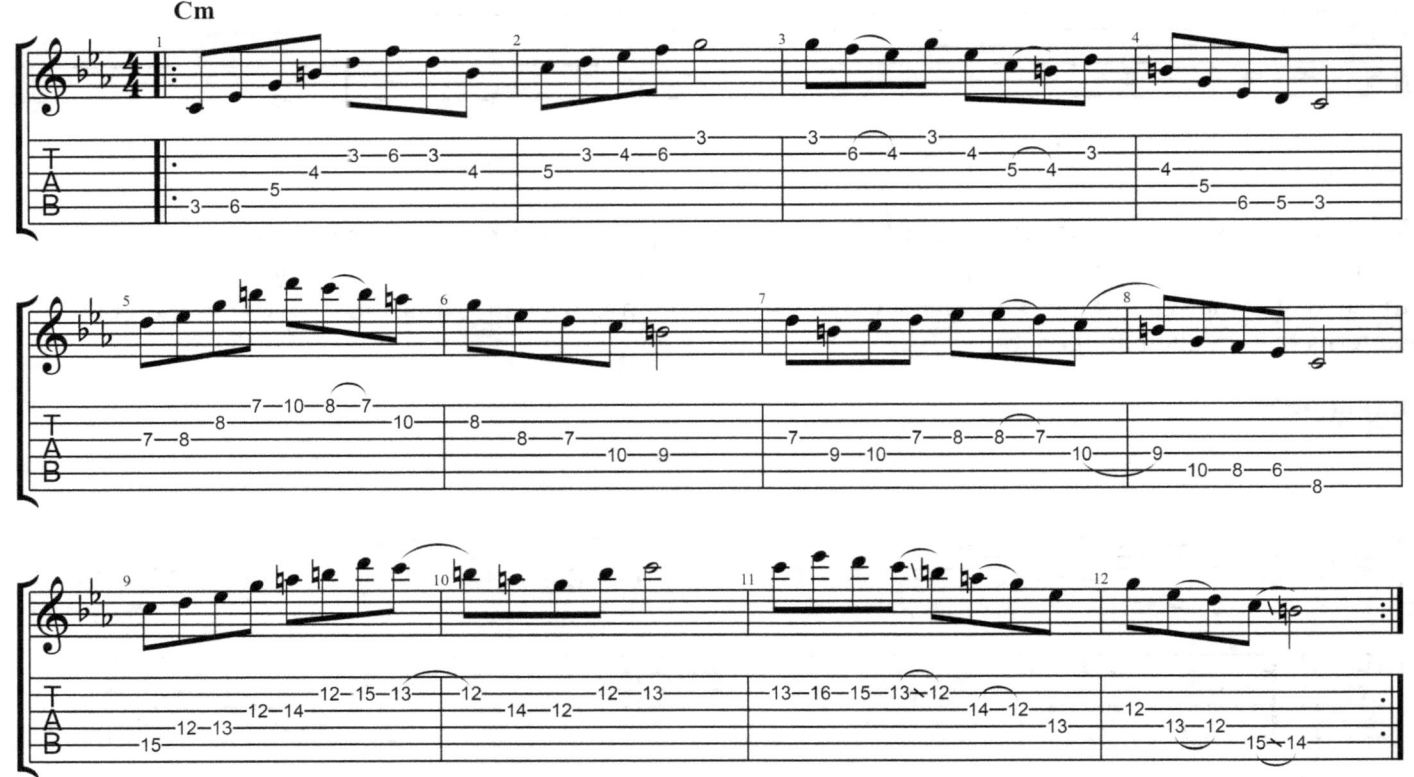

As a final idea, I want you to see just how much the melodic minor and Dorian sounds coexist in musical context. It's totally OK to use some of the melodic minor flavour (with that natural 7th) then slip back into Dorian.

Example 9m

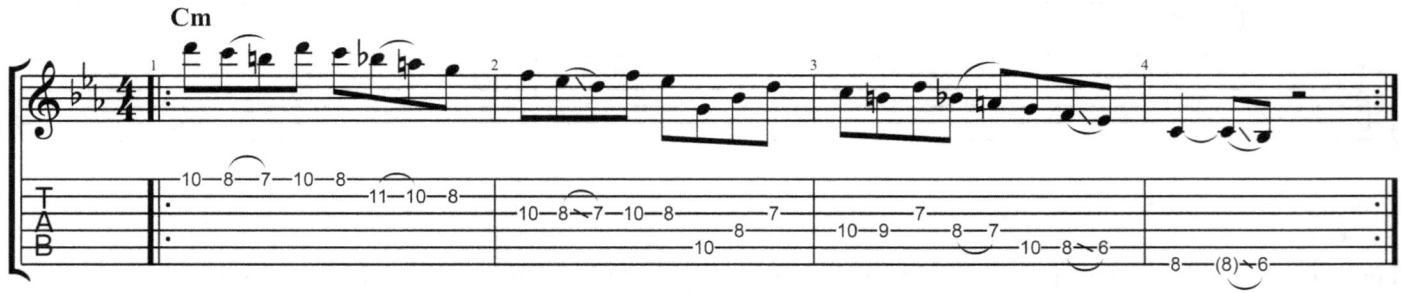

89

Or you can play something like this.

Example 9n

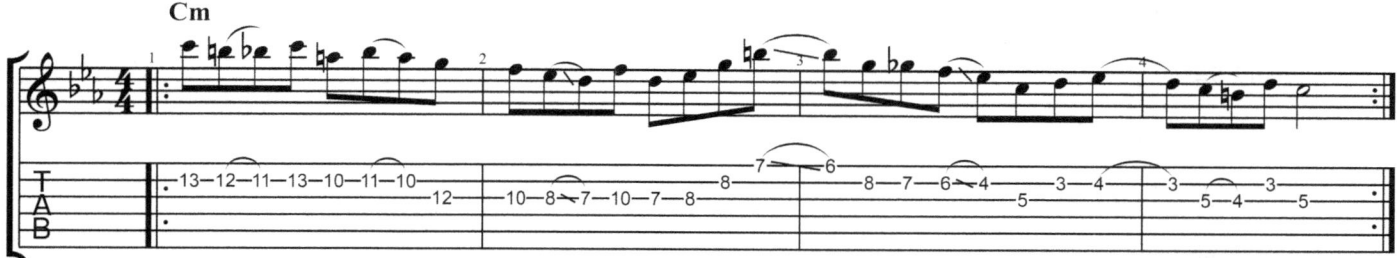

Take your time with all these patterns because next time we'll look at the important modes of the melodic minor scale – and there are a few of them!

Routine Nine – Melodic Minor Modes

Like any seven-note scale, the melodic minor scale has seven modes:

- Melodic Minor
- Dorian b2
- Lydian Augmented
- Lydian Dominant
- Mixolydian b6
- Locrian Natural 2
- Super Locrian

Your personal mileage may vary with these, depending on the contexts you play in, but I use *five* of these quite regularly.

We've already covered the parent, melodic minor. The others I use regularly are:

Lydian dominant – a Mixolydian mode (i.e. dominant) but with a #4 (giving it a Lydian quality). This is a great sound on a dominant 7 chord.

Mixolydian b6 – as the name suggests, it's a Mixolydian mode with a b6, which creates a cool, yearning sound over a dominant chord.

Locrian Natural 2 – once again, as the name suggests, it's a Locrian mode with a natural 2nd rather than a b2. This adjustment makes it a much more practical sound to play over minor 7b5 chords than Locrian. The natural 2nd is a much more pleasing sound than the b2.

Super Locrian – also known as the altered scale, this is a catch-all scale for dominant 7 chords with jazzy altered tensions (b5, #5, b9, #9).

It was when I was learning the melodic minor modes that the whole interval thing began to click for me. At first, I tried to learn a bunch of new shapes and that was hard work. When I focused on them as things I already knew, but containing a different note, that was the key to nailing the sound of the new mode.

Let's look at these five modes in order, starting with the Lydian dominant. It has the formula:

1, 2, 3, #4, 5, 6, b7

Here it is played from a fifth string root.

Example 10a

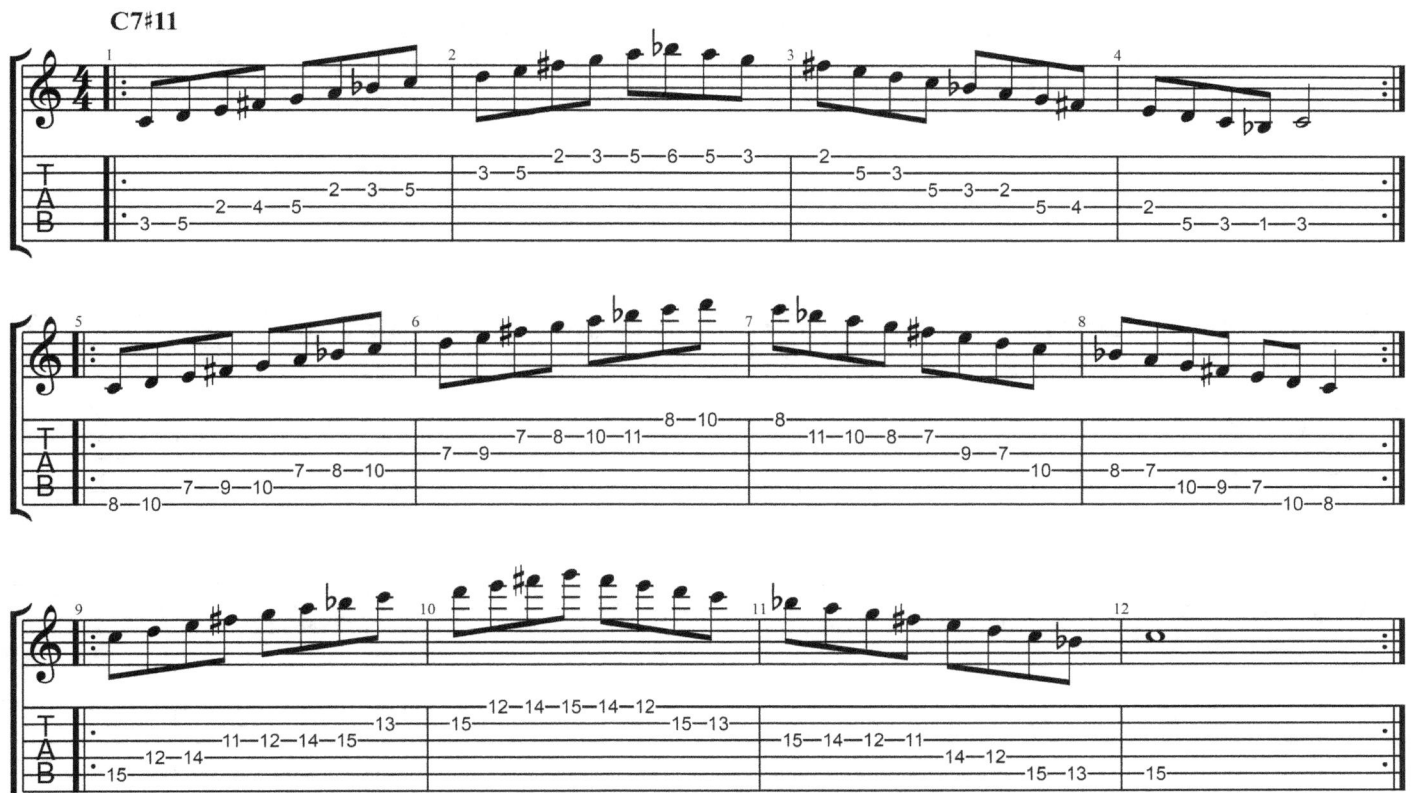

Let's look at a common context for this scale. You'll hear players like Robben Ford use it over the IV chord in a blues. If we play just C7 to F7, and use C Mixolydian over the C7, then switch to F Lydian Dominant for the F7 chord, you'll immediately hear how ear catching the #11 is over F7.

Example 10b

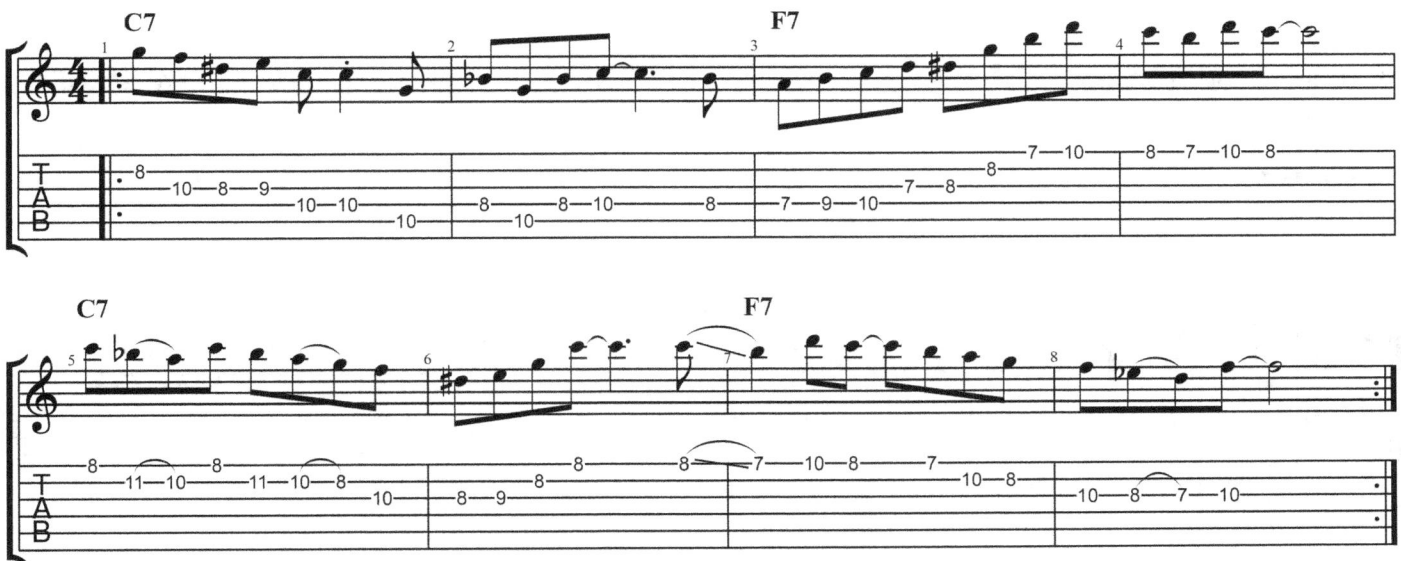

Alternatively, you can use the Lydian dominant scale when playing over extended dominant 7 chords to add a bit of intrigue to your lines.

Here's a short etude using G Lydian Dominant that shows how I like to put lines together from this scale. In my practice, I make an effort to set up a chord loop for a short period and just see what happens. The more I do this, the less I think about it.

Example 10c

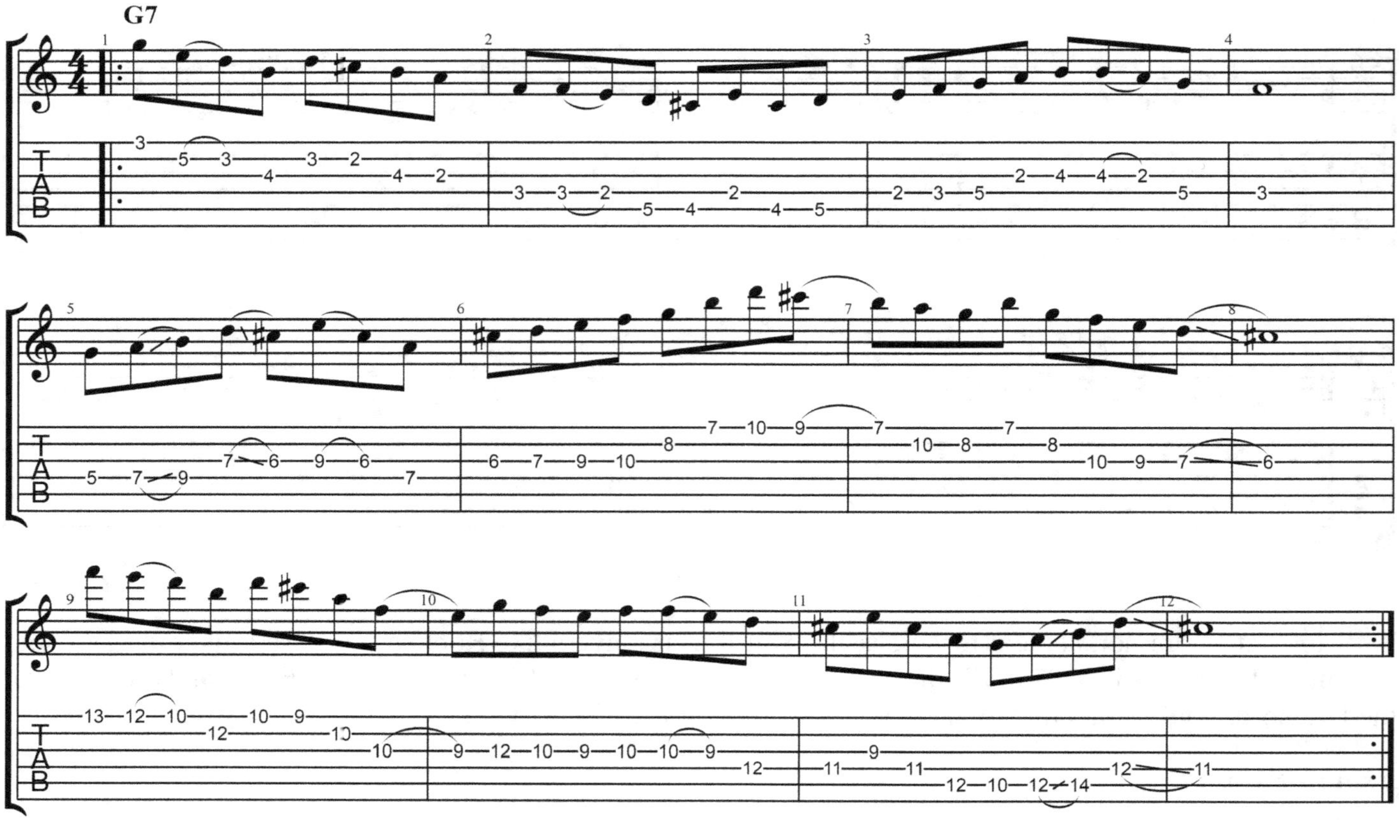

Next, let's look at Mixolydian b6. As the name suggests, this scale's formula is 1, 2, 3, 4, 5, b6, b7. Here's how it sounds over C7.

Example 10d

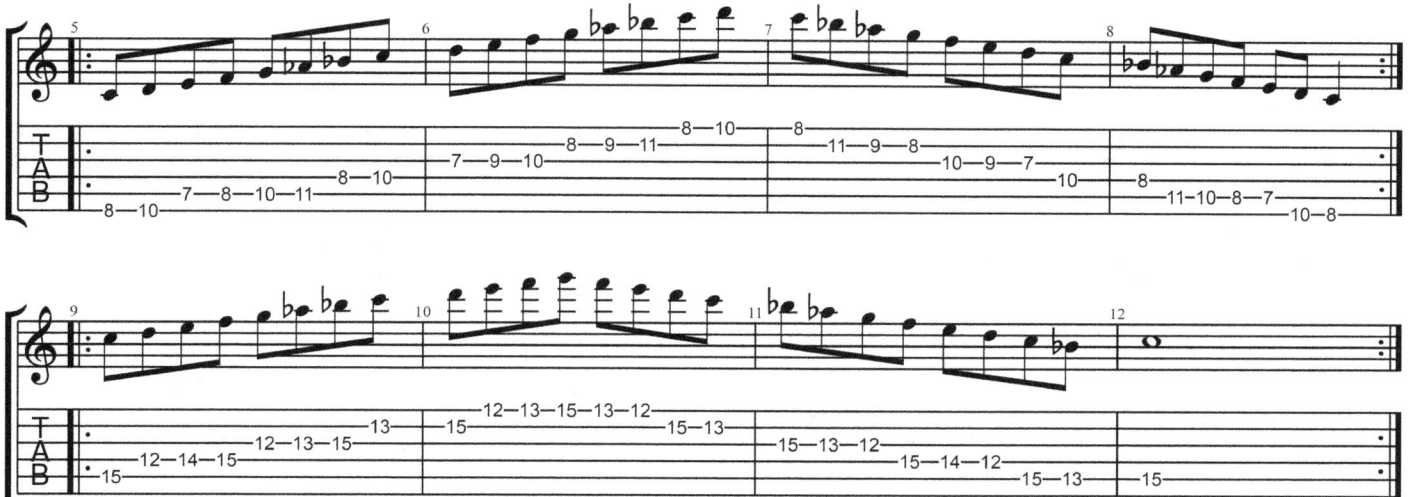

Isn't it wild that both of these modes are sounds that work over dominant chords, yet they have dramatically different vibes?

We can attempt to use this scale in a blues, though I don't really like this sound. To me, the Mixolydian b6 sounds like a minor scale due to its b6 and b7, but with a major 3rd. That's a bit of a juxtaposition, and not quite what we expect to hear over a blues, but it's still a good exercise! Here, we're using the same licks for C7, then plugging in the F Mixolydian b6 mode over the F7 chord.

Example 10e

Here's a longer etude showing how beautiful this scale sounds in a static Mixolydian b6 setting.

Example 10f

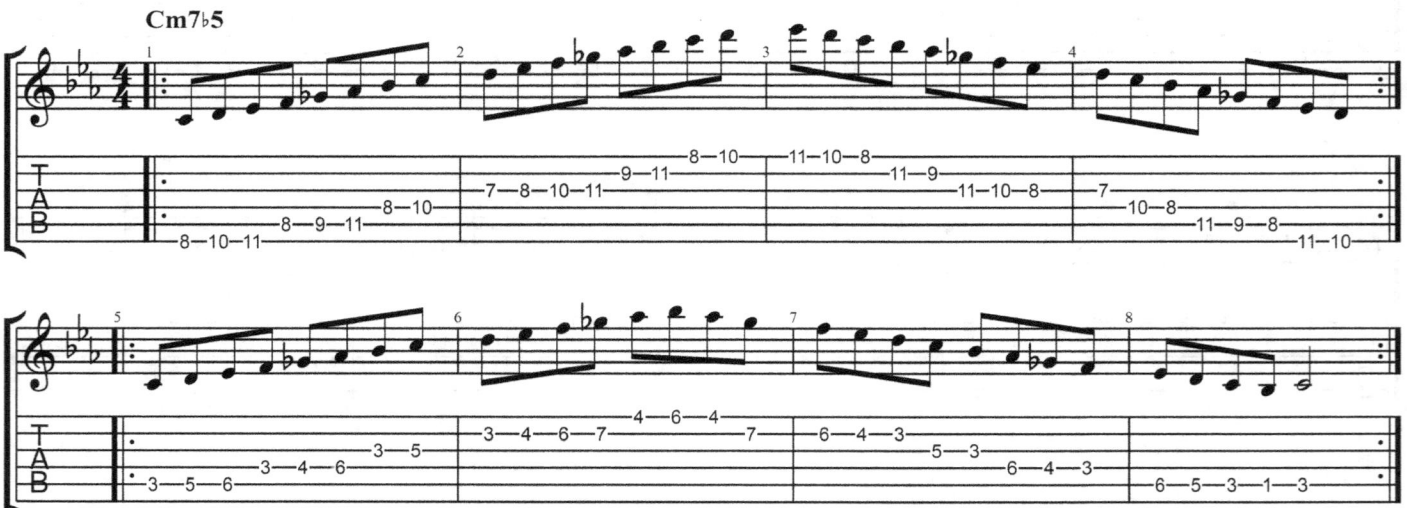

Next up is Locrian Natural 2 (sometimes called Aeolian b5). As the name suggests, we have a formula of 1, 2, b3, 4, b5, b6, b7. Here's the scale played around the neck.

Example 10g

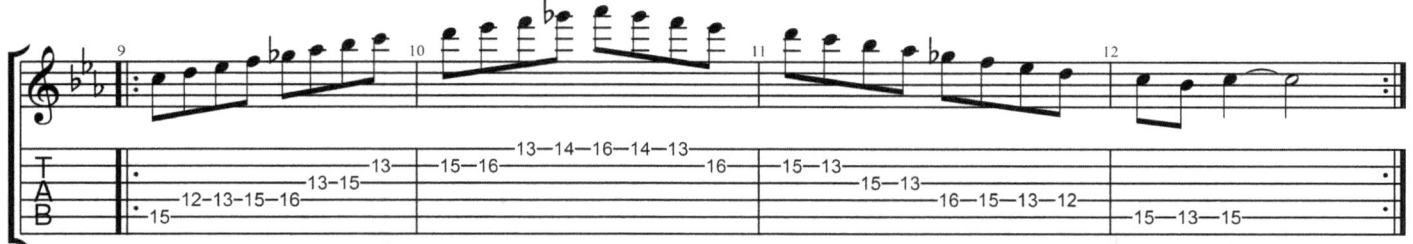

You might listen to this and wonder why this scale is so useful to us. Admittedly, it's a little more jazz, but it's still useful! The minor 7b5 chord is part of the major scale, built from its 7th degree, but playing the associated Locrian scale over it always sounds a little dull, mainly because of the Locrian's b2 interval. With this mode, suddenly we have a pleasing sounding natural 2nd which is much more stable.

In this example, using the chord progression Dm7b5 – G7b9 – Cm, we are linking together D Locrian Natural 2, G Phrygian Dominant, and C Minor sales.

Example 10h

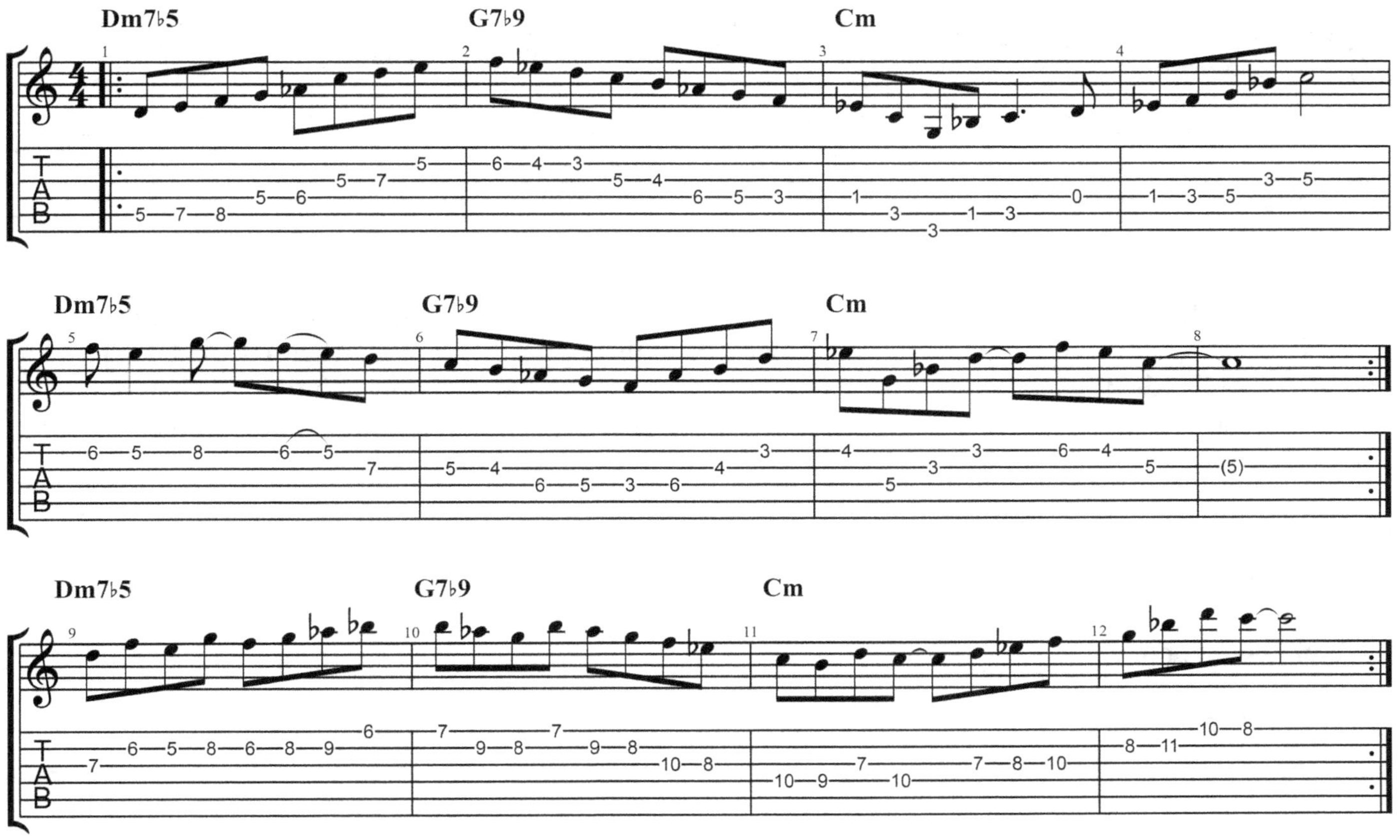

Now let's play a slightly longer etude that explores just the Locrian Natural sound.

Example 10i

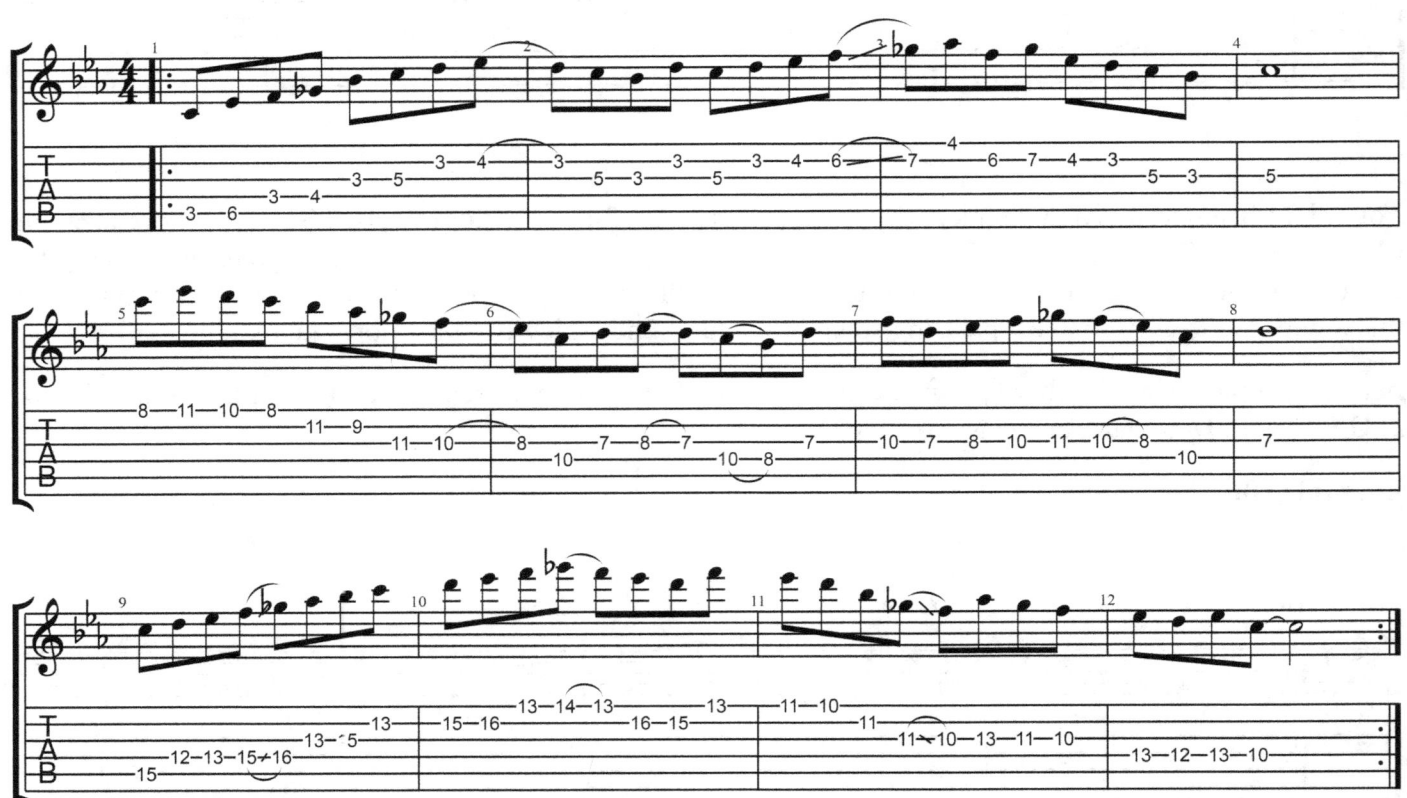

Thus far, when looking at the melodic minor modes, we've only considered them from a parallel, rather than derivative, standpoint, and that is how I tend to approach them. In other words, when I see a C7 chord and want to play C Lydian Dominant over it, I'm not thinking "G Melodic Minor". Similarly, when playing C Mixolydian b6, I'm not thinking F Melodic Minor, or Eb Melodic Minor when I want to access C Locrian Natural 2.

The Super Locrian mode is the exception to this rule.

Super Locrian consists of the following intervals:

1, b2, b3, b4, b5, b6, b7

These intervals can also be viewed as:

1, b2, #2, 3, b5, #5, b7

In other words, a dominant 7 chord shell and all the possible alterations that can be made to it.

If you want, you can *try* and think of these intervals and visualise them, but I've always found this particularly nightmarish compared to the common hack used to access this scale: just play the melodic minor scale up a semitone from the root of the dominant 7 chord. In other words, to play C Super Locrian over a C7alt chord, we play Db Melodic Minor.

Example 10j

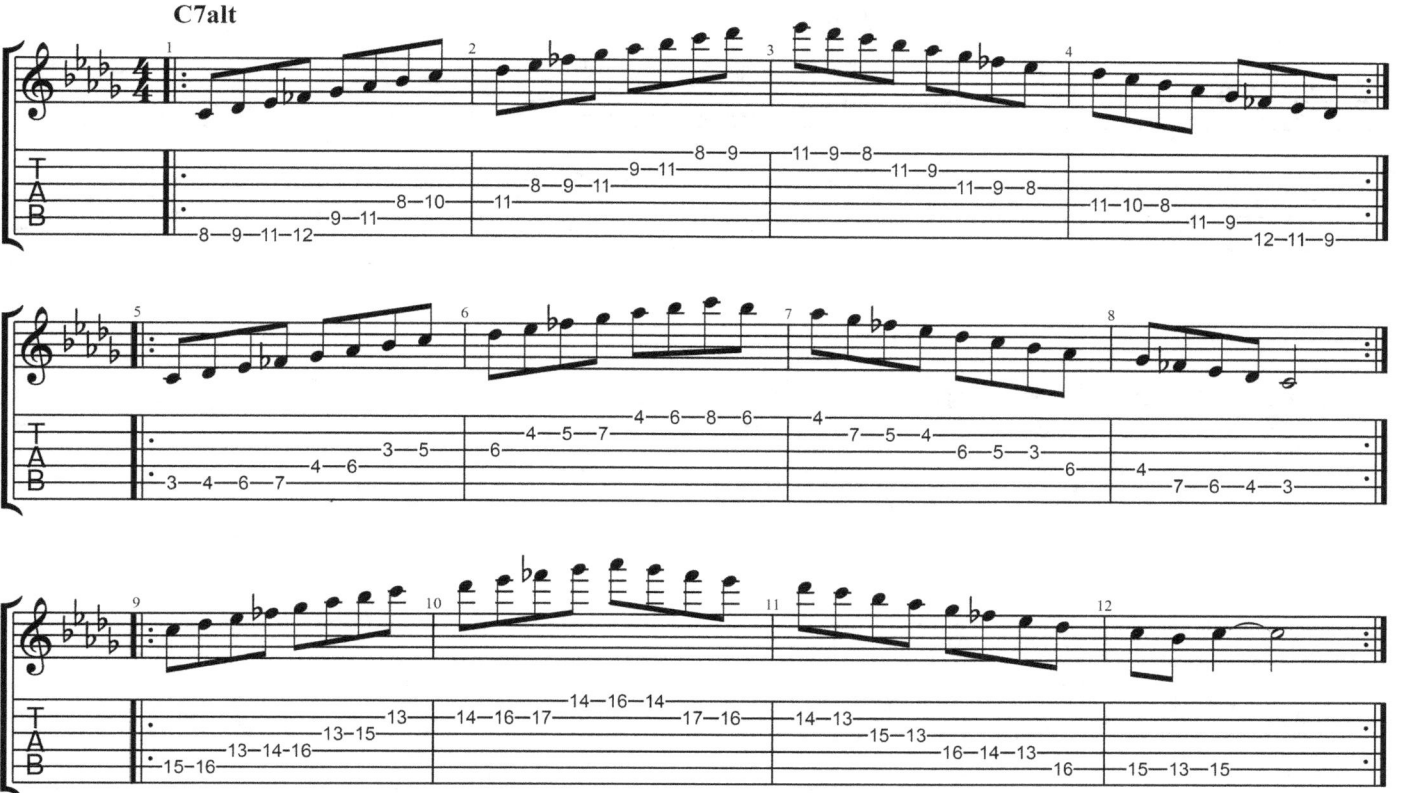

Super Locrian might be the most important mode of melodic minor, as it's the go-to sound for adding tension to functioning dominant chords (i.e., chords that resolve to a tonic chord).

In order to really practice this scale, ensure that you focus on how each pattern resolves up a 4th to the I chord.

So…

C Super Locrian always resolves to F Major.

F Super Locrian always resolves to Bb Major.

Bb Super Locrian always resolves to Eb Major, and so on.

In this exercise we practice that movement going from C7alt to Fmaj7.

Example 10k

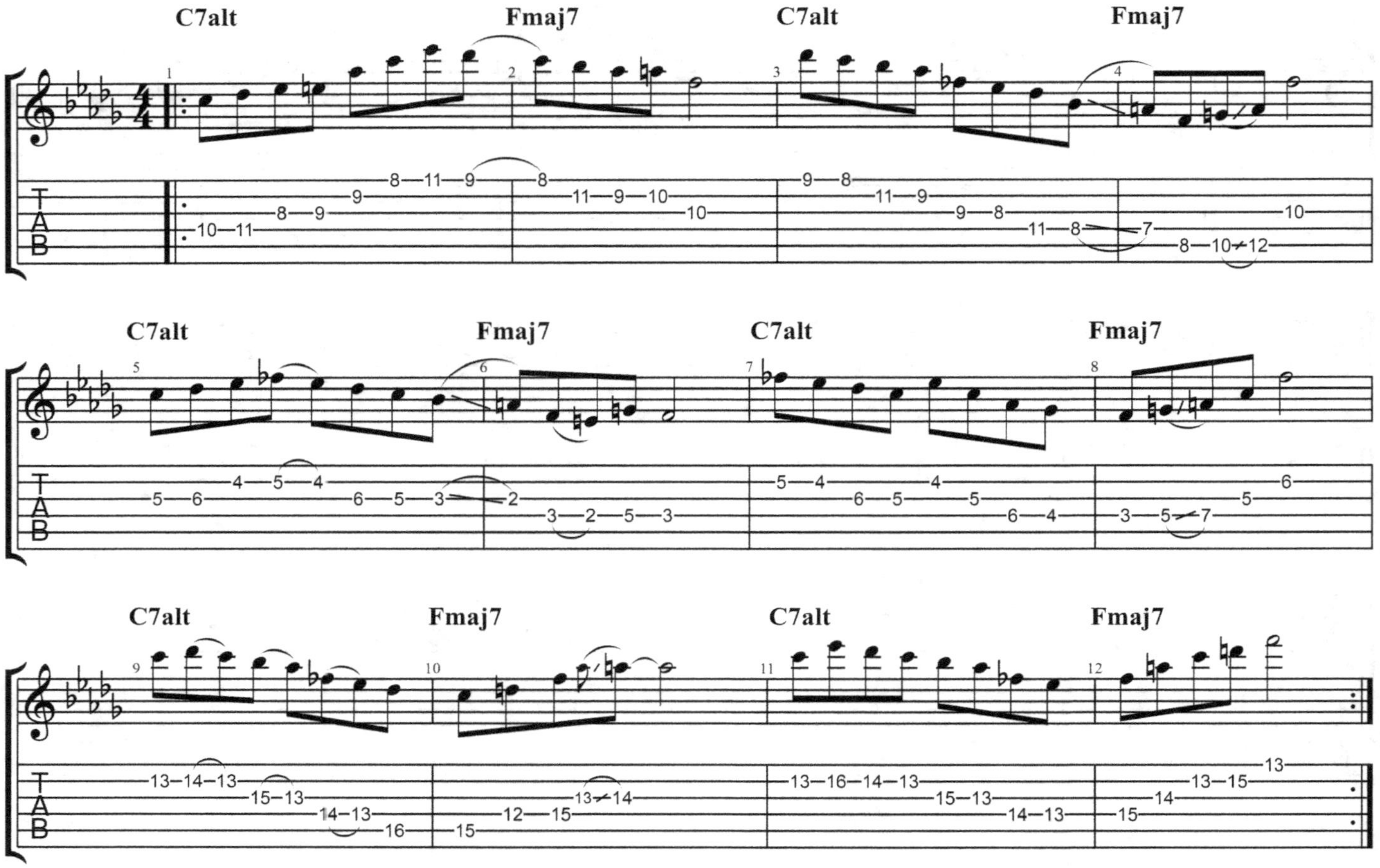

And here's an extended C7alt vamp where we're playing longer lines, staying in that Super Locrian sound. Even though our ears expect this to resolve, I still think it sounds cool!

Example 10l

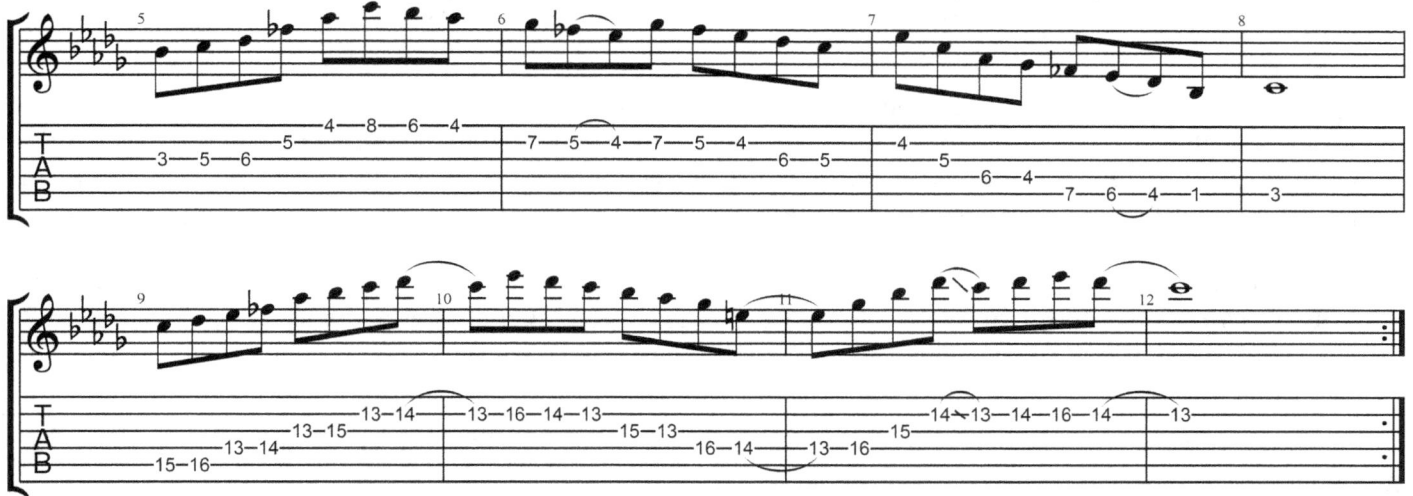

Again, we're just scratching the surface of these modes and what we can do with them musically. You can explore them more on your own, but for now, our focus is still upon how quickly we can put these sounds together and play them. Are you seeing them as new patterns that you need to learn, or are you viewing them as intervals and beginning to see them as variations of scales you already know?

Get to work and I'll see you in a week!

Routine Ten – Chromatic Scale

Many years ago, when I was just a teen with a dream of music, I was obsessed with knowledge. I needed to know as much as I could! Because then I'd have it all figured out, right? I was part of a great little online community that had some really accomplished players who were generous with their time for us up-and-comers. I still vividly remember one particular conversation I had with one of those guys. It went like this:

[Me] "So, what scales are you using over this chord… and this chord… and when this happens, are you thinking like *this* or like *this*… and how do you work out how to play melodies and what the right notes are?"

[Him] "You know there's only one scale, right? The Chromatic scale."

At the time I considered this to be bad advice because I took it very literally. As good a player as he was, surely he didn't just think in terms of chromatic scales?

As time has gone on, I've come to understand what he was trying to tell me, and now I want to pass that on to you.

First, stop thinking so much! Music isn't science and you can't calculate everything. Music is art. Focus more on the music and less on musical strategies and you'll get better at music.

Second, there are only 12 notes (or intervals) in our Western tonal system of music. If you are in control of those 12 notes, then you've got access to all your sounds.

The chromatic scale gets its name from the Latin word *chroma*, which in turn came from the original Greek word *khrōma*, meaning "colour". We can therefore think of the chromatic scale as the scale of "all colours".

Because of the tuning of the guitar, there are fundamentally two practical ways to lay out the chromatic scale on the guitar. First, as a pattern that moves down the neck as we cross strings.

Example 11a

And we can also stay in position by including shift slides on strings that are tuned a 4th apart from each other.

Example 11b

The nature of the chromatic scale makes it pointless to play the kinds of sequences we've used on previous scales. Playing in 3rds or using ascending "4s" doesn't achieve much. Instead, we can use it to work on improving our dexterity, as this descending triplet idea shows.

It might seem easier to try and play most of this with two fingers, but we're going to use a specific fingering to give the fretting hand a workout.

In each bar, play the first group of three notes with the third and fourth fingers, the second group with the second and third fingers, the third group with the first and second fingers, and the last group with the fourth and first fingers.

Example 11c

You can really give yourself a test if you take that same pattern but now play it legato, picking just the first note of each long single-string group.

Example 11d

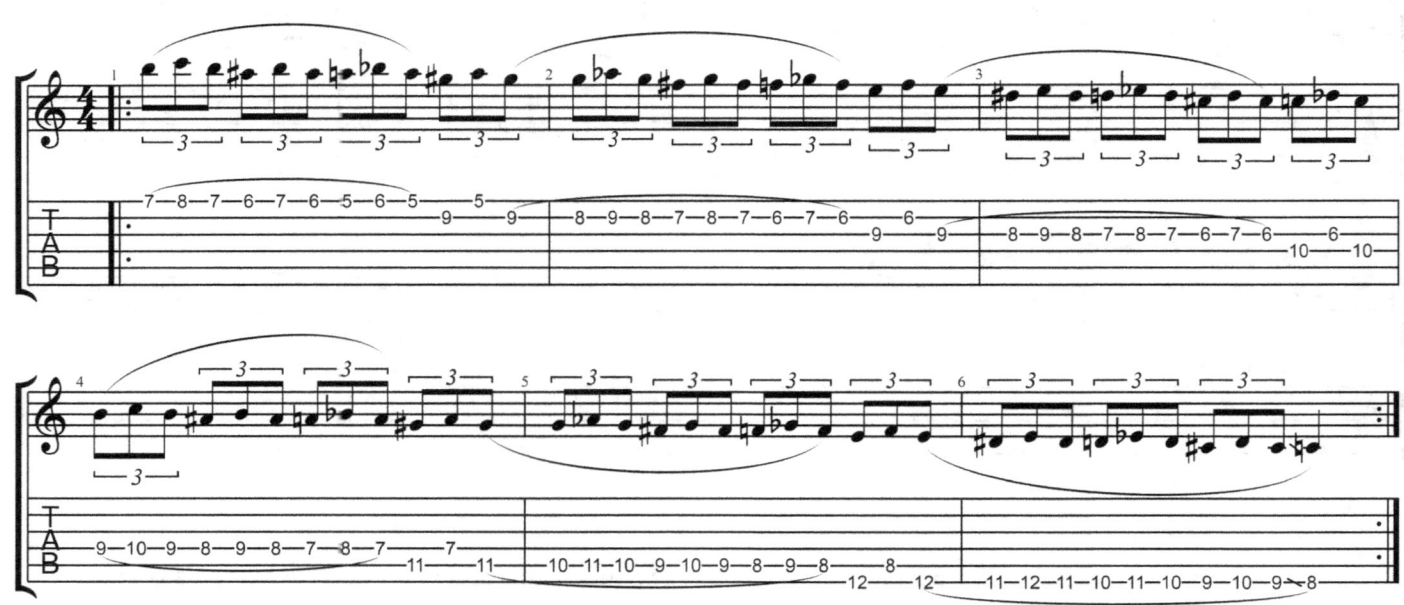

My first lightbulb moment with chromatics was a pretty simple one, and came when I saw John Petrucci fill in the blanks of a minor pentatonic scale.

This exercise uses a C Minor Pentatonic framework, but we're connecting up each of the notes with chromatic notes.

Example 11e

We can apply the same idea, but this time thinking C Dorian, which might look like this.

Example 11f

Of course, this is an idea that needs to be developed to become more musical. There's a huge difference between playing a scale connected with chromatic notes and playing actual melodic lines. So here are two lines based around a C Dorian/melodic minor framework, with some chromatic ideas thrown in to add colour and make things sound more interesting.

Example 11g

The more I've studied the playing of the great jazz improvisers, the more I've seen similar patterns coming up again and again. As guitarists, any time we play the following pattern on a string, we can turn it into a chromatic idea.

Example 11h

This will be true no matter what position we play in, as shown here, this time using C Mixolydian at the 3rd fret.

Example 11i

Or up at the 12th fret area.

Example 11j

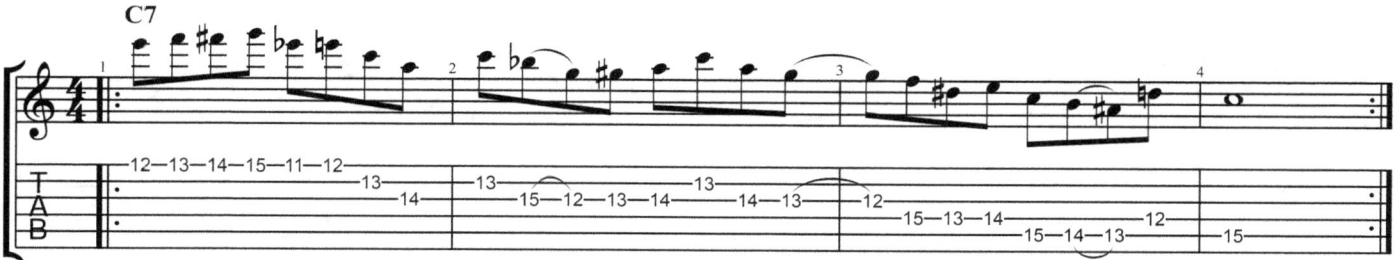

We're going to finish this routine with some chromatic examples played over one of my favourite chord sequences: the bridge of the "rhythm changes" progression. This is taken from the tune *I Got Rhythm* by George Gershwin, a popular jazz standard that he wrote for the musical *Girl Crazy*. While this song is still played a fair amount in its own right, its chord changes were so popular with jazz musicians that many *contrafacts* were written using them (i.e., a new melody written over the harmony borrowed from another song).

Songs based on *I Got Rhythm* are so common they're now just referred to as Rhythm Changes tunes, and some of the best include,

- *Rhythm-A-Ning*
- *Oleo*
- *Lester Leaps In*
- *Cotton Tail*
- *Moose The Mooche*
- *Straighten Up and Fly Right*

The A section of the rhythm changes has lots of fast moving chord changes that can be a real challenge to solo over, but the B section consists of a series of static dominant chords moving through the Circle of 4ths:

| D7 | % | G7 | % | C7 | % | F7 | % |

The rhythm changes are nearly always played in Bb Major and the bridge begins with the III7 chord (D7) then cycles down to F7, the V chord that resolves back to Bbmaj7.

Working on this part of the tune allows us to stretch out with some of our dominant 7 vocabulary, while adding chromatic embellishments.

Here's a simple idea using chromatics over those changes. In order to make things a little easier, I've stayed on the last note of each chord for two beats to give you time to think about where you're going next.

Example 11k

Things begin to flow much better if we connect our chords more.

Example 11l

Here's another exercise to challenge yourself!

Example 11m

And here's one final run at it to see just how many chromatics we can throw in there.

Example 11n

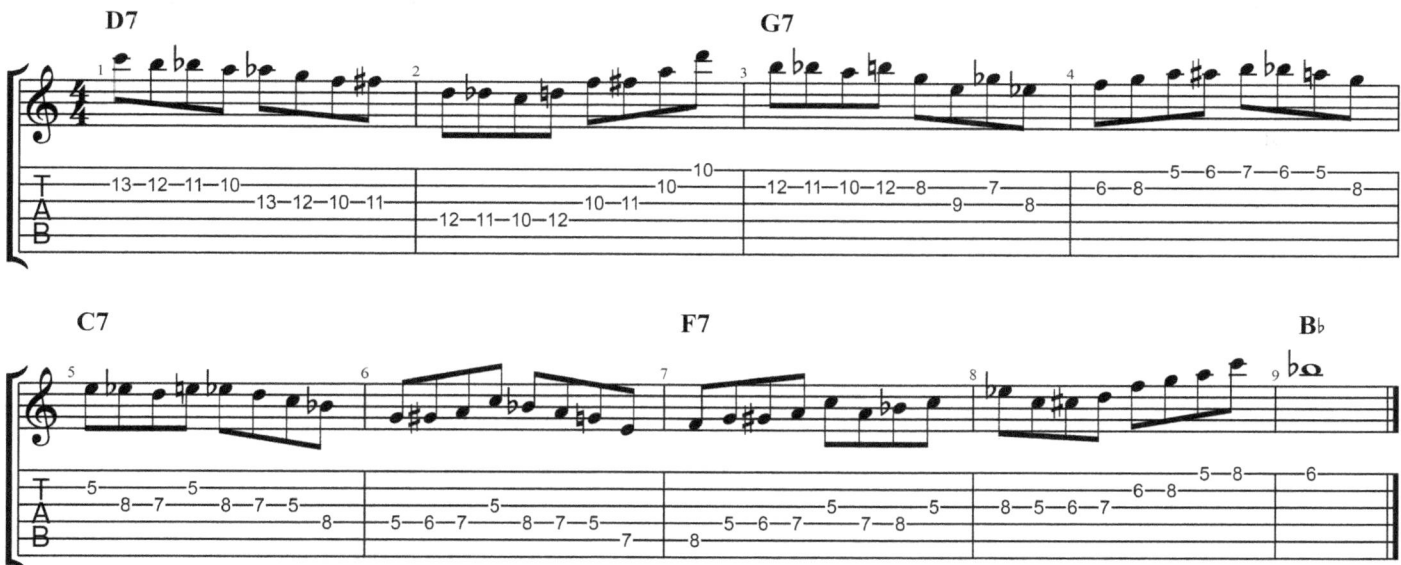

While we can play the chromatic scale as a scale in its own right, the best way to view it is as a source of non-diatonic notes we can draw on when improvising. Chromatic notes are just "colours" that live next to the notes you usually play. The deeper you dig into this concept, the more you'll begin to develop a unique voice as a player. So, get to work and go experiment with these ideas!

Conclusion

And there we have it! We've done ten weeks of practice getting to grips with scales, and we've focused on developing a deeper understanding of intervals – the ingredients that make up every scale. But there are still many months of work ahead, as you take these ideas and develop them further!

No matter what place you were at when you began this course, I hope you've learned a lot more about scales, including how best to practice them, all the while simplifying the process of understanding and constructing new scales.

Now that you have a solid method for building a scale and identifying/comparing its intervals, you should be able to learn new scales much more easily.

The Whole Tone scale? 1, 2, 3, #4, #5, b7. Easy!

Harmonic Major? 1, 2, 3, 4, 5, b6, 7. Easy!

Half-Whole Diminished? 1, b2, b3, 3, b5, 5, 6, b7. Easy!

When you come to work on the books that will follow on from this one (chords, then arpeggios), you'll already be armed with most of the skills you need to make them feel as effortless as possible.

We have covered a LOT of different ideas in this book: scale construction, patterns, sequences, chord progressions, limitation exercises, etc. Don't be afraid to go back, take one idea at a time, and thoroughly explore and apply it.

Once you understand this stuff, applying it is just letting your fingers do the things your brain has already learned. And the more you take the ideas in this book and apply them to other scales you might want to play, the faster you're going to develop as a player.

Get to work and I'll catch you next time!

Good luck,

Levi.

GUIDED GUITAR CHORD PRACTICE ROUTINES

Master Every Essential Guitar Chord in this Comprehensive 10-Week Course

LEVI CLAY

FUNDAMENTAL CHANGES

Guided Guitar Chord Practice Routines

Master Every Essential Guitar Chord in this Comprehensive 10-Week Course

www.fundamental-changes.com

For over 350 free guitar lessons with videos check out:

www.fundamental-changes.com

Join our free Facebook Community of Cool Musicians

www.facebook.com/groups/fundamentalguitar

Tag us for a share on Instagram: **FundamentalChanges**

Cover Image Copyright: Author photo used by permission.

Contents

Introduction 113

How To Use This Book 114

Get the Audio 115

Routine One – Chord Grips 116

Routine Two – Major Triad Workout 123

Routine Three – Minor Triads & Beyond 131

Routine Four – Chord Scales 141

Routine Five – Open Voiced Triads & Inversions 151

Routine Six – 7th Chords & Triad Mutation 159

Routine Seven – Drop 2 Voicings 171

Routine Eight – Drop 3 & Beyond! 181

Routine Nine – Chord Naming Rules & Extensions 189

Routine Ten – Slash Chords 199

Conclusion 210

Introduction

Congratulations on making the step towards taking chords more seriously. I know it sounds hyperbolic, but the day I switched my perspective on music to be more harmony focused, that was the day my musical life changed completely.

We might think of chords as being the domain of the rhythm guitarist (like that's a bad thing!) but the truth is, chords and harmony hold all the power of melody too. Any melody will sound completely different depending on the chord it's being played over, so having an in-depth knowledge of harmony, and understanding how we hear melodies in relation to it, will influence our melodic decisions and make us better soloists.

Most guitar players have a sense of the importance of chords, and over the 20 years I've been teaching, I've often been asked what books I studied to learn all the chords I know. The truth is, I didn't read any! I remember Joe Pass talking about chord books, referring to them as huge compendiums with page after page of chord diagrams that don't help us learn anything. The reality is, trying to learn a thousand chord diagrams is plain silly – and that's before we consider that many voicings just aren't usable in the real world.

So, you won't find page after page of diagrams here. Instead, I'll show you how I worked on harmony. Here you'll find a systematic series of week-long routines, each introducing a new harmonic concept. These routines aren't just about showing you lots of chord shapes to add to your arsenal, they aim to grow your understanding of chord construction, theory, and practical application.

By the end of this book, you should never need another lesson on chords. You'll have all the tools you need to be able to build any chord you like and find your own voicings.

That said, chords are built from scales, so having a solid understanding of scales is going to be essential to your progress in this pursuit. This book is number two in a series, so I'll assume (or at least hope) that you've already worked through the first book, *Guided Guitar Scale Practice Routines*.

The routines contained here might feel like a lot of work at first, but remember, this is all about a complete shift in perspective – one that will revolutionise your playing. If you feel like you're wading through mud at first, that's completely normal. You are reprogramming the way you think. We're not just buying a house here, we're learning how to think like architects and engineers!

But I promise you it'll be worth it. So let's get on with it.

Levi

How To Use This Book

I've gone out of my way to make the books in my guided practice series different from every guitar book you've read before, and this one is no different.

Not only is there a full description of each exercise and downloadable audio for every example, there's also an additional full-length recording of each entire routine, with all the repeats, and with me talking you through it as we play it together. If you prepare yourself to play these full routines with me every day, I guarantee you will see growth.

There are only three rules for how to use this book…

First, learn the material, then practice the routines!

Although the routines are designed to each span one week, it's likely that they'll take longer. I always talk about the difference between learning and practice. We learn a thing, then we practice it. If you already know all the material, then you can jump straight into practicing it and be done in a week. However, if you're learning things that are new to you, that information must be solidly in place before you leap into the practice routine.

Don't feel the need to rush, otherwise you'll get discouraged. Take a week or two just to learn the exercises if you need. Rushing will just lead to roadblocks in your playing later. There's a lot of stuff here, so take your time with it.

Second, while this book will arm you with every concept you'll ever need to master chords, it's not possible to notate every possible permutation of each exercise in every key. We didn't want to publish an intimidating 750-page book. Talk about off-putting! I'll hold your hand for the journey but there will come a point where you'll need to take a chord type you've learned and apply the principles of practice for yourself. The more you put in, the more you'll get out.

Lastly, let me briefly mention songs too. We have to remember that playing music is ultimately about playing songs. There are a ton of exercises here that are applied to various chord progressions, but nothing beats using the chords/concepts in this book by applying them to real songs that you know or want to learn.

My main gig is in the Soul genre, so I'm deep into that traditional RnB, Blues and Gospel sound – but you can apply these ideas to whatever style is your bag. Be sure to do that, because that's what's going to make you a real musician – someone who can get up and play songs and make them sound good.

That's about it, so let's start our routines!

Get the Audio

The audio files for this book are available to download for free from **www.fundamental-changes.com**.

The link is in the top right-hand corner. Click on the "Guitar" link then simply select this book title from the drop-down menu and follow the instructions to get the audio.

We recommend that you download the files directly to your computer, not to your tablet, and extract them there before adding them to your media library.

For over 350 free guitar lessons with videos check out:

www.fundamental-changes.com

Join our free Facebook Community of Cool Musicians

www.facebook.com/groups/fundamentalguitar

Tag us for a share on Instagram: FundamentalChanges

Routine One – Chord Grips

In this first chapter, I want to address what I call *chord grips*. The guitar is an interesting instrument because it combines the ability to play chords like a piano with portability. It's quite unique in this respect, which is why it has a long history of being the go-to tool for singer-songwriters.

Above all other instruments, the guitar is also incredibly shaped based. I've met countless guitarists who can play chords that they can't name. Typically, they have learned a bunch of open chords, maybe a few barre chords, then they just move them around to get the sound they want. That doesn't happen with pianists. That's not to say I think it's wrong, though. In fact, I think it's awesome. It means we're able to learn chords on the guitar quickly, whereas on the piano we have to learn the notes that go into a chord before we can play it.

I wanted to write this book in a way that celebrates the accessibility of the guitar, so we're going to start there. We're going to use the familiar open chord shapes as reference points from which we'll build and explore. Don't worry, we'll learn the theory that backs up every idea too, but having clear reference points from which we can work on harmony will give our practice some real focus.

You may have heard these open chords affectionally referred to as "cowboy chords". If you know these chords and own a capo, then you'll be able to strum a lifetime of songs around the campfire! You won't be thinking about issues like chord construction, key signatures or harmony theory, but at least you'll have a selection of grips your hand can effortlessly jump to.

The five most important open chords are E major, D major, C major, A major, and G major.

To warm up, we're going to cycle through them, just thinking of them as physical grips and focusing on achieving good fretting technique and clean execution.

Example 1a:

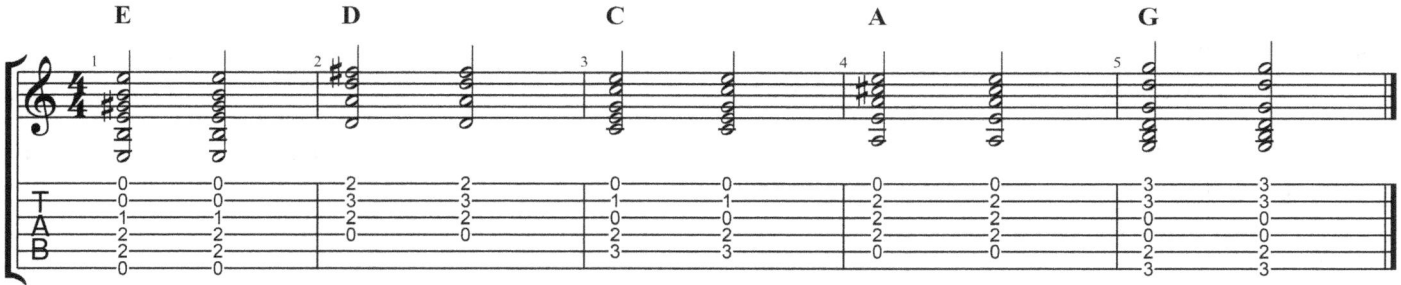

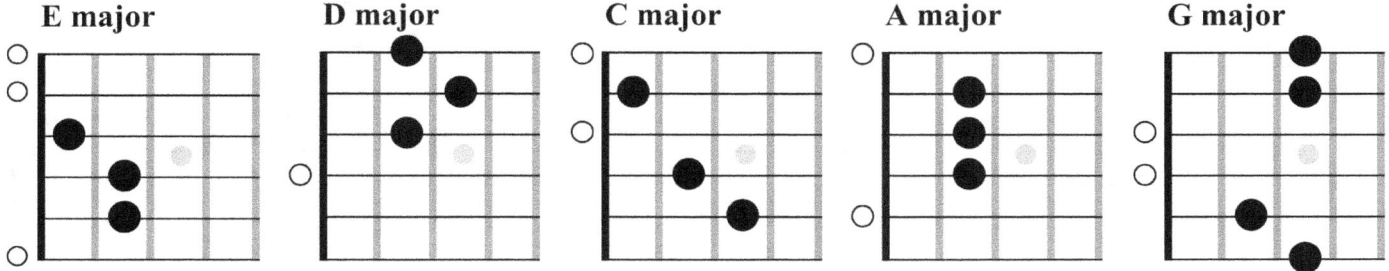

Some of you may have made the connection to the CAGED system (or EDCAG as I laid it out). We'll delve deeper into that soon, but for now we're making sure we have the most common chord grips under our hands.

Moving on, what about open position minor chords?

Example 1b:

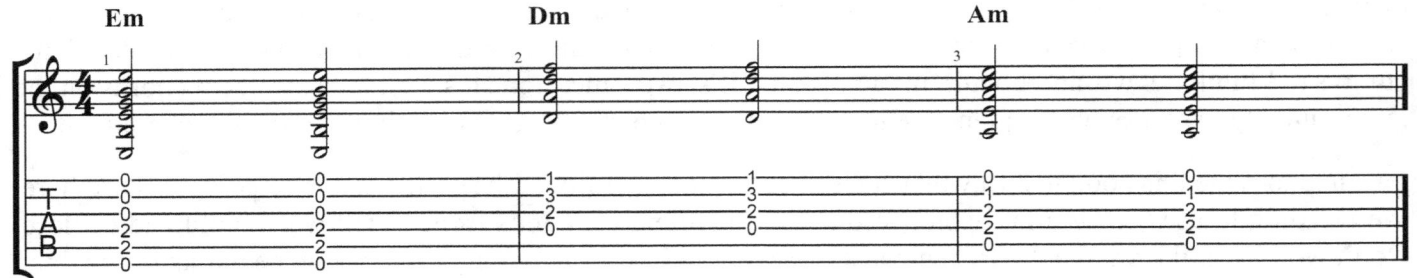

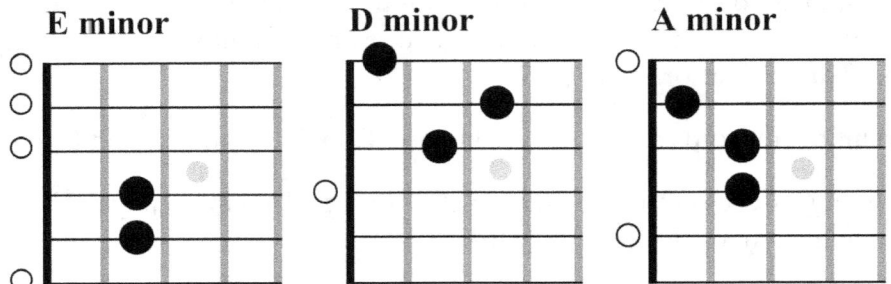

You'll notice there's no open C minor or G minor. These are theoretically possible to play, but hard work on the hand, so they are never played in the real world.

Of course, there are lots more open chords to learn – 7th chords, inversions, suspended chords, slash chords and more – but they are all based on the five chords in Example 1a. For example:

Example 1c:

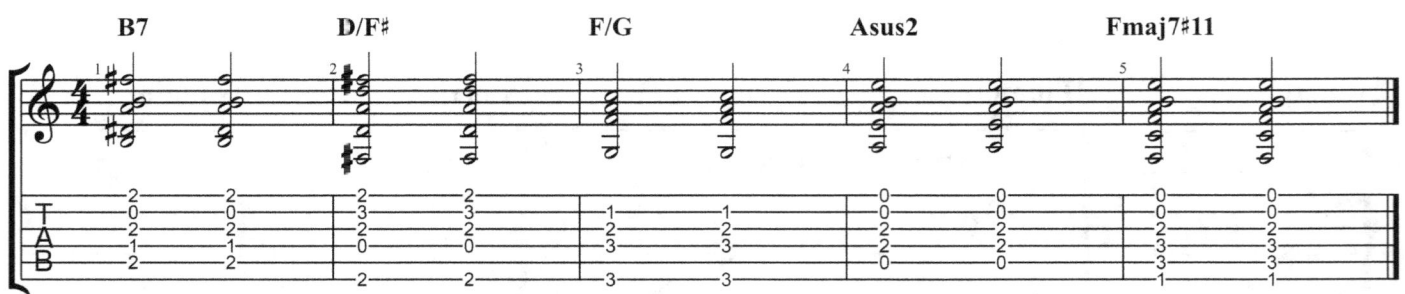

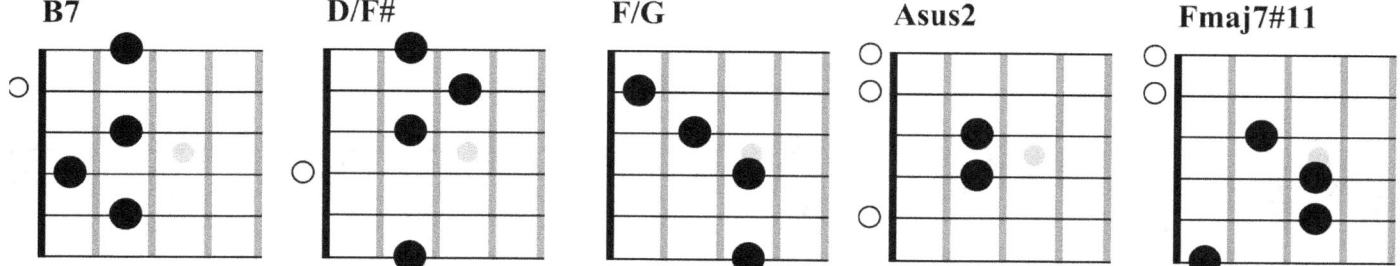

How many singer-songwriters have managed to write entire libraries of material using just three of these basic chords? The secret is making sure we can transition effortlessly between the common chord grips, as in the next example.

Example 1d:

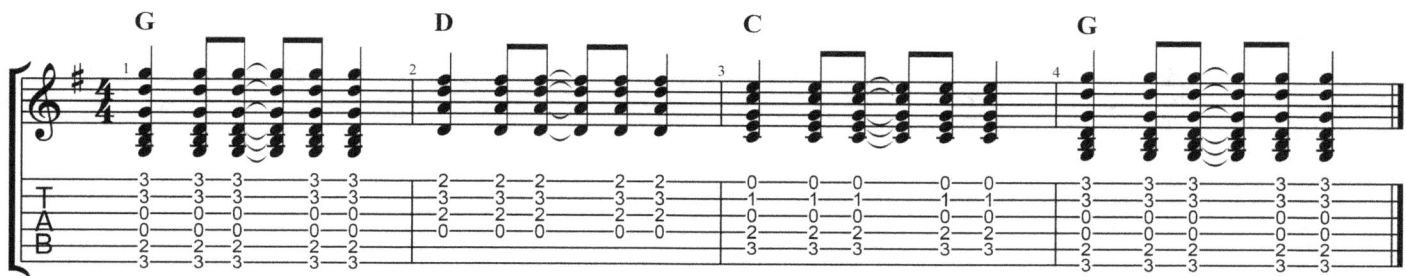

The next step in developing the basic open shapes is turning them into their barred forms. The most commonly used is the E major chord, moved up the neck one fret at a time. For that reason, we call this the "E shape".

Example 1e:

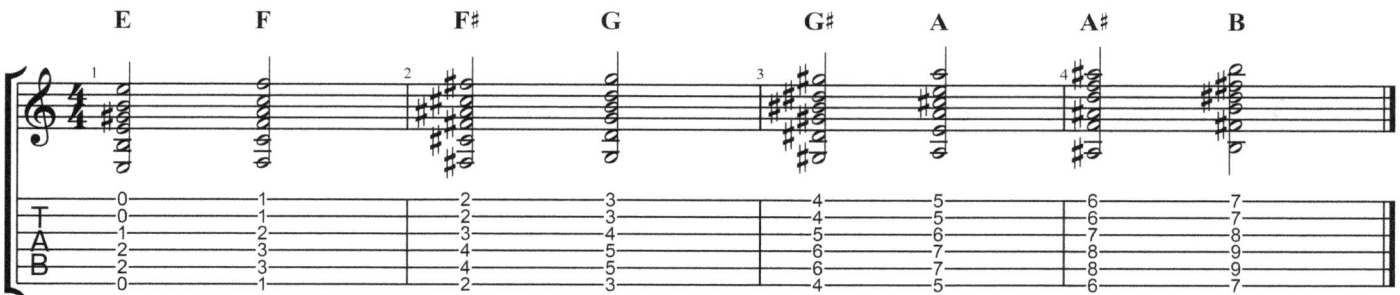

We can move each open chord in the same way. Here's the A shape moved up the neck. Notice that I don't try to get the note on the high E string when barring. Instead, I use the ring finger to barre the D, G, and B strings, but I know that top note could be there if I wanted.

Example 1f:

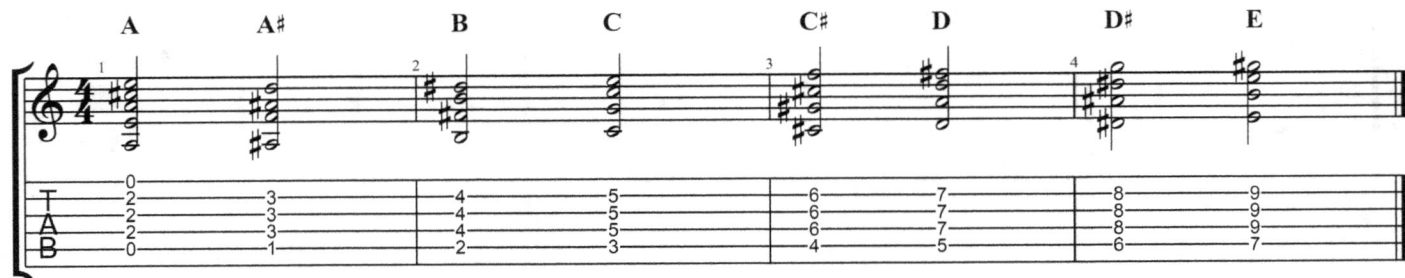

Next, here's the C shape. This one in incredibly important and is the shape every one of my new students struggles with. Sort it out!

Example 1g:

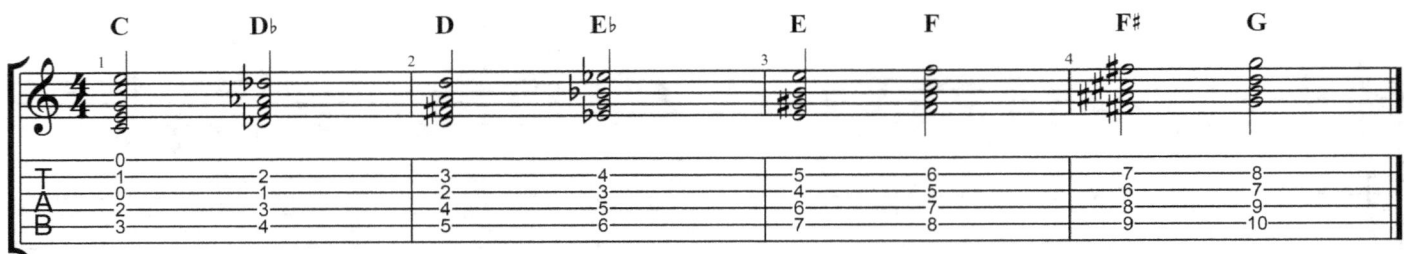

When it comes to moveable D and G shapes, they are possible, but I can honestly say the last time I played these was when I was recording the audio for a different book. There's a difference between what's possible and what's practical in the real world. I always veer towards the pragmatic! Try them anyway.

Example 1h:

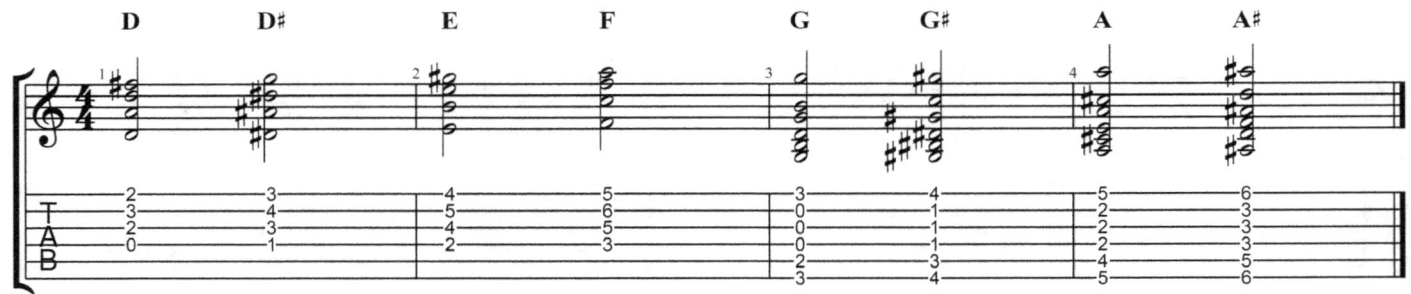

So the most important of our shapes are the E, A, and C shapes. The following exercise cycles through three G major chord voicings, first in the E shape, then the C shape, then the A shape.

When doing this, it's incredibly important to focus on one thing only: the root note on the E or A string. That's all I'm seeing. I look for that note, then I put the correct chord grip on top of it.

Example 1i:

Here's the same idea applied to a C major chord. Focus on the C root note on the 3rd fret of the A string, then the 8th fret of the low E, jumping up to the 15th fret on the A string for the higher octave.

Example 1j:

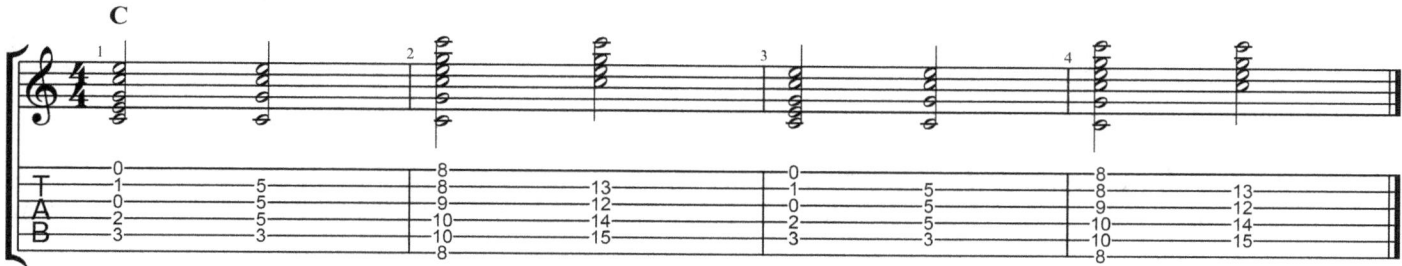

When we think like this, we can identify the root note movements for a progression like E – G#m – A – B and plug chord grips on top of them. Here's that progression using E shape chords, but on the repeat we're throwing in a C shape for the E major, just to mix things up.

Example 1k:

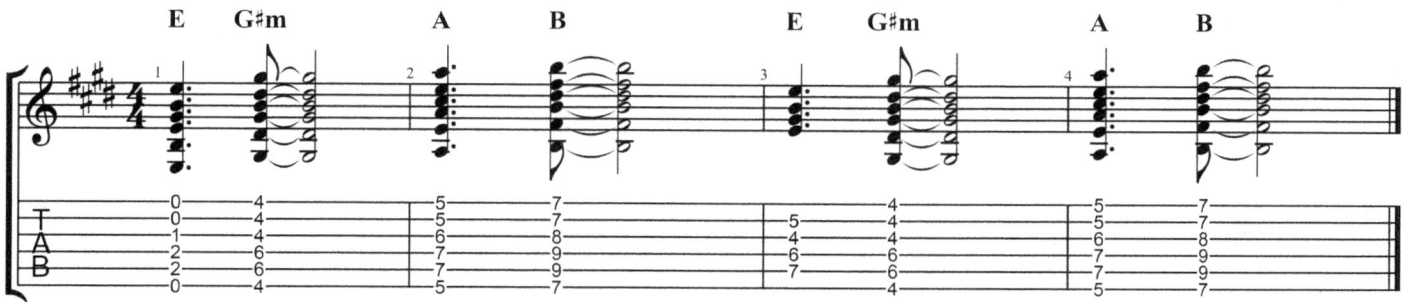

I made a big deal in my previous book about the use of the Circle of 5ths as a tool for practicing in twelve keys, and nowhere is that more useful that here.

As a reminder, starting on C, the Circle of 5ths pattern is:

C – F – Bb – Eb – Ab – Db – Gb – B – E – A – D – G – C

Apply that to the fretboard using our E, A, and C grips, and we have the following

Example 1l:

There are a lot of ways we could play through this progression. Just focus on looking for the root note of each chord on the E or A string, then apply the chord grip that fits on that root note. Here's a pathway starting down in the A shape.

Example 1m:

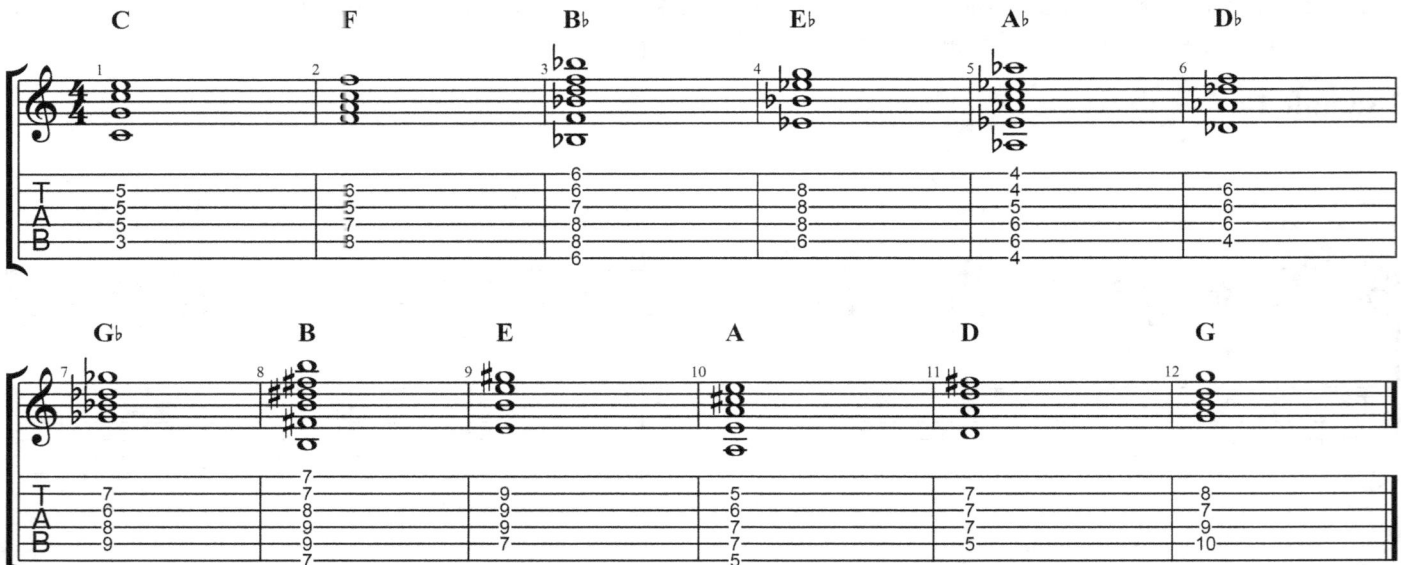

For one final example, we could move through our three chord grips on each chord to keep us on our toes, always looking for the next chord change while developing the fretboard relationship between different voicings of the same chord.

Example 1n:

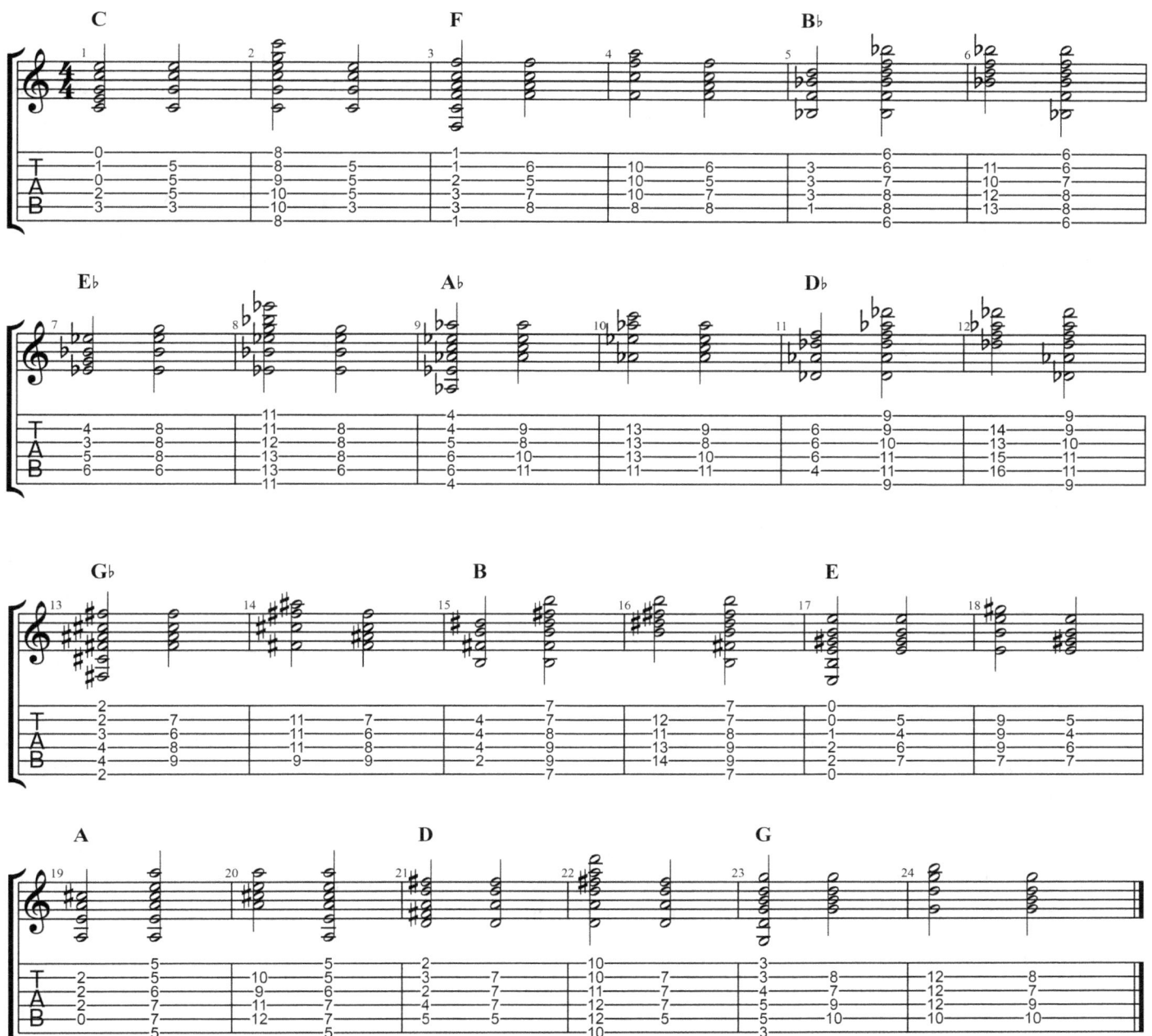

Spend some time getting used to these shapes because we're going to be using them as visualisation tools to help focus our study of chord construction.

See you there!

Routine Two – Major Triad Workout

Now we're going to start thinking about chords from the perspective of chord theory and construction. Chords are built from the notes of scales, so a sound knowledge of scales is essential. In my guided scale practice book, I placed huge emphasis on knowing your intervals, because that's how we hear notes – the distance between the note we're playing and the root note of the scale. It's that interval relationship that gives each note its emotional impact.

Our Western system of harmony is based on the principle of *tertian* harmony. In other words, we form chords by stacking them in 3rds. Let's take the C Major scale (C D E F G A B C). If we take the first note, then a note a 3rd higher, then a note another 3rd higher, that gives us C, E, and G. Together they form a C major triad – the tonic chord of the scale.

Let's apply that to the guitar. Here is the C Major scale played on the A string, followed by the notes of the triad (the 1st, 3rd and 5th degrees of the scale).

Example 2a:

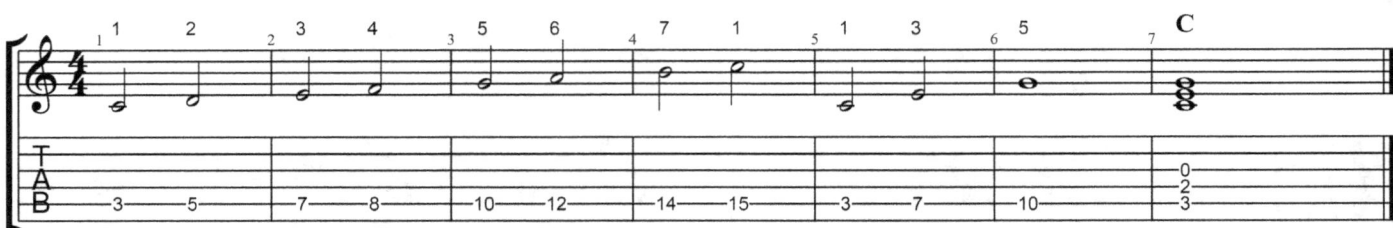

So, the root, 3rd and 5th of the major scale are the ingredients of a major triad. Knowing those intervals feels much more useful than trying to remember the pitches of each note. And the formula is the same whatever key you happen to be playing in.

Sticking with C major (C E G), it doesn't matter where those notes are played, or in what order (C doesn't have to be the lowest note), they will always spell a C major triad. And there are lots of ways we can play those three notes on guitar. Here's a small selection of them:

Example 2b:

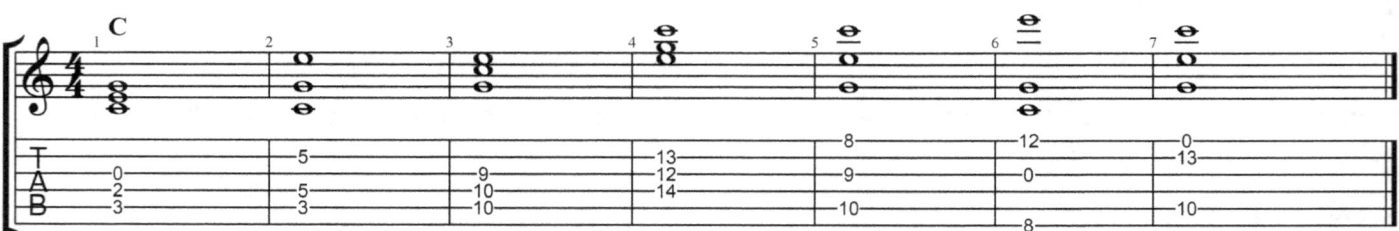

It wouldn't be practical to memorise every possible triad voicing that can be played on guitar. Instead, we need a system of organisation to help compartmentalise different areas of the fretboard. Fortunately, we've already done the bulk of the work by learning our E, A, and C grips. Here is an easy way to break down those shapes into triads.

It's possible to play C major in the C shape utilising every string, as in bar one of Example 2c. Then, if we break that big shape down into several smaller shapes, each one arranged on three adjacent strings, we get this:

Example 2c:

Let's take a look at what just happened.

Remember that it's a C major triad (C E G), even if the notes appear in a different order. On the top three strings we have the notes G, C, E, low to high. On the next string set we have E, G, C. Then we have C, E, G, and finally G, C, E on the bottom three strings.

The thing to notice about this pattern is that each new triad is formed by taking the highest note of the previous one and moving it to the bottom.

We took the high E note from the triad on the top three strings, and moved it to the bottom of the triad on the next string set. Then we took the high C note from that triad and moved it to the bottom of the next one, and so on.

We call these *closed voiced* triads. This means that all the notes in the chord are arranged as close together as possible (usually on adjacent strings), fit within an octave, and are stacked in 3rds.

If we do the same with the A shape, we get the following.

Example 2d:

The main mistake students tend to make when working on this is not grasping the idea of moving from one triad to the next by taking the *top note* and moving it to the *bottom*.

For example, after playing the second triad in bar two above, arranged on the D, G and B strings, they will just move every note across a string at the 5th fret. But this means they're now playing the notes C, G, C and it's no longer a triad. Instead, the E note on top of that shape needs relocating to the 7th fret of the A string. It's crucial to get into our heads this idea of taking the top note and moving it to the bottom!

Let's do the same with the E shape, focusing on the top note moving to the bottom each time.

Example 2e:

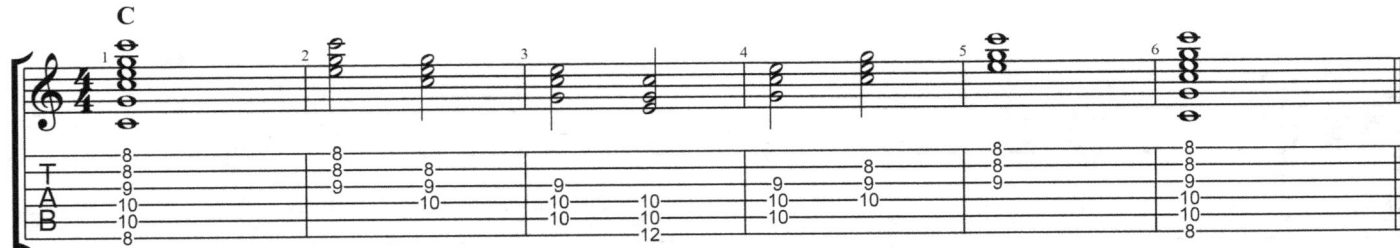

If we put all of this into diagram form, it immediately becomes clear how the major triads lay out across the neck in three distinct areas. I call them the A, E, and C shapes, because I visualise them around those CAGED patterns. These are my "master patterns".

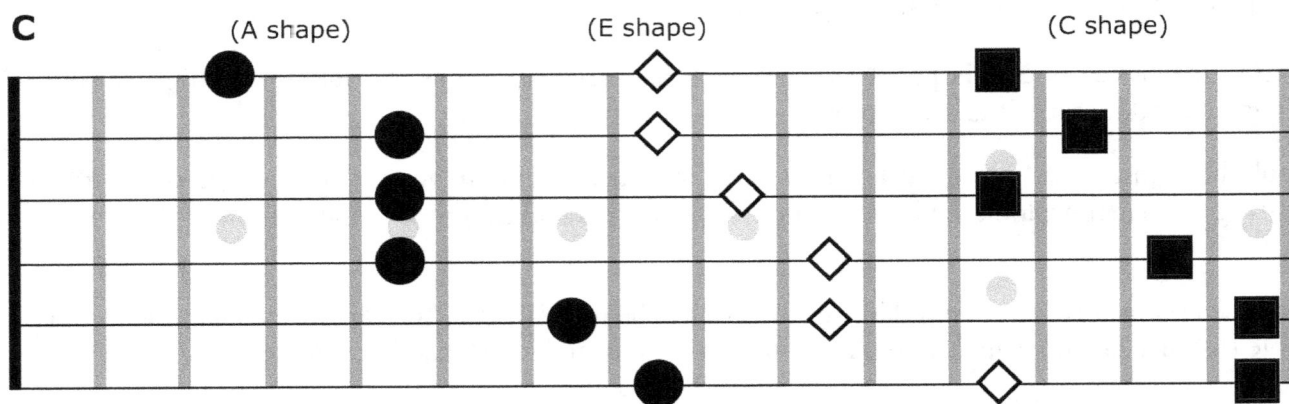

The goal we are working towards is to effortlessly play triads across all string sets in any key – and to be able to do so because we can *see* those bigger barre forms. Let's switch to a G major triad. Think about the larger barre shapes and pick out the closed voiced triads.

Example 2f:

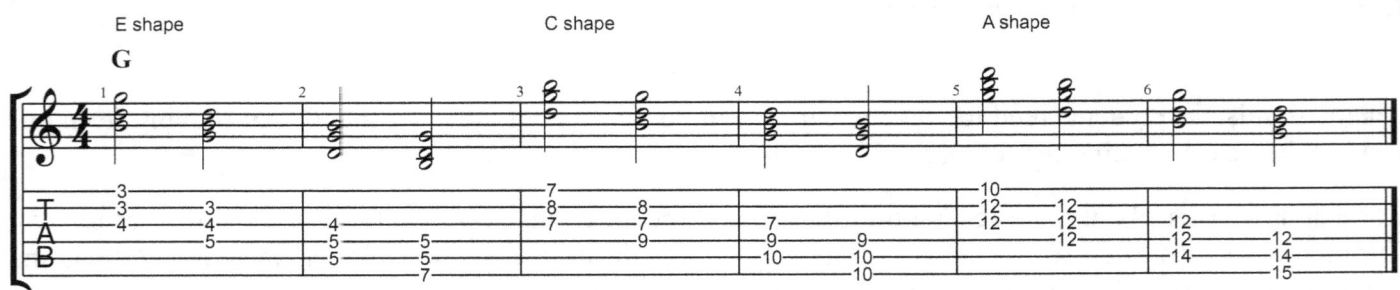

I call this approach *vertical* because we're moving triads across the strings in a single area of the fretboard. But we can also take a *horizontal* approach, where we play along the length of the neck.

In Example 2g, we take the first E shape G major triad and move it on the same strings to the C shape, then the A shape. Then we play the E shape again in the higher octave before descending. This tests our ability to immediately visualise the big barre forms in each zone of the neck, while picking out the smaller triads.

Then we move to the E shape G major triad voiced on the D, G and B strings, repeat the process, and so on.

Example 2g:

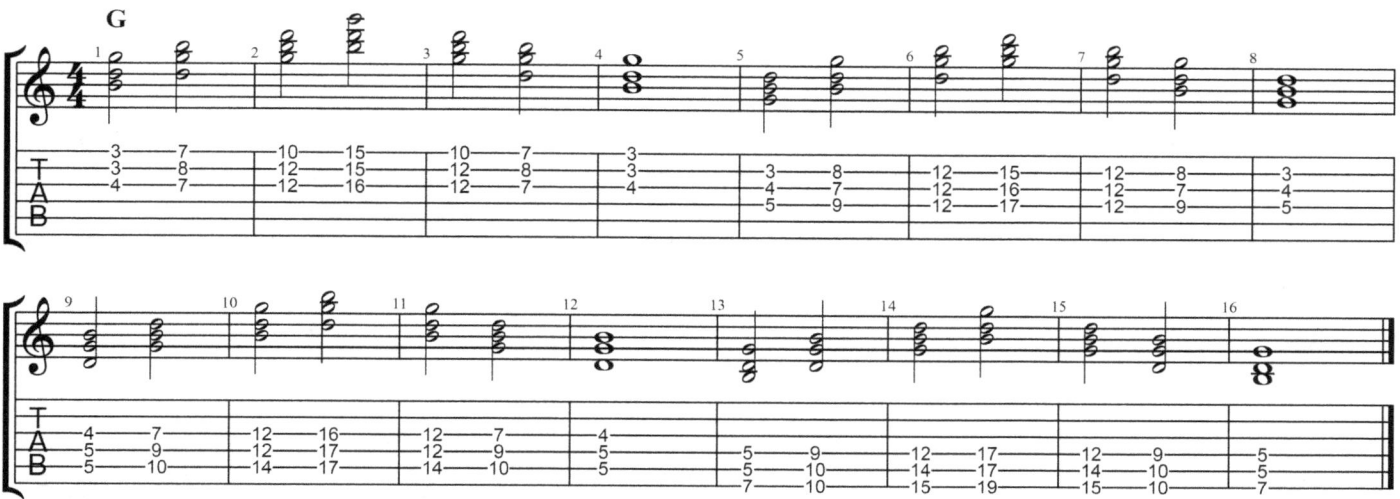

There are lots of ways to practice these three positions, and I'm a firm believer in the idea that the more we stress our brains in the practice room, the more results we'll see. So, I like to combine horizontal and vertical approaches to test myself.

In the following example, we start with a G major triad on the low strings. To move to the next voicing, we have two choices:

Vertical – stay in position and change string set.

Horizontal – change position using the same string set.

The goal we're working towards is to always be able to *see* these two options, so that we can choose one and, when we move to it, visualise the *next* two options. This exercise isn't easy!

Example 2h:

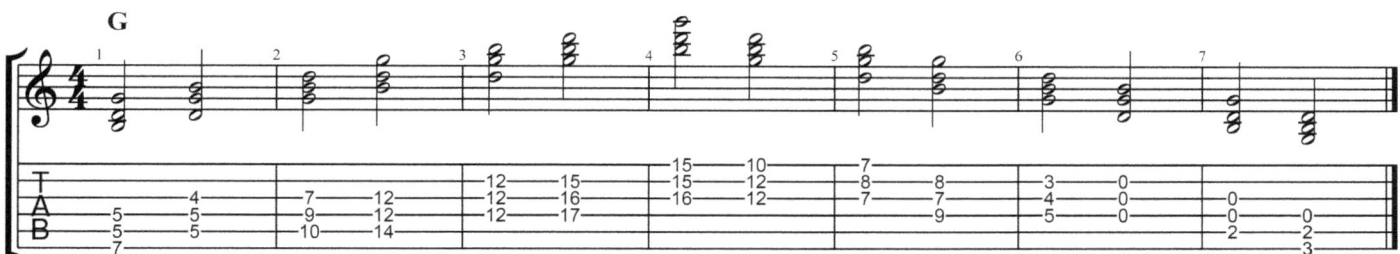

We can do this with any major triad. The key is visualising our three larger "master patterns", so we can confidently pick out the smaller, closed voiced triads. Here's the same idea outlining a C major chord.

Example 2i:

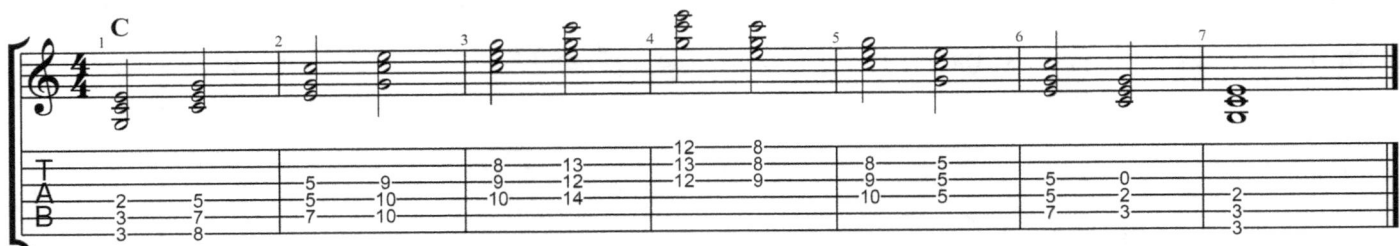

At this stage, we're still mostly thinking about closed voiced triads as shapes. We'll focus much more on their intervals in next week's routine. But first, we have to learn to confidently see them.

Let's work around the Circle of 4ths this time and only play triads on the D, G, B string set. It's the same idea as the previous routine: we're looking for the big barre chord, then playing a smaller triad within it.

Example 2j:

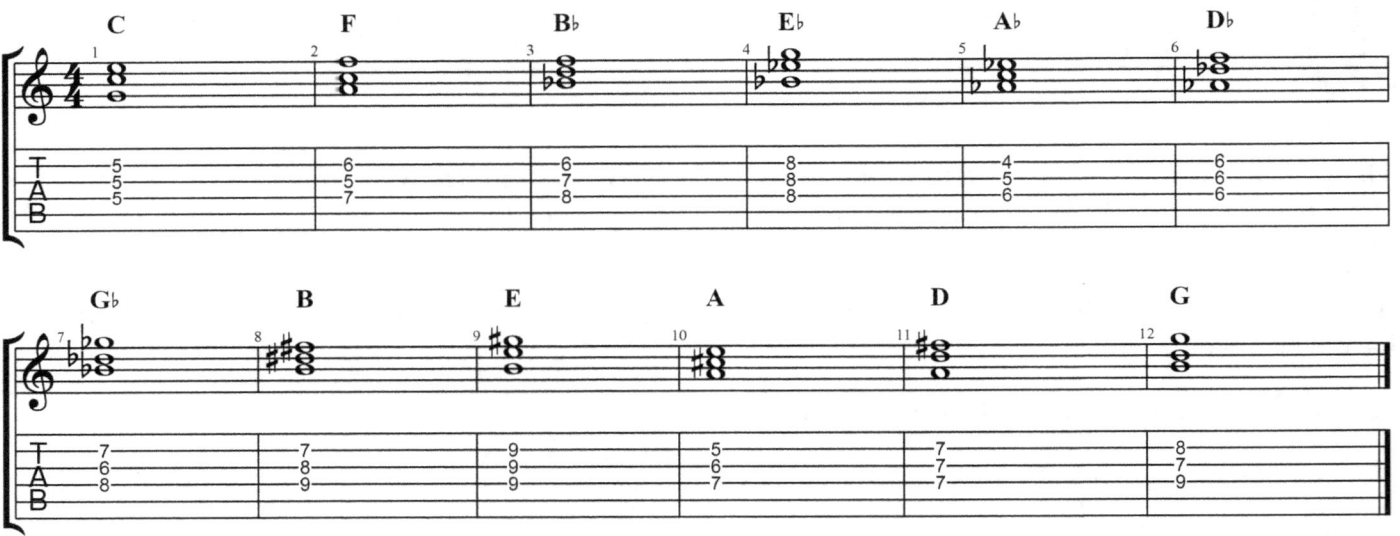

To keep us on our toes, let's repeat that but play two triads in horizontal fashion for each chord.

Example 2k:

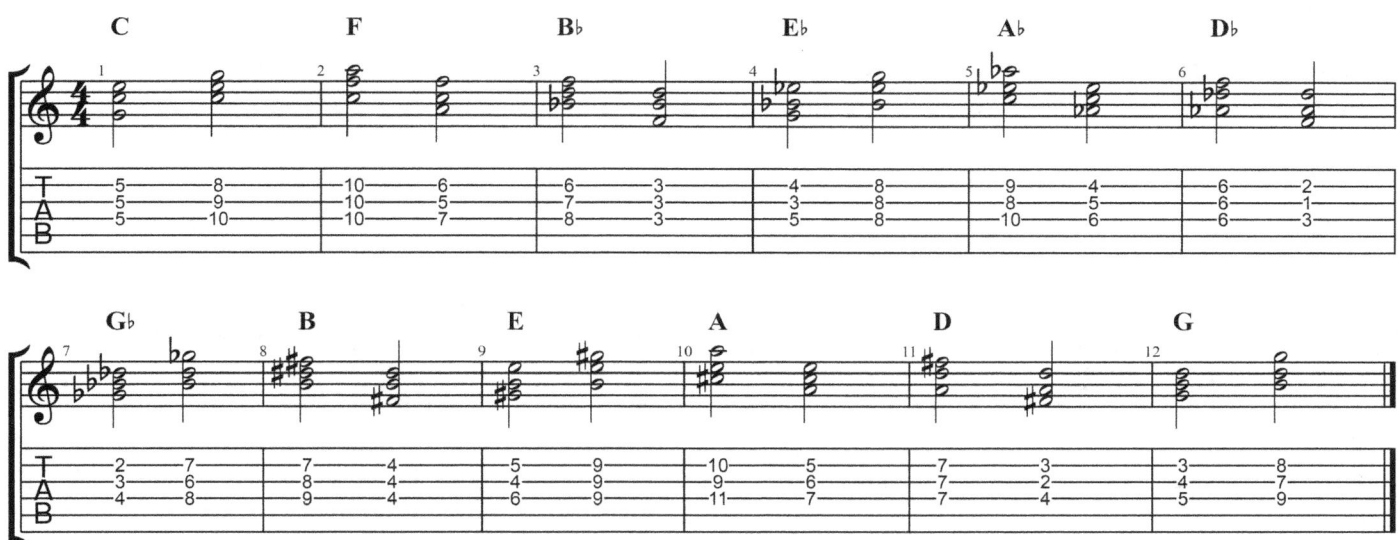

You could (and should!) be working on this in your own practice times, aiming to do the same thing on different string sets – like this example, where we play only the top three strings.

Example 2l:

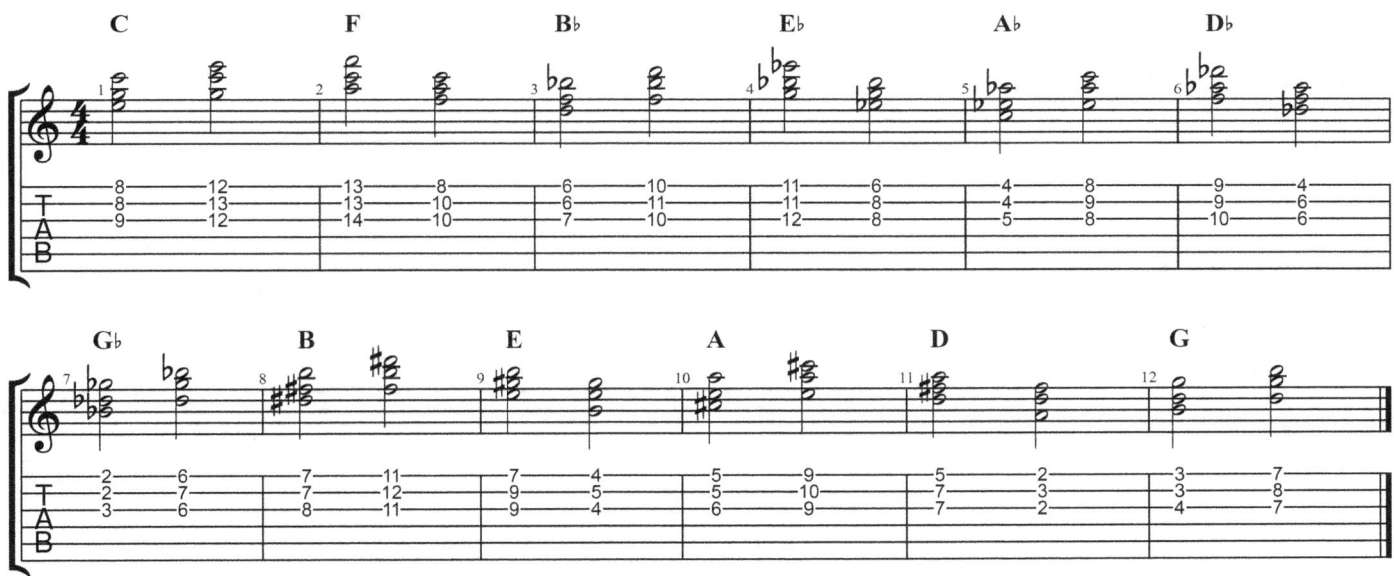

Now I want you to do that on all string sets, breaking them up horizontally and vertically! Challenge yourself. Stress your brain!

Thankfully, you're not likely to have to do anything as stressful as this in real world music, so now I want to look at some practical chord progressions. To begin with, I–IV–V patterns.

If that terminology is new to you, let's quickly decode it.

In a major key (let's take C Major), the chords built on the 1st, 4th and 5th scale degrees are all major chords. Every chord in a key is assigned a Roman numeral, hence we have a I–IV–V sequence (1 4 5). In C Major those chords are C, F and G.

We can learn the pattern of a sequence like this. If you know where your I chord is located, the IV will always be in the same place in relation to it, as will the V chord.

Example 2m:

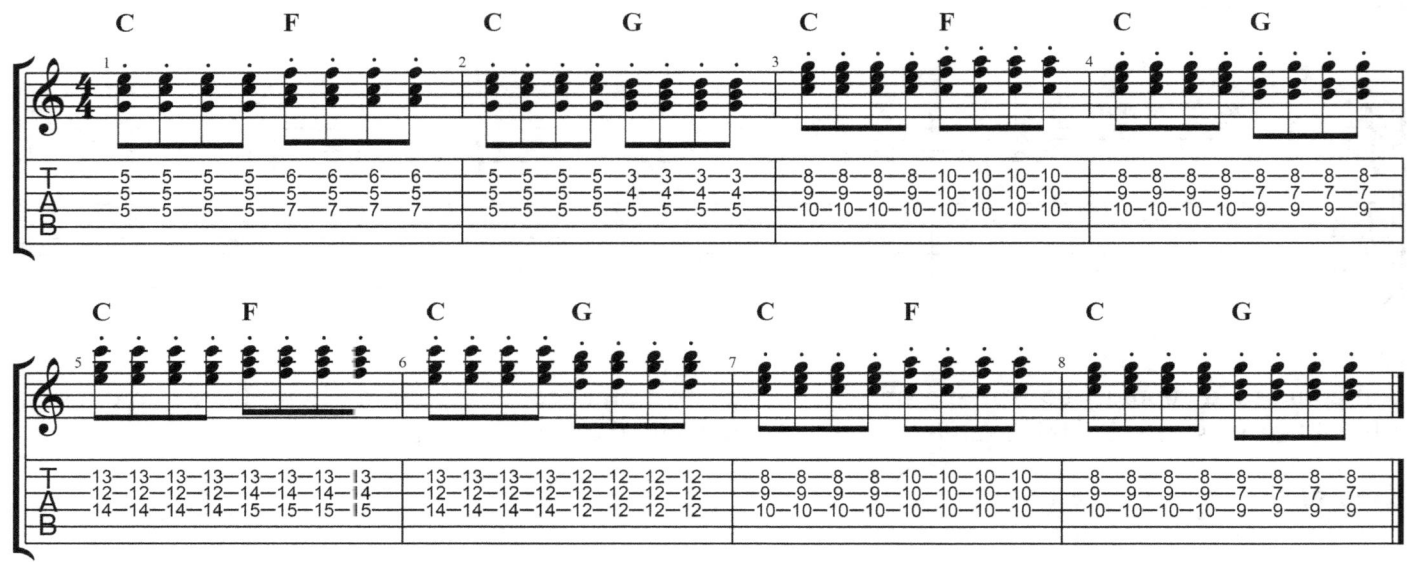

Here's the same idea played on the A, D, G string set.

Example 2n:

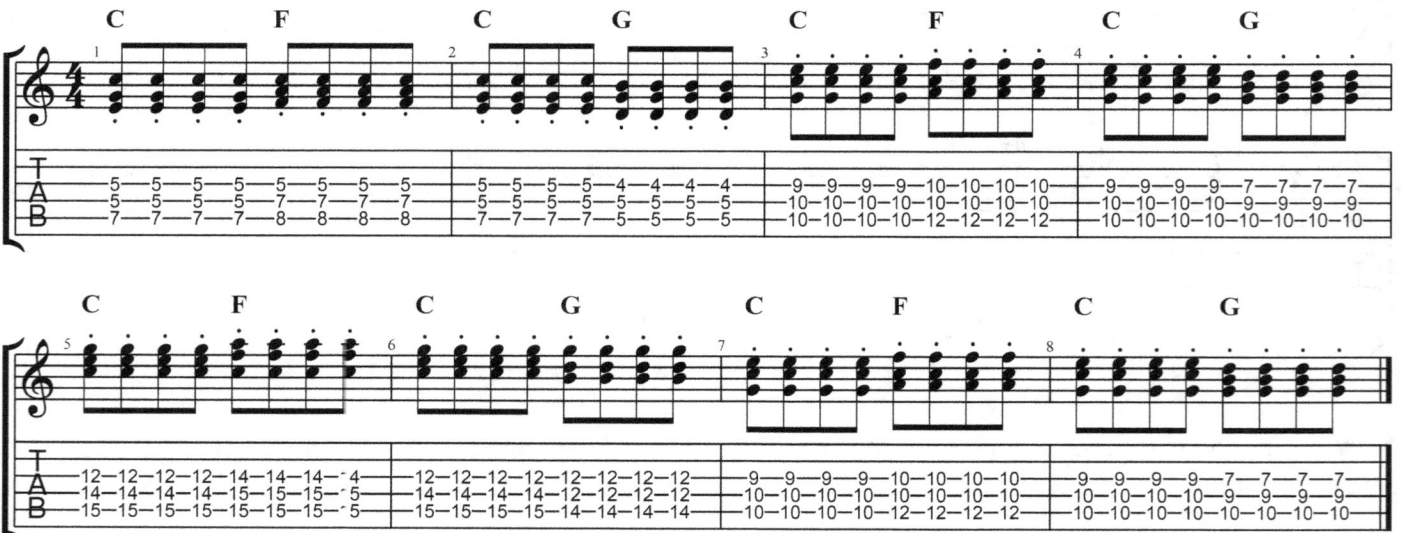

The relationship between a major chord and a chord a 4th higher can be called a "I–IV move". I use this idea all the time to add a little colour to a major chord. So, in the following example, we play C *and* F triads over a C major harmony. We do the same for the F major chord, using F and Bb triads, and the same for G major, using G and C triads. You can create an instant riff with this idea.

Example 2o:

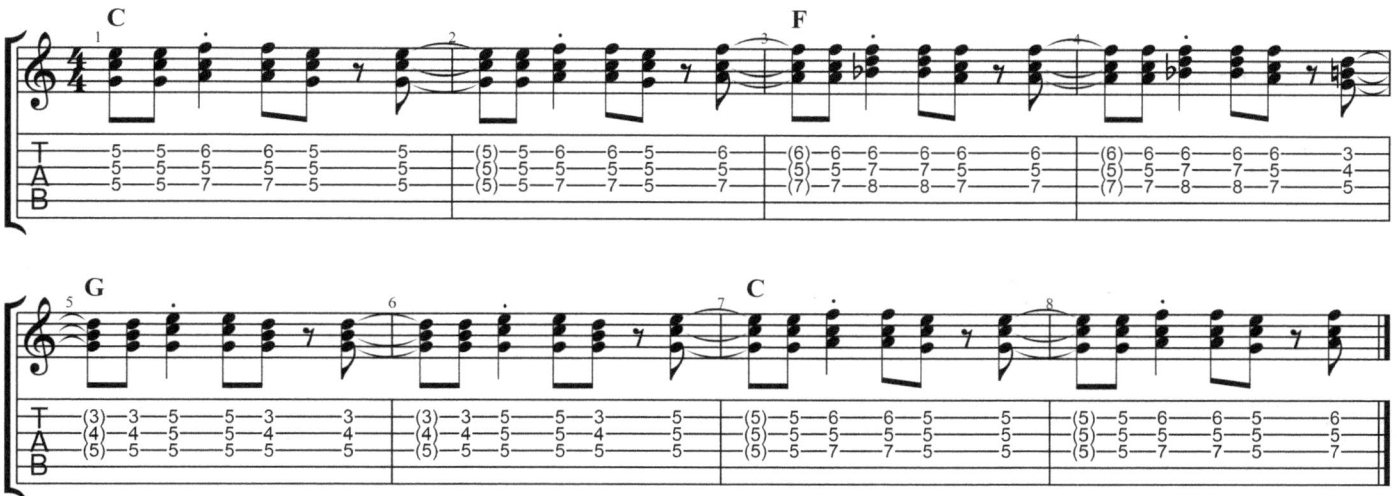

Here's the same I–IV movement on the top strings, using a slightly different rhythmic idea.

Example 2p:

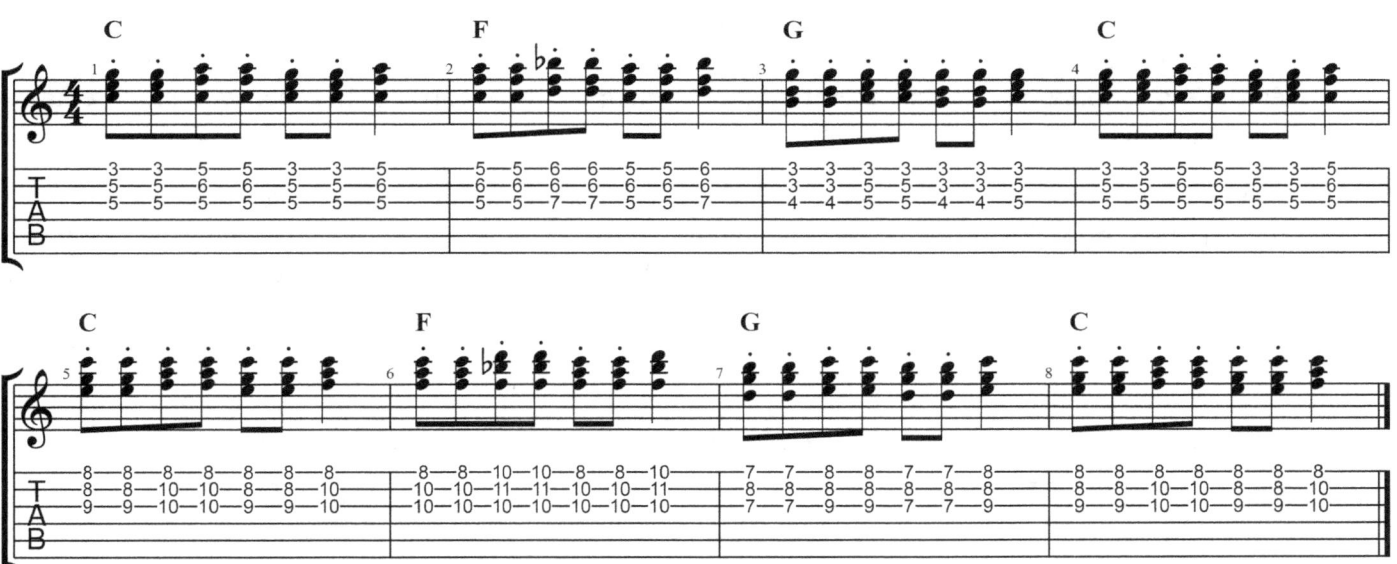

As we continue to study, you'll notice that major triads come up time and again. Not just on the I, IV and V chords in a key, but on lots of others. So, don't underestimate the importance of this week's routine. Major triads are incredibly versatile and we need to know their voicings inside out, without hesitation, in any key.

Routine Three – Minor Triads & Beyond

Everything we've done so far can be repeated with the major scale's sibling, the natural minor scale.

C Natural Minor has the notes C D Eb F G Ab Bb C

Using the principle of tertian harmony we can take the first note, skip the next, then skip another note, and we have C, Eb, G – a C minor triad.

This the principal triad in the minor scale and it's the pepper to the major triad's salt.

Example 3a:

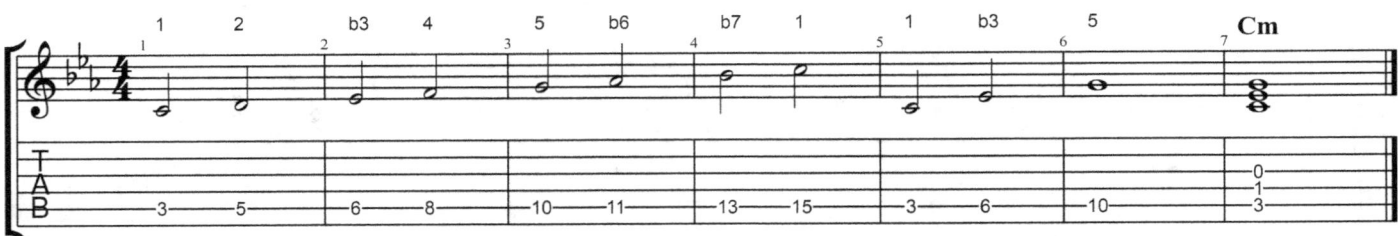

The important thing to spot here is that the difference between a major triad and a minor triad is just one note – the b3. We can take *any* major triad, lower its 3rd to a b3, and we'll have a minor triad.

In order to be able to do this effortlessly, we need to know where the 3rd is located in any of our major triad voicings. At this point, we shift away from *shapes* and begin to think much more about *intervals*.

In our chord grips routine, we put a lot of emphasis on finding the root note on the E and A strings. This is a great starting point, because if we can confidently see the root note, we can work out where other intervals are located. I always apply my "If this, therefore this" principle when learning. In other words, if we know one thing, we can use it to deduce another thing.

You're probably very proficient in locating root notes on the E and A strings, but we need to know where all the root notes are to apply this principle. So, take another look at the E, C and A shape major barre chords. Start by looking at the root notes on the E and A strings, then focus on learning the octave patterns to locate the higher root notes.

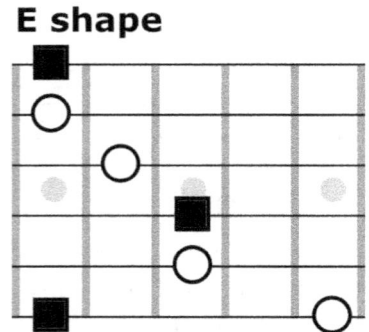
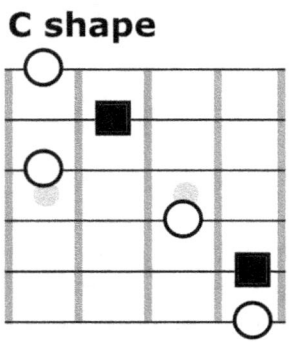
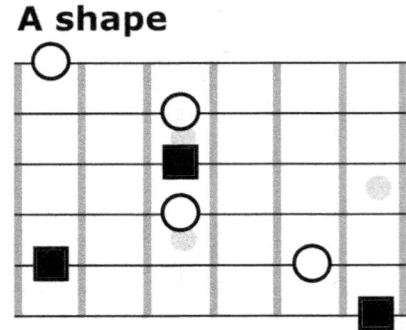

Practice locating all the root notes until you can drop on them at will in all three shapes. It might take a little while to commit to memory, but it's an important step. If we know where the root notes are, we can use them to work out where the 3rd interval is located.

Here's the key: if you know where the root note is, the next note up will *always* be the 3rd.

Let's work through this using a G major chord (G B D). In bar one of Example 3b, we play a G major triad on the top three strings. We know from studying the E shape diagram that the root is located on the D string, below this voicing. Therefore, we know that the note on the G string must be the 3rd. We can then flatten this note to a b3 (Bb) to make a G minor triad.

In bar two, we move onto the next string set. The G root is there on the D string, and we know that the note above it on the G string is the 3rd, which we flatten to make G minor.

The 3rd is still located on the G string when we move down to the next string set.

Finally, when we're on the lowest string set, we're not using the G string anymore, so the 3rd must be located on a new string. In this instance, it's the Bb note on the E string, 6th fret.

Example 3b:

Now let's apply this idea to the C shape.

Example 3c:

And the A shape.

Example 3d:

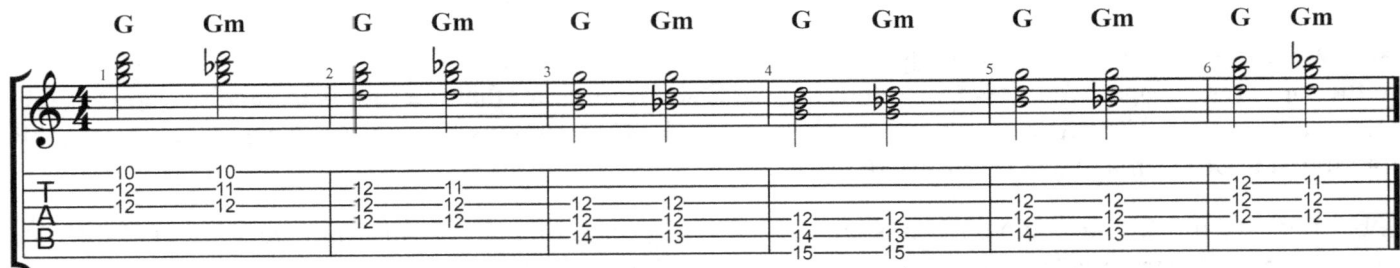

Converting major triads into minor triads is important interval training for us, but once we know this, we can begin drilling minor triads in their own right, without needing to play the major triad first. The diagram below shows all three large minor barre shapes at a glance.

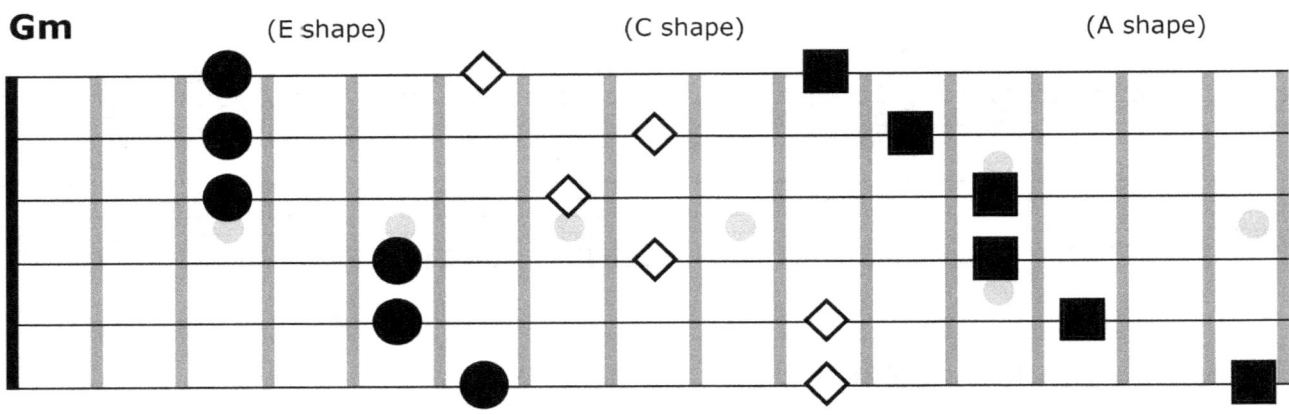

Here are the smaller G minor triads contained within the large shapes, played consecutively.

Example 3e:

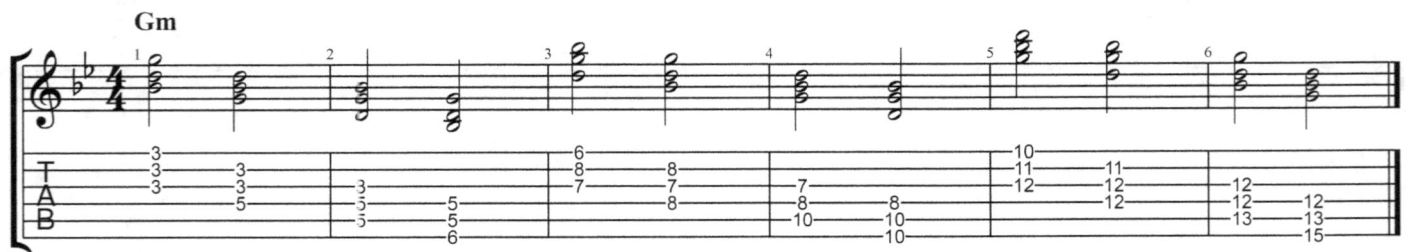

The obvious next step is to be able to do this in any key. Here we're playing C minor triads.

Example 3f:

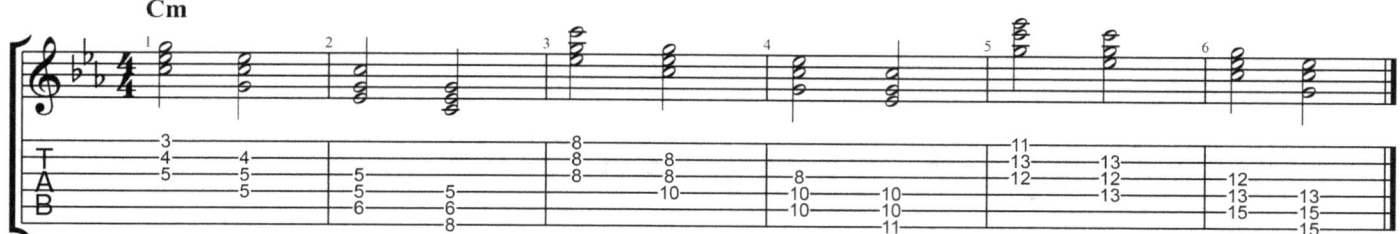

Let's stay with C minor but combine vertical and horizonal approaches.

Example 3g:

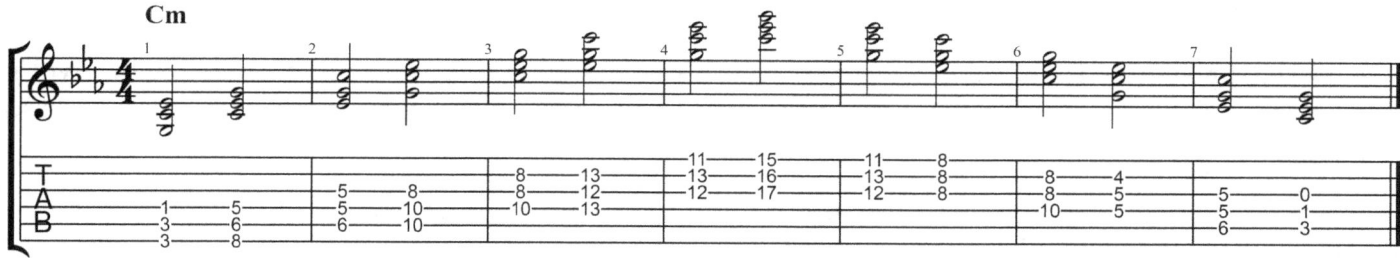

Minor chords are also found in the major scale, not just the minor scale. Using the C Major scale (C D E F G A B C) we built a major triad from the root note (C E G). If we build a triad from the 2nd, we get a D minor triad (D F A). The second chord in a major key is always a minor triad.

A common chord move that I use all the time over a major chord is to combine these major and minor triads. So, over a C major chord, I'll combine C major and D minor triads. This works, even though the harmony stays on C.

Example 3h:

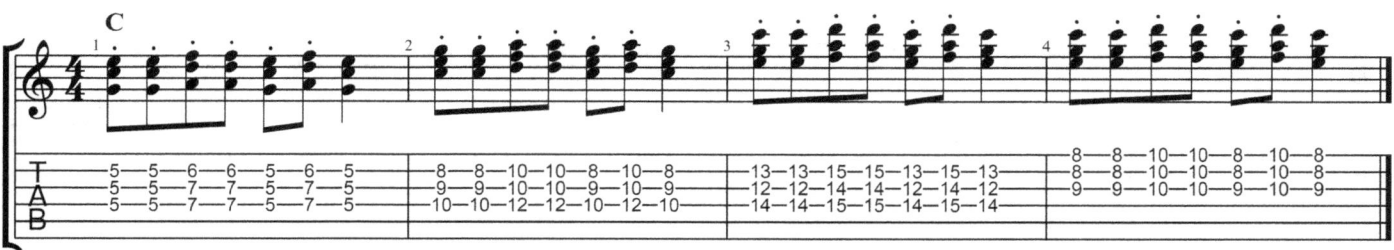

In the previous example, we played each measure on the same string set, but we could also combine string sets in a vertical fashion, as shown in the following idea that works over C and F chords. This means we're playing C major and D minor triads over C, and F major and G minor triads over F.

Example 3i:

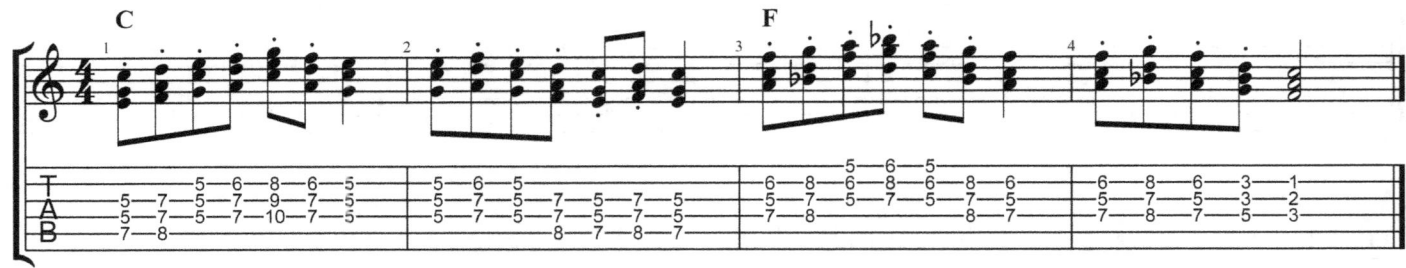

Now let's look at some chord progressions that combine major and minor triads to give ourselves some vehicles to practice with.

First up, let's play a I–vi–ii–IV chord progression. This comes up in tons of songs, such as Taylor Swift's *Blank Space*. (Notice that the Roman numeral system uses lower case letters for minor chords and upper case for major).

In the key of C Major, the I–vi–ii–IV is C major, A minor, D minor, F major. Here are a few ways I might voice that on the fretboard. Make sure you can visualise the bigger shapes of each triad!

Example 3j:

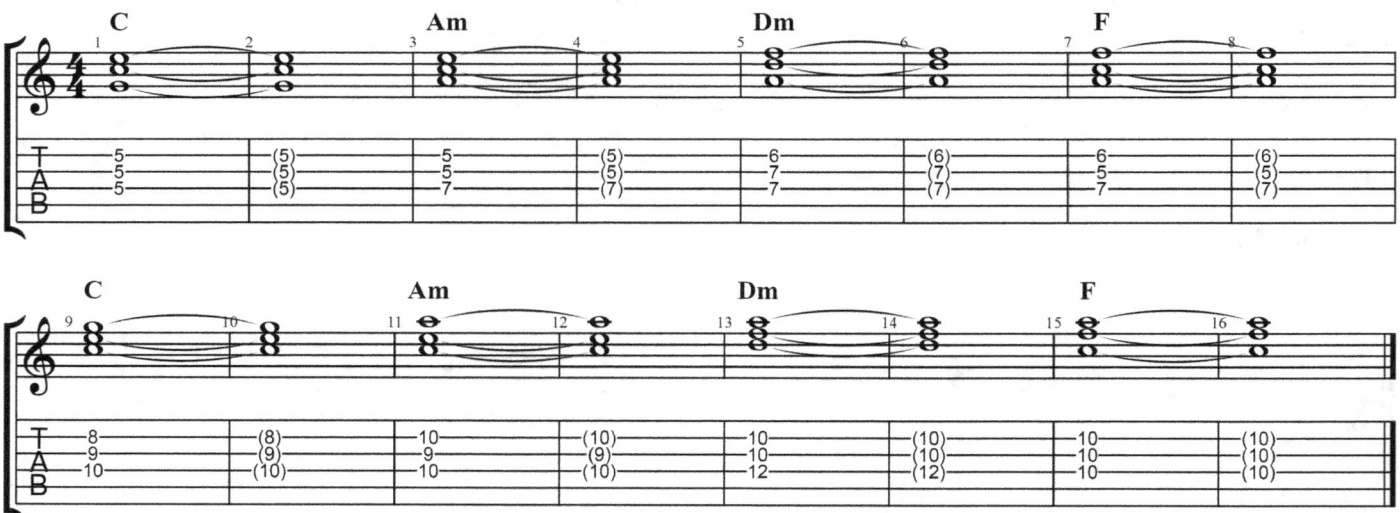

We can achieve a lot using triads like this. For example, if we add some volume swells using a pedal or the volume knob, and add a bit of delay, we can create some nice textures.

Example 3k:

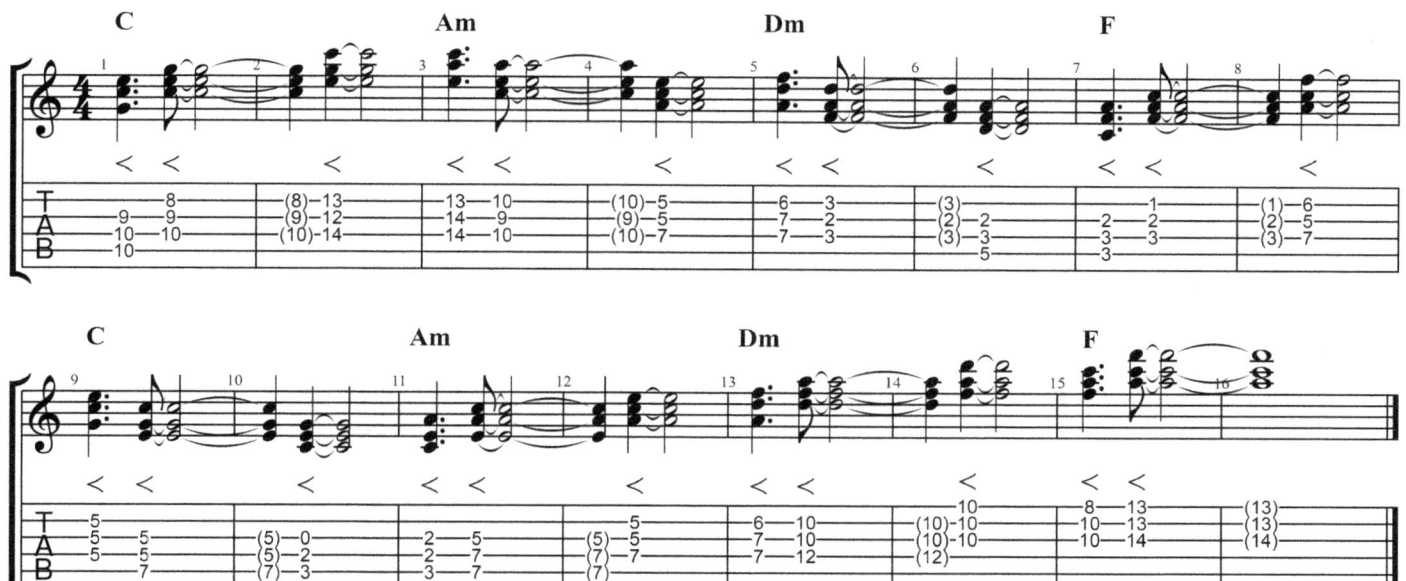

The previous example is a great approach to take if you want to simulate the sound of strings. If you're playing a tune like *Freebird* by Lynyrd Skynyrd, and don't have an organ player, you can replicate that sound too using triads. Here, we play through the progression twice on the D, G, B strings, then twice on the A, D, G string set. Of course, you can (and should) come up with different places to play this every time you practice.

Example 3l:

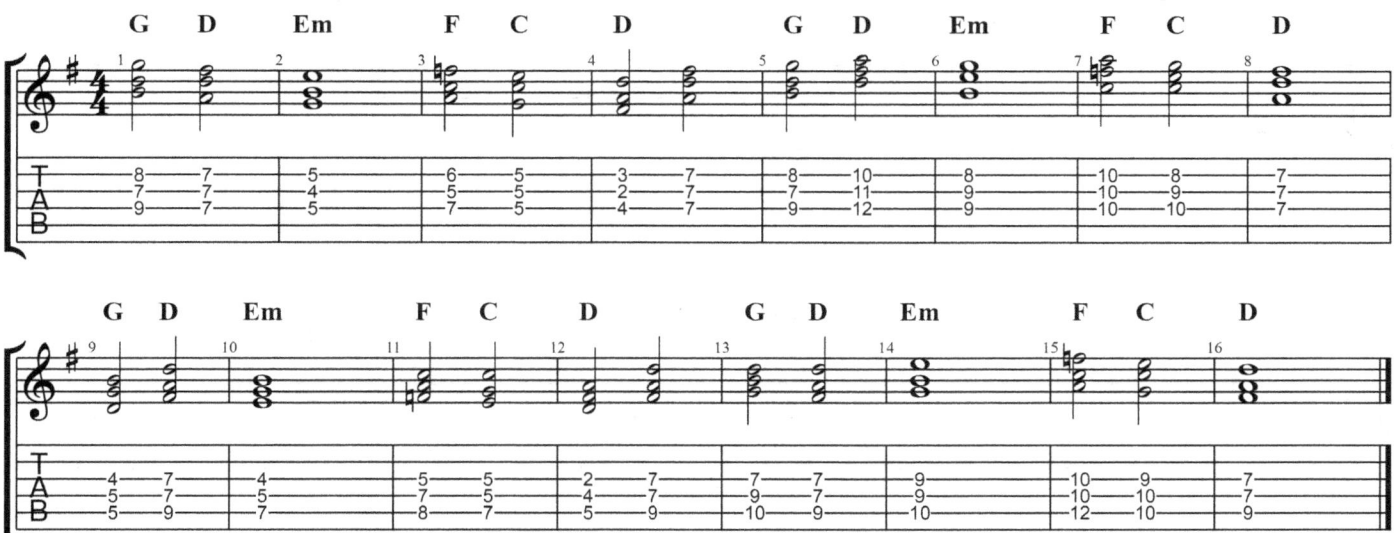

Before we conclude this routine, I want to briefly introduce two more triads to complete our musical palette. We've covered…

- Major – 1 3 5
- Minor – 1 b3 5

But from those two triads we can also make:

- Diminished – 1 b3 b5
- Augmented – 1 3 #5

The diminished triad is a minor triad with a flattened (diminished) 5th. Here's an example where we play minor triads from the E shape of G minor, followed by G diminished triads. This allows us to focus on where that b5 is located.

Example 3m:

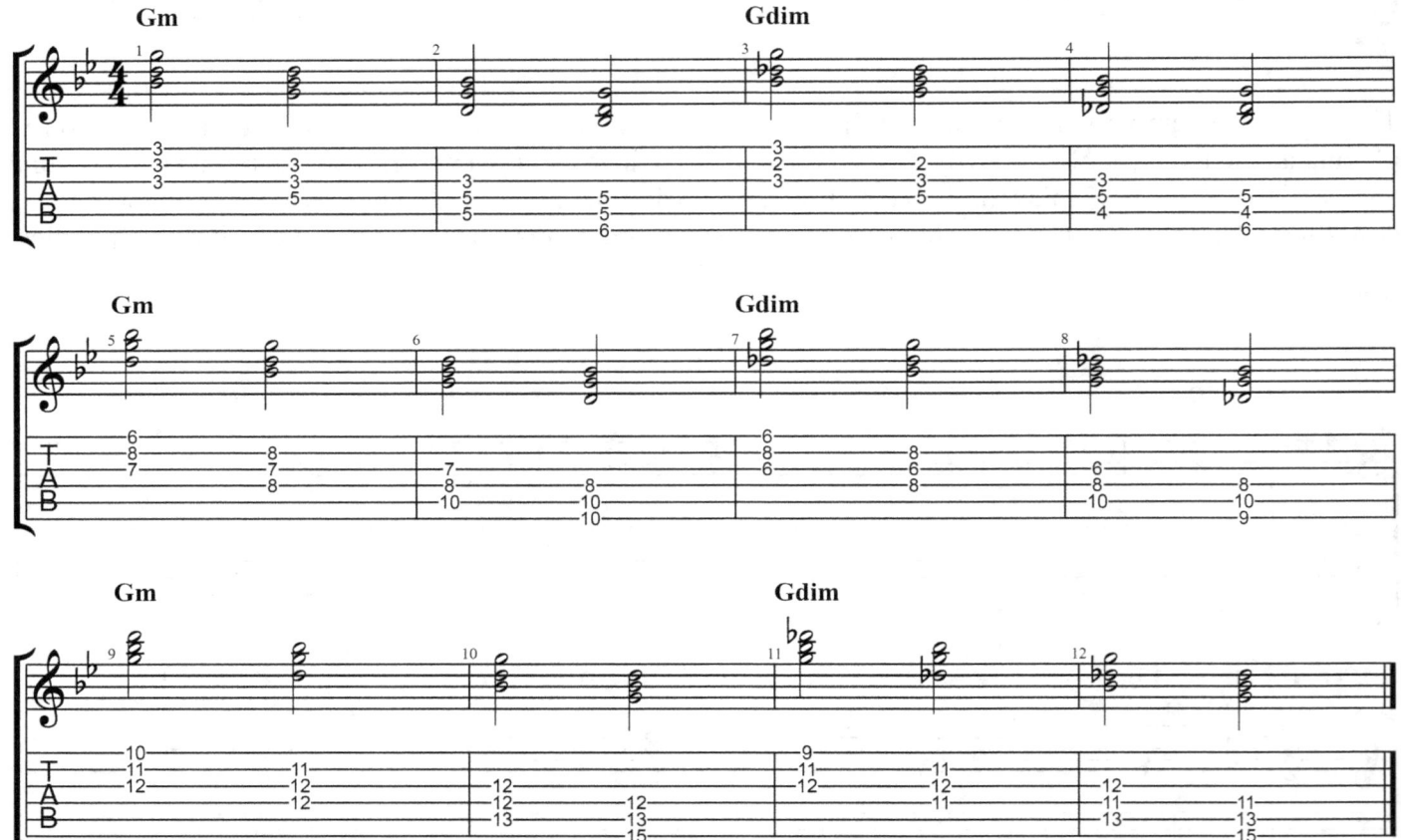

The augmented triad is a major triad with a raised (augmented) 5th. Play the full major triads, then switch to augmented to see where the #5 sits.

Example 3n:

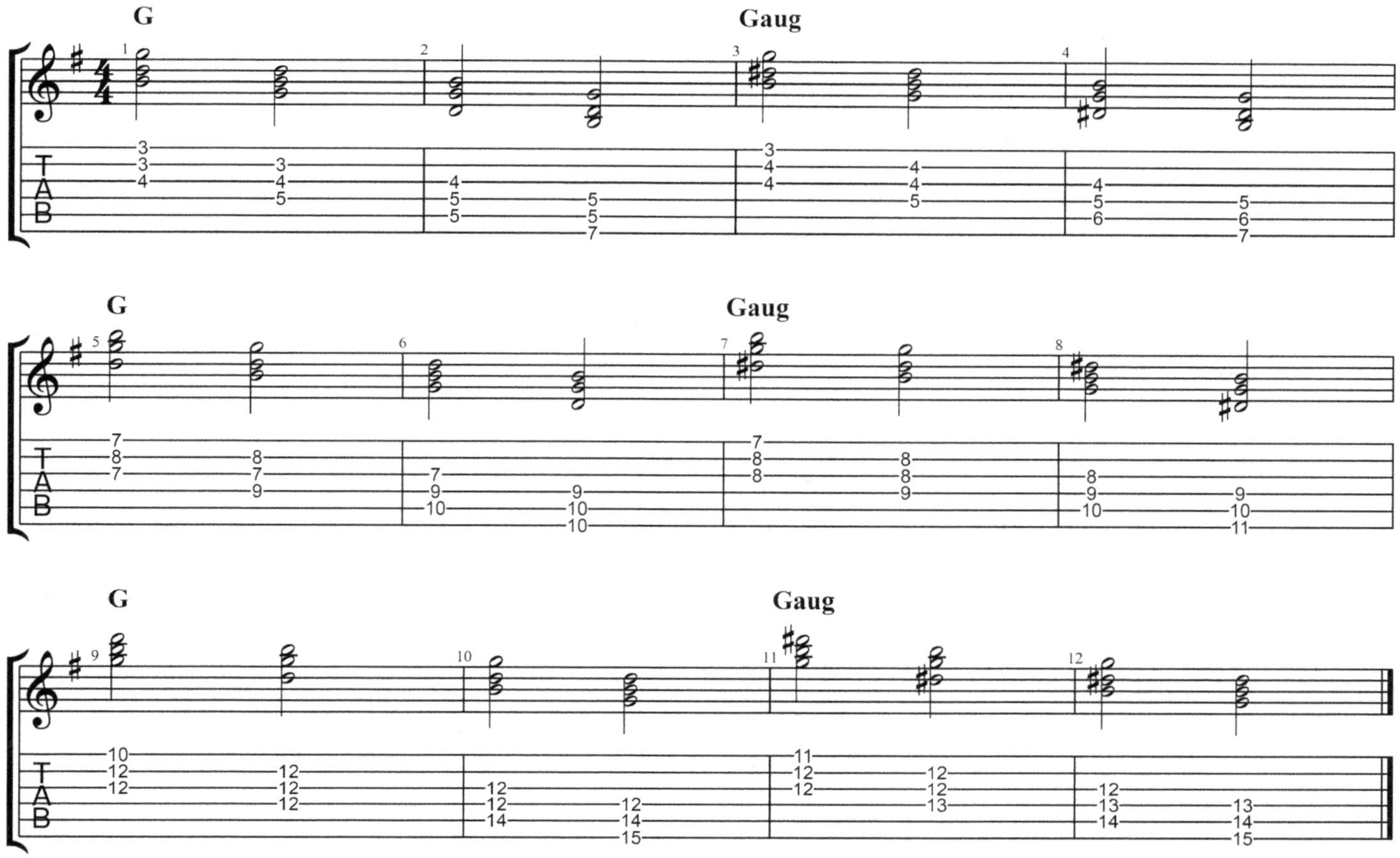

The augmented triad is an interesting sound because it doesn't appear in the major scale. Plus, all the notes in the augmented triad are a major 3rd away from each other, so it's symmetrical. This becomes even more apparent when we play it in horizontal form. Each of the three triads on any given string set are the same!

Example 3o:

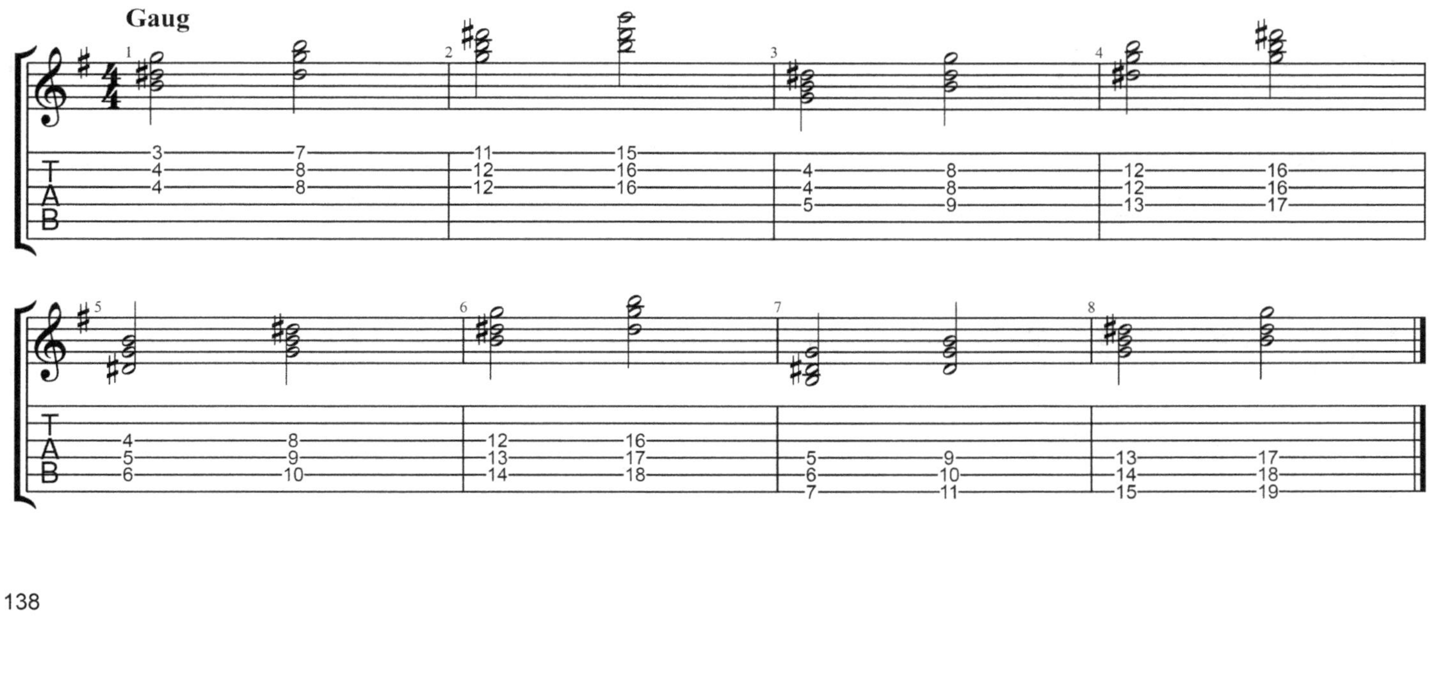

For one final exercise, I'd like to present my patented (it's not patented!) "hardest triad exercise in existence". This entails putting all twelve major, minor, diminished and augmented triads into a random list generator to randomise the order. For a non-techie approach, you could do the same using cue cards with chord names written on them, shuffled into a random order.

The result is a chaotic series of 48 chords of different types. Now we pick an area of the neck and work on playing the triads in the order presented. Here's one randomly generated sequence!

Ab, F#aug, Adim, Bbdim, A, G, Fdim, Eb, Bbaug, Fm, Dbdim, Ebaug, Gdim, F#m, Abdim, Caug, Eaug, Dm, Abm, Gm, Ebm, B, Em, Daug, F, Dbm, Bm, F#dim, Baug, D, Cm, Db, Ddim, Aaug, Ebdim, C, Gaug, Am, Bb, Edim, Bbm, Cdim, Faug, Bdim, Dbaug, E, Abaug, F#.

It's impossible to remember all of that, so we have to work on being able to read it. The result might look something like this.

Example 3p:

Randomising those triads wasn't particularly musical, but it's the kill or cure approach to knowing your triads inside out. If you're still with me, well done, because that one was nuts! There's nothing else in this book that's harder or as unmusical, but sometimes you just have to take your medicine. Take some time with this exercise and try your own randomised sequences. In the next routine we're going to focus on chord scales. See you there!

Routine Four – Chord Scales

We've spent three weeks working on chord construction and now have the knowledge to build all the essential triads we're likely to come up against. Next, I want us to look at the relationships between chords and how they work with each other. We'll do this by looking at diatonic chord scales.

Not only will this give you a deeper understanding of which chords work well together, it's a great way of making sure you know all the chords we've already looked at.

In last week's routine, I mentioned the first two chords that can be built from the C Major scale. If we harmonise every note of C Major, then we get the following "chord scale".

C Major (C D E F G A B C) gives us:

  C E G – C major (I)

  D F A – D minor (ii)

  E G B – E minor (iii)

  F A C – F major (IV)

  G B D – G major (V)

  A C E – A minor (vi)

  B D F – B diminished (vii)

This pattern of chords is consistent for *every* major scale. Chords I, IV and V are always major. Chords ii, iii and vi are always minor, and chord vii is always diminished.

Let's look at this on the fretboard. Here we have a C Major chord scale played on the A, D, G strings. After playing the C major triad, I say to myself, "Chord ii is minor" as I move up to D minor. Then I say, "Chord iii is minor" as I move to E minor, and so on. Speaking it out helps us to memorise the chord types, understand their position in the scale, and know what we're looking for next.

Example 4a:

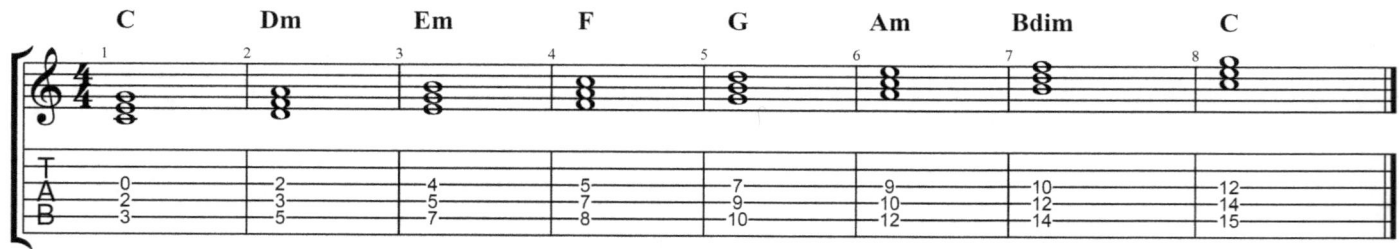

We can do this on any string set. Here's the same exercise on the D, G, B strings.

Example 4b:

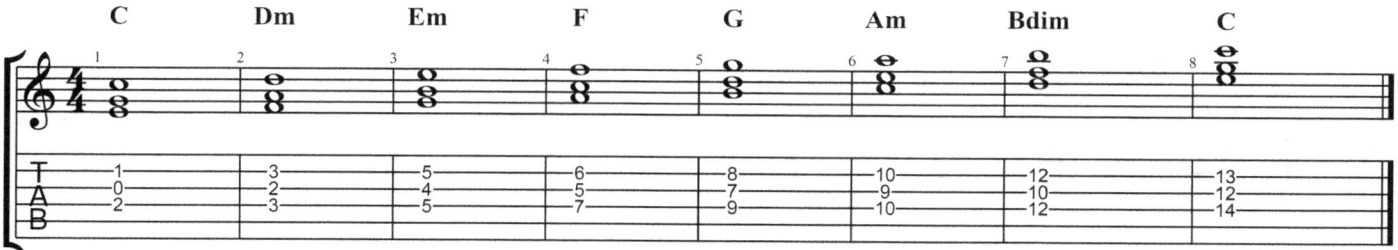

And on the G, B, E string set.

Example 4c:

Now let's change key to F Major (F G A Bb C D E F) and play the chord scale starting in the E shape. This time we're playing all four triads in position for each chord.

Example 4d:

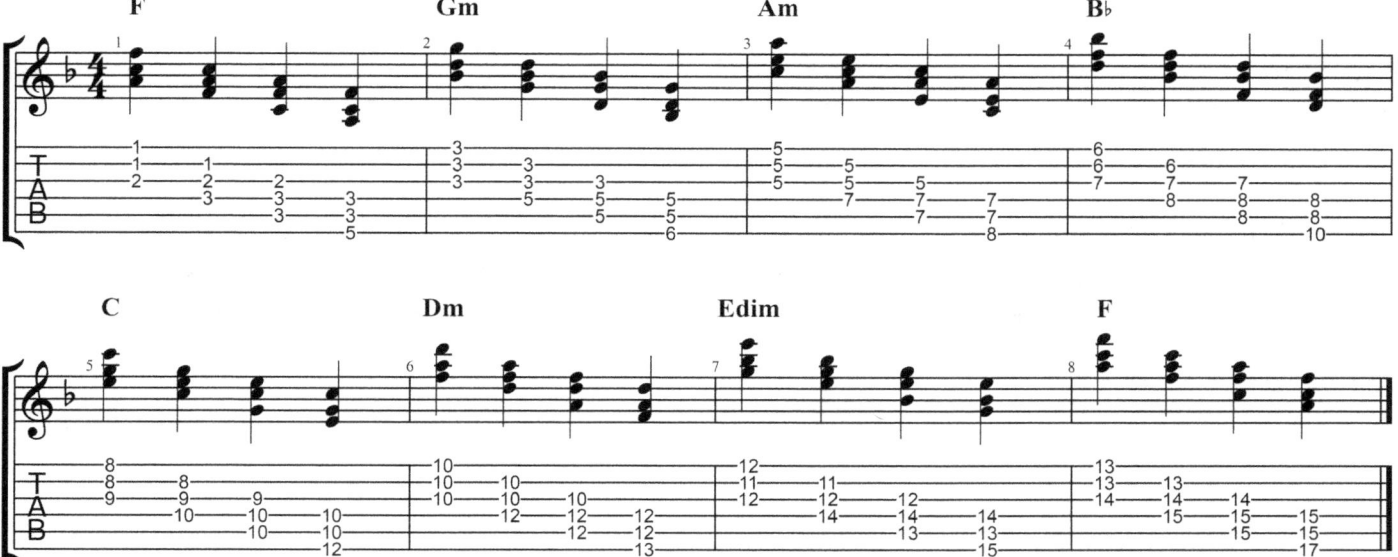

Let's change again. Here's a Bb Major (Bb C D Eb F G A Bb) chord scale starting in the A shape.

Example 4e:

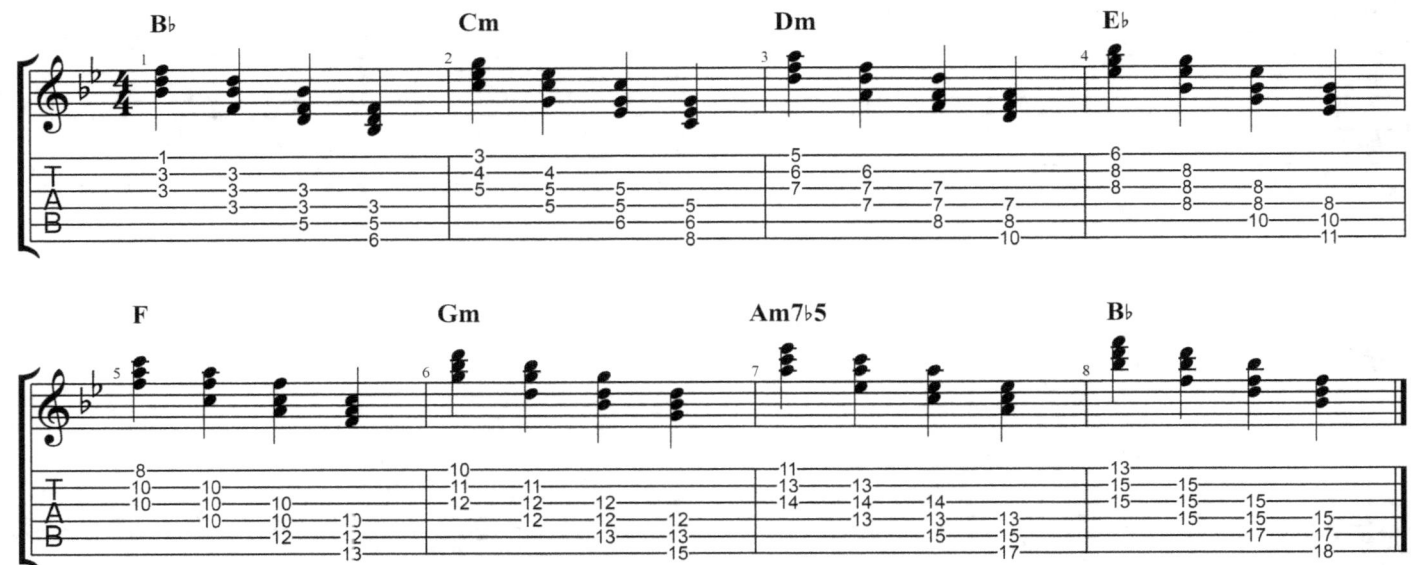

Getting good at this just means picking different keys and getting it done. Here's an E Major chord scale on the top strings starting in the C shape.

Example 4f:

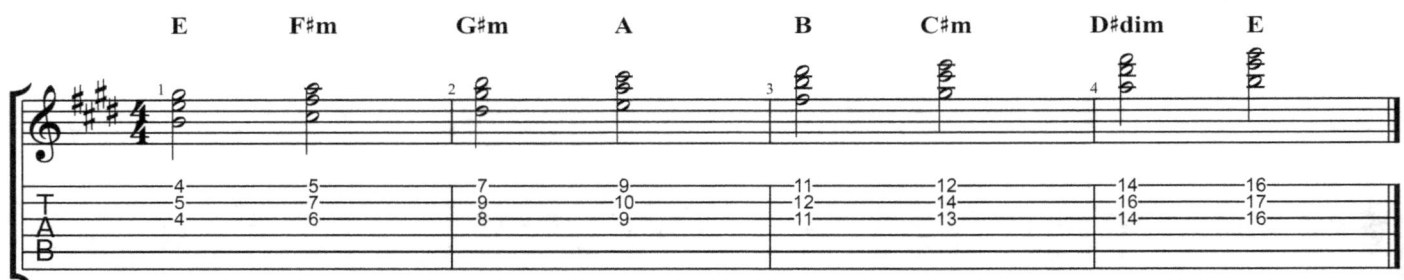

The challenge when playing these chord scales is that panic often sets in when we reach the diminished triad. We can work on hearing/seeing the diminished triad better by starting high and descending. Here's an E Major chord scale descending, starting in the E shape, and moving through three different string sets.

Example 4g:

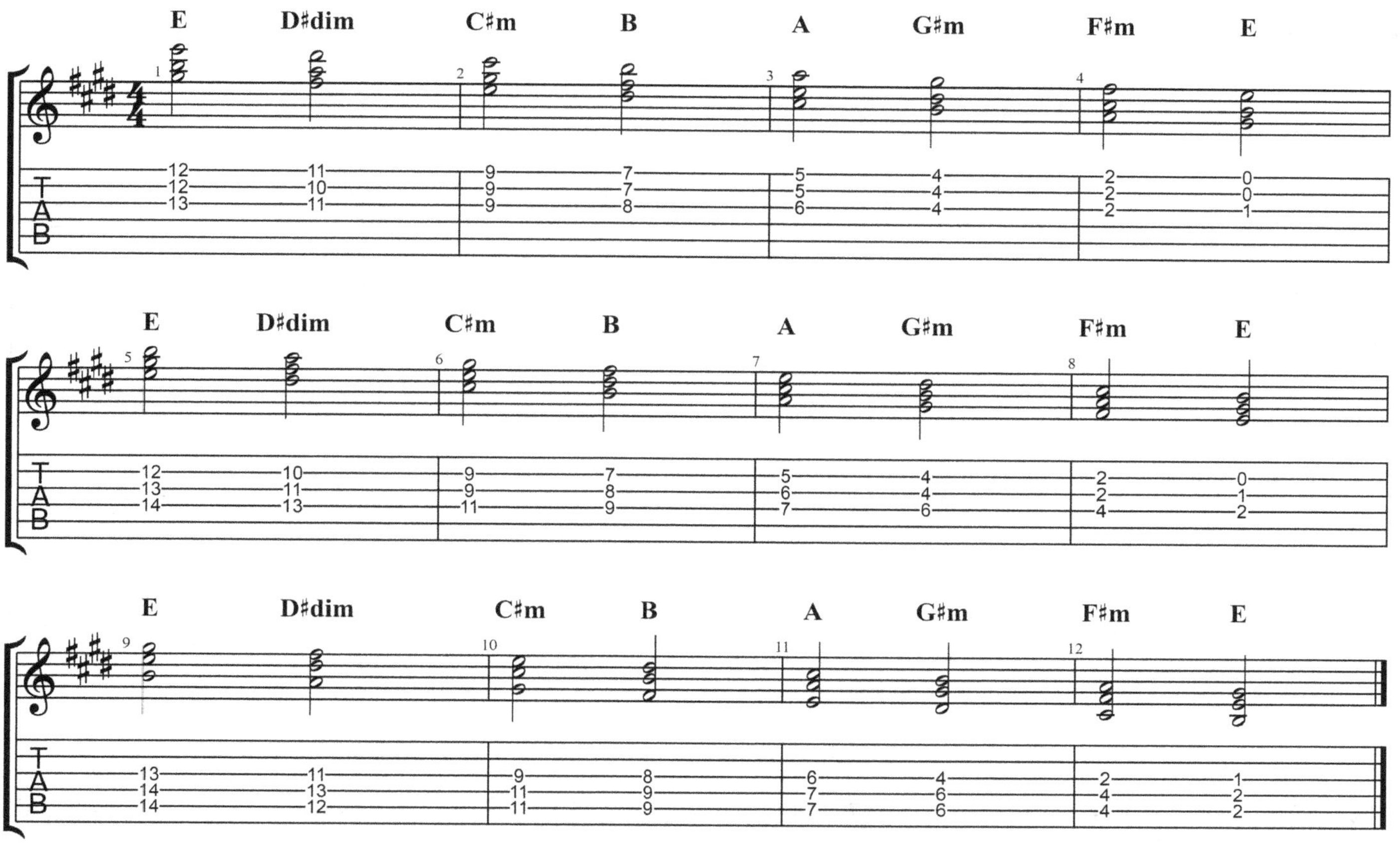

Let's go back to the C Major scale. A good exercise to practice our triads is to play them ascending and descending. Here, we play a C Major chord scale on the top string set using the C shape.

Example 4h:

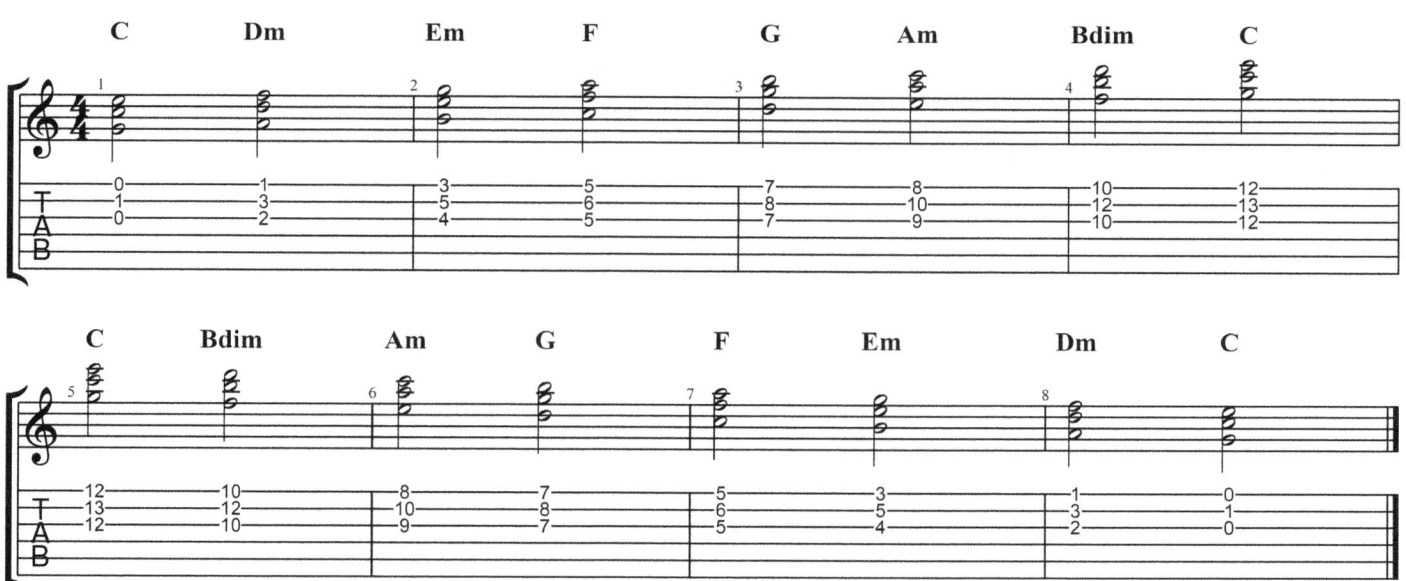

I like to take this idea to the extreme by ascending the scale on one string set, descending on the set below, ascending on the set below that, and then descending on the final set!

Example 4i:

Then, we can take this idea around the Cycle of 4ths by moving to F Major in the E shape.

Example 4j:

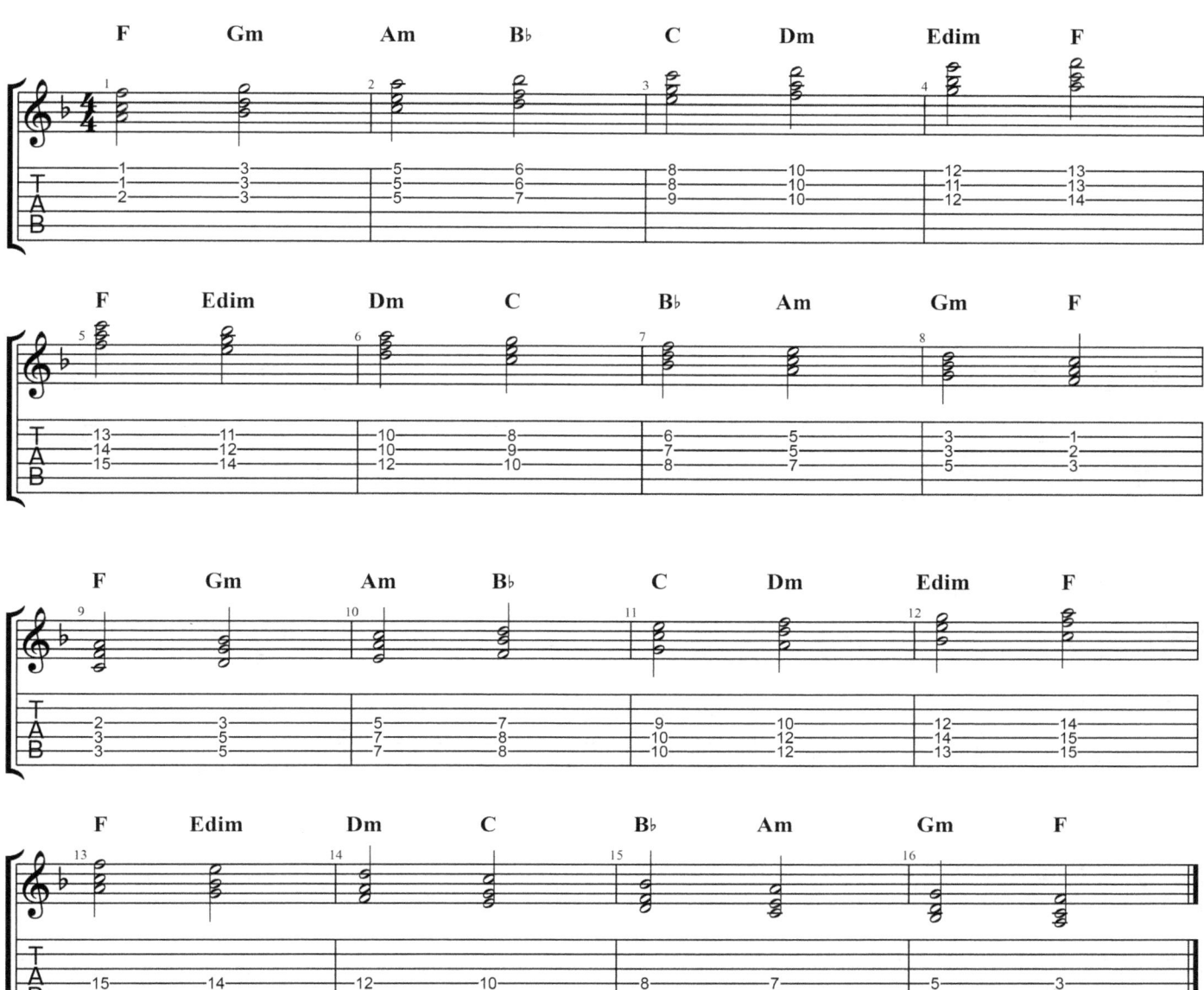

And continue round the Circle to Bb using the A shape.

Example 4k:

For the sake of space, I'm not going to write out all twelve keys using three triad shapes – that would eat up about 20 pages. But, each time you sit down to work on this concept, add a new key and a new position.

For completeness, I want to use the last part of this routine to give you a crash course in chord scales that are not derived from the major scale. There are three useful ones – all of them minor.

C Natural Minor – C D Eb F G Ab Bb C

C Harmonic Minor – C D Eb F G Ab B C

C Melodic Minor – C D Eb F G A B C

The natural minor scale has a symbiotic relationship with the major scale. It contains the same notes, just from a different starting point, so it's known as the *relative minor scale*. You locate the relative minor by going to the 6th degree of the major scale, so in the key of C Major, the relative minor is A Minor.

If we're talking about the C Natural Minor, that shares notes with Eb Major. (C minor is chord vi in the key of Eb Major). Here it is played as a chord scale.

Example 4l:

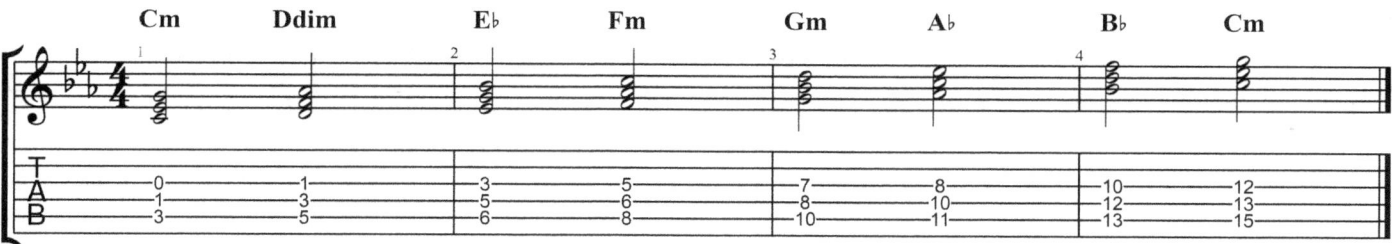

As an aside, in Roman numerals, some might describe this chord scale as i, ii, iii, etc. That's not wrong, but it makes more sense to learn it as:

i – iidim – bIII – iv – v – bVI – bVII – i

Although initially this might seem more complicated, it accurately describes what each chords is. In a minor key we have a ii diminished chord; we have a major chord built on the b3 of the scale; a major chord on the b7, and so on.

These are true-to-life chord functions. When you see a chord progression that mixes chords from both major and minor keys, using this naming convention will help you to identify them. For example, the progression…

C – Am – Bb – Dm – C

…can be described as I–vi–bVII–ii–I.

Example 4m:

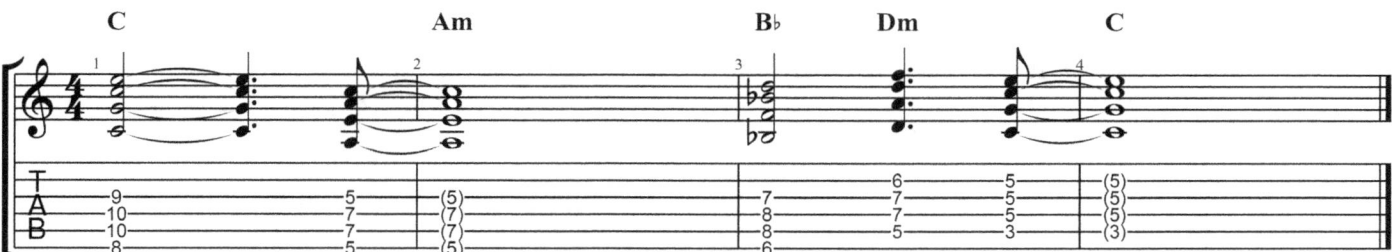

Or, C – G – Ab – Bb – C, would be:

I–V–bVI–bVII–I.

Example 4n:

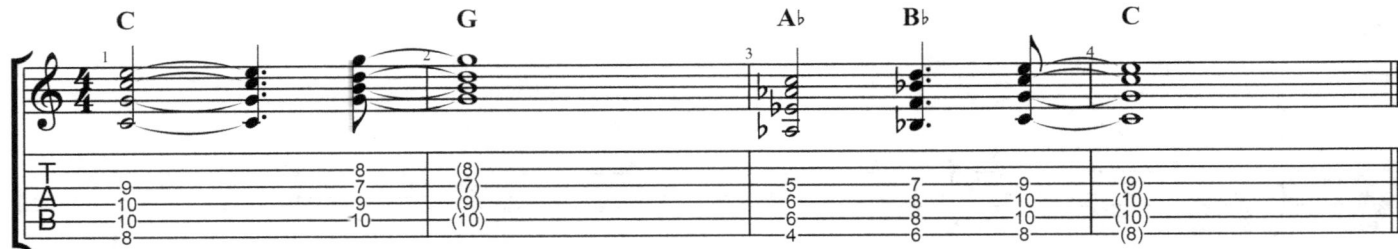

Or, C – Em – F – Fm – C, would be:

I–iii–IV–iv–I.

Example 4o:

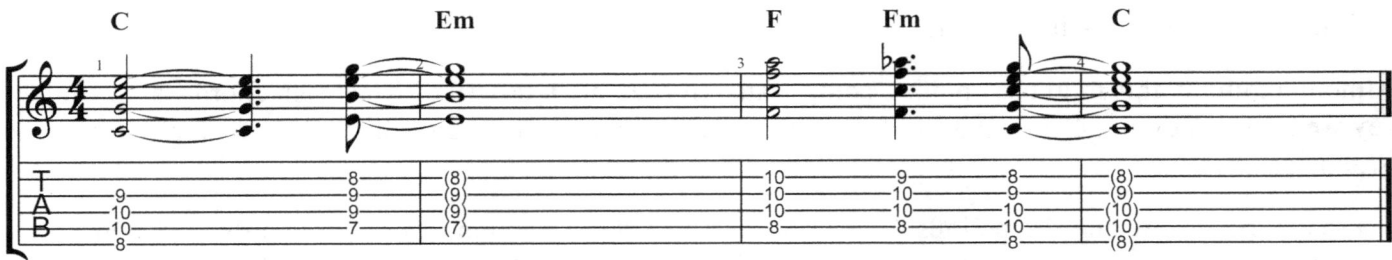

All of the above chord progressions were in the key of C Major, but we borrowed commonly used chords from the key of C Minor.

Technically, the idea of borrowing chords from another key/scale is called *modal interchange*, but 100s of tunes use this idea, and I'm sure the composers weren't led by theory – they just heard a cool sound they liked! However, using the correct Roman numerals to label them is a big help.

Moving on to the C Harmonic Minor scale, harmonising the scale gives us this set of chord designations:

i – iidim – bIII+ – iv – V – bVI – viidim – i

This scale contains two diminished triads and even an augmented triad (the + sign means #5). Let's play through the triads.

Example 4p:

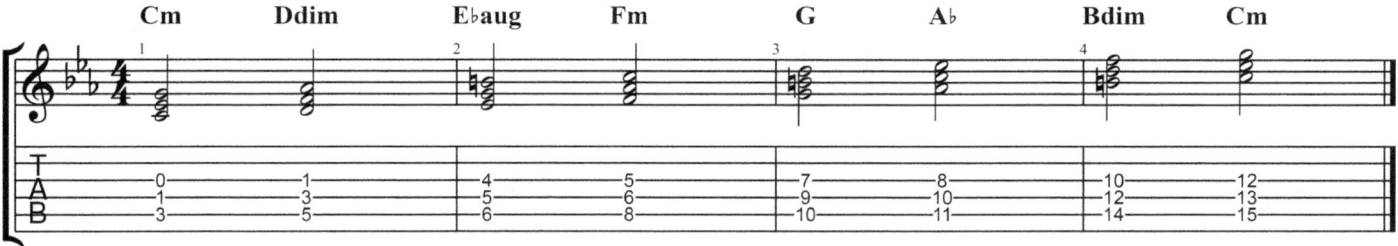

Finally, the C Melodic Minor scale gives us:

i – ii – bIII+ – IV – V – vidim – viidim – i

This scale also has two diminished triads and an augmented triad, but in different places.

Example 4q:

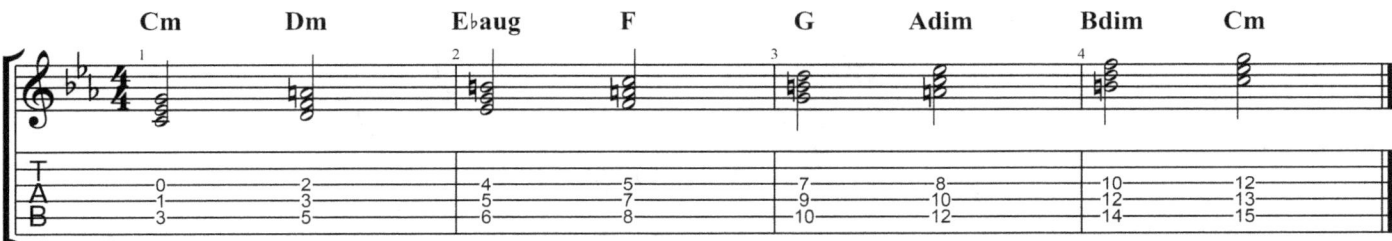

Many tunes have been written based on harmonic minor scale progressions, or by blending harmonic and natural minor scales. *Paint it Black* by the Rolling Stones, *Bury a Friend* by Billie Eilish, *Infinity on High* by Fall Out Boy, and *I Should Have Known Better* by the Beatles are all examples. The same is true of the melodic minor, with tunes like *Yesterday* by the Beatles and more.

This means it's worth your while exploring these scales in more depth. We've played them here only on the A, D, G string set, using just the C shape. You can, of course, work on them in all twelve keys, on all four string sets, using all three shapes! That's a LOT of work, but it'll keep your practice times fresh. Remember, it's not a race, and one day you'll just know all this stuff.

Until next time, get practicing!

Routine Five – Open Voiced Triads & Inversions

So far, all of the chord voicings we've played have been "closed voiced" triads. In other words, the notes are located as close together as possible, and they fit within the span of an octave. Closed voicings have a focused sound and are "dense" compared with the other voicing options we have at our disposal.

In this chapter we're going to expand our triads into *open* voicings. As the name suggests, an open voicing is one that is spread out and spans more than an octave. They sound much more spacious and delicate than their closed counterparts.

Thankfully, they are pretty easy to conceptualise. The diagram below shows a closed voiced C major triad (left) with the root note on the D string (C E G). We'll take the middle note (E) and move it down an octave (E C G). I've left the original E note in the chord grid on the right, so you can see where it was, but it's not played.

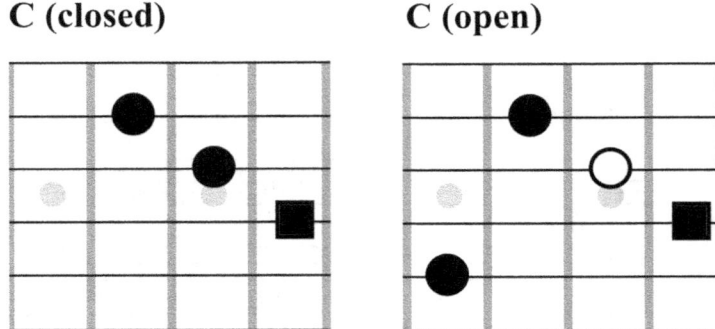

I call this voicing a "2 1" pattern, because we have two notes on adjacent strings, then we skip a string and have one note on its own. We can use the same shape to play C major triads across the neck like this:

Example 5a:

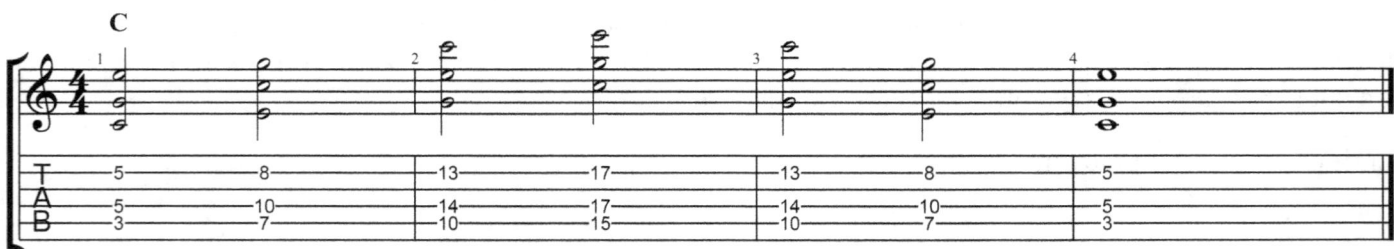

If we want, we can reorganise all of those voicings as "1 2" patterns: one note on its own, a string skip, then two adjacent notes.

Example 5b:

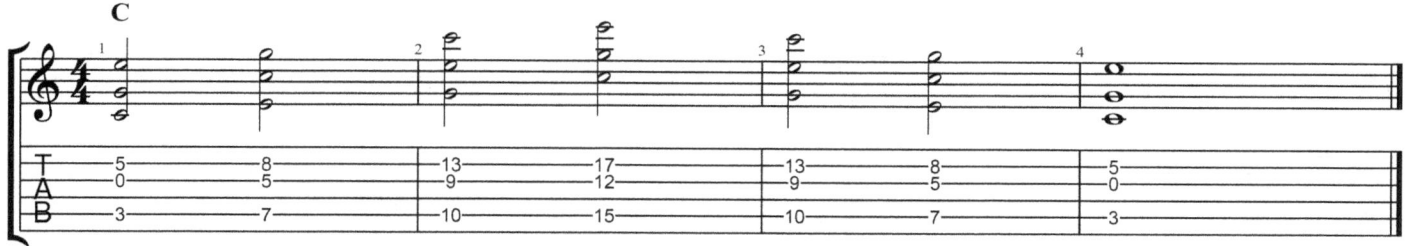

It's worth working on both fingering configurations and deciding which you prefer. Something I like to do is ascend with one pattern and descend with the other, to get a feel for which fingerings are easier. Here's that exercise with a C major on the top string set.

Example 5c:

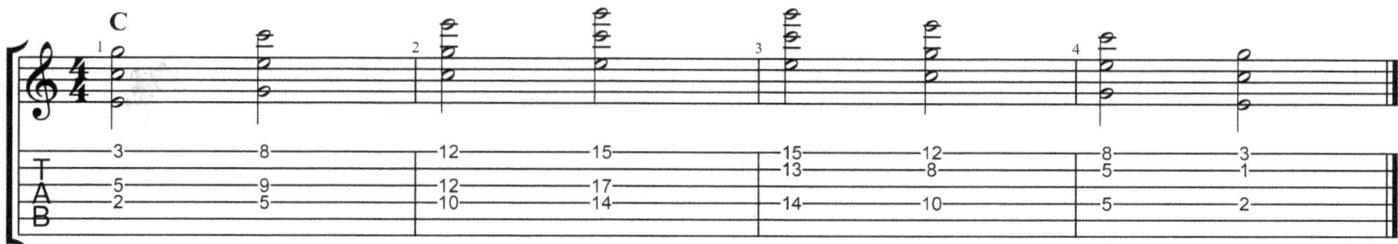

And, as you might expect, this can also be done on the lower string set too.

Example 5d:

So far, we've only looked at things horizontally, but we can stay in position and work on vertical open voicings using our large barre shapes for reference. Here's a C major played vertically in all three shapes. Play around and experiment to see what fingerings you prefer.

Example 5e:

Just as we did with closed voiced triads, we can change notes in these open voicings to make major, minor, diminished or augmented sounds. I won't make you sit and work on all the diminished and augmented sounds because we'll be here all day, but minor triads are always useful. The following exercise works through alternate open voiced major and minor triads.

Example 5f:

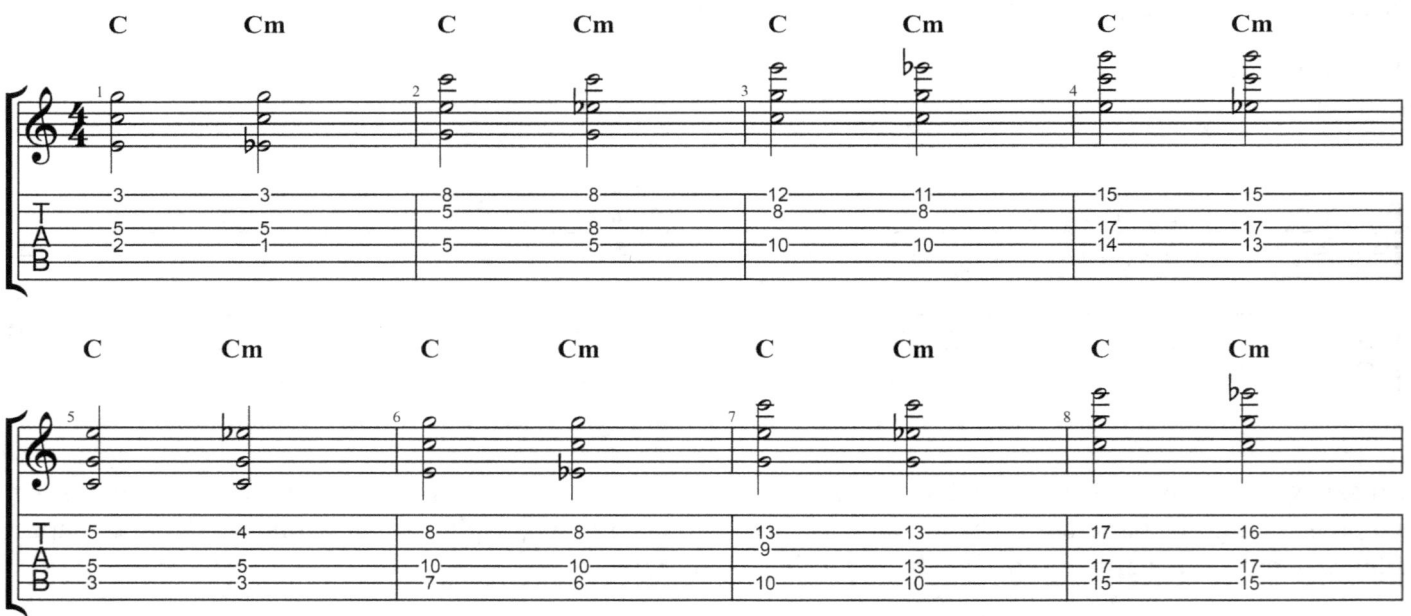

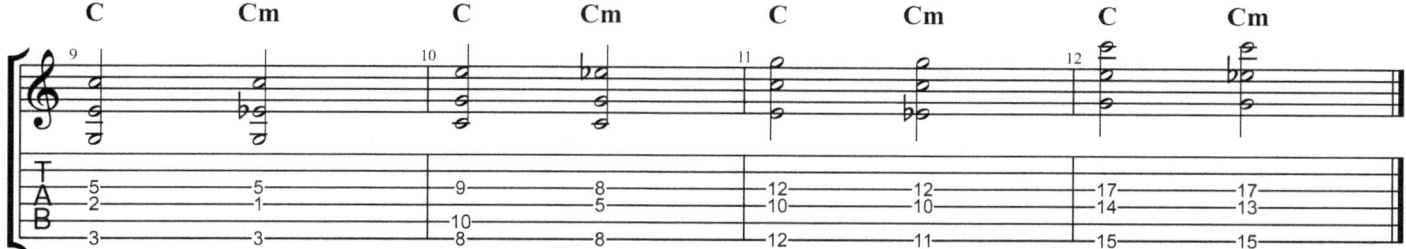

Here's a cool little chord progression inspired by the great Steve Morse. It uses both major and minor triads in open voicings and has an undeniable classical edge to it.

Example 5g:

There's something different about that progression which we've not yet discussed: *inversions.*

If you've studied any music theory, you may have viewed our closed voiced triads as different inversions of the same chord. But you may also have noticed that I never once used that term.

An inversion simply means that you have a note other than the root of the chord in the bass. To me, the most important part of that description is "in the bass". We hear chords in context, in relation to a root note that we either imagine, or perhaps the bass or keys are playing. A C major triad played on the top three strings with E as the lowest note doesn't sound like an inversion, because we hear it in relation to the C harmony we're playing over. That's the reason why I don't really see those closed voiced triads as "inversions".

Look at the following example to understand my reasoning.

In bar one we have a closed C major triad with E as its lowest note. The bass on the audio track is playing a C root note, so it feels wrong to call this chord an inversion and label it C/E, because it isn't being played over an E note.

In bar two, we have a root position closed C major triad spelled (C E G). This time, however, the bass is playing an E underneath it. It doesn't matter that the guitar is not playing an inversion – it has been *made* an inversion because of the E bass note which gives it a specific sound.

In bars 3-5, I've moved to playing open voiced triads. The F/A chord definitely does sound like an inversion, especially when put in the context of F moving to F/A moving to Bb.

Example 5h:

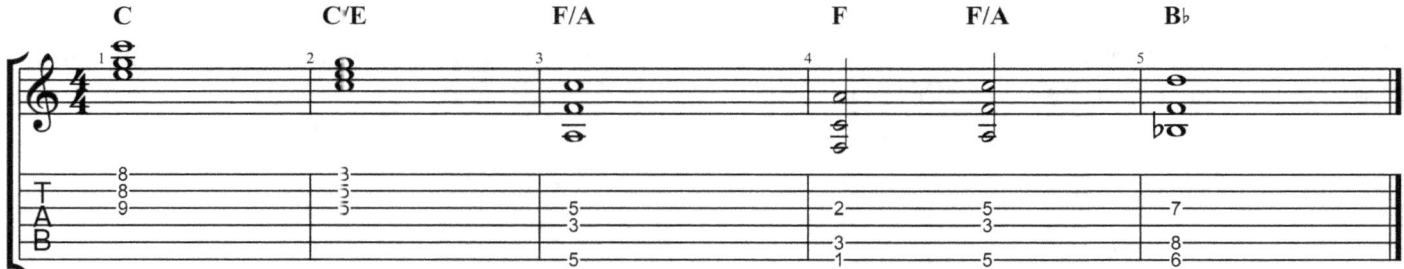

Now, if we revisited Example 5g, we could write out those chords more accurately as:

| Dm A/C# | Dm C/E | F C/E | F D/F# |

| Gm D/F# | Gm F/A | Bb | A |

What do all these inversions have in common?

They all have the 3rd of the chord in the bass. We call this "first inversion". First inversion chords have a powerful sound and feel quite "unstable". They are still major chords, but that bass note feels ready to move!

Notice in Example 5g that every time a first inversion chord is played, the bass note resolves up a semitone. Once you've played this movement a few times, you'll begin to hear it used all over the place.

The chorus of *Anyhow* by the Tedeschi Trucks Band is a good example of first inversion use. It uses an obvious E/G# that it sits on for a long time before resolving up to A.

Check out the following progression and see how the G/B chord always moves up to a C.

Example 5i:

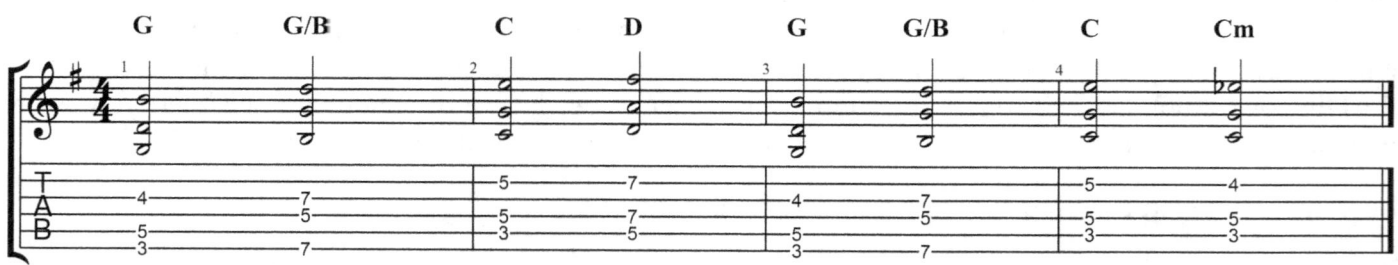

This is not the only way in which first inversions work though. Often you'll see inversions used that don't belong to the key. That's because they are also a great way to fill the gaps in a chord progression chromatically, but in a way that still logically ties the progression together. Maroon 5 use the following idea in one of their songs:

Example 5j:

Inversions help to take us from one chord to the next and are used in classic songwriting all the time. Just ask someone like ABBA!

Example 5k:

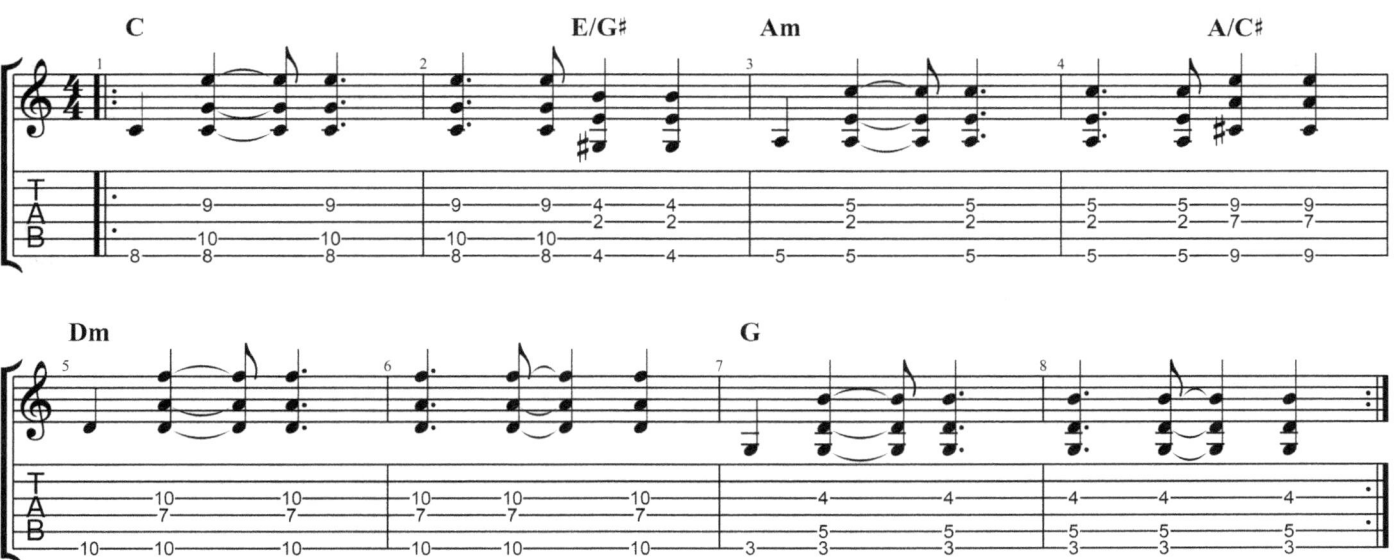

If we invert a chord by moving its 5th into the bass, we call that a "second inversion". These chords have a denser sound. They are not quite as stable as root position chords, but don't sound like they want to resolve in the same way as first inversion chords.

I think of the introduction to *Your Song* by Elton John for the sound of the second inversion. Here's that idea played in the key of G Major. In it we have a G chord followed by C/G. The 5th (G) of the C chord has been moved to the bass to create a second inversion, and it keeps that G bass note going throughout.

Example 5l:

It's worth noting that what we play on guitar will never supersede the bass player. They have the casting vote on how our chords are perceived by the audience. The inversions we play with different notes in the bass are nice ways to reinforce what the bass is doing. The previous example could, for example, be played using basic closed voiced triads, or open voiced ideas higher up the neck. They will have the same effect if the bass is holding down that G, like this:

Example 5m:

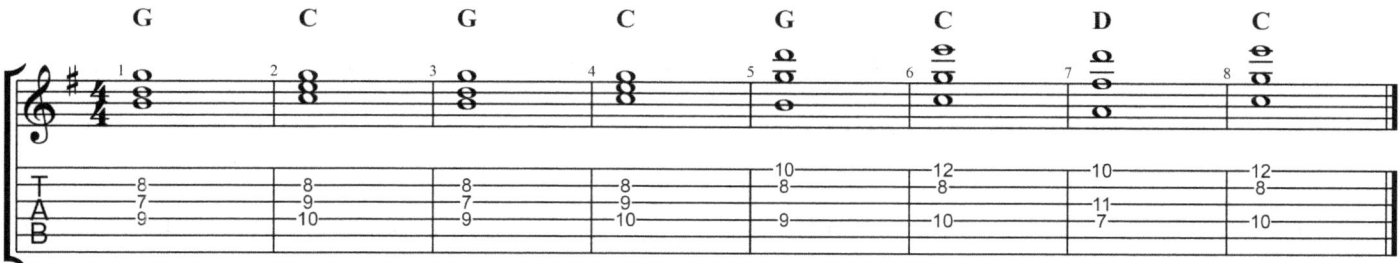

Here's one final example that combines open voiced triads and inversions to outline a longer chord progression.

Example 5n:

As I've mentioned, practice means taking an idea like open voicings and applying it to other concepts we've already studied – such as moving them around the Circle of 5ths, or simply applying them to any chord progression we know. The more we apply chords practically, the more they'll become part of our long-term, subconscious chord vocabulary. We just have to stick with them and put in the time.

Remember, the harder you're sweating while practicing, the more progress you're going to make. See you in the next routine!

Routine Six – 7th Chords & Triad Mutation

We've reached the halfway point in our chord routines and so far we've only talked about triads. That's because I genuinely believe they are *that* important to your personal development and study of harmony.

Moving on, we're going to talk about 7th chords. We'll look at the theory, how to construct them, and how we can apply them to the fretboard.

Using our tertian system of harmony, we built triads by stacking 3rds, using the 1st, 3rd and 5th degrees of the scale. If we continue that pattern and stack one more 3rd on top we have a 7th chord (1 3 5 7).

Technically, there are three different types of 7th we can add to a chord. The most common are the natural 7th of the major scale and the b7 of the natural minor scale. It's also possible to add a bb7 (yes, a double flat 7th!) which comes from the diminished scale, but we won't worry about that for now.

Before we play any chords, let's talk theory. We'll take the triads we know and add a 7th to each one, then see if we can name them. First, the major triad:

If we add a natural 7th to a major triad we get a major 7 chord. If we add a b7 we get a dominant 7 chord.

- 1 3 5 7 – Major 7
- 1 3 5 b7 – Dominant 7 (also just called a 7 chord)

Next, the minor triad. Add a b7 and we get a minor 7 chord. Add a natural 7th and we get a minor-major 7 chord.

- 1 b3 5 b7 – Minor 7
- 1 b3 5 7 – Min(Maj7)

It's also worth considering some other options.

Add a b7 to a diminished triad and we get a minor 7b5 chord (also called a half-diminished). Add a natural 7th and we get the very rare diminished major 7.

- 1 b3 b5 b7 – Min7b5
- 1 b3 b5 7 – DimMaj7

Finally, there's the augmented triad. Add a natural 7th to the augmented triad and we get a major 7#5 chord. Add a b7 and we get a dominant 7#5.

- 1 3 #5 7 – Maj7#5
- 1 3 #5 b7 – Dom7#5 (more commonly written as 7#5)

Spend some time committing these to memory, then we'll work on putting sounds to the names.

We'll start with what I call the *additive* approach. In other words, we'll play a triad then add a 7th on top of the chord. For example, we can take a C major triad and add a B note on top to give us a closed voiced Cmaj7.

Example 6a:

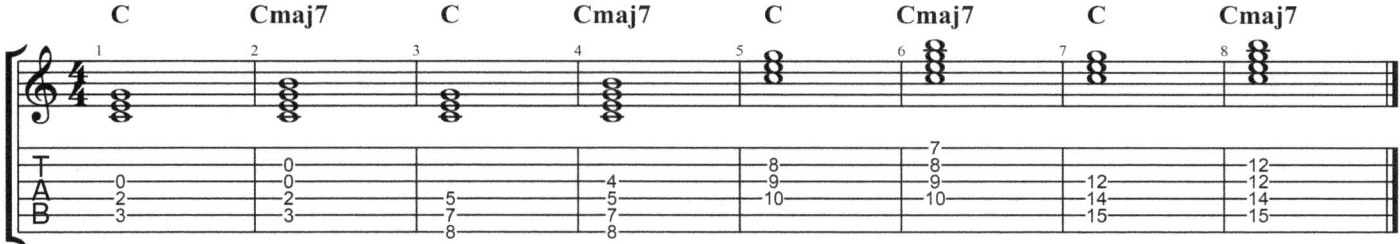

We can do the same using the C major triad but adding a b7 note, to give us the grittier sounding dominant 7 chord. Note that we can't achieve this in open position because we can't flatten the open B string.

Example 6b:

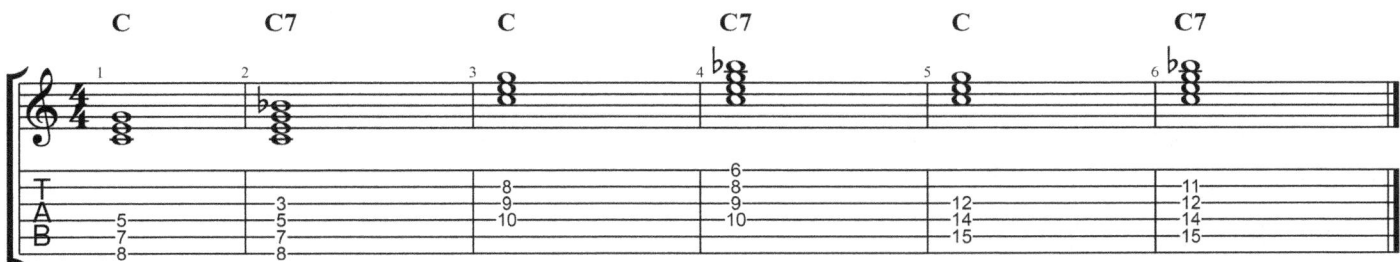

If we keep the b7 interval but lower the 3rds in all those chords, we convert them to Cm7.

Example 6c:

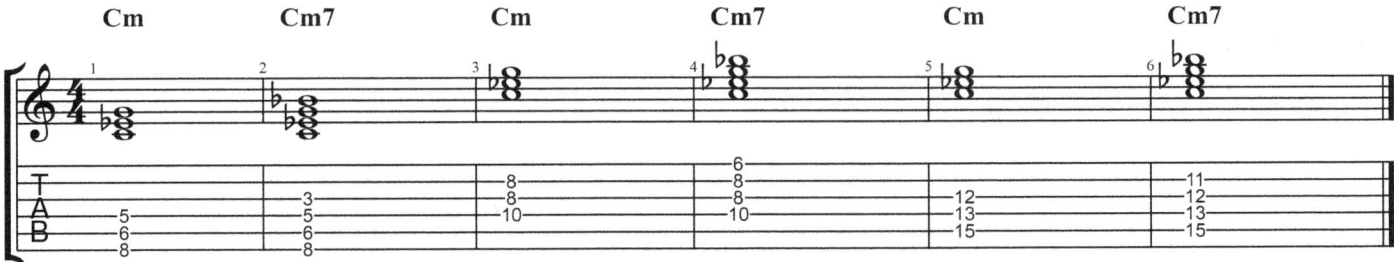

You'll notice that the more we delve into 7th chords, the harder it becomes on the hands. So it makes sense to have some standard grips for these 7th chords that we can pull out quickly to play songs. Below are the most common voicings for the most important 7th chord types. We'll discuss where they come from later – for now, we just need them under our fingers.

Example 6d:

If we go back to our chord scales, we can quickly see where these 7th chords come from. When we harmonised the C Major scale into triads it produced:

C – Dm – Em – F – G – Am – Bdim – C

The C Major scale harmonised into 7th chords gives us all of the chord types in Example 6d.

Cmaj7 – Dm7 – Em7 – Fmaj7 – G7 – Am7 – Bm7b5 – Cmaj7

Notice that,

- All the minor triads (ii, iii, and vi) are now minor 7 chords
- Chords I and IV are now major 7 chords, but chord V is a dominant 7
- Chord vii is now a half-diminished or minor 7b5 chord

Using the first chord grip from the previous example, we can play the harmonised C Major scale like this:

Example 6e:

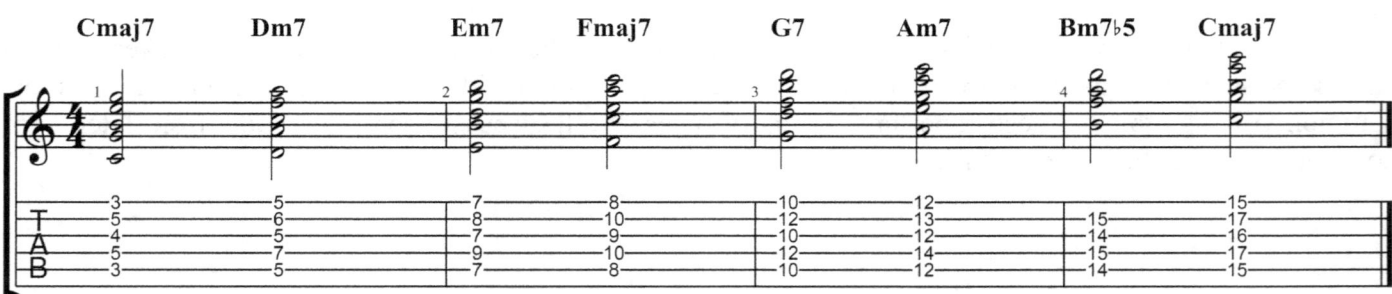

If we switch back to using closed voicings now, you'll suddenly see why having chord grips is a huge help for us. Here is the G Major chord scale played using closed voicings on the top strings. It's not easy!

Example 6f:

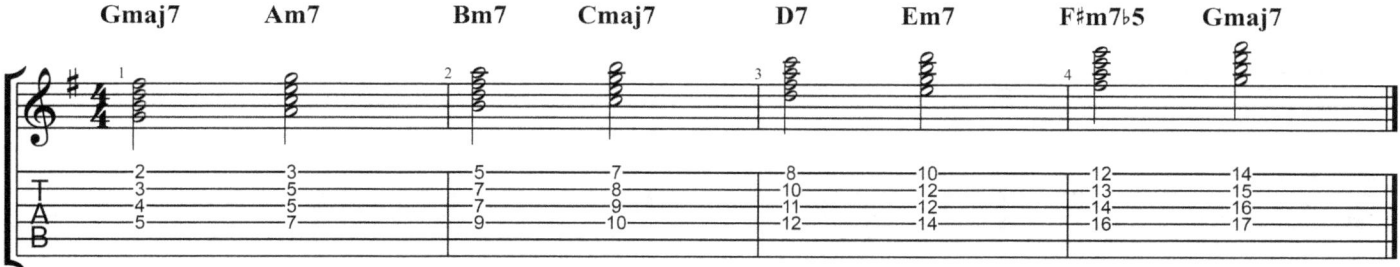

And what happens when we start to invert these chords? You'll quickly realise that it's impossible. Try the following idea, where I play the first Gmaj7 chord, then move each note up to the next note in the chord. Only pianists can play this stuff. We guitarists need a better solution!

Example 6g:

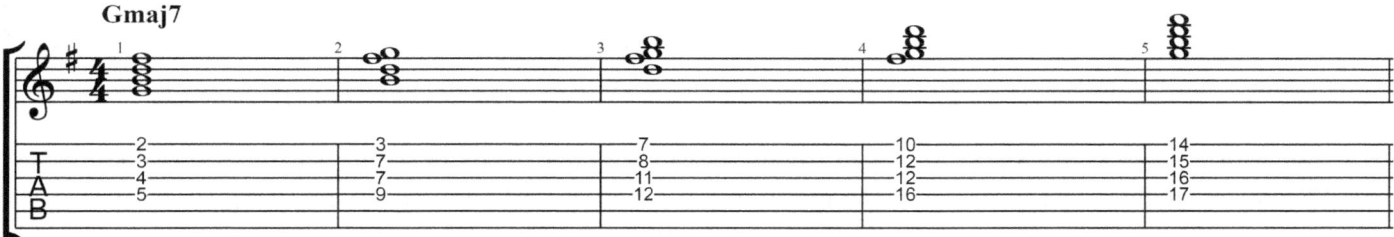

Clearly we need a different approach to practicing 7th chords – ideally one that's based on the triad knowledge we already have. This is where my "triad mutation" approach comes in!

The principle of this approach is to take a triad voicing and change one note for another to create the richer 7th chord sound we're looking for.

For example, we can take a C major triad and move the 5th interval up to the 7th. By doing that we change its 1 3 5 voicing (C E G) to a 1 3 7 voicing (C E B) which creates the sound of Cmaj7.

First have a listen to how this simple "mutation" sounds, then I'll explain why we can do it. Play it in all three of our triad positions, each time taking the 5th (G) and moving it to the 7th (B).

Example 6h:

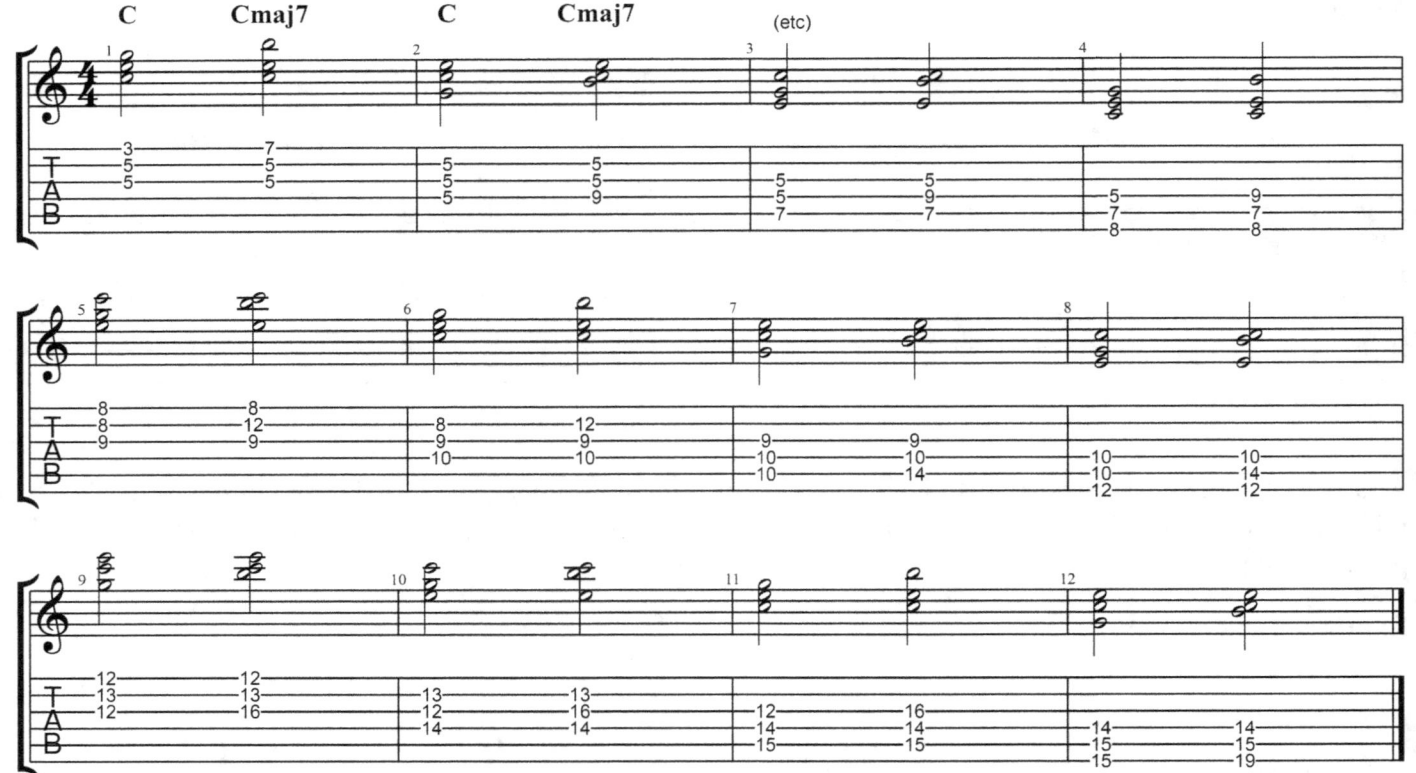

To know why this mutation works, we need to understand how each note in a 7th chord functions. Let's look at each interval and consider which are the really important ones and which ones could be sacrificed.

Root: this is the note we hear the chord in relation to. You might think it's important, but it's very likely that the bass/keys player will be playing this note, so we don't have to. Rootless chord voicings are very common in jazz.

3rd: this note is a key ingredient – it tells us whether the chord is major or minor.

5th: this note doesn't help us to identify the chord, it just makes the sound a little thicker. It can't tell us whether the chord is major, minor or dominant.

7th: like the 3rd, the 7th is the other important note that tells us the quality of the chord. For this reason, the 3rd and 7th of any chord are called the "guide tones".

When we mutated our C major 1 3 5 voicing to 1 3 7, we used the root and the two guide tones. Combined, they fully describe the sound of Cmaj7.

Some of the mutated voicings are more useful than others. Some just sound great and some are easier to play than others. We tend to gravitate towards the ones that suit our personal taste.

Now let's perform another mutation!

If we drop all those 7s down to b7s (1 3 b7) then we'll create a set of C7 voicings. These are all easier on the hands, but some still sound a little better than others.

Example 6i:

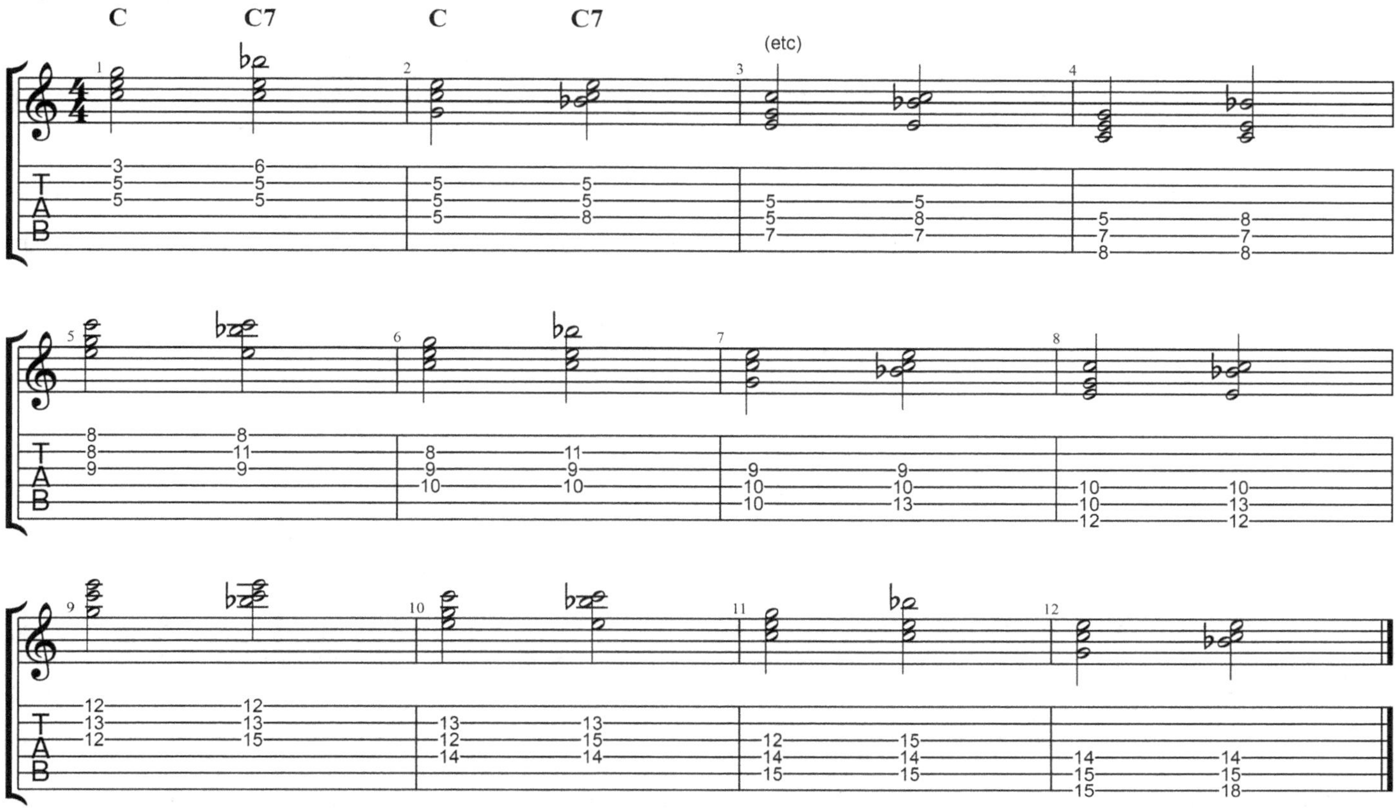

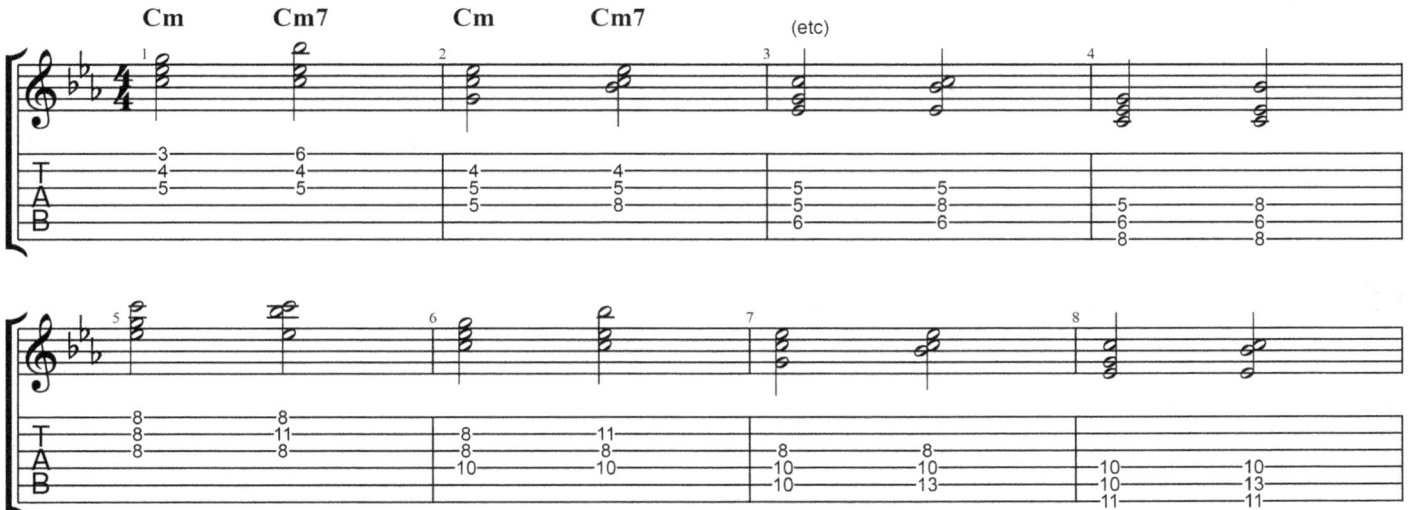

Let's mutate the voicings again. If we now lower all the 3rds in these voicings to b3s we'll have minor 7 chords. Importantly, these voicings will also work in place of minor 7b5s, because they don't contain a 5th.

Example 6j:

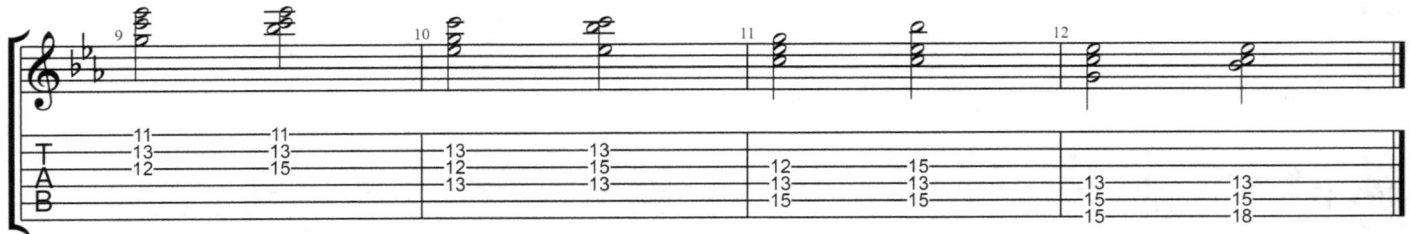

Let's take just ONE of these 1 3 7 voicings and use it to play a Bb Major chord scale. I don't want to scare you but there are 12 voicings. Played through all 12 keys that's 144 options! I won't write them all out here, but you can work on them in your practice sessions. Don't tell me you've run out of things to practice!!!

Example 6k:

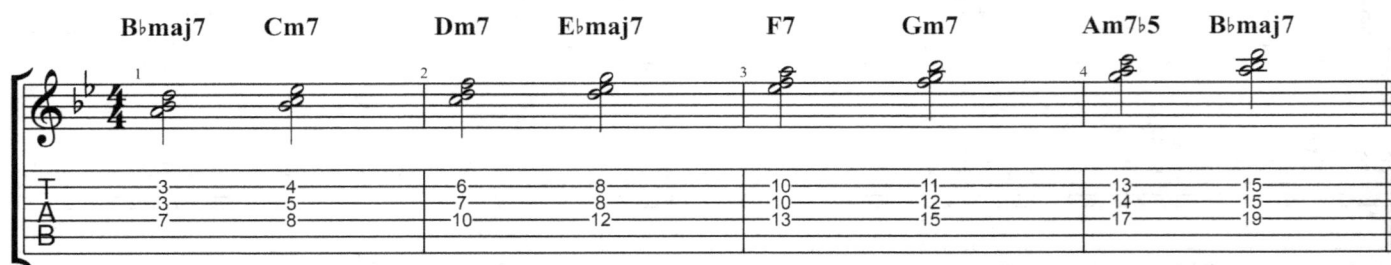

We've discovered that there are endless options available to us with 1 3 7 voicings, but we're only halfway in exploring triad mutations. There is another important one to consider! So far, we've created 7th chords by raising the 5th, but we can also mutate triads by lowering the 7th, so that 1 3 5 becomes 7 3 5.

Remember, our chord voicings don't need a root note – someone else is playing that!

We'll follow the same process as before, playing all twelve 1 3 5 triad voicings, lowering the root note each time to make 7 3 5 voicings. Let's do that now with C major – Cmaj7.

Example 6l:

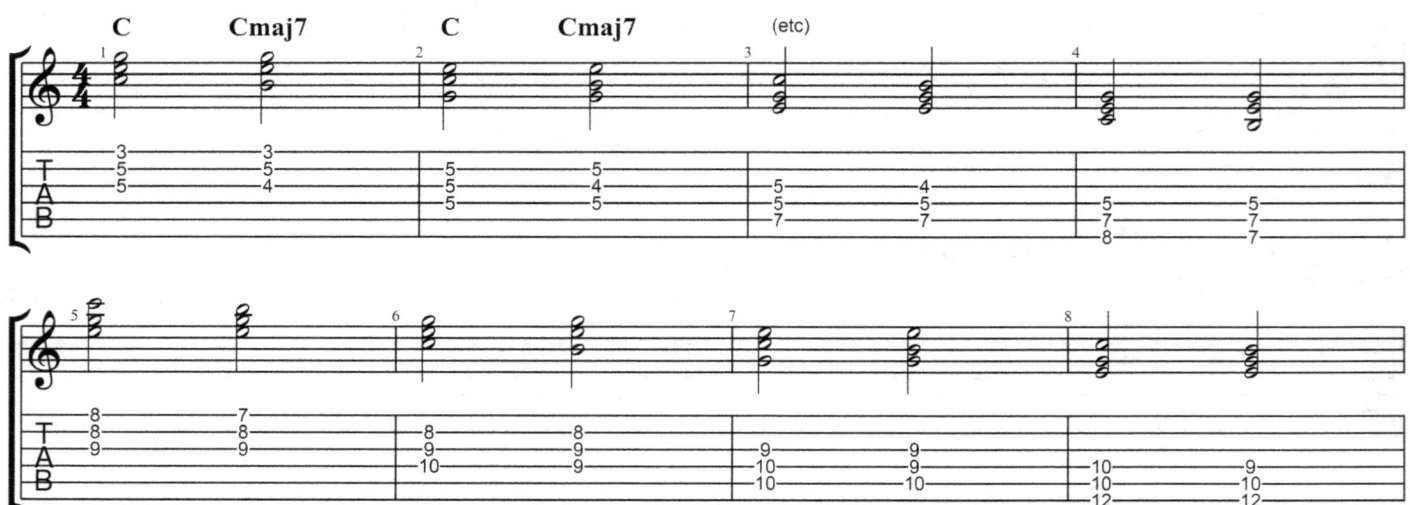

165

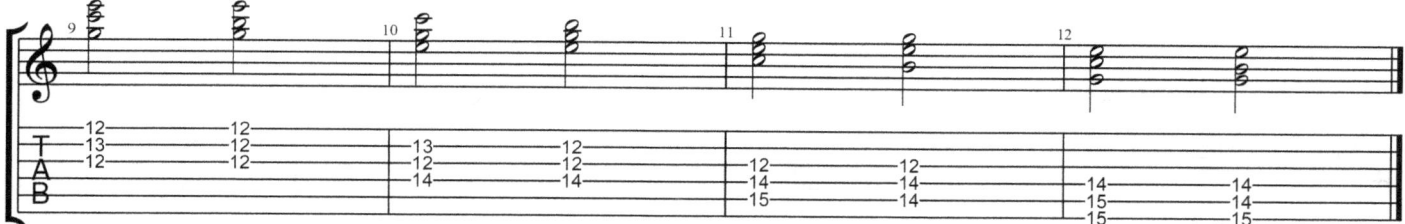

As we did before, let's now lower the 7ths to b7s to change the voicings to C7. If you recognise the sound, they are just the diminished triads you've been working on.

Example 6m:

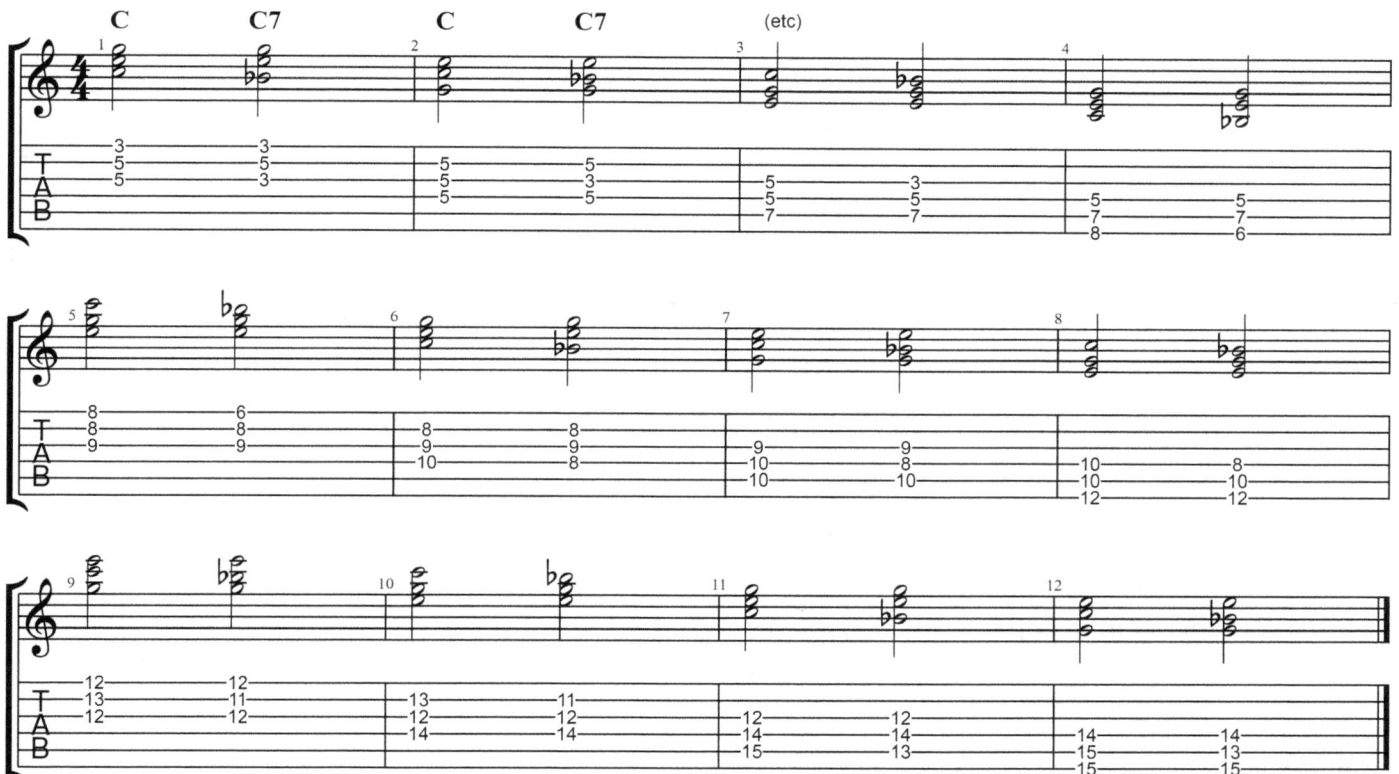

By lowering the 3rds to b3s we get to our minor 7 voicings. Do these look familiar? Yep, they are just Eb major triads! (NB: these minor 7 voicings won't work in place of minor 7b5s this time, because the chord contains the natural 5th).

Example 6n:

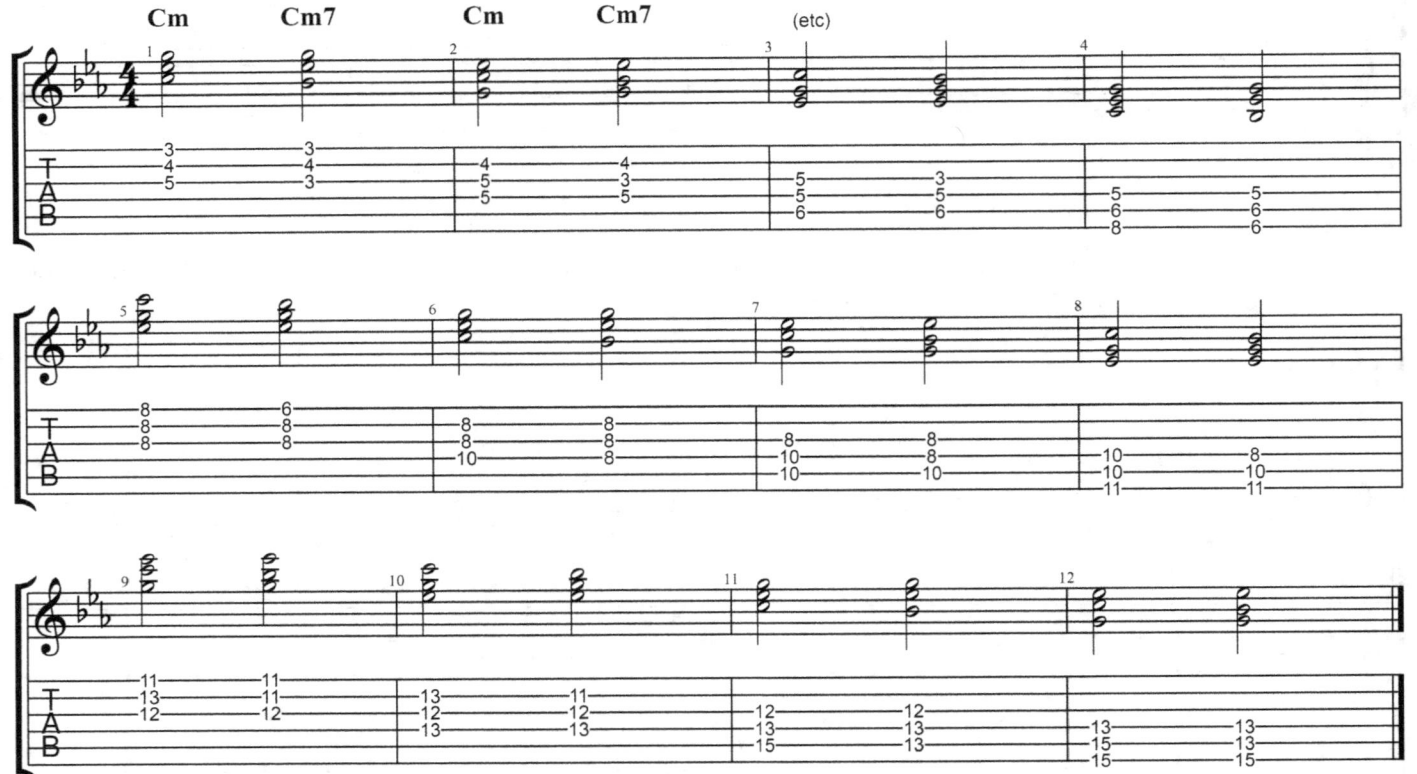

Now that we've completed our study of 1 3 7 and 7 3 5 shapes let's spend some time on musical context. I've said it 1,000 times and I'll keep saying it: I'm not a jazz musician, but I *think* like one.

That means I often use jazz standards for practice because they usually contain a lot of chord/key changes. So, to conclude this chapter, we'll look at the chords to the popular standard, *All of Me*.

I use the *Real Book* or an app like iReal Pro to reference the chord changes. A quick glance will show you that this tune is full of 7th chords. However, to begin with, we're going to ignore every 7th chord and just use major and minor triads to spell out the changes.

Example 6o:

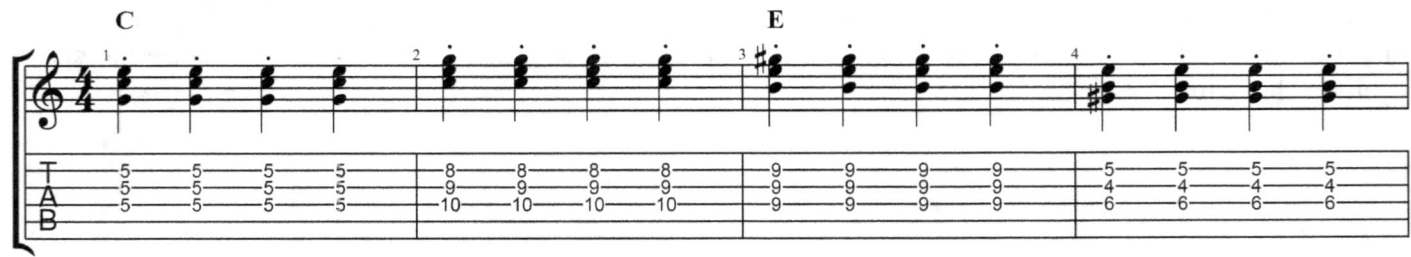

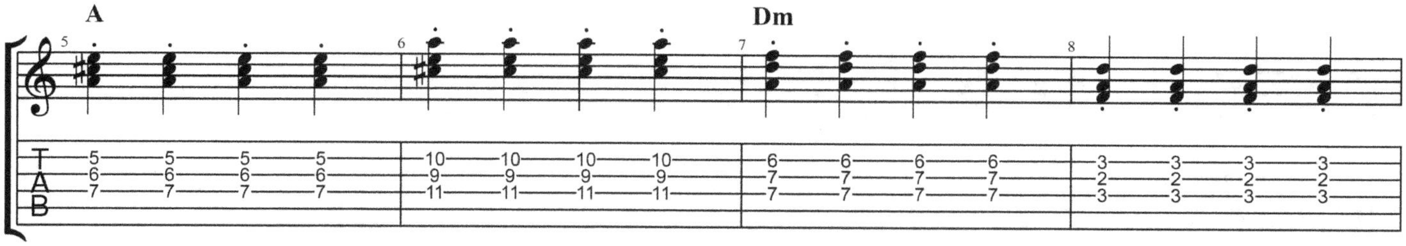

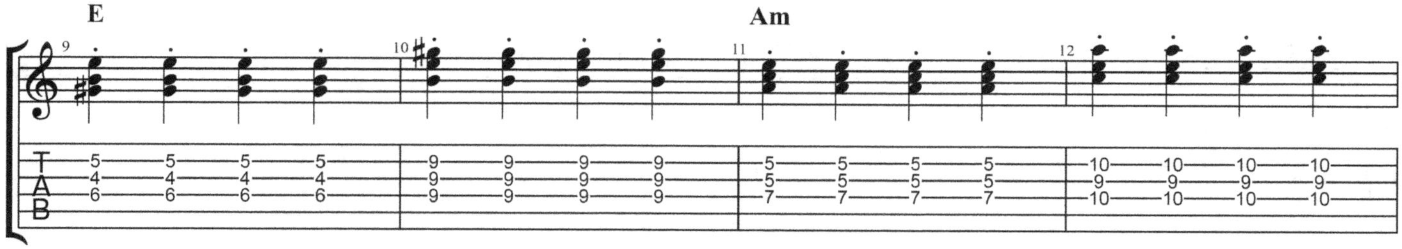

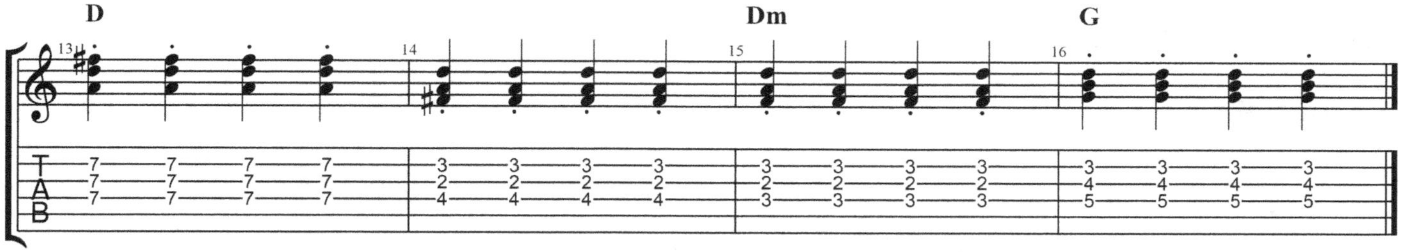

Using those same triads, I'll now turn them into 7th chords, either by lowering the root note or raising the 5th. Here's how it sounds.

Example 6p:

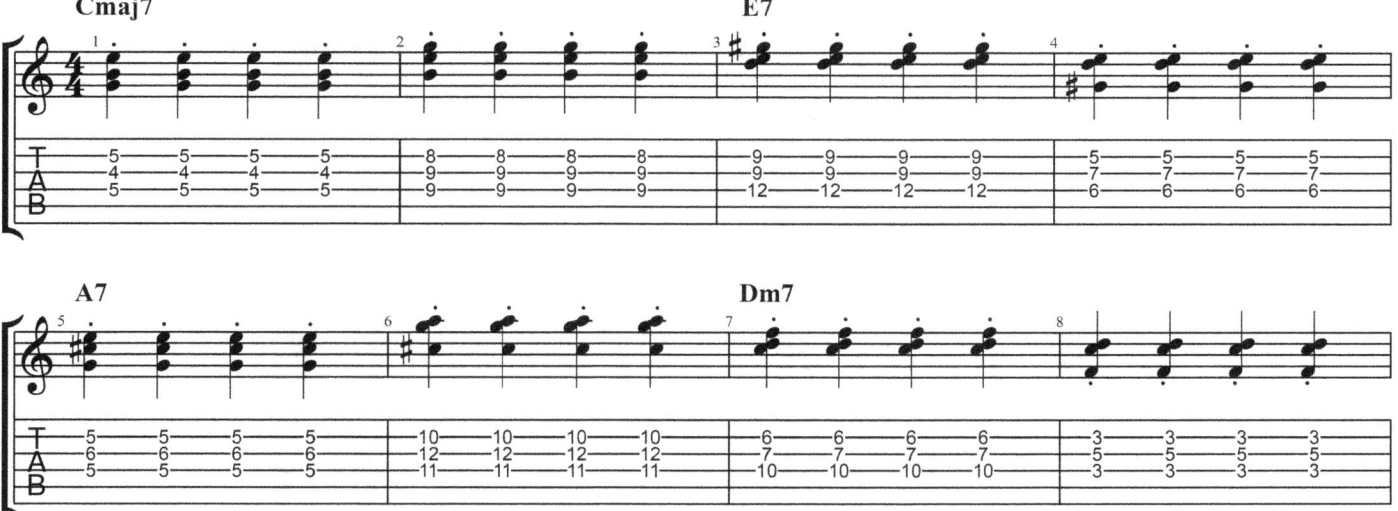

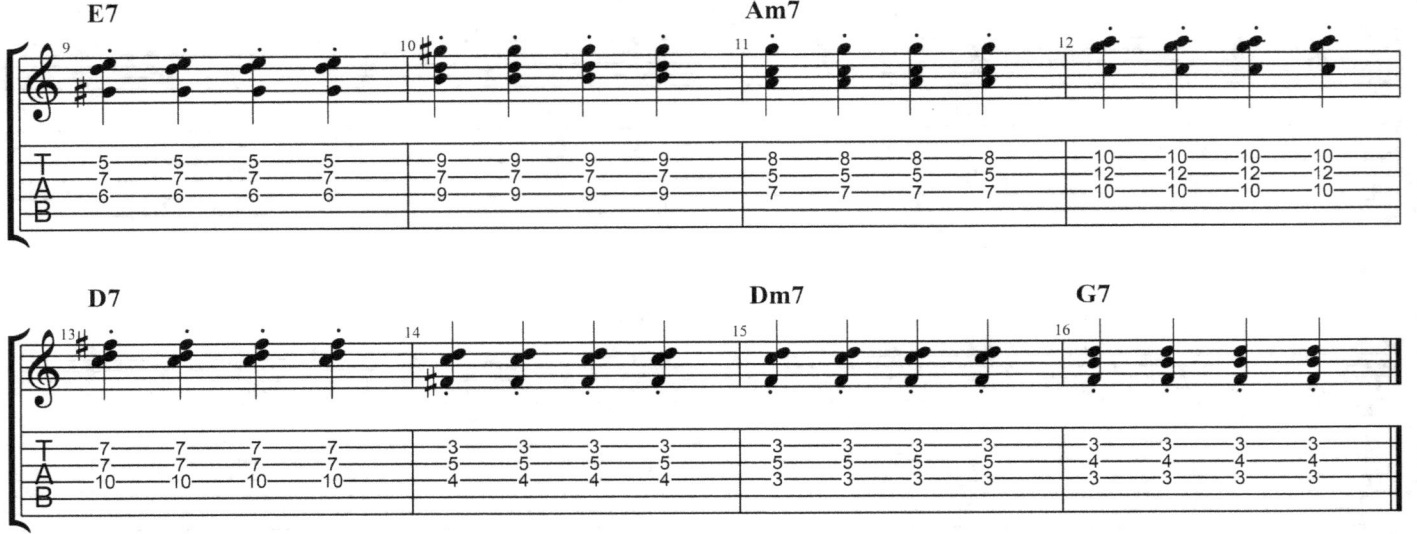

The sky is the limit here; we could also play it like this:

Example 6q:

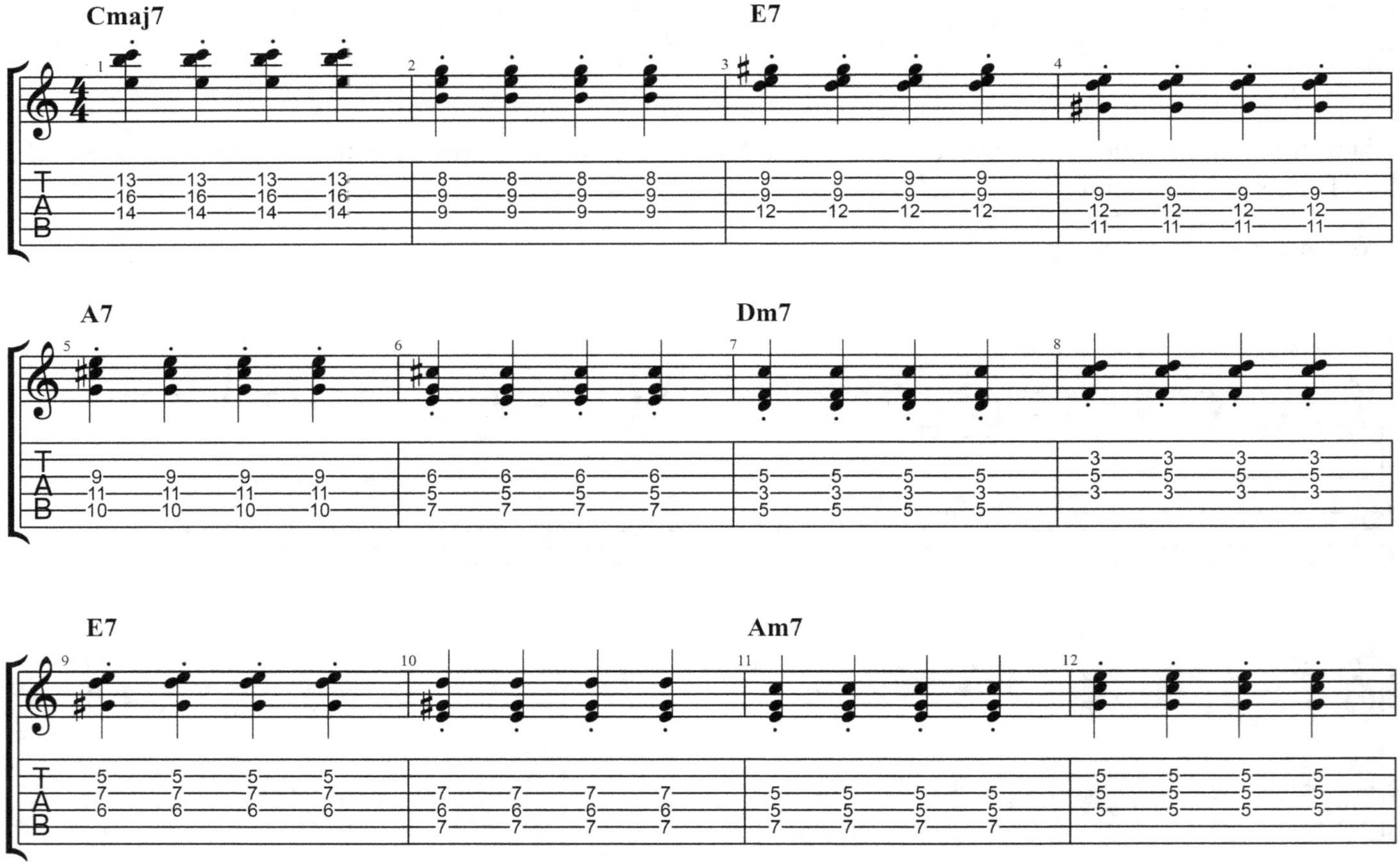

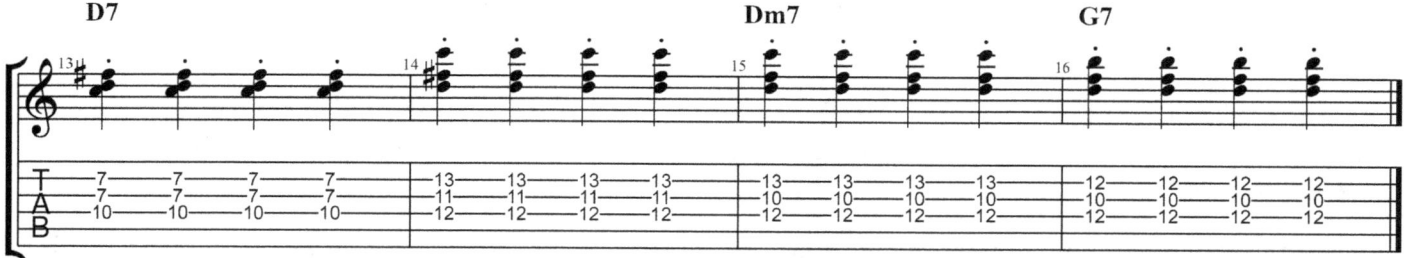

We have to remember that this book isn't just about learning, it's about practice, and about how *I* practice. We've looked at some of the possibilities on one tune, but there are countless others to work on.

By taking a song – even a random one you've never heard before – you are developing your brain's ability to work things out, rather than just memorise things. Playing the same song over and over quickly becomes an ineffective use of your practice time, so mixing things up is important. Try these other great jazz standards and work through them using the process we've established.

All The Things You Are

Polkadots And Moonbeams

Misty

Skylark

Stella By Starlight

All of these tunes have rich chord changes to work on, but we're just dipping our toe in the water. There are more songs out there than we can ever learn, so let's keep studying!

Routine Seven – Drop 2 Voicings

We've arrived at Routine Seven and we now know how to construct 7th chords, which are the most important intervals, and we have some tools for voicing them. However, the options at our fingertips thus far are a bit of a compromise.

Some of the chord grips omit notes, and we don't have good voicings for all chord types. The triad mutations are missing a note, and as soon as we begin inverting closed voiced 7th chords they quickly become unplayable. While all these chord options sound great and have their place, we still need a bit more flexibility – and this is where *drop voicings* come in.

Drop chords take closed voicings and spread them out in a way that creates a more open sound.

Remember when we took a C major triad (C E G) and dropped the middle note down an octave so that we had E C G?

That's all a drop voicing is!

There are various types and in this chapter we're looking at Drop 2 voicings.

A Drop 2 voicing takes a closed voiced chord and drops the *second note from the top* down an octave. Let's illustrate this with a Cmaj7 chord (C E G B).

In the Cmaj7 voicing below (left diagram), the second note from the top is G. So, we take that G and move it to the bottom (middle diagram).

However, the result is a voicing with a string skip, which can be hard to play, so we can reorganise the Drop 2 voicing to fit on adjacent strings (right diagram).

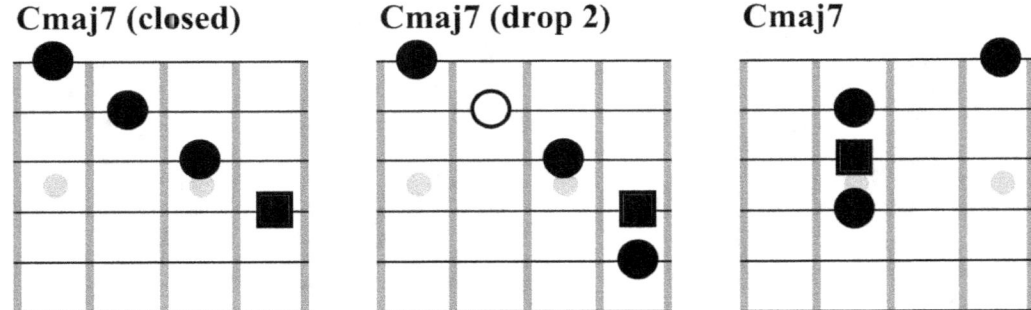

Rather than taking all four closed voiced major 7 chords, dropping down the second note from the top, then re-fingering them, it's much more efficient to take the reorganised Cmaj7 voicing on the right and move each note up to the next note in the chord. If we do that for Cmaj7, we get the following.

Example 7a:

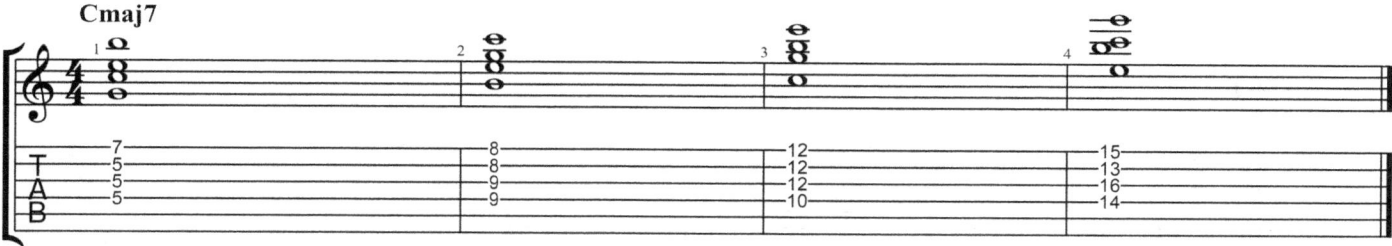

I think about these chords in terms of the note that is on top. This is our melody note. The first voicing is Drop 2 with the 7th of the chord on top. The next voicing has the root on top. The remaining two voicings have the 3rd and 5th respectively on top. Knowing this will help you down the road when you want to harmonise melodies with chords.

We can take these voicings and move them down to the two lower string sets too. Remember that as we introduce lower notes into our voicings, they start to sound like inversions. It's tough to find a place for voicings with the 7th in the bass when playing with other musicians, but that's not a reason to not know them.

Example 7b:

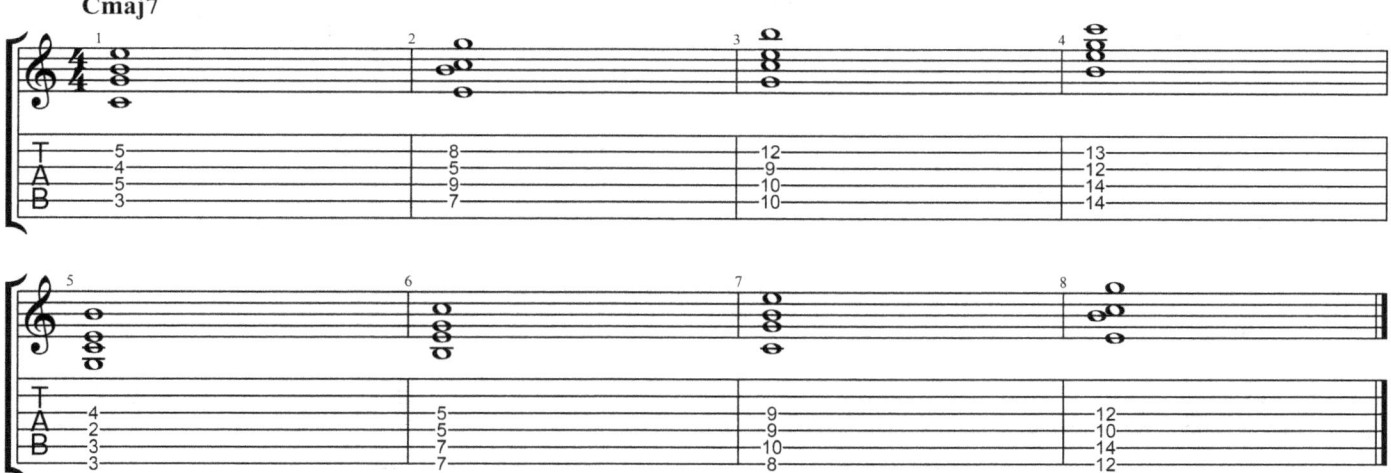

Let's play those voicings again but move them around the Circle of 5ths by going to the key of F.

Example 7c:

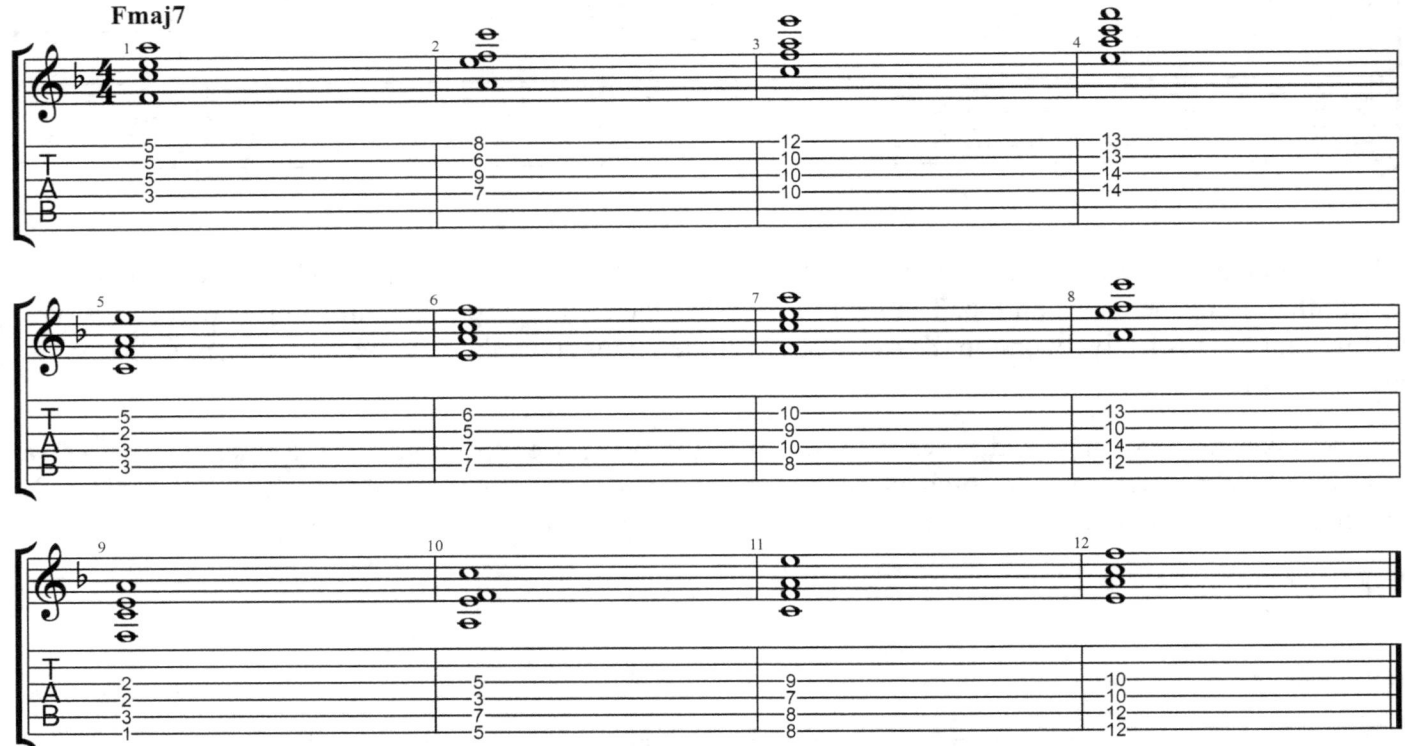

Now let's take those Fmaj7 voicings and turn them all into F7 chords by lowering the 7ths to b7s.

Example 7d:

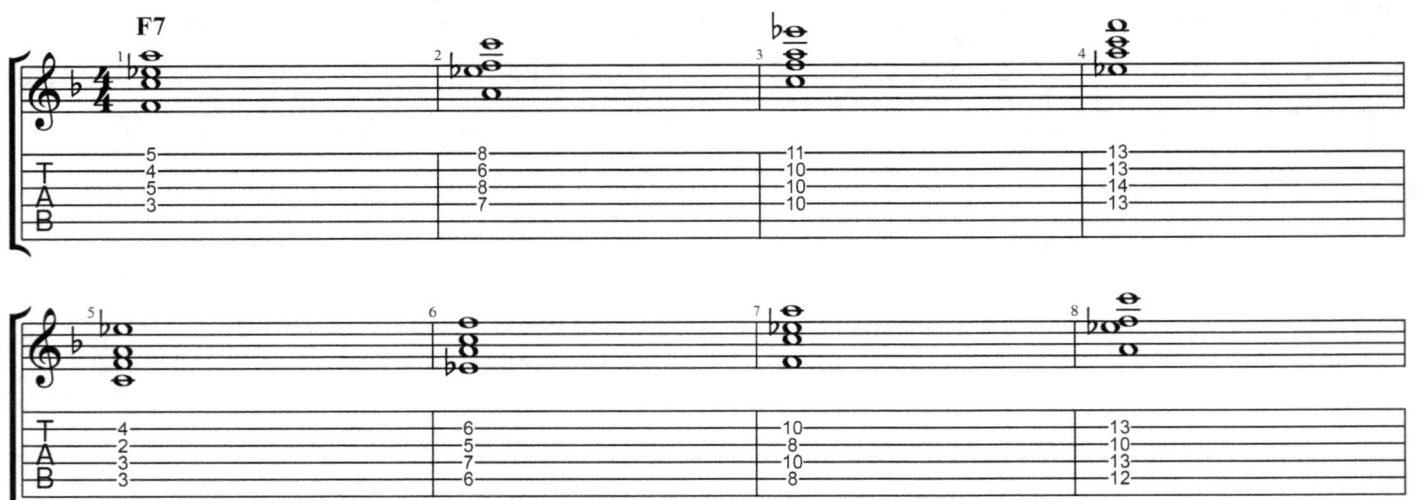

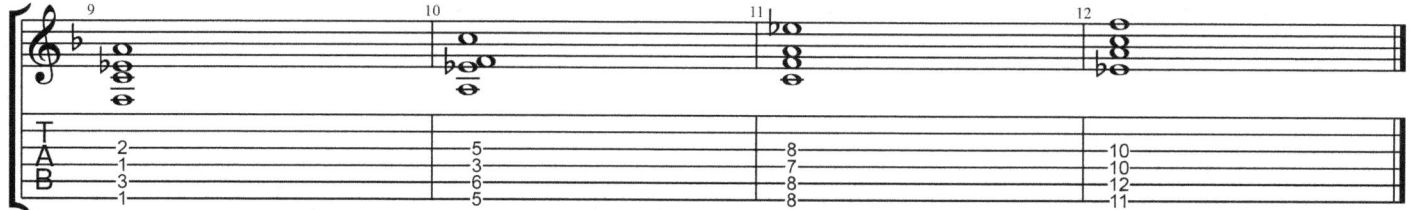

We're applying the same learning process here that we've followed throughout. Now we take those F7 voicings and move them around the circle to Bb. Being confident to play any of these voicings in any key is an essential part of chord mastery.

Example 7e:

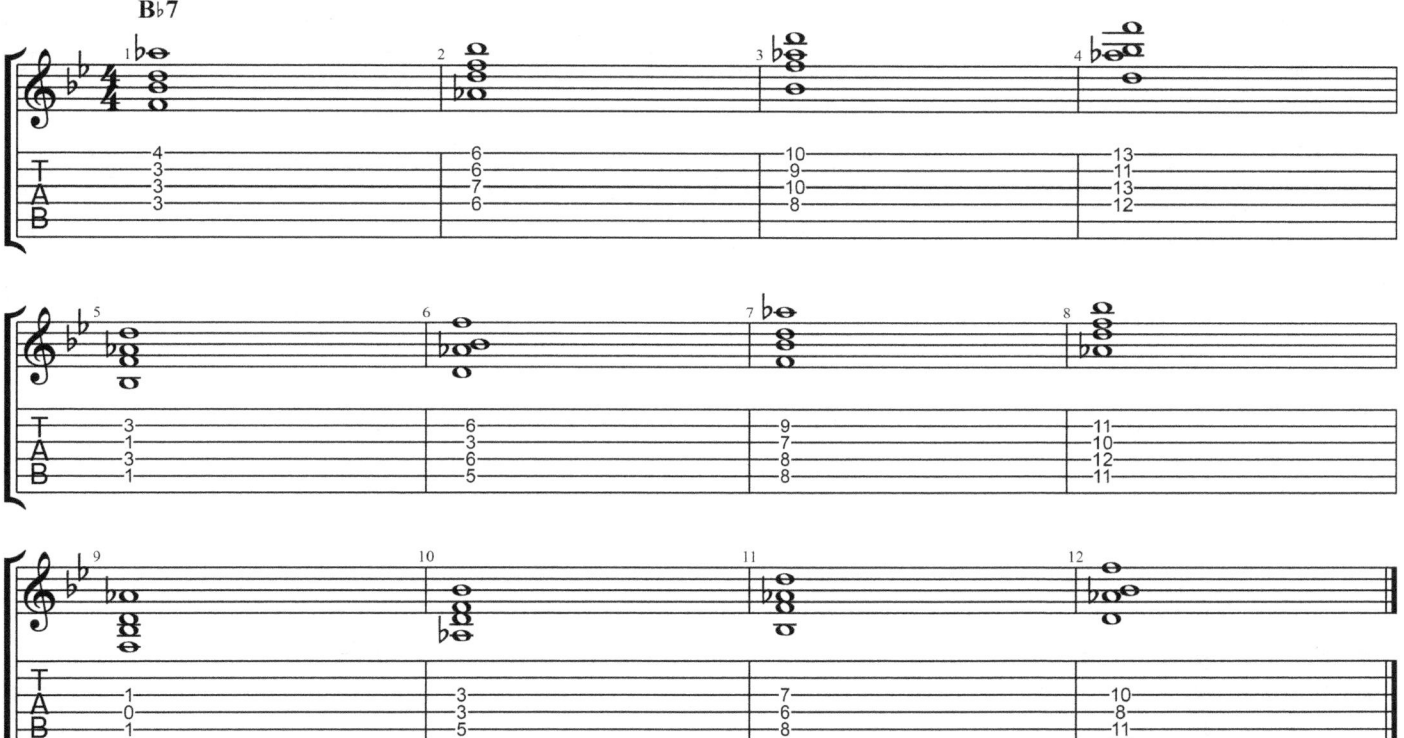

Now let's take those B7 chords and lower the 3rds to b3s to make Bbm7 chords.

Example 7f:

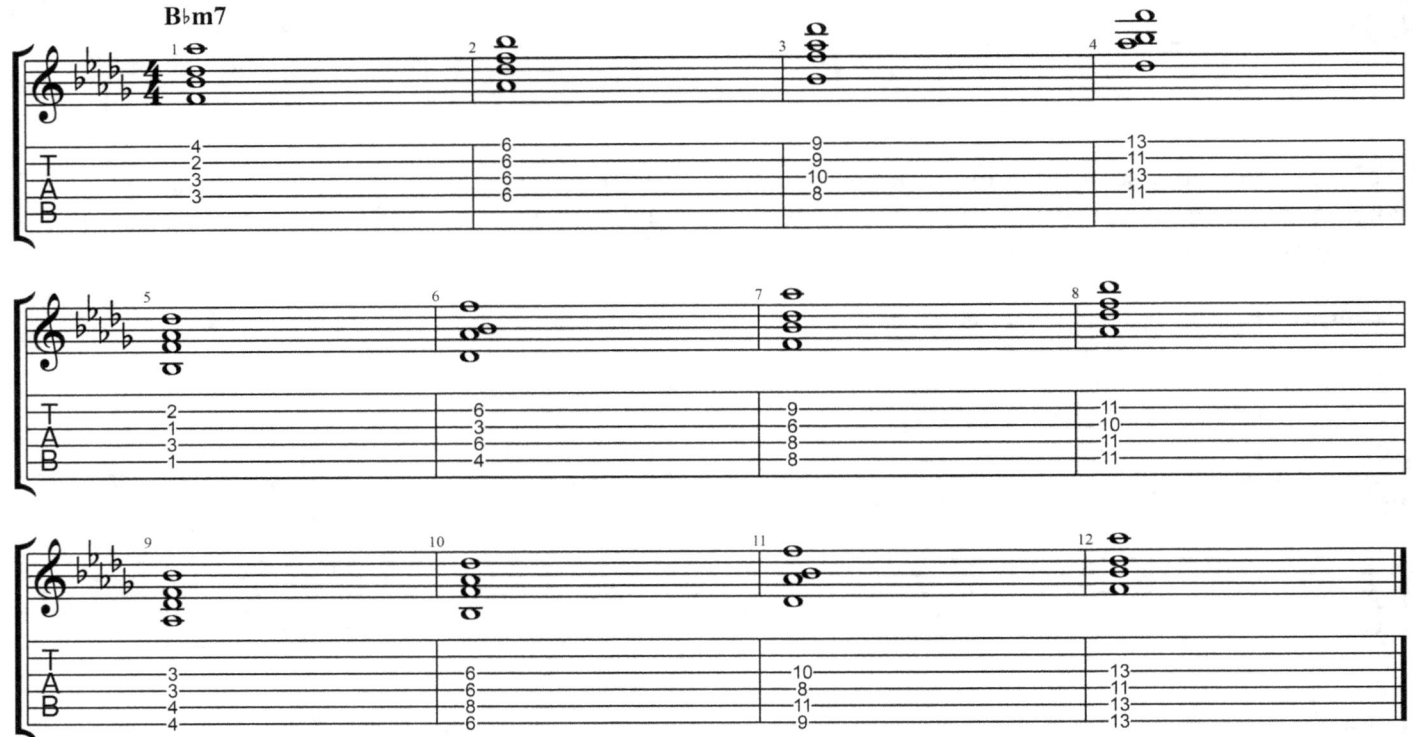

And if we move this around the circle again we end up playing Ebm7 voicings.

Example 7g:

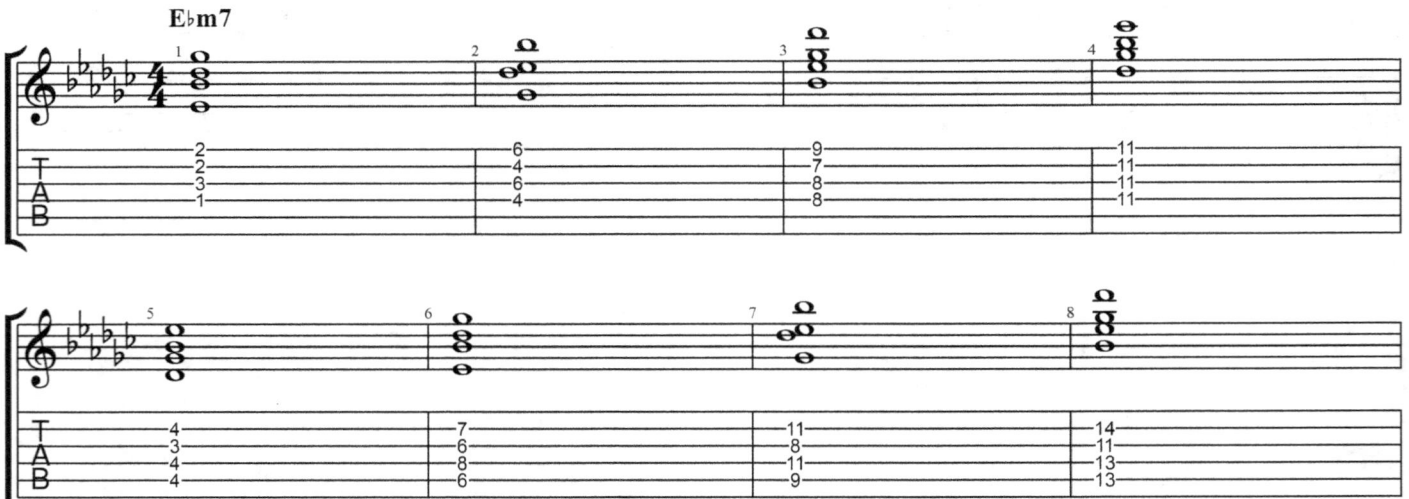

175

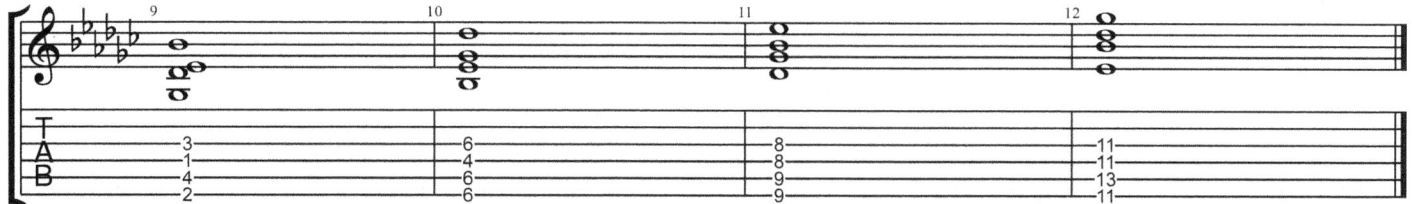

Hopefully, you can guess where we're going with this now! Let's lower all the 5ths to b5s to make Ebm7b5 voicings.

Example 7h:

Using a Drop 2 chord to generate more voicings just opened up our options even more. Let's use this idea to play diatonic chord scales with different note intervals on top. You know the drill: you can practice these using all the possible voicings in all keys. I won't write them all out, but we'll do some of them.

First, an A Major chord scale played with the 7th on top.

Example 7i:

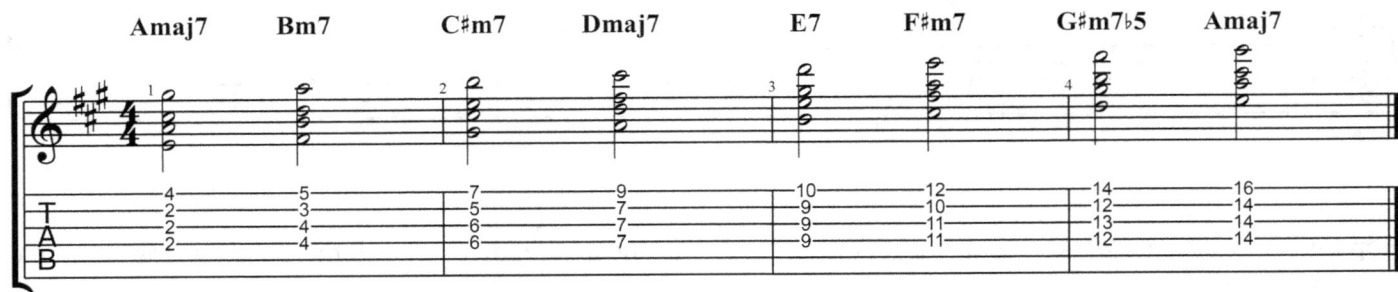

Here's C Major played with the 5th on top.

Example 7j:

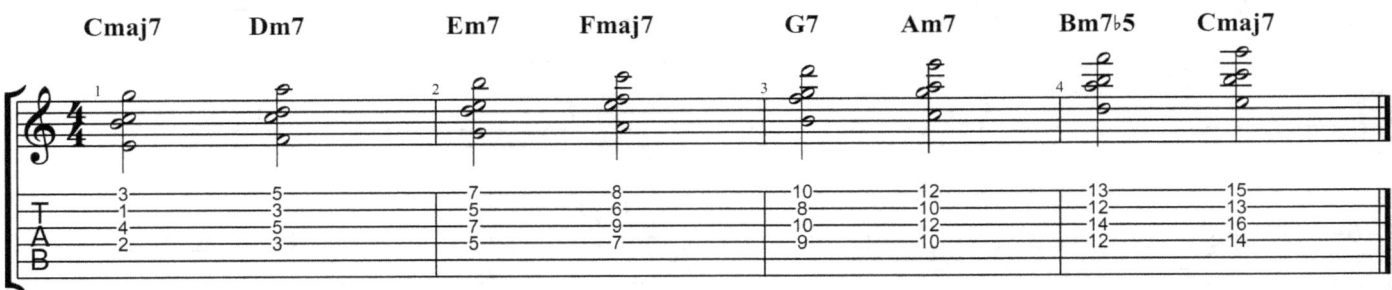

While there isn't a whole lot of use for drop voicings on the lowest string set, the middle set is viable. Here's a B Major chord scale played with the 3rd on top.

Example 7k:

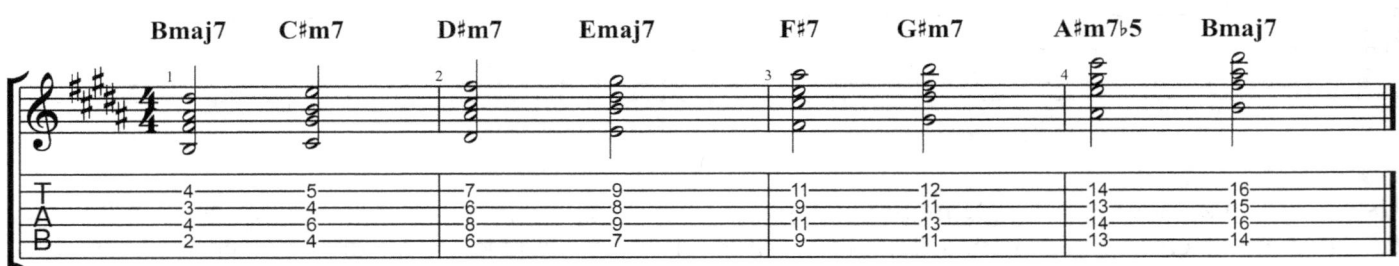

Let's apply what we've learned to a common chord progression: the major I–VI7–ii–V.

Astute readers will immediately look at this and think, "It should be I–vi–ii–V in a major key" and you'd be right, but a common change to the I–vi–ii–V (Cmaj7 – Am7 – Dm7 – G7) is to switch out the vi chord for a dominant 7 to give us Cmaj7 – A7 – Dm7 – G7.

This works on the principle of musical gravity. Dominant chords always want to resolve, and by changing Am7 to A7 (called the subdominant) we create a stronger resolution to the Dm7 chord.

Let's play those chords in position, first with the 7th on top, then the root, then the 3rd, then the 5th.

Example 7l:

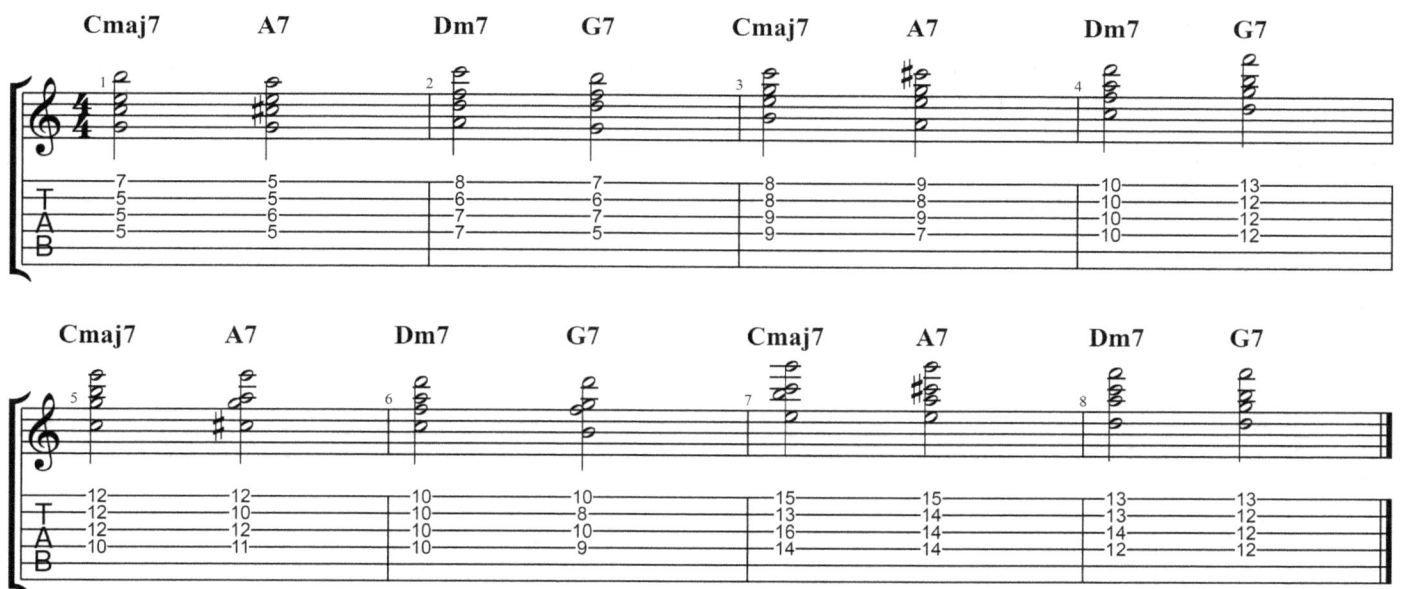

We can also work on this chord progression on the middle string set. First with the 3rd on top, then the 5th, then the 7th, then the root.

Example 7m:

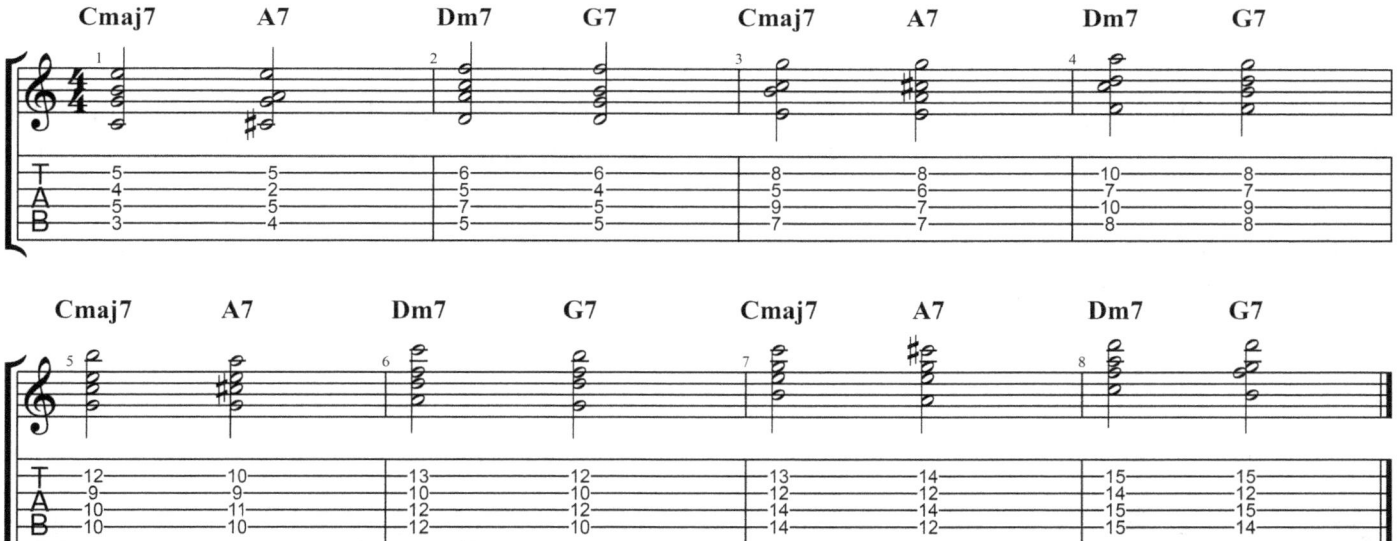

To conclude this routine, I want to give you one new chord type that sits adjacent to the chords we've learned so far. That's the diminished 7 chord and it has the formula:

1 b3 b5 bb7

Rather than learning it as an entity in its own right, it's better to adapt something we already know. It's tempting to think of taking a minor 7b5 voicing and moving the b7 down to a bb7, but there is an easier way. Instead, we take a dominant chord and raise the root a semitone.

The sharpened root becomes our new "1" interval and now we have the desired 1 b3 b5 bb7. Let's work this idea across the fretboard turning C7 chords into Dbdim7 voicings.

Example 7n:

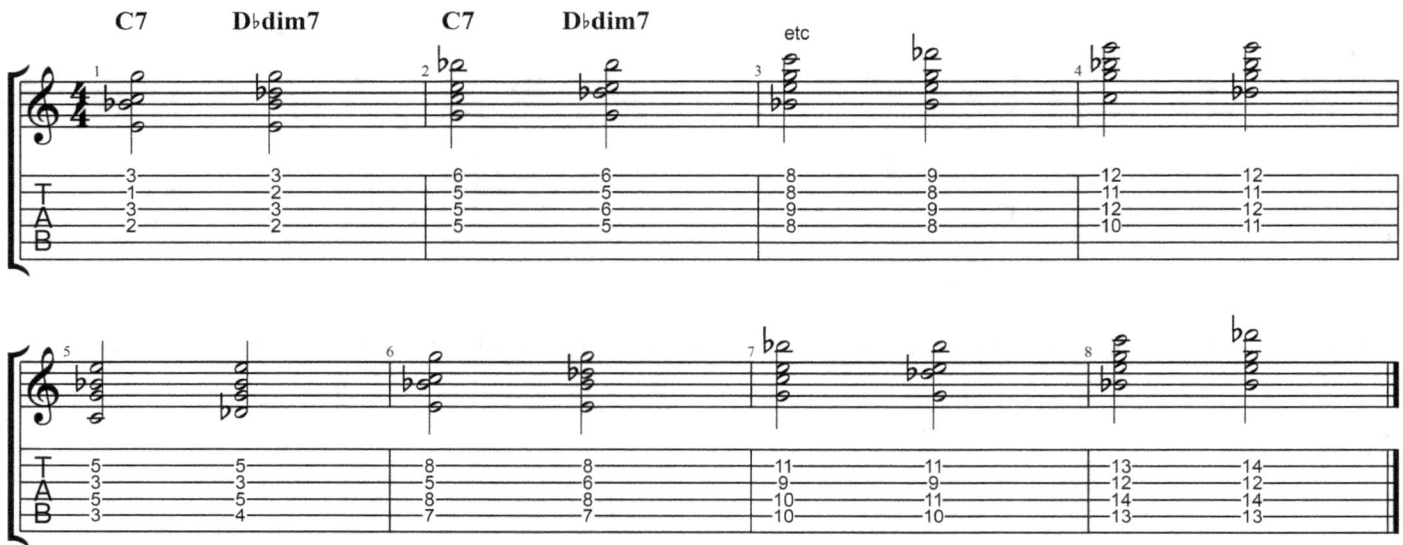

There is something very interesting about this idea. If we look at the diminished 7 chord in isolation, we realise that we can move *any* note in that chord down a semitone and it will create a *different* dominant 7 chord.

Practice the visualisation skill of playing a diminished 7 chord, lowering one of its notes a half step, then naming the dominant chord. It's a good workout!

Example 7o:

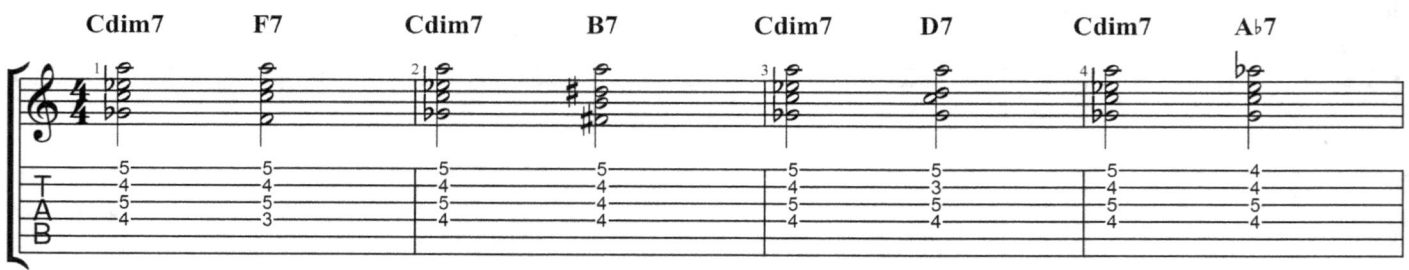

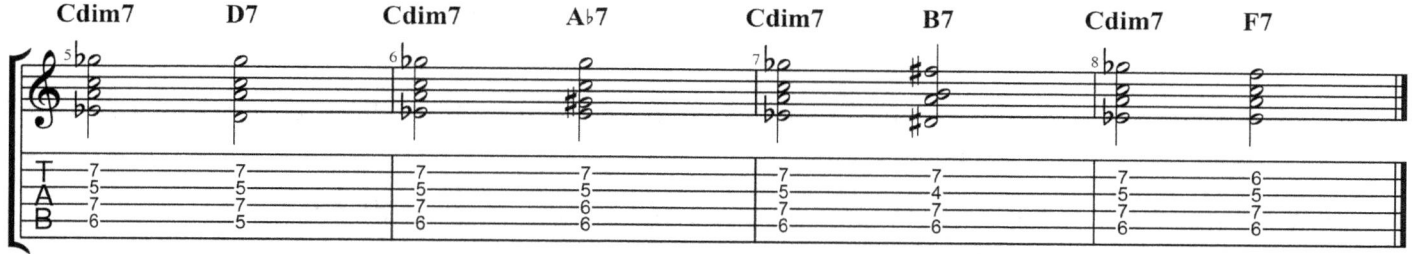

This chapter has been a good example of how a practice routine can generate much more than a week's work. You can spend a *lot* of time working these ideas through your playing, but as always, no rushing! You're only short-changing yourself if you skip ahead too quickly, so get to work on this stuff!

Routine Eight – Drop 3 & Beyond!

If you're still with me and have followed everything until this point, the title of this chapter shouldn't present a mystery. Here, we're going to look at Drop 3 voicings.

To create a Drop 3 we take the *third* note from the top in a closed voicing and drop it down an octave. Let's view this using the same diagram as the previous chapter.

Here, we take the E note of the chord and move it down an octave (middle diagram). Just like Drop 2 chords, it helps to have a consistent fingering system. Drop 2s were always played on four adjacent strings, but Drop 3 chords have a low note, a string skip, then three notes on adjacent strings (right diagram).

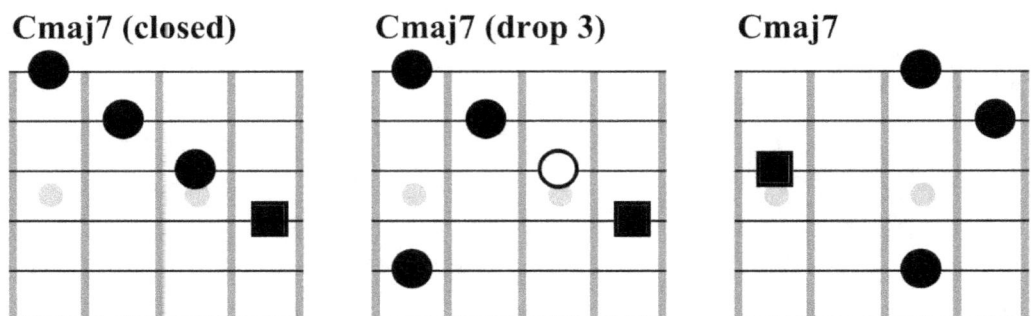

Drop 3 chords have a more open sound than Drop 2s. To my ears, Drop 2 voicings are piano-like, but drop 3s feel more guitar-centric.

When we spell out all the possibilities for Cmaj7, we have the following eight voicings.

Example 8a:

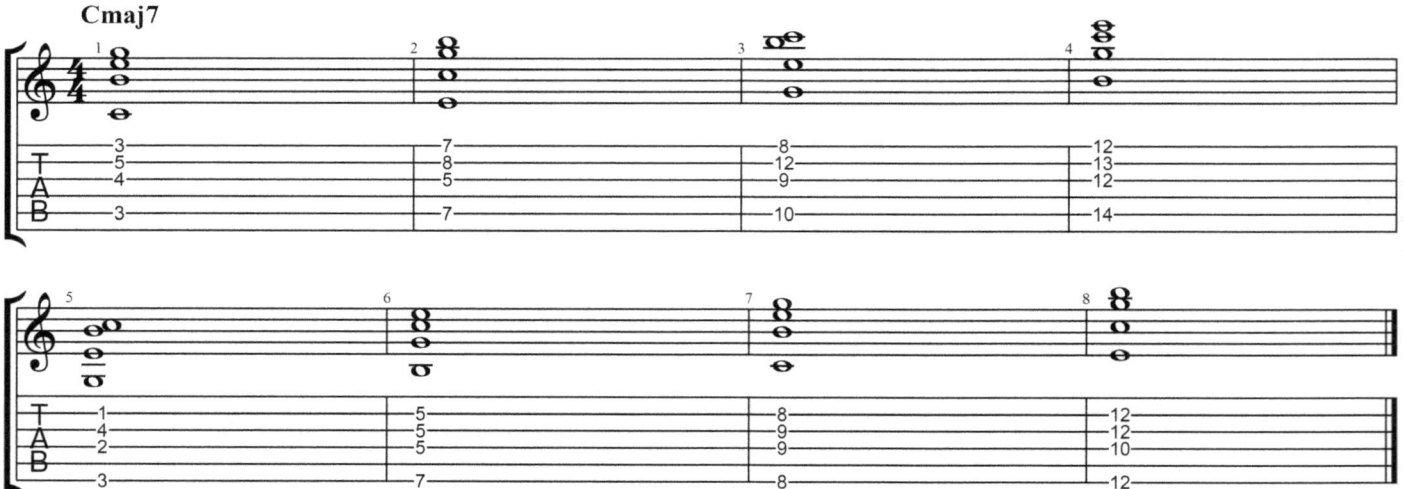

Practice until you have these voicings down. When you're comfortable with them, we can move onto other chord types. The first is the dominant 7.

Example 8b:

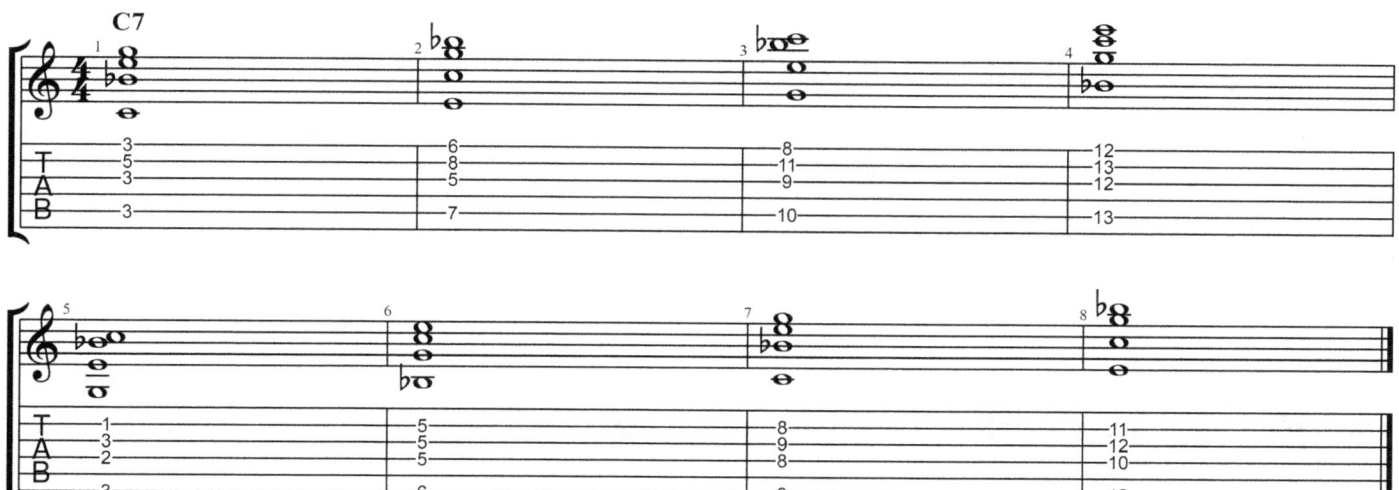

Let's make those voicings minor 7s by lowering the 3rds to b3s.

Example 8c:

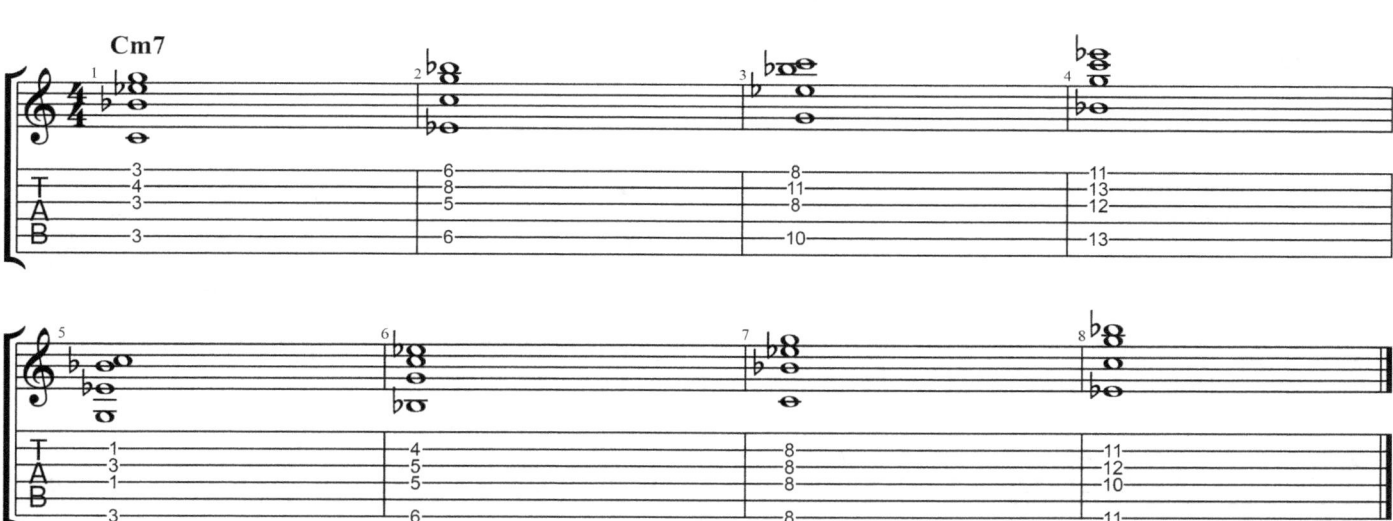

Then we can turn the minor 7s into minor 7b5s by lowering the 5ths to b5s.

Example 8d:

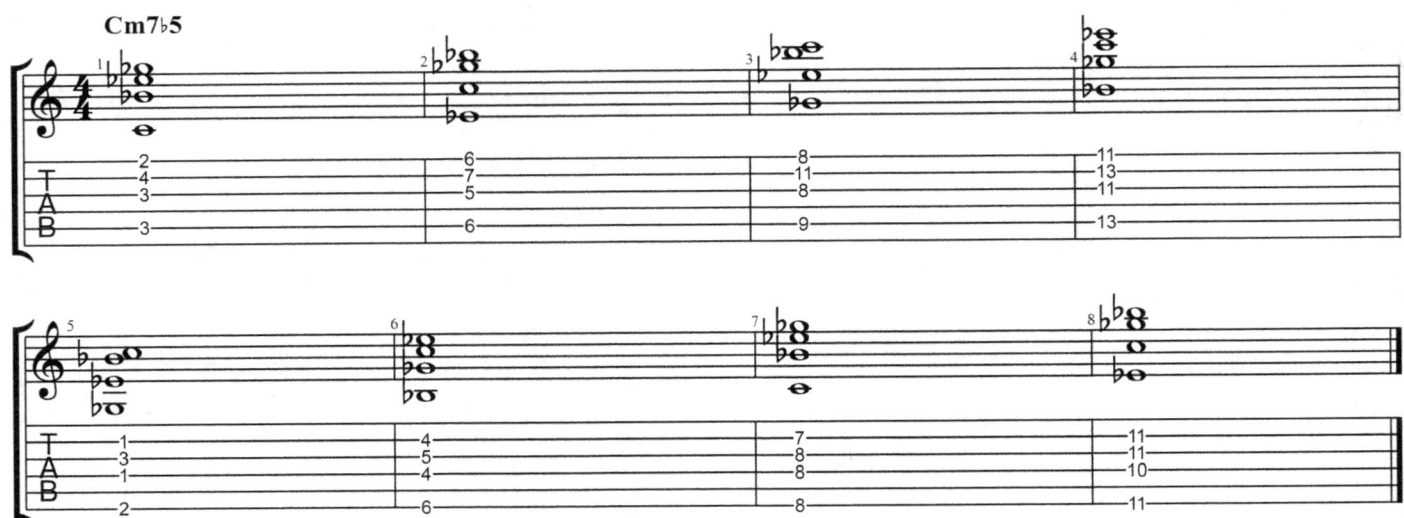

Now let's look at Drop 3 diminished 7 chords. In this arrangement, we can see just how symmetrical they are, with each voicing moving up three frets (a minor 3rd).

Example 8e:

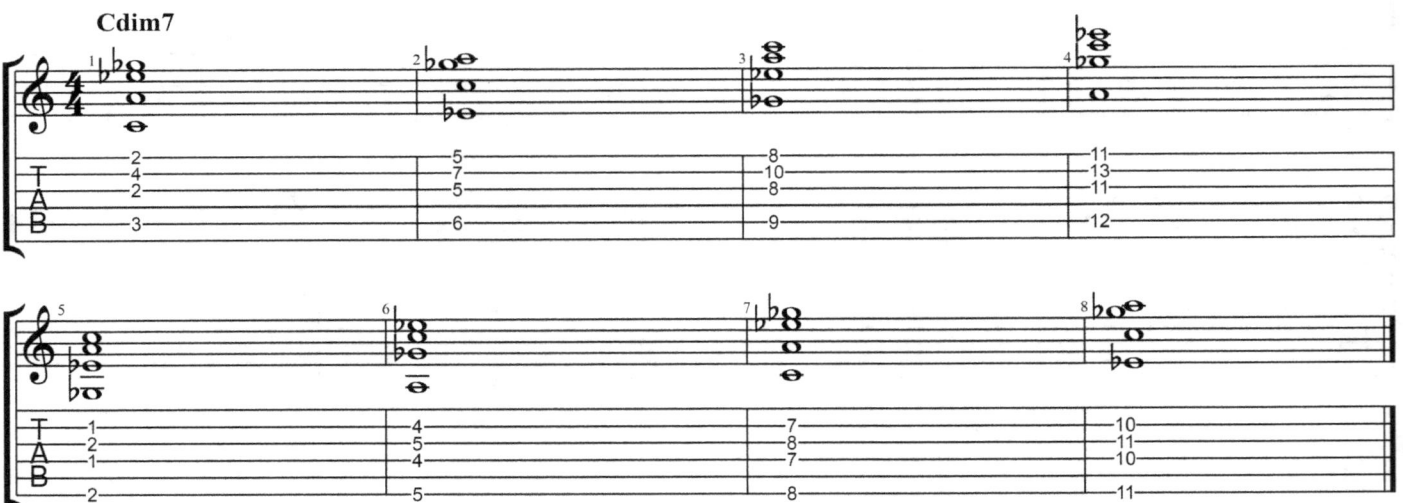

Now let's think of chord scales for a moment and play the most common Drop 3 voicing, with a root note on the low E string, through the G Major scale.

Example 8f:

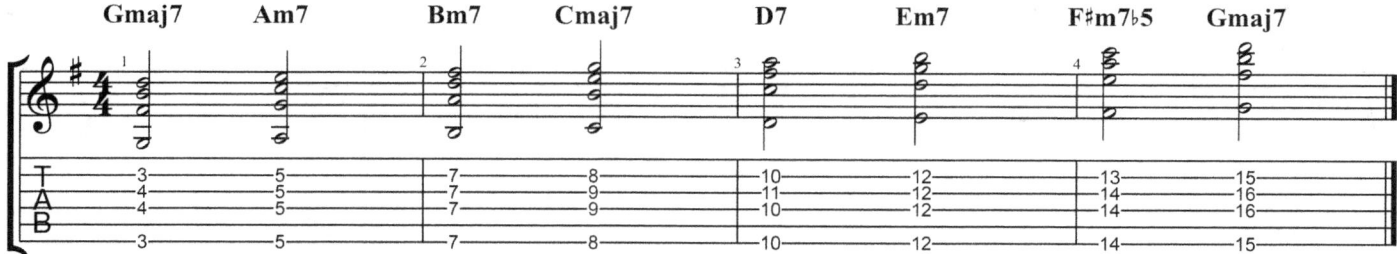

Now let's try an F Major chord scale, this time using first inversion voicings that move the 3rd to the bass. These Drop 3 chords do sound like inversions!

Example 8g:

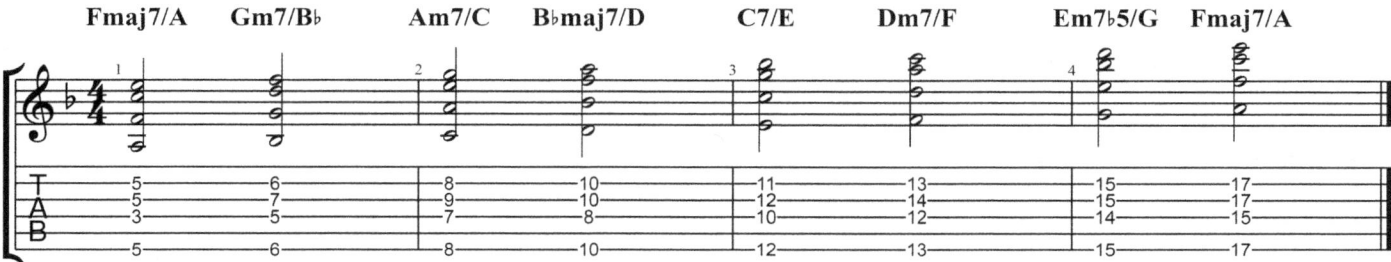

To test our comfort level with the drop chords we've learned so far, let's pause and use them to play through a Bird blues progression. We're going to limit ourselves to Drop 3 chords on the lowest string set (E D G B), and Drop 2 chords on the middle string set (A D G B).

Let's start with root position Drop 3 and 2 chords. We could call these our E and A shapes from earlier in the book.

Example 8h:

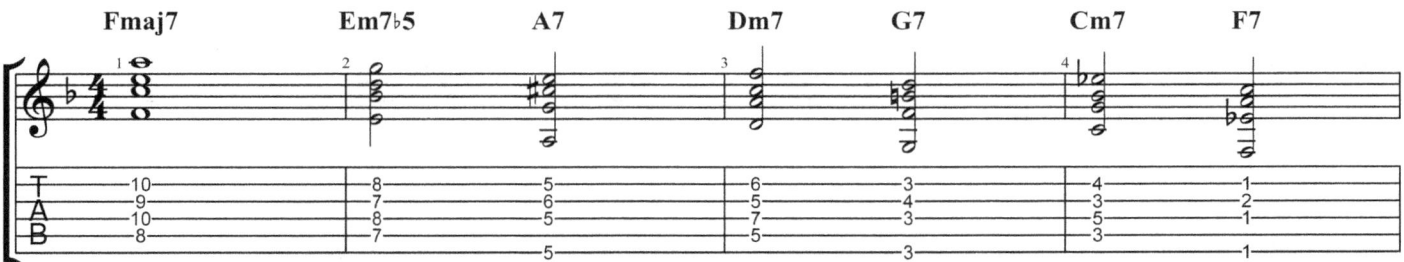

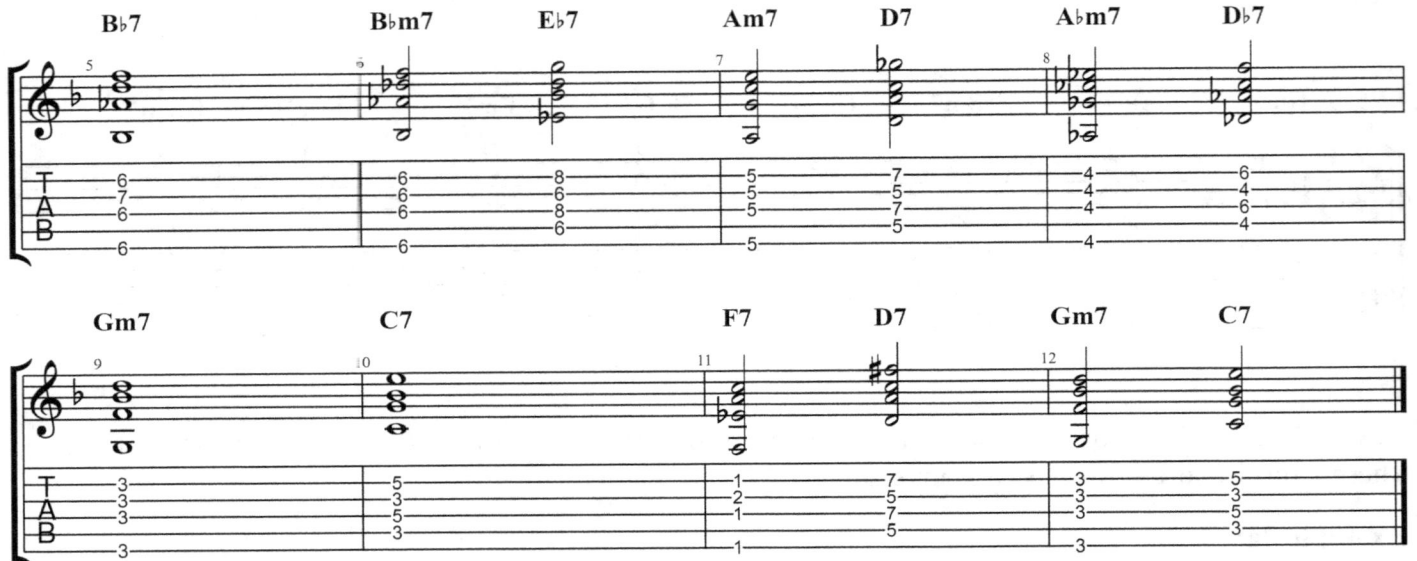

Here's a sunnier chord progression. Again, we're just limiting ourselves to the Drop 3 E shape and Drop 2 A shape.

Example 8i:

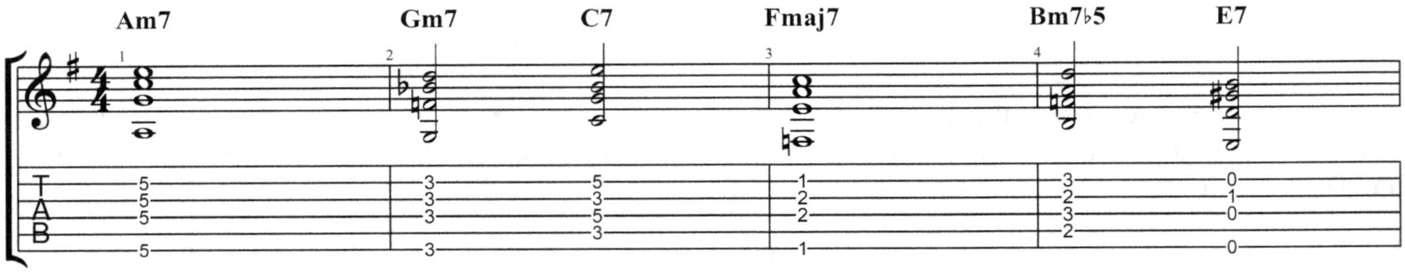

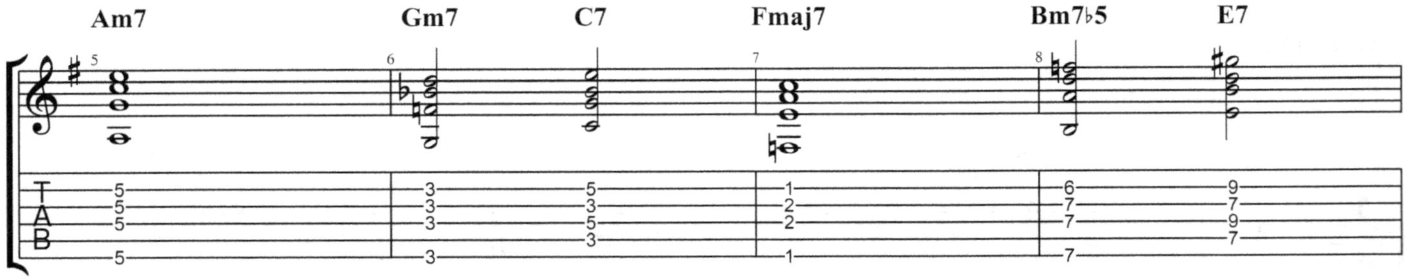

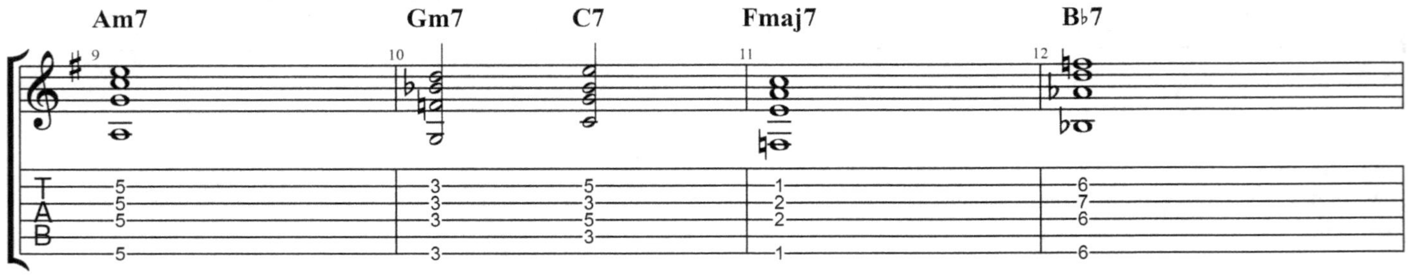

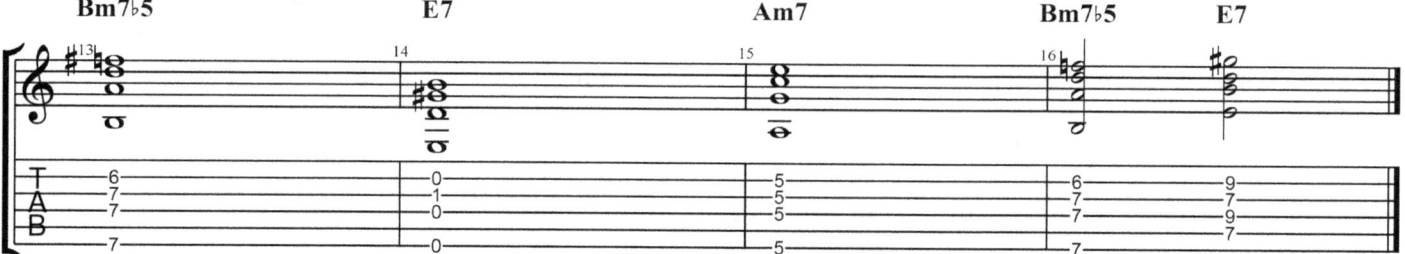

If we combine these voicings with our C shape closed voiced chords and grips, we can start developing some real flexibility when we play. I'm looking for my root notes, then sticking a chord voicing on top.

Example 8j:

We've played through a few chord progressions using drop voicings, but to test yourself apply this idea to any progression/song you know. Growth is all about keeping your brain working, so keep on mixing things up. I don't want you to copy the same path that I've used, I want you to work out your own.

To close out this chapter, I want to put one more idea in front of you: the concept of Drop 2&4 voicings. As the name suggests, this is when we take a closed voiced chord and drop both the 2nd and 4th notes from the top down an octave. Let's return to our diagram to visualise it.

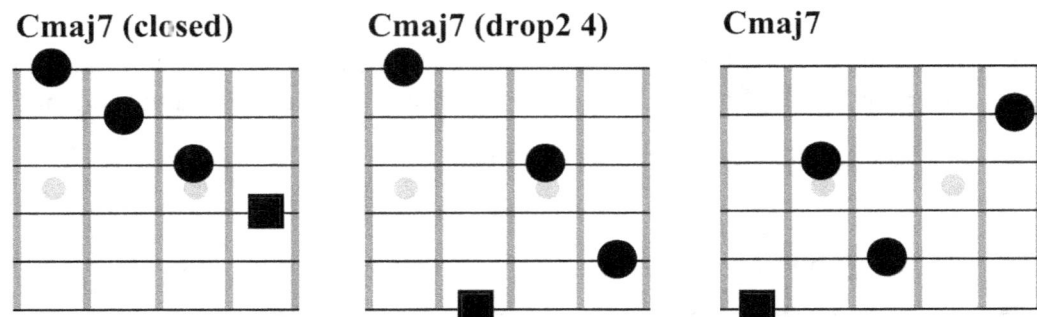

To organise these notes on the fretboard in a sensible way, I recommend playing two notes on adjacent strings, skipping a string, then playing two more adjacent notes, as in the right hand grid above.

These chords sound even more open than Drop 3 voicings and are a feature in the playing of many "out there" modern jazz/fusion icons such as Allan Holdsworth.

Here are Drop 2&4 voicings on the lowest string set for Cmaj7.

Example 8k:

You'll probably notice that most of these voicings sound like they don't work too well. Why is that?

Well, a chord only needs to contain the right intervallic ingredients to be considered a chord, and the way in which we voice it has a big impact on how we hear it. These Drop 2&4 voicings sound like inversions. Plus, any chord voiced with its 7th in the bass on the low E string is going to sound muddy.

However, transfer them onto the top strings in the higher register and suddenly they're quite nice!

Example 8l:

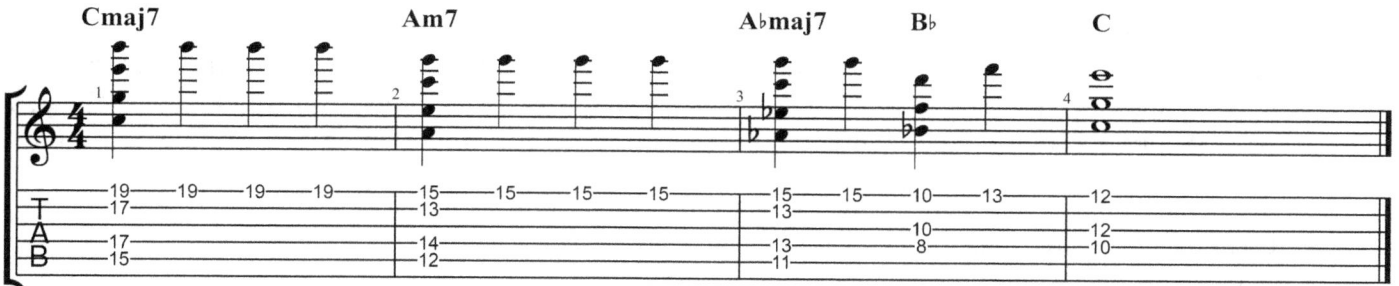

This throws up the topic of *voice leading*. The study of voicing chords and voice leading them (how we move from one chord to the next) is a lifetime's work and not something we can pursue here. There are some notable texts on the subject, like George Van Eps' *Harmonic Mechanisms* – three volumes clocking in at 900 pages! In other words, it's not something that can be mastered in ten weeks. However, as long as we focus on getting a little better each day, we're heading in the right direction.

Routine Nine – Chord Naming Rules & Extensions

I'll warn you up front: we're going to cover a lot in this routine and there will be a fair bit of theory amidst the examples! The most important aspect of this session will be learning about chord naming conventions. The reason we're looking at this is because I want to arm you to be able to interpret any chord symbol that is put in front of you in the future. So, when you see a Sus2 or Sus4 chord written on a chart, to give a simple example, you'll know exactly what it is and how to play it.

Let's start with triad naming rules.

From our studies, we know that triads contain variations of intervals 1, 3 and 5.

- 1 3 5 – Major
- 1 b3 5 – Minor
- 1 b3 b5 – Diminished
- 1 3 #5 – Augmented

We've talked about the function of these intervals. We hear a chord in relation to the root (1). The 3rd gives us information about the chord's quality (major or minor). The 5th just adds some density to the chord sound.

The first variation we should talk about is suspended chords. Suspended chords (usually written "sus") delay the commitment to a major or minor sound by switching out the 3rd for either the 2nd or 4th of the scale.

- 1 2 5 – Sus2
- 1 4 5 – Sus4

To play them, we can take any of our triads and move the 3rd up (to the 4th) or down (to the 2nd) to form a suspended chord.

Example 9a:

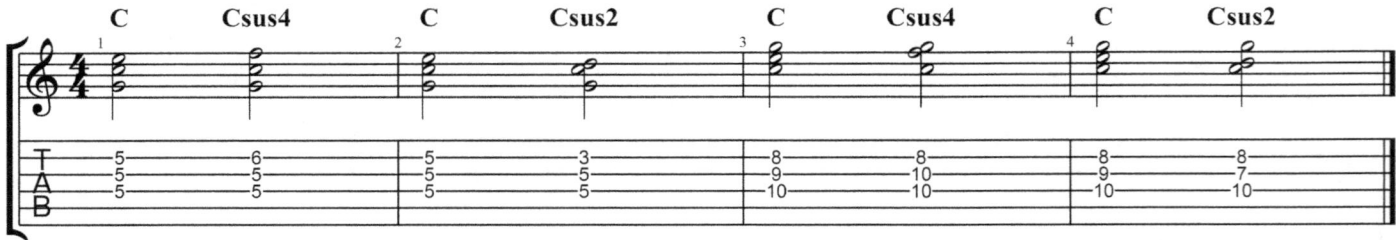

You should be able to play *any* of our twelve closed voiced triads and turn them into sus2 or sus4 voicings. I'm not going to write them all out here, because if you need them written out nine routines in, you need to go back for a refresher!

Sus chords are beautiful because they're so ambiguous in nature. They can be used to add inner voice movement to your chords for colour. One voicing I play a lot is the E shape triad on the D, G, B string set, and I'll hammer from the 2nd up to the 3rd.

If you want to get real serious with this chord, you can also add the root note on the low E string with your thumb! Here's me alternating between an Asus2 to A and Dsus2 to D.

Example 9b:

Sus chords are an example of where we change a note in a triad to turn it into something else, but we can also *add* notes to chords to create more colourful versions of the basic triad.

For instance, we can add the 2nd or 4th to a triad, and they are (aptly) called "add" chords.

The 2nd and 4th can also be called the 9th and 11th. They are the same pitches moved up an octave. So, common "add" chords are:

- 1 3 5 9 – add9 (sometimes called add2)
- 1 b3 5 9 – madd9 (minor add9)
- 1 3 4 5 – add11 (sometimes called add4)

There are lots of ways to play these chords, but not easily in the same octave, so we might omit some notes. The bass player will be covering the root, so we can, for example, move the root note up to the 2nd to create an add9 chord. Let's play A to Aadd9 now.

Example 9c:

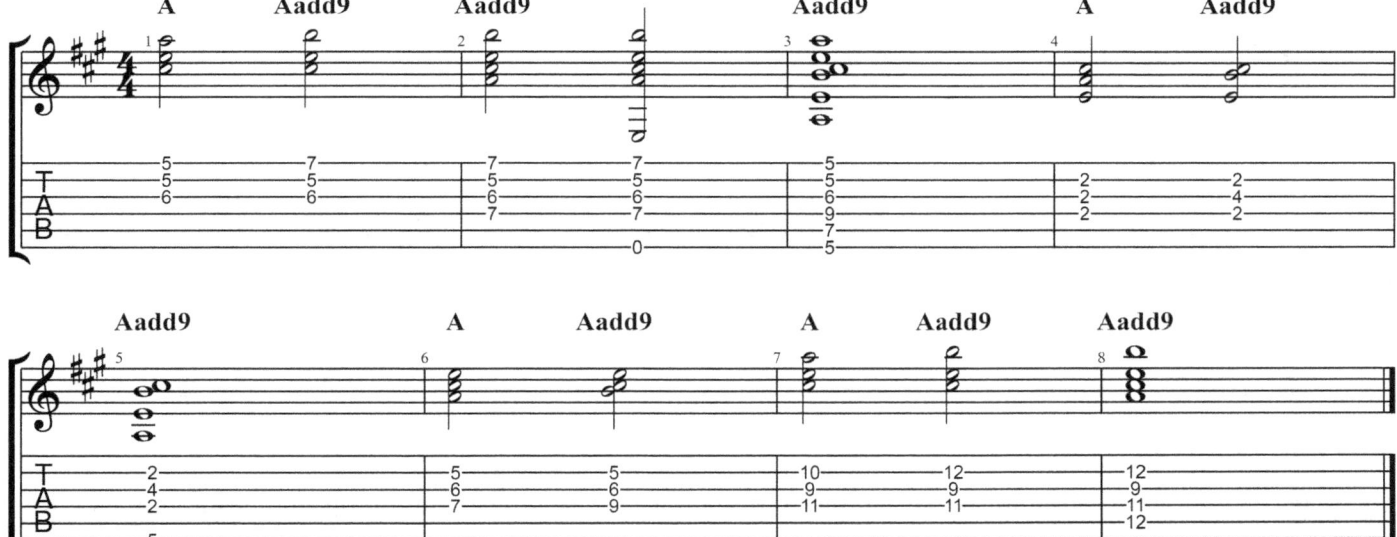

While the add11 is less common, these are beautiful chords if you can make the stretches. In order to play them, we'll take triads we know then drop the 5th down to the 4th. These chords work best when the 11th is higher up in the chord. We don't want it in the bass!

Example 9d:

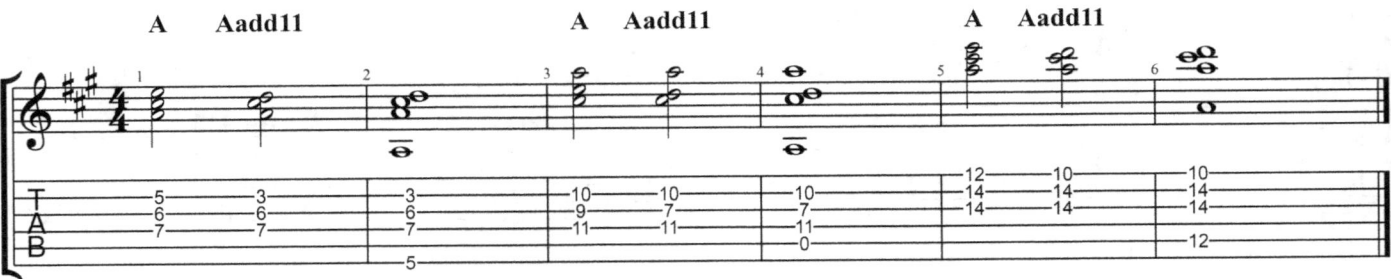

Now comes the 6th, a note added to triads so frequently that we stop saying "add"!

- 1 3 5 6 – Maj6
- 1 b3 5 6 – m6 (or min6)

Note that both of these chords have a major 6 (the 6th from the major scale). The minor 6 chord doesn't take the 6th from the minor scale.

These can be played as four-note voicings, but we can also play triads with the 5th moved up to the 6th. Here are some Maj6 voicings:

Example 9e:

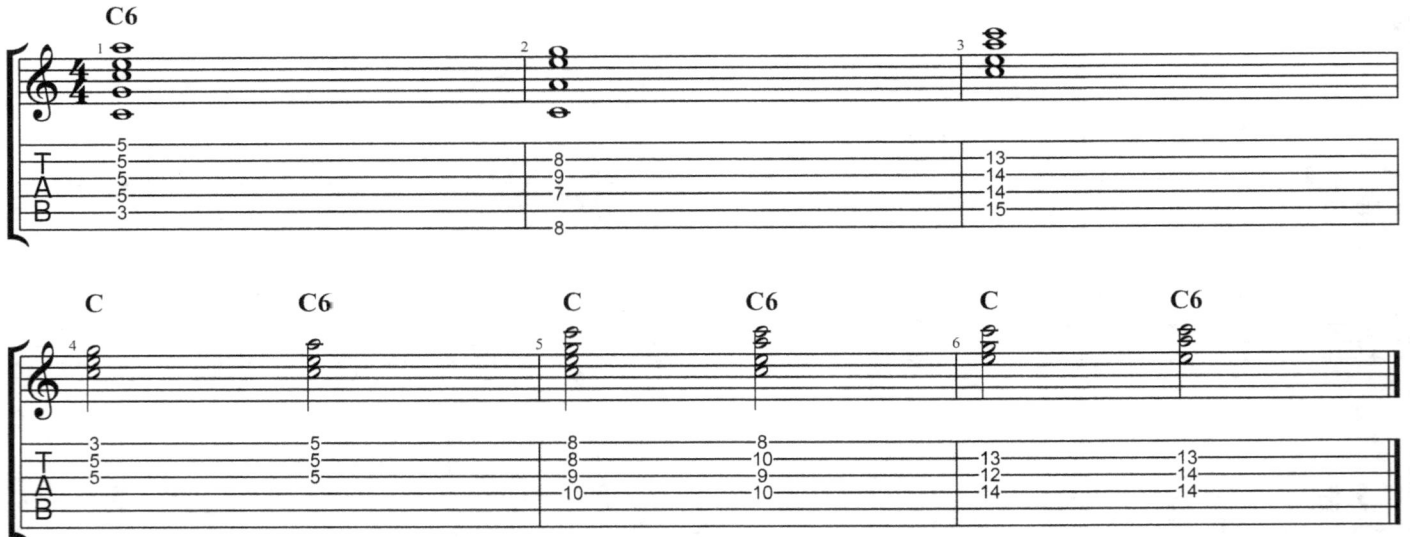

And here's our super cool minor 6 chord sounds. For these, we will raise the 5th up to the 6th, but also drop the root down to the 6th!

Example 9f:

You might see combinations of 6th and 9th chords (written "6/9"), which are major chords with the 6th and 9th added:

- 1 3 5 6 9 – 6/9

It's rare that all five notes are played, so giving the listener the important notes (3rd, 6th and 9th) will do the job.

So, we've looked at adding more colourful notes to a triad, but what happens to the naming conventions when we add them to a 7th chord?

Let's take the 9th interval. We'll never see written Maj7add9. Occasionally I'll see Maj7(9) written with the added note in brackets but I don't like that. I prefer to see Maj9. To cite another example, nobody needs to see C7(9, 11, 13) when C13 will do.

We name a chord according to its highest extension. Maj9 implies we've taken a major 7 chord and added the 9th to it. If it simply said "add9" we'd know it was a triad-based chord.

When we see a Maj11 chord, it's implied that 9th is already in the chord. If we see a Maj13, it's implied that both the 9th and 11th are in the chord.

Let's briefly note the construction of major and minor 9th chords then play them.

- 1 3 5 7 9 – Maj9
- 1 3 5 b7 9 – 9
- 1 b3 5 b7 9 – m9
- 1 b3 5 b7 9 – m9b5

When you play these voicings, you should be able to stop and list off each interval in the chord in relation to the root note. If you can't, pause and take some time to do that.

Example 9g:

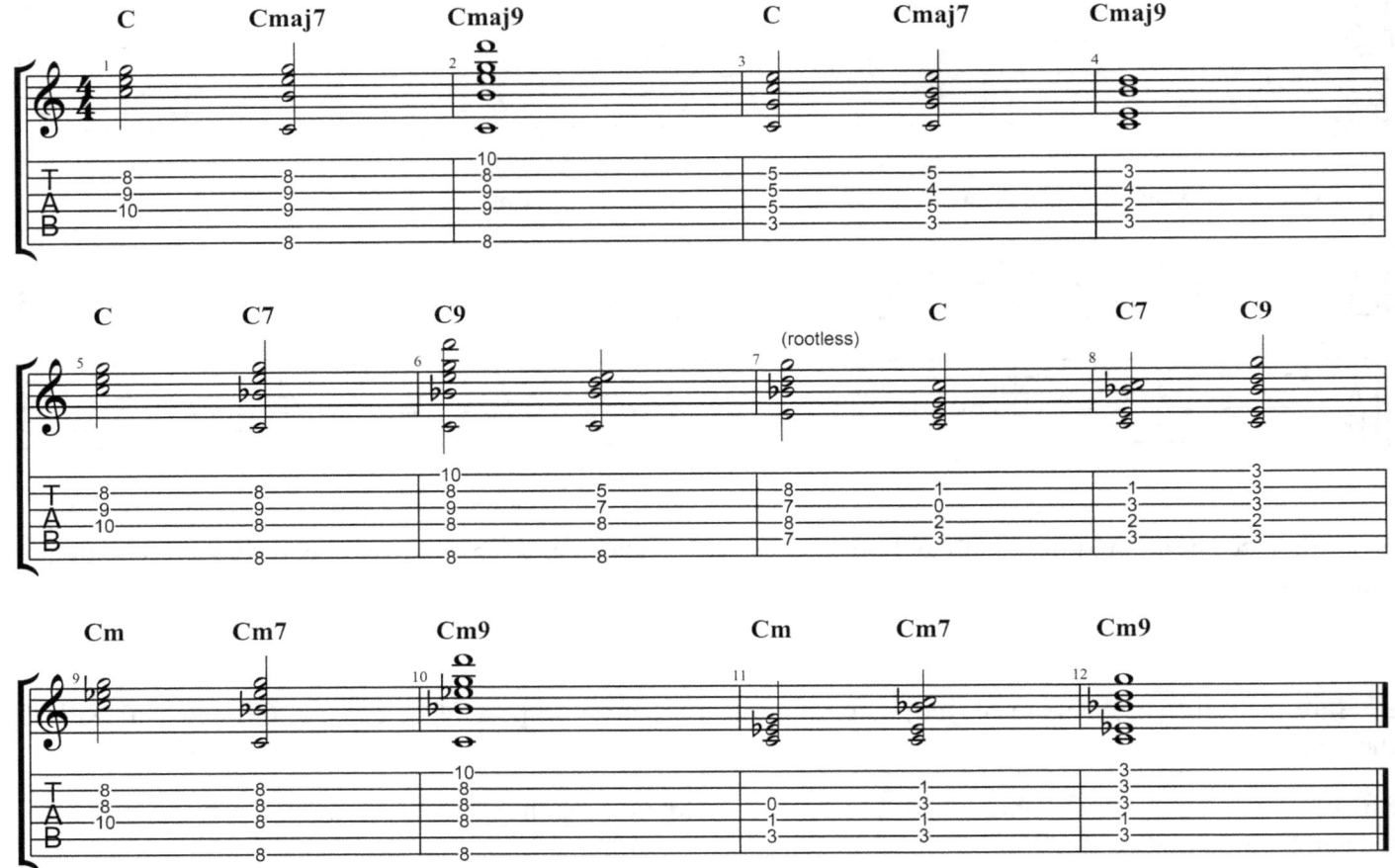

The 11th interval doesn't sound good on a major 7 chord, so it's often left out, but it works on dominant and minor chords.

- 1 3 5 b7 9 11 – 11
- 1 b3 5 b7 9 11 – m11

13s follow all the same rules.

- 1 3 5 7 9 13 – Maj13
- 1 3 5 b7 9 11 13 – 13
- 1 b3 5 b7 9 11 13 – m13

Occasionally, you'll see a 7th chord that contains the 11th but not the 3rd. What do we call that? It has a suspended quality, but still has the 7th, so "7sus" does the trick. Sometimes you'll see "9sus" chords too.

Example 9h:

We've covered almost all of the intervals you're likely to come across. All that's left are the alterations we can make to dominant chords: the b9, #9, b5/#11 and #5.

Let's start with the #9 because it's the ever-popular "Hendrix chord".

- 1 3 5 b7 #9 – 7#9

In fact, any of these intervals can be added to a dominant chord in any combination to make an altered dominant:

- 1 3 5 b7 b9 – 7b9
- 1 3 #5 b7 – 7#5
- 1 3 #5 b7 #9 – 7#5#9
- 1 3 #5 b7 b9 – 7#5b9

And there's nothing to stop us combining natural and altered extensions, such as:

- 1 3 5 b7 b9 13 – 13b9
- 1 3 #5 b7 9 – 9#5

The key to using these intervals is to know where they sit around your E and A shapes. Then you'll be able to add them without thought. Each one has its own flavour, but they all add tension and want to resolve like a standard dominant 7 chord.

Here are some altered dominant chords in the key of F Major. We're playing C7alt in the E shape.

Example 9i:

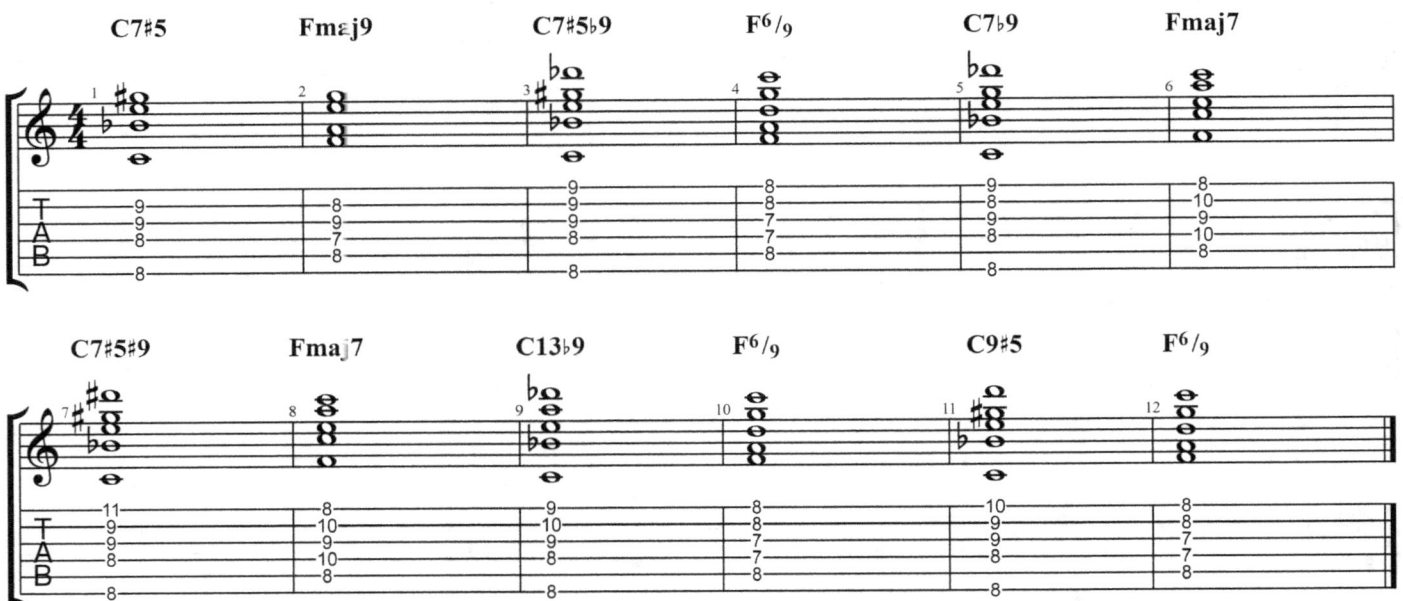

Here are some more altered dominants, now in the key of C with G7alt in the A shape.

Example 9j:

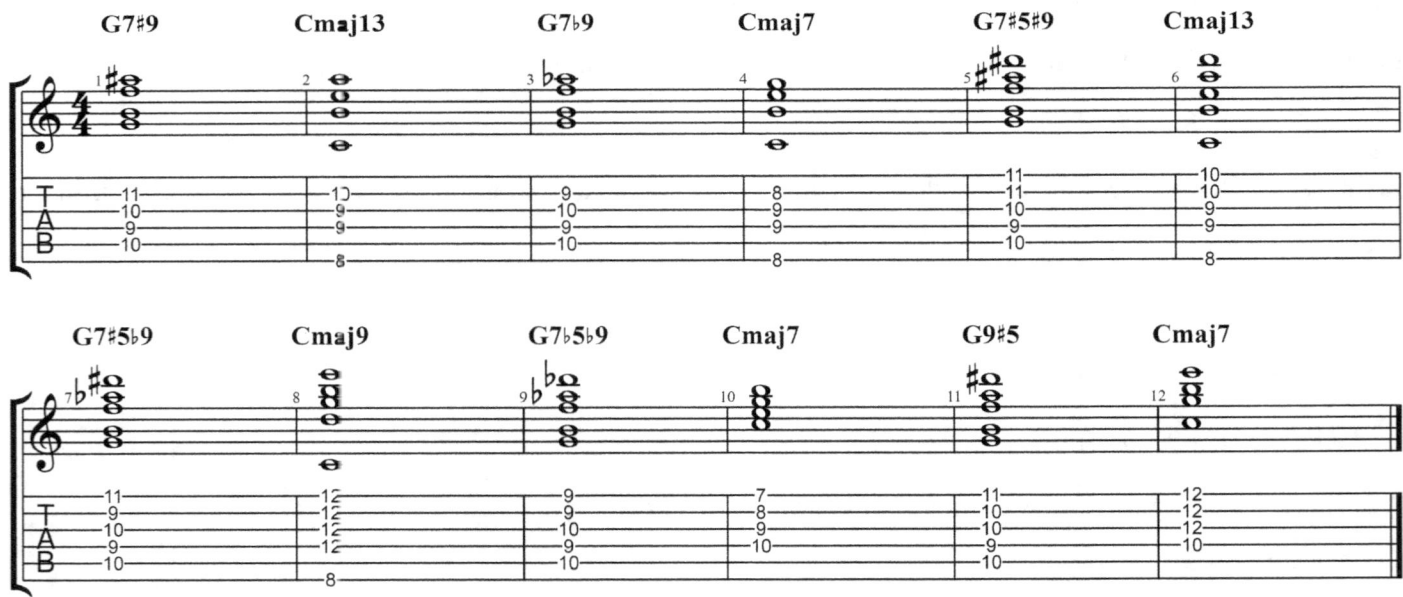

These alterations aren't commonly found on chords other than dominant 7s, with the exception of the #11 on major 7 chords. This makes sense because the 11th interval on a major 7 chord is incredibly sour! Raising it a semitone adds a nice, mysterious sound. And we can add natural extensions too:

1 3 5 7 #11 – Maj7#11

1 3 5 7 9 #11 – Maj9#11

1 3 5 7 9 #11 13 – Maj13#11

These chords work great either as the IV chord in a key (where they are diatonic) or as a bit of a surprise on a I chord.

Example 9k:

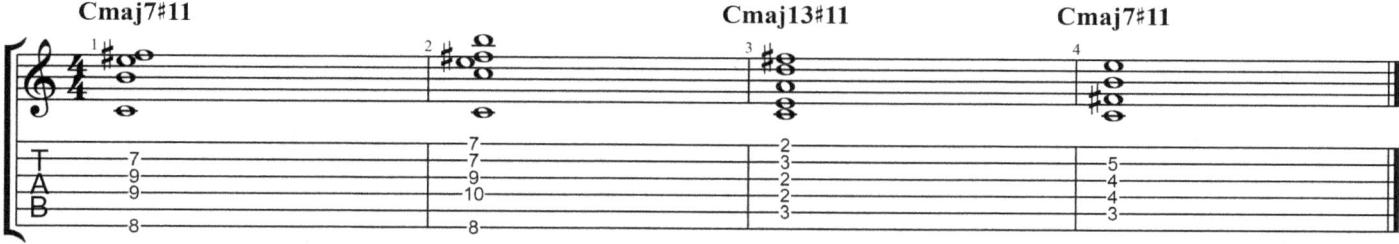

Experimentation is the key to becoming confident using chords like these. I don't get out my theory book when I want to play them, I just put them in chord progressions and see what sounds work.

One of the best ways to experiment with them is to play chromatic melodies on the top of our chords. This forces us to use extended and altered chords to find the melody note we're looking for.

For example, I'll take a ii–V–I progression in C Major (Dm7 – G7 – Cmaj7) and add a descending chromatic line on top.

I might play a Dm9 for the ii chord with the E on top. Then the E note needs to drop down a semitone to D# over the G7 chord, so it has to be a G7#5. Then the D# will drop down to D, so the I chord has to be a Cmaj9.

Here's that done with a descending chromatic line on the B then E string.

Example 9l:

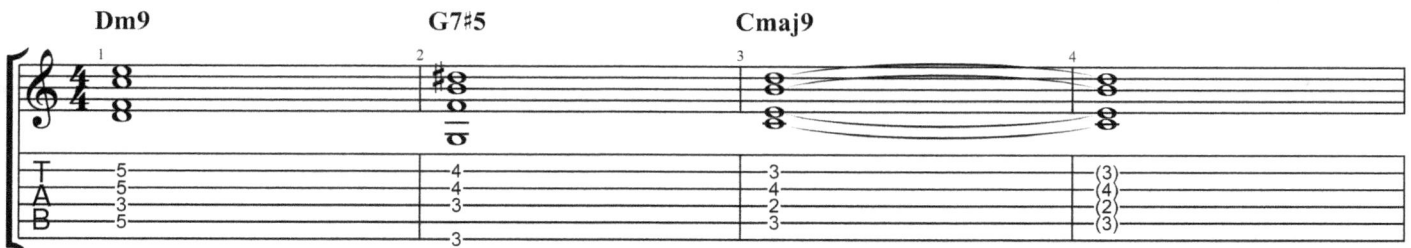

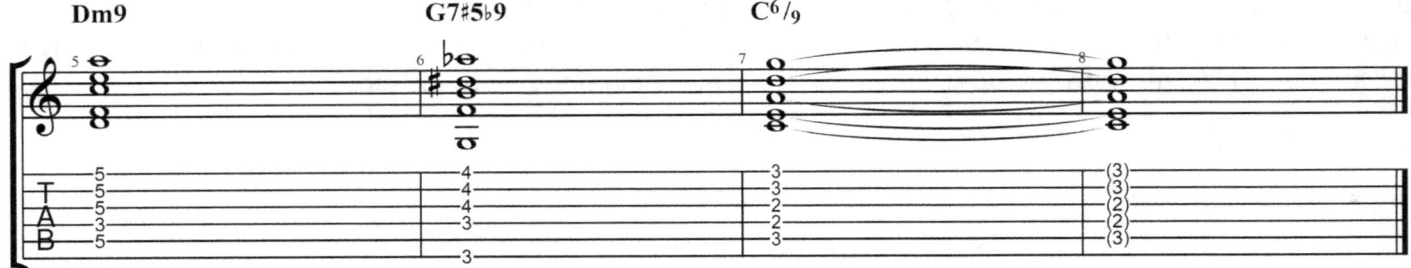

You could do the same with an ascending chromatic line too.

Example 9m:

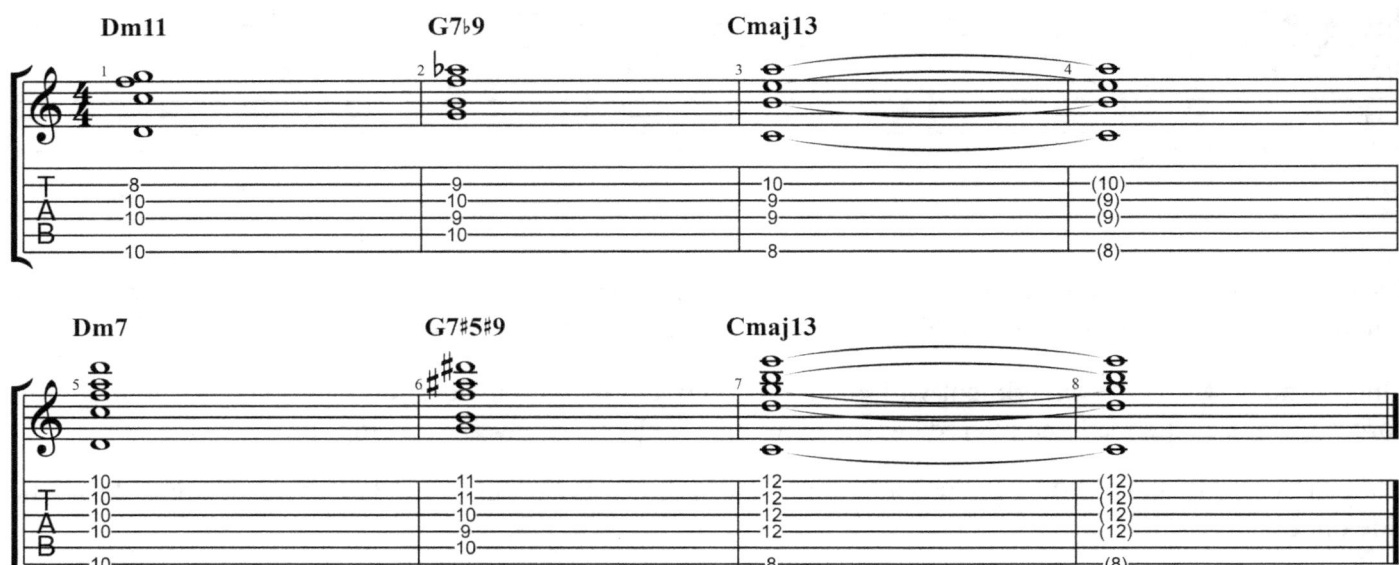

If we jump back to look at one of our previous chord progressions, we can try out some of these extended chords in place of vanilla 7th chords.

There is an element of focusing on the melody notes for these chords, but essentially I'm just having fun adding different extensions to see what I like and what I don't. In a practice routine, I'd sit and come up with many different ways to get through this progression.

Example 9n:

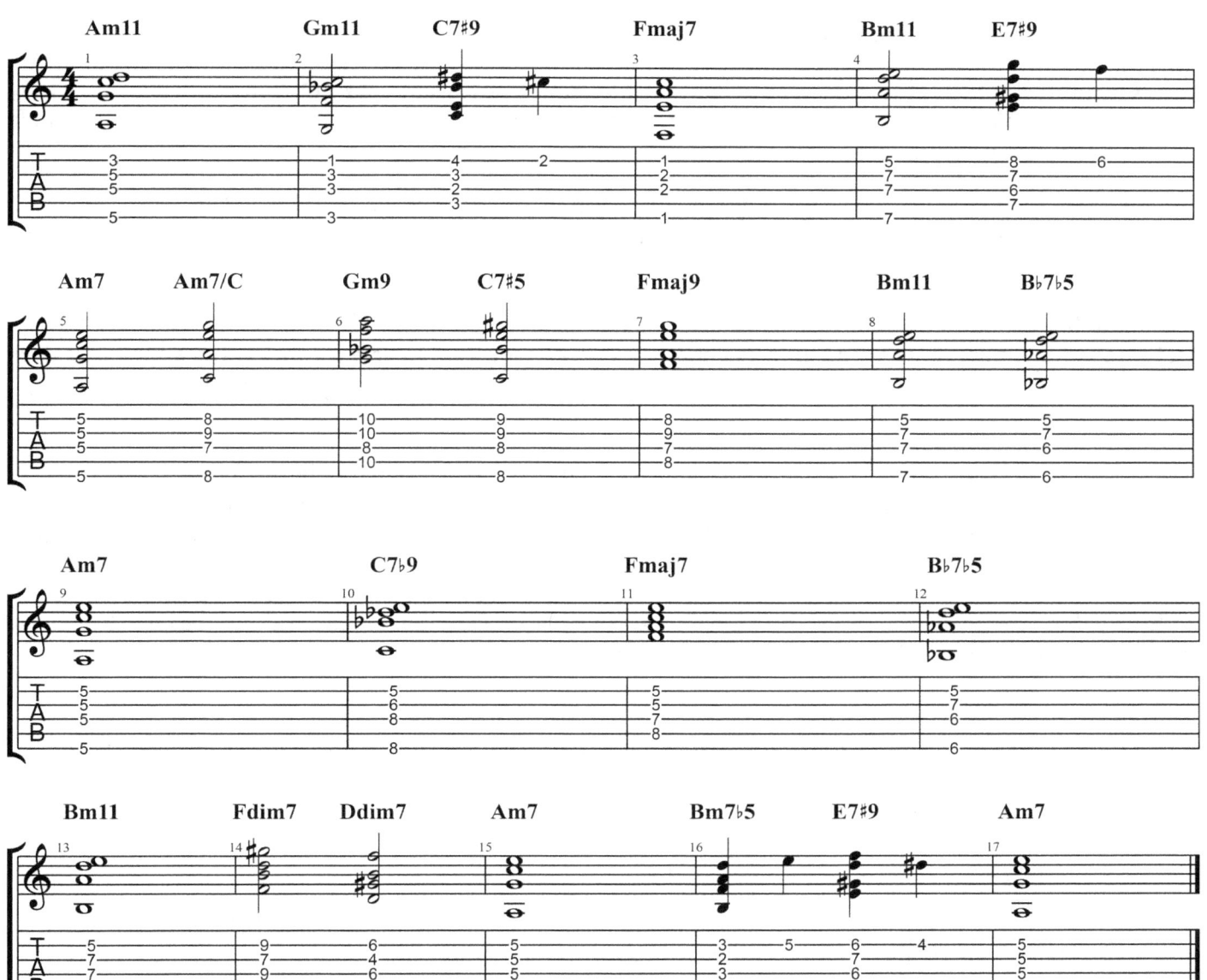

And, when I'm done with that, I'll pull up other progressions and work my way through those – jazz standards, RnB tunes, soul – it doesn't matter. Time spent thinking about and experimenting with harmony will always help develop our minds and ears, so dig deep, and I'll see you for the final routine!

Routine Ten – Slash Chords

If you thought the last routine was a lot of work, I have some good and bad news…

The good news is, this is the last routine! The bad news is, this one will have you thinking the most by a long shot. However, don't be afraid to focus on small ideas and keep revisiting this routine. I wanted to include this chapter to get you thinking about, and experimenting with, harmony on a deeper level.

You've probably heard the term "slash chord" and seen chords written down like G/B or F/G. The chord names contain a slash, so they're slash chords! Most often they mean a chord played over a specific bass note. E.g., G/B means a G triad played over a B bass note.

You might think, "Sure, we saw that chord when we looked at inversions" and you'd be both right and wrong. Technically, an inversion is a form of slash chord, but that's not what people mean when they refer to slash chords. Usually, they are written on chord charts because a chord is being played over an unexpected bass note.

We've learned that we hear chords in relation to the bass note. We can play a beautiful sounding C major triad (C E G), but the bass player holds all the power. And if the bass note changes to a note that's not in the chord, such as Bb, suddenly our chord doesn't sound like C major anymore. We hear chords from the bottom up, not the top down.

Let's take that exact scenario. At this point, to figure out what's happening in the harmony, we have to analyse our C major triad in the light of the new Bb bass note. Bb effectively becomes our new "1" so…

- C is the 2nd over Bb
- E is the #4 over Bb
- G is the 6th over Bb

Expressed as a formula, this new chord is 1 2 #4 6.

It's tricky to name this chord. There is a 2nd instead of a 3rd, so it's a sus sound. There is no 7th to tell us whether it's major, dominant or minor, but there is a #4 which suggests a Lydian chord. Here are a few ways we can play it:

Example 10a:

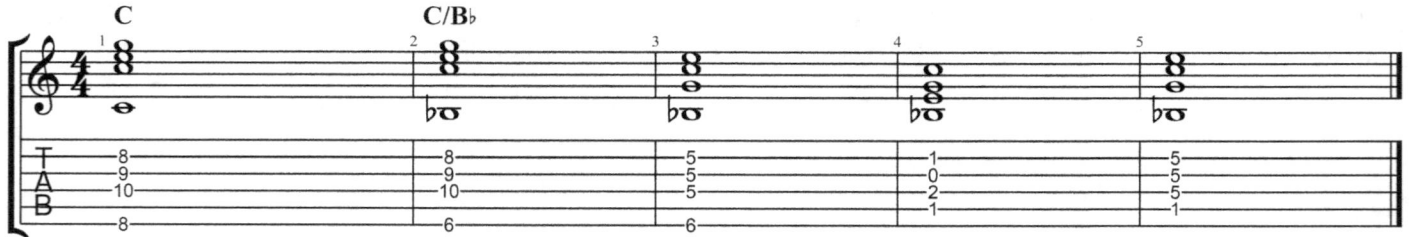

That's one slash chord, but we can put *any* triad over *any* bass note. In fact, we don't have to limit ourselves to triads, we can add alternative bass notes to 7th chords too. The question is, what works and what doesn't? And where do we start?

We need a system in place to help us "audition" and process this stuff in a comprehensive manner, and that's where my *chromatic superimposition* exercise comes in.

The idea is simple: we take a triad and play it over all twelve chromatic bass notes. Then we make a note of the intervals that are created. Finally, we try playing each chord and name the results (if possible).

You can do this just sitting with your guitar. Play a C major triad on the D, G, B strings with a C root under it, and work out the intervals visually. Then, shift the bass note up a semitone and repeat the process, working out the intervals in relation to the new root note, and so on.

Or, to make the process easier, write it all down. I've completed the exercise for the C major triad and put the results in the table below. The triad notes appear across the top, and every chromatic note is listed down the left-hand column. So, we can see, for example, that if we put an F bass note under the C triad, the F becomes the new 1, the C note is now the 5th, E is the 7th and G is the 2nd. The result is an Fma7sus chord.

Bass Note	C	E	G	Chord Name
C	1	3	5	Maj
C#/Db	7	b3/#2	b5/#4	
D	b7	2	4	7sus
D#/Eb	6	b2	3	
E	b6/#5	1	b3/#2	(inversion)
F	5	7	2	Maj7sus
F#/Gb	b5/#4	b7	b2	7alt
G	4	6	1	(inversion)
G#/Ab	3	b6/#5	7	Maj7#5
A	b3/#2	5	b7	m7
A#/Bb	2	b5/#4	6	Lydian/Maj13#11
B	b2	4	b6/#5	(inversion)

When it comes to naming these chords, we'll often be able to view them in a few ways. We might take a few liberties and sometimes the description will be helpful and sometimes not! The really important thing is to take note of the voicings you feel are usable and remember how to find them.

There are a couple in the above table that I'd want to know.

7sus – major triad played from the b7.

Maj7sus – major triad played from the 5th.

m7 – major triad played from the b3.

Maj7#11 – major triad played from the 2nd.

The only way to test these out is to immediately apply them to a simple chord progression. Let's go with a ii–V–I in C Major (Dm7 – G7 – Cmaj7) and let's focus on viewing each chord as a triad over a bass note.

For the Dm7 I'll play Dm7, which can also be viewed as an F major triad over D. F is the b3 of Dm7.

For the G7 I'll play G7sus. This can be seen as an F major triad over G – F/G.

For the Cmaj7 I'll make it a Maj7sus. That's a G major triad over C. G is the 5th – G/C.

Another option for Cmaj7 is the colourful Cmaj13#11. That's a D major triad over C. D is the 2nd – D/C.

Have a listen to how these ideas sound.

Example 10b:

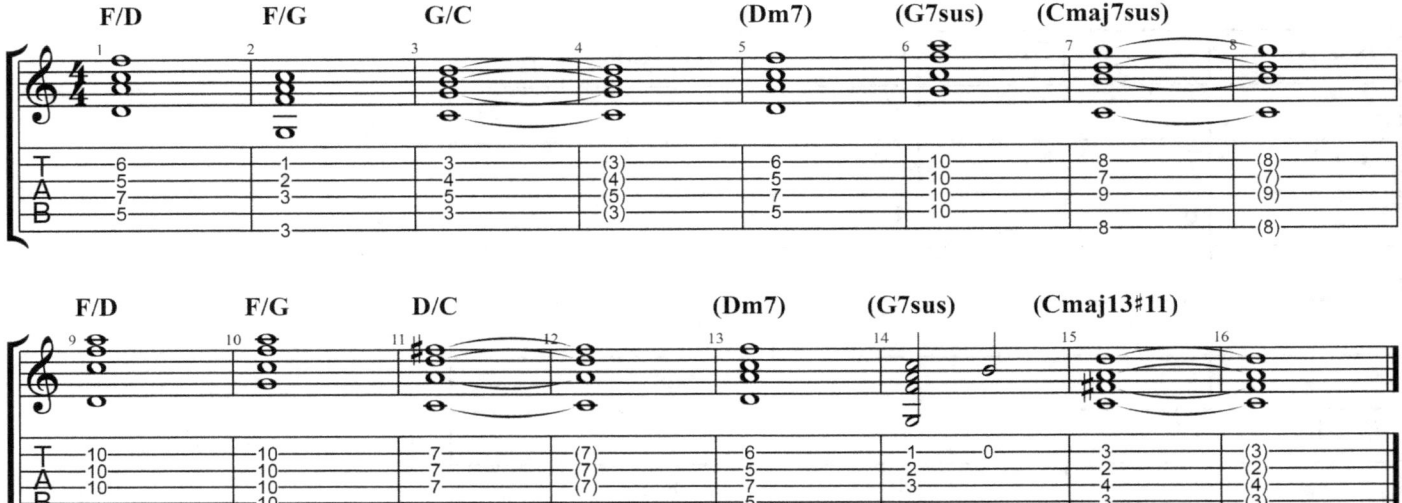

The most valuable thing you can do with voicings you like is to slot them into chord progressions. From that list, the 7sus is the most useful one to me. I use it all the time in chord progressions in place of a V moving to a I, as it's a little softer than the classic V–I sound. This is so common it's often written as IV/V.

Here's a chord progression where I've switched out the two dominant chords for 7sus sounds. Eb/F in place of F7 and Bb/C in place of C7.

Example 10c:

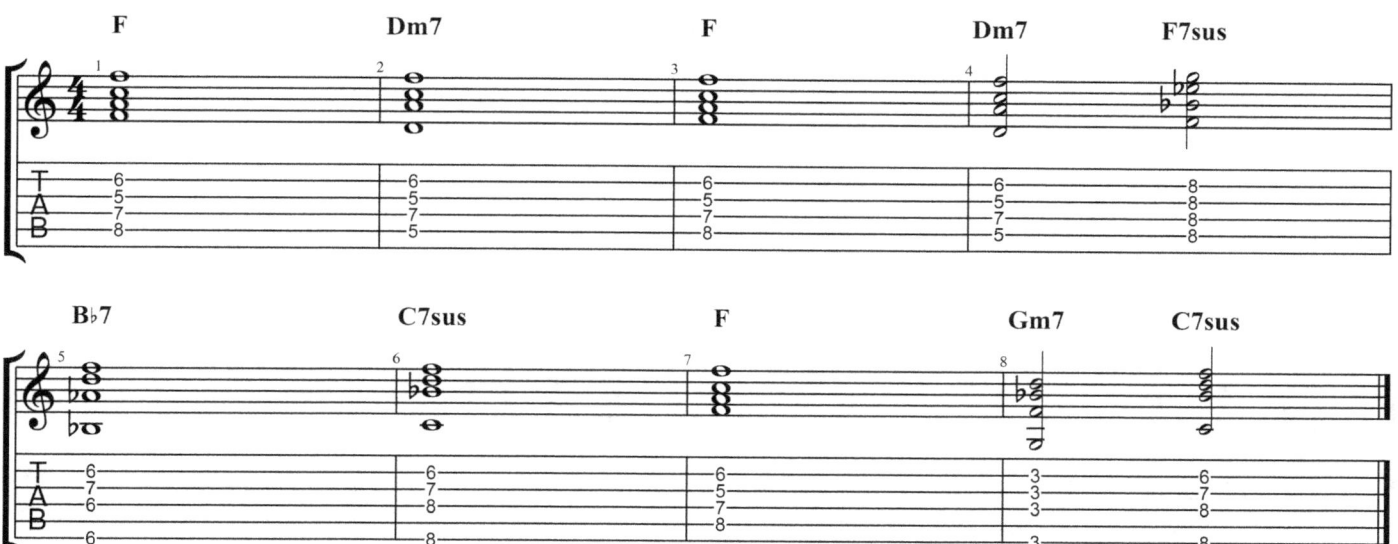

We've done the *chromatic superimposition* exercise with a major triad, but we can do it with a minor triad too. Here is the table of results for a C minor triad.

Bass Note	C	Eb	G	Chord Name
C	1	b3	5	min
C#/Db	7	2	b5/#4	
D	b7	b2	4	
D#/Eb	6	1	3	(inversion)
E	b6/#5	7	b3/#2	
F	5	b7	2	7sus
F#/Gb	b5/#4	6	b2	
G	4	b6/#5	1	(inversion)
G#/Ab	3	5	7	Maj7
A	b3/#2	b5/#4	b7	m7b5
A#/Bb	2	4	6	6sus
B	b2	3	b6/#5	

I like all of the named chords here. The 7sus as a minor triad from the 5th is a nice alternative to the major triad from the b7. Here's an example where I combine the two, also using a minor 7 built from the 3rd to make a major 7 chord.

Example 10d:

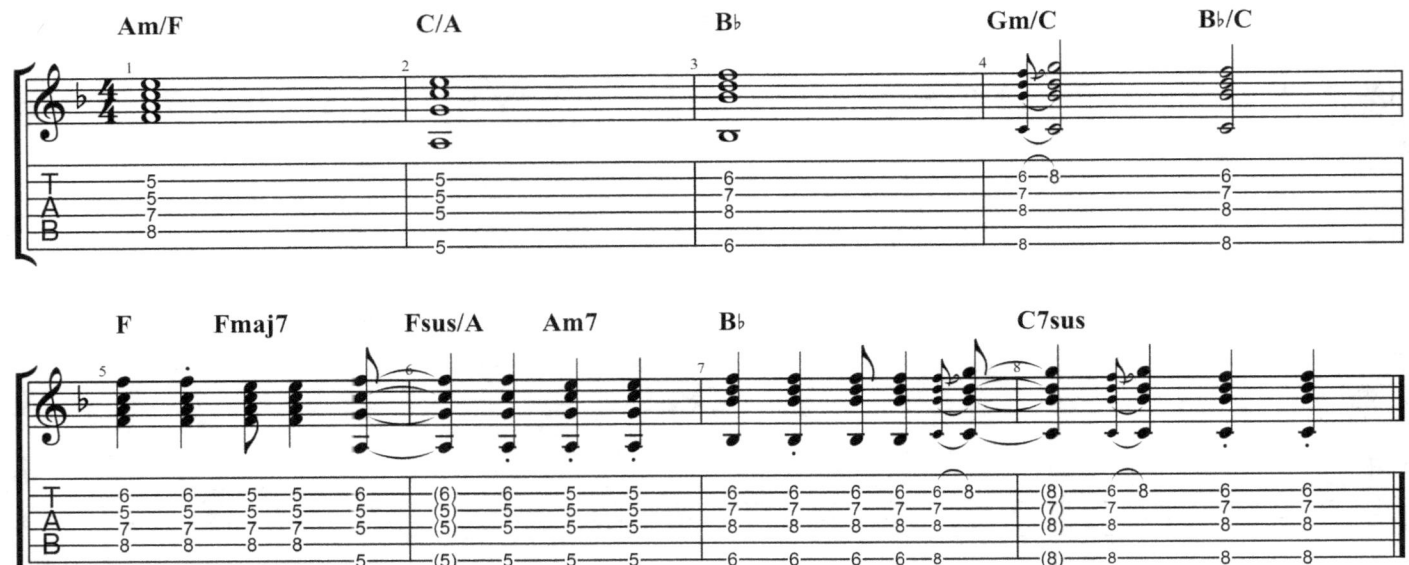

Another great use of these minor triads is alternating between the I and ii over a major chord/bass note. Over a C root note, I could alternate between C major and D minor triads. The C will sound like a major triad, while Dm/C gives us a suspended sound. It's a nice little shift from an inside sound to a more colourful sound and back.

Example 10e:

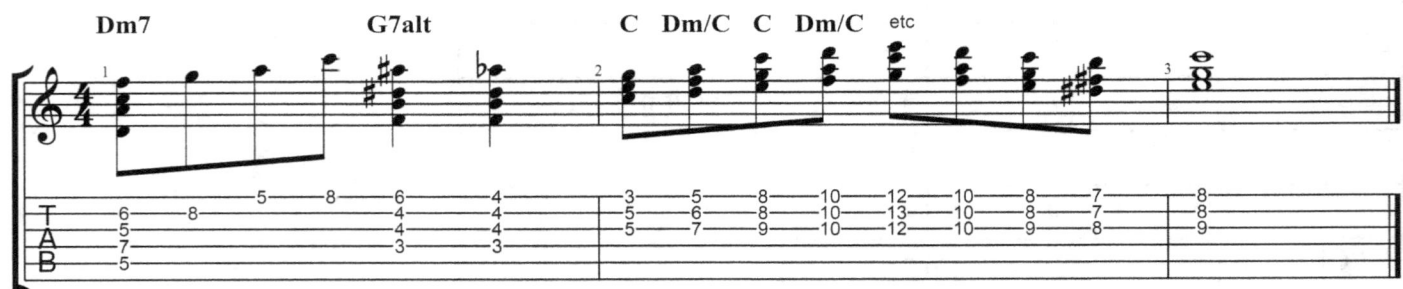

I want you to get on board with the idea of chromatic superimposition and the process of working it all out! Draw up a table, work through it, then do another one the next day. I've done this countless times and each time I get a bit quicker at it. It really helps to embed the useful note relationships.

For example, from my study of chromatic superimposition I know that playing an augmented triad from the 5th of a chord will give me a beautiful min(Maj7) sound.

First, I'll play the slash chords with bass notes, then I'll just play the triads and let the bass guitar deal with the bass notes. In the real world, that's how I'm using this stuff. We work with the bass to create the sound we want.

Example 10f:

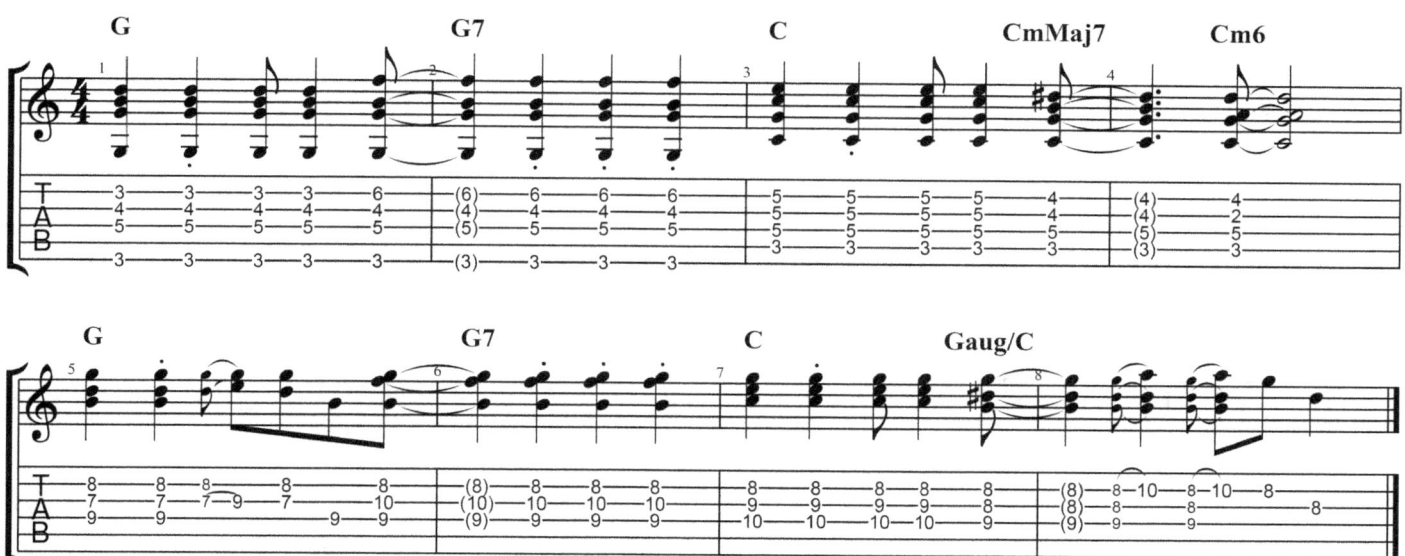

I won't make tables for diminished and augmented chords – it's over to you to work through that process. Instead, I want us to look at 7th chords because there is so much rich harmony to be found when we start with four notes rather than three. Below is a chromatic superimposition table for major 7 chords.

Bass Note	C	E	G	B	Chord Name
C	1	3	5	7	Maj7
C#/Db	7	b3/#2	b5/#4	b7	
D	b7	2	4	6	13sus
D#/Eb	6	b2	3	b6/#5	
E	b6/#5	1	b3/#2	5	(inversion)
F	5	7	2	b5/#4	Maj9#11(no 3rd)
F#/Gb	b5/#4	b7	b2	4	
G	4	6	1	3	(inversion)
G#/Ab	3	b6/#5	7	b3/#2	
A	b3/#2	5	b7	2	m9
A#/Bb	2	b5/#4	6	b2	
B	b2	4	b6/#5	1	

Because major 7 chords have more notes in them to begin with, it can be hard to voice them with different bass notes, but here are some that work well:

- C13sus (Bbmaj7/C)
- Cmaj9#11 (Gmaj7/C)
- Cm9 (Ebmaj7/C)

Example 10g:

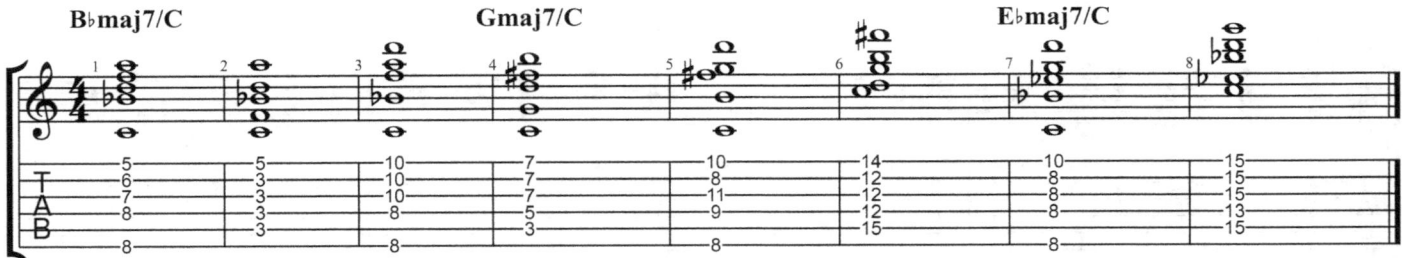

The skill in the application of this idea is knowing where you can place a major 7 voicing in order to create one of these richer sounds. For example, to turn a Dm7 into Dm9 we can play a major 7 from the b3, a.k.a. Fmaj7/D.

Example 10h:

In the previous example, we also had slash chords with minor 7 and minor 7b5 sounds played over different bass notes, so let's look at those briefly. Here's the table for C minor 7.

Bass Note	C	Eb	G	Bb	Chord Name
C	1	b3/#2	5	b7	m7
C#/Db	7	2	b5/#4	6	
D	b7	b2	4	b6/#5	
D#/Eb	6	1	3	5	6
E	b6/#5	7	b3/#2	b5/#4	(inversion)
F	5	b7	2	4	11sus
F#/Gb	b5/#4	6	b2	3	
G	4	b6/#5	1	b3/#2	(inversion)
G#/Ab	3	5	7	2	Maj9
A	b3/#2	b5/#4	b7	b2	
A#/Bb	2	4	6	1	sus
B	b2	3	b6/#5	7	

All of the named slash chords are usable sounds. I particularly like that 11sus sound and use it over dominant 7 chords, which I'll then shift into an altered voicing to create a nice bit of tension.

Example 10i:

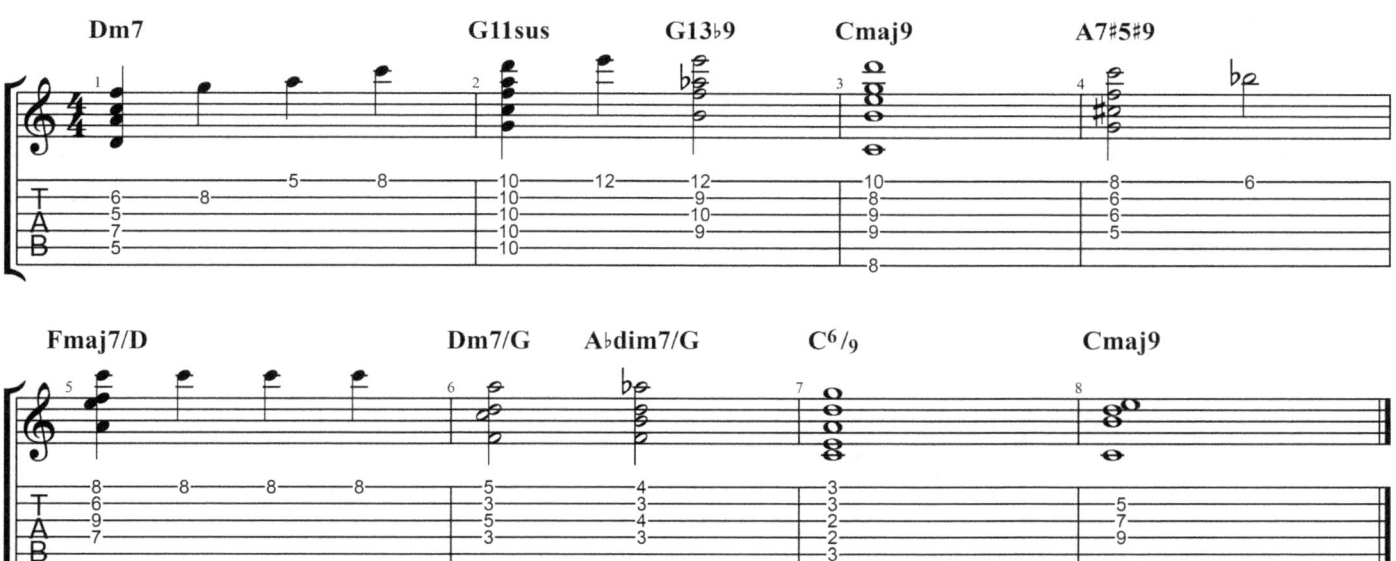

There aren't as many applications for the dominant 7 chord, because it's such a strong sound on its own, but before moving on I'd still encourage you to draw out a chart and work on the skill of identifying the intervals and trying to name the chords.

The minor 7b5 chord is a little more useful.

Bass Note	C	Eb	Gb	Bb	Chord Name
C	1	b3/#2	b5/#4	b7	m7b5
C#/Db	7	2	4	6	Maj13sus
D	b7	b2	3	b6/#5	7#5b9
D#/Eb	6	1	b3/#2	5	(inversion) – m6
E	b6/#5	7	2	b5/#4	
F	5	b7	b2	4	Sus4b9
F#/Gb	b5/#4	6	1	3	(inversion)
G	4	b6/#5	7	b3/#2	
G#/Ab	3	5	b7	2	9
A	b3/#2	b5/#4	6	b2	
A#/Bb	2	4	b6/#5	1	
B	b2	3	5	7	

Here's a blues that combines minor 7b5 voicings with different bass notes.

Example 10j:

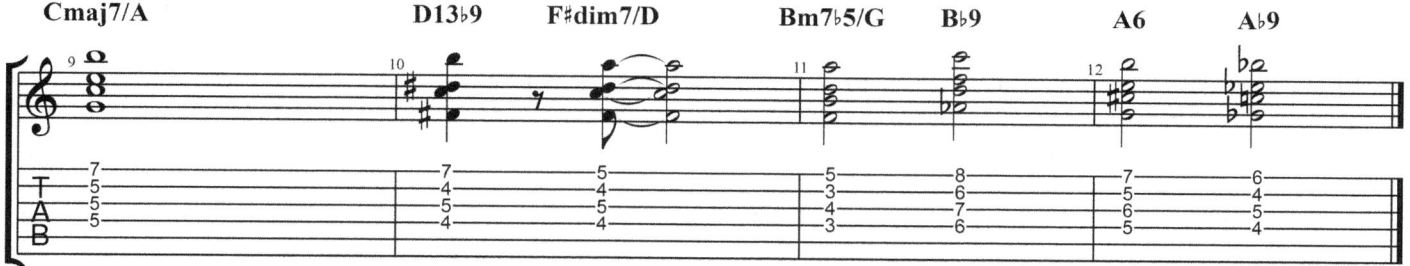

Finally, here's an example that makes use of the interchangeability of minor 6 and minor 7b5 sounds, which are essentially just inversions of each other. The IV chord (F) moving to a iv6 (Fm) is a nice sound in itself, but if we play the latter as a slash chord we can create a richer harmony.

Dm7b5 has the same notes as Fm6. If we superimpose that over a G bass note, we get the beautiful sus4b9 sound you'll hear in the music of the great Stevie Wonder. You can only really discover ideas like this through harmonic exploration!

Example 10k:

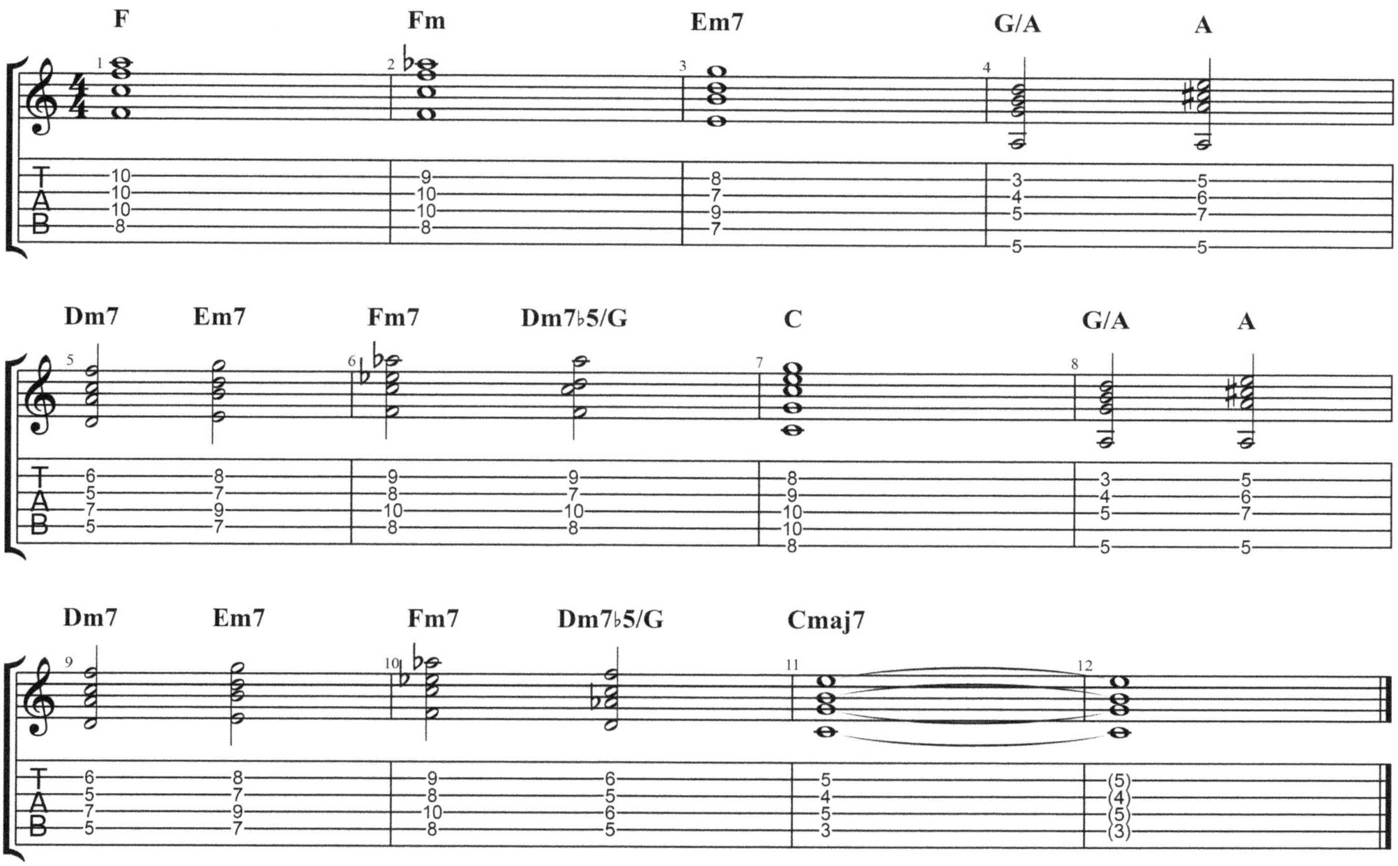

Work on this idea on your own for all possible 7th chords. When I was at university, we did this exercise for all the common 7th chord types, then moved onto more exotic chords such as Maj7#5, 7b5 and a bunch of others that felt like busy work! What this process achieved was to expand my ears to new sounds, and it gave me the ability to pick out sounds that I couldn't hear before. (Like the ending of John Coltrane's *Naima*, where he goes from an Abmaj7/Eb to Gmaj7#5/Eb!)

The more you dig into harmonically rich music the more you'll discover wild chords like these. Only now, you'll be better equipped to decode and play them. This isn't a week's work, of course, it's a lifetime's journey, but week by week you can learn new sounds and, in time, they'll become as familiar to you as a major chord.

Conclusion

Well, that got in depth pretty quickly!

Hopefully, you are now in a position to confidently build any chord that you see on a chart, and have a better idea of how to name any chord that you find on your guitar.

This book has laid an important foundation for us before we move on to look at arpeggios in the next book – because arpeggios are all about using chord sounds in a linear fashion to create melodies. Without the knowledge of what the chord is, what it sounds like, and why we play it, an arpeggio won't make any sense.

With this study under your belt, you should be shifting your perspective to think in a more *vertical* manner about chords, and be able to consider how the things you play are impacted by the bass note you're playing over, and how that changes what the listener hears.

Ultimately, music is near infinite. There are so many approaches to harmony and plenty of music out there that contains rich sounds. I mentioned Stevie Wonder, who is a huge influence on me, but anything that has a jazz influence is going to require a deeper understanding of harmony and an ear for hearing it.

Whether it's Michael Brecker's work with the Brecker Brothers, or Scott Henderson with Tribal Tech, many musicians have explored the concepts we've looked at with wonderful results. The more you learn about harmony, the further you can delve into the world of music and find things you'll be better equipped to understand.

I hope you enjoy your new-found understanding of harmony, and that it lights a fire of excitement under you. I trust that it will serve you as well as it has served me.

Good luck!

Levi

GUIDED GUITAR ARPEGGIO PRACTICE ROUTINES

Master Every Essential Guitar Arpeggio in this Comprehensive 10-Week Course

LEVI CLAY

FUNDAMENTAL CHANGES

Guided Guitar Arpeggio Practice Routines

Master Every Essential Guitar Arpeggio in this Comprehensive 10-Week Course

Join our free Facebook Community of Cool Musicians

www.facebook.com/groups/fundamentalguitar

Instagram: **FundamentalChanges**

For over 350 Free Guitar Lessons with Videos Check Out

www.fundamental-changes.com

Cover Image Copyright: Author photo used by permission.

Contents

Introduction 214

How To Use This Book 215

Get the Audio 216

Routine One: Right Hand Technique 217

Routine: Two Vertical Triads 225

Routine Three: Horizontal Triads 235

Routine Four: Triad Progression Workouts 243

Routine Five: Diatonic 7th Arpeggios 254

Routine Six: 7th Chord Progression Workouts 263

Routine Seven: Chord Scale Arpeggios 275

Routine Eight: Combining Arpeggios & Scales 284

Routine Nine: Extended Arpeggios 295

Routine Ten: Putting It All Together Etudes 307

Conclusion 321

Introduction

It may seem strange to start an introduction by talking about what came before, but the book you're reading now is the final volume in a trilogy that builds on specific skills progressively over time, helping you to develop a deep understanding of music from an intervallic perspective.

In the first book we explored scales – the most linear form of melody – and learned that we can think of a scale simply as a set of ingredients from which we can build chords and play melodies and solos.

In the second book, we took this knowledge of intervals and applied it to chords. Chords can be thought of as harmony expressed in *vertical* form. They are a snapshot of a particular sound – collections of intervals stacked up to create different musical colours. A deep understanding of chords and how they interact with each other helps us determine which scales fit best over them.

Now, we come to the focus of this book: *arpeggios*.

So, what exactly is an arpeggio and how does it fit into this picture?

The term "arpeggio" comes from the Italian word *arpa*, meaning harp, and *arpeggiare*, meaning to play on a harp. It captures the idea of playing rich chordal sounds as individual notes. An arpeggio is a chord (vertical harmony) played in a linear manner.

The difference between arpeggios and scales lies in their relationship to the underlying harmony. When you play a scale over a certain chord, only some of the notes will belong to that chord. When you play an arpeggio, *every note* belongs to the chord, so every note is a strong melodic choice.

When students ask me, "What should I play over X chord?" I always give them the same answer: "Play X arpeggio."

Thinking in arpeggio terms takes away some of the complexity of scalic thinking. If it's an A minor chord, you can play an A minor arpeggio. If it's D7, you can play a D7 arpeggio. If it's a more complex chord like G7#9, you can play that arpeggio too. While we can also add scale tones to make our melodies more interesting, a great starting point for any solo is to just let the chords dictate what we should play.

Here we are going to explore arpeggios on the guitar in great detail. This will allow us to dig deeper into our understanding of the fretboard, but we'll also tackle the challenges of being able to play arpeggios on guitar to a high technical level. These challenges are one of the main reasons guitarists give up exploring arpeggios when they reach a certain level, but together we'll overcome them by the end of this book.

Finally, we'll bring everything full circle by examining how scales and arpeggios can work in harmony with each other (pun intended!) to help you break out of tired licks and patterns, so that you can create more dynamic, musical ideas.

How To Use This Book

As with the previous instalments in this series, the goal here is to approach the material like an old aerobics VHS tape! We're working through a set of exercises designed to focus on a key concept, then practicing it together in full.

One thing that's become clear throughout these books is that the weekly format doesn't work as well for beginners. The idea of progressing weekly is more of a long-term goal, and something you'll achieve as you develop as a player.

I've been playing guitar for over 20 years, so when I open a book like this, I'm already familiar with the concepts in each chapter and can jump right into practicing the routine. But I realise that many readers aren't at that stage yet. You may need to spend some time just learning the material before you move onto practicing each routine. And that's just fine – don't stress yourself out thinking that you're not keeping up or that everything is taking too long. Learning is a deeply personal experience, and everyone progresses at their own pace. It's perfectly fine if it takes you a little longer to master certain exercises.

You may find yourself going through this book several times, and each time it will become easier as you become more familiar with the concepts. This is the long-term goal and the reason why we practice – so that things become second nature to us. Eventually, when you're on stage, or hitting the record button in the studio, you won't have to think about what chord comes next or what arpeggio to play over it, you'll just know it.

To help the learning process go as smoothly as possible, I've recorded audio for every individual example here, as well as the full weekly routines with me talking you through the practice session. Take your time, learn the individual exercises, then move on to playing the full routine with me. When you reach the end of the book, go back to the beginning and see how much easier it feels the second time through. That's progress.

Remember, your only goal is to be better today than you were yesterday. If you keep that up, day after day, the only outcome will be reaching your goal.

Good luck!

Levi

Get the Audio

The audio files for this book are available to download for free from **www.fundamental-changes.com.** The link is in the top right-hand corner. Click on the Guitar link then simply select this book title from the drop-down menu and follow the instructions to get the audio.

We recommend that you download the files directly to your computer, not to your tablet, and extract them there before adding them to your media library. On the download page there are instructions, and we also provide technical support via the contact form.

For over 350 free guitar lessons with videos check out:

www.fundamental-changes.com

Join our free Facebook Community of Cool Musicians

www.facebook.com/groups/fundamentalguitar

Tag us for a share on Instagram: **FundamentalChanges**

Routine One: Right Hand Technique

I was playing arpeggios almost as soon as I picked up the guitar. If you hold down a C major chord and randomly pick (or fingerpick) the strings, you're literally arpeggiating the chord. Some of the first things I ever wrote were simply me picking through chords and turning them into arpeggios with my fingers.

As I hinted in the introduction, one of the biggest challenges when mastering arpeggios on the guitar is the technical skill required to play them smoothly. Think back to the work we did with chords and you'll realise that we didn't put much effort into what our picking/strumming hand was doing – it just sort of happened.

Arpeggio picking technique presents a bigger challenge. Arpeggios become more difficult to play cleanly and precisely when the playing speed increases. So, to ensure that in the future you can play anything fast that you can play slowly, I want to set you on the path of *alternate picking*.

In Example 1a we're going to arpeggiate a simple C major chord, ascending and descending. You could play this idea with sweep picking, using a series of downstrokes then upstrokes, and it would sound fine, but if the speed increased, you'd find that this method really hurt your timekeeping. So, instead we will alternate pick our way through this arpeggio. While this might feel awkward at first, you're laying a great playing foundation for future you.

I won't lie, picking one note per string using alternate picking is one of the hardest things to do on guitar. In fact, many teachers come up with systems to help their students avoid this weakness. But, here we're about facing the things we find difficult and overcoming them.

Notice the pick direction indicated above the TAB in this example. It's important to follow the symbols. The square-like symbol represents a downstroke, and the "V" symbol is an upstroke.

Example 1a:

In the next example, we'll keep the alternate picking motion but change the order of the strings we play. Although we're still using alternate picking, this change introduces a new challenge in keeping your picking consistent.

Although Example 1a could be played using a sweep picking motion, you'll see how quickly that technique falls apart when tacking Example 1b where the string order changes. Alternate picking is the way forward for good note separation and clarity.

Example 1b:

If you need further proof that alternate picking is best, let's exaggerate this idea by including more string skips in the pattern.

Example 1c:

By adding a hammer-on and altering the rhythm slightly, we can give this idea more of a bluegrass feel. Even though we're still arpeggiating a C major chord, we've introduced some rhythmic variation.

This type of picking is known as *cross-picking* in the bluegrass world and is a skill that takes time to develop. It won't improve without focused practice, but it's worth the effort.

Example 1d:

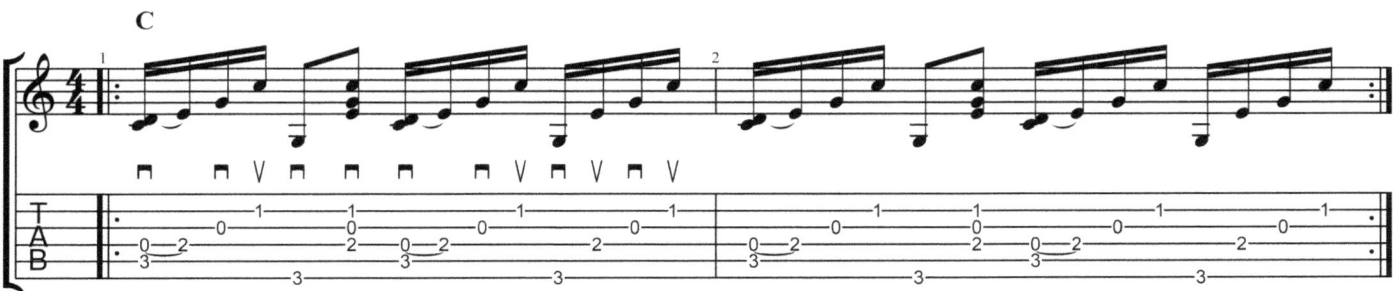

One exercise I like is to play an ascending group of three notes played four times, followed by a group of four notes on the D, G, and B strings.

As you practice, you'll notice that anchoring your hand to the bridge makes this technique harder. Instead, aim for a more free-floating hand, allowing for smoother transitions across the strings.

Start slowly, and build up speed as you go.

Example 1e:

To increase the challenge, try moving your groups of three across different sets of strings. This requires even more flexibility in your picking hand and further develops your cross-picking ability.

Example 1f:

To put this technique into a musical context, let's use it on an actual chord sequence. Here's a simple progression of G – D/F# – F – C, played with ascending arpeggios.

Example 1g:

We can make things more challenging by applying some of those three-against-four patterns to a chord movement from C major to A minor.

Example 1h:

The beauty of this technique is that once you're comfortable moving across the strings you can apply it to any chord grip. For example, try picking across an E minor with an added 9th, and a G major with an added 9th.

Example 1i:

Although alternate picking will give us the most consistent rhythmic results, we can still sweep through an open position arpeggio like that in Example 1j, and that's a valuable technique for your toolbox.

When sweeping an arpeggio like this, don't play it as a series of separate downstrokes. The motion comes from a *rest stroke*. This means, instead of picking the string in the normal way and lifting the pick away, you sound it by pushing the pick through the string so that it briefly comes to rest on the adjacent string, ready to push through to the next string. So, the sweep is a single, controlled motion that pushes through all the strings.

The best way to develop this technique is by strumming the chord normally then gradually slowing down the motion until you produce a more distinct, arpeggiated chord. We'll do this in the following example, and once the motion feels natural, focus on repeating the pattern with as much rhythmic consistency as possible.

Example 1j:

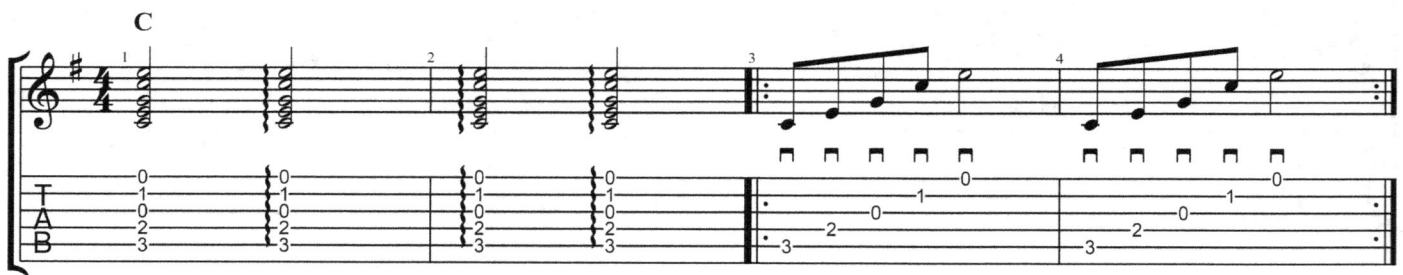

We can take this idea and apply it to just the middle of an arpeggio to create a pattern similar to *The House of the Rising Sun* by The Animals. Here, I've applied it to A minor and C major chords.

Example 1k:

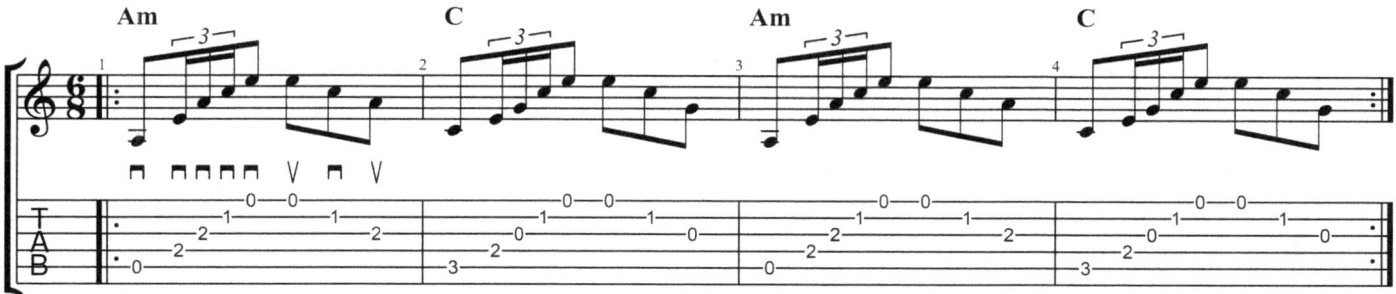

To finish up this routine, I've included some longer examples that will help you work on both rhythmic evenness and left-hand stamina.

The first example is something I covered in my *Hybrid Picking Guitar Technique* book, which is Bach's Prelude in C. I suggest alternate picking this for rhythmic accuracy but feel free to experiment with rest stroke sweeping (notated in bars 1-2) as well.

Example 1l:

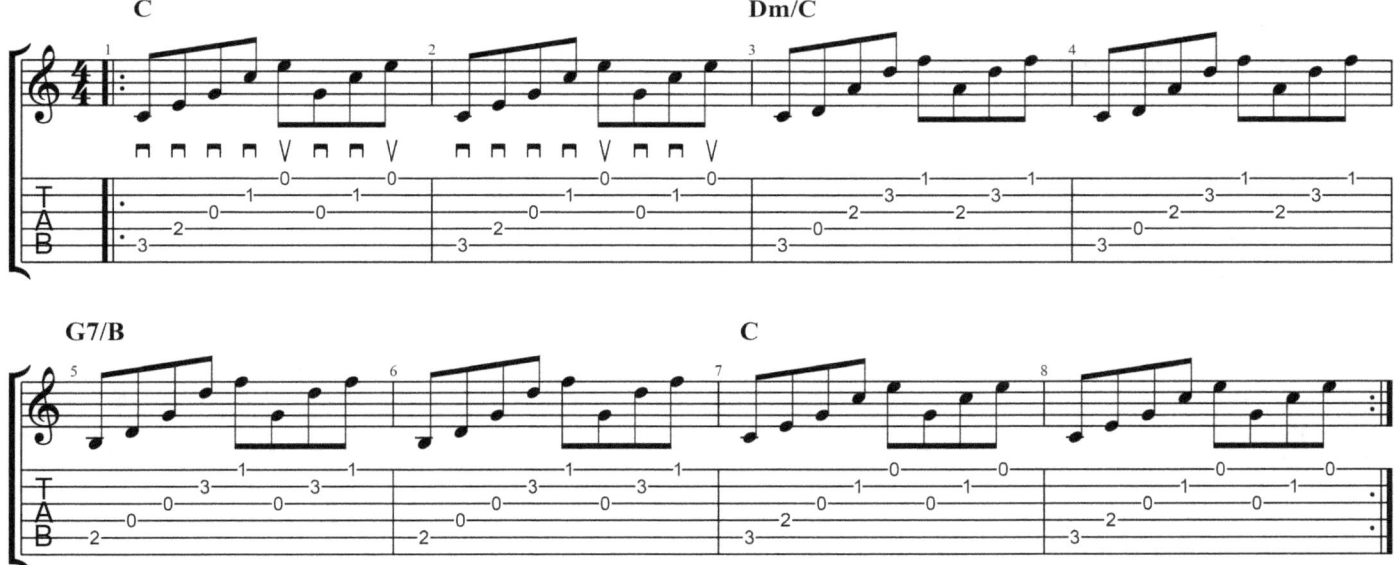

Next is an eight-bar idea that follows a chord progression with more of a bluegrass picking pattern, combining single-note arpeggios with chord strums. Remember, your fretting hand is simply holding down a chord while the picking hand creates melodic interest by arpeggiating.

Example 1m:

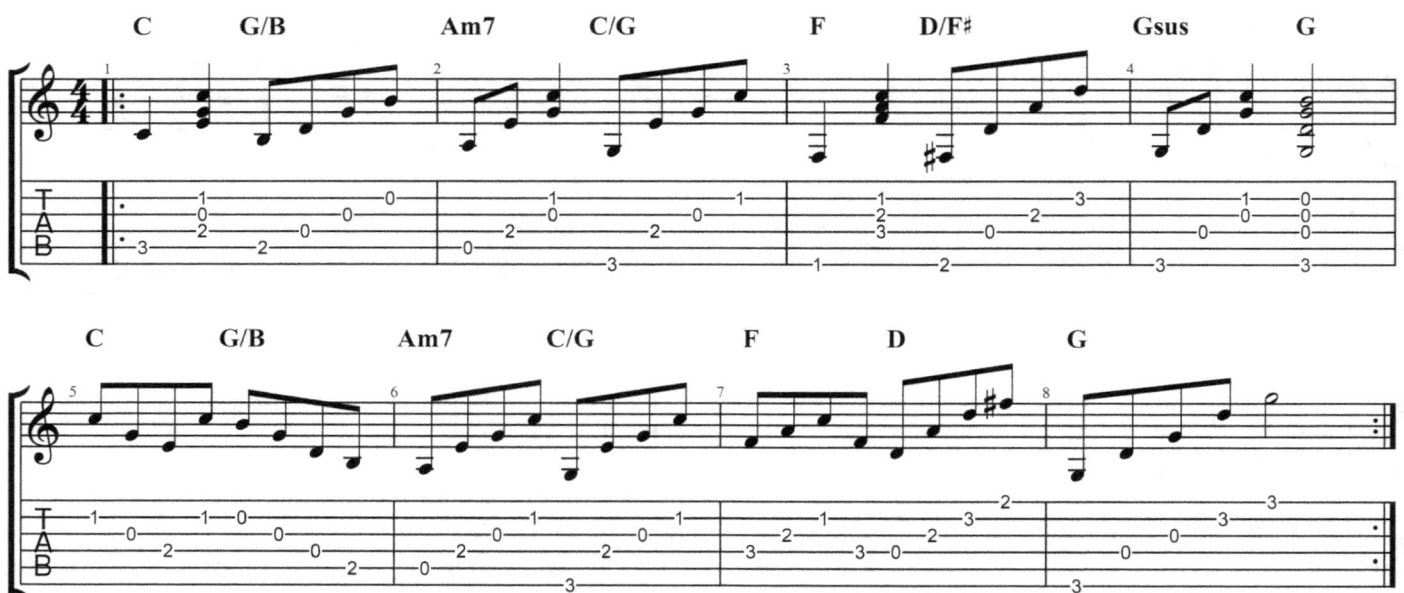

Another useful warm-up for the picking hand that creates some beautiful sounds is to take a basic CAGED E shape barre chord and, leaving the top two strings open, move it around the fretboard. I remember hearing guitarists like Alex Lifeson and John Petrucci do this and loving the effect. Let the open strings ring out and you'll get some lovely harmonies.

Example 1n:

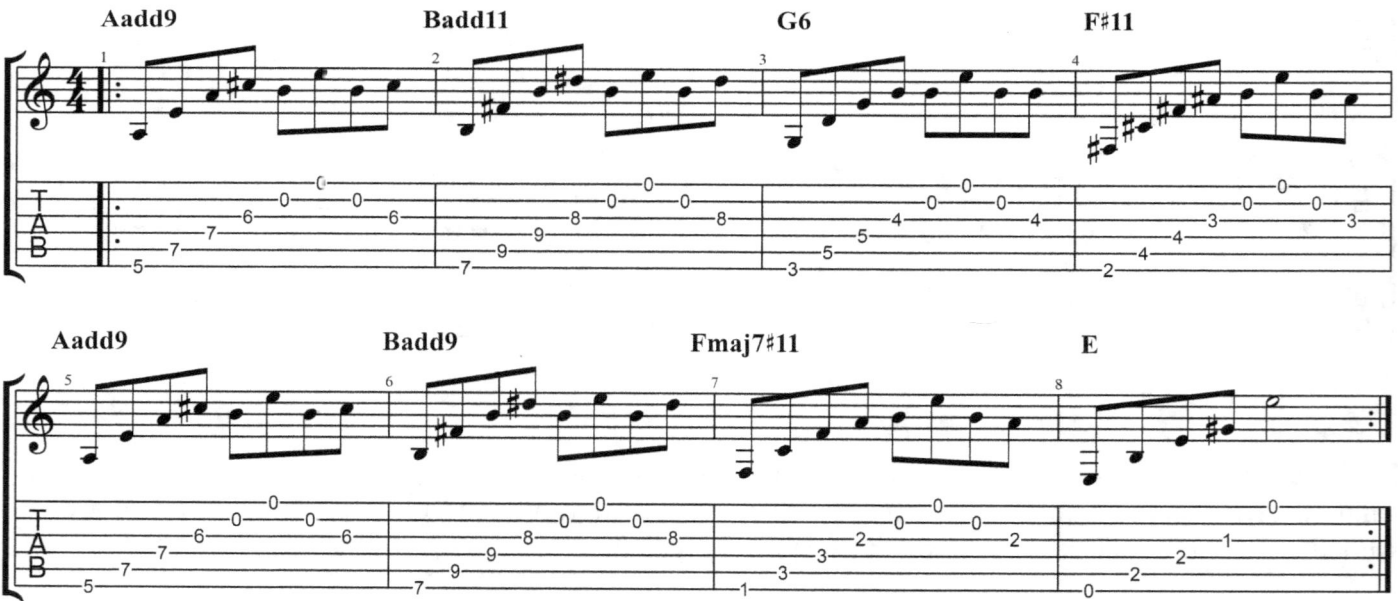

That's it for the first routine. There's plenty to get your teeth into here and it's a good introduction to the techniques you'll need for upcoming chapters. You really can't spend too much time on these techniques. Everything you invest here will lead to greater confidence on the guitar and the ability to play ideas that many players avoid.

Take your time with these picking exercises, and try applying them to your own chord progressions to gradually build proficiency.

Get to work, and I'll see you next week!

Routine: Two Vertical Triads

We've spent some time getting the basic picking technique in place and applying it to chords. Throughout the rest of the book, keep applying that alternate picking approach and you'll be well on the way to mastering it thoroughly. Now we've put that foundation in place, it's time to start thinking about how we organise arpeggios on the fretboard.

As with scales and chords, the key to gaining a deep, practical understanding of arpeggios lies in applying a system of organisation to the theory. If you understand how arpeggios are constructed and have a good method for organising them on the fretboard, you'll be pretty unstoppable.

We'll start by reviewing triads and applying them in three basic positions. These arpeggios will move across the strings rather than along them, so I think of these as *vertical* configurations. Just as we visualise scales around chord forms, we want to do the same with our arpeggios.

Let's begin with major triads, which consist of a root (1), a 3rd (3), and a 5th (5). For example, if we take an E shape C major chord in its barre form, as in Example 2a, and examine its intervals, we have:

R 5 R 3 5 R.

This is almost a complete triad arpeggio and all we need to do is add the missing 3rd between the first root and the 5th to get all the triad notes in order.

When we reach the top of the arpeggio we land back on the root note. When playing this type of major triad shape, if the root is at the 8th fret, then the 3rd will be four frets higher at the 12th fret.

Our first exercise uses this pattern to create a looping arpeggio. While playing it, actually speak the names of the intervals out loud to reinforce your understanding.

Example 2a:

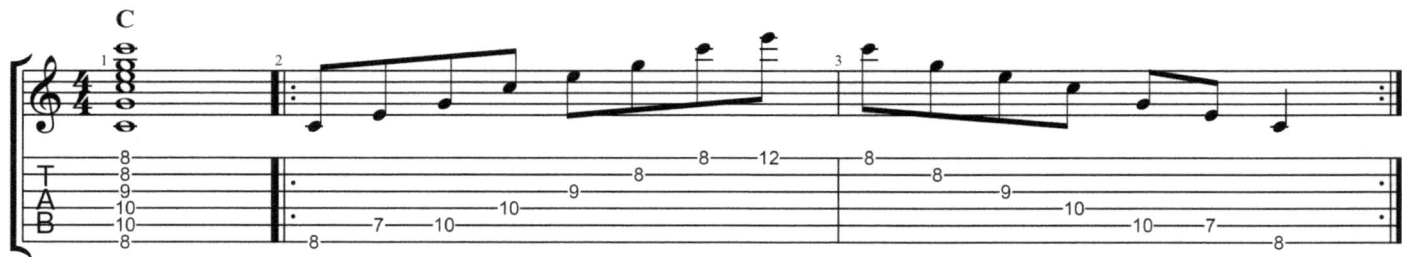

One of the best ways to start integrating arpeggios into your playing is by breaking them into smaller fragments. One approach is to use sequences where the arpeggio is played in groups of four notes. These sequences are challenging for both your picking and fretting hands, so take your time to ensure each note is cleanly separated. We're playing melodies, not strumming chords.

Example 2b:

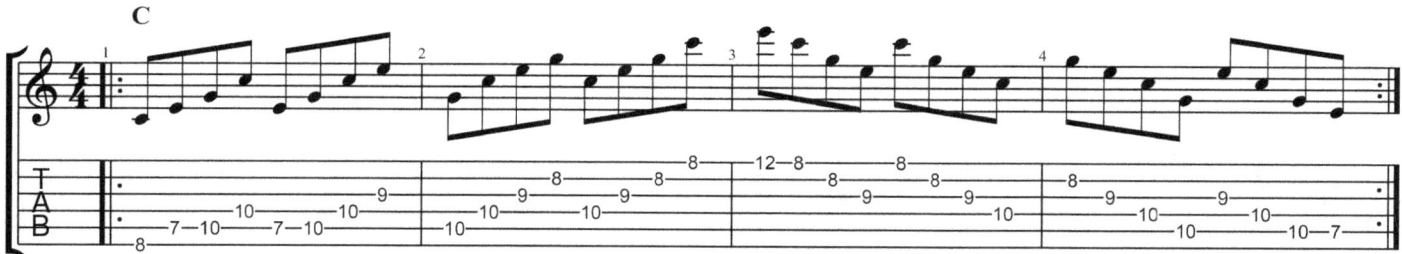

Another great way to practice this concept is to re-finger the arpeggio so that it includes all the closed-voiced triads I covered in *Guided Guitar Chord Practice Routines*. In this example, we will add some rhythm to break the arpeggio into three-note groupings, making it easier to distinguish from the full six-string pattern.

Example 2c:

We can apply the same idea to different chord positions. For instance, if we move down the neck to the A shape, we can play another C major triad arpeggio that fits around this chord form.

Example 2d:

The stretch from the 3rd to the 8th fret can be difficult if you have smaller hands and part of playing guitar is recognising your physical limitations and what you can and can't pull off. If the A shape C major triad feels too much, try shifting up to a G major arpeggio, which you'll find a lot easier. As always, these stretches will become easier with practice.

For an extra challenge, play the A shape arpeggio and, when you reach the top, shift up and descend using the E shape arpeggio.

Example 2e:

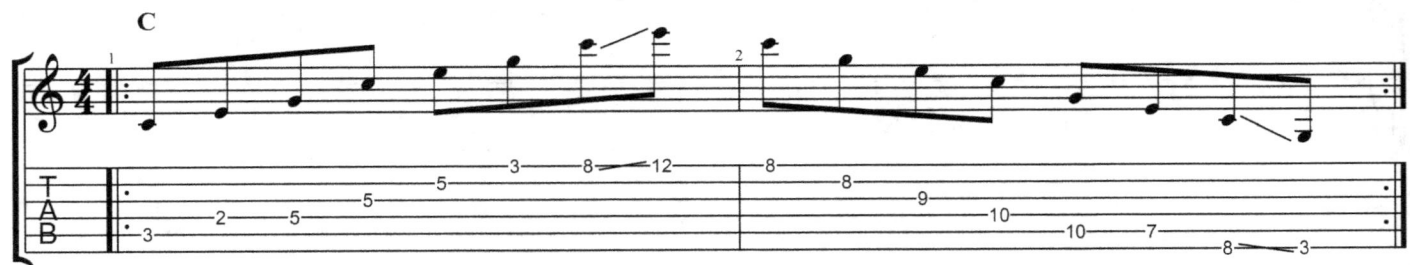

The C shape arpeggio is probably the most comfortable as it doesn't require any awkward rolling motions with the fretting hand.

Example 2f:

Let's now ascend through the E shape, shift into the C shape, and descend.

Example 2g:

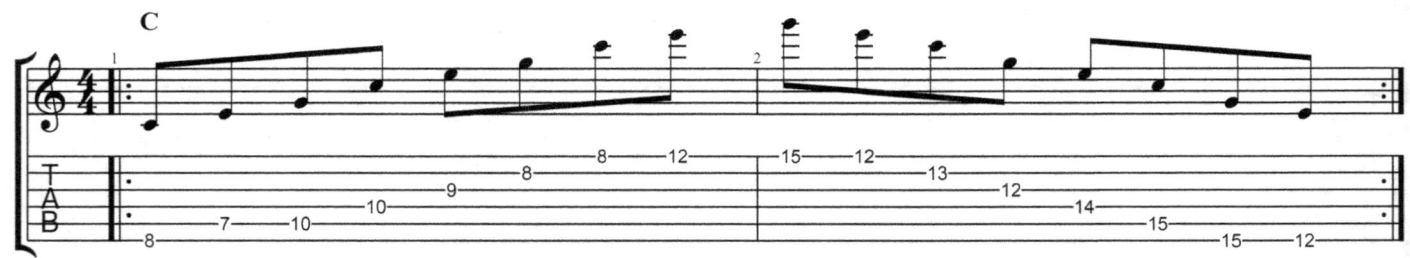

Position shifting through arpeggios across multiple octaves can be tough on your hands and isn't necessarily how we'd play arpeggios in a real-world setting, but they provide a great technical workout.

Remember that when we're practicing, we're exercising our minds not just our hands, so let's practice arpeggios through the Circle of Fifths to keep mentally engaged. To start, we'll just play them ascending with a held note at the end, so we can mentally prepare for the next chord.

The Circle of Fifths pattern is:

C F Bb Eb Ab Db Gb B E A D G

You may notice that when I play an A shape arpeggio, sometimes I'll play the 3rd on the A string and other times on the D string.

Example 2h:

To really develop your ability to think and visualise faster on the fretboard, you need to put your brain under a bit of stress during practice. We'll do that here by adding the descending version of the arpeggio as you think about which key comes next.

Example 2i:

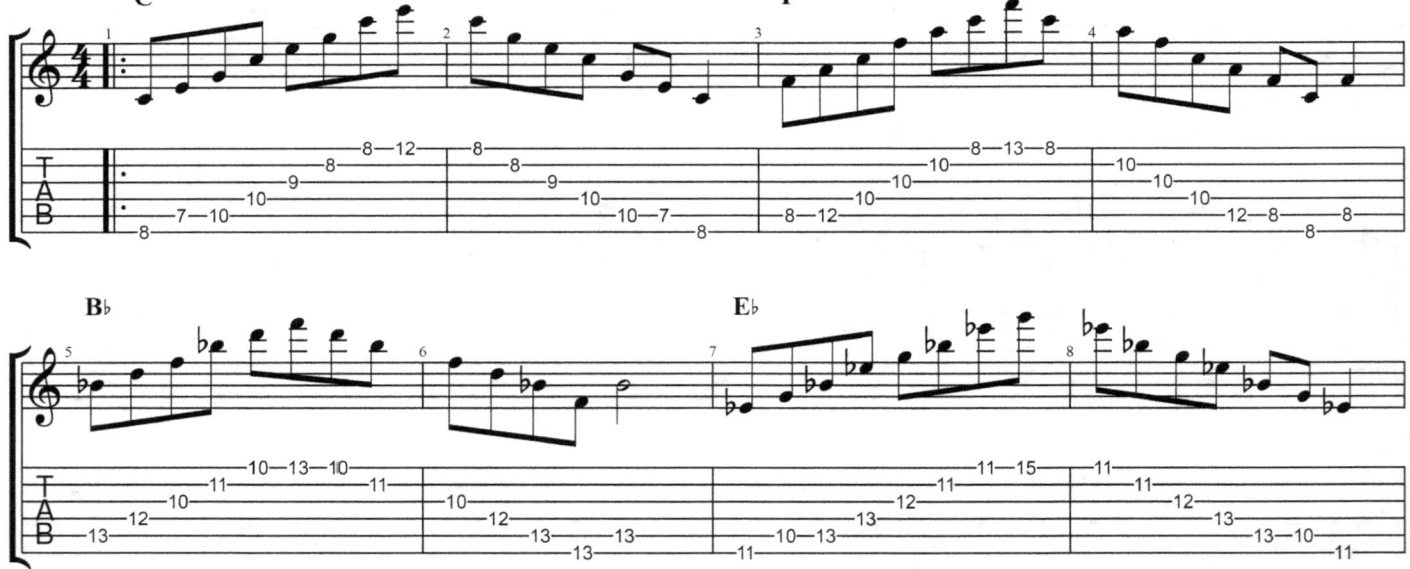

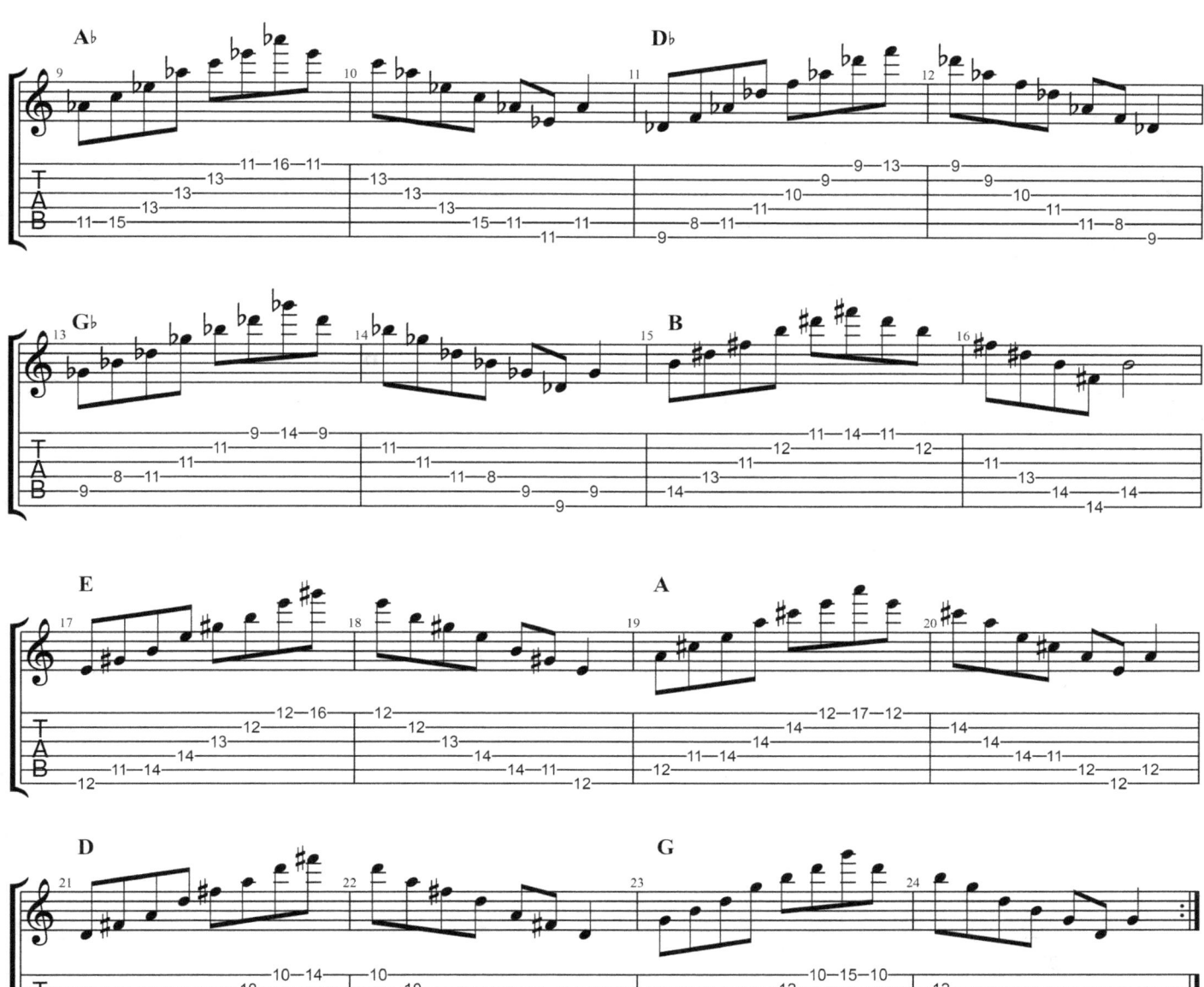

If you want to take this idea to the next level, you need to practice changing from one arpeggio to the next on any string. A good way to do this is to slow down the pulse to 1/4 notes and focus on connecting to the nearest note in the next arpeggio when the chord changes.

Example 2j:

Now let's change things up by converting these major triad arpeggios into minor triads. Instead of thinking of these as "new" shapes, think of them as the major shapes you already know, but you're lowering the 3rds (E) to flat 3rds (Eb). Here's an example using the E shape, with a triplet rhythm for some variety.

Example 2k:

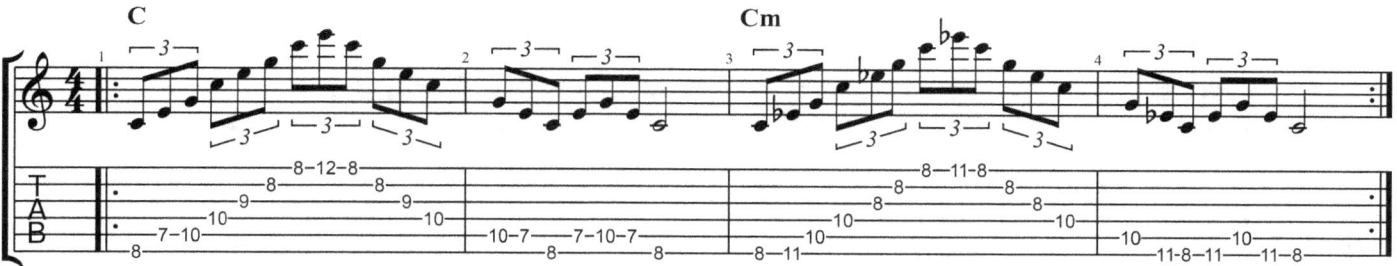

Here's the same idea, now moved up to the C shape.

Example 2l:

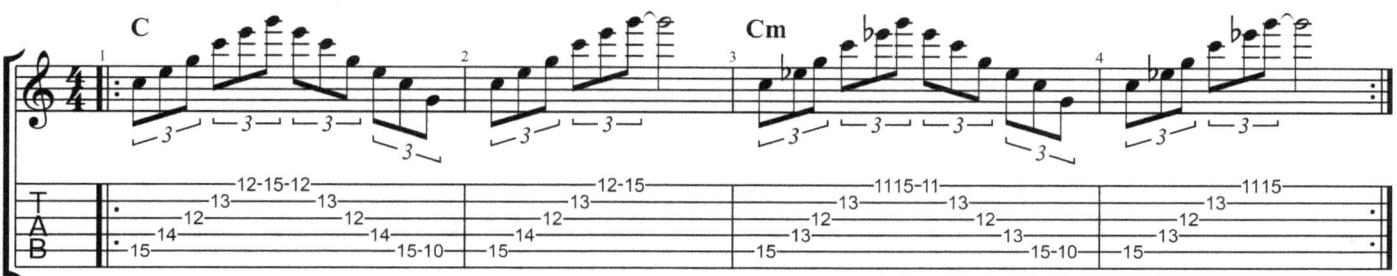

And finally, here it is in the A shape.

Example 2m:

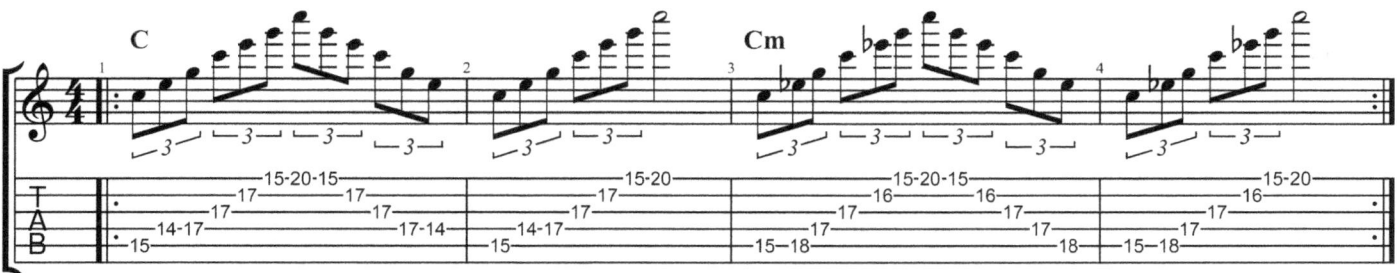

These exercises will help get your fretting hand in sync with solid alternate picking. Once you're comfortable with these shapes, a good challenge is to link them up by ascending one position and descending the next. Here's an example with a C minor chord.

Example 2n:

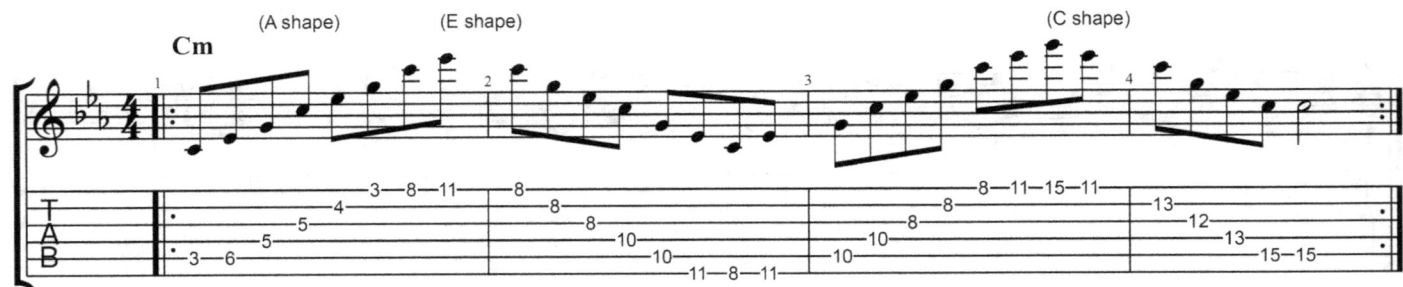

Major and minor triads are essential to know, but there are also three other types of triad you need to know: diminished (1 b3 b5), augmented (1 3 #5), and suspended (1 2 5 and 1 4 5).

Here are the three C diminished triad arpeggios. To play these, I visualise a C minor arpeggio and lower the 5ths (G) to b5s (Gb). These shapes don't come up too often, but they're great for interval practice.

Example 2o:

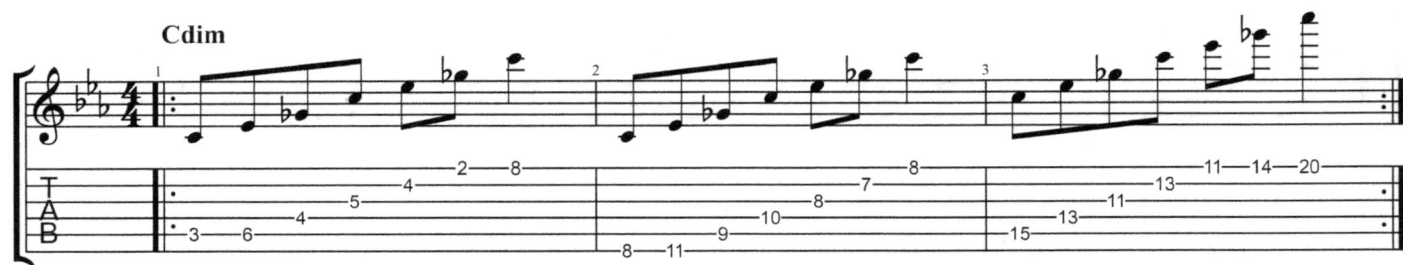

Next, here are the three C augmented triads. To play these, I visualise C major and raise all the 5ths (G) to #5s (G#) You'll notice that these shapes are essentially identical as the augmented triad is symmetrical – each note is the same distance (two tones) apart.

Example 2p:

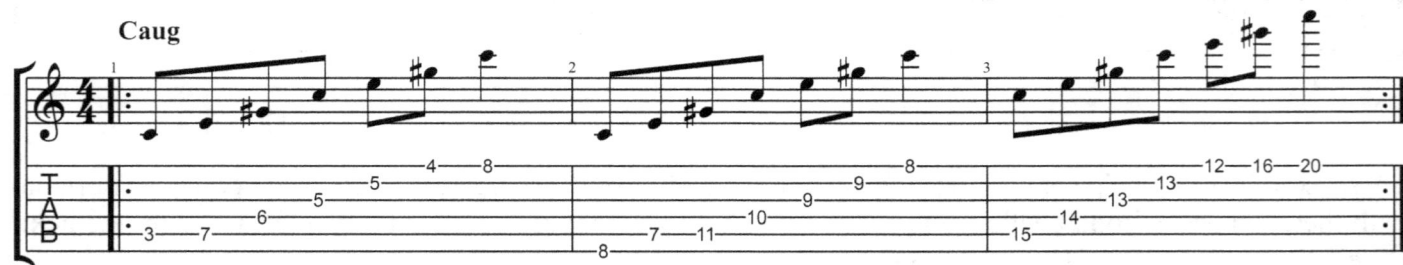

Now, let's look at the three Csus2 arpeggios. These are great for adding a more ambiguous sound to your solos.

Example 2q:

Finally, here are the three Csus4 arpeggios.

Example 2r:

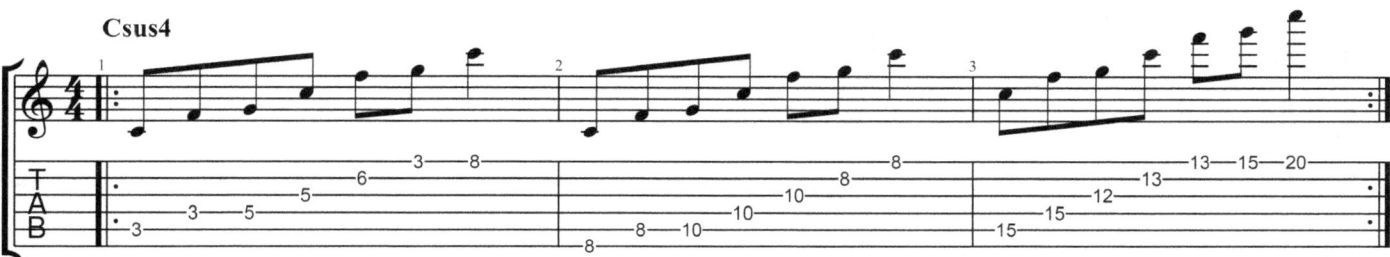

It's important to acknowledge that a lot more work can be done on the ideas we've covered here. For example, once you feel comfortable, you could incorporate sequences of fours, take the arpeggios through the Circle of Fifths, or link positions into one long example.

The first step is making sure you know all these arpeggios in their most common forms and can play them automatically. Once that becomes second nature, you'll have more mental energy to focus on applying them in different musical contexts.

Routine Three: Horizontal Triads

True mastery of the fretboard comes when you start breaking free of the limitations of the box patterns you learned as a beginner. In the last chapter, we worked with triad arpeggios using the E, A, and C shapes, and briefly touched on the horizontal approach by shifting between positions as we moved up the fretboard. Horizontal movement along the string is an important skill, and it's something we want to be able to do seamlessly at any time on any string.

We can develop this skill in a methodical way by playing intervals and varying the number of notes we play on each string. A simple pattern-based approach is to take a C major triad and organize it in a 1-2-1-2-1-2 pattern across the strings, so that we play one note on the first string, two on the next, one on the following, and so on.

To finger this, use the middle, index and pinkie finger, then shift up to play the note on the D string with the middle finger, then repeat.

Example 3a:

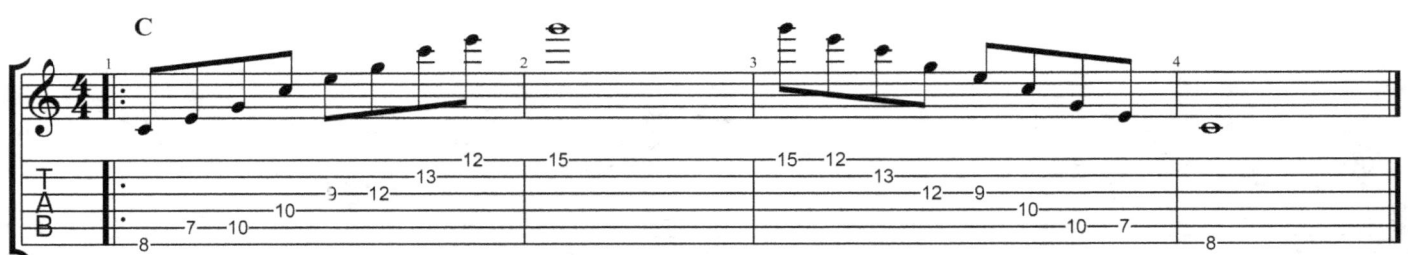

We can also arrange this triad in a 2-1-2-1-2-1 pattern.

Example 3b:

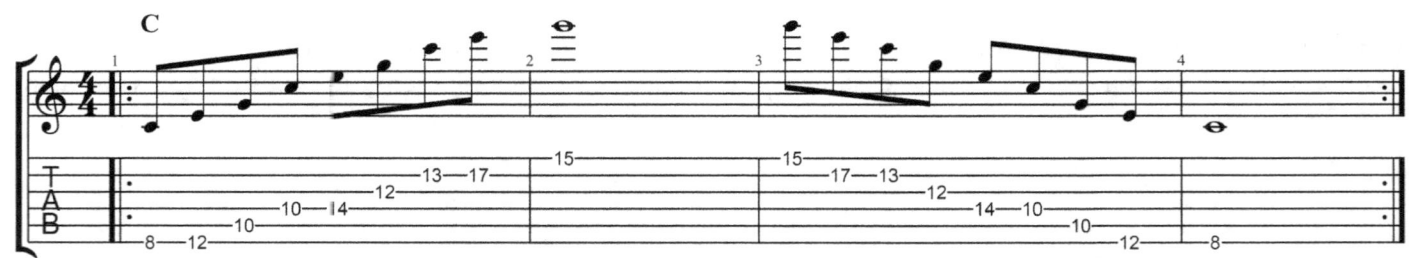

Let's turn the C major triad into a C minor triad by flattening all the E notes to Eb. Now practice ascending and descending through both finger patterns with this new minor triad.

Example 3c:

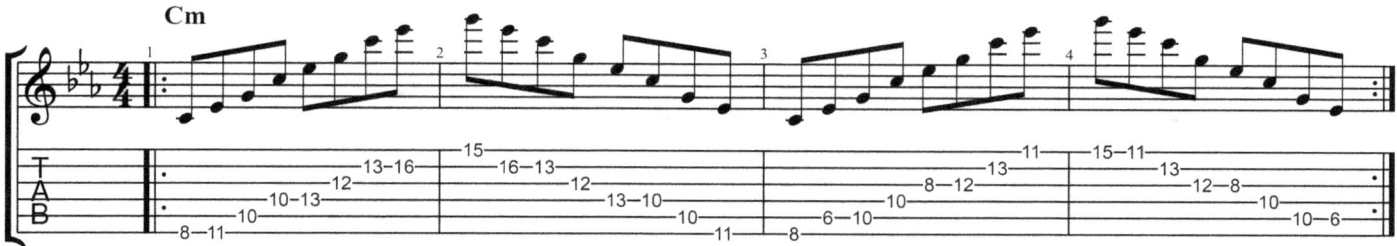

If we pause to consider the intervals and the relationships between them, it opens up new possibilities for fingering these triads.

In a major triad, we have a root, 3rd, 5th, then we add the root an octave higher. The interval between the root and 3rd is a major third (four frets); the interval between the 3rd and 5th is a minor third (three frets); and the distance from the 5th to the higher root is a perfect fourth (five frets).

When we play a triad, we can think of it as the movement, "up a major 3rd, up a minor 3rd, up a perfect 4th" and repeat. If we play this for G major on a single string, it looks like this, played first on the E string, then on the D string, then on the B string.

Example 3d:

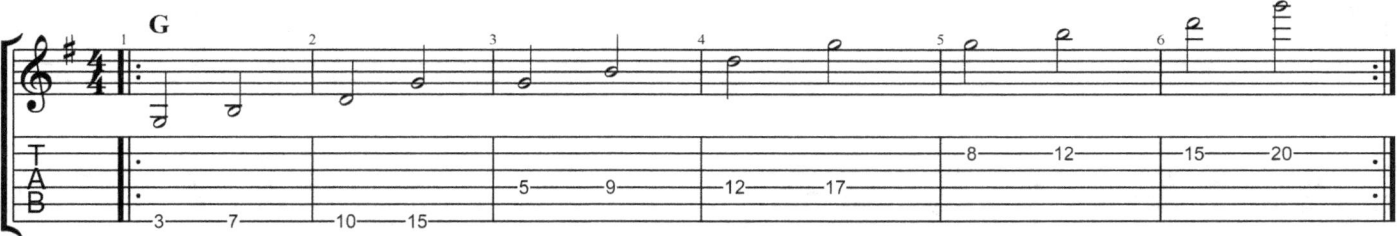

It's not practical from a musical point of view to play triads as four-note-per-string patterns, but the previous exercise helped us to learn the intervals. Once we can clearly "hear" those intervals, and know which note to go to next, we can finger triads in many different ways.

I've written out three possible fingerings for G major in Example 3e. As you play through them, pay attention to both the sound of the intervals and where they're located.

Example 3e:

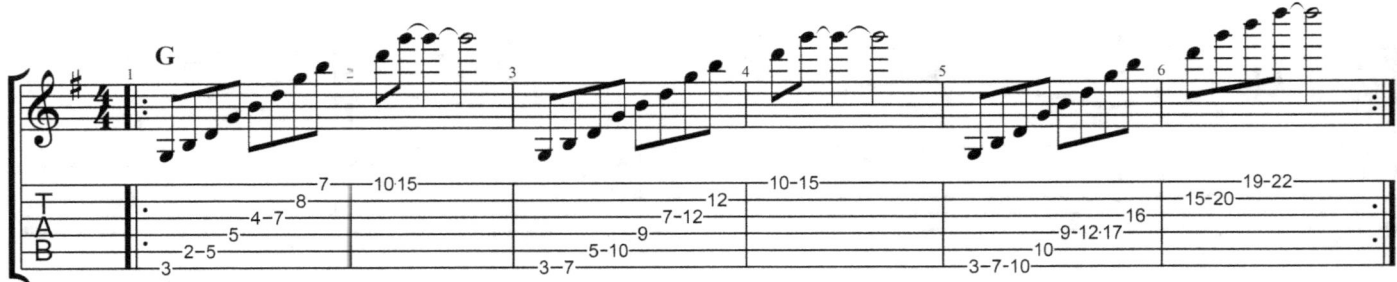

To become more fluent on the fretboard, let's focus on transitioning at different points on each string. In this next exercise, we'll move from the E shape to the C shape, first transitioning on the E string, then the A string, then the D string, and so on.

We'll do this in both ascending and descending patterns.

Example 3f:

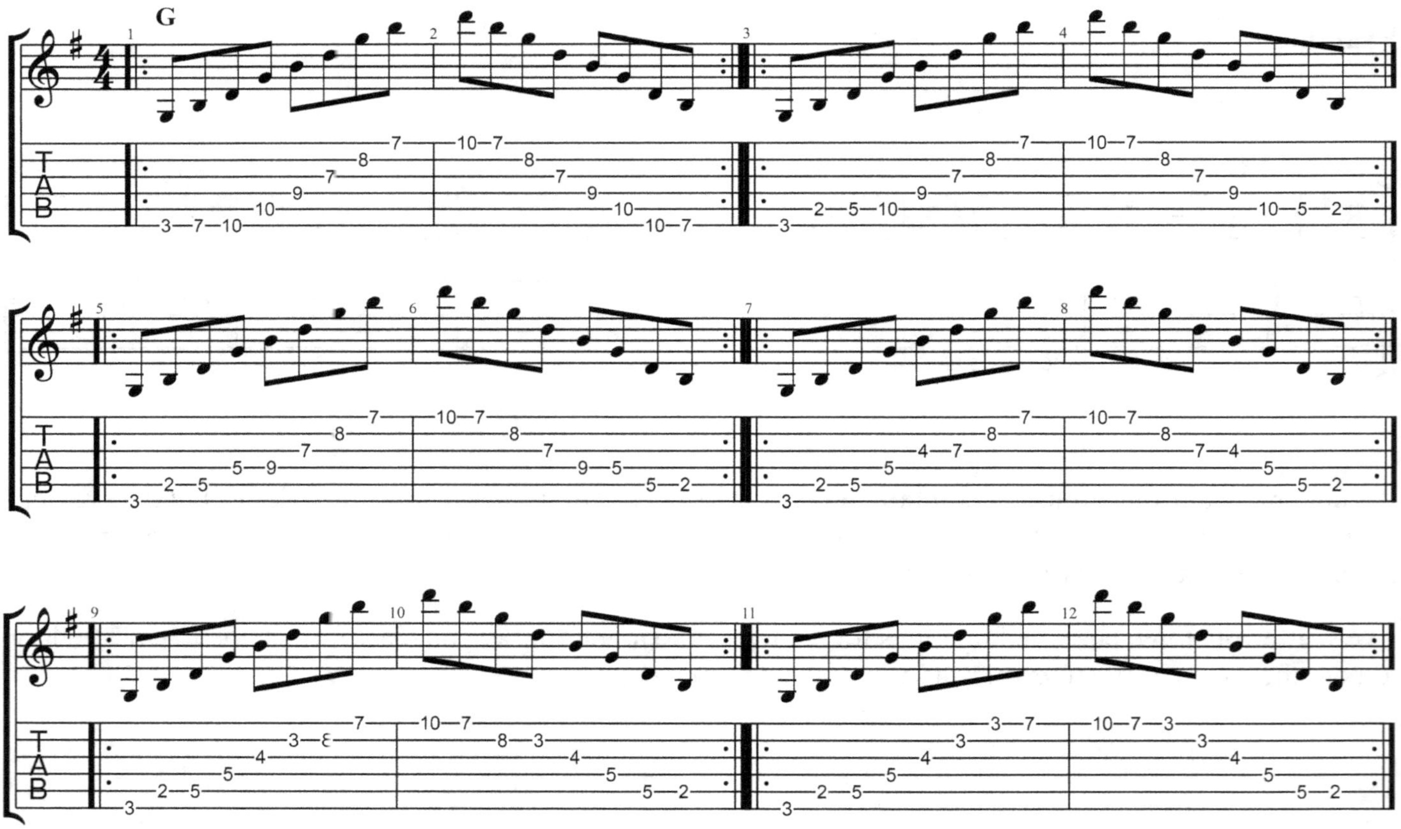

Now do the same exercise moving from the C shape up to the A shape.

Example 3g:

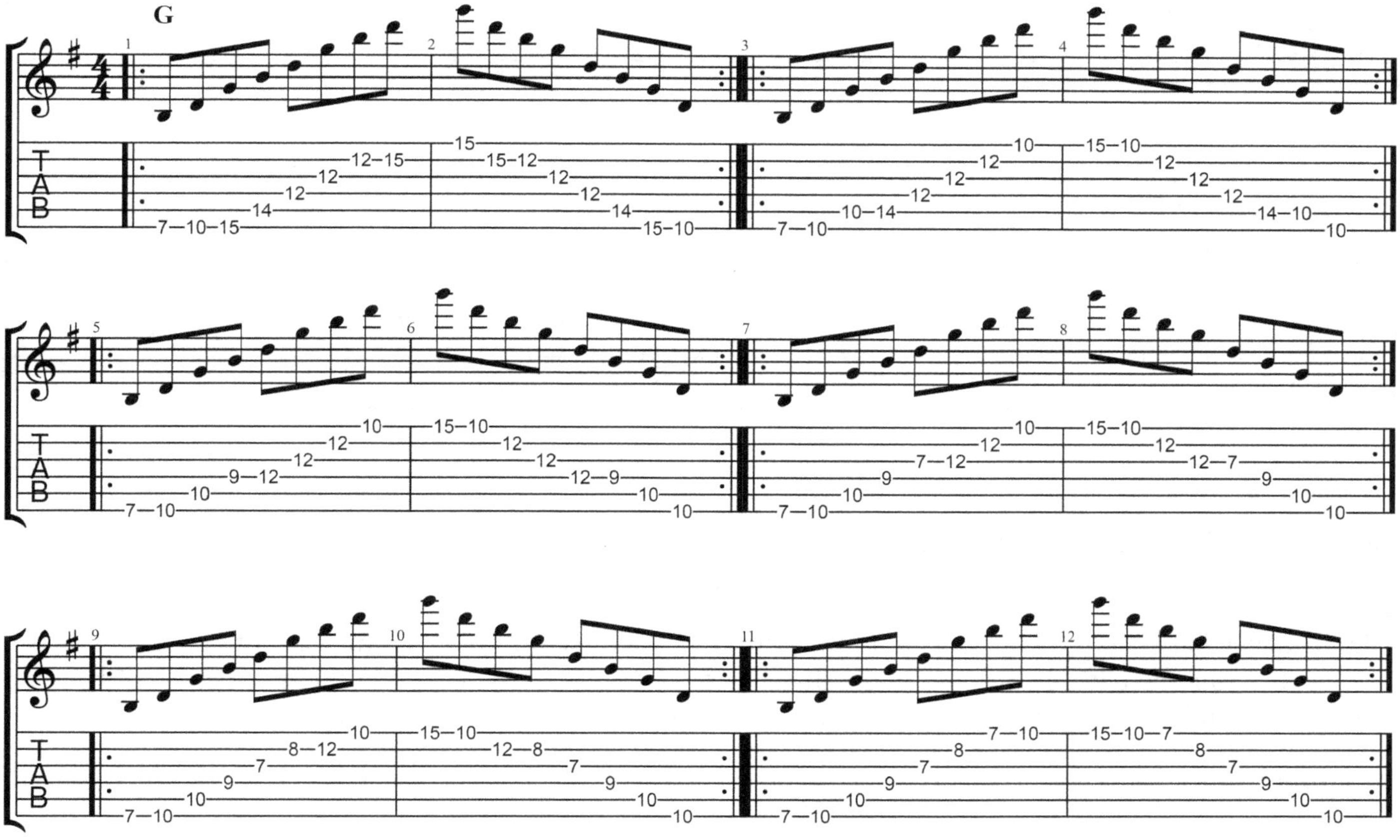

And finally, let's practice moving from the A shape to the E shape.

Example 3h:

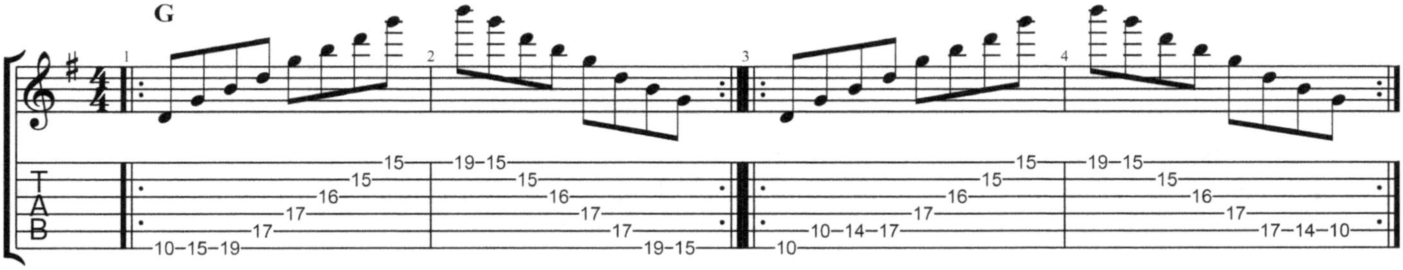

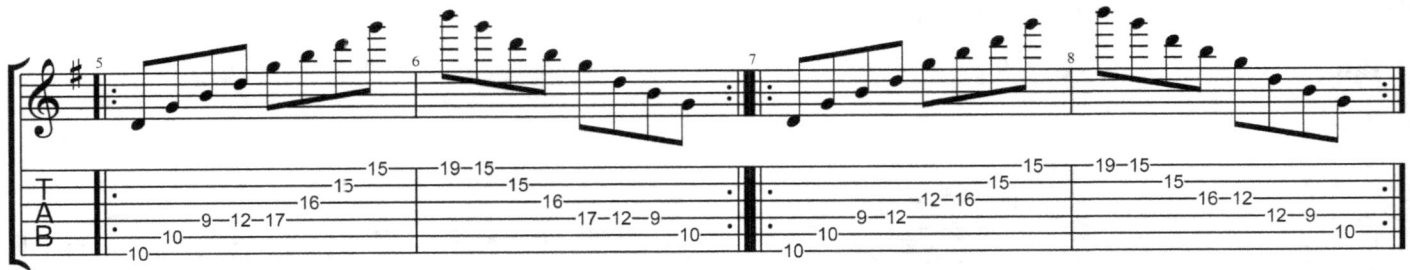

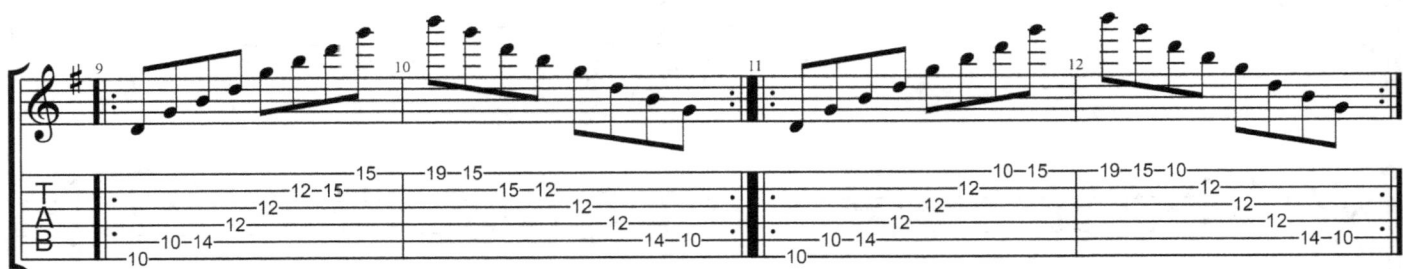

Instead of writing these exercises out again for minor triads, I want you to apply the same concepts as earlier to the following triads and work them into your practice routine.

The distances between the intervals in a minor triad are slightly different. From the root (1) to the b3 is a minor 3rd. From the b3rd the 5th is a major 3rd. From the 5th back up to the root the distance is a 4th. We'll start with a G minor arpeggio in the E shape, and make transitions on the D, G, and high E strings.

Example 3i:

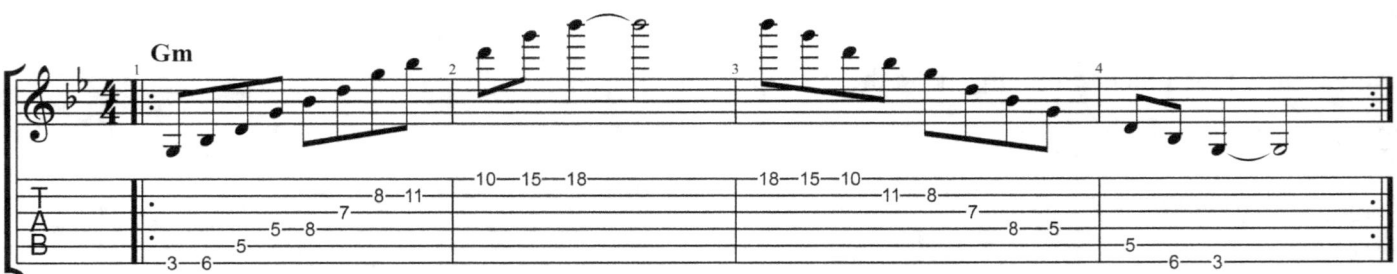

It's worth noting that the more you work on ideas like this, the more you'll discover which patterns feel natural to play, and which ones you can safely discard. I favour transitions that feel comfortable to my hand because those are the ones I'll be able to play effortlessly in the midst of a solo.

If we move to a C minor triad in the A shape, we can begin low on the neck and transition up into the higher position. This approach mirrors the octave patterns we discussed earlier in the chapter, where we played a three-note idea and shifted it up in octave patterns across two strings.

Example 3j:

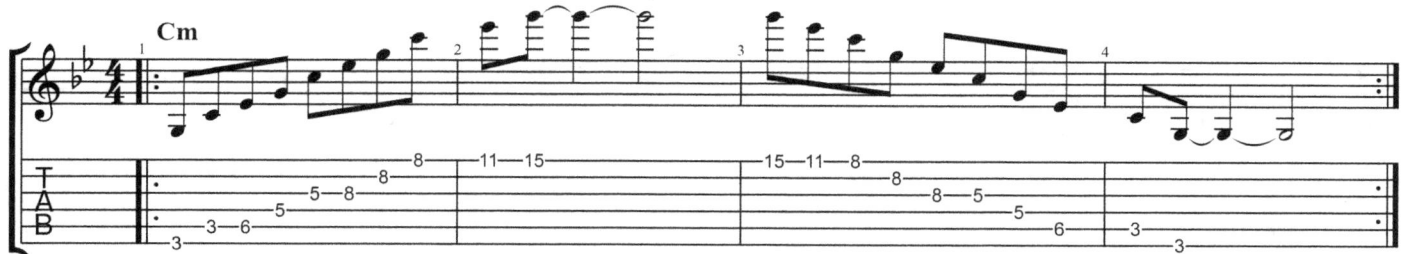

But we don't have to stick to those patterns, and we can create something with even more range, as in the following example. Notice how I ascend and descend slightly differently. This variation helps to keep me on my toes.

Example 3k:

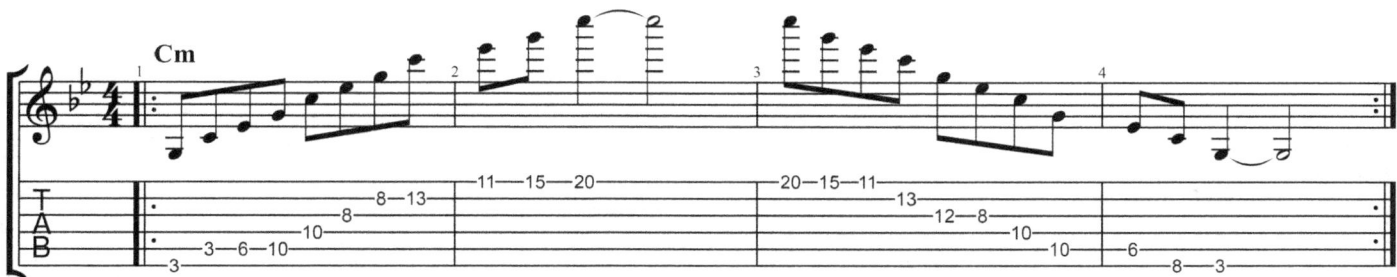

If we switch to a D minor triad, we can start in the C shape and move all the way up the neck to the E shape which gives us another useful position shift.

Example 3l:

For an even wider range, we can use an E minor triad. With the open E string available, we can extend the arpeggio even further. If you have a guitar with 24 frets there's nothing stopping you from taking this arpeggio up to the highest notes, creating a full four-octave spread.

Example 3m:

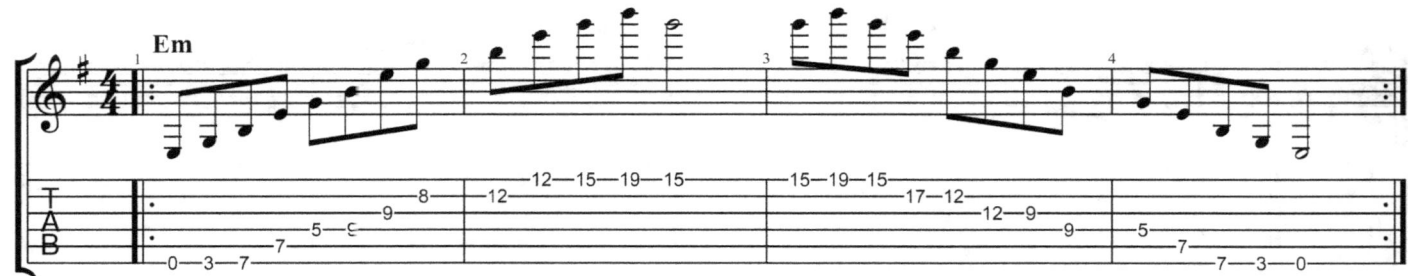

To wrap up this routine, I want to push you a bit further by applying a melodic sequence to these horizontal patterns and combining both major and minor triads.

In the following example, we'll use a C major to A minor progression and play an ascending sequence of fours.

Example 3n:

If we transpose this progression to the key of G, we have a G major to E minor sequence which gives us a completely different pathway up and down the neck.

Example 3o:

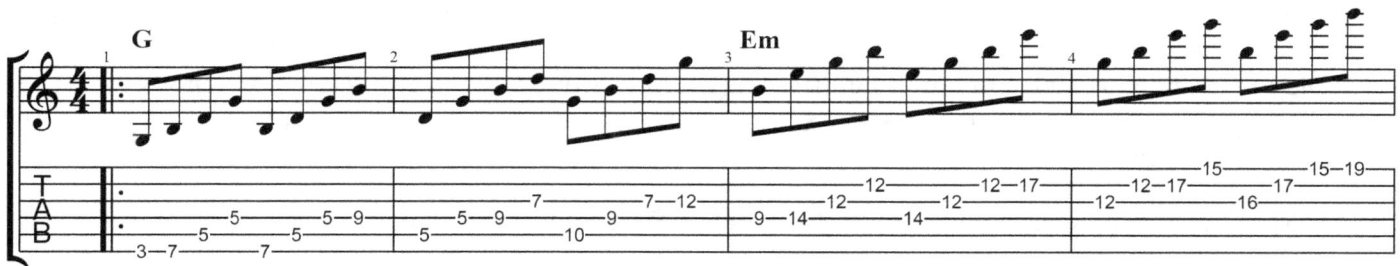

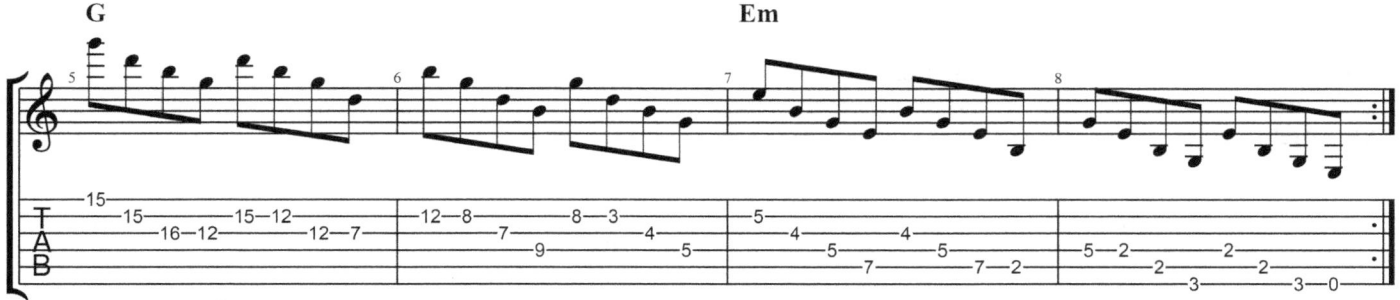

We haven't discussed picking in this chapter, but these ideas have to be alternate picked. With so many position changes, they go against the different systems guitar players use to sweep pick. But, the great benefit of these exercises is that they will increase your fretboard knowledge and give you a greater level of melodic control.

The more you can break out of traditional box patterns, the more freedom you'll have when playing melodically using both arpeggios and scales.

There's no shortcut with this stuff! You just need to improve your brain's ability to visualise these pathways and train your hands to keep up with where they need to be.

Routine Four: Triad Progression Workouts

We've looked at a little bit of technique and worked through a series of fingering options for triad arpeggios, but one of the best ways to get to grips with arpeggios is to apply them in a musical way. So, in this chapter we'll play some longer etudes that outline different chord positions in various ways. Sometimes we'll stay within a single position, while other times we'll challenge ourselves to break out of the usual box patterns and cover more of the neck.

Let's start with the classic arpeggios found at the end of *Sultans of Swing*. The chord progression is:

Dm – Bb – C – C

There are countless ways to arpeggiate this progression, but a good starting point is to use two-string arpeggios, which is how Mark Knopfler plays them.

Example 4a:

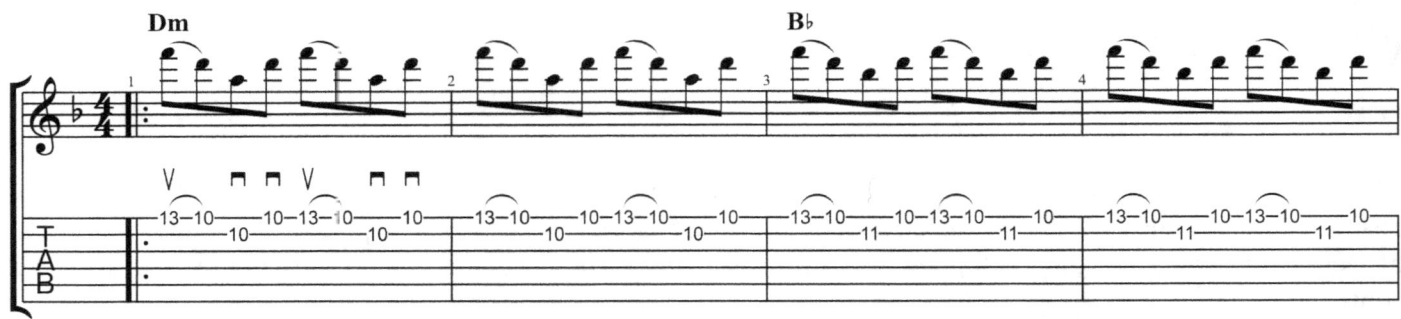

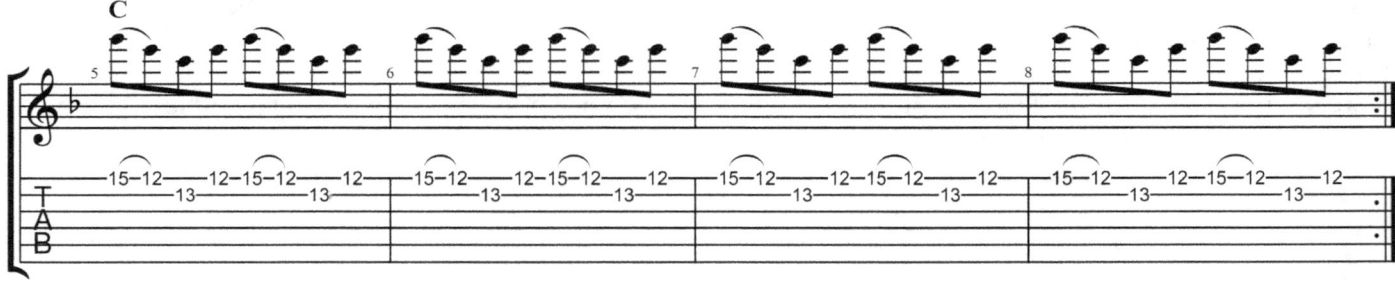

From here, let's expand the chord progression into a three-string looping arpeggio pattern that stays in the same position.

Example 4b:

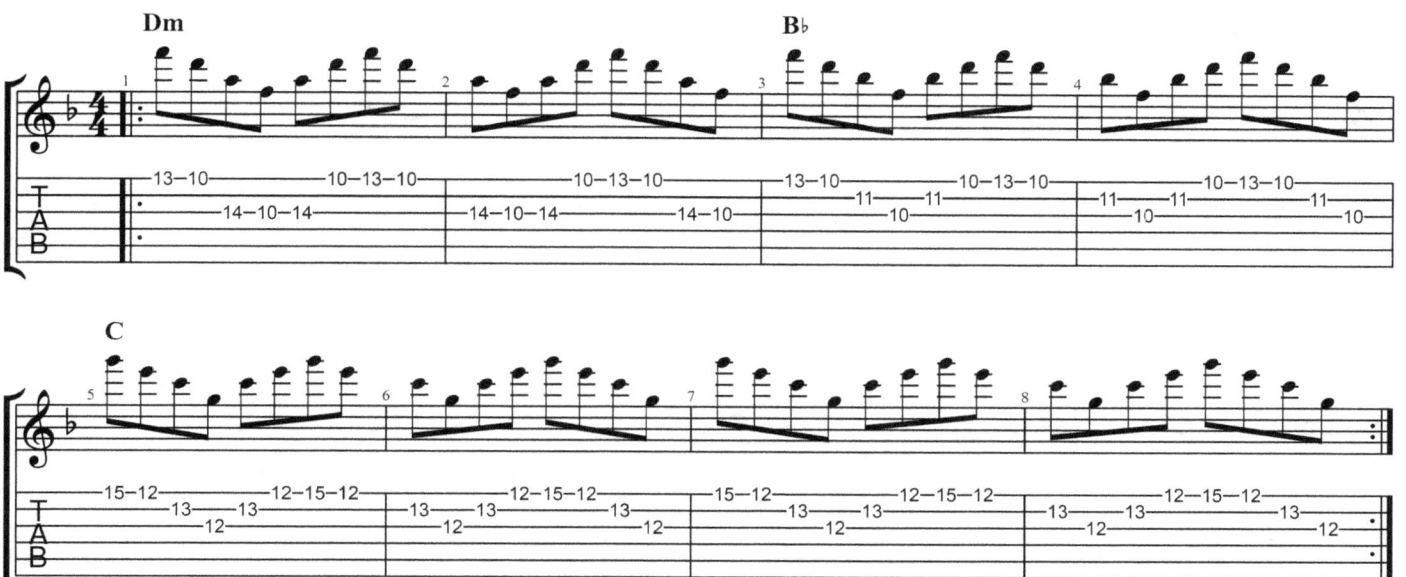

For a more challenging approach, we can jump between different positions and inversions, still using three-string patterns but adding some complexity. I've ended this example with a big descending D minor arpeggio.

Example 4c:

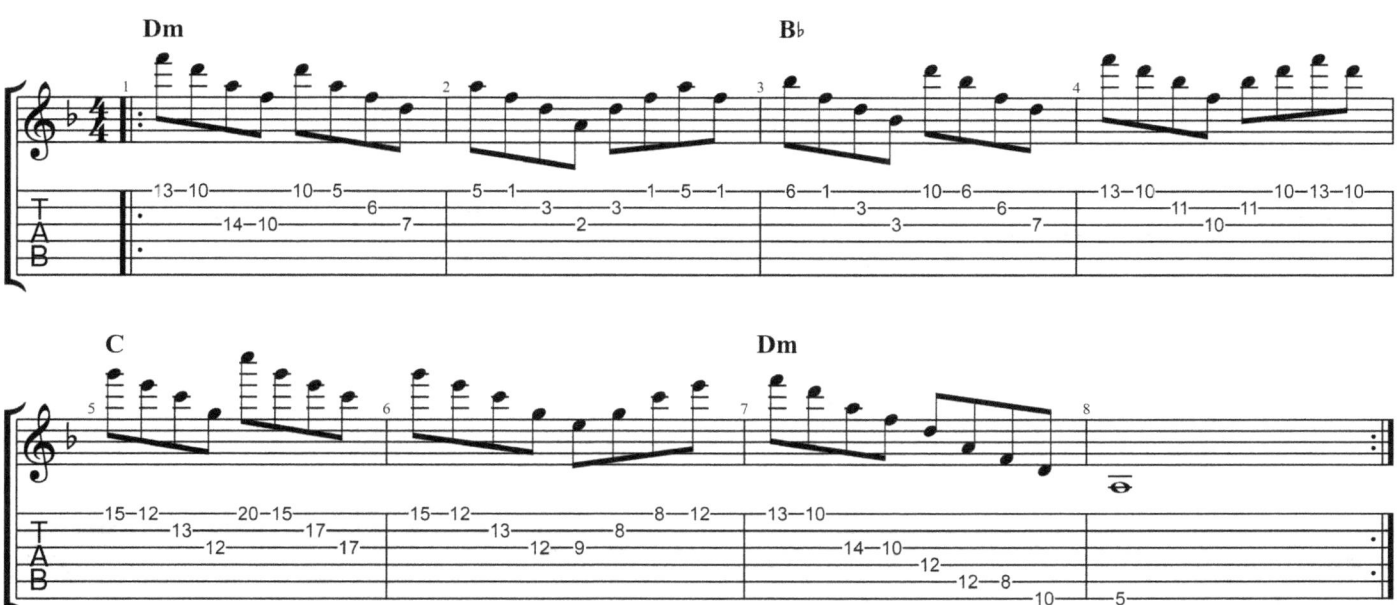

Example 4d is a much trickier etude as we play the chord changes twice as quickly and cover all six strings in the process.

Example 4d:

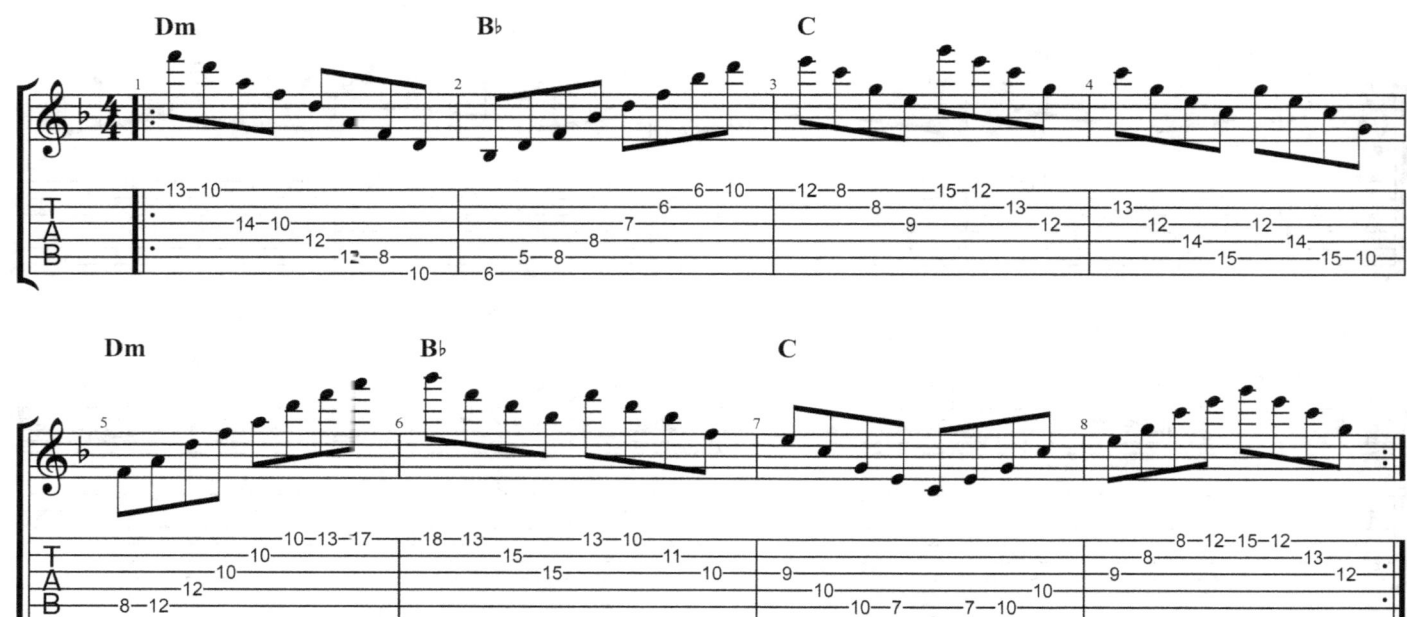

It's common in rock and metal tunes to have a section with a set chord progression, which the guitarist will outline with an arpeggio pattern. You could stick with familiar patterns used by players like Yngwie Malmsteen or Jason Becker, but there's no reason why you can't write your own arpeggio lines that incorporate more intricate points of transition.

Example 4e:

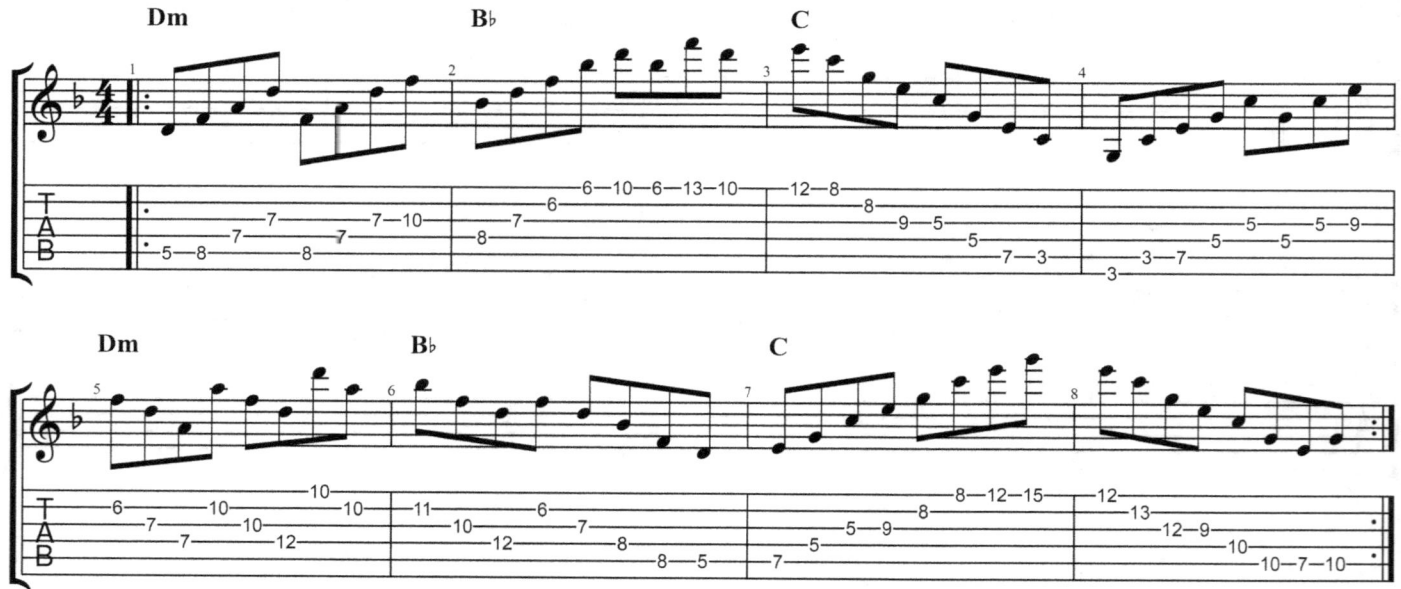

While classic rock offers great progressions for arpeggios, looking to the world of classical music is a great way to find progressions to work on. One of the most well-known examples is Johann Pachelbel's *Canon in D*, a piece so famous that it arguably makes Pachelbel the original one-hit wonder!

Canon in D follows a repeating chord sequence of D – A – Bm – F#m – G – D – G – A.

This progression is perfect for warming up with full six-string arpeggios, either starting from the top or bottom of each arpeggio.

Example 4f:

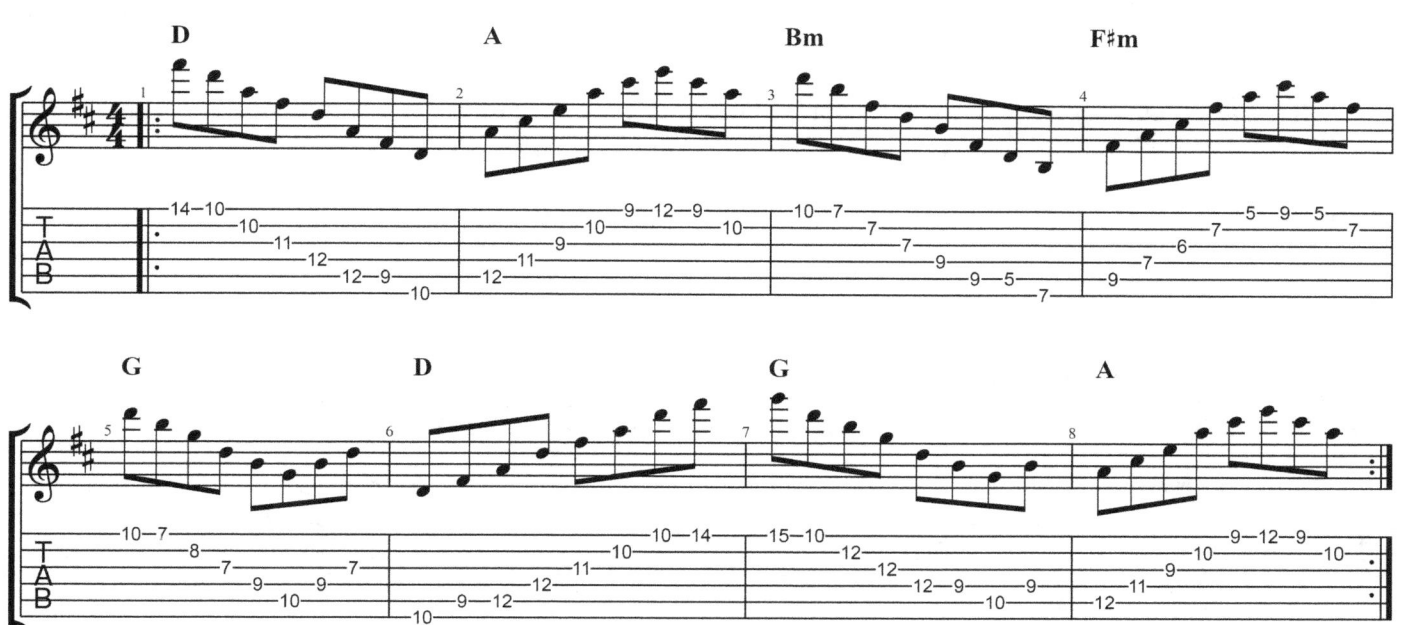

But there are countless ways to approach arpeggios and here's another variation you can explore.

Example 4g:

We can raise the difficulty level by channelling some Jason Becker influence and play triplets with sweep picking to create a more technical feel.

After all the alternate picking you've been doing, take your time with this one. Learn it slowly and make sure you control the picking hand well to keep the sweeps smooth and consistent.

Example 4h:

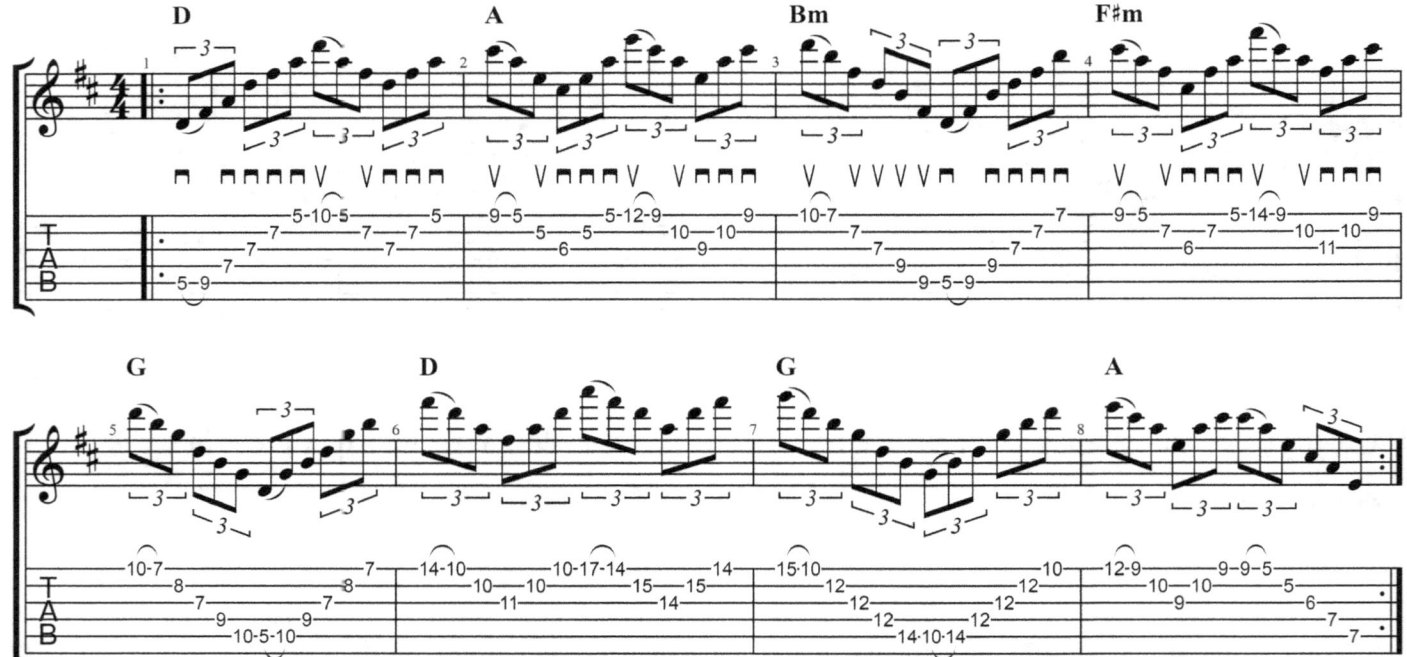

As with any arpeggio idea, the real challenge is to break out of predictable patterns and become comfortable with changing chords on any string. Here's a more melodically engaging etude that shifts between chords in less expected ways.

Example 4i:

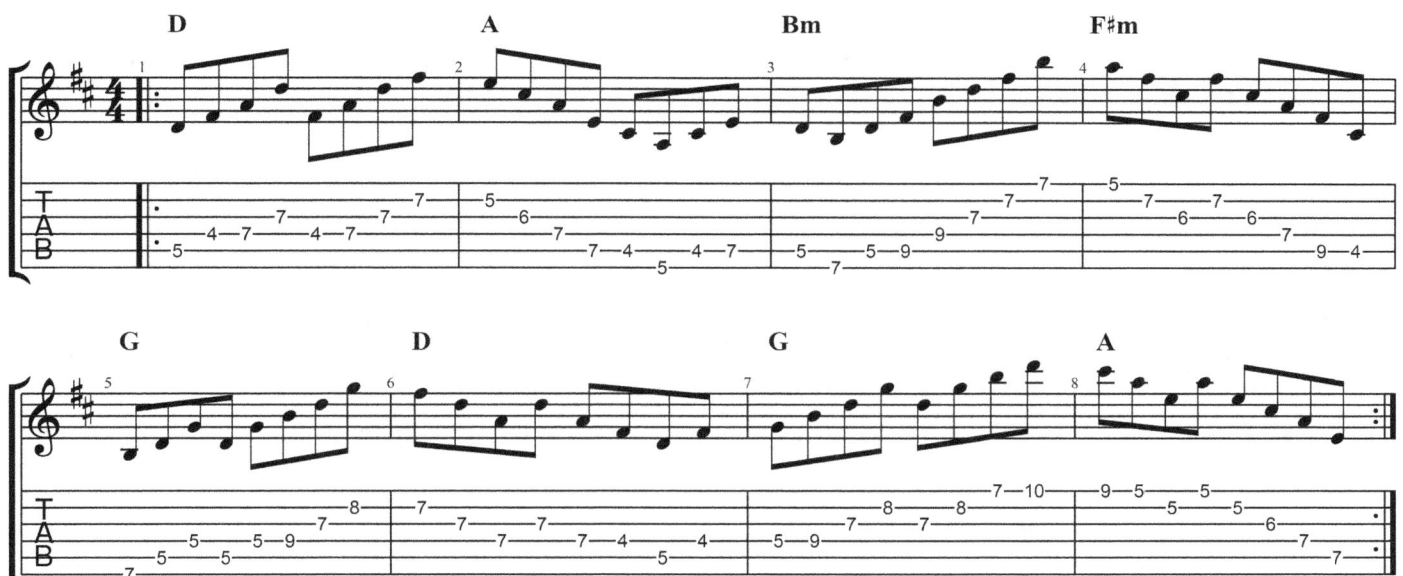

Here's another etude based on the Canon played higher up the neck with more challenging transitions. I love working on etudes like this. Though I've only included two here, I could easily fill a book with these kinds of studies.

Once you're comfortable with the examples I've provided, try composing some of your own. Since we're only using notes from the triads, the limited note pool should mean you can come up with something fresh if you take your time.

Example 4j:

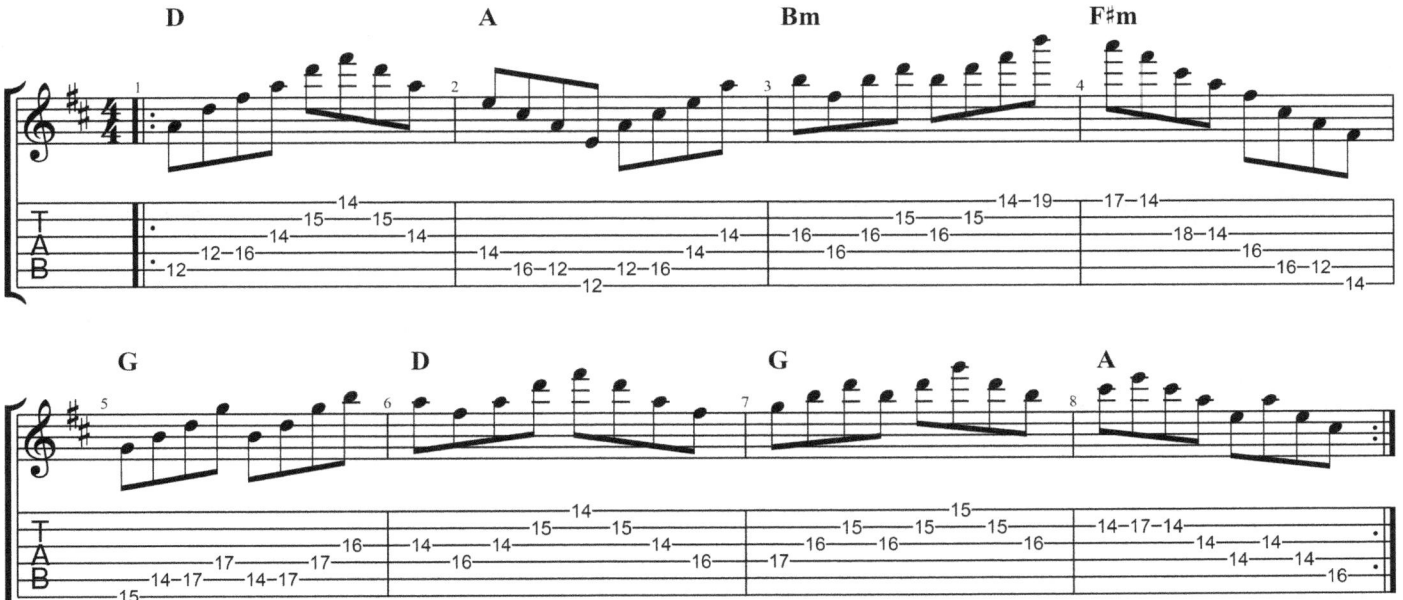

For our final progression we'll stay in the classical world, this time drawing inspiration from Beethoven's famous *Moonlight Sonata*. I've simplified it by treating the dominant chords as major triads, but it's still a wonderful way to practice arpeggios.

Unlike the previous progression, we're now in a minor key (C# Minor) and in 12/8 time, so each bar contains four triplet groupings. To start, we'll play simple ascending and descending arpeggios.

Example 4k:

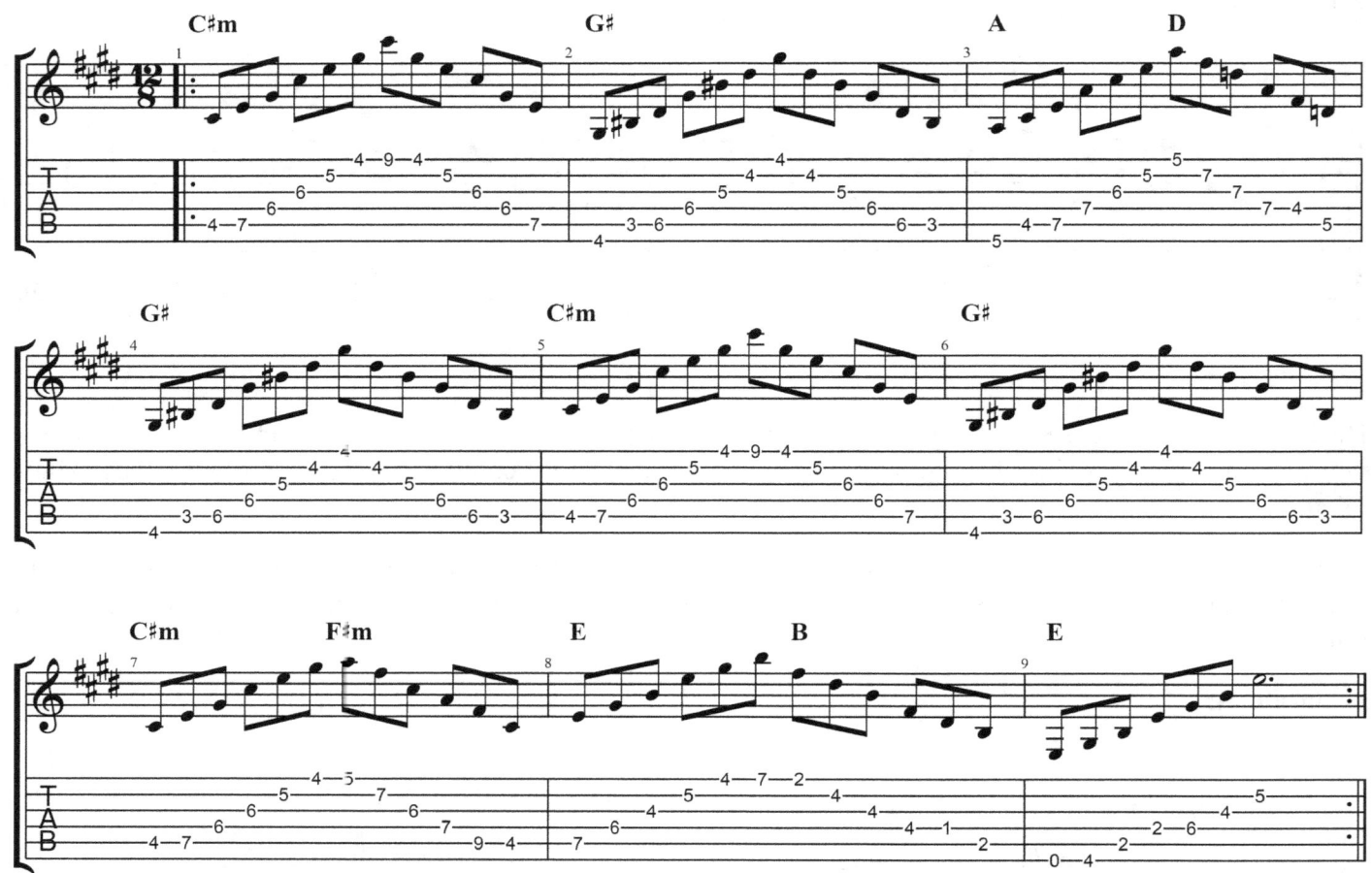

Now, let's embrace the triplet feel of the piece by playing three-note groupings of closed-voiced triads that outline the chord changes.

Example 4l:

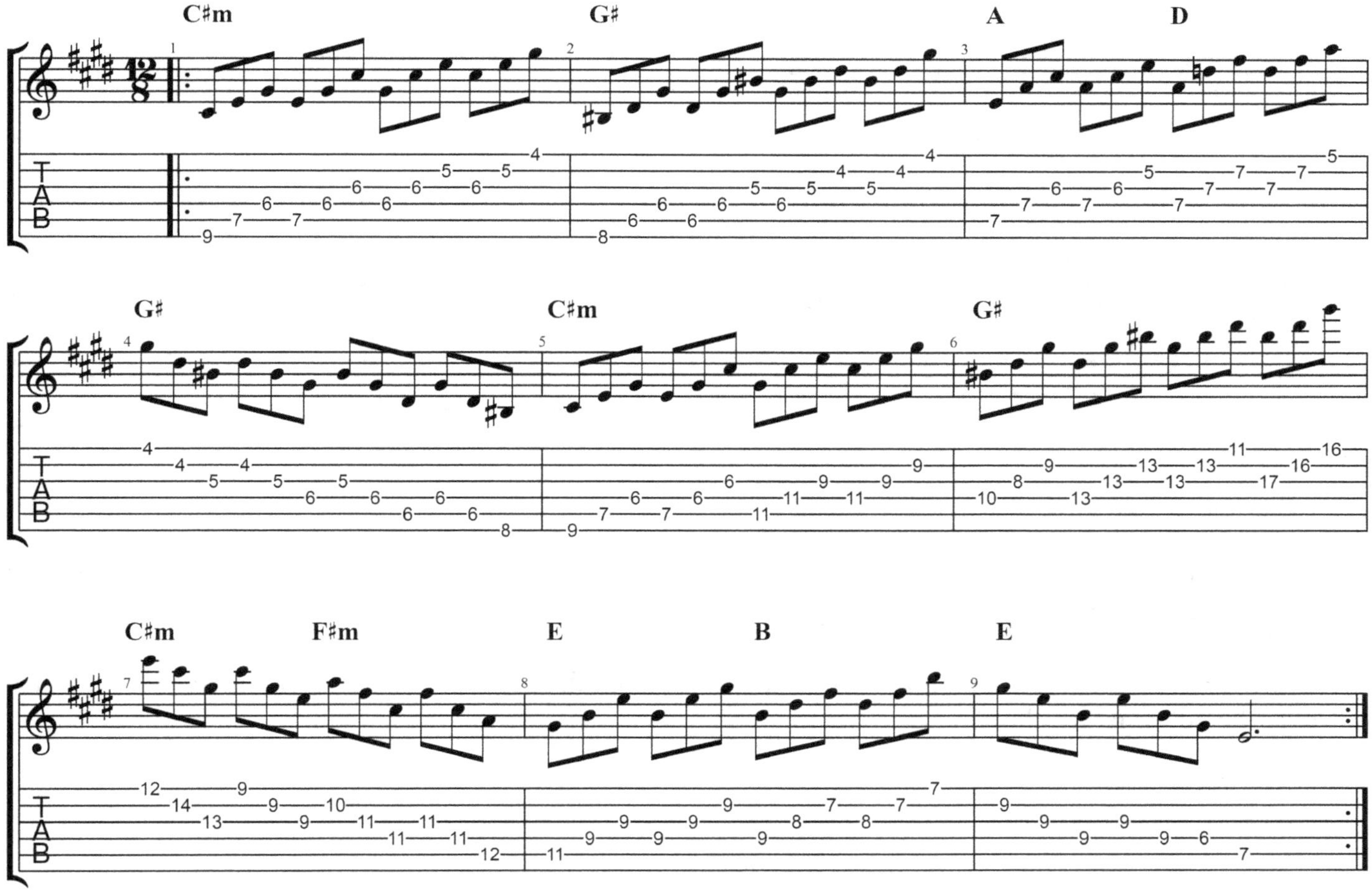

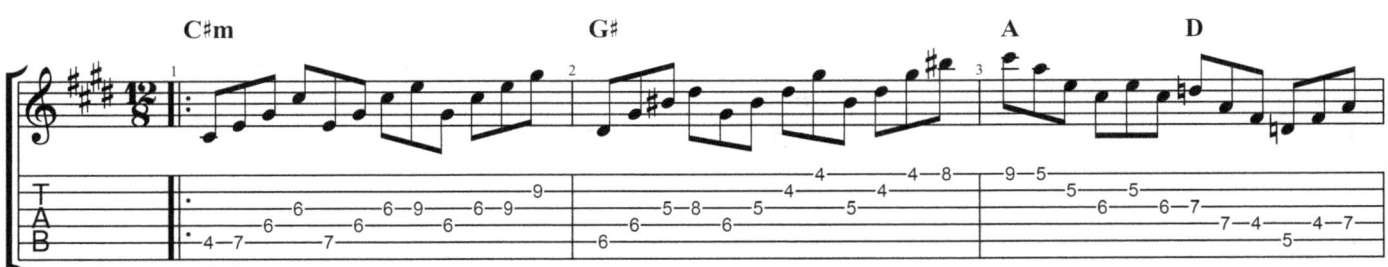

Even though the piece has a triplet feel, we don't have to limit ourselves to three-note groupings. In fact, it can be interesting to play groups of four, creating a rhythmic feel of four-against-three.

Example 4m:

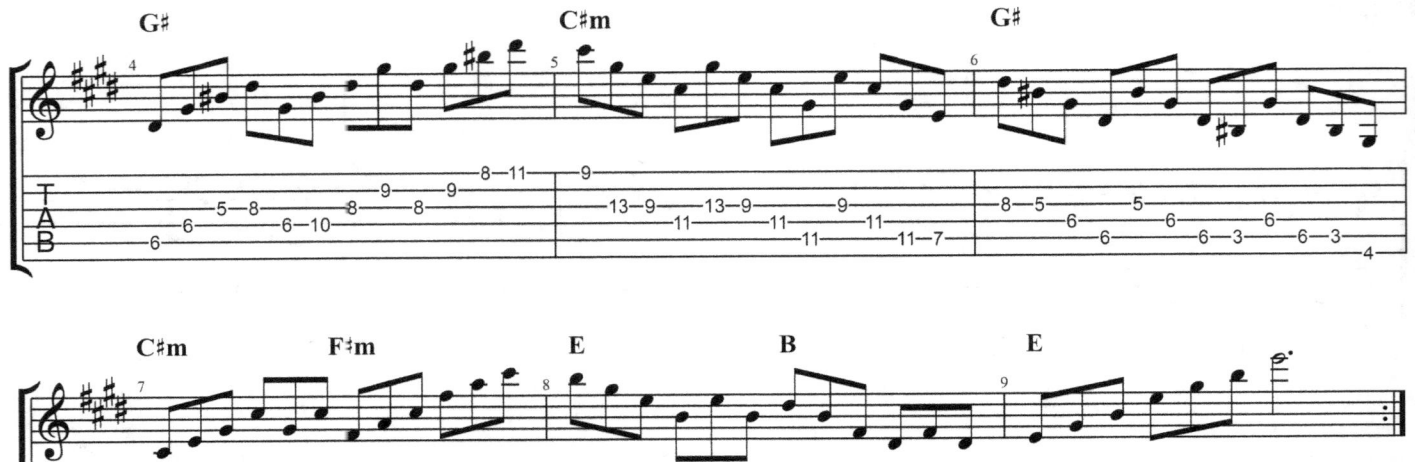

To really stretch our arpeggio muscles, it's fun to play etudes that cover the entire neck while twisting and turning through unexpected positions. These studies require deep fretboard control, and while you can learn etudes like this by heart, your long-term goal is to develop enough fretboard freedom to improvise through chord changes seamlessly. That might seem intimidating, but the concept is simple: when a chord happens, just play the notes in that chord!

Example 4n:

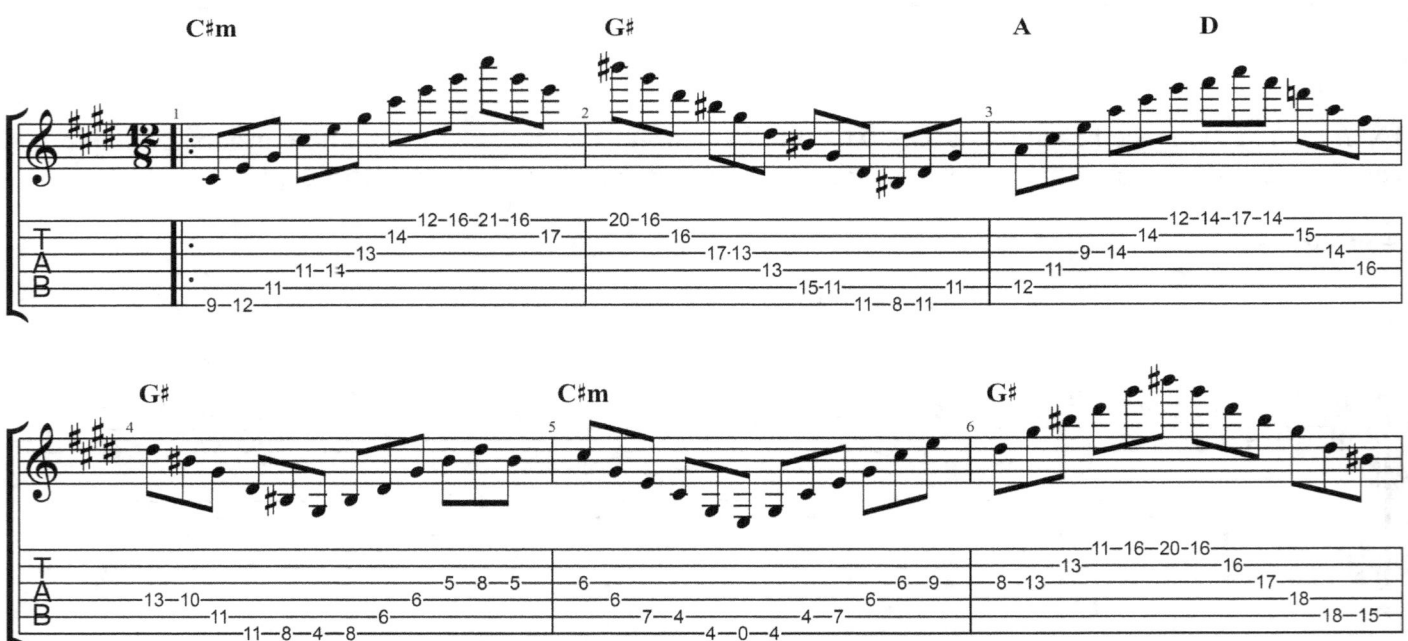

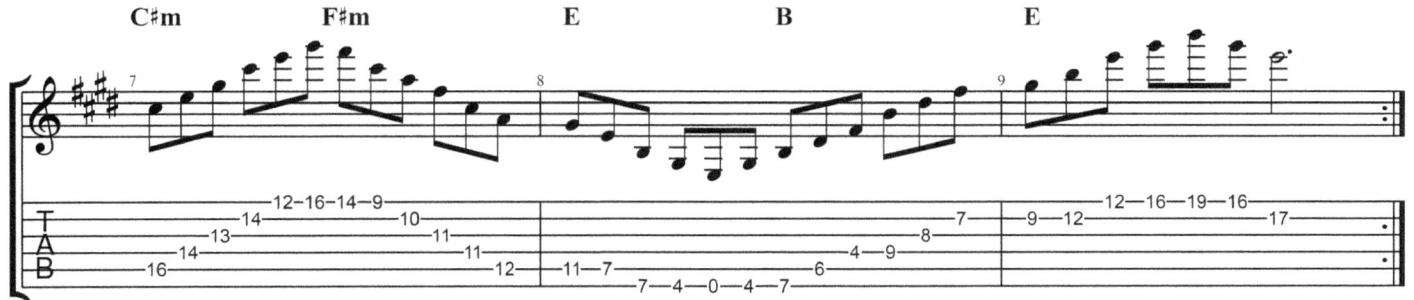

Finally, I wanted to come up with something even more challenging for you. Instead of sticking to stepwise motion with our arpeggios, we'll break them into wider spread, open-voiced triads. These are much harder to navigate because we have to skip strings between each note.

You'll find it difficult to memorise this etude if you haven't spent enough time learning your chord voicings, but these are all open-voiced grips we covered in my guided chord practice book. If you struggle with this, it might be a sign that you need to revisit some of that foundational work. Don't hesitate to go back and reinforce those basics!

Example 4o:

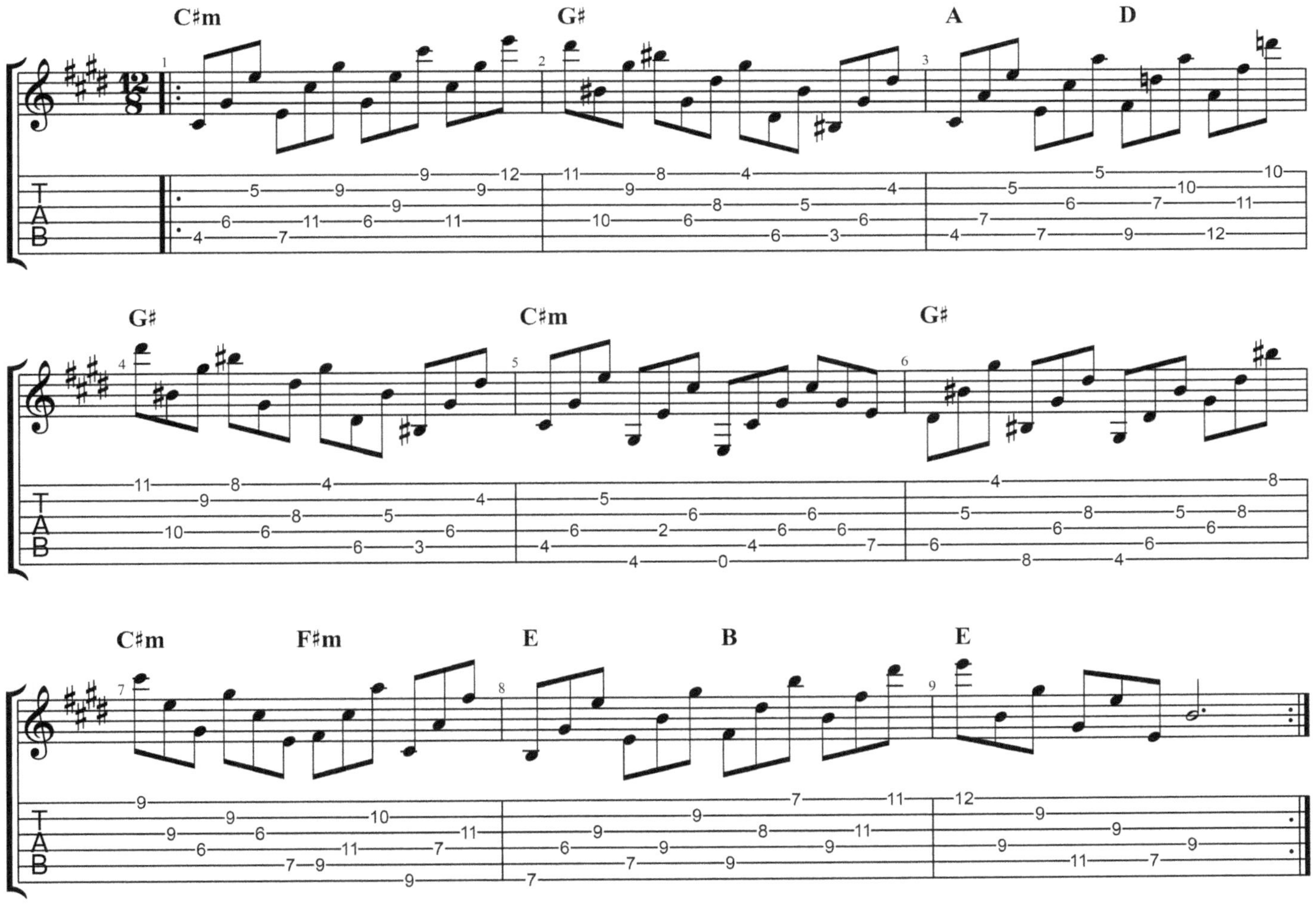

That's plenty of triad work for now. There's much more to arpeggios than just three-note chords, but I wanted you to master these before moving on to the richer, more complex chords in the following chapters.

Routine Five: Diatonic 7th Arpeggios

With our triad workout complete, it's time to get a little jazzier by adding an additional note to turn our triads into 7th chords.

In this routine, we'll build on the triad knowledge we've developed, exploring all the 7th arpeggios we're likely to need, using both vertical and horizontal fingering systems.

Let's start by brushing up on the theory behind 7th chords.

In the key of C, a C major triad consists of the intervals 1 (root), 3 (major 3rd), and 5 (perfect 5th). These notes are chosen by selecting every other note from the major scale (C D E F G A B). I.e., we take the first note (C), skip the second, take the 3rd note (E), skip the 4th, and take the 5th note (G).

If we continue this pattern and add a fourth note, we get the intervals:

1 3 5 7

This forms a Cmaj7 chord.

Major 7 chords are a major triad with an added 7th from the major scale. It's useful to know that the 7th is always located a semitone below the root note.

As we work through this chapter, we'll look at how each type of 7th arpeggio is constructed, but first let's work with the major 7th.

Major 7 Arpeggios

Let's play a Cmaj7 arpeggio based around our triad E shape. Note that there are two options for where we play the 7th interval at the top of the arpeggio: either on the high E string or the B string.

Example 5a:

As you work through the arpeggios in this chapter, focus on where the new note (7th) is located and memorise its position relative to the rest of the arpeggio. Get familiar with the placement of this interval, so that you never forget where it is.

Here are two options for playing a Cmaj7 arpeggio around the A shape.

Example 5b:

For the C shape chord there's only really one practical way to play the Cmaj7 arpeggio.

Example 5c:

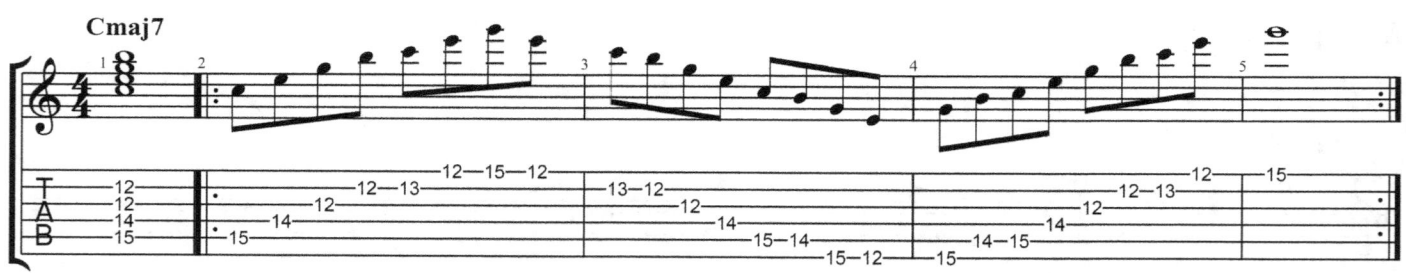

One of the beautiful things about 7th arpeggios is that they lend themselves really well to creating small, two-string motifs that can be moved up and down the neck in octaves. It's a great way to incorporate horizontal movement and position shifts.

Example 5d:

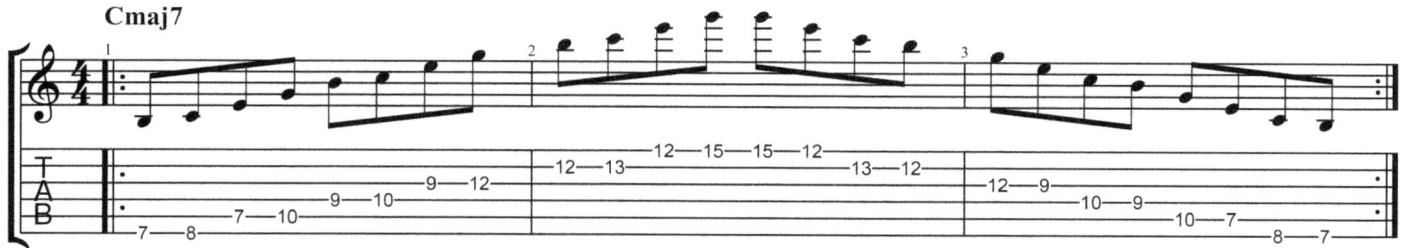

There are lots of two-string patterns that work well when moving in octaves and finding these can quickly help to expand your fretboard knowledge.

Example 5e:

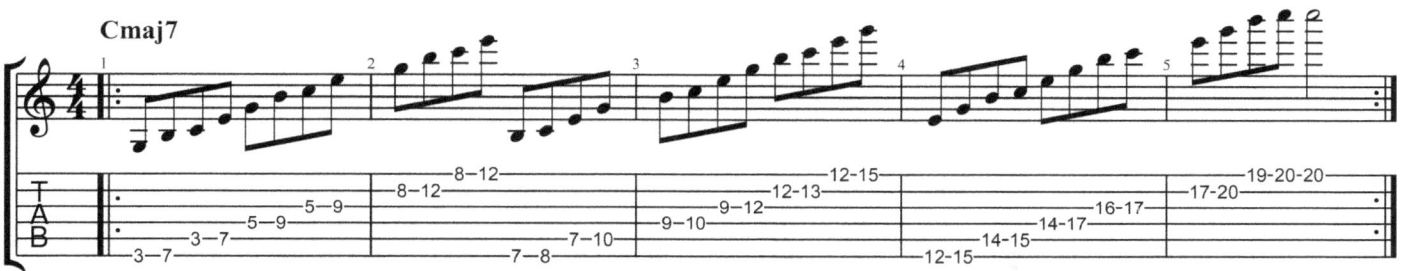

The best way to really get to grips with arpeggios on the fretboard is to come up with some of your own long, flowing etudes that cover the entire neck. As in previous chapters, the aim of such exercises is to work on seeing/hearing the distance from one arpeggio tone to the next. Once you can do this on adjacent strings and with position shifts, you'll be able to do anything!

Here's an example of a flowing Cmaj7 arpeggio etude.

Example 5f:

Here's a similar idea that begins higher up the neck and descends.

Example 5g:

Dominant 7 Arpeggios

If we take a Cmaj7 arpeggio and lower the 7th by a semitone we create the intervals 1 3 5 b7, which is the formula for a C dominant 7 (C7) arpeggio and gives us the notes C E G Bb.

It's useful to know that the b7 is a tone below the root.

Example 5h:

If we apply that formula to our A, E, and C shapes, we create the following arpeggios. When learning these shapes, view them as the major triads you already know, but with an added b7.

Example 5i:

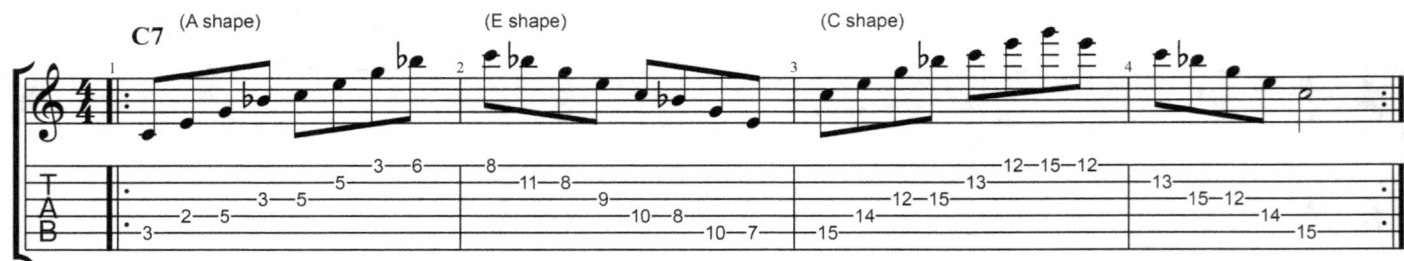

You could also play these arpeggios in each of the five CAGED forms.

Example 5j:

This is the part where things get interesting, because when I use dominant 7 arpeggios to solo over dominant 7 chords, I almost always add a chromatic note to the shape. Chromatic notes are very useful in an arpeggio context, just to add a bit of movement and interest.

A typical thing I do is to add the b3 as a chromatic approach note to the 3rd. This b3 often occurs on a weak part of the bar (an off-beat) and resolves to the 3rd on a stronger beat.

This begs the question: is it still an arpeggio?

Technically, we're adding notes that aren't in the chord, but the idea of using the notes of the arpeggio to outline the chord remains. For me, this chromatic note just helps to make this arpeggio sound more musical.

It's worth noting that this movement always occurs as an ascending idea (i.e., b3 ascending to the 3rd, and never 3rd descending to b3), even when the actual melody descends the arpeggio.

So we would play,

1 b7 5 *b3-3* 1

Not,

1 b7 5 *3-b3* 1.

You can see this in the idea below.

Example 5k:

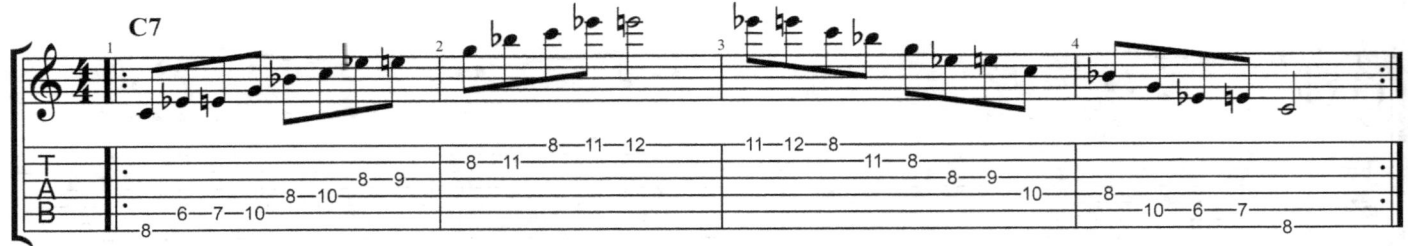

We can actually add several notes and still think of it as an arpeggio, as long as targeting arpeggio notes is the core concept.

The next example begins with a chromatic connection from the 3rd up to 5th, followed by a b3 to 3rd motion, and ends with a phrase that goes 4th, b3, 3rd. While this isn't a pure arpeggio, it's certainly an arpeggio-based idea and definitely not a scale line!

After playing this in the C shape, move it down an octave and play it around the E shape.

Example 5l:

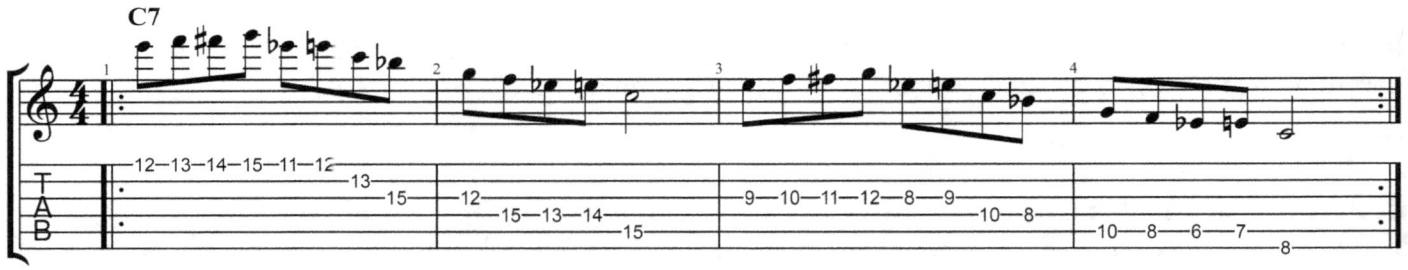

This may all seem like a bit of a detour, but it's been a valuable exercise because it's helped to reinforce the location of the b3 interval, which brings us onto the minor 7 (m7) arpeggio.

Minor 7 arpeggios

If we take a dominant 7 arpeggio (1 3 5 b7) and lower the 3rd, we create the intervals 1 b3 5 b7.

This forms a minor triad with a b7, which is a minor 7 chord. In the key of C that gives us the notes C Eb G Bb.

Here's how that looks around the E shape.

Example 5m:

Once you know the intervals that make up the arpeggio, you can easily apply them to our three basic A, E, and C chord forms.

Example 5n:

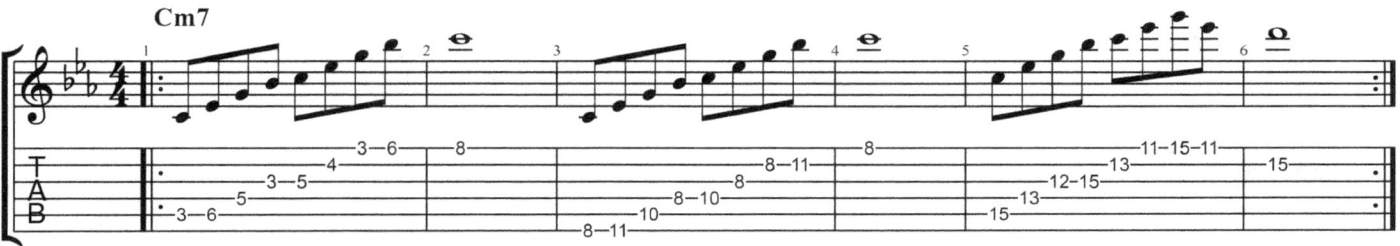

A great exercise to reinforce your knowledge of an arpeggio is to apply a pattern of ascending and descending "fours", where we ascend four notes of the arpeggio, jump back down to the second note we played, and repeat this pattern as we gradually ascend.

This exercise is not just musical, it quickly helps you to identify any technical issues you have with fingering the arpeggios in each position.

Here's the ascending and descending fours pattern around the E shape. Once you've mastered it here, apply it to the other three positions of every arpeggio type in this chapter.

Example 5o:

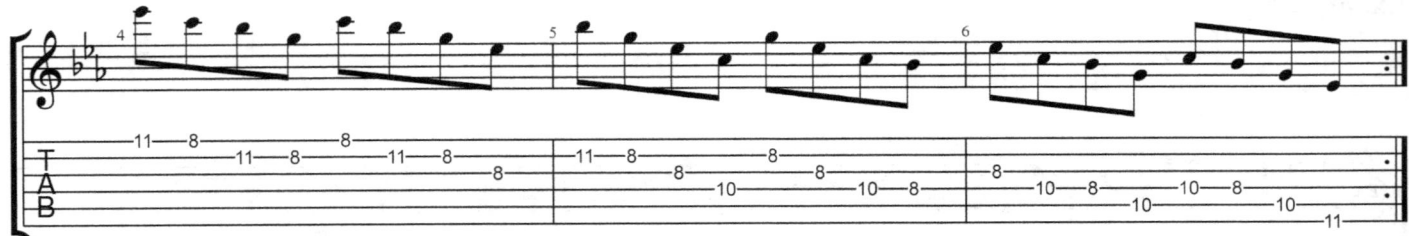

Another fantastic way to break up a position is by playing a note-skipping idea. Play the first note of the arpeggio, skip the second, and jump to the third note. Now return to the note you skipped and repeat the process.

Again, ideas like this will immediately bring up technical issues for you to overcome. Apply this pattern to every arpeggio voicing in this chapter.

Example 5p:

m7b5 arpeggios

The final arpeggio we'll cover is the minor 7b5. This could be considered the ugly stepsister of our diatonic arpeggios, but while it may feel awkward at first, it has many great uses.

To create it we take a minor 7 arpeggio (1 b3 5 b7) and lower the 5th to build an arpeggio that has the intervals 1 b3 b5 b7.

This arpeggio exists naturally in the major scale and is formed when we harmonise the 7th degree.

Here's it is played around the E shape.

Example 5q:

Now let's play it around the A, E, and C shapes.

Example 5r:

It may feel like we've rushed through these arpeggio types, but we're just laying foundations here. We'll be getting into them in much more detail over the coming weeks as we look at how to apply them.

For now, practice these arpeggio patterns in different keys. Once you're comfortable, try the sequencing ideas you learned above and try to create your own pathways from the bottom to the top of the neck.

Don't rush the process, as familiarity with these patterns will allow you to apply them musically to chord progressions when soloing. Put in the time, and you'll see the results!

Routine Six: 7th Chord Progression Workouts

There's no better way to work on your arpeggio skills than by applying them to real music. I grew up listening to heavy metal and later got into country, and the truth is, there aren't that many 7th chords found in those genres. So, to practice your fluency, you might need to step outside your usual listening habits.

Jazz is the perfect place to go for this. Now, I know what you're thinking, "Jazz?! Eww!" But don't worry, I'm not talking about smoky clubs and abstract jazz, where the only people listening are other musicians with their arms folded. I mean the *old* jazz standards, often referred to as the Great American Songbook.

These were the popular songs of their day, often sung by iconic artists like Nat King Cole, Bing Crosby, Tony Bennett, Dean Martin, or Chet Baker. Songs like *Fly Me to the Moon*, *The Way You Look Tonight* and *Summertime* are still loved today because they have beautiful melodies and interesting harmonies.

The main way I work on my arpeggios today is by opening an app like iReal Pro and picking one of the thousands of jazz standard chord charts. Then, I will arpeggiate my way through it. The best approach is to listen to the song you're going to work on first, so that your ear can connect with the harmony and you have an idea of the sound you're aiming for, then work through it.

In my guided chord routine book, I used the progression to *All of Me* as a reference. Let's start with that tune, since you might already be familiar with it. However, you can (and should) take all these exercises and apply them to as many songs as possible.

Start by arpeggiating each chord, beginning from the root note on the E or A string.

Example 6a:

Once you feel you're getting to grips with this, move on to ascending one arpeggio and descending the next. I'm sticking to 1/4 notes here to keep things simple and not overload our brains.

Example 6b:

In the previous example, we changed arpeggio at the top or bottom of each pattern, which is easier to do, but sticking to that approach won't give us the freedom we're looking for – we need to challenge ourselves. So, now we'll move to 1/8th notes and change arpeggios mid-pattern, on whatever string we happen to be playing when the chord changes.

Example 6c:

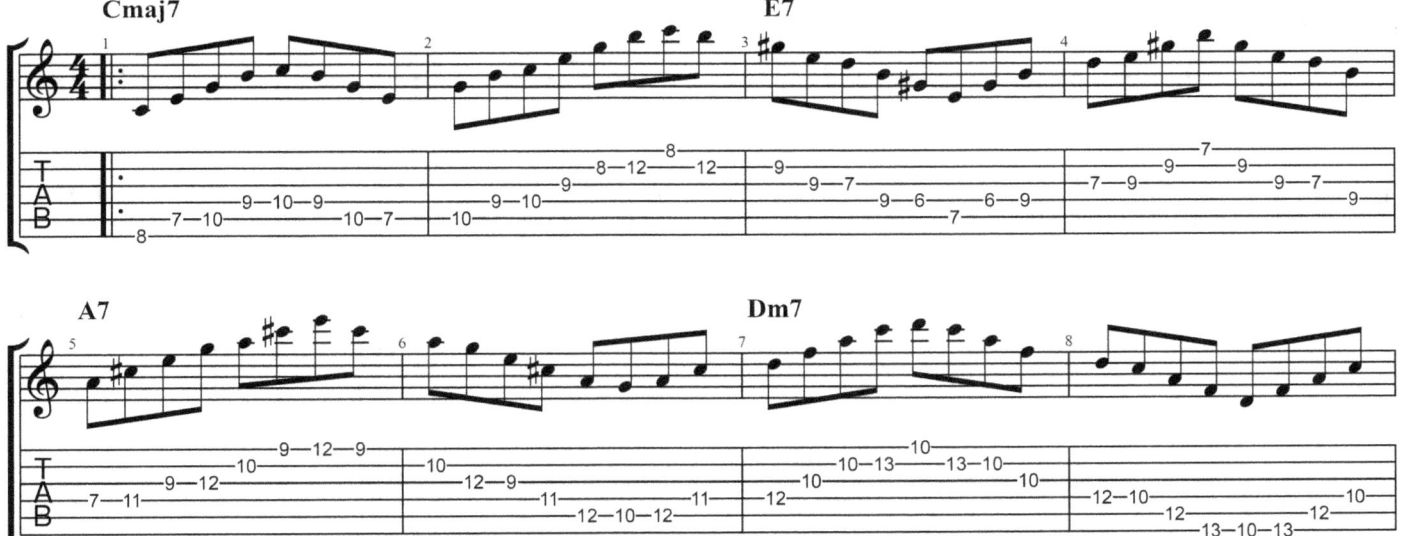

Another way to push yourself is by adding a limitation. For example, playing the arpeggios on only the top three strings will force you to visualise the fretboard differently.

Example 6d:

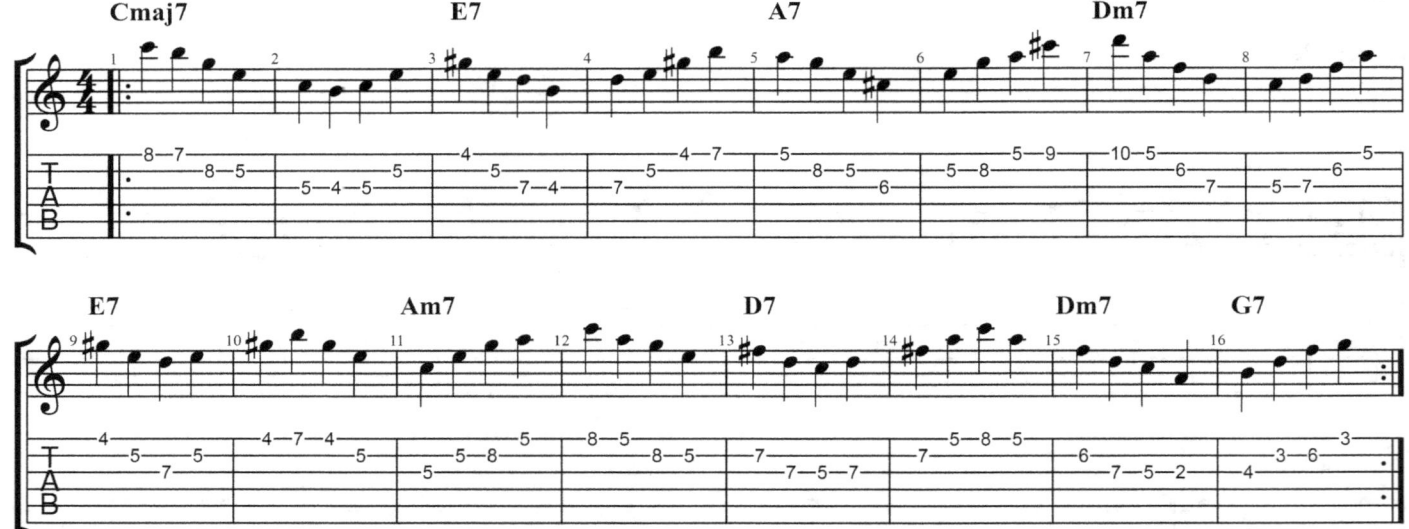

Now let's switch to the Jerome Kern standard *All the Things You Are*. I like this one because the chord changes happen more frequently (almost every bar), and it covers all four basic chord qualities.

As before, the first step should be listening to some recordings of the song to get familiar with how it sounds. Then, review the chord symbols to understand the harmony. Just like *All of Me*, we'll start by arpeggiating each chord in an ascending pattern.

Example 6e:

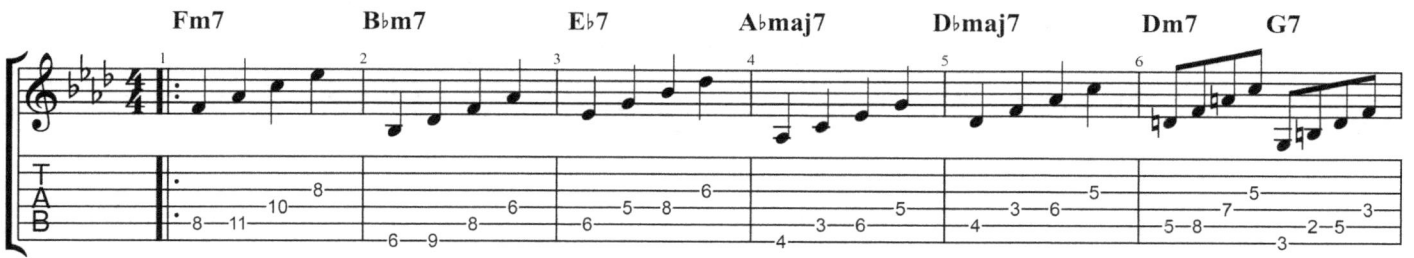
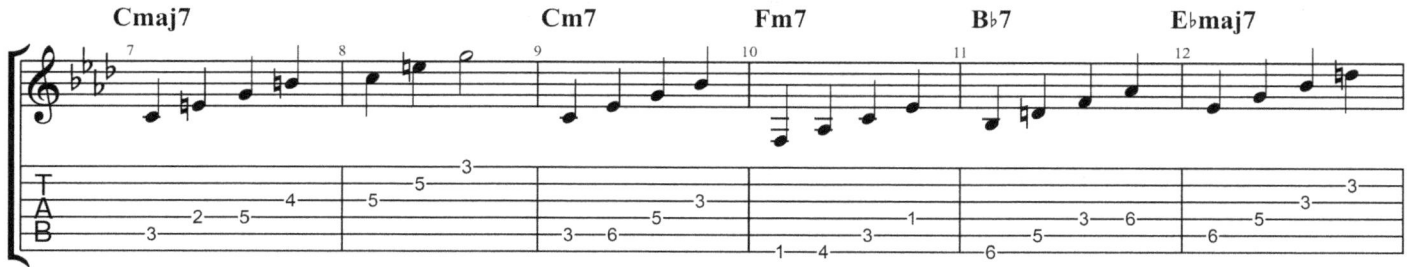
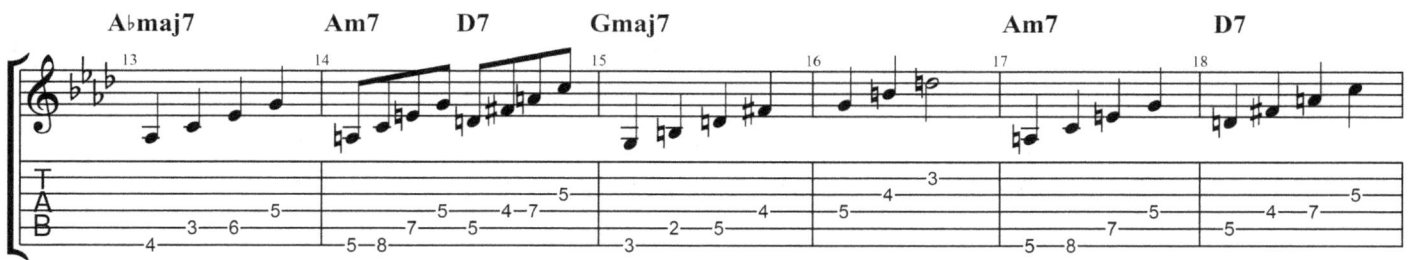
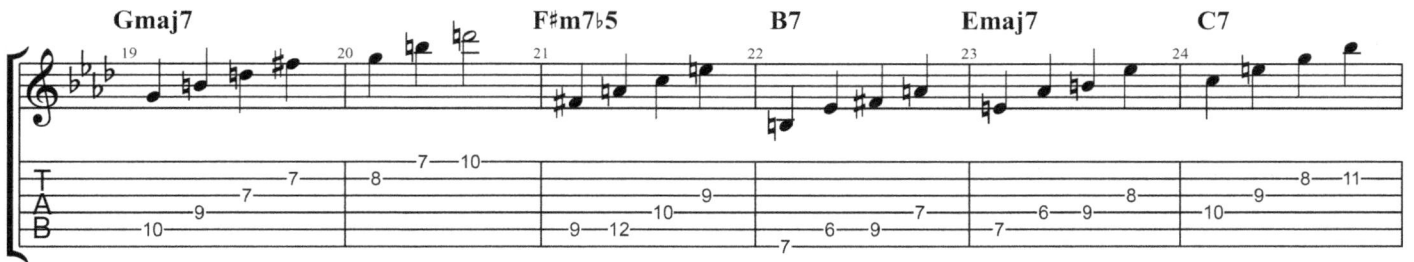
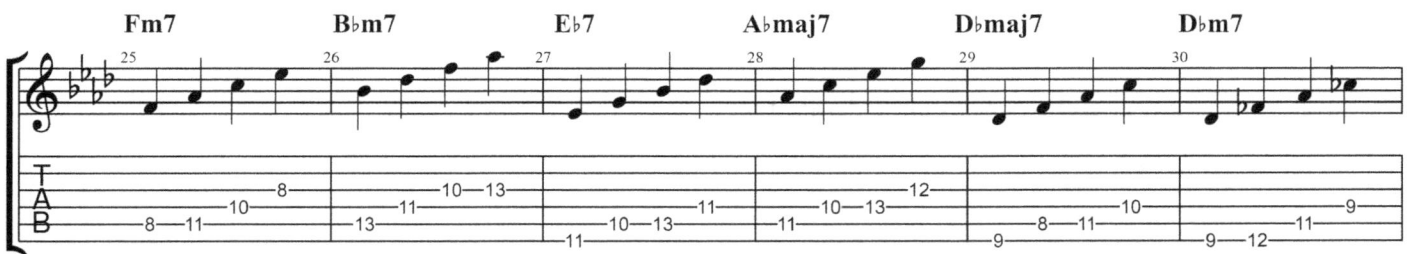

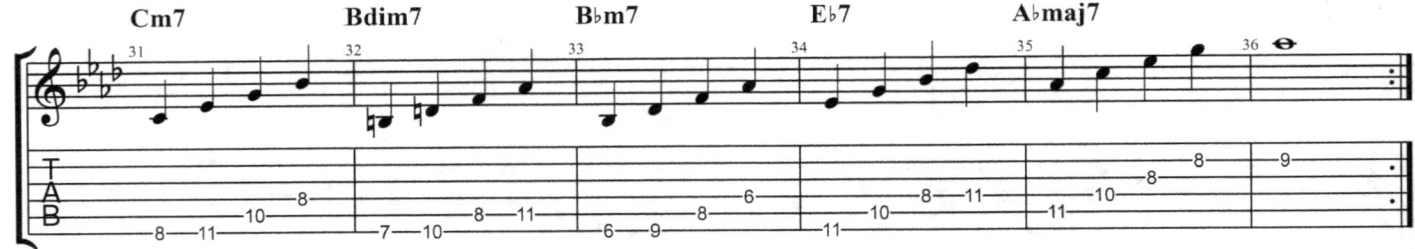

That's a lot of chords to remember! The task can be made much easier if we break the progression down into manageable eight-bar chunks and look for patterns that we recognise, so there's less to think about while we're playing.

Think back to the Circle of Fifths pattern we discussed and you'll spot some clear patterns here.

Starting on F and moving around the circle, we get:

F Bb Eb Ab Db

These are the first five chords of the progression!

Then there is a Dm7 chord. Moving from there we have D G C – another three consecutive notes on the Circle of Fifths.

When looking at chord charts like this, dominant chords can help us to identify the key, since each key has only one dominant chord. The Eb7 in bar three tells us we're in Ab Major. So, the first five chords form the sequence:

vi – ii – V – I – IV

Or,

Fm7 – Bbm7 – Eb7 – AbMaj7 – DbMaj7

Then, we modulate to C Major and play:

ii – V – I

Or,

Dm7 – G7 – Cmaj7

Let's play through this eight-bar chunk in 1/8th notes.

Example 6f:

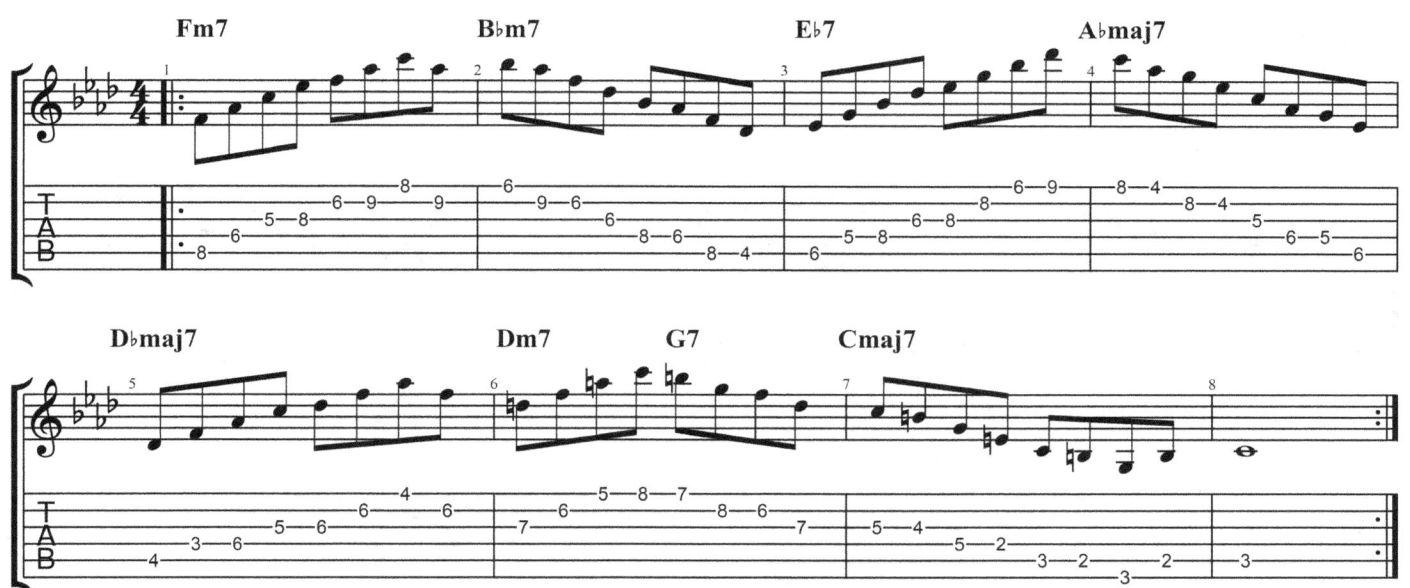

We should aim to be able to play this anywhere on the neck.

Example 6g:

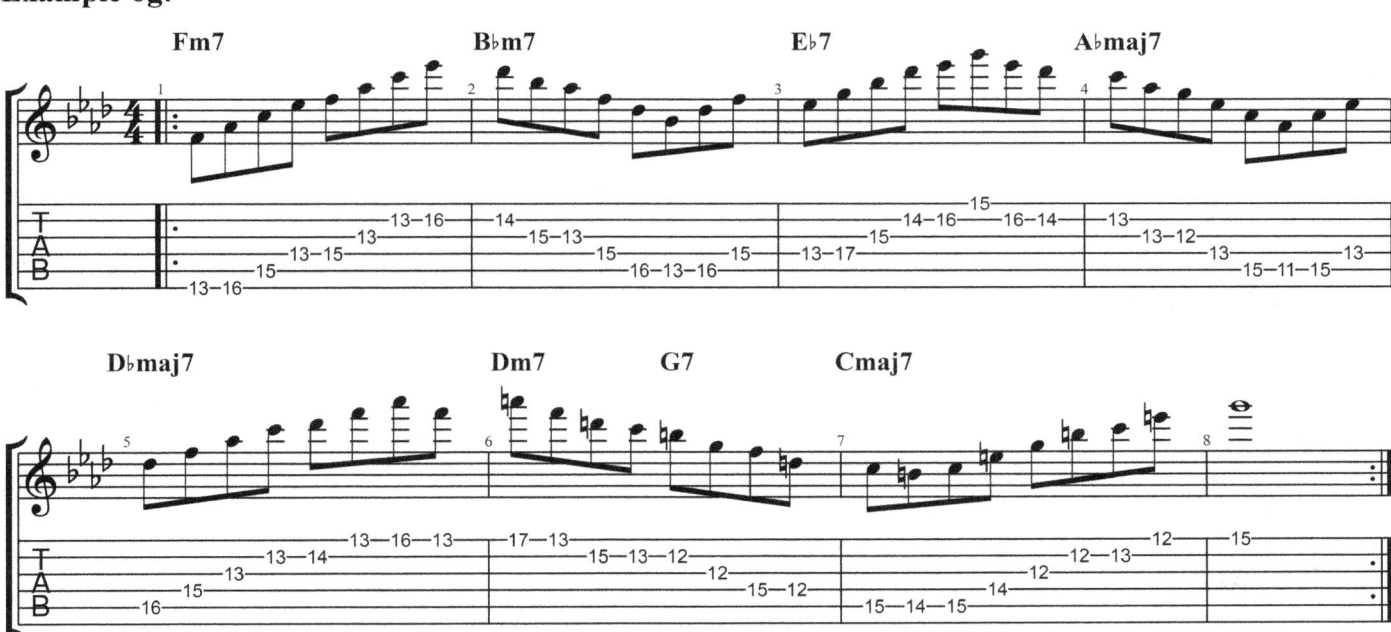

The next eight bars of the tune are actually just a repeat of the previous eight bars but played a 4th higher. Without looking at the chords, we can simply follow the Circle of Fifths:

Cm7 – Fm7 – Bb7 – EbMaj7 – AbMaj7

Then, we move up a semitone and play another ii – V – I, this time in G Major:

Am7 – D7 – Gmaj7

Example 6h:

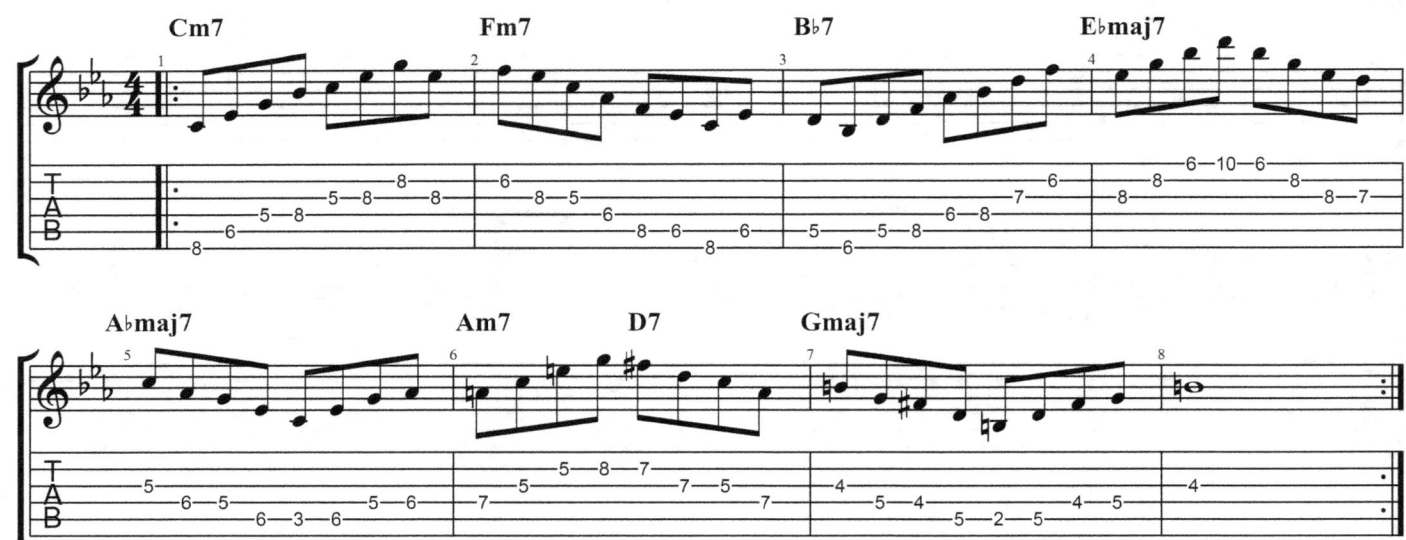

Here's another run through those arpeggios, this time higher up the neck.

Example 6i:

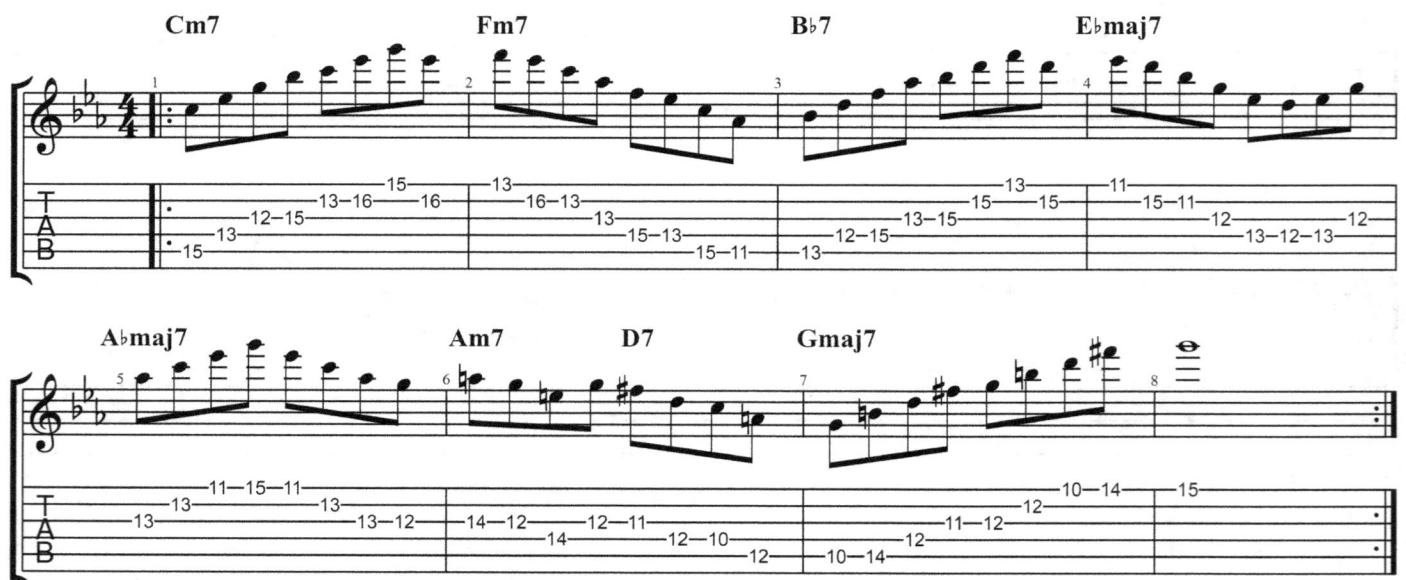

The next eight bars contain two ii – V – I progressions, one in G and one in E:

Am7 – D7 – Gmaj7

Then,

F#m7b5 – B7 – Emaj7

Notice that the second ii – V – I starts with a m7b5 ii chord, but resolves to a *major* rather than a minor chord, which creates an unexpected but pleasant variation in the song.

The section ends with a C7, which sets up the Fm7 in the next bar.

Example 6j:

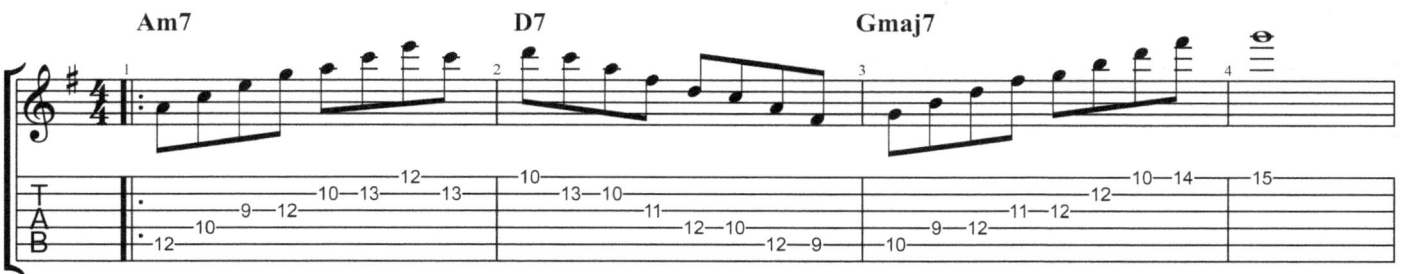
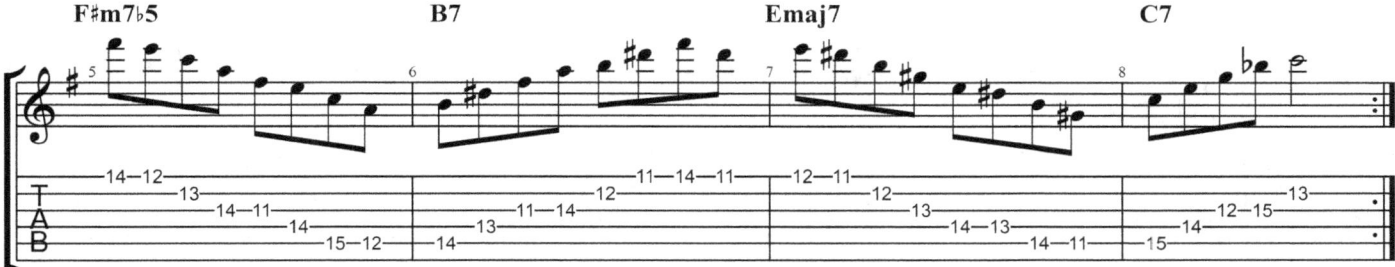

Being able to arpeggiate through ii – V – I progressions like this is incredibly beneficial. It will do wonders for both your fretboard knowledge and your ear as you internalise what it sounds like to navigate functional harmony.

Example 6k:

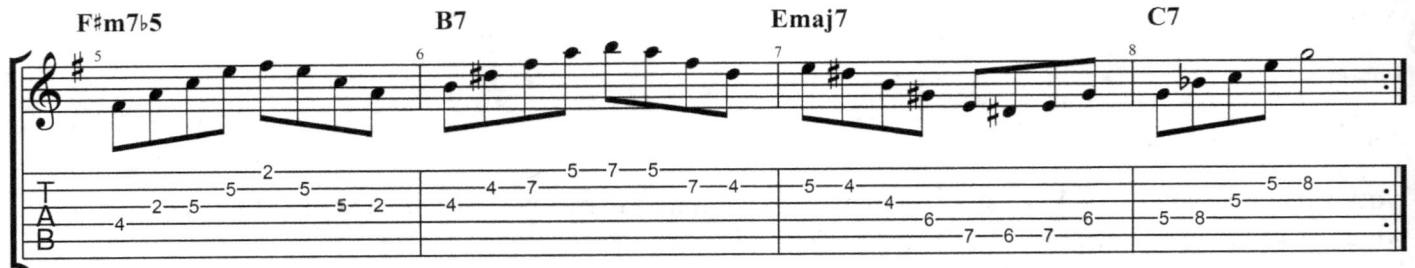

The final section mirrors the first, but with a little diversion when we arrive at Dbmaj7. From there, the chord quality shifts to a minor 7, followed by a chromatic descent to Bbm7 (the ii of the key) and resolves home to the I chord via the V chord, another ii – V – I sequence. So, that is:

Fm7 – Bbm7 – Eb7 – AbMaj7 – DbMaj7 – Dbm7 – Cm7 – Bdim7 – Bbm7 – Eb7 – AbMaj7

Let's arpeggiate through that.

Example 6l:

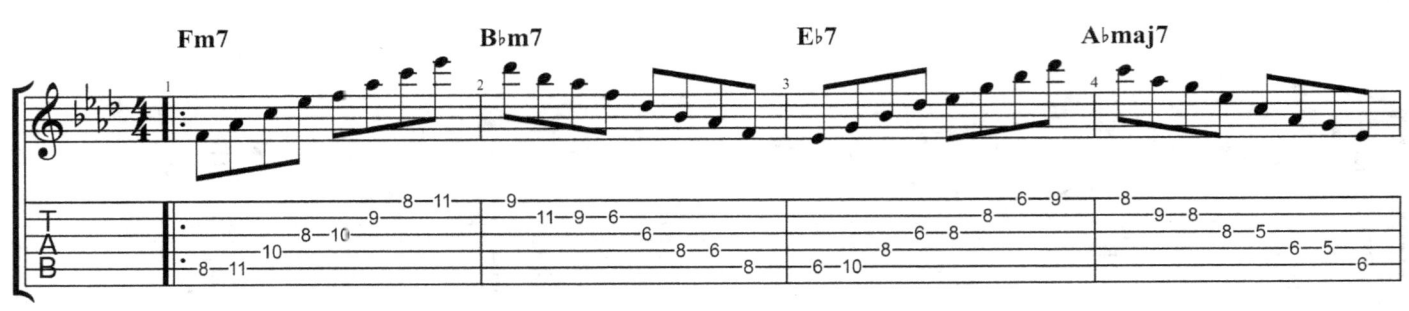

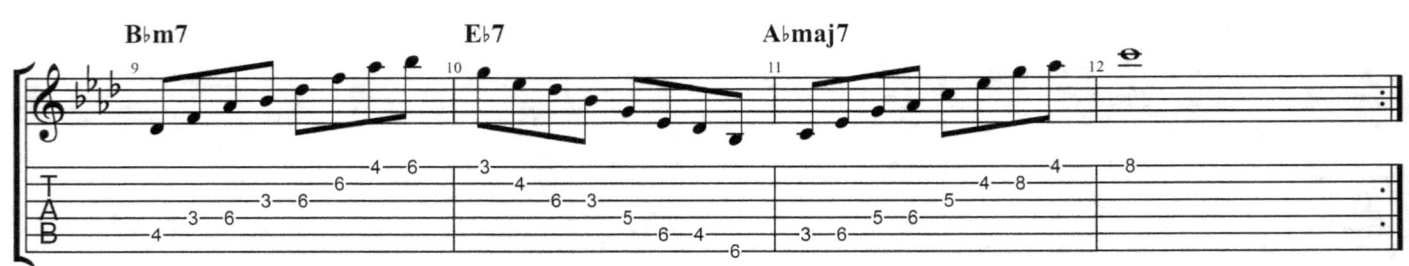

So far, we've played everything as long runs of 1/8th notes. While that is a great challenge for the mind, it's not the most rewarding exercise for the ear, so let's take the final ii – V – I and add some rhythmic variety to make it more musical.

Simple syncopation can transform these arpeggios into something much more expressive.

Example 6m:

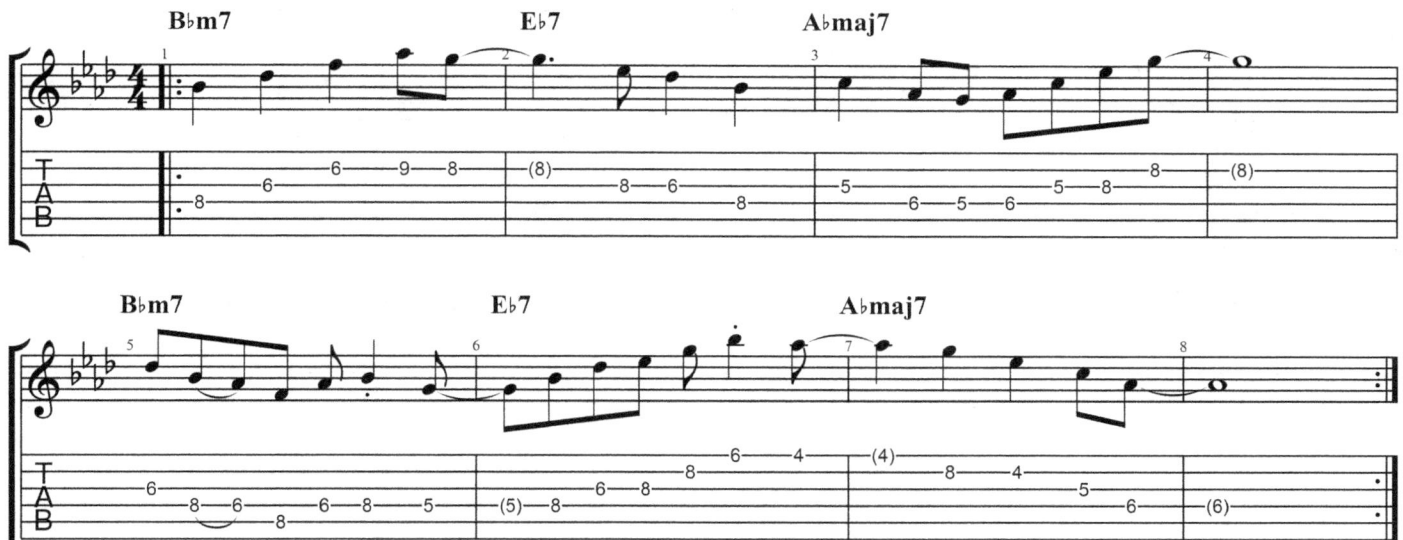

Here's another example in a higher position on the neck.

Example 6n:

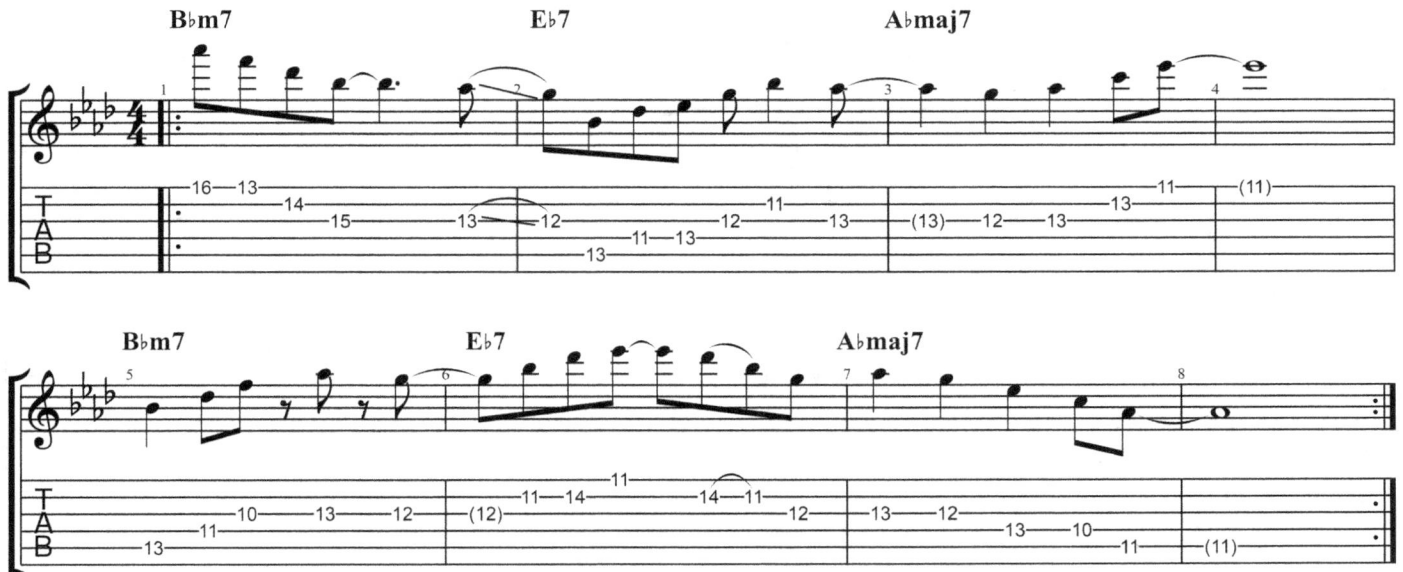

To finish up this routine, I'll improvise through the entire progression, playing only notes from the arpeggios and breaking them up with rhythmic variations.

Example 60:

Of course, we're still only scratching the surface of what's possible. We haven't even started adding in notes outside of the arpeggios! While it might be tempting to rush ahead, spending time mastering the basic four-note arpeggios, and figuring out as many ways as possible to lay them out on the neck, will feel like a superpower when we begin incorporating more advanced ideas later.

I've said it before and I'll say it again, we're building on solid foundations here, not quicksand, so, get to work!

Routine Seven: Chord Scale Arpeggios

Until now, we've only played arpeggios that match the chord we're playing. For example, if the chord is Cmaj7, we've played a Cmaj7 arpeggio. But this isn't the only way to approach arpeggios. In fact, we can play other arpeggios that are built from the notes of the parent scale that the chord belongs to.

This approach requires both a strong knowledge of the chords that belong to a key and solid fretboard visualisation.

First, we're going to learn how to move between all the arpeggios and triads that can be built on each note of a scale as the chords change, but later we'll learn how we can play these ideas over different chords to create rich solos that contain *extensions* on the original chord.

Let's start by refreshing our memory of the diatonic chords in a key. In the key of C Major, the chords are:

Cmaj7 – Dm7 – Em7 – Fmaj7 – G7 – Am7 – Bm7b5

The pattern of chord *qualities* (major 7 and minor 7 etc) is consistent in any major key:

- Chords 1 and 4 are always major 7
- Chord 5 is always dominant 7
- Chords 2, 3, and 6 are always minor 7
- Chord 7 is always minor 7b5

Let's play these diatonic arpeggios consecutively in the A shape.

Example 7a:

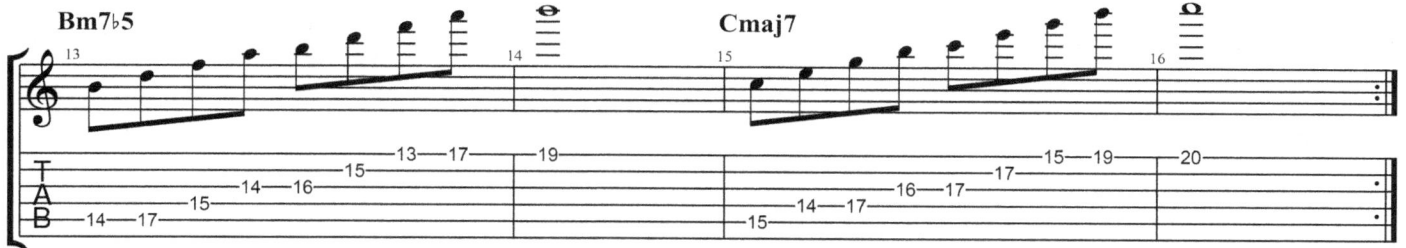

If we move to the key of G Major, we can apply the same formula to the notes in the G Major scale:

Gmaj7 – Am7 – Bm7 – Cmaj7 – D7 – Em7 – F#m7b5

Let's play these arpeggios in the E shape.

Example 7b:

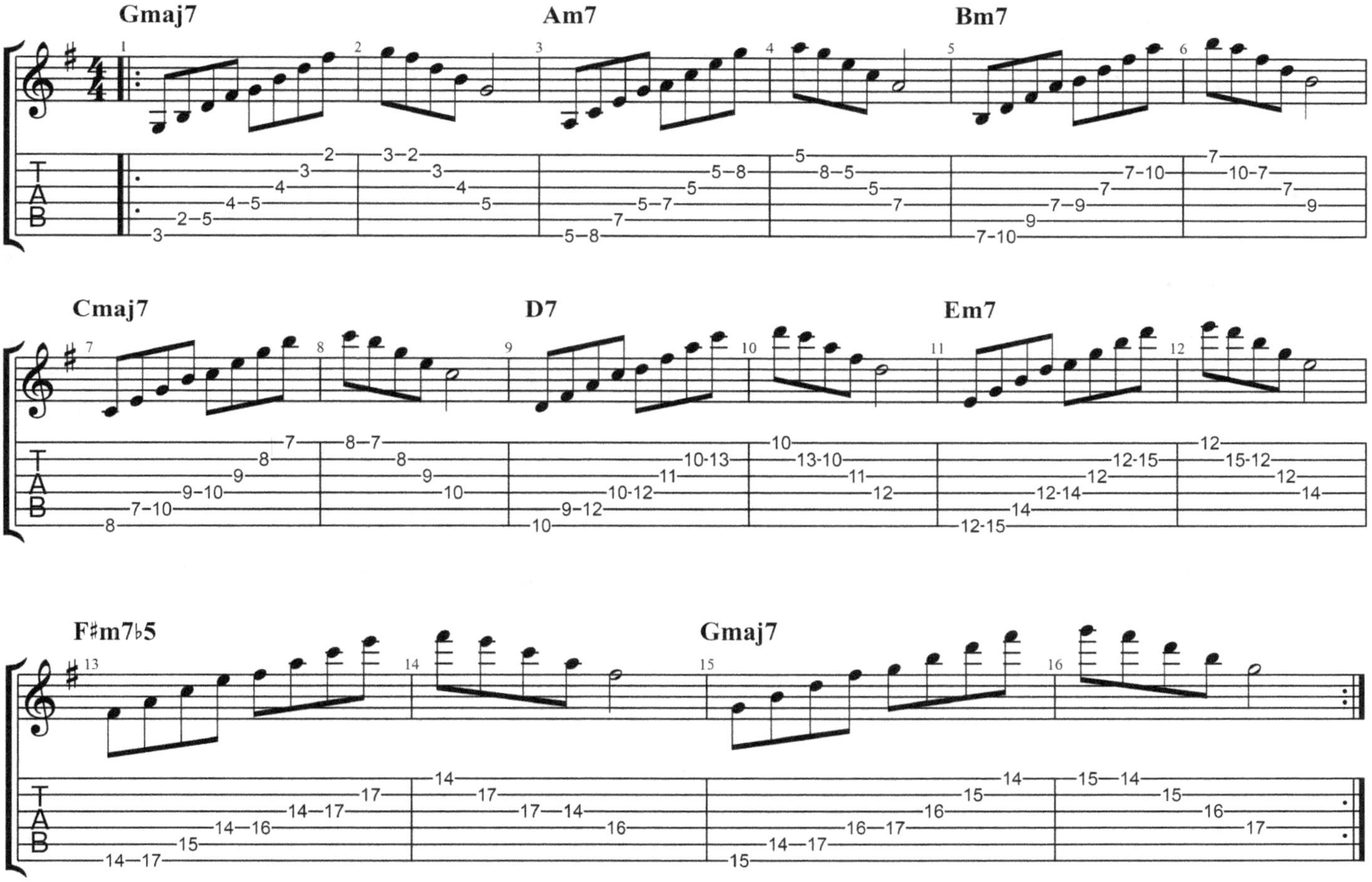

Now, let's jump back to the key of C and stay in the E shape. This time we'll ascend through each of the diatonic arpeggios but stay in position. This exercise will teach you to build arpeggios from any finger on any string.

When I do this, I like to say the name of the arpeggio I'm moving to. Try it – it connects the name of the arpeggio with its fingering pattern, making the process more about visualisation than memorising a long string of notes.

Example 7c:

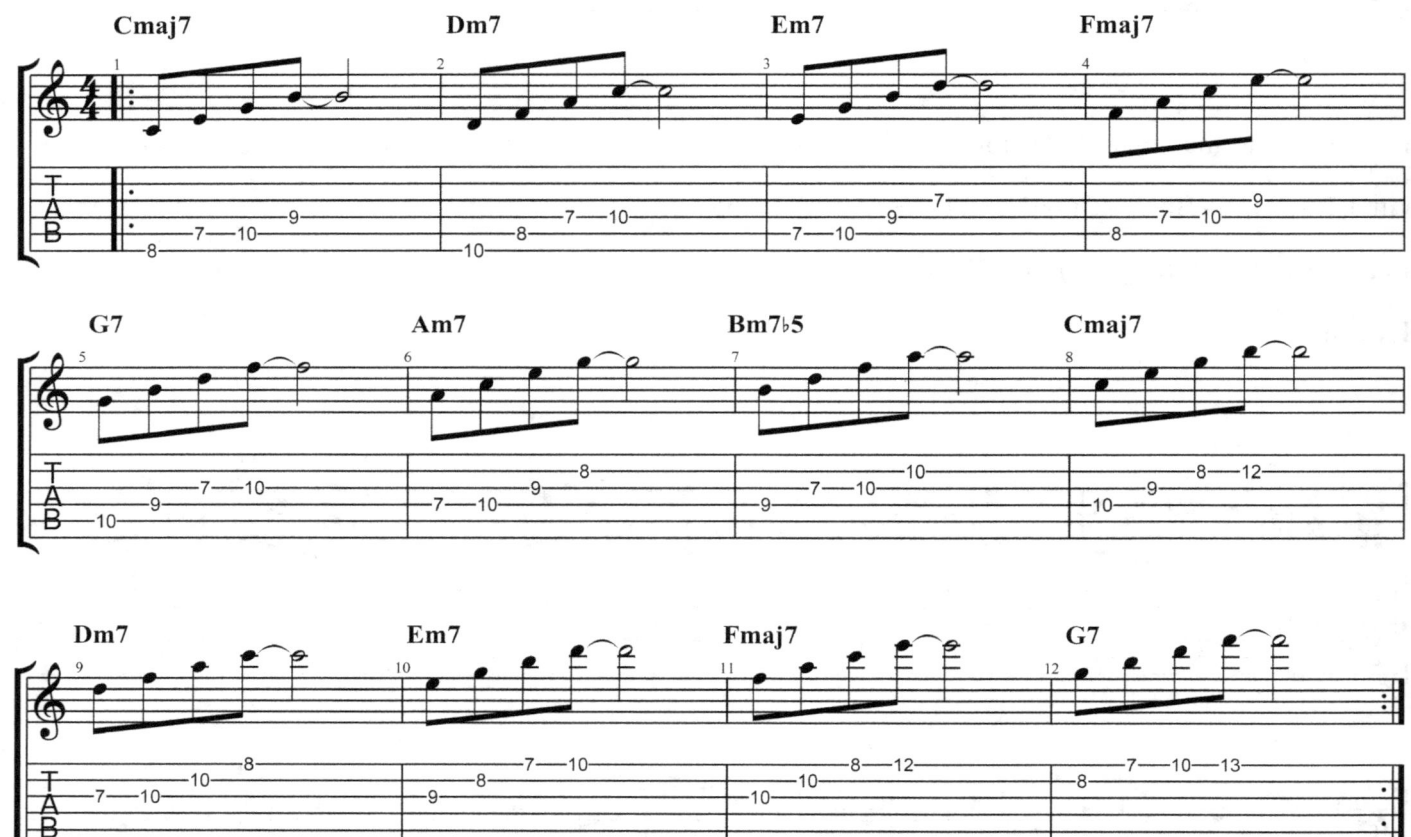

In the previous example, I made things easier by allowing you two beats of rest between each chord change. Let's now remove those rests and connect all the arpeggios as one continuous stream of 1/8th notes so it sounds a bit more fluent.

Example 7d:

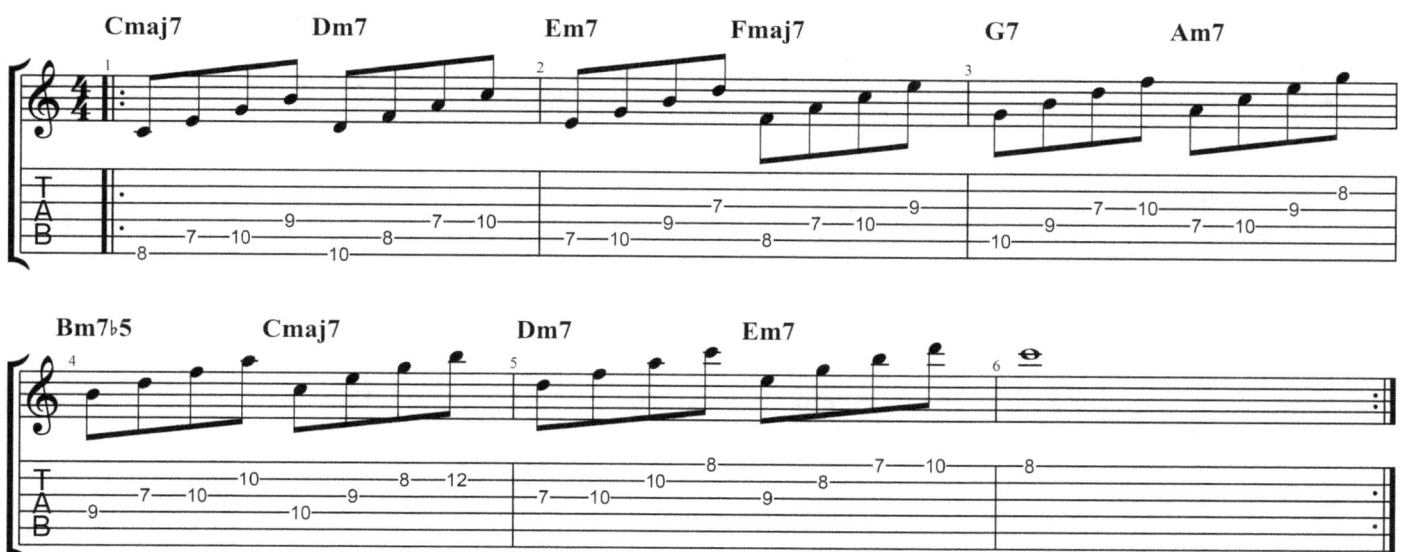

Another approach is to ascend one arpeggio and descend the next. Try this descending from the top strings too.

Example 7e:

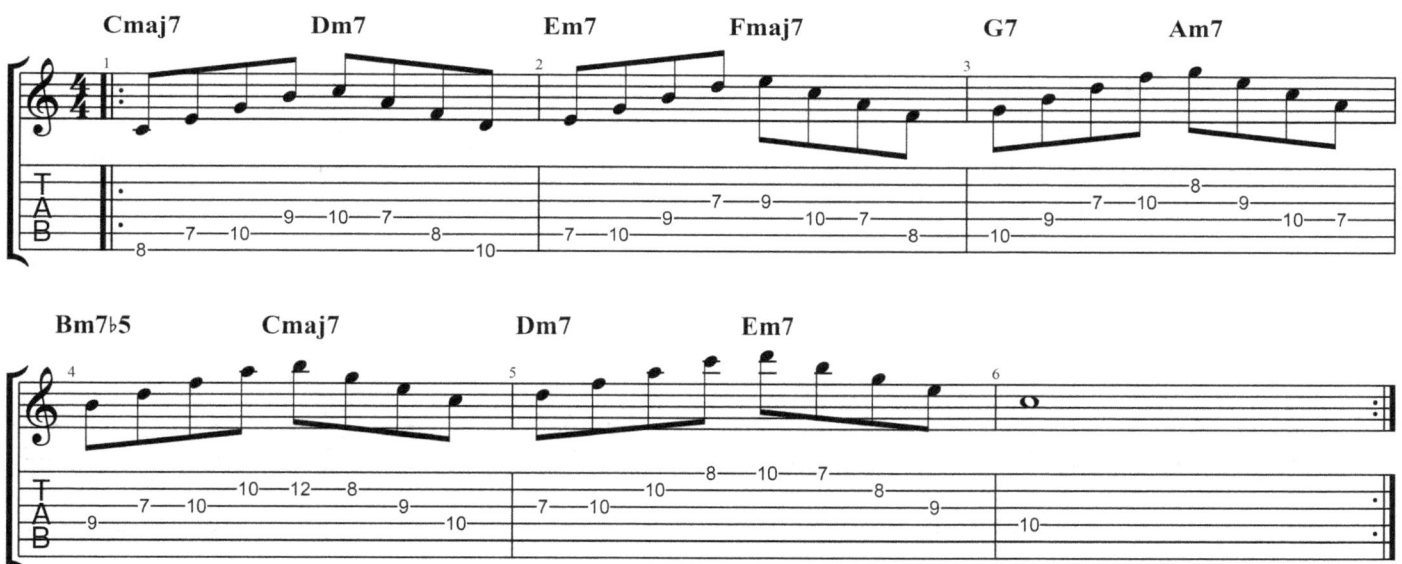

This is something you should be able to do in any position on the neck. Let's play our ascending arpeggios in the A shape.

Example 7f:

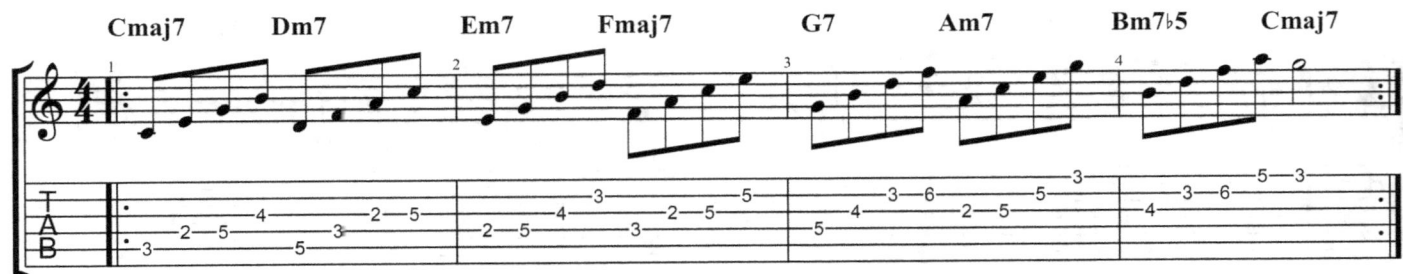

Or try playing them around the C shape. Again, figure out how to begin from different strings and ascend or descend from wherever you start. This can form hours of musical practice.

Example 7g:

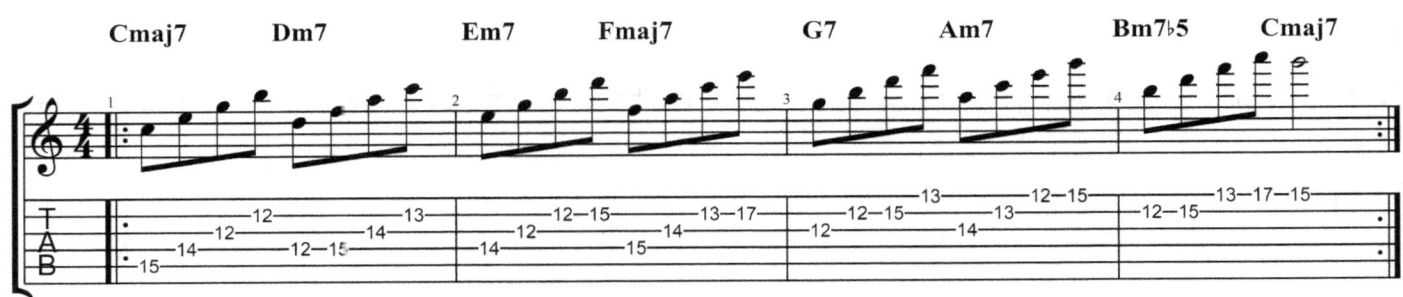

We don't have to limit ourselves to 7th arpeggios as triads work just as well! If we go back to the E shape and play a mix of ascending and descending triads, it looks like this. Notice how the rhythm of two 1/8th notes followed by a 1/4 note places each triad into its own two-beat phrase.

Example 7h:

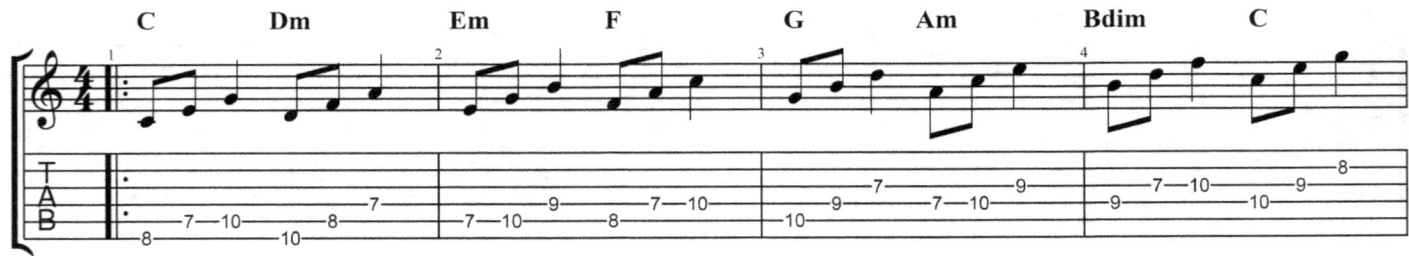

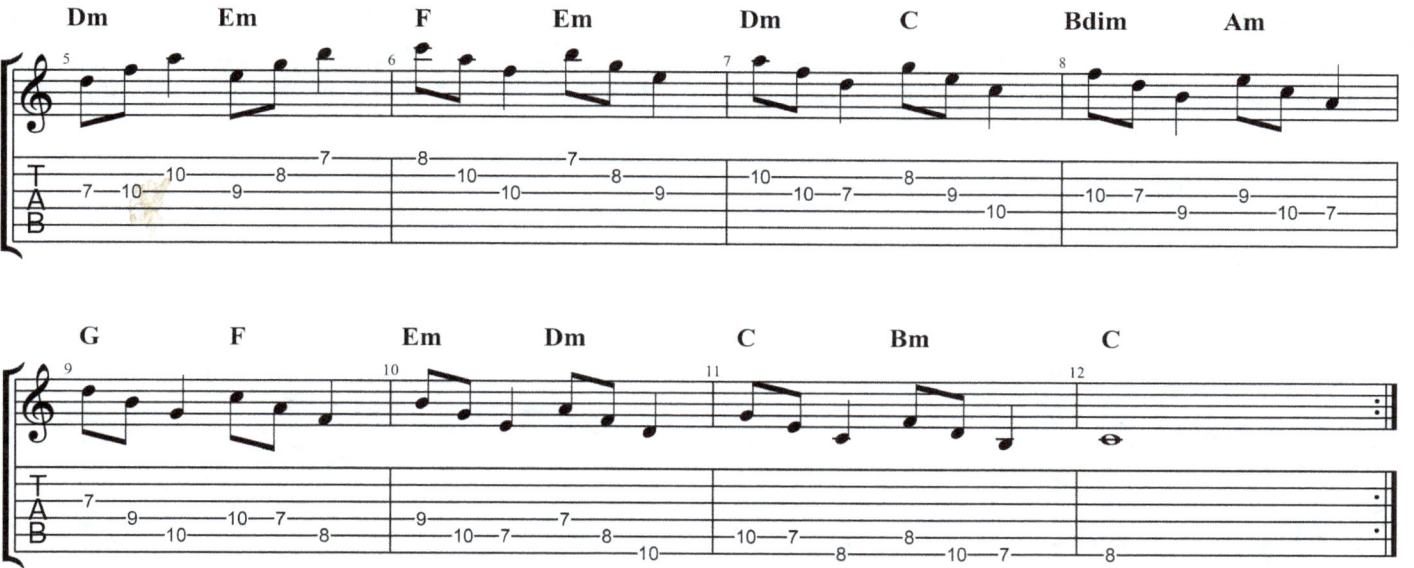

If we play this series as straight 1/8th notes, we create an interesting three-against-four feel.

Example 7i:

So, here's an interesting question… Are we playing arpeggios, triads, or scales? Well, we're playing triad arpeggios but we're also playing all seven notes of the major scale.

Remember that the goal of this book is ultimately to blur the lines between chords, scales and arpeggios, allowing for complete freedom in your playing. So, while I'm thinking of all these examples as arpeggiated ideas, since I'm focusing on triads, they could easily be viewed as scale patterns too. Neither is wrong.

We can push this concept even further by adding a chromatic approach note leading into each triad. In the next example, the chromatic approach notes are shown in brackets.

Example 7j:

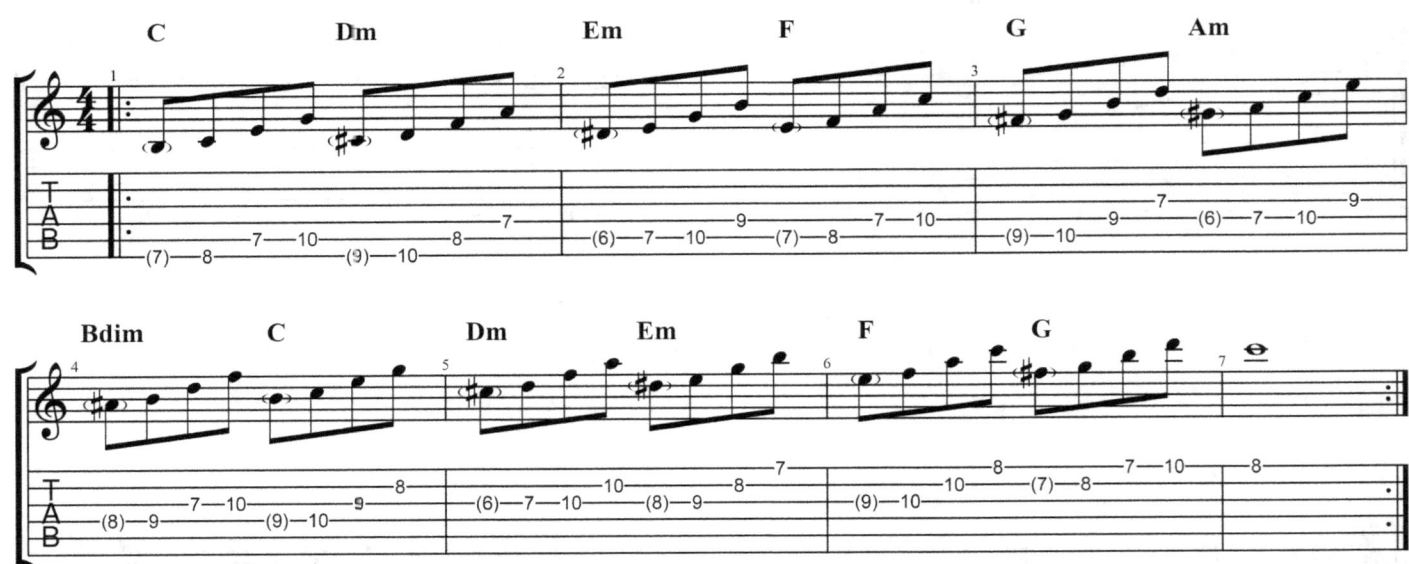

When descending, we still add a chromatic approach below the first note of each triad. You can also slide when you need to shift position with the index finger. For example, when targeting the 7th fret on the D string, you can slide up from the 6th fret with the index finger.

Example 7k:

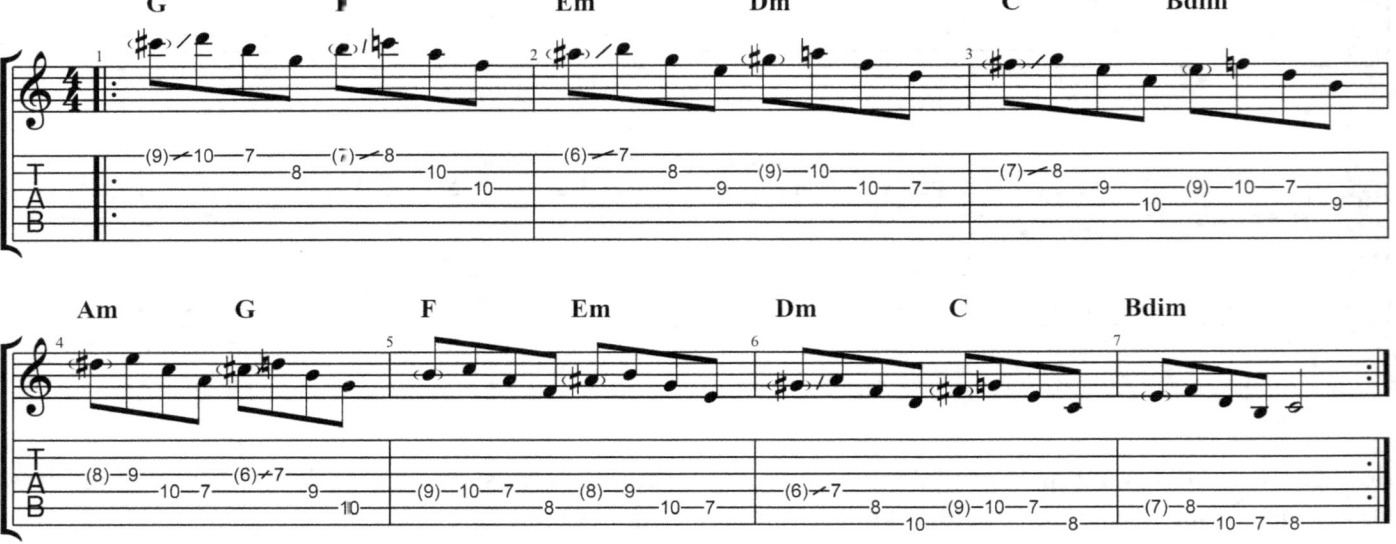

Here's an example of ascending and descending triads around the A shape with added chromatic approach notes.

Example 7l:

Now, let's add chromatic approach notes to 7th arpeggios. A common method is to place the chromatic note right before the beat, sliding up into the arpeggio, then ascending with a triplet feel. Here's how that sounds with the diatonic chords of C Major.

Example 7m:

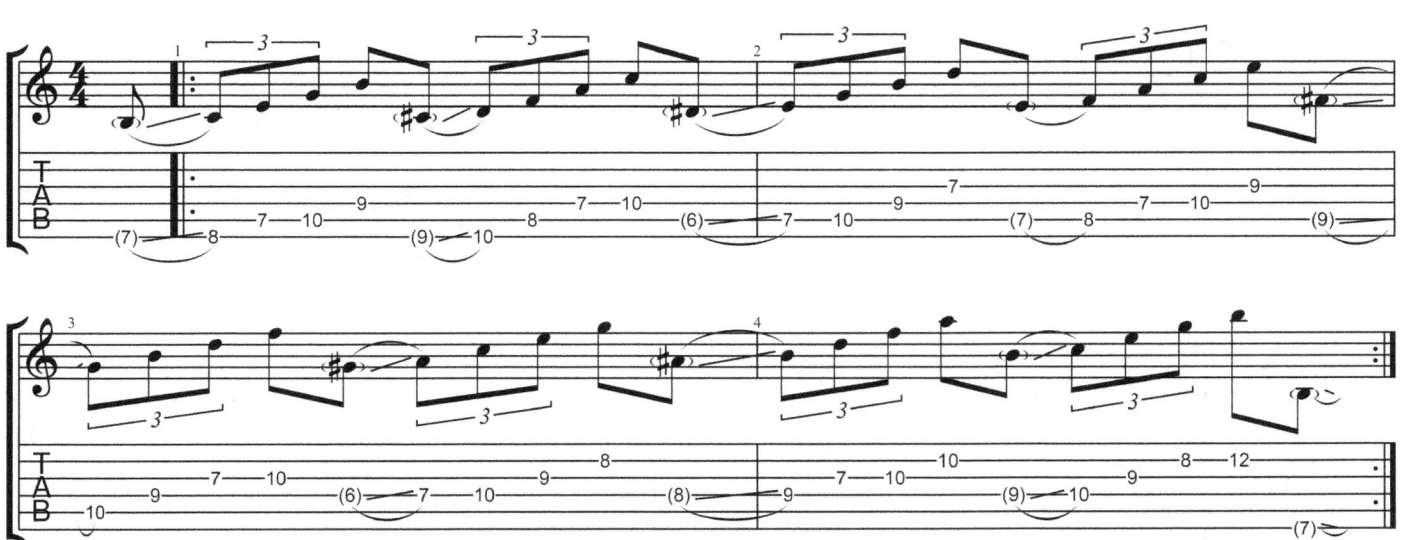

Staying in one position is more challenging than shifting up and down the neck. Neither approach is better, they're just different ways to navigate the fretboard. However, to become a more fluent player you'll need the freedom to do both.

Here's an example of diatonic arpeggios in C Major ascending the neck without any chromaticism.

Example 7n:

Now, let's add chromatic tones to connect these positions. Even if you don't consider yourself a chromatic player, practicing these ideas will help you move around the fretboard with more fluidity and less fear.

Example 7o:

As with everything in this book, we're only scratching the surface of what's possible with arpeggios. There are countless ways to outline chords, and you don't have to stick to only the notes of the chord you're playing. We'll explore this more later.

Spend some time with these concepts then we'll dive deeper in the next routine where we'll explore how to combine arpeggios and scales in a more fluid way.

Routine Eight: Combining Arpeggios & Scales

Now we're getting into the really interesting stuff. You might be wondering, "If this is a book on arpeggios, why are we talking about scales?"

Well, one of the worst things you can do in your musical development is to think of arpeggios, triads and scales as separate "boxes", when the reality is that beautiful music blurs the lines between them so seamlessly that it's hard to say where one ends and the other begins.

I spent many years working on scales and arpeggios separately, and when it came to playing, everything sounded formulaic and predictable. I was just cycling through things I'd learned with no real freedom, and it became a bit of a prison for me.

It just wasn't very musical, yet this is a mentality that many guitarists get trapped in. I always felt that the worst shred guitar solos were the ones where the guitarist mentally checked off the techniques on a list… "Here are my tapping ideas … here's my legato ideas … here's my picking bit…" The guitarists who spoke to me were the ones who didn't use solos to demonstrate their technique, but the ones who used their technique to make powerful music.

So, I began working on exercises that allowed me to combine the things I knew more seamlessly, and before I knew it, music became magical again.

Let me show you what I mean.

First, we need to make sure that we know both our arpeggio and our scale. Here they are for a Cmaj7 chord.

Example 8a:

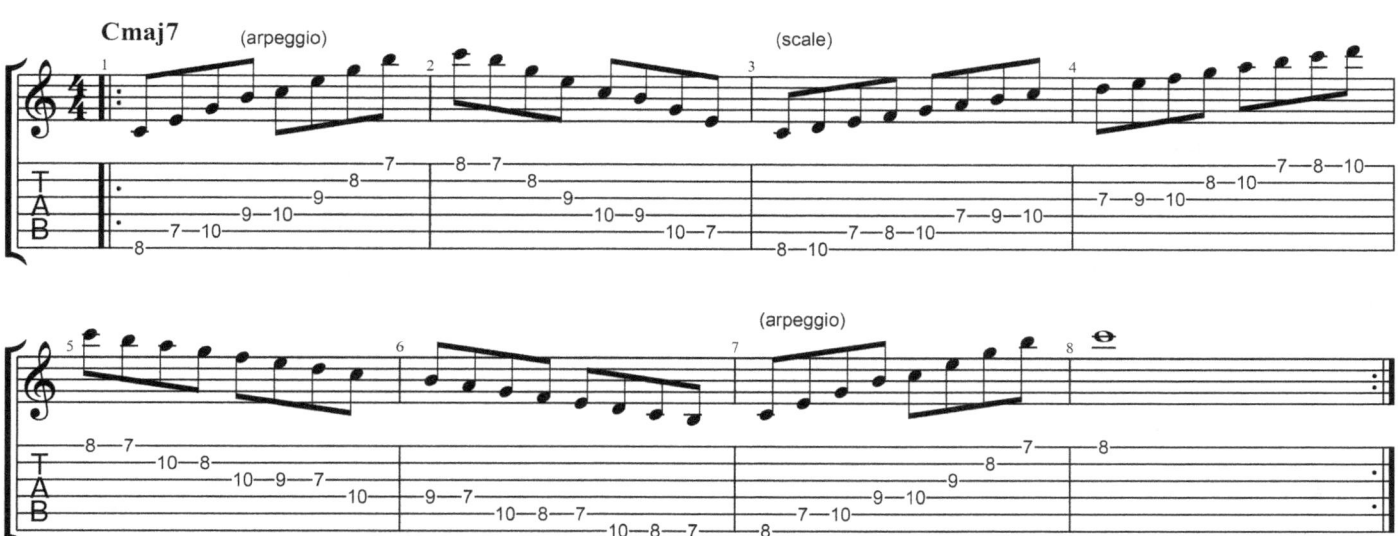

Many people like to think of arpeggios as something you "take out" of a scale. I.e., the notes of a Cmaj7 arpeggio are found within the C Major scale:

(C) D (E) F (G) A (B) (C)

But I prefer to think of scales as the notes that *connect* my arpeggios. The arpeggio notes are the target notes, and the scale notes fill in the gaps between them. It's a subtle shift in perspective, but it's incredibly useful when it comes to thinking about note choice when we're soloing.

Let's explore this idea by playing parts of the arpeggio and filling in the gaps with scale tones.

Example 8b:

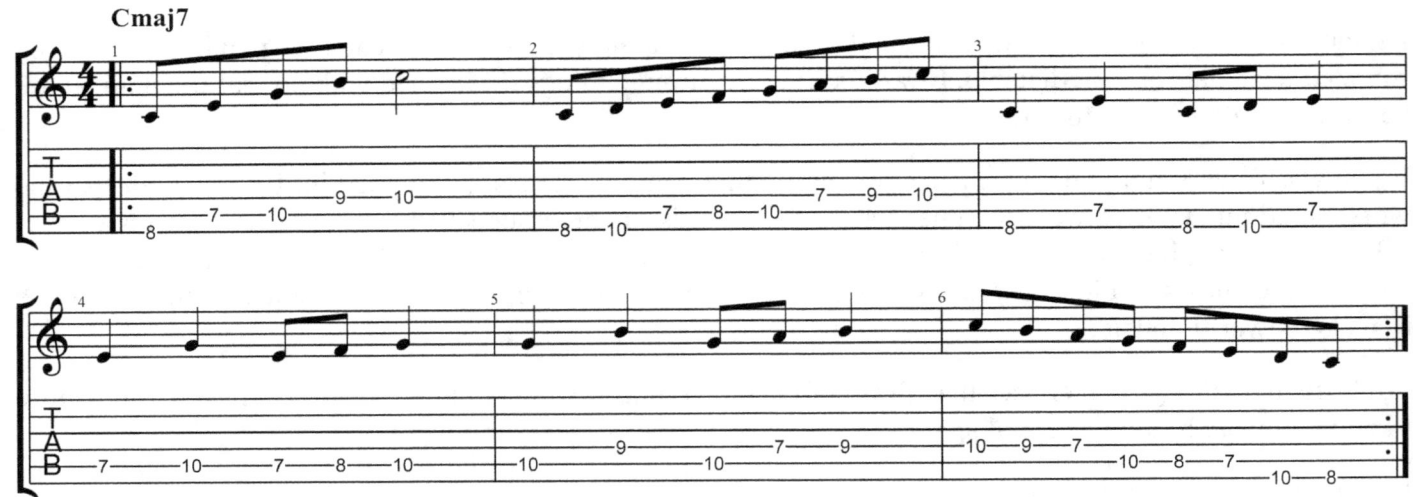

The secret exercise that will supercharge your visualisation here is to ascend four notes of the arpeggio, then descend four notes of the scale.

For example, we ascend the arpeggio notes:

1 3 5 7

Then descend the scale intervals:

6 5 4 3

Next, we return to the arpeggio and ascend again. Since we finished on the 3rd (an arpeggio tone), we don't want to repeat that note, so we jump to the 5th and ascend:

5 7 1 3

Then we descend the scale:

2 1 7 6

Here, I prefer to jump up to the root rather than the 7th because the 7th can sound weak. This causes us to repeat the whole patten an octave higher. The entire exercise looks like this:

Example 8c:

This exercise is fascinating because even though we're playing all seven notes of the major scale, it still feels like an arpeggio idea because four of the seven notes are chord tones, so the lines naturally outline the sound of the chord. This doesn't just train your fingers, it trains your ear as well.

Of course, we need to be able to do this across the neck. Here's the same idea played around the A and C shapes.

Example 8d:

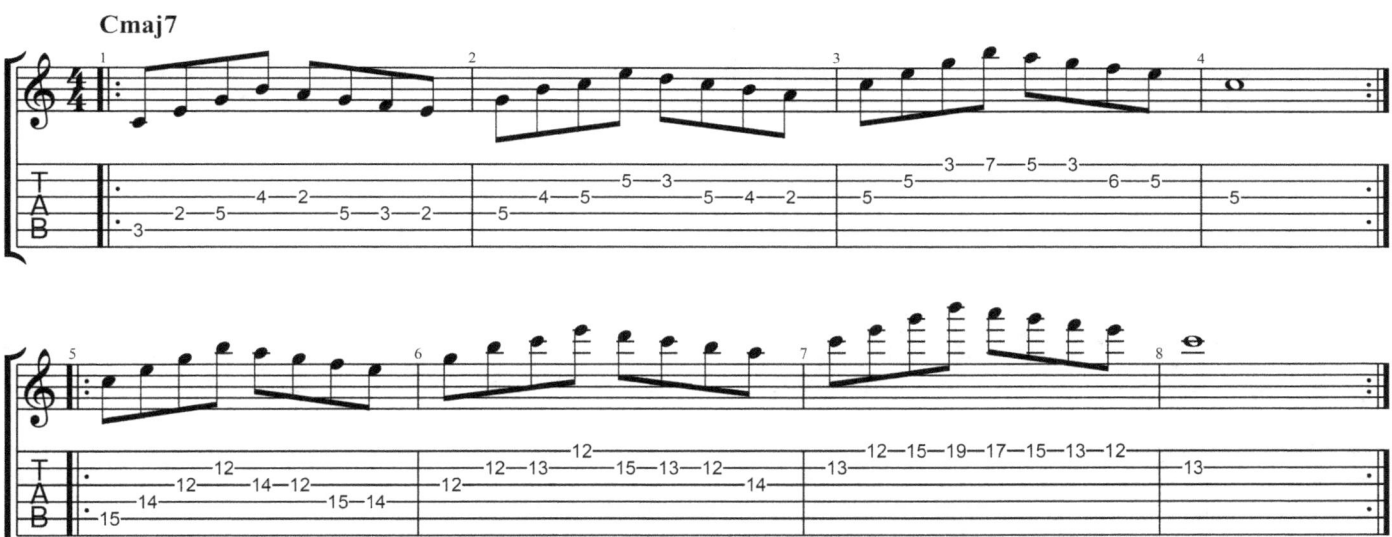

The real magic of this exercise is how it subconsciously trains your ear. If we switch to a C7 chord and connect the arpeggio and scale with the same approach, we're suddenly playing the Mixolydian mode.

Let's do this but include a descending version this time. It's the same principle as before, but now we'll descend four notes of the arpeggio and ascend four notes of the scale in the second half of the exercise.

Notice all the B notes are now Bb.

Example 8e:

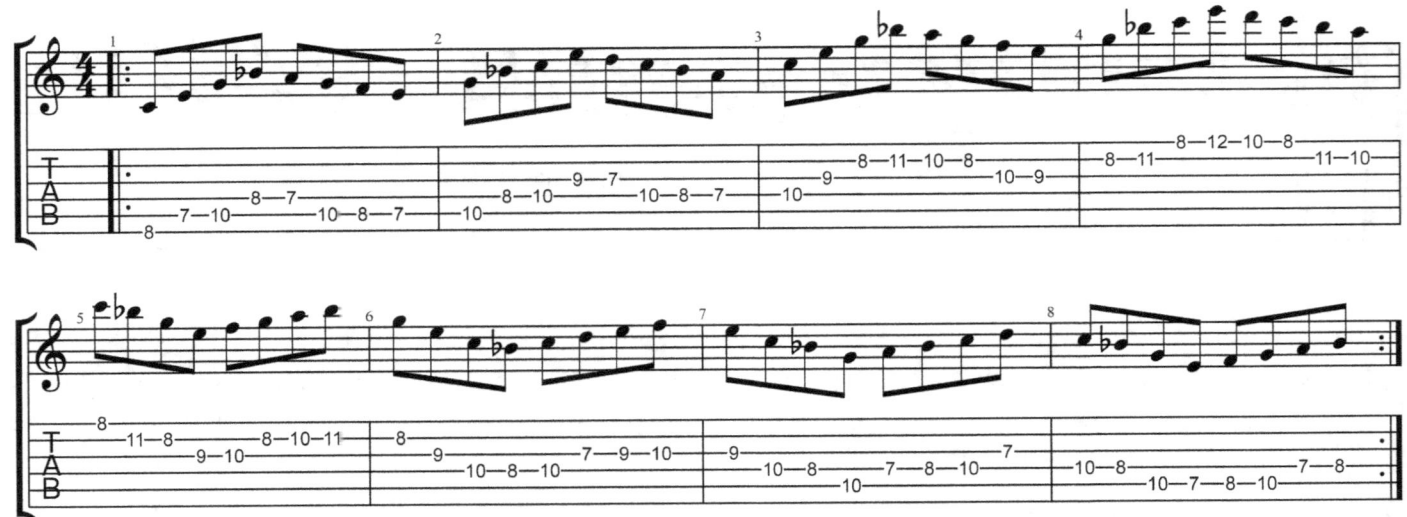

This exercise not only develops your fretboard fluency, it helps blur the line between arpeggios and scales in a natural, musical way, so you can combine them organically in your solos.

As an aside, if we add a chromatic tone before the ascending arpeggio and mix up the rhythm, we can instantly create some really cool-sounding vocabulary that works great over a blues chord sequence. I use these kinds of ideas as springboards for improvisation because they're perfect for establishing the tonality and setting a line in motion.

Example 8f:

Here's that C7 sound, but now outlined in both the A and C shapes.

Example 8g:

Mixolydian is the most commonly associated scale sound with a dominant 7 chord, but it's not the only one we can use. Another option is Phrygian Dominant. Instead of learning this as a new scale with new fingerings, we can simply adjust the descending scale notes to match the scale formula: 1 b2 3 4 5 b6 b7.

So, let's connect our arpeggio notes with a b2, 4, and b6 instead.

Here's that idea laid out on the fretboard around the E shape. Try to hear the intervals before you play them.

Example 8h:

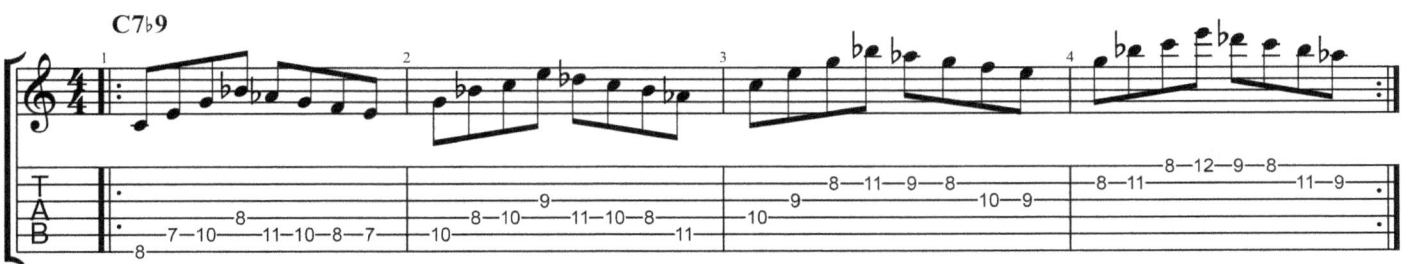

This approach can be applied to any scale as long as we understand the intervals (which I assume you have a reasonable grip on if you're reading this book).

For example, there's nothing to say we *must* connect major 7 arpeggios with notes from the major scale. We could use the Lydian scale instead (like the major scale but with a #4). Listen to how the one small change of adding the #4 (F#) changes the sound of a Cmaj7 vamp.

Example 8i:

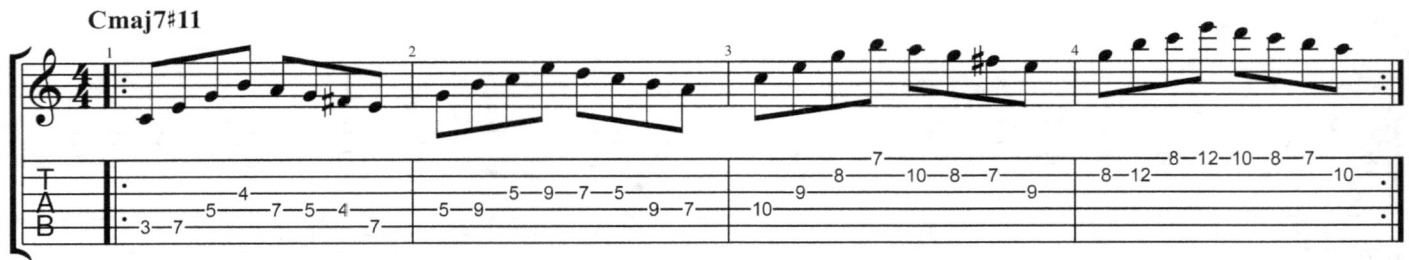

Now we know we can connect arpeggios that spell out the chord using different notes, let's look at what we can do on a minor 7 chord.

Minor chords can be confusing at first because they work differently depending on their function in a key. For instance, sometimes they function as the ii chord in a key and sometimes as the vi.

The ii chord is a Dorian scale sound (1 2 b3 4 5 6 b7), and the vi chord is Aeolian (1 2 b3 4 5 b6 b7). The chord function affects which notes we use to connect our arpeggios.

As Dorian is slightly more common, we'll start there. Dorian has a natural 6th, so our connecting scale tones will be the 2, 4, and 6.

Example 8j:

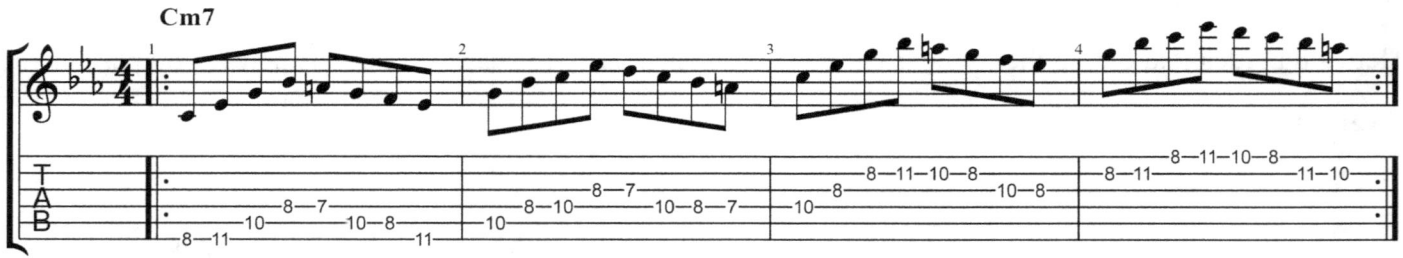

If we replace the natural 6th with a b6, we create the darker Aeolian sound. You already know where the b6 is from the Phrygian Dominant earlier in the routine, we're just using it in a minor chord now.

Example 8k:

Let's extend these ideas a bit. In this next exercise, we'll play through each of the diatonic chords in the key of C Major, using scale notes to connect them when descending. For example, we'll ascend Cmaj7, descend the scale, ascend Dm7, descend the scale, and so on.

This exercise is a perfect blend of scales and arpeggios and shows how they can coexist.

Example 8l:

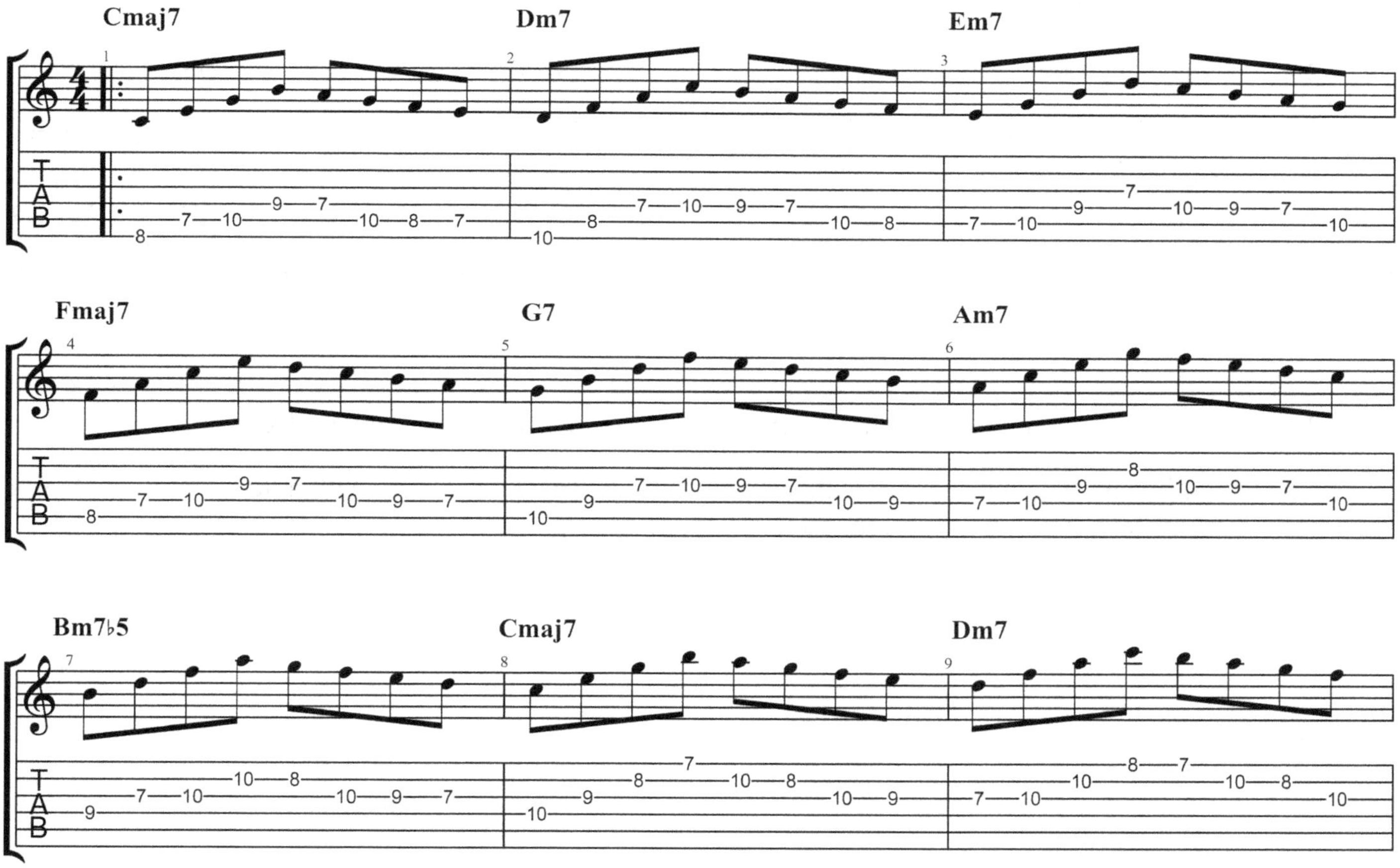

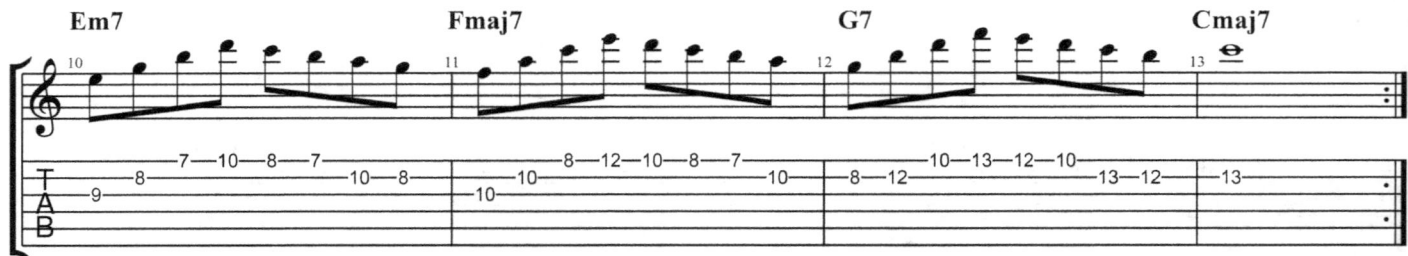

You can do this same idea in different positions, like around the A shape.

Example 8m:

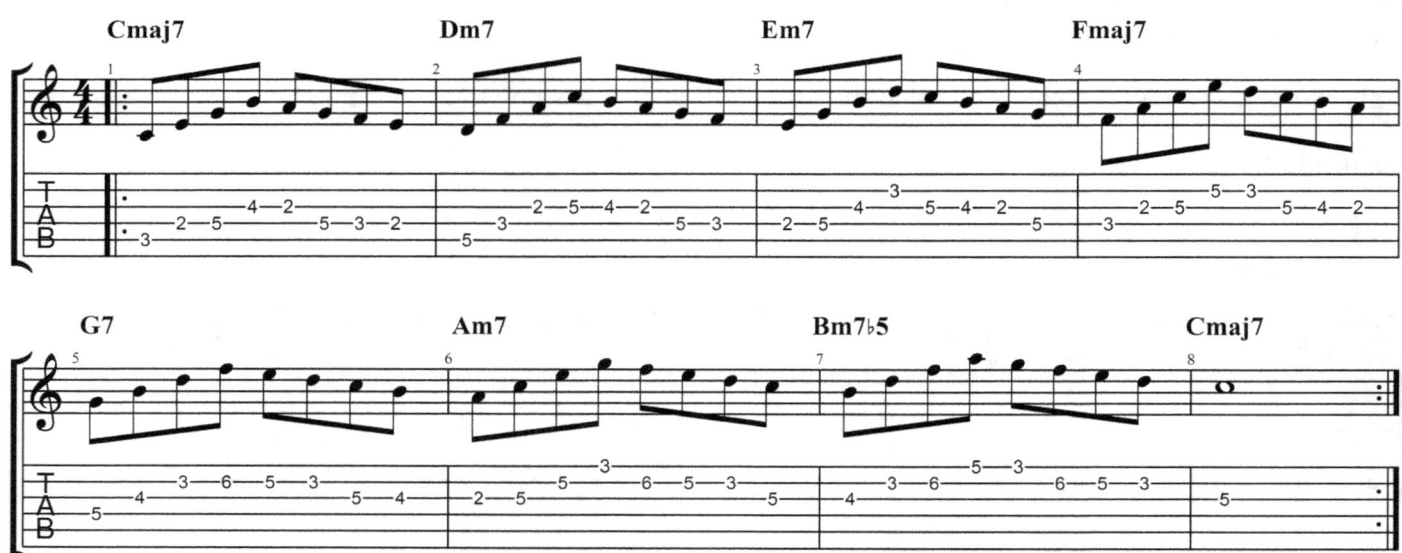

This idea also works horizontally across the neck, which can really test your fretboard knowledge.

As you do this, think about and visualise each chord in the key and connect them with notes from the C Major scale, rather than thinking about a different mode for each chord.

Example 8n:

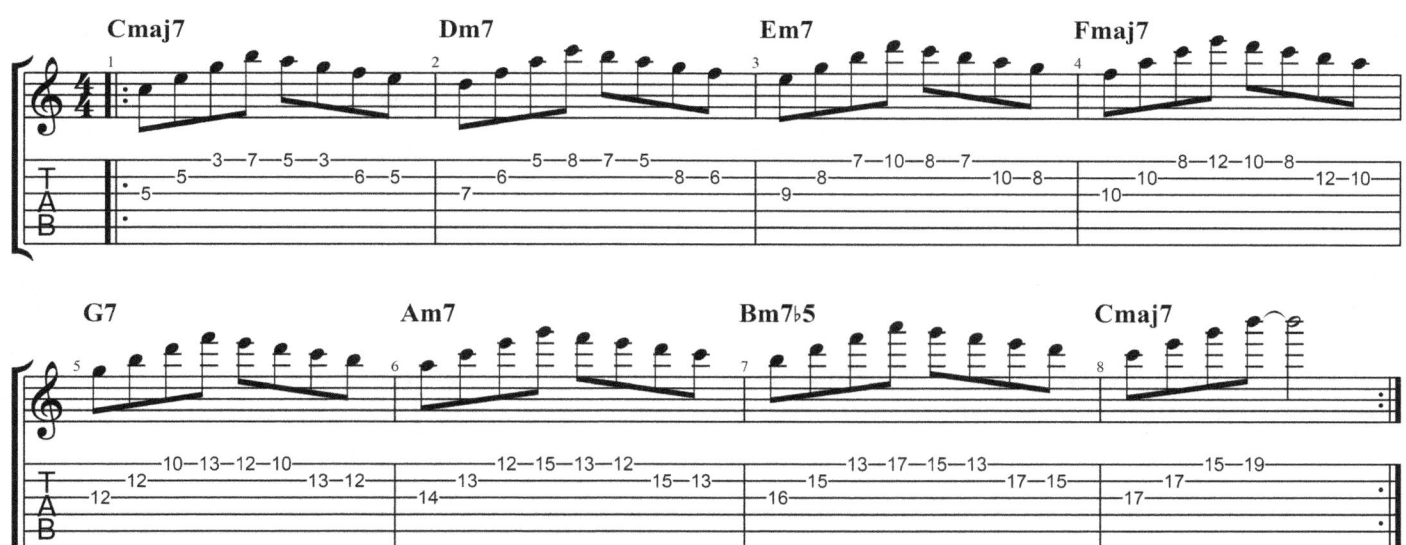

To finish this week, let's take the chord sequence from *Fly Me to the Moon* and learn how we can combine our arpeggios and scales in a more fluid manner.

The first step is outlining the chord progression with only arpeggios. Here, I played through the progression in just one of the infinite ways possible. Copying this example will help you to learn, but figuring out your own approach will be the most valuable practice, so make sure to explore your own creative approaches.

Example 8o:

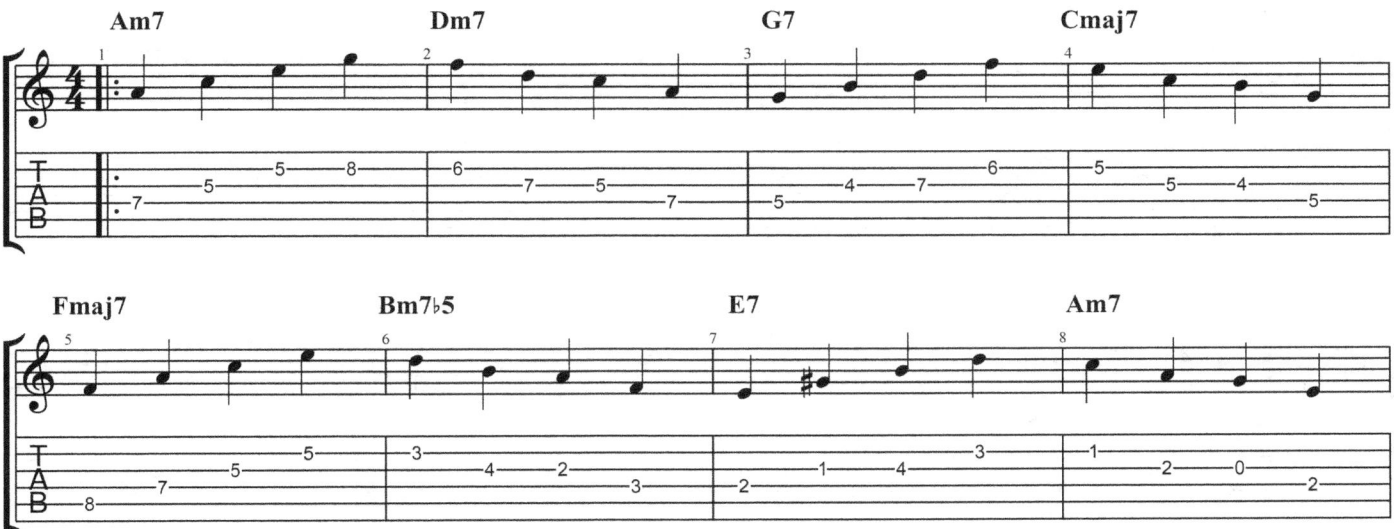

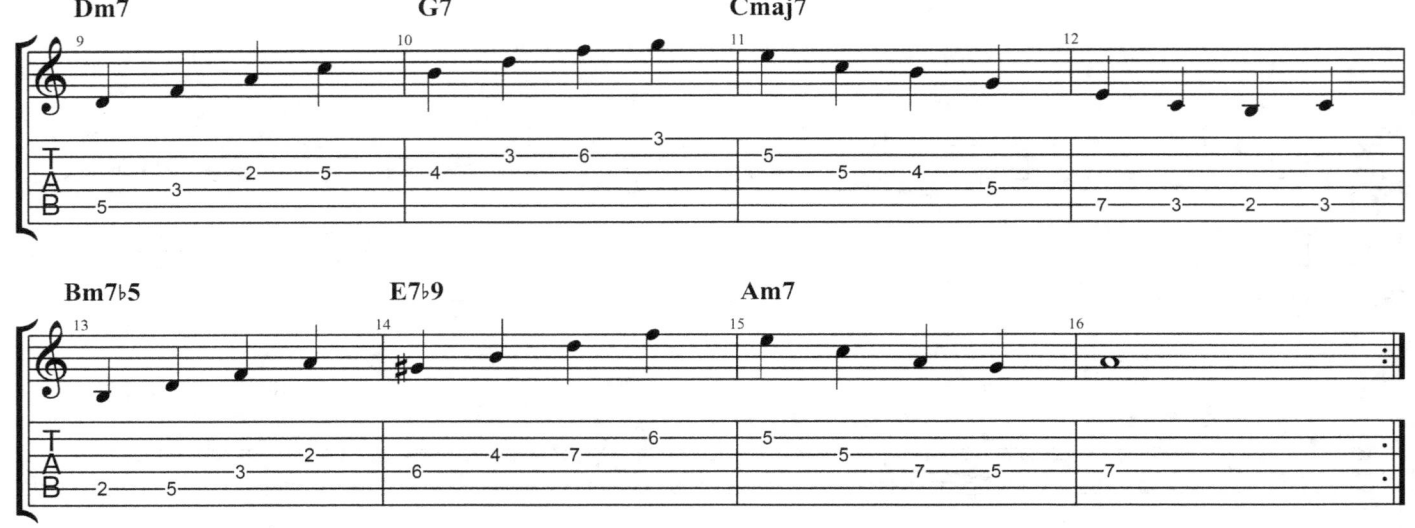

Now, if we add rhythmic variety to some arpeggio and scale combinations we can create a more melodic approach.

You could spend a lifetime refining your phrasing with this concept, and that's the journey most of us end up on in our playing, as we constantly practice these ideas over more tunes.

Normally, the melody of the tune we're playing guides the shape and rhythmic ideas in our solos. It's all about repeating this process until you can smoothly outline your chord changes in a convincing way that relates to the melody of the song.

Example 8p:

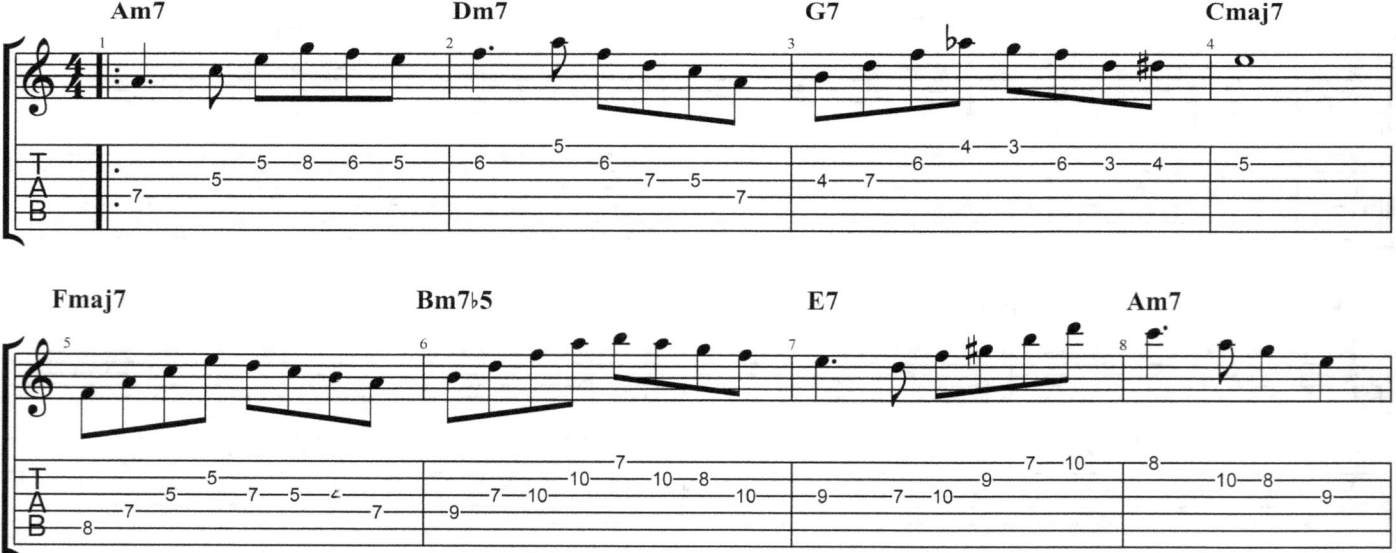

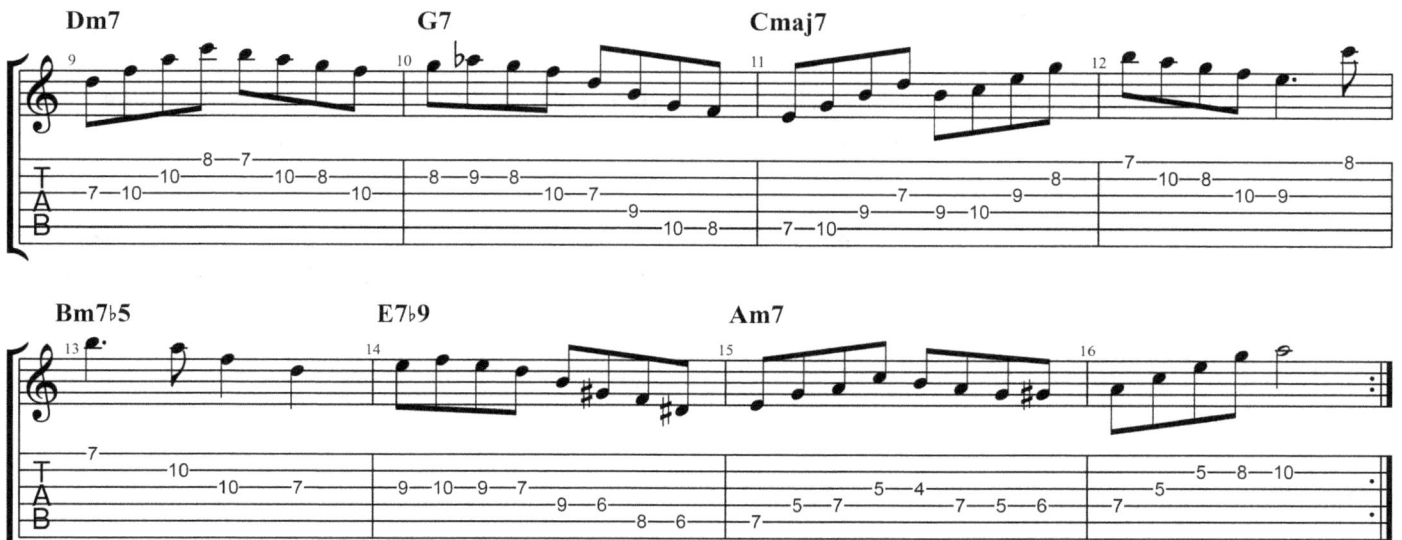

There are no shortcuts here, you just need to put in the time. Minutes turn into hours, hours into days, and days into weeks. But if you focus on getting a little better each day, mastery becomes inevitable.

Keep at it!

Routine Nine: Extended Arpeggios

As we discovered in the chord book in this series, one of the most interesting ways to create complex sounds in harmony is to look to extended chords. The same goes for arpeggios, where we have multiple options for incorporating richer sounds.

A very simple way of extending an arpeggio and adding colour is to take the triad and add just one more note. For example, we can add a 9th interval to a C major triad to turn it into a Cadd9 arpeggio, giving us the intervals:

1 3 5 9

Or, if we confine those intervals to a single octave:

1 2 3 5

This idea creates the simplest form of extended arpeggio, but they sound wonderful. These should be learned around our three basic positions so that we can play them comfortably in any key.

Example 9a:

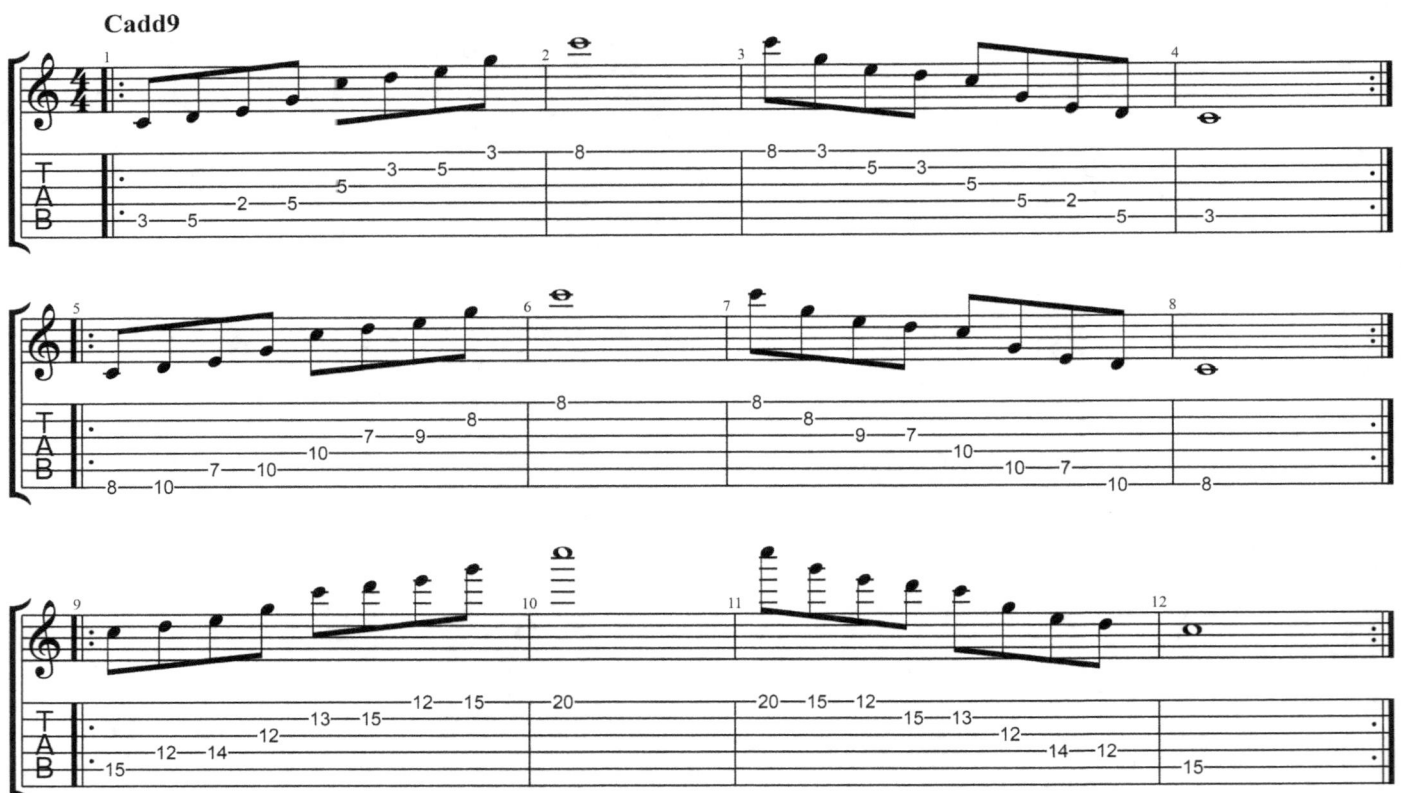

The previous example showed the extended arpeggio in vertical form, but they also work well in horizontal form. In fact, they allow us to cover a little more range and sound a bit like the iconic *Final Fantasy* prelude arpeggios!

Learn these starting on both the E and A string.

Example 9b:

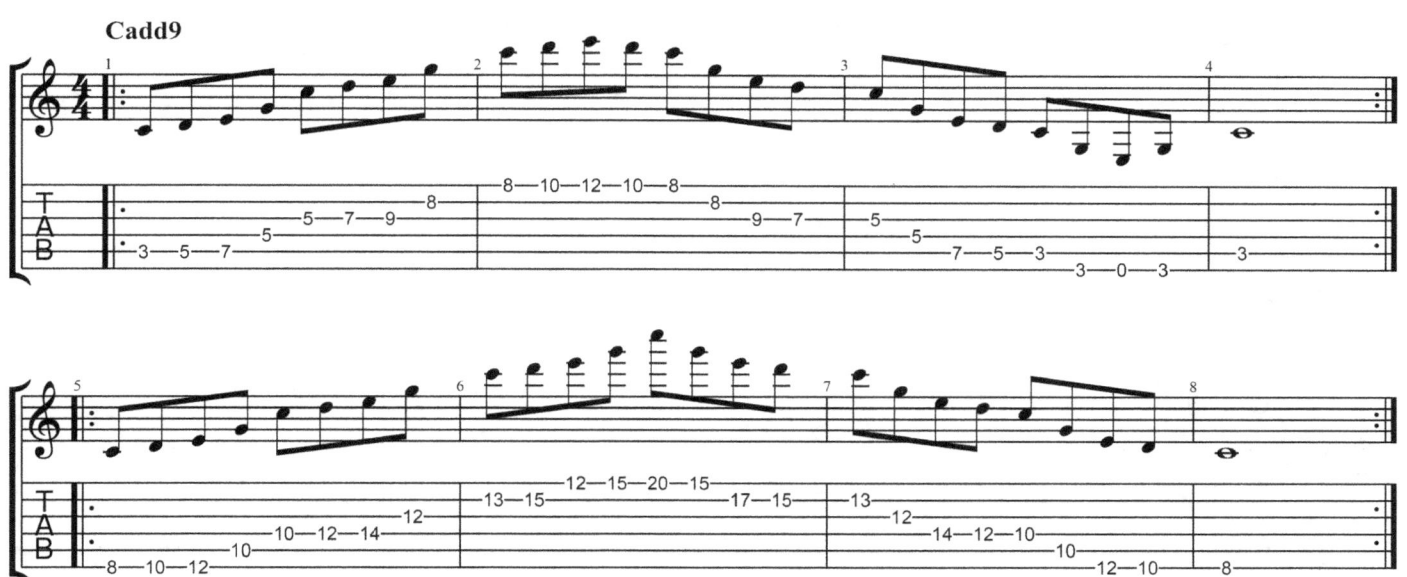

We can apply the same concept to minor triads by adding the 9th, resulting in the intervals:

1 2 b3 5

So, a C minor add9 arpeggio across three positions looks like this:

Example 9c:

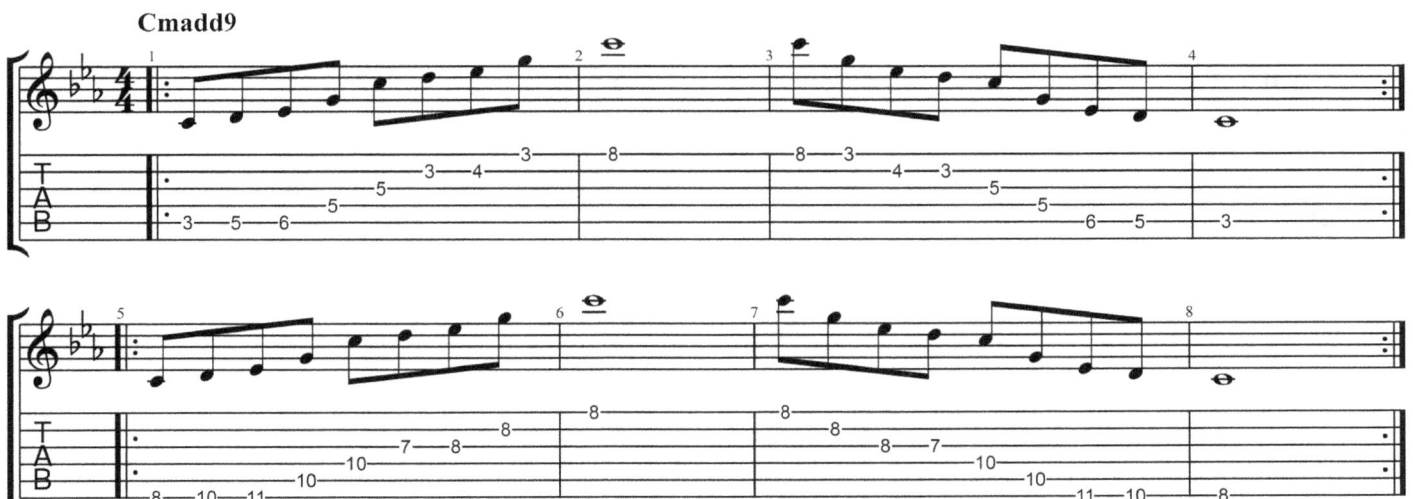

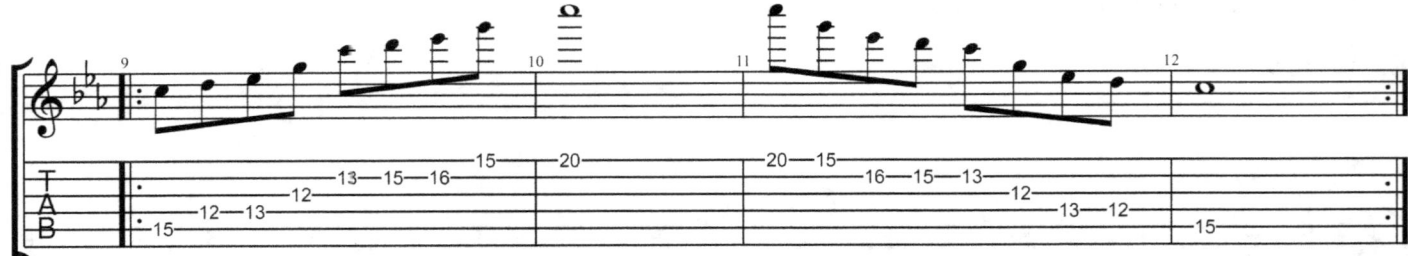

When played in horizontal patterns, they lay out on the fretboard like this.

Example 9d:

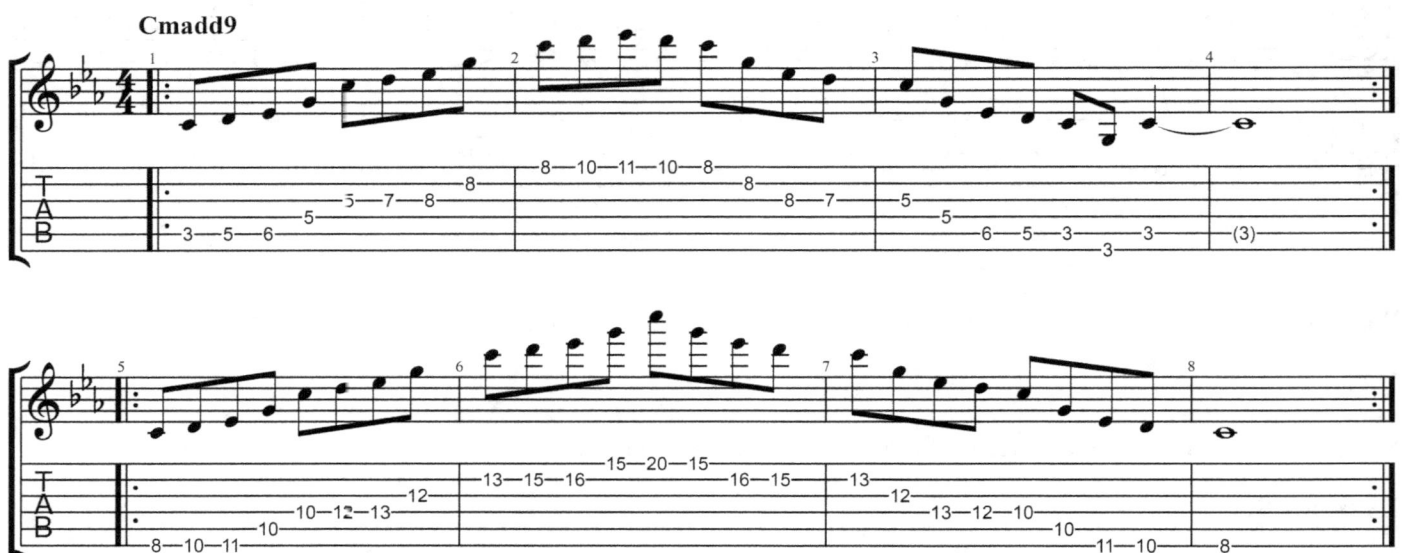

At this point, it's worth considering again: when does an arpeggio start to feel like a scale?

Even though these arpeggio patterns contain three consecutive scale tones, they still function as arpeggios in my view. For example, in a chord progression like A – F#m – D – E, you can outline each chord with an add9 arpeggio starting from the root. Over the course of the progression, you play all seven notes of the A Major scale, but you're breaking them up into arpeggios that correspond directly to the harmony.

Example 9e:

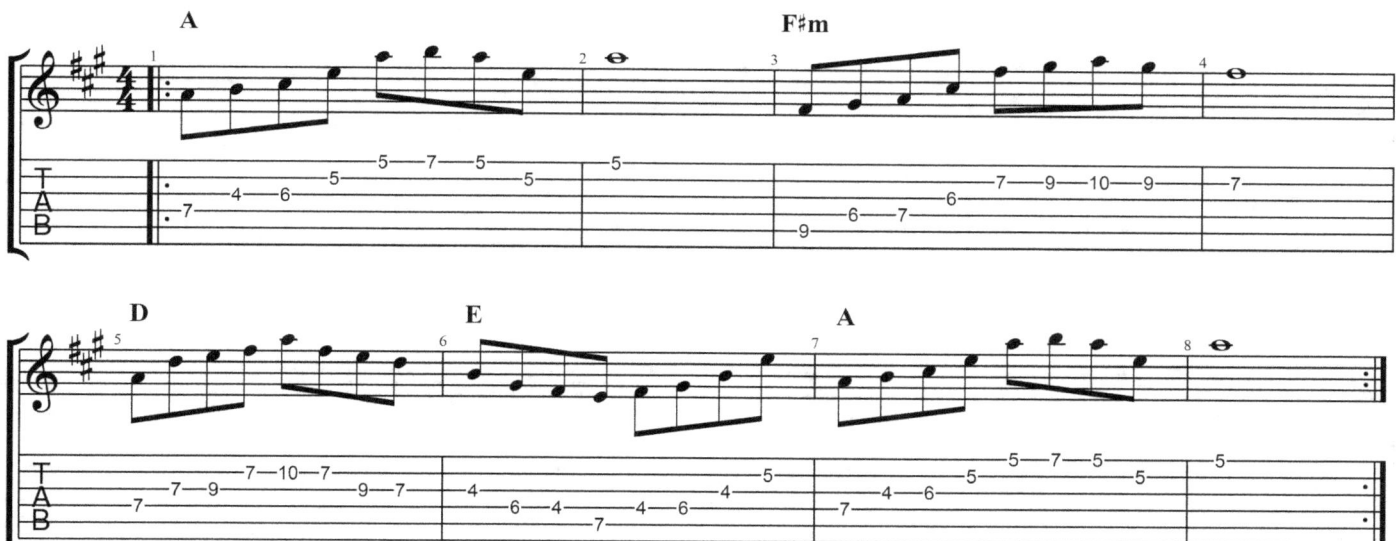

Here's a longer example outlining that same progression twice. This time, I've added a few notes outside of the basic add9 arpeggios to make it more melodic. Let's break down this idea:

- In bar one, I use the b3 as a passing tone to approach the 3rd, and a 4th to connect the 5th down to the 3rd

- In bar three, there's a bluesy b5 to 4 slide that transitions down the F#m triad

- Bar five features a descending scale, leading to the 3rd of the E major chord in the next bar

- In bar 7, I use a 4th–b3–3rd targeting idea, plus a 4th to connect the 5th and 3rd again

- Bar 11 introduces the b7 of F#m, leading into the root in bar twelve, which could be interpreted as part of an F#m9 arpeggio

- Finally, bar fourteen ends with either the b7 of E major or another 4th–b3–3rd figure leading into the 3rd of A major in the next bar, depending on how you choose to view it

What I want you to take from this is that we don't have to be rigid with arpeggios. We can add embellishment notes to make our lines more dynamic and interesting.

Example 9f:

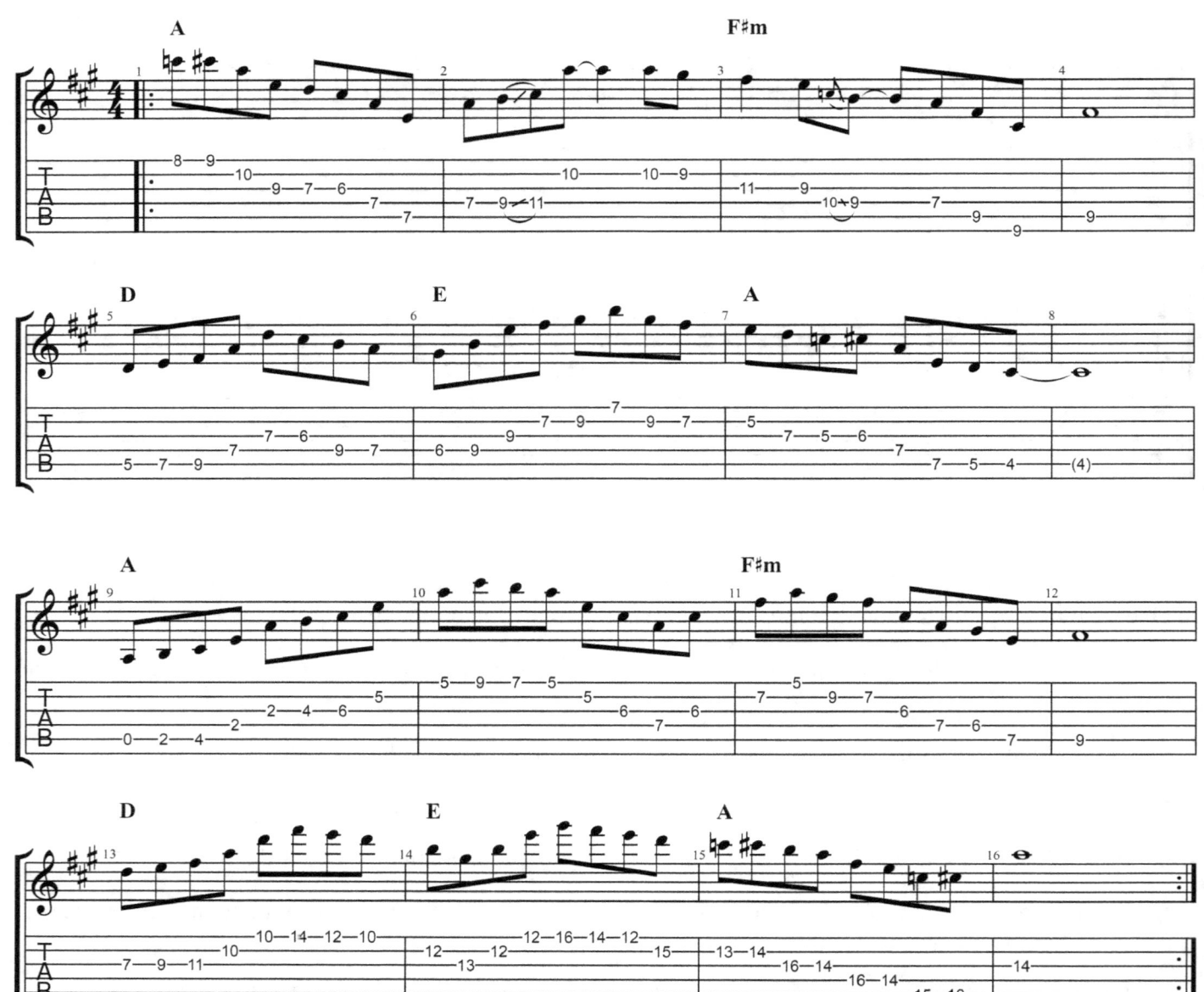

Why am I calling these add9 arpeggios, rather than just major 9 and minor 9?

Think back to the chord book and you'll recall that we learned the names of chords based on the highest extension when the 7th is present.

A chord built from the intervals 1 3 5 9 is simply a triad with an added 9th (no 7th).

If we include the 7th, so that we have 1 3 5 7 9, that's a major 9 chord.

So, we can make the major 9 sound either by adding one note to a major triad, or by playing a five-note arpeggio. Here we're playing a Cmaj9 (C E G B D) five-note arpeggio:

Example 9g:

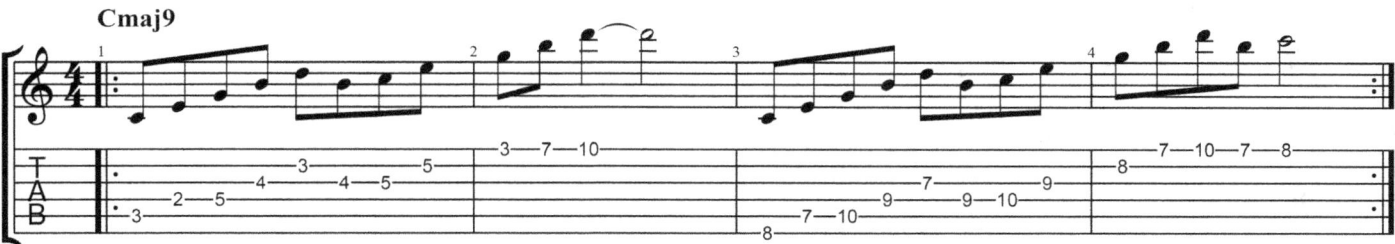

We can extend this to a ii–V–I progression by playing minor 9, dominant 9, and major 9 arpeggios for each chord type.

Example 9h:

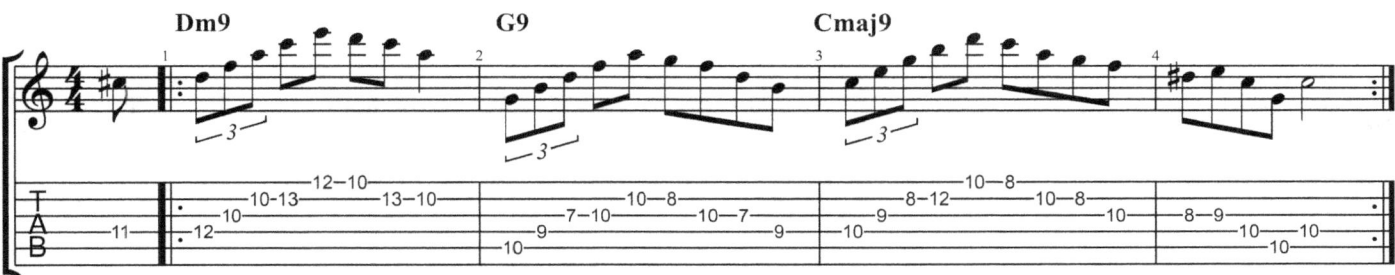

If we look at five-note arpeggios more closely, we can also view them as slash chords. In other words, an arpeggio superimposed over a bass note. For example, a Cmaj9 arpeggio can be viewed as an Em7 arpeggio played over a C bass note, or Em7/C in chord terms.

(C) E G B D

How does this information help us? Well, it allows us to play something we already know well (an Em7 arpeggio) and use it to create a different sound.

The key is to understand where to place this arpeggio relative to the root. In this case, to create a major 9 sound, we play a minor 7th arpeggio starting from the 3rd of the major chord (for C, that's E).

To understand why this works, we have to shift our perspective of the intervals. In the case of an Em7 arpeggio (1 b3 5 b7), the context changes when played over a C root. Here, E no longer sounds like the root (1), because now it's the 3rd of C. Similarly, G is no longer the b3, it's the 5th of C, and so on.

This is such a common arpeggio that we give it a name – the 3-to-9 arpeggio – because we're arpeggiating from the 3rd to the 9th of the chord.

Let's apply this idea to the three most basic chord types.

For each one I'll play the 1, then I'll say, "3 5 7 9" on the recording and play those intervals in relation to the chord.

Over a major 7 chord it will be 3 5 7 9.

Over a dominant 7 chord it will be 3 5 b7 9.

Over a minor 7 chord it will be b3 5 b7 9.

Example 9i:

You may have noticed that I didn't include a minor 7b5 chord in that demonstration. Why? The minor 7b5 chord gives us more options to explore. In a major scale, the 9th on a minor 7b5 chord is actually a b9, which doesn't always sound pleasing. So, when playing a 3-to-9 arpeggio over a minor 7b5 chord, I often play it as b3 b5 b7 9, turning it into a minor 9b5 arpeggio.

These kinds of choices always exist. For example, over a dominant chord, we can play 3 5 b7 9, but if we want a darker sound, we can instead play 3 5 b7 b9 for a 7b9 arpeggio.

Example 9j:

Now, let's revisit the *Fly Me to the Moon* progression from earlier, but this time we'll ascend 3-to-9 arpeggios over each chord:

- For major 7 chords we'll play a minor 7 arpeggio from the 3rd
- For minor 7 chords we'll play a major 7 arpeggio from the b3
- For dominant chords we'll play a diminished 7th arpeggio from the 3rd (for a 7b9 sound)
- For minor 7b5 chords we'll play a minor 7 arpeggio from the b3

Example 9k:

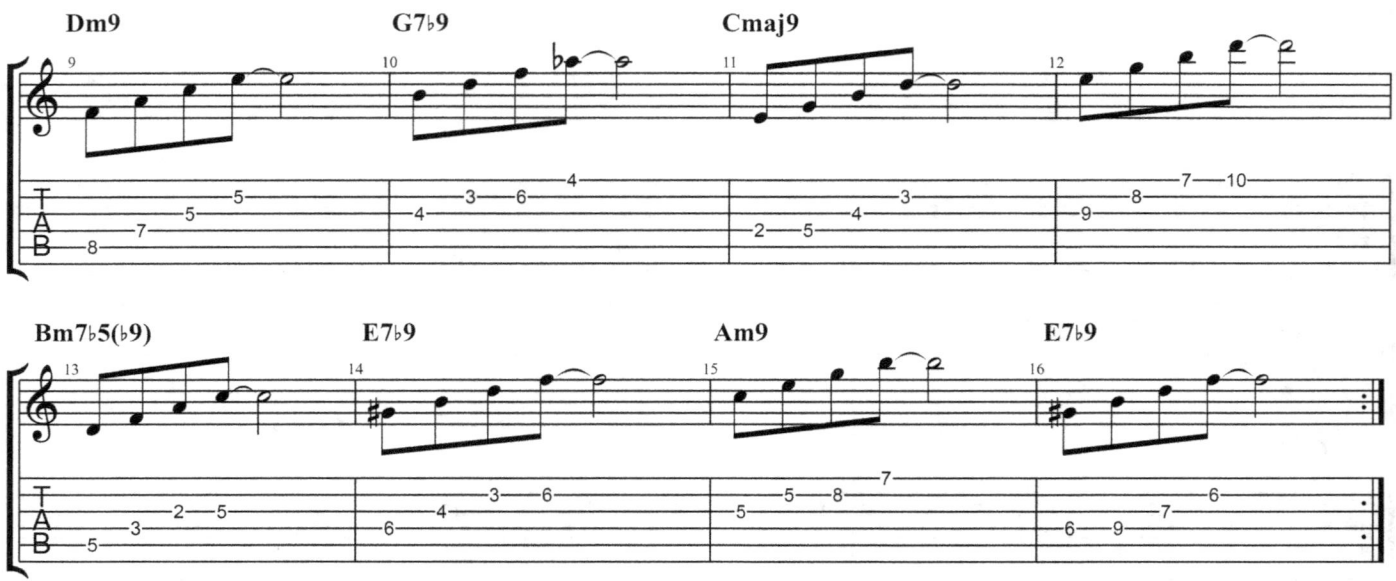

Exercises like this are great because they force our brain to work out what we have to play, while we're playing it.

In the last example, we played the 3-to-9 arpeggios in ascending order, but keep in mind, as long as you're using the 3rd, 5th, 7th and 9th, it's still considered a 3-to-9 arpeggio, no matter the note order.

One way I like to break up this pattern is with octave displacement. Instead of playing the 3rd then ascending through 5, 7 and 9, I'll play the 3rd, followed by the 5th an octave lower, then ascend 5 7 9.

This time I'll play two beats of a chord tone, then play our 3-to-9 arpeggios with octave displacement.

Example 9l:

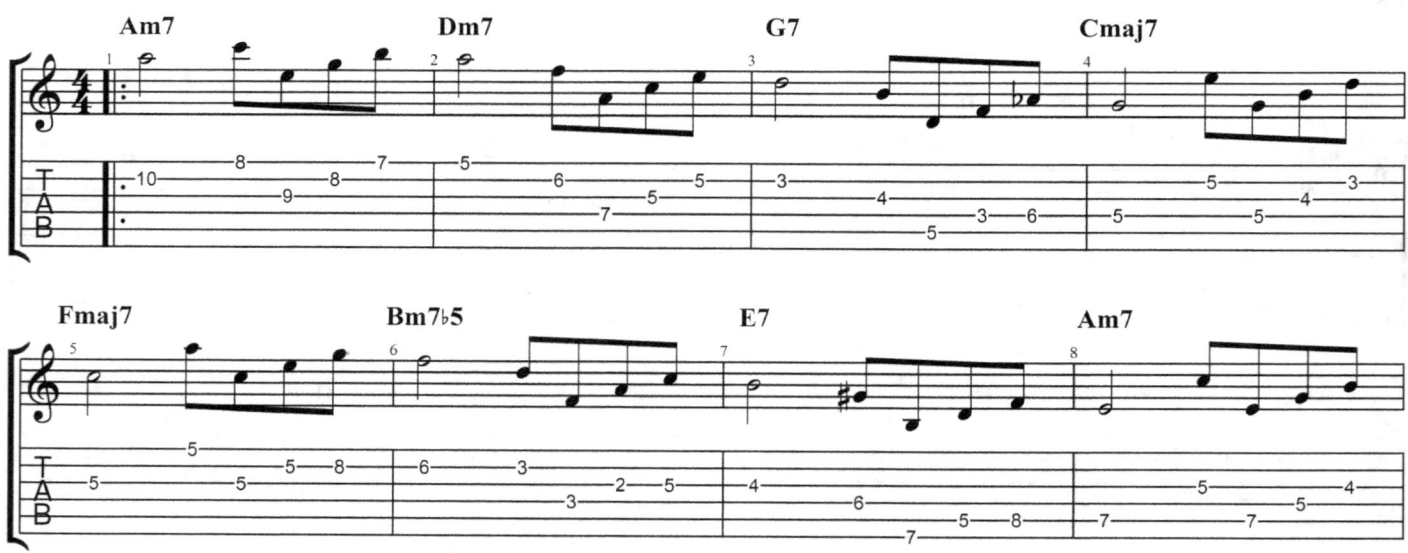

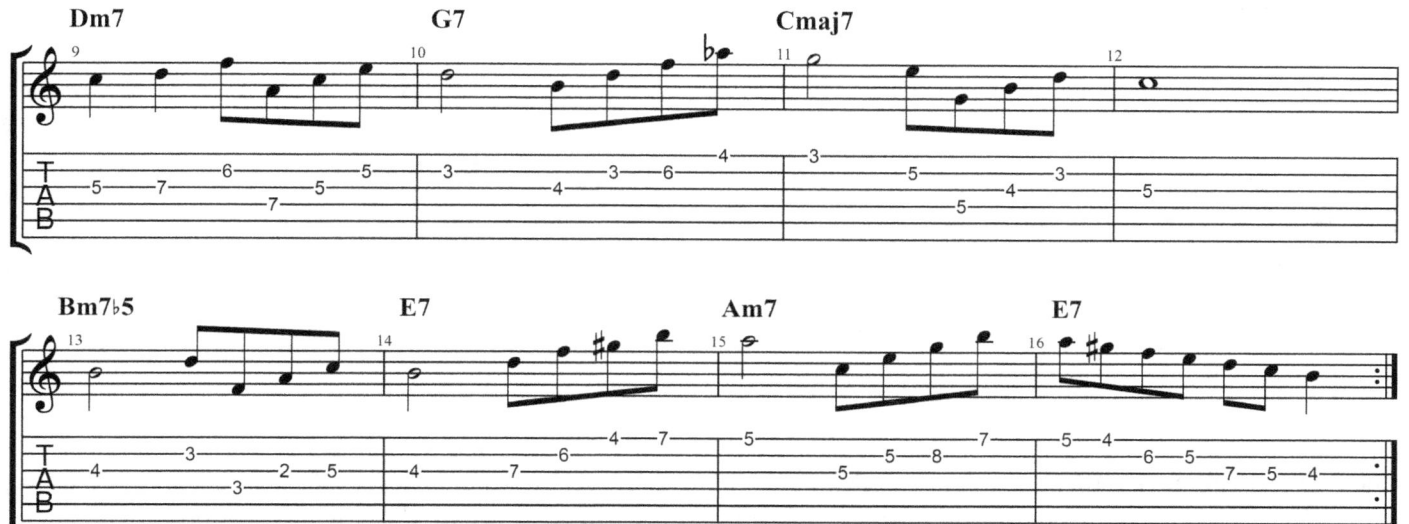

This approach opens up new melodic possibilities and helps us to break free from repetitive patterns.

Now that we've discussed 9th arpeggios, it's time to explore 11th and 13th arpeggios. These extended arpeggios allow us to further enrich our sound, and while there are various ways to approach them methodically, I want to introduce what I call my "ultimate arpeggio patterns".

Our harmonic system is based on stacking 3rd intervals, called *tertian harmony*. If we build a 7th chord and continue stacking up the 3rds, we get:

1 3 5 7 9 11 13

This sequence covers all seven notes of the scale.

But if we're playing all the notes of the scale, how is this different from simply playing the scale itself? The distinction lies in thinking vertically – structuring these notes as stacked intervals rather than running them sequentially, as we would for a scale.

Let's take the C Mixolydian scale as an example. Here are the notes of the scale:

C D E F G A Bb

If we stack the notes in 3rds we get:

C E G Bb D F A

That forms a C13 arpeggio.

To me, this is the best way to internalise any scale, because it allows us to hear the harmony as a *vertical structure*.

When you think "C Mixolydian", I want you to hear the sound of C13. That's what this mode represents sonically – a rich, extended C dominant sound.

Let's apply this to the fretboard now.

Example 9m:

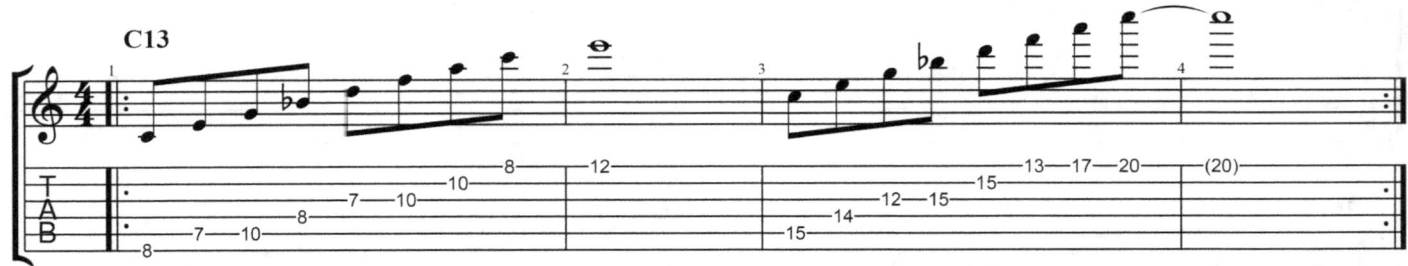

The key is to focus on the concept of stacking 3rds. No matter where you are on the neck, if you're playing over a C7 chord, you can stack thirds from the C Mixolydian mode to create that lush C13 sound.

In the next example, I'm using all seven notes of the scale, but the line emphasises stacked 3rds and we're playing through fingering fragments you've worked on in this book.

Example 9n:

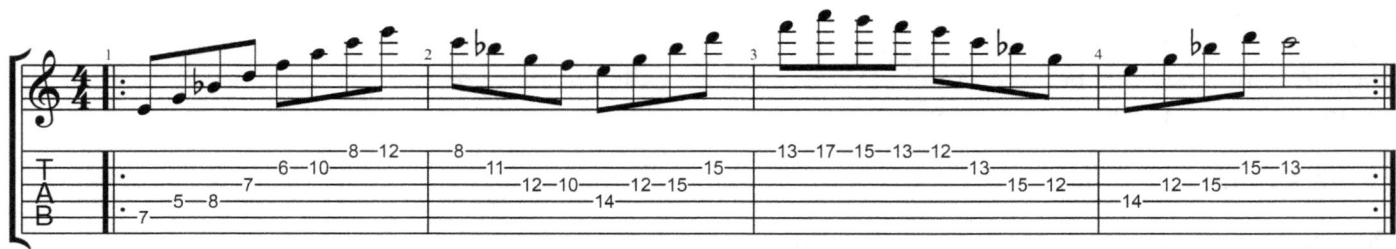

The best way to practice this concept is to pick a key – let's stay in C to keep things simple –and, starting on each note of the C Major scale (C D E F G A B), stack notes in 3rds as you move up the neck.

This exercise has a double payoff. First, it helps you develop the ability to think vertically and create these extended arpeggios. Second, it trains your fingers to navigate these patterns efficiently. Remember, a concept is only as useful as your ability to execute it quickly, without hesitation.

Example 9o:

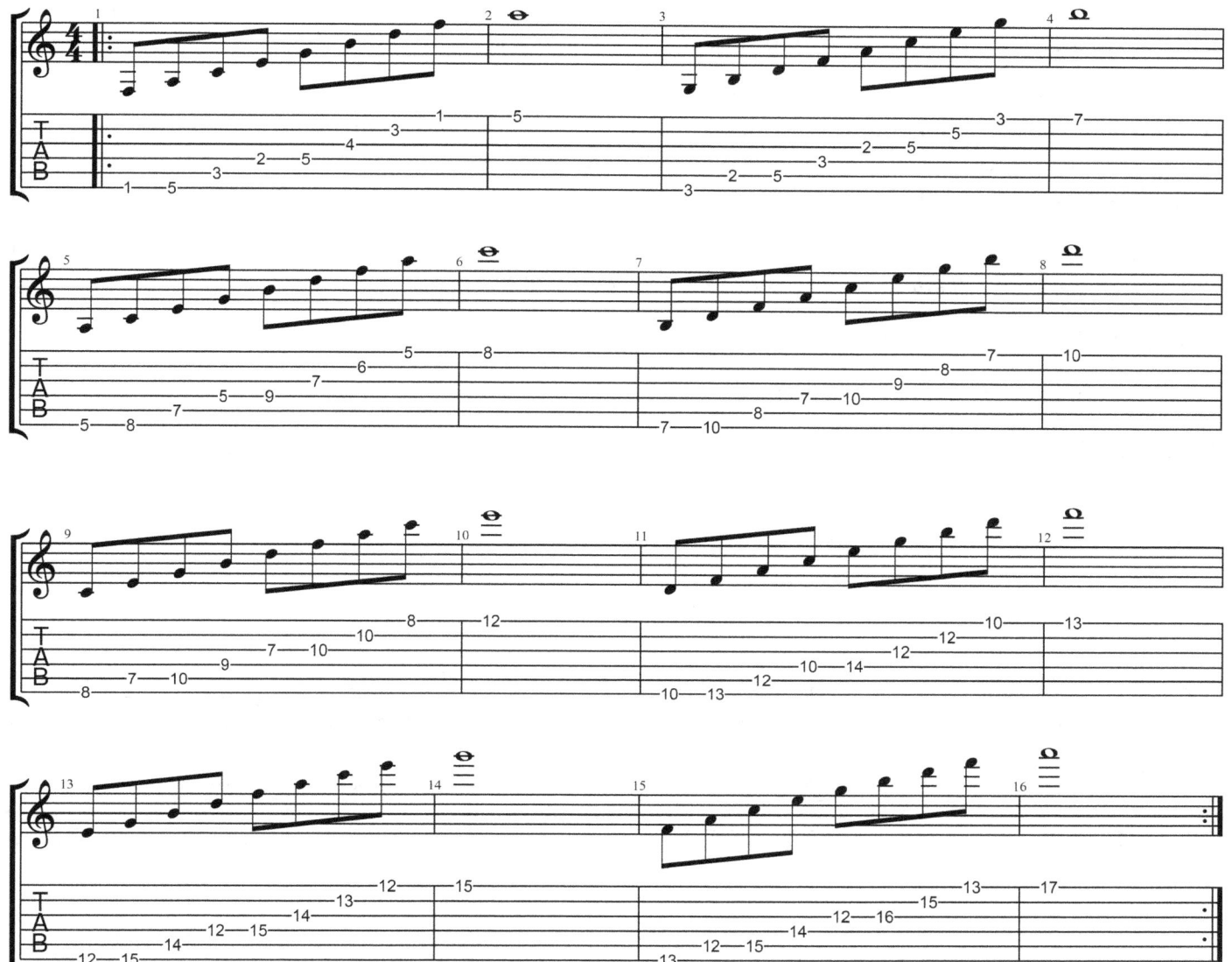

There's a lot to unpack here, and we're still just scratching the surface, but I don't want to go too much deeper. It makes more sense to master the core concepts you'll use regularly in your playing. However, you can take away these ideas and work on them whenever you want to explore further.

Take your time working on stacking 3rds and incorporating different extensions into your playing. When we return for the final week, we'll be working on etudes that will pull together all the concepts in the previous routines, so you better be ready!

Routine Ten: Putting It All Together Etudes

So, you've made it to the final week! Here's where we bring everything together and apply what we've learned with a collection of etudes over different chord progressions.

Any time you run into a problem with this routine, don't be afraid to go back to the where the concept was first introduced and refresh your memory. Remember, mastery of this subject is all about *knowing* the stuff. You won't have nailed this routine until you instinctively understand and *know* the concepts in it. If that means going back because you found a weak spot, excellent! That's just you working to eliminate your weaknesses.

We'll start this routine with the simplest of progressions, based on a classic pop-rock progression you might hear in a song like *Sweet Child O' Mine* or *Sweet Home Alabama*.

We're going to outline the following chords:

D major – C major – G major – D major

Our first etude will stick just to the notes of the triads, but we'll cover a lot of the neck doing it. Limitations like this really put our knowledge to the test.

Example 10a:

Some people say triads are boring, but that's not fair. It's not even right to call them simple – they are harmonically strong and the purest sound of a chord. Sure, you might want to add more complexity, and that's fine, but triads give you a solid foundation to build on.

We could, for example, treat each of those major chords as add9 chords and mix in our 1 2 3 5 arpeggio ideas.

Example 10b:

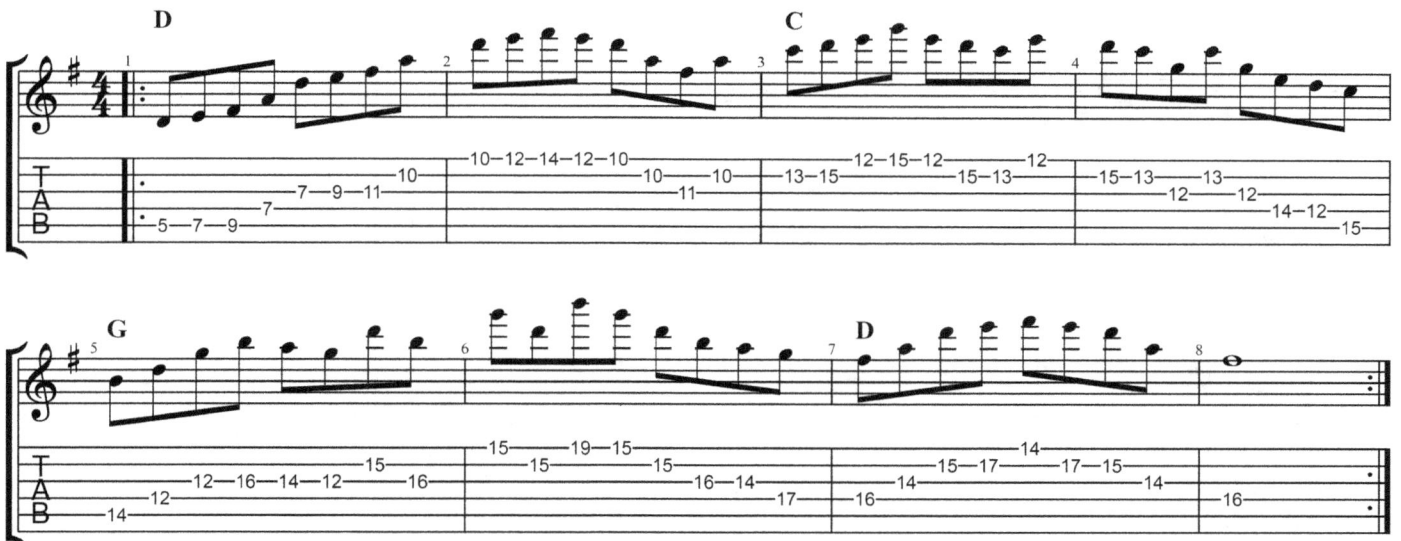

To make these etudes more musical, we can break up the rhythm a little. Long runs of 1/8th notes can get monotonous. I'll also introduce chromatic approach notes, often targeting the 3rd by approaching it with a b3 a semitone below.

Example 10c:

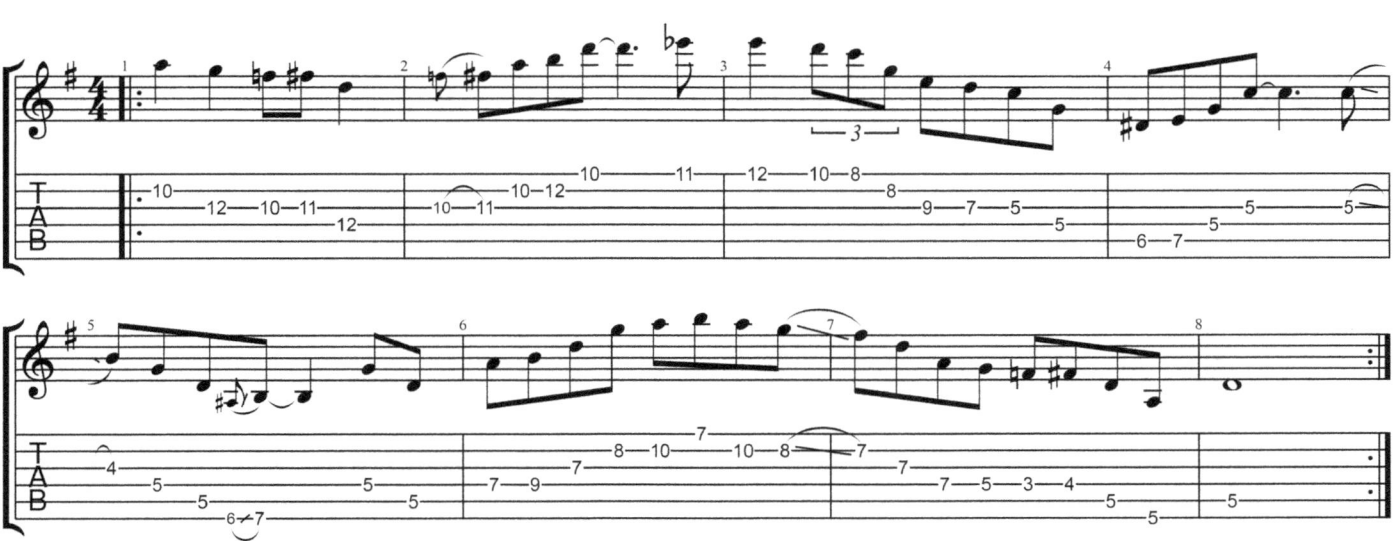

In the last etude for this progression, we'll throw theory out the window and treat all three chords as dominant chords. Technically, there should only be one dominant chord in a key, so how can we play three different dominant chord sounds here? The easy answer is that making everything dominant is a very blues or gospel thing to do – it's a familiar sound, even if it's not strictly "correct".

Example 10d:

Now let's move on to a different chord progression. This time it's a slightly jazzier take on a 12-bar blues. I've added a move to the VI chord in bar eight and replaced the V–IV move in bars 9-10 with a ii–V progression. This allows us to target a few more chords with our arpeggios.

We'll start by outlining the progression with arpeggios from the root note.

Example 10e:

[Musical notation and tablature for Example 10e, 12 bars over chords A7, D7, A7, D7, A7, F#7, Bm7, E7, A7, E7]

If we decide to start every new chord from the 3rd, we can work on applying our 3-to-9 arpeggios. These can be played as straight ascending ideas, or with octave displacement.

Outside of those obvious 3-to-9s, I've also included some chromatic passing tones and scalar ideas because arpeggios should never exist in a vacuum – we're always looking to combine things to make them musical.

Example 10f:

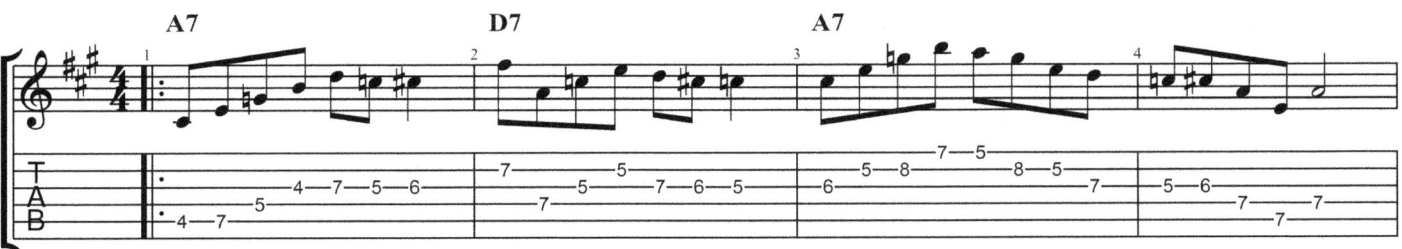

Our next etude expands on this 3-to-9 idea by alternating between 1-to-7 and 3-to-9 arpeggios over each chord. The big difference is we're going to focus on outlining the 7b9 chords by using diminished 7 arpeggios when they happen. So, you're getting to work on two things now.

Example 10g:

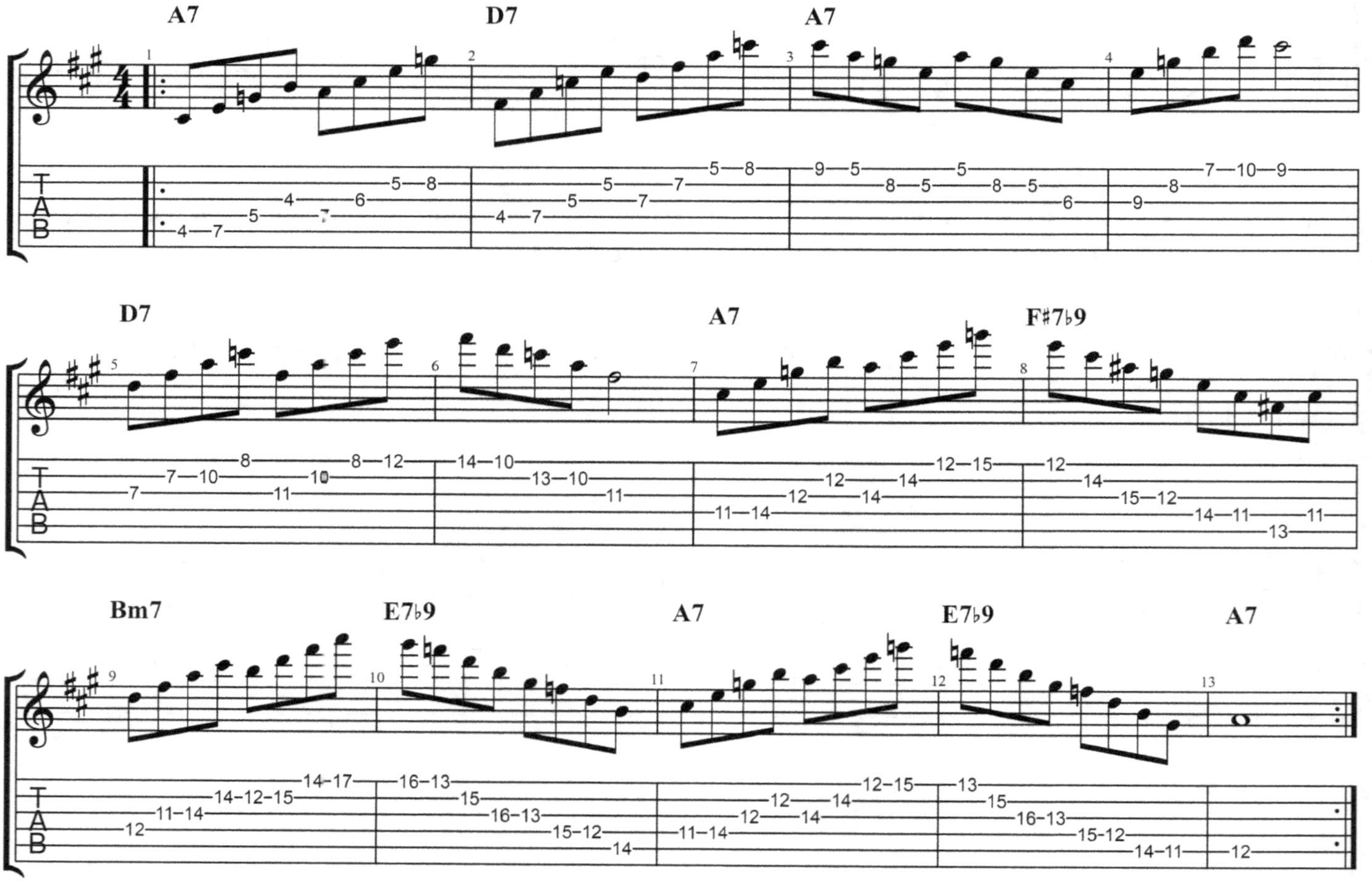

Now I'm going to blend our arpeggios and scalar ideas in a bit more depth.

We're using 3-to-9 arpeggios in the first two bars, then something a little closer to a straight A7 in bar three.

In bar four, I use a diminished 7 arpeggio to make the A7 an A7b9.

Bars five and six both use 3-to-9 arpeggios, both with octave displacement, and straight arpeggios.

Over the A7 in bar seven, we're playing a C#m7b5 in descending groups of four, which we transition into a Gdim7 in fours over the F#7b9.

Example 10h:

To finish up looking at arpeggios on the blues progression, I want to limit us to the "ascending arpeggio descending scale" concept we looked at in Routine 8. We don't always have to ascend up from the 1 either. If you look in the first measure, we ascend up a 3-to-9 arpeggio then come down the Mixolydian scale. We want to be able to do this with arpeggios starting on any note in the chord.

Example 10i:

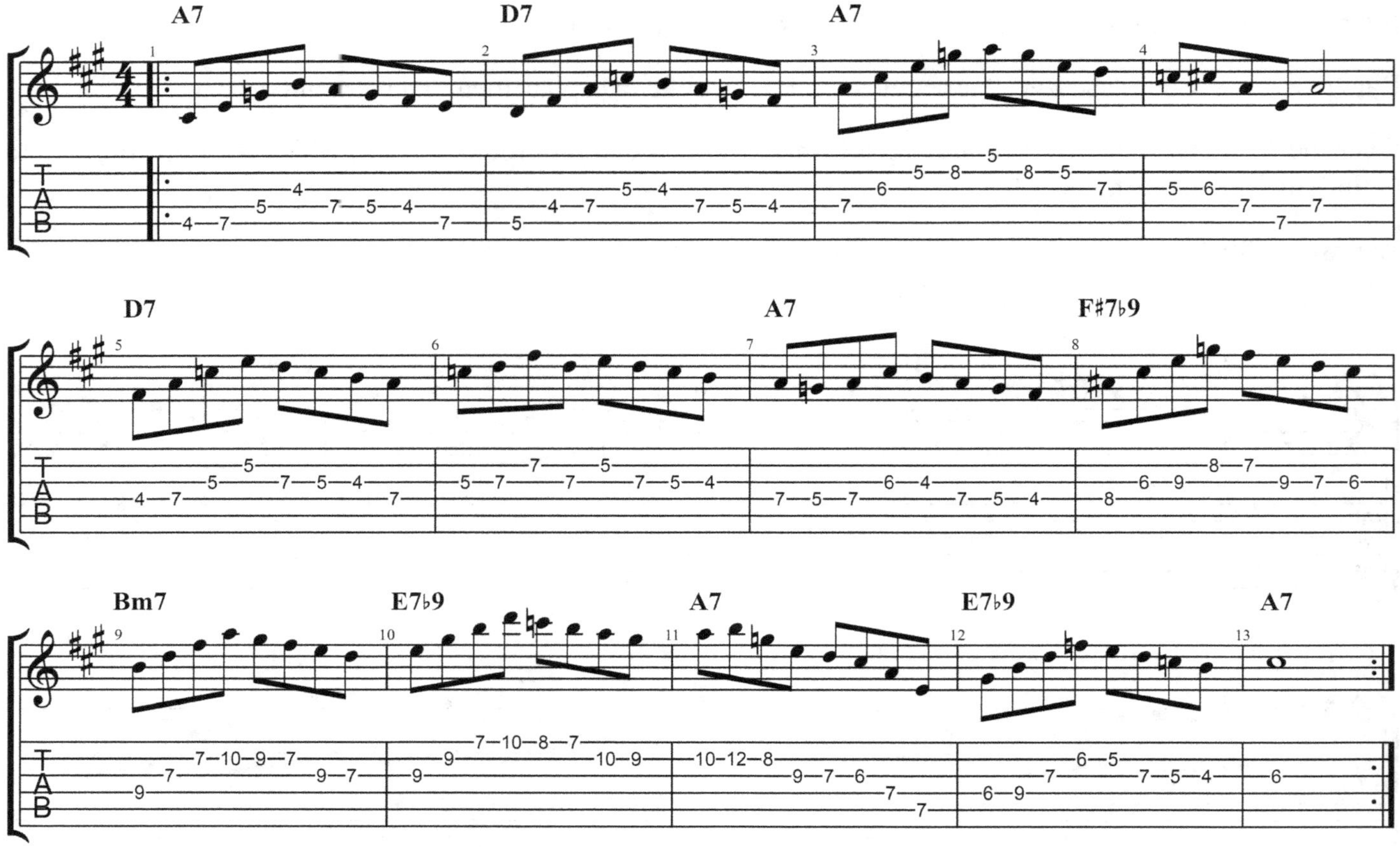

Now I'd like to move on to the first sixteen bars of the progression for *Back Home Again in Indiana*. This is a great little progression that includes three of our important chord qualities, and has both functioning and non-functioning dominant chords. Your first step should be to memorise the chord progression, both as named chords and how it sounds. The best way to do this is always with just straight ascending arpeggios, so we'll start there.

Example 10j:

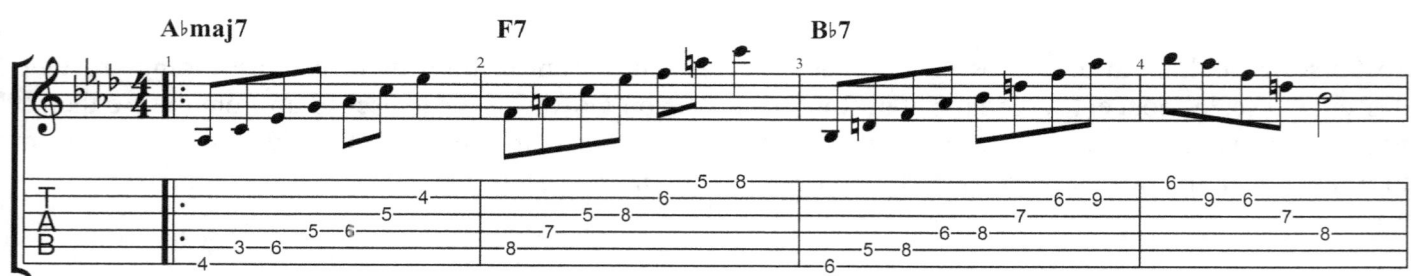

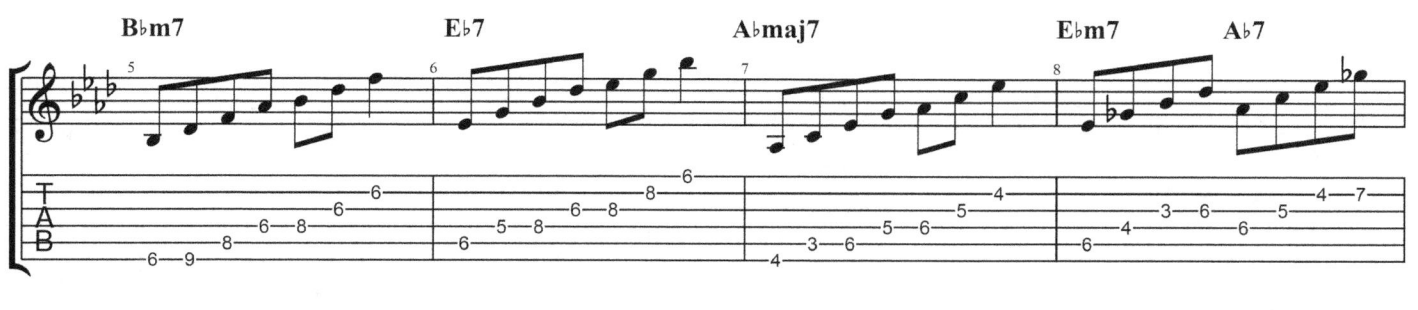

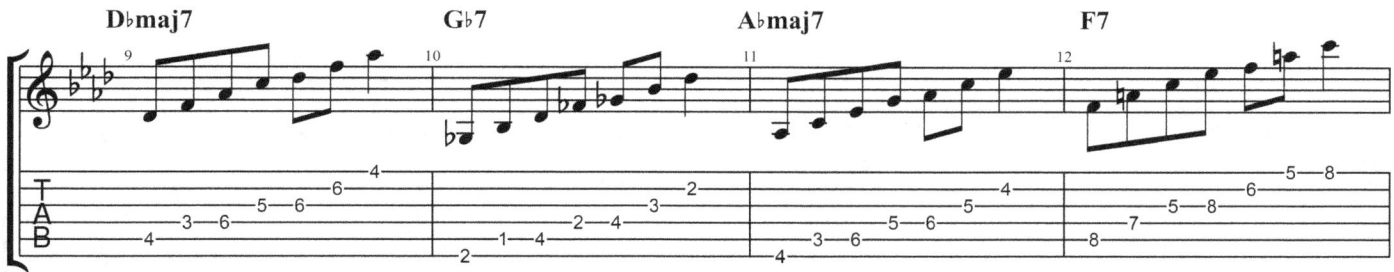

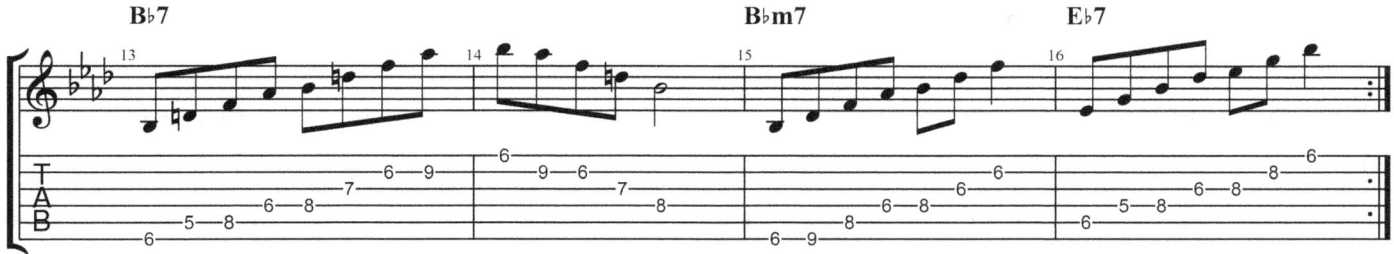

When you have this down, it makes sense to shift up to 3-to-9 arpeggios. When doing this, I'll treat the Eb7 and F7 as 7b9 chords, because they're resolving dominant chords, so we're using diminished 7 arpeggios on those. This is a great way to delve a little further into a chord progression before developing your lines over it in more detail.

Example 10k:

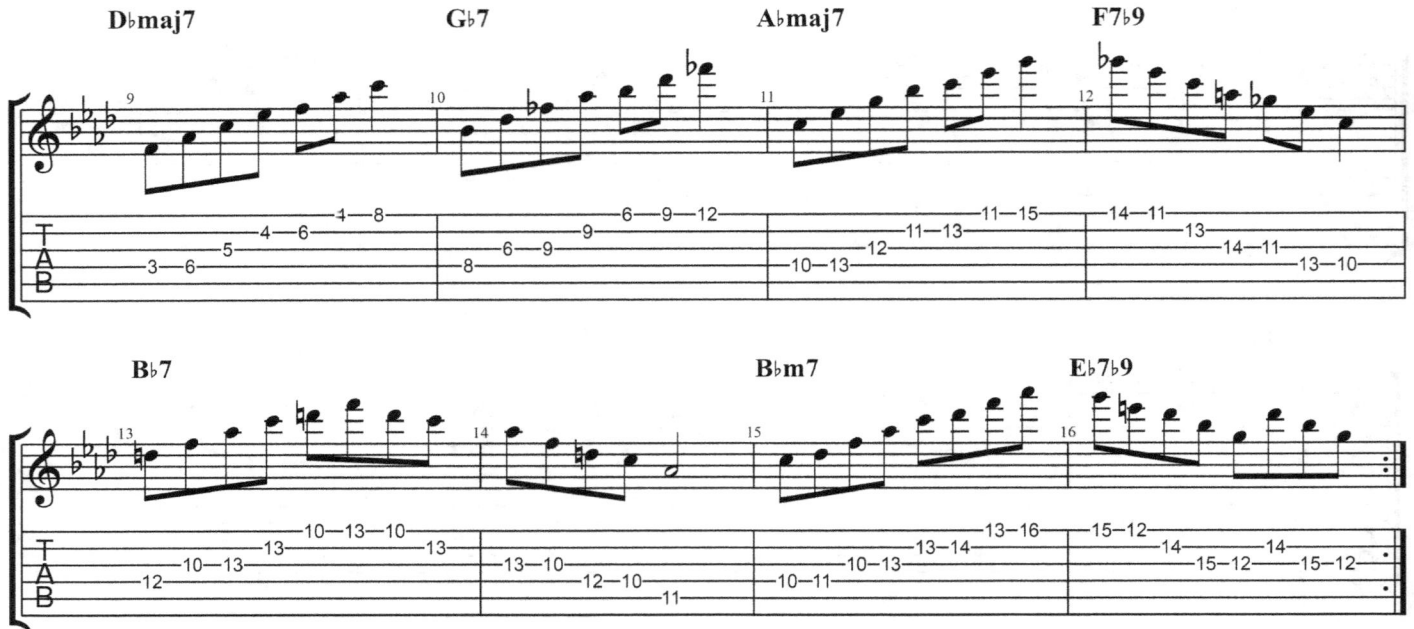

That might have felt like a lot of brain work, right? But we can dial back the mental stress by breaking up our rhythms and leaving a little more space.

Here, I'll start with a 3-to-9 over the Abmaj7 with 1/4 notes, then a straight F7b9 arpeggio over the F7, and an arpeggio-scale combination over the Bb7.

Over the Bbm7, I play a 3-to-9 idea with both octave and rhythmic displacement. This leads us to the Eb7 chord, and over this, I'm actually playing the #5, 3, #9 and b9 – that's a lot of tension! Drawing altered chord ideas from the Super Locrian mode always gives us options. Bar nine outlines the Dbmaj7 chord with a Db major triad, and I add chromatic approach notes, which happen to also be in the key.

Example 10l:

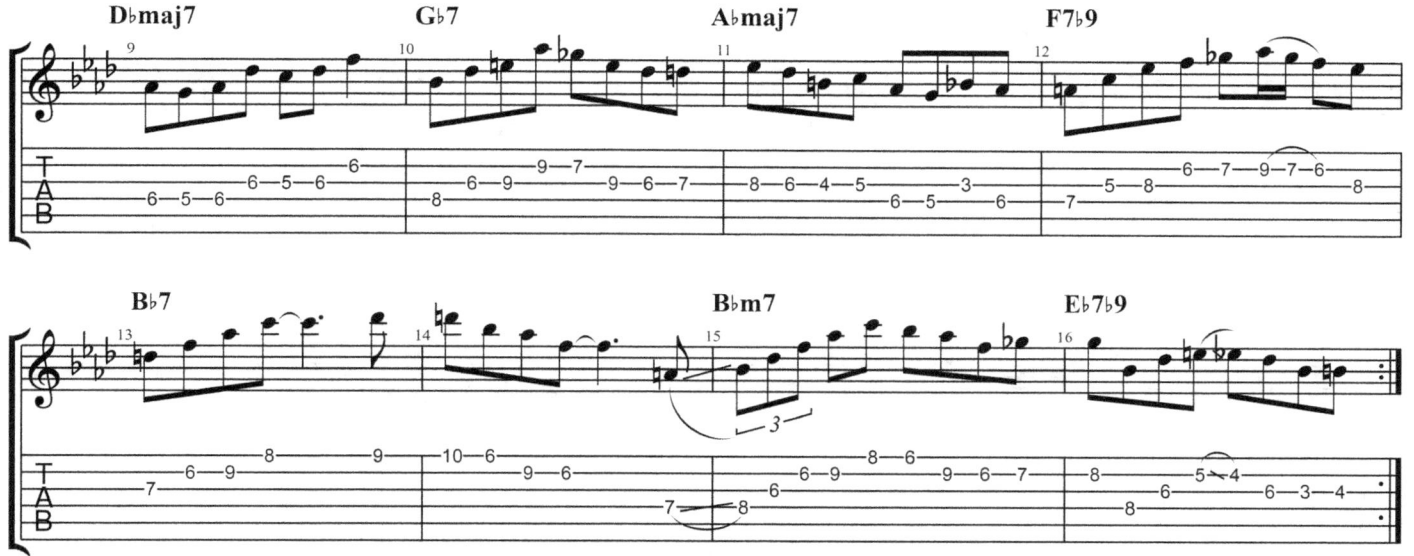

Now let's look at one of the more popular melodies played over these changes. I'm particularly fond of bars five through eight. If you look closely, you'll see a Bbm9 arpeggio, the 3-to-9 Bbm7 with octave displacement, an Eb+ triad, a Cm7, and an Ebm9 arpeggio. That's a lot of cool arpeggios woven together!

Example 10m:

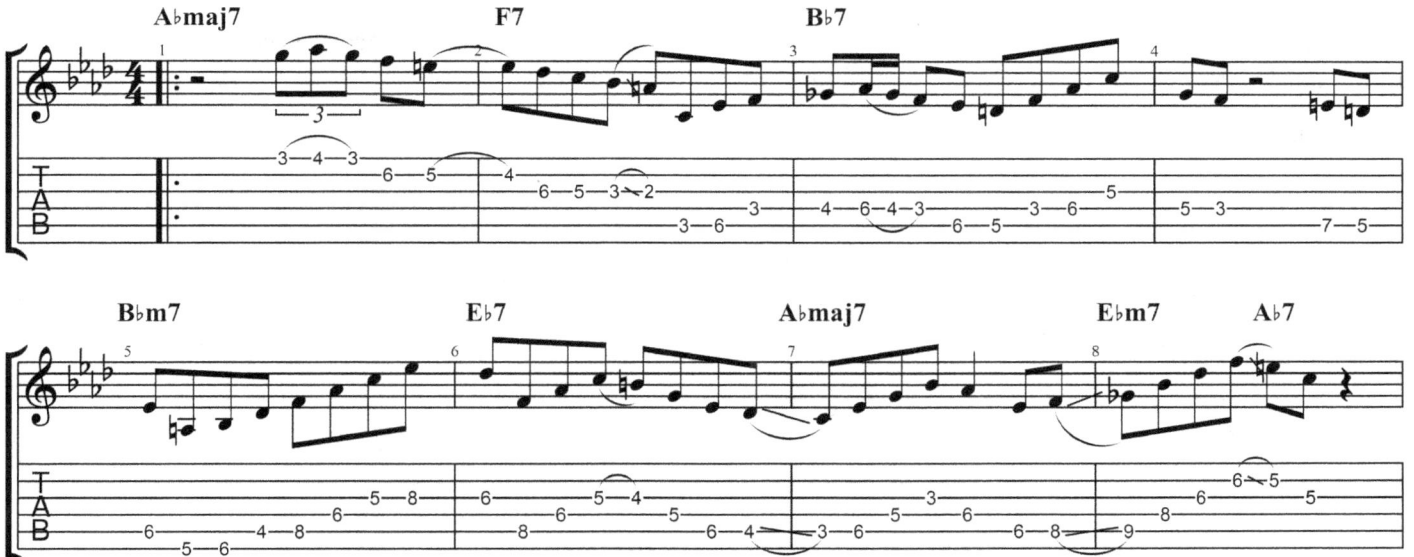

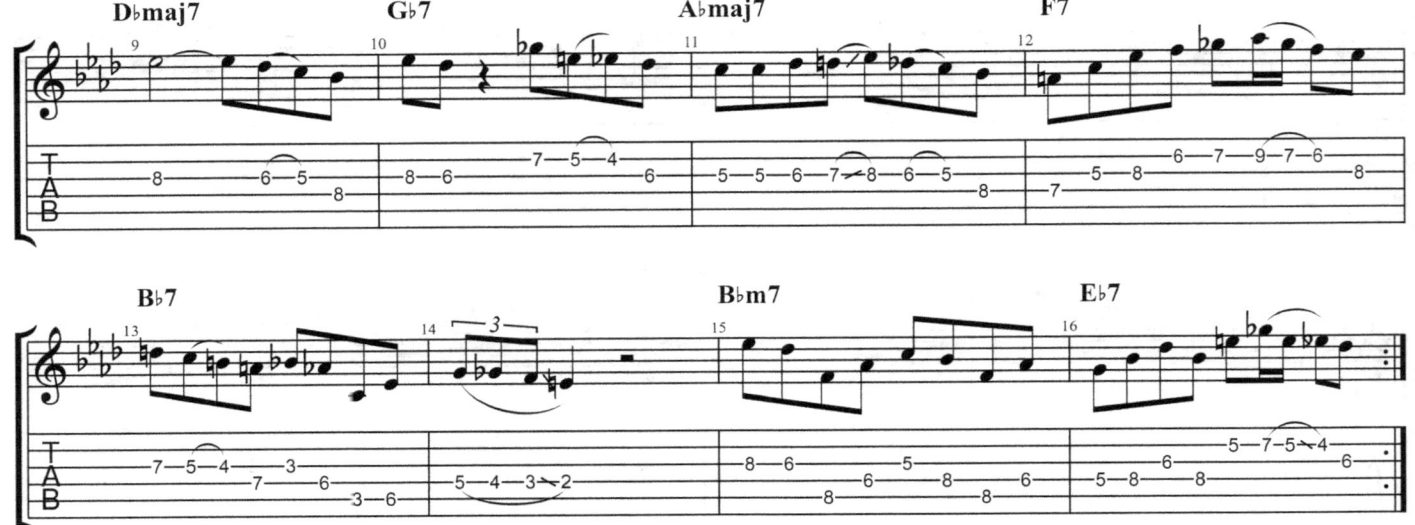

For our last couple of examples, I want to up the challenge by focusing on something where we need to play two chords per bar. There are lots of examples of that, but we're going to look at John Coltrane's iconic *Giant Steps*.

This is a tune that has a reputation for being one of the big bogeyman of jazz, but I like to think about Joe Pass's take on it. He said people sometimes ask for *Giant Steps*, but they don't really know what they're asking for – it's just a challenge. He didn't like to work too hard, so he'd play it as a bossa!

As with all the previous examples, the best place to start is by playing ascending arpeggios. This is going to be much harder now because there's no breathing room between chords.

Example 10n:

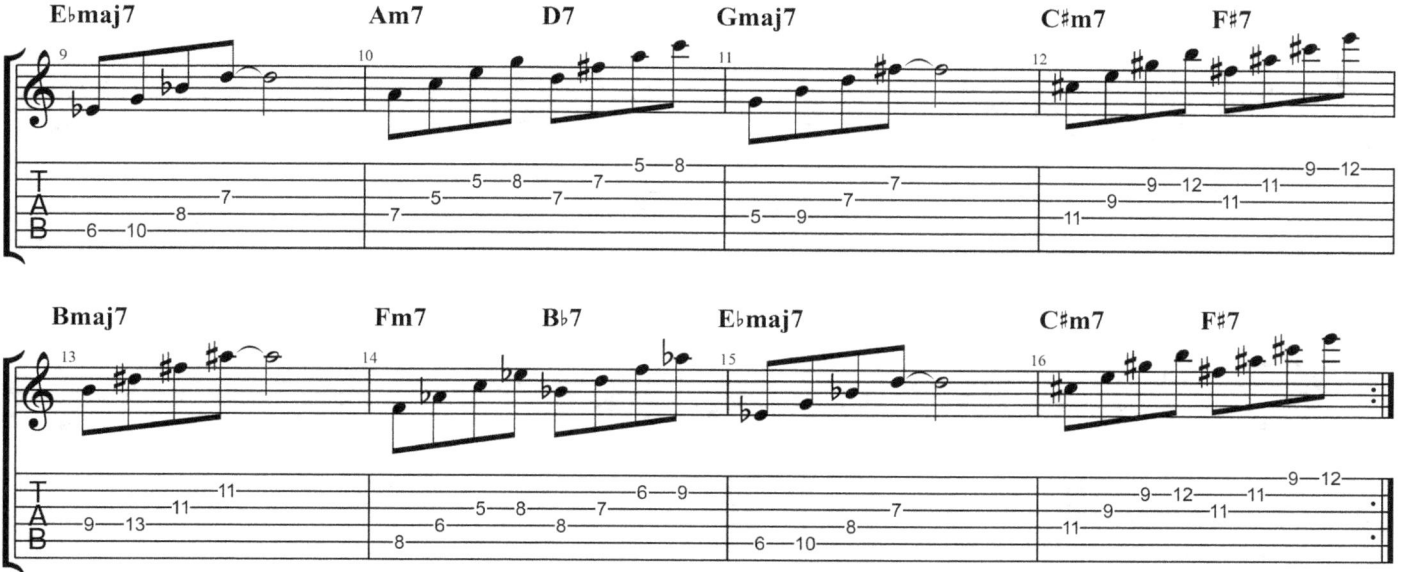

Now let's up the ante by ascending one arpeggio then connecting it to the nearest note in the next arpeggio and descending. We're not worried about playing in root position here, we're just focusing on connecting one arpeggio to the next. It's a real visualisation nightmare!

Example 10o:

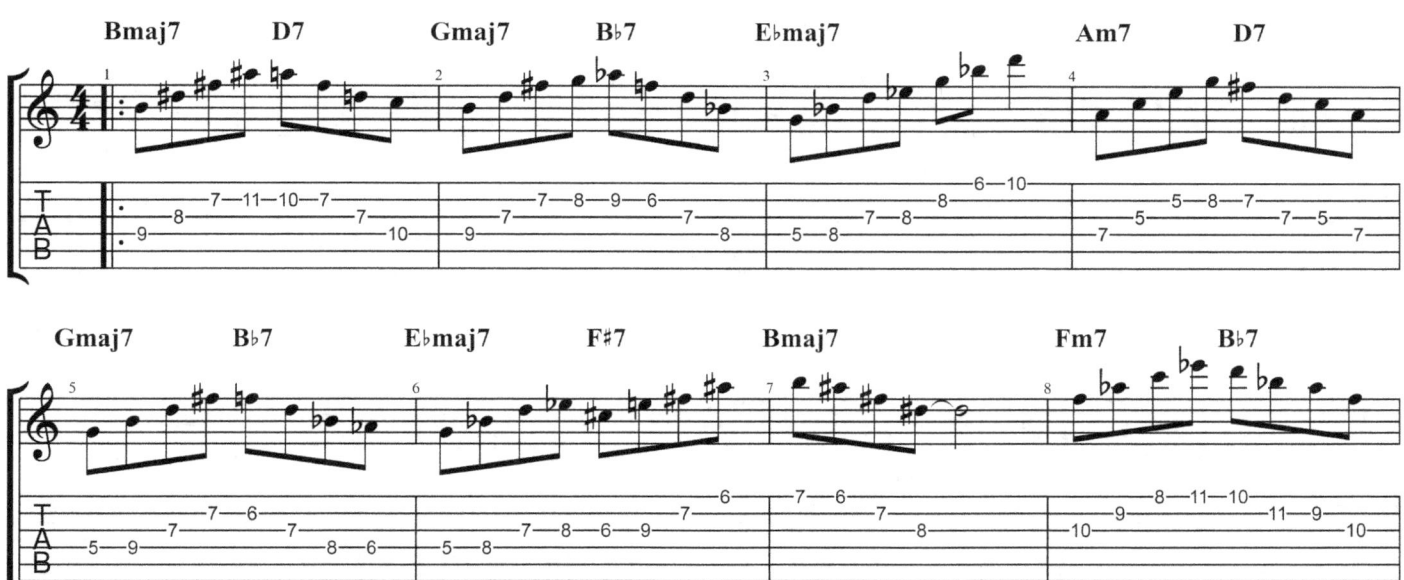

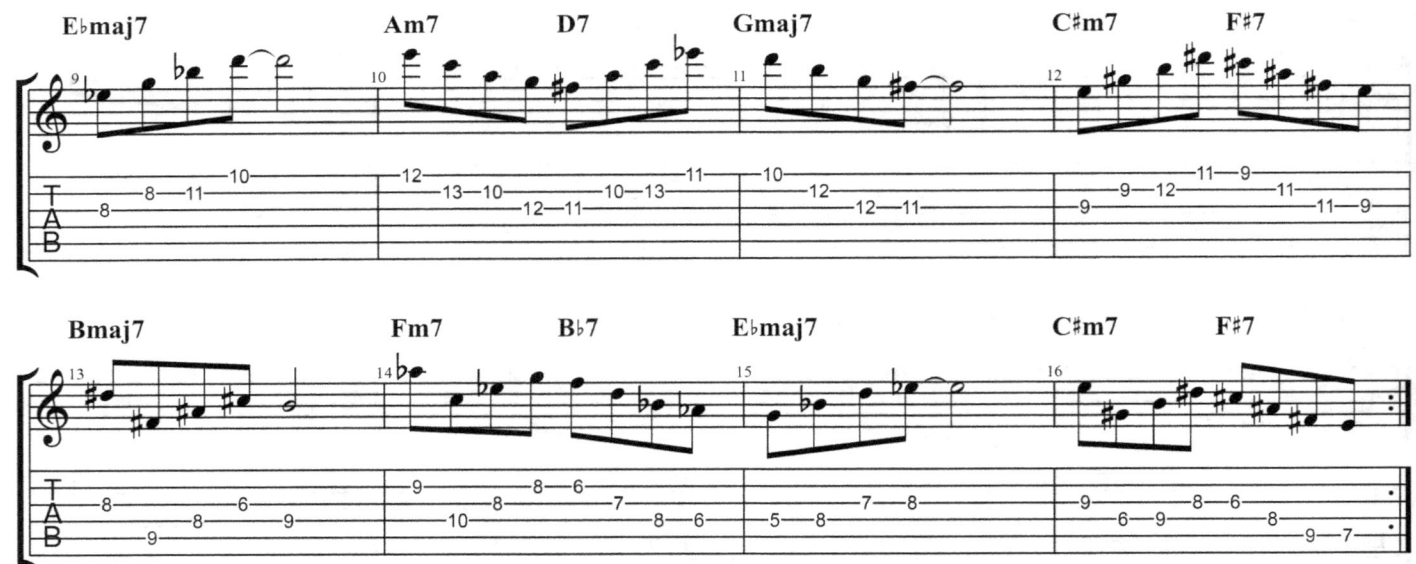

There are obviously limitless ways to outline these changes. I like to think of it like a gigantic plinko board: you drop your token in at the top, and you never quite know which path it's going to take to the bottom. That's the exciting part: knowing that anything can happen.

Example 10p:

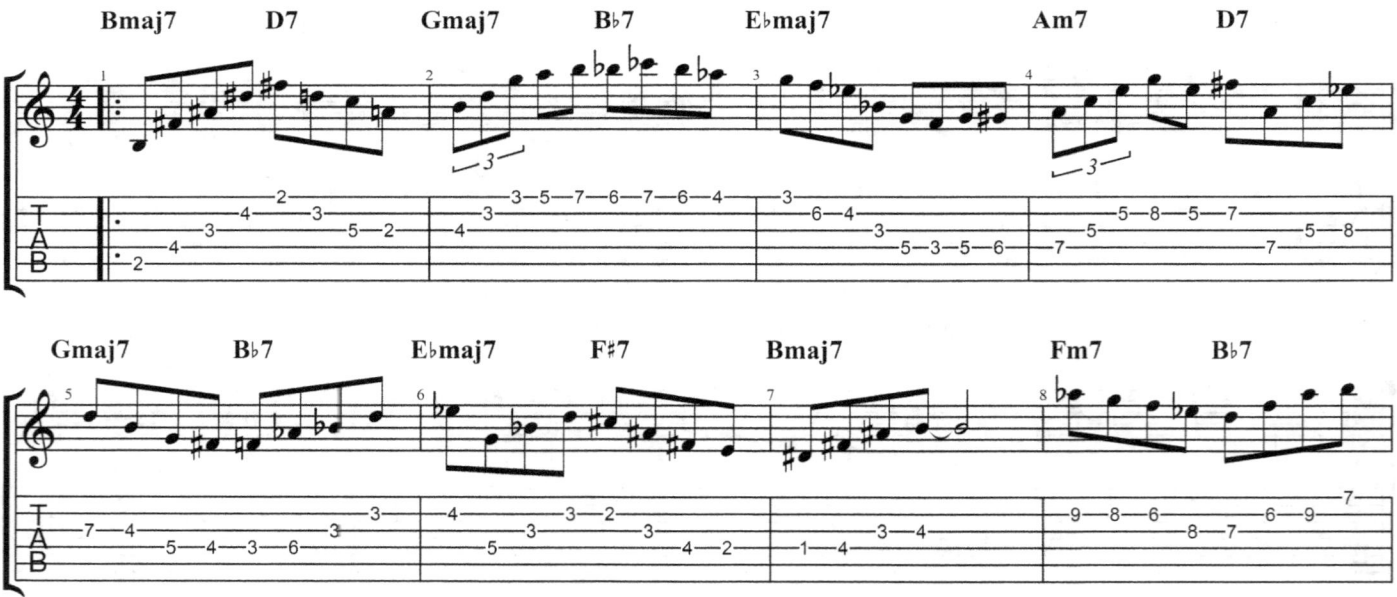

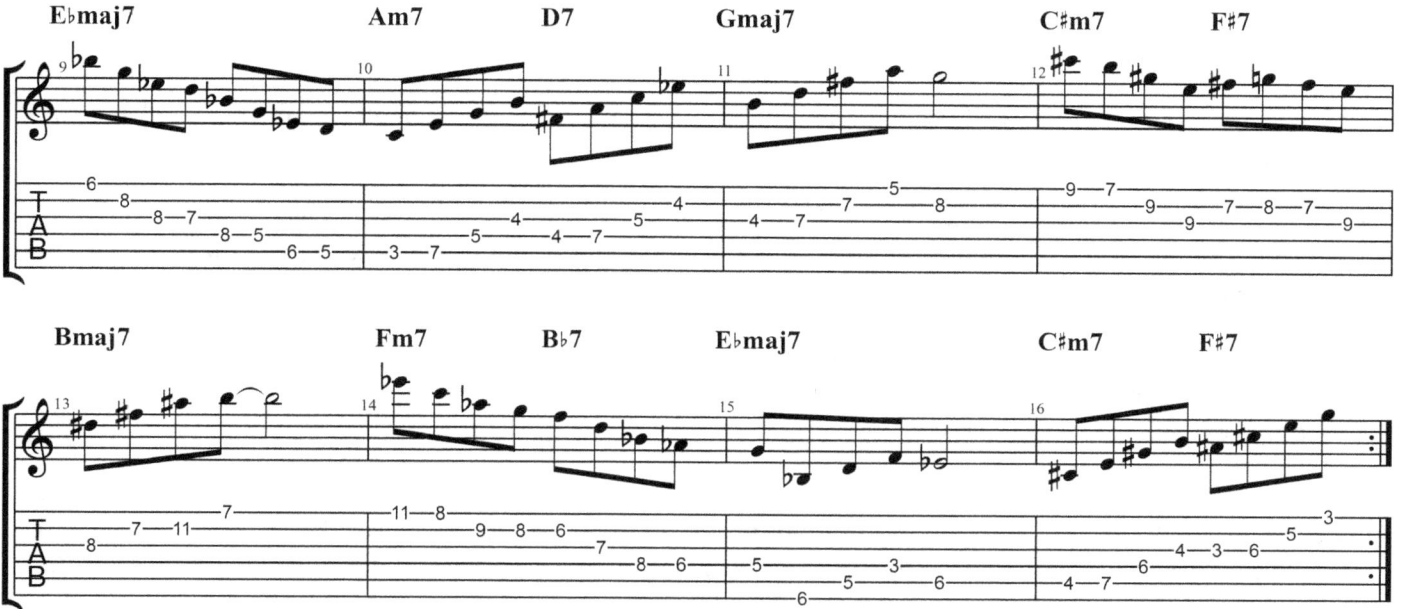

In that example, I tried to be even less tied down. There are some chromatic connections and scalar ideas, plus a cool drop 2 voiced arpeggio to start. I might use that as a springboard to arpeggiate through the whole progression with drop 2 voicings, or play 3-to-9s on every chord, or focus on approaching all the chords chromatically.

Whatever takes my fancy, as part of my own practice sessions I will sit down with pen and paper and write out a new etude, then work on that idea. I'll learn it, then I'll throw the paper away and forget it. For the next session, I'll write something new. That's because it's always about working on the skill of creating, never just remembering something composed. If we keep pushing like that, our brains will never stop improving.

And there we have it, the end of 10 weeks! But it's not over… it's never over!

Conclusion

It's been a long road, but you've finally made it! If you've been working through this for ten weeks or more, give yourself a pat on the back, you've certainly earned it.

Now, with that out of the way, let's get real. Real-life music isn't like a book with a neat, tidy ending. Music is an ever-evolving art form, a way to express ourselves, and it's an unending task – the learning never stops. But here's the thing: you've now got the tools to continue forward and be your own guide in your studies.

You can now pull up the chord progression to any song and dig into it; play the chords, mess around with the arpeggios, explore the scales. You can think about how the chords work together and what options they offer you as a player.

Remember, music is a language, and the best way to learn it is to listen to how it's spoken, to speak it yourself, and ideally to speak it with others. Study the greats. Whether it's Jason Becker or Pat Martino, it doesn't matter. Listen to how your favourite players use these words to speak and you'll hear scales, chords, and arpeggios being used in all different ways. The more you listen, the more your ears will get trained, and soon enough you'll be able to hear something on a record or in your head, and instantly connect it to your guitar. You'll hear an idea and *bam*, you'll be able to play it.

It all comes down to knowing your intervals inside-out and having a solid relationship with your instrument, so that applying those intervals becomes second nature. Yes, that takes time! But you've already put in months of work, training this stuff subconsciously, so trust me, you've got what it takes.

If there's one thing I believe after twenty years of playing, teaching countless students, and rubbing shoulders with some of the best players in the world, is that there's no such thing as talent. The only people who talk about talent are the ones looking for excuses to explain why they can't do something.

The truth is, it all comes down to hard work, passion and repetition. Keep working at it, day after day. Every time you pick up the guitar, just aim to be a little bit better than you were yesterday. With that approach, success isn't just a possibility, it's guaranteed.

Get out there, keep playing, and good luck!

Levi

www.ingramcontent.com/pod-product-compliance
Lightning Source LLC
Chambersburg PA
CBHW051146290426
44108CB00019B/2629